STUDIES IN PLATO'S METAPHYSICS

International Library of Philosophy and Scientific Method

A Catalogue of books already published in the *International Library of Philosophy and Scientific Method* will be found at the end of this volume.

Studies in PLATO'S METAPHYSICS

edited by

R. E. Allen

LONDON
ROUTLEDGE & KEGAN PAUL
NEW YORK: THE HUMANITIES PRESS

First published 1965
by Routledge & Kegan Paul Ltd
Broadway House, 68–74 *Carter Lane*
*London, E.C.*4

Printed in Great Britain
by Compton Printing Ltd
London and Aylesbury

Second impression 1967
Third impression 1968

SBN 7100 3626 4

CONTENTS

CONTENTS

PREFACE

MY thanks are due to the Clarendon Press for permission to publish articles XI, XVI, XVIII, XX, which originally appeared in *The Classical Quarterly*; to The Johns Hopkins Press for articles I and XVII, which originally appeared in *The American Journal of Philology*; to the Harvard University Press for article VII, which originally appeared in *Harvard Studies in Classical Philology*; to the Institute of Classical Studies, University of London, for article IX, which originally appeared in their *Bulletin*; to the Editor of *Mind* for articles II, III, V, and VI; to the Editors of *The Philosophical Review* for articles IV, XII, XIII, XIV, XIX; and to the Society for the Promotion of Hellenic Studies for articles VIII, X, and XV, which originally appeared in *The Journal of Hellenic Studies*.

Bibliography may be found in Professor Cherniss' articles in *Lustrum*, 4 (1959) 5–308, and 5 (1960) 321–615. These contain a survey of the literature on Plato from 1950 to 1957, annotated and conveniently arranged by topic; they mention the main contributions to Platonism in this century.

I should like to express my gratitude to Mr. John L. Ackrill, Professor Alan H. Donagan, Mr. David J. Furley, and Professor Gregory Vlastos, for helpful criticism, encouragement, and advice; to Professor W. K. C. Guthrie and Mr. E. J. Kenney, for other kindnesses; to Mr. Martin Mueller for the *index locorum*; and to Indiana University, which kindly put at my disposal secretarial facilities which made the mechanical burdens of editing much lighter. My greatest debt, as always, is to Ann Usilton Allen, my wife.

R.E.A.

INTRODUCTION

R. E. Allen

THE articles which follow have been selected for their bearing on Plato's metaphysics, especially the metaphysics of the later dialogues and, however one proposes to date it, the *Timaeus*. All of them have been previously published in British and American journals, none before 1930 and most since 1950. It is hoped that, by bringing them together within the covers of a single book, they may be more readily available to a wider public.

These articles speak for themselves, and require no introduction; more accurately, perhaps, they are their own best introduction. The questions they raise are nearly as various as the questions of philosophy itself, for there is no neat budget of issues, precisely circumscribed, in contemporary discussions of Plato, and the reader who wishes to know what is in this book must read it.

There is, however, a general issue which runs through many of the articles which follow, and which may well bear remark. It has to do with the question of whether Plato abandoned or sharply modified the Theory of Forms in later life; or if he did not, whether he consigned it to the back of his philosophical lumber-room, an outworn piece of machinery whose workings his developing and increasingly sophisticated interests had rendered largely obsolete.

This is a historical question; but the answer one gives to it is liable to be much influenced by philosophy. If one believes that the Theory of Forms is in some sense true, and the questions it answers philosophically important, one will naturally be reluctant to think that Plato ever abandoned or discounted it. One will be less reluctant to think this if one supposes the theory false, or more than false, irrelevant—an answer to mistaken questions; for it will then seem reasonable to suppose that a philosopher of Plato's acumen came to see this for himself.

The later view has grown increasingly prominent in recent

years, and is liable to become still more prominent in future. Its growth has been encouraged by recent developments in philosophy. The present century has seen extraordinary advances in formal logic and logical theory, and increased concern for the bearing of logic on philosophy. The effect of this has been to direct attention once again to the classical problem of universals, to the ancient issues of realism, nominalism, and conceptualism, and, among students of Plato, to prompt new debate on the nature and viability of the Theory of Forms. That debate has been complicated, in recent years, by the rise, primarily in Britain, but also to some degree in America, of conceptual, or non-formal linguistic, analysis. This movement has been heralded as a revolution in philosophy, and perhaps it is; but it is a revolution with a sense for the past, and many of its exponents have come to see in Plato's later dialogues, particularly the *Parmenides*, *Theaetetus*, and *Sophist*, an anticipation of their own methods and results.

The temper of this movement is diffuse. It does not lend itself to summary statements of doctrine, and its slogans, in so far as it has had slogans, have been mainly expressive of what it is against, not what it is for. In this it is perhaps like most other revolutions, and like them too in that its essence lies rather in an attitude of mind than in a body of doctrine. That attitude is inclined to treat the traditional problems of metaphysics, and especially problems of universals, as problems to be resolved rather than solved, problems which arise from misleading questions, and which yield, or generally yield, to analyses of concepts.

The critic of Plato who shares this temper of mind is liable to view the Theory of Forms as a simple mistake, and to suppose that Plato himself came to think it so. If he did, then the development of his thought in some measure recapitulated, or perhaps better, precapitulated, the development of philosophy in this century. In the *Phaedo*, *Symposium*, and *Republic*, or so it is generally agreed, Plato held that universals exist, that they exist both independently of the mind and of the individuals which partake of them, and that abstract nouns are names of which those universals are the *nominata*. In short, the Theory of Forms in the middle dialogues was a realistic theory of universals, a theory with a strong family resemblance to the realistic theories which were prominent in philosophy in the early years of this century. But in the *Parmenides*, Plato subjected that theory to criticism; and the revolutionary interpreter is inclined to believe that those criticisms were valid, and that Plato knew that they were valid. If this is true, the *Parmenides* marks a turning point in his thought, and a turning whose direction can be specified. Negatively, it may be argued, Plato came to realise that the Theory of Forms involved a confusion, in that it treated concepts as though they were somehow like the individuals to which concepts apply; he came to realise that concepts are not individuals, however lofty, that abstract nouns are not names, however strange. Perhaps he even came to realise that meaning is not itself a form of reference or naming. Positively, it may be argued, Plato became aware that there are radical differences in the logical behaviour of concepts, that concepts such as existence and unity, for example, differ in important ways from concepts such as justice or triangularity; and the later dialogues are the record of his attempt to analyse those differences. Plato's thought, then, moved in a new and vitally important direction after the *Parmenides*. It had been dominated in the beginning by a status question, by the question of how concepts were to be located in the world *vis-à-vis* the individuals to which they apply. It turned to a series of network questions, to questions of logical behaviour, logical relations, logical types. At the end of his life, Plato had begun to ask the questions that many philosophers ask today; speculative ontology had largely given place to logic—not formal logic, but the informal logic of concepts in ordinary use. The founder of the *ancien régime* had himself become a revolutionary.

To the revolutionary in philosophy, this portrait of Plato is liable to seem plausible, and perhaps more than plausible, natural. To more conservative critics it will seem implausible, the portrait of a man who abandoned a voyage of discovery for essays in county cartography. But matters of taste or philosophical preference apart, the revolutionary interpretation raises a variety of concrete and specific issues in scholarship. It may be that the *Theaetetus*, *Sophist*, *Politicus*, *Philebus*, and *Laws* may be so construed as to support it, or at least not contradict it. In large measure, that remains to be seen. But any view of Plato's development which implies that he abandoned the Theory of Forms, or radically modified it, or ceased to view it as crucial to his philosophy, must deal with the *Timaeus* and the *Seventh Epistle*, and in dealing, it must deal radically. If the *Seventh Epistle* is genuine, as almost all editors in this century have thought, it was written towards the close of Plato's life; in it, the Theory of Forms, construed very much as in the *Phaedo*, is central in Plato's view of reality. Similarly, the *Timaeus* has been universally regarded as a late dialogue, written well after the *Parmenides*; in it, the Theory of Forms is made central to Plato's cosmology. Thus, if the revolutionary interpretation, even in attenuated form, is to be made good, the *Seventh Epistle*, or at least its 'philosophical digression', must be proved a forgery, and the *Timaeus* either shown to be mythical in such a way as to imply no literal commitment to Forms, or redated to a period before the *Parmenides* and ranked as a middle dialogue. Either that, or the revolutionary must proceed by *tour de force*, and undertake to show that the Theory of Forms was not a realistic theory of universals after all.

These claims will not pass unchallenged; they have already provoked debate and will provoke further debate in future. All of this is to the good. Issues in the scholarship of philosophy have always tended largely, though by no means wholly, to be governed by issues in philosophy itself, and nowhere has this been more true than with Plato. No doubt this has often placed obstacles in the way of learning what Plato actually meant; it has led to anachronism. But it has also immensely deepened our understanding, and in the end, the good outweighs the evil. In late antiquity, Plato became a Plotinian. In the middle ages, he became a Christian. In the last century he first became a Kantian and then a Hegelian. In this century, he became a realist, and then moved towards conceptual analysis. This need not be any matter for surprise. It is part of the genius of Platonism, which makes it perennial, that it can, like a leaping spark, kindle fire in minds of widely different outlook and impel interpretations of widely different kinds. And it is part of the genius of Platonic scholarship that it can absorb those interpretations, take from each of them something of value, and leave it as a permanent deposit for the future. Santayana once remarked that Platonism, if it were ever lost as a tradition, would presently be revived as an inspiration. The reason, perhaps, is that Plato, more than a philosopher, is philosophy itself. So long as men reflect, they will disagree about what he meant, and in their disagreement, or so one may believe, there is health and hope for the future.

I

THE PHILOSOPHICAL ECONOMY OF THE THEORY OF IDEAS

(1936)

H. F. Cherniss

THE objection with which in the *Metaphysics*[1] Aristotle introduces his criticism of the theory of Ideas expresses a difficulty which has tended to alienate the sympathy of most students who approach the study of Plato. The hypothesis, Aristotle says, is a superfluous duplication of the phenomenal world; it is as if one should think it impossible to count a number of objects until that number had first been multiplied. This objection, even tacitly entertained, distorts the motivation of the hypothesis; that it misrepresents Plato's express attitude towards scientific problems, the well-known statement of Eudemus quoted by Simplicius on the authority of Sosigenes amply proves.[2] The complications of the planetary movements had to be explained, Plato asserted, by working out an hypothesis of a definite number of fixed and regular motions which would 'save the phenomena'. This same attitude is expressed in the *Phaedo* where Socrates explains the method of 'hypothesis' which he used to account for the apparently disordered world of phenomena;[3] the result of this method, he says, was the Theory of Ideas.[4]

The phenomena for which Plato had to account were of three kinds, ethical, epistemological, and ontological. In each of these spheres there had been developed by the end of the fifth century doctrines so extremely paradoxical that there seemed to be no

[1] *Met.*, 990a 34 ff. It is repeated almost exactly at 1078b 34–6.

[2] Simplicius, *in De Caelo*, p. 488, 18–24 (Heiberg).

[3] *Phd.*, 99d 4–100a 8.

[4] *Phd.*, 100b 1–102a 1.

possibility of reconciling them with one another or any one of them with the observable facts of human experience.[1] The dialogues of Plato, I believe, will furnish evidence to show that he considered it necessary to find a single hypothesis which would at once solve the problems of these several spheres and also create a rationally unified cosmos by establishing the connection among the separate phases of experience.

The interests of Socrates,[2] the subject-matter of the early dialogues, the 'practical' tone of Plato's writings throughout make it highly probable that he took his start from the ethical problems of his day. It is unnecessary to labour the point that he considered it fundamentally important to establish an absolute ethical standard; that the bearing on this point of the 'inconclusive', 'exploratory' dialogues could not have been obscure to his contemporaries is obvious to anyone who looks at such evidence of the time as is furnished by the Διασοὶ Λόγοι (which discusses the relativity of good and evil, fair and foul, just and unjust, true and false, and the possibility of teaching wisdom and virtue) or by the papyrus fragment of Antiphon the Sophist[3] (where conventional justice is called adventitious and generally contradictory to natural justice which is defined as that which is truly advantageous to each individual). The necessity for an absolute standard of ethics which would not depend upon the contradictory phenomena of conventional conduct but would be a measure of human activities instead of being measured by them was forcibly demonstrated by the plight into which Democritus had fallen. He had bitterly opposed the relativism of Protagoras;[4] yet two of his own ethical fragments show how vulnerable he must have been to counter-attack. 'They know and seek fair things,' he said, 'who are naturally

[1] Note the criticism and warning in *Phd.*, 101e: ἅμα δ' οὐκ ἂν φύροιο ὥσπερ οἱ ἀντιλογικοὶ περί τε τῆς ἀρχῆς διαλεγόμενος καὶ τῶν ἐξ ἐκείνης ὡρμημένων, εἴπερ βούλοιό τι τῶν ὄντων εὑρεῖν; ἐκείνοις μὲν γὰρ ἴσως οὐδὲ εἷς περὶ τούτου λόγος οὐδὲ φροντίς. ἱκανοὶ γὰρ ὑπὸ σοφίας ὁμοῦ πάντα κυκῶντες ὅμως δύνασθαι αὐτοὶ αὑτοῖς ἀρέσκειν. They do not keep the 'universes of discourse' clearly defined but think it is legitimate, for example, to drag an epistemological difficulty into an ethical problem before they have completely canvassed the ethical phenomena and have set up an hypothesis to explain them. An example of this 'childish' confusion is outlined in the *Phil.*, (15d–16a; 17a).

[2] Cf. e.g. Aristotle, *Met.*, 987b 1 ff.

[3] *Oxyrh. Pap.*, XI, 1364; Diels, *Fragmente der Vorsokratiker*, 4th ed., vol. II, pp. xxxii ff.

[4] Plutarch, *Adv. Colot.*, 1108f–1109a.

disposed to them.'[1] And, attempting to reconcile conventional law and natural good, he remarked, 'The law seeks to benefit the life of men but can do so only when they themselves desire to fare well. For to those who obey it it indicates their proper goodness.'[2] This bald assertion of a difference between fair and foul things, virtuous and vicious actions offers no standard whereby to determine the difference, no reason for the similarity of all fair things quâ fair and for their difference from all that are foul. So long as these are only characteristics of material individuals no standard can be found, for to measure individuals against one another is to succumb to relativism. To compare and contrast one must have a definite standard of reference which must itself be underivative lest it become just another example of the characteristic in question and so lead to an infinite regress. The 'dialogues of search', by demonstrating the hopelessness of all other expedients, show that the definitions requisite to normative ethics are possible only on the assumption that there exist, apart from phenomena, substantive objects of these definitions which alone are the source of the values attaching to phenomenal existence.[3] The possibility of ethical distinctions, then, implies objective differences which can be accounted for only by the hypothesis of substantive ideas.

While this hypothesis makes an ethical system possible in the abstract, the problems raised by conscious human activity involve the construction of a complete ethical theory in the questions of epistemology. That a consistent and practical ethical theory depends upon an adequate epistemology, Plato demonstrates in the *Meno*. The subject of that dialogue is *virtue*, but it is with one of the popular practical questions about virtue that Meno opens the discussion. Socrates protests that such questions as the teachability of virtue must wait upon a satisfactory definition of

[1] Democritus, *fragment* 56 (Diels): *τὰ καλὰ γνωρίζουσι καὶ ζηλοῦσιν οἱ εὐφυέες πρὸς αὐτά.*

[2] Democritus, *fragment* 248 (Diels): *ὁ νόμος βούλεται μὲν εὐεργετεῖν βίον ἀνθρώπων. δύναται δὲ ὅταν αὐτοὶ βούλωνται πάσχειν εὖ. τοῖσι γὰρ πειθομένοισι τὴν ἰδίην ἀρετὴν ἐνδείκνυται.*

[3] *Euth.*, 15c 11–e 2; *Laches* 199e (cf. 200e–201a); *Lysis*, 222e (N.B. 218c–220b 5: necessity of finding a *πρῶτον φίλον* which is the final cause of *πάντα φίλα*); *Charm.*, (176a); *Hippias Minor* (376b: if *anyone* errs voluntarily, it must be the good man [who, of course, as good would not err at all]). Cf. *Prot.*, (361c: the difficulties into which the argument has led show that it is necessary first to discover what *ἀρετή* is and *then* discuss its teachability).

virtue;[1] but Meno's failure to produce a definition makes him fall back upon the 'eristic argument' that one cannot search for either the known or the unknown.[2] To the implication here that ethical problems are not susceptible of investigation Socrates answers that one can escape this difficulty only by supposing that learning or discovering is really recollection of that which has already been *directly* known.[3] Here Socrates is not concerned with the details of the process; his contention is simply that, since determination of the characteristics of virtue presupposes a definition of its essential nature and to give such a definition presupposes knowledge of the essence, we must assume that essential virtue exists and has been directly known unless we are to surrender all possibility of considering ethical problems. Socrates is forced by Meno's insistence to discuss his question anyway, but his repeated objection that such questions demand a prior determination of the nature of virtue itself is a warning and an explanation of the paradoxical outcome of the consequent discussion.[4]

If men act virtuously without being able to teach virtue (that is, without being able to give a consistent account of the causes of their actions), it is because they have 'right opinions' and so are virtuous by a kind of 'divine grace'.[5] But such right opinions, though having results speciously identical with those of knowledge, are unstable, for they are haphazard, being unconnected by a chain of causality with the final cause. The recognition of this causal relationship, however, is knowledge and this is just recollection.[6] Consequently until one bases his reasoning upon the knowledge of essential virtue, there can be no adequate solution of the problems of ethics.[7] So it is that by argument and example the *Meno* demonstrates how, having to distinguish knowledge and right opinion in order to save the phenomena of moral activity, the ethical philosopher is forced to face the problems of epistemology.

But Plato was not satisfied with having proved that considera-

[1] *Men.*, 71a 3–7. It is in the light of this that I find the key to the riddles of the *Protagoras* in Socrates' remarks at the end of that dialogue (*Pro.*, 361c 2–d 2).

[2] *Men.*, 80e–81a.

[3] *Men.*, 81d 4–5. Note the word used for acquiring the knowledge in the first place: ἑωρακυῖα (81c 6).

[4] *Men.*, 86c 6–87b 5.

[5] *Men.*, 99a–d.

[6] *Men.*, 97e–98b.

[7] *Men.*, 100b.

tions of ethics require the assumption of substantive ideas and an epistemology consistent with such an hypothesis. The pragmatic relativism of Protagoras' ethics was, after all, a necessary result of his subjective realism; and Plato had before him the example of Democritus who, though insisting upon the reality of definite moral standards, could not finally refute Protagoras since he had no adequate reason for giving mind the sovereignty over sensations. There is a winsome sadness in his confession of defeat expressed in the reply he makes the sensations give to the strictures of mind: 'unhappy Intelligence, with evidence we give you you attempt our overthrow; your victory is your defeat'.[1] The saving of the phenomena of intellection and sensation is the primary duty of epistemology; if, however, it should appear that these phenomena can be saved in their own right only by setting up the same hypothesis as was found to be essential for ethics, the coincidence of results would by the principle of scientific economy enunciated in Plato's phrasing of the astronomical problem lend added validity to the hypothesis in each sphere.

The epistemological necessity for the existence of the Ideas is proved by the same indirect method as was used in establishing the ethical necessity. Since the phenomena to be explained have first to be determined, it is essential to proceed by analysis of the psychological activities, to decide the nature of these activities and their objects. In brief, the argument turns upon the determination of intellection as an activity different from sensation and opinion. In the *Timaeus*,[2] in an avowedly brief and casual proof of the separate existence of Ideas, it is stated that if intellection is other than right opinion it follows that there exist separate substantive Ideas as the objects of intellection. The indications of the essential difference of intellection and right opinion are there said to be three. Knowledge is produced by instruction, is always accompanied by the ability to render a true account or proof, and cannot be shaken by persuasive means, whereas right opinion is the result of persuasion, is incapable of accounting for itself, and is susceptible of alteration by external influence. The difference here mentioned is vividly exemplified in the myth of Er[3] by the horrible choice of the soul concerning whom it is said: 'he was one of those who had come from heaven, having in his former life lived in a well-ordered city and shared in virtue out of habit

[1] Democritus, *fragment* 125. [2] *Tim.*, 51d–e. [3] *Rep.*, 619b ff.

without philosophy'.[1] The *Theaetetus*, in its attempt to define knowledge, treats as the last possibility considered the suggestion that 'true opinion' may be a constitutive element of knowledge, may in conjunction with a λόγος or 'account' *be* knowledge itself.[2] As this proposal is tested, it is shown that, of the various possible meanings which λόγος might here have, the most satisfactory is 'knowledge of the proper difference of the object known'.[3] But if this 'knowledge of the difference' is not to be, in turn, mere 'right opinion' about the difference, an empty tautology, the definition is vitiated by a 'circulus in definiendo'.[4] In short, if 'true opinion' and knowledge are not identical, the former can not be an essential element of the latter, either. The common assumption of a relationship between 'right opinion' and knowledge is due to the external similarity of their results,[5] but the rightness of any particular opinion is simply accidental as Plato succinctly shows.[6] Right opinion is still essentially opinion; and this, the *Theaetetus* has already proved, cannot be knowledge, for it involves the possibility of error or wrong opinion which can be explained only as a mistaken reference to something known, although it is difficult to see how—if the term of reference be known—a mistaken identification is possible.[7] Opinion, then, is different from knowledge and secondary to it, for no satisfactory account of error can be given until the process of intellection has been explained.[8] Similarly the earlier part of the *Theaetetus* proved that knowledge can not be sensation or derived from sensation,[9] because sensation itself implies a central faculty to which all individual perceptions are referred and which passes judgement on them all.[10] As in the *Republic*[11] the proof that knowledge and opinion are different faculties is conclusive evidence for the fact that the objects with which they are concerned must be different, so here from the observation that the mind functioning directly without any intermediate organ contemplates the notions that are applicable to all things[12] proceeds the conclusion that knowledge is not to be found in the perceptions but in the reflection upon them, since

[1] In the parallel passage of the *Phd.* (82a–b) 'philosophy' is glossed by 'intelligence': ἄνευ φιλοσοφίας τε καὶ νοῦ.

[2] *Tht.*, 201c 8 ff.

[3] *Tht.*, 208d.

[4] *Tht.*, 209d 4–210a 9.

[5] *Tht.*, 200e 4–6.

[6] *Tht.*, 201a–c.

[7] *Tht.*, 187b 4–200d 4.

[8] *Tht.*, 200b–d.

[9] Cf. *Tht.*, 186e 9–187a 6.

[10] *Tht.*, 184b 5–186e 10.

[11] *Rep.*, 477e–478b 2.

[12] *Tht.*, 185e 1–2.

only in this process is it possible to grasp reality and meaning.[1] The attempt of the *Theaetetus* to define knowledge fails, and this failure demonstrates that the λόγος, the essential characteristic of knowledge, cannot be explained by any theory which takes phenomena to be the objects of intellection. That this is the purpose of the dialogue is revealed by the *Timaeus* passage above which shows that the λόγος is the δεσμός of the *Meno*,[2] the mark which distinguishes knowledge from right opinion in that dialogue and which was there identified with ἀνάμνησις. The *Theaetetus*, then, is an attempt to prove that the theory of Ideas is a necessary hypothesis for the solution of the problems of epistemology; the constructive doctrine of the *Sophist* demonstrates that it is a sufficient hypothesis for that purpose.[3] The process of abstraction and generalisation which Aristotle thought sufficient to account for knowledge[4] was recognised by Plato,[5] but he considered it to be inadequate. In the *Parmenides*,[6] after advancing all his objections to the hypothesis, Parmenides is made to assert that it is still necessary to assume the existence of Ideas if thought and reasoning are to be saved; and in the *Phaedo*[7] Socrates outlines the theory of abstraction almost in the very words which Aristotle was to use, connects it with the theories of the mechanistic physics, and rejects it in favour of the theory of separate Ideas. The possibility of abstraction itself, if it is to have any meaning, Plato believes, requires the independent reality of the object apprehended by the intellect. That is the basis of his curt refutation of mentalism in the *Parmenides*.[8] So the process of abstraction and analysis outlined in the *Philebus*, which is there said to be possible because of the participation of the phenomena in real Ideas,[9] and which in a simple example of its use in the *Republic*[10] is called 'our customary method', is in the *Phaedrus*[11] designated as ἀνάμνησις and said to require the substantial existence of the Ideas and previous direct knowledge of them by the intellect. The successful 'recollection' of the Ideas by means of the dialectical process is in the *Republic*[12]

[1] *Tht.*, 186d 2 ff.

[2] *Men.*, 98a.

[3] Cf. *Soph.*, 258d–264b and note the triumphant tone of 264b 5–7.

[4] *De Anima* 432a 3–14; *Post. Anal.*, 100a 3–b 17; cf. *Met.*, A, 1.

[5] *Charm.*, 159a 1–3; *Phil.*, 38b 12–13.

[6] *Parm.*, 135b 5–c 3.

[7] *Phd.*, 96b.

[8] *Parm.*, 132b–c.

[9] *Phil.*, 16c 10 ff. N.B. 16d 2: εὑρήσειν γὰρ ἐνοῦσαν.

[10] *Rep.*, 596a.

[11] *Phdr.*, 249b 5–c 4. Cf. the extended demonstration of *Phd.*, 74a 9–77a 5 which is based upon epistemological considerations.

[12] *Rep.*, 479e–480a.

said to constitute intellection as distinguished from opinion, and the man who is capable of such activity is there described in terms parallel to the 'mythical' description of the 'wingéd intellect' of the *Phaedrus*.[1]

The nature of the mental processes, then, can be explained only by the hypothesis of Ideas. Since no mere addition to right opinion from the sphere with which it itself deals can produce knowledge or make intelligible the fact of error and since no combination of sensations can account for apperception, knowledge cannot be synthetic or derivative. Knowledge as a special faculty dealing *directly* with its own objects must be assumed in order not only to explain the fact of cognition but also to make possible opinion and sensation as they are given by experience. The special faculty of knowledge, however, is characterised by direct contact of subject and object; since phenomena cannot enter into such a relationship with the subject, mediating organs being required in their case, it is necessary that the objects of knowledge be real entities existing apart from the phenomenal world and that the mind have been affected by them before the mental processes dealing with phenomena occur. Only so can one avoid the self-contradictory sensationalism of Protagoras, the psychological nihilism of Gorgias, and the dilemma of Democritus.

The effort to save the phenomena of mental activity leads to the same hypothesis as did the attempt to explain human conduct, and the ethical hypothesis is supported by the independent requirements of epistemology. There is, however, another sphere naturally prior to knowledge and sensation and by which finally all epistemological theories must be judged. The Ideas are necessary to account for the data of mental processes; but the physical world and its characteristics are not dependent upon these mental processes, and it is no more sufficient to assume an ontology which will fit the requirements of epistemology than it is to construct an epistemology in order to account for the phenomena of ethics. It is with this in mind that Timaeus, when in a physical discourse he uses a résumé of the epistemological proof of the existence of Ideas, apologises for his procedure with the excuse that the magnitude of his main subject requires him to give the briefest possible demonstration.[2] The very language of this passage shows that Plato considered it as a requirement of sound method

[1] *Phdr.*, 249c. [2] *Tim.*, 51c 5 ff.

to develop his ontological hypothesis according to the data of the physical world itself. This requirement is explained in the *Theaetetus* where a detailed theory of psychological relativism is expounded[1] by way of considering the thesis that knowledge is sensation. Such a doctrine, in spite of the objections that can be brought against its epistemological and ethical consequences, may still present a correct account of the nature of existence as nothing but a flux of motions. What seem to be individual objects and characteristics would then be merely the transitory resultants of the component motions. In that case, knowledge would really be vivid sensations which are the functions of clashing and passing movements.[2] To argue that no practical ethics or adequate epistemology can be developed from such an account is pointless, for there could be no *naturally* valid criterion by which to evaluate the different moments of evidence.[3] Such a theory as that of Ideas would be a merely pragmatic hypothesis, and distinctions of good and bad, true and false would be at best only conventional and artificial. It is, then, necessary that the study of ontology be undertaken independently of the requirements of ethics and epistemology to discover what hypothesis will explain the data of physical phenomena as such.[4] The data with which the investigation has to work are the constantly shifting phenomena of the physical world, and Plato accepts this unceasing flux as a characteristic of all phenomenal existence.[5] This flux, however, is the datum which has to be explained, and his contention is simply that change itself is intelligible and possible only if there exist entities which are not themselves involved in the change. The argument in the *Theaetetus*[6] attempts to show that the constant flux of phenomena involves alteration as well as local motion but that alteration requires the permanent subsistence of immutable abstract qualities. The relativism that asserts the constant change of everything, however, makes attributes and perceptions the simultaneous resultants of the meeting of agent and patient, while agent and patient themselves are merely complexes of change without independent existence,[7] with the result that not only are all things constantly changing their characteristics but the characteristics themselves are constantly altering, and 'whiteness' can no more

[1] *Tht.*, 156a–160e. [2] *Tht.*, 179c. [3] *Tht.*, 158b–e.
[4] *Tht.*, 179d. [5] Cf. *Tim.*, 27d 5–28a 4. [6] *Tht.*, 181c–183b.
[7] *Tht.*, 182b.

be really 'whiteness' than any other colour.[1] Similarly, if the qualities themselves are always altering, the sensations which are defined by these constantly altering qualities are undifferentiated.[2] Such an account of the world involves the denial not only of fixed states and determinable processes but also of the laws of contradiction and the excluded middle.[3] The data of phenomenal change, then, logically require the hypothesis of immutable and immaterial ideas. The argument occurs again at the end of the *Cratylus* (where, however, it is connected with one form of the epistemological proof);[4] and Aristotle accuses the Protagoreans, in the same terms as does Plato, of denying the laws of logic.[5] In a passage obviously influenced by the *Theaetetus*,[6] he explains the difficulties of the relativists as due to their failure to recognise immaterial existences and to note the distinction between quantitative and qualitative change. Like Plato, Aristotle felt that a logical account of physical nature required some hypothesis of qualitative existence as underived from quantitative distinctions.

The digression on mensuration in the *Politicus*[7] has the same intention. There Plato distinguishes between quantitative and qualitative 'measurement', the former being only relative measurement and the latter measurement against a norm,[8] and castigates those who think all the world susceptible of quantitative measurement; their error lies in the supposition that all difference can be reduced to quantitative distinctions.[9] For this reason in the *Timaeus*, where the quantitative determinations of the minima of phenomenal air, fire, water, and earth are elaborated in great detail,[10] Plato still insists that there must be substantive Ideas of air, fire, water, and earth, apart from phenomena, immutable, the objects of intellection only,[11] and that phenomenal objects are what they are because they are imitations of these real Ideas.[12] Indications of the ontological necessity of the hypothesis are not lacking in this dialogue either. The most certain and evident characteristic of phenomena is their instability; they are all in-

[1] *Tht.*, 182d 1–5. [2] *Tht.*, 182d 8–e5. [3] *Tht.*, 183a 4–b5.
[4] *Crat.*, 439d 3–440c 1.
[5] *Met.*, 1008a 31–34; cf. 1009a 6–12.
[6] *Met.*, 1010a 1–37. [7] *Pol.*, 283d–287a. [8] *Pol.*, 283d 7–284b 2.
[9] *Pol.*, 284e 11–285c 2; cf. Rodier, *Études de philosophie grecque*, p. 48, note 1.
[10] *Tim.*, 53c 4–55c 5; 55d 7–57c 6. [11] *Tim.*, 51a 7–52a 4.
[12] *Tim.*, 50c, 51a 7–b 1 (cf. Shorey in *Class. Phil.*, XXIII [1928], p. 358).

volved in the process of generation[1] and so imply a cause external to themselves.[2] Apart from the 'mythical' form of the explanation to which this leads, the argument is the same as the indirect proof of the *Theaetetus*. The instability of phenomena can be explained only by assuming a world of Ideas as the source of phenomenal characteristics. To dispense with such a superphenomenal world is not only to identify right opinion and knowledge but, in fact, to say that phenomena are stable.[3] This brief remark of Timaeus sums up the results of the demonstration in the *Theaetetus* which shows that the relativistic ontology transgresses the law of the excluded middle and so can no more say that all is in motion than that all is at rest. To do away with stable qualities is tantamount to denying the possibility of change.[4] Yet it is the possibility of phenomenal alteration that was to be saved, for phenomena have no stability at all;[5] they are fleeting phrases without persistent substantiality,[6] but such they can be only if apart from them there are substances of which somehow the phenomena partake.[7]

The physical phenomena, then, considered in themselves and not as objects of sensation or cognition still can be saved only by the hypothesis of separate, substantive Ideas. That the necessary and sufficient hypothesis for this sphere turns out to be the very one needed for ethics and epistemology makes it possible to consider the three spheres of existence, cognition, and value as phases of a single unified cosmos.

The apparently disparate phenomena of these three orders, like the seemingly anomalous paths of the planets, had to be accounted for by a single, simple hypothesis which would not

[1] *Tim.*, 28b 8–c 2.

[2] *Tim.*, 28c 2–3.

[3] *Tim.*, 51d 6–7.

[4] Aristotle reproduces the argument in his own language in *Metaphysics*, 1010a 35–7.

[5] Cf. *Tim.*, 49d 4 ff. (*βεβαιότητα*-d 7) and 51d 5–7.

[6] *Tim.*, 49c 7–50a 4.

[7] *Tim.*, 50b–c. That the mere configuration of space is not enough to produce phenomenal fire, etc., 51b 4–6 shows (N.B. *καθ' ὅσον ἂν μιμήματα τούτων δέχηται*). All this, I think, makes Shorey's interpretation of 56b 3–5 certain (*Class. Phil.*, XXIII [1928], pp. 357–8). To interpret *στερεὸν γεγονός* here as 'having received a third dimension' would be tautological, for the pyramid is *eo ipso* three-dimensional. Cf. also A. Rivaud in his introduction to his edition of the *Timaeus* (p. 26) in the Budé series.

only make intelligible the appearances taken separately but at the same time establish the interconnection of them all. The problem which Plato set others in astronomy he set himself in philosophy; the resulting theory of Ideas indicates by its economy that it proceeded from the same skill of formulation which charted for all time the course of astronomical hypothesis.

II

LOGOS AND FORMS IN PLATO (1954)

R. C. Cross

IN the *Theaetetus*, in the search for an answer to the question What is knowledge? the suggestion is made at 201d that true belief with the addition of a logos is knowledge, while belief without a logos is not knowledge. Where no logos can be given of a thing, then it is not knowable; where a logos can be given, then it is knowable (ὧν μὲν μή ἐστι λόγος, οὐκ ἐπιστητὰ εἶναι . . . ἃ δ' ἔχει, ἐπιστητά (201d)). This view is then elaborated in Socrates's 'dream'. It is the view that the first elements (στοιχεῖα) out of which every thing is composed have no logos. Each of them taken by itself can only be named. We can add nothing further, saying that it exists or does not exist. None of the elements can be told in a logos, they can only be named, for a name is all that they have. On the other hand, when we come to the things composed of these elements, then just as the things are complex, so their names when combined form a logos, the latter being precisely a combination of names. Thus the elements have no logos and are unknowable, but can be perceived (ἄλογα καὶ ἄγνωστα εἶναι, αἰσθητὰ δέ (202b)), while the complexes (συλλαβάς) are knowable and statable (ῥητάς) and you can have a true notion of them. The view is then summed up at 202b ff.—'whenever then anyone gets hold of the true notion of anything without a logos his soul thinks truly of it, but he does not know it; for if one cannot give and receive a logos of anything, one has no knowledge of that thing (τὸν γὰρ μὴ δυνάμενον δοῦναί τε καὶ δέξασθαι λόγον ἀνεπιστήμονα εἶναι περὶ τούτου), but when he has also acquired a logos, then all these things are realised and he is fully equipped for knowledge.'

Theaetetus expresses satisfaction with this view. Socrates himself, it is interesting to note, remarks (202d) that the statement (that true belief with a logos is knowledge) taken just by itself may well be satisfactory; for, he asks, how could there ever be knowledge apart from a logos and right belief? He objects, however, to the 'most ingenious' feature of the theory, namely, that the elements are unknowable, while the complexes are knowable. On this point, using the model of letters and syllables, Socrates presents the theory with a dilemma which, cashing the model, runs like this; if the logos just is the names which compose it, each name being the name of an unknowable element, then it itself conveys no more than do its several words—it is a mere congeries of unknowables. On the other hand, if the logos is something more than the nouns out of which it is composed, a new linguistic unit which somehow conveys something more than is conveyed by the bare enumeration of the individual names in it, then this something more will itself be a new simple, which as such will be unknowable (as having no logos), and the logos will stand in the same naming relation to it as the individual nouns did to the original elements. Thus the logos will no more convey knowledge than do the names with which we began.

In a paper read to the Oxford Philological Society Professor Ryle has related the theory of Socrates's dream and the criticism of it in this part of the *Theaetetus* to logical atomist theories about words and sentences such as are to be found in Russell's early writings and elsewhere. With the larger bearing of this part of the *Theaetetus* on modern versions of logical atomism I am not here concerned, but with some remarks Professor Ryle made about its relevance to Plato's own theory of Forms. He argued that 'if the doctrine of Forms was the view that these verbs, adjectives and common nouns are themselves the names of simple, if lofty, nameables, then Socrates's criticism is, *per accidens*, a criticism of the doctrine of Forms, whether Plato realised this or not', and he added that 'if a Form is a simple object or a logical subject of predication, no matter how sublime, then its verbal expression will be a name and not a sentence; and if so, then it will not be false but nonsense to speak of anyone knowing it (savoir) or not knowing it, of his finding it out, being taught it, teaching it, concluding it, forgetting it, believing, supposing, guessing or entertaining it, asserting it, negating it or questioning it'. It is these remarks I want to discuss.

What then are we to say of this criticism of the theory of Forms which Professor Ryle develops from the discussion in the *Theaetetus*? A number of possibilities suggest themselves. In the first place, we might say that what Plato is concerned with in the *Theaetetus* is knowledge in relation to perception. The unknowable elements there are, as he himself says, *αἰσθητά*, and he is not thinking of anything but perceptual 'simples', nor of any relation the argument might have to the theory of Forms. Still, it seems clear that the argument does hold for any simple nameables, whether objects of perception or objects of thought. Further, it is not easy to believe that Plato could have missed this, especially when so much of the language here echoes the language he has used elsewhere in setting out his own philosophical views. (Cf. e.g. *Tht.*, 202c *τὸν γὰρ μὴ δυνάμενον δοῦναί τε καὶ δέξασθαι λόγον ἀνεπιστήμονα εἶναι περὶ τούτου* with *Rep.*, 531e where the dialectician is contrasted with those who *μὴ δυνατοὶ . . . δοῦναί τε καὶ ἀποδέξασθαι λόγον (οὐ δοκοῦσιν) εἴσεσθαί ποτέ τι ὧν φαμεν δεῖν εἰδέναι*.) In any case, whether or not Plato was himself at this point aware of the possible effects of the argument on the theory of Forms, we ought to consider them.

It might be suggested, secondly, that Plato himself was aware that the arguments here were damaging to the theory of Forms, but was undisturbed by this, because he had already abandoned, or was about to abandon, the theory. Some scholars have certainly thought that the theory was either abandoned or fundamentally altered in the later dialogues. Burnet, for instance, maintains that 'the doctrine of Forms finds no place at all in any work of Plato later than the *Parmenides*'.[1] How much alteration there must be before we say that the theory is 'fundamentally altered' or 'abandoned' is, of course, a pretty problem. Stenzel sees a change from the form as a 'representative intuition' to the Form as something approaching a 'concept', but he would certainly not have wanted to say that Plato had abandoned his theory of Forms. So far as verbal expressions are concerned the language still occurs in the later dialogues which was used in the earlier in connection with

[1] Burnet, *Platonism*, p. 120. Cf. also p. 119, 'in the *Laws* there is no trace of the theory of "ideas" '.

the theory of Forms. This is true even of the *Laws*, e.g. 965b–c where there is the familiar contrast of the one and the many, and the necessity is insisted on of being able πρὸς μίαν ἰδέαν ἐκ τῶν πολλῶν καὶ ἀνομοίων . . . βλέπειν. Too much cannot be made of verbal similarities and we have Lewis Campbell's warning that 'in Plato ... philosophical terminology is incipient, tentative, transitional'.[1] Still, they are there. Further, some of the familar notions of the earlier dialogues are there too, e.g. knowledge and Forms, opinion and sensibles, and so on. The theory may have evolved, but the evidence suggests that there is enough left both linguistically and in content to make it rash to say that Plato had abandoned it. If, however, we are not prepared to say that Plato abandoned the Forms, we cannot adopt the device of reconciling Professor Ryle's interpretation of the arguments in the *Theaetetus* with the theory of Forms by the simple procedure of annihilating the latter.

A third possibility suggests itself, arising out of some things Mr. Robinson has said. His interpretation of this part of the *Theaetetus* is this—and here I quote from his article 'Forms and Error in Plato's *Theaetetus*' (*Phil. Rev.*, lix, (1950), 16): 'Here at the end of the *Theaetetus* he (Plato) offers strong arguments to show that logos does not entail knowledge, and, much worse, that some aloga must be knowable if there is any knowledge at all.' On the other hand, just above he has pointed out that is was 'one of Plato's own favourite doctrines', both before and after the *Theaetetus*, 'that knowledge entails logos'. Now two things about this. First, it is clear that Mr. Robinson interprets this part of the *Theaetetus* differently from Professor Ryle—he treats it as a sort of *reductio ad absurdum* argument in favour of the conclusion that 'a thing's being alogon does not make it unknowable'. Thus on page 15 he writes: 'the examination of the three senses of "logos" is immediately preceded by a discussion of uncompounded elements, the tendency of which is to conclude that, if elements are unknowable because they have no logos, everything is unknowable, from which anyone who thought that knowledge does occur would have to conclude that a thing's being alogon does not make it unknowable.' I myself am prepared to reject this interpretation and accept Professor Ryle's, partly for reasons which will, I hope, be obvious later, partly because within the *Theaetetus* passage itself

[1] *Plato's Republic*, Jowett and Campbell, vol. ii, p. 292.

the emphasis of the argument seems to be not that we should substitute for the low-grade 'pool' atoms of the sensationalist new high-grade 'branded' atoms, but that no sort of atoms or atomistic nameables will do. Secondly, Mr. Robinson reconciles his own interpretation with his admission that it continues to be a favourite doctrine of Plato elsewhere that knowledge entails logos, by the suggestion that this is a smaller example of what we find in the *Parmenides*—'namely a searching critique of one of Plato's own favourite doctrines, which he nevertheless continued to hold after writing the critique in spite of the fact that he does not appear ever to have discovered the answer to it'. We might then, while rejecting Mr. Robinson's interpretation of the argument, accept this self-criticism explanation for our own interpretation. We would then say that the doctrine of Forms does lead to the logical atomist difficulties which Plato exposed in the *Theaetetus*. Plato had no answer to these difficulties, but still went on holding his doctrine. But while it may be that there are parts of Plato's writing which defy any other explanation, this self-criticism story cannot but create some feeling of uneasiness. If a philosopher exposes damaging difficulties in central doctrines that he holds, and nevertheless, and this is the important point, apparently continues to hold them without ever answering the difficulties, his procedure is, to say the least, puzzling, and in the end might lead us to suspect his credentials. It looks then as though the self-criticism explanation should be adopted only in default of a better. There is, however, in the present case a fourth possibility. Professor Ryle's argument was that 'if the doctrine of Forms was the view that these verbs, adjectives and common nouns are themselves the names of simple, if lofty, nameables, then Socrates's criticism of logical atomism is . . . a criticism of the doctrine of Forms'. If we are already convinced that this *was* the doctrine of Forms, and if we accept, as I have been prepared to do, Professor Ryle's interpretation of the implications of the passage for that doctrine, it looks as if we must perforce fall back on the self-criticism explanation. But if on other grounds we were not so sure that this was the doctrine of Forms, the *Theaetetus* passage would encourage us further to see if the theory of Forms is not capable of a different interpretation. I want to suggest some other grounds for hesitation in accepting the interpretation of the doctrine of Forms indicated in the quotation from Professor Ryle.

Before, however, we come to these, let us first state the interpretation somewhat more fully.

It would maintain (no doubt among other things) that on Plato's view, apart from proper names, which stand for particulars, other substantives, adjectives, prepositions, and verbs stand for Forms or universals, are the names of these. Ross puts this clearly when he says: 'The essence of the theory of Ideas lay in the conscious recognition of the fact that there is a class of entities, for which the best name is probably "universals", that are entirely different from sensible things. Any use of language involves the recognition, either conscious or unconscious, of the fact that there are such entities; for every word used, except proper names—every abstract noun, every general noun, every adjective, every verb, even every pronoun and every preposition—is a name for something of which there are or may be instances.'[1] These universals exist timelessly in their own right apart from the sensible world; they are 'real entities', 'substances' (the phrases are from Professor Cherniss);[2] and to know them is, or involves some form of immediate apprehension in which we are directly acquainted with them. In Professor Cherniss's words again 'the special faculty of knowledge is characterised by direct contact of subject and object'.[3] This is the interpretation of some of the essential features of the theory of Forms that is to be found, whether explicitly or implicitly, in the writings of a large number of the most distinguished modern Platonists—Ross, Cherniss, Taylor, I think Cornford, and many others. In fact, it is accepted orthodoxy. Two things may be said about it. First, it must be allowed that there is much in Plato's actual language that could be construed to support this interpretation. Secondly, if this is what Plato was saying, the theory of Forms is less illuminating than perhaps it once seemed. This remark is, of course, irrelevant to the question of the correctness of the interpretation, but it is worth making for this reason. A number (and I suspect a large number) of the propounders of this interpretation—and Ross is a clear and distinguished example of this—have not merely believed that this is what Plato meant by his theory, but that it is, by and large, a good theory. If it can be

[1] W. D. Ross, *Plato's Theory of Ideas*, p. 225.

[2] 'The Philosophical Economy of the Theory of Ideas', *Amer. Journ. of Phil.*, vol. lvii, 1936, pp. 452, 456. See above, pp. 8, 11.

[3] Loc. cit., p. 452. See above, p. 8.

seen, and I think it can be seen, that as a theory it is unworkable and in the strict and non-abusive use of the word largely meaningless, we may be the less inclined to father it on Plato unless we must, and the more inclined to re-examine what he actually says. Since the merits of the orthodox interpretation as a piece of philosophy are irrelevant to the question of whether it is the correct interpretation, it would be out of place here to elaborate its demerits. It is enough to say that the suggestion that it is an unworkable and largely meaningless theory arises not merely from the logical atomist difficulties developed from the *Theaetetus*, but from many other considerations as well—e.g. to mention only one, the difficulty of giving any cash value to a phrase like 'timeless substantial entities'. I repeat, however, that the merits or demerits of the theory are strictly irrelevant to its correctness as a piece of interpretation. There are, however, things in Plato that seem to me to suggest that he may have had other ideas in mind, and I shall now try to mention a few of them, turning first to the *Meno*.

Meno opens the dialogue by raising certain questions about the the acquiring of virtue, and Socrates says he cannot possibly answer them until he knows what virtue is—*τί ἐστιν ἀρετή*. Meno thinks this an easy question and proceeds to enumerate the virtues of a man, of a woman, and so on. Socrates objects (72a-b) that this is to give him a swarm of virtues when he asks for one, and carrying on the figure of the swarm points out that when the question is about the nature of the bee it is not a proper answer to say that there are many kinds of bees. Bees do not differ from one another as bees, as Meno readily admits, and what the questioner wants to know is what this is in respect to which they do not differ, but are all alike—*ᾧ οὐδὲν διαφέρουσιν ἀλλὰ ταὐτόν εἰσιν ἅπασαι, τί τοῦτο φῂς εἶναι*; Similarly with the virtues—they have all one common form which makes them virtues, and on this he who would answer the question, what is virtue, would do well to keep his eye fixed. (*ἕν γέ τι εἶδος ταὐτὸν ἅπασαι ἔχουσι δι' ὃ εἰσὶν ἀρεταί, εἰς ὃ καλῶς που ἔχει ἀποβλέψαντα τὸν ἀποκρινόμενον τῷ ἐρωτήσαντι ἐκεῖνο δηλῶσαι, ὃ τυγχάνει οὖσα ἀρετή* (72c).) Meno is still not altogether clear about the existence of a common characteristic in the case of virtue, though he seems not to feel any difficulty in other cases—74a-b *οὐ γὰρ δύναμαί πω, ὦ Σώκρατες, ὡς σὺ ζητεῖς μίαν ἀρετὴν λαβεῖν κατὰ πάντων, ὥσπερ ἐν τοῖς ἄλλοις*. Socrates explains further by taking the example of figure. What we want to know here is what that is which is common to the round, the straight, and all the other figures—*τί ἐστιν ἐπὶ τῷ στρογγύλῳ καὶ εὐθεῖ καὶ ἐπὶ τοῖς ἄλλοις, ἃ δὴ σχήματα καλεῖς, ταὐτὸν ἐπὶ πᾶσιν;* (75a). Socrates then gives two answers to this question *τί ἐστι σχῆμα*, either of which he would regard as a satisfactory reply to the question. The first is that figure is the only thing which always follows colour (75b), and he adds that he himself would be satisfied if Meno would give him an answer of the same sort about virtue. Meno asks what answer Socrates would have given if a person were to say that he did not know what colour was, and Socrates then produces his second answer (76a), that figure is the limit of a solid. This is the sort of answer he wants to this sort of 'what is it' question; and Meno is encouraged to try, with no more success than before, to produce a similar type of answer to the question 'What is virtue?'.

Now there are three points of interest in this section of the *Meno*. First, Meno himself is not represented in the dialogue as being particularly acute or particularly skilled in philosophy—rather the reverse. Yet he does not seem to find any difficulty or anything particularly striking in the fact that we do use a word like 'bee' or 'figure' as a general term for any one of a group of particulars. No fuss seems to be made on this point either by Meno or Socrates. They both just seem to take it for granted that we do use words that way, or, to use the language of the present context, that there is something common to a group of particulars which are called by one name. Yet this something common is, on the orthodox view of the theory of Forms, a 'universal', and the discovery of universals and their relation to particulars is hailed as one of the achievements of the theory. But neither Meno nor Socrates seem much interested in this revelation. It is true that Meno is not so sure (73a) that virtue will be the same in a child as in an adult, in a woman as in a man, but his worry is apparently confined to the special case of virtue. He seems to have no difficulty over the one and the many elsewhere (cf. 74a–b quoted above). Secondly, what he has difficulty over, and what both he and Socrates are interested in, is in trying to discover what this one, in the case of each group of particulars—bees, figures, virtues—is. The whole emphasis is on this—i.e. not on the point that there is one over against the many, but on what this one, in the case of each group of particulars, is. Thirdly, Socrates by the example of 'figure' illustrates the way in which he expects Meno to cope with this 'what is it' question. If he is asked 'what is figure?' the appropriate response is to say that, e.g. figure is the only thing which always follows colour, i.e. to use deliberately vague language, the appropriate response is to say something, to tell the questioner something, to make some sort of statement.

Now in all this the *Meno* is in no way peculiar. This 'What is X?' question appears in the *Republic*—'What is justice?', in the *Theaetetus*—'What is knowledge?', in the *Sophist*—'What is a sophist?', and so on, as well as in many of the early dialogues, and it is quite plain that Plato attaches the greatest importance to it. In the *Theaetetus* too, Theaetetus makes just the same sort of mistake as Meno does—when asked what knowledge is, he enumerates the different sorts of knowledge—knowledge of geometry, of cobbling, of carpentry, and so on, and Socrates makes just the same objection—146d 'you are generous indeed, my dear Theaetetus—so open-handed that, when you are asked for one simple thing, you offer a whole variety'. Further, here too Socrates, after remarking at 147b that a man cannot understand the name of a thing when he does not know what that thing is, gives an illustration of the sort of answer he wants; if he is asked what clay is, the simple and ordinary thing to say is that clay is earth mixed with moisture (147c). Theaetetus mentions a mathematical example, where he has been able to do this sort of thing in the case of roots (δυνάμεις), and Socrates exhorts him similarly περὶ ἐπιστήμης λαβεῖν λόγον τί ποτε τυγχάνει ὄν (148d) adding, in what I think an important remark, 'just as you found a single character to embrace these many roots, so now try to find a single logos that applies to the many kinds of knowledge'—ὥσπερ ταύτας πολλὰς οὔσας ἑνὶ εἴδει περιέλαβες, οὕτω καὶ τὰς πολλὰς ἐπιστήμας ἑνὶ λόγῳ προσειπεῖν (148d). Mr. Robinson in *Plato's Earlier Dialectic*, chapter 5 has some excellent remarks on the pitfalls and the vagueness of the 'What is X?' question. As he has shown, unless the question is put in some specific context, a number of quite different answers to it would all be equally legitimate, and as he says, quoting from G. E. Moore, 'the vague form "What-is-X?" is an especial temptation "to answer questions, without first discovering precisely *what* question it is you desire to answer" '.[1] The important thing for our present purposes is that there is evidence both in the *Meno* and elsewhere that when Plato asks this 'What is X?' question, e.g. as in the *Meno* 'What is virtue?', he will be far from content with the announcement that 'there is a Form of virtue' or that 'virtue is a Form or universal', or that 'there are Forms as well as particulars, and virtue is a Form'. As I pointed out above both Meno and Socrates make practically no fuss at all of the point that there is an εἶδος for the group. To keep telling them that there is would be merely infuriating. This is not to deny that Plato elsewhere also raises what might be called status questions in connection with Forms in general—questions about their separation from particulars and so on. But it is quite clear in the *Meno* and elsewhere that when he asks this 'What is X?' question, he is taking it for granted that there is a form of X, and wanting to know what that form is. And as I have already insisted, from what he says it seems that he hopes to achieve this coming to know the Form by way of statements, logoi. I suggest, therefore, that it is misleading when Shorey writes: 'except in purely mythical passages, Plato does not attempt to describe the ideas any more than Kant describes the Ding-an-sich or Spencer the "unknowable". He does not tell us what they are, but that they are.'[2] From the early dialogues to the late it is, I suggest, one of Plato's main motifs to try to tell what the εἴδη are. It may be that he never succeeds, but failure to emphasise that that is certainly one of the things he is trying to do, and that he hopes to do it by logoi, is liable to lead to the obscuring of an important element in this theory. In fact it leads to the orthodox view that Plato has discovered, and is well satisfied with the discovery of, universals—good sound entities of only too too solid flesh, of which words are names, and of which the fundamental mode of awareness is some kind of direct insight, Professor Cherniss's 'direct contact of subject and object' or Russell's 'knowledge by acquaintance'.

Now in connection with this notion of knowledge by acquaintance in Plato, Diotima's speech in the *Symposium*, which is usually taken as embodying views of Socrates or Plato, is of interest. As befits the speech of a priestess, it is highly enthusiastic, and here, if anywhere, we would expect the language of insight or direct contact or acquaintance. And this is what we do in fact find when

[1] Op. cit. (first edition), p. 62. [2] *Unity of Plato's Thought*, p. 28.

Diotima describes how the soul after a long training comes to see beauty itself. It is a sudden vision—*πρὸς τέλος ἤδη ἰὼν τῶν ἐρωτικῶν ἐξαίφνης κατόψεταί τι θαυμαστὸν τὴν φύσιν καλόν* (210e), an act of contemplation and communion *θεωμένου καὶ συνόντος αὐτῷ* (212a). What is of interest, however, is that this moment of acquaintance with beauty itself, the goal of human life, is so strongly marked off from all ordinary experience. In particular in 211a, where this supreme beauty is being described, we are told that of this there is *οὐδέ τις λόγος οὐδέ τις ἐπιστήμη*—there is no logos of it and no knowledge of it. The suggestion is that it is above knowledge in any ordinary sense, and that with knowledge in its ordinary sense there always goes a logos. Beauty itself, on the other hand, is nameable, but not in any ordinary sense knowable. It is true that in the same passage there is a reference to a *μάθημα* of *αὐτὸ τὸ κάλον*, but here again this quite special *μάθημα* is distinguished from what are ordinarily known as *μαθήματα*—*ἀπὸ τῶν μαθημάτων* (not *τῶν ἀλλῶν μαθημάτων*) *ἐπ' ἐκεῖνο τὸ μάθημα τελευτῆσαι* (211c); true also that there is a reference to the vision of a 'single science, if it may be called that', which is of beauty itself, but this special sort of science or knowledge is marked off from knowledge or the sciences as ordinarily meant, and from the logoi to which the lover of wisdom is usually confined—*πολλοὺς καὶ καλοὺς λόγους καὶ μεγαλοπρεπεῖς τίκτῃ καὶ διανοήματα ἐν φιλοσοφίᾳ ἀφθόνῳ, ἕως ἂν ἐνταῦθα ῥωσθεὶς καὶ αὐξηθεὶς κατίδῃ τινα ἐπιστήμην μίαν τοιαύτην, ἥ ἐστι καλοῦ τοιοῦδε* (210d). I agree with Festugière[1] that this *μάθημα* and this *ἐπιστήμη* belong only to the moment of *ἐποπτεία* and go beyond the ordinary norms of knowledge. Ordinarily knowledge and logos go hand in hand, and of the ideal beauty *οὐδέ τις λόγος οὐδέ τις ἐπιστήμη*. If we like we can call this special knowledge of *αὐτὸ τὸ καλόν* knowledge by acquaintance, and there is no reason why we should grudge Plato his special moments of acquaintance. But these are not ordinary moments, nor is the knowledge the knowledge with which he is usually concerned. The knowledge that interests him in his non-enthusiastic moments is the knowledge in which logos is inextricably involved; it is of this knowledge that he primarily speaks in connection with the Forms; and it is not, I contend, knowledge by acquaintance. The point is frequently made that 'Plato constantly uses metaphorical

[1] Festugière, *Contemplation et Vie Contemplative selon Platon*, p. 231 (especially note (2)).

expressions taken from the senses of sight and touch to denote the immediate character of his highest knowledge'.[1] Lutoslawski, e.g., from whom I have just quoted, cites ἰδεῖν, ἅπτεσθαι, ὁρᾶν, and so on from the *Republic*. This is a fair and scholarly point, but too much can be made of it. We too, in our language, talk, for example, of 'seeing' a problem, 'handling' it, 'grasping' it, 'grappling' with it, and so on, without wishing to convey anything about 'the immediate character of our highest knowedge' of the problem. Two examples may perhaps suffice to show how difficult it is to rely too much on Plato's 'seeing' and 'touching' language. Professor Cherniss, in his article in *American Journal of Philology*, to which I have already referred, in explaining the passage in the *Meno* 81d, where Socrates produces his theory of learning as recollection, says that on Socrates's hypothesis 'learning or discovering is really recollection of that which has already been directly known', italicising 'directly'; and in a footnote he adds 'note the word used for acquiring knowledge in the first place: ἑωρακυῖα (81c6)'.[2] But it should also be noted that four lines below Socrates remarks that it is not strange if the soul can remember what it knew before, where the Greek is οἷον τ' εἶναι αὐτὴν ἀναμνησθῆναι, ἅ γε καὶ πρότερον ἠπίστατο where the verb ἐπίστασθαι would not suggest direct knowledge by acquaintance. Again Lutoslawski[3] quotes ἅπτεσθαι in *Republic* 511b as an example of the metaphorical use of sight and touch expressions to convey the notion of immediate knowledge; but in the passage, which runs τοῦτο (this segment of the line) οὗ αὐτὸς ὁ λόγος ἅπτεται τῇ τοῦ διαλέγεσθαι δυνάμει the emphasis seems to be on hard argument rather than immediate knowledge, and to press the metaphor in ἅπτεσθαι coming as it does between λόγος and διαλέγεσθαι seems highly dubious. The truth seems to be that here, as I think often in Plato, it is dangerous to make too much of the particular linguistic expressions he uses. This linguistic argument then is not decisive enough to lead to our abandoning the contention that in Plato knowledge and logos go together, and that, except in exceptional cases like αὐτὸ τὸ καλόν which he specially marks off for us, he is not relying on the device of knowledge by acquaintance.

Two further points require attention. First, it must be stressed

[1] Lutoslawski, *Origin and Growth of Plato's Logic*, p. 294.

[2] Op. cit., p. 448; above, p. 4. [3] Op. cit., p. 294.

how constantly throughout the dialogues knowledge, forms, and logos turn up together. We have already seen this in the *Meno* and have noted the ἐπιστήμη-λόγος connection in the *Symposium*. The same is true in the *Phaedo*, e.g. 78d αὐτὴ ἡ οὐσία ἧς λόγον δίδομεν τοῦ εἶναι καὶ ἐρωτῶντες καὶ ἀποκρινόμενοι, or again the famous passage 99e ff: ἔδοξε δή μοι χρῆναι εἰς τοὺς λόγους καταφυγόντα ἐν ἐκείνοις σκοπεῖν τῶν ὀντῶν τὴν ἀλήθειαν, and so on; similarly in the *Republic*, cf. e.g. the description of the dialectician 534b: ἦ καὶ διαλεκτικὸν καλεῖς τὸν λόγον ἑκάστου λαμβάνοντα τῆς οὐσίας; καὶ τὸν μὴ ἔχοντα, καθ' ὅσον ἂν μὴ ἔχῃ λόγον αὑτῷ τε καὶ ἄλλῳ διδόναι, κατὰ τοσοῦτον νοῦν περὶ τούτου οὐ φήσεις ἔχειν; so again in the *Theaetetus*, e.g. 148d in discussing knowledge Theaetetus is told προθυμήθητι . . . λαβεῖν λόγον τί ποτε τυγχάνει ὄν; in the *Parmenides*, e.g. at the beginning of the exercise (135e) where Parmenides says that the exercise must not be directed to visibles but forms—ἀλλὰ περὶ ἐκεῖνα ἃ μάλιστά τις ἂν λόγῳ λάβοι καὶ εἴδη ἂν ἡγήσαιτο εἶναι; *Sophist* 260a τούτου (sc. τοῦ λόγου) γὰρ στερηθέντες, τὸ μὲν μέγιστον, φιλοσοφίας ἂν στερηθεῖμεν; *Politicus* 266d τῇ τοιᾷδε μεθόδῳ τῶν λόγων and 286a διὸ δεῖ μελετᾶν λόγον ἑκάστου δυνατὸν εἶναι δοῦναι καὶ δέξασθαι· τὰ γὰρ ἀσώματα, κάλλιστα ὄντα καὶ μέγιστα, λόγῳ μόνον ἄλλῳ δὲ οὐδενὶ σαφῶς δείκνυται. It would be tedious to continue this list into the later dialogues. As Mr. Robinson says in the article I mentioned earlier 'it was one of his (Plato's) firm convictions . . . that knowledge entails logos'. This trinity of knowledge, forms, logos appears throughout. Further, where Mr. Robinson shortly afterwards refers to 'the big matter of the Forms' and 'this little matter of logos', I want to insist that 'this little matter of logos' is just as big as 'the big matter of the Forms'—in fact, that the two are of equal importance and cannot be separated.

Secondly, before I try to amplify this, a little must be said about logos itself. I want to translate this word in a wide and indefinite way, keeping it closely connected with the verb λέγειν as 'to tell', 'state', 'say', and translating it as something like 'discourse' or 'statement' in a very wide sense in which hypothesis e.g. would be included. It would be foolish indeed to say that this is *the* meaning of logos in Plato; but perhaps less foolish, in tracing the intricacies of his use of the word, to insist on remembering the saying and statement connection. Brice Parain in his book *Essai sur le Logos Platonicien*, from which I have borrowed suggestions in what follows, suggests the translation 'opération de langage'[1]—I suppose 'linguistic operation'. This seems to me to have certain objections —in particular that one might call 'naming' a linguistic operation, whereas I want in Plato to attach logos to saying—but I agree with him in trying, if one likes as a hypothesis, but I think a salutary one, to keep logos, to put it vaguely, in the domain of language, and in emphasising the point he makes that 'le logos est un phénomène de langage'.[2] It is perhaps worth noting, as Parain does, that where Plato himself defines or describes logos (at *Crat.* 431b, *Tht.* 202b, *Soph.* 262d) he keeps it to the linguistic domain —e.g. in the *Cratylus* a σύνθεσις of ῥήματα καὶ ὀνόματα; though I do not think too much can be made of this, since the context in these passages demands some linguistic sense. More important are Aristotle's references to the Platonists, for example, as οἱ ἐν τοῖς λόγοις *Met.* 1050b 35—'the people who occupy themselves with verbal discussions' (Ross) (cf. 987b 31 of Plato: διὰ τὴν ἐν τοῖς λόγοις . . . σκέψιν (οἱ γὰρ πρότεροι διαλεκτικῆς οὐ μετεῖχον)); or again the interesting passage in Book XII of the *Metaphysics*, 1069a 28 ff. where he remarks that 'the thinkers of the present day (Ross says "evidently the Platonists") tend to rank universals as substances (for genera are universals, and these they tend to describe as principles and substances, owing to the abstract nature of their inquiry)'—δὶα τὸ λογικῶς ζητεῖν, where a better translation might be 'through pursuing their inquiry by means of logoi—cf. the οἱ ἐν τοῖς λόγοις in *Met.* 1050b 35 quoted above. What is of interest here is that Aristotle is contrasting people who get down to the brass tacks of things, with the Platonists who interest themselves in talk. It is also very clear that λογικῶς does not mean 'logically' in the sense of 'rationally', as though the others with whom he contrasts the Platonists proceeded irrationally in the sense of being poor at reasoning. To connect logos in Plato too closely with 'reason' or 'thought' seems to me likely dangerously to obscure the point of what he is saying. Jowett is an arch-offender in this,[3] and I give three examples which are important in themselves: (1) *Phd.* 99e εἰς τοὺς λόγους καταφυγόντα ἐν ἐκείνοις σκοπεῖν τῶν ὄντων τὴν ἀλήθειαν; Jowett's translation: 'I had better have recourse to the world of mind and seek there the

[1] p. 10. [2] Op. cit., p. 200.

[3] References are to *The Dialogues of Plato*, translated by B. Jowett (third edition).

truth of existence', where I should want to translate 'I had better have recourse to statements, etc.' (2) *Parm.* 135e περὶ ἐκεῖνα ἃ μάλιστά τις ἂν λόγῳ λάβοι καὶ εἴδη ἂν ἡγήσαιτο εἶναι; Jowett 'in reference to objects of thought, and to what may be called ideas', and my translation 'in reference to those things which are especially grasped by statement' (or 'discourse' (Cornford)) and etc. (3) *Pol.* 286a τὰ γὰρ ἀσώματα, κάλλιστα ὄντα καὶ μέγιστα, λόγῳ μόνον ἄλλῳ δὲ οὐδενὶ σαφῶς δείκνυται: Jowett 'for immaterial things, which are the noblest and greatest, are shown only in thought and idea, and in no other way', and the suggested translation 'are shown only in discourse (or statement), and in no other way'. All these translations of Jowett's blur what I think is the essential point, namely, the connection of knowledge, forms, and statement.

I shall now try to sum up, and set my suggested interpretation of the theory of forms over against the orthodox view. What lay at the basis of that view was, I said, the notion of the forms as simple nameables known ultimately by acquaintance. Now let us go right back to the *Meno* and take the very simple example there which we discussed in detail, when Plato asks what is figure, i.e. asks for the εἶδος of figure. How does he think this request should be met? Not, it is clear, by, as it were, holding up a substantial entity and saying: now look at this, this is named 'figure', have a good look at it, get thoroughly acquainted with it, and then you will know figure. Not at all. The move in giving the εἶδος of figure, in answering the question 'What is figure?', is to make a statement—'figure is the limit of a solid', and this is regarded as a satisfactory answer. The εἶδος of figure has been displayed in the logos, and displayed in the predicate of the logos. It is the same in the passage I quoted earlier from the *Theaetetus* where Theaetetus is proud of finding an εἶδος of mathematical roots, and Socrates says ὥσπερ ταύτας πολλὰς οὔσας ἑνὶ εἴδει περιέλαβες, οὕτω καὶ τὰς πολλὰς ἐπιστήμας ἑνὶ λόγῳ προσειπεῖν. Cornford translates 'just as you found a single character to embrace all that multitude, so now try to find a single formula that applies to the many kinds of knowledge'. It will be noticed that ἑνὶ λόγῳ is parallel with ἑνὶ εἴδει, i.e. to give an εἶδος involves giving a logos which embodies, using Cornford's word, 'a formula'. Thus we might say that a form, so far from being 'a substantial entity', is much more like 'a formula'. It is the logical predicate in a logos, not the logical subject. It is what is said of something, not something about which something else is said. Thus it would be incorrect to say that we talk about εἴδη, but correct to say that we talk with εἴδη, and logoi, pieces of talk, are are necessary to display εἴδη to us.

A. E. Taylor in his Varia Socratica essay on the words εἶδος, ἰδέα (*Varia Socratica*, pp. 178 ff.) tried to show that in the Hippocratic writings εἶδος came to mean 'primary body', 'element', and, to quote Taylor himself, *Varia Socratica*, p. 243 'often appears to take on the associations we should connect with such terms as "monad", "thing in itself", "real essence", "simple real" '; and he believed Plato was influenced in his use of the word by these associations (pp. 243 ff.). Without going into the evidence here, I should myself say that, as Gillespie showed,[1] Taylor was wrong in seeing any meaning like 'simple real', 'thing in itself' in the Hippocratic use. An εἶδος there was an εἶδος *of* something, not a simple real. Ross in his introduction to his edition of Aristotle's *Metaphysics* seems to approve of Gillespie's view, and adds that 'as regards Plato's usage it is important to notice that both words as used by him employ a dependent genitive, and he speaks of "the Forms" with an implied reference to the things of which they are the Forms';[2] and H. C. Baldry (in the *Classical Quarterly*, vol. xxxi, 1937, pp. 141–150) while agreeing with Gillespie detects a fairly general use of εἶδος and ἰδέα for 'quality'. Of course argument from the Hippocratic use cannot be pressed, because Plato may have been uninfluenced by this use, or have deliberately given εἶδος a new use. Still it is curious that Ross, with his insistence in the passage quoted that εἶδος implies a dependent genitive, i.e. cannot function in its own right, should then go on to say in the next sentence 'the Forms are for Plato simple entities, but that is not what the word *means*'. If, however, the word εἶδος always requires or implies a dependent genitive, and if Baldry is right in detecting a use where εἶδος means quality, I suggest that in both cases we might expect that an εἶδος would function as a logical predicate, not as a logical subject; and I suggest that that is what it does in Plato.

Suppose then that when we ask, what is figure or what is

[1] *Class. Quart.*, vol. vi, 1912, pp. 179 ff.: cf. especially p. 200, 'There is no case in which the word is an absolute name; it always requires a dependent genitive to complete its meaning.'

[2] Op. cit., p. xlviii.

virtue or what is justice, i.e. when we ask for the εἶδος of any of these, the correct move is to produce a logos, in the predicate of which the εἶδος is displayed—suppose, that is, taking the rough illustration of figure which Plato uses, that when we ask what is figure, what is the εἶδος of figure, the correct move is to make the statement 'figure is the boundary of a solid', where the εἶδος of figure is displayed in the predicate of the statement. An interesting question now arises about the logical subject, about what the statement is about. We are clear that the logos is not about the Form figure. The Form is displayed in the predicate. The question then is still on our hands, and the simple and unsuspecting answer still seems to be that it is about figure, justice, and so on. But this tends to prompt the old question: what is figure, what is justice, and to start us again on the old process, in which we make a statement where the answer to the question is in the predicate of the statement which displays the Form of whatever is under discussion. When then we say that the sentence is about figure or about justice it looks as if what we must mean is that the sentence is about the word 'figure', 'justice', and so on. But then, of course, the whole process is ceasing to be 'real definition' and is becoming like 'nominal definition'—not, that is, defining a thing, justice—the thing justice has slid away into the predicate—but defining the word 'justice'. In this way we will arrive at necessary statements, but necessary because logically necessary, because it would be self-contradictory to deny them. They will no longer be truths about things, but logical truths about the way we talk about things. The 'What is X?' question is inherently ambiguous from the start. It may mean tell me about the thing X, or it may mean tell me about the word X—and Plato never clears up the ambiguity. I think it is pretty clear that he sets out with the idea that it is a 'thing' question, in some sense of thing; but it is also clear that he sets out with the determination to reach certainty, and if you want certainty you must pay its logical price.

This is, however, in some degree a digression. The main argument has been that in the end the forms are logical predicates displayed in logoi and not simple nameables known by acquaintance. This is not to deny that there are many things Plato says that can be construed to fit the 'simple nameables' view; and in particular I am not pretending that the view of the Forms as logical predicates displayed in logoi is to be found explicitly formulated in Plato. Indeed, at any rate in the earlier dialogues, before he had begun his conscious examination in the *Theaetetus* and *Sophist* of the notion of logos, with its attendant notions of subject and predicate, he could hardly have had even the technical equipment for such a formulation. I have argued, however, that the view is there implicitly in the way in which Plato actually develops and operates with the theory of Forms. It might be suggested that it was because he himself was becoming conscious of this aspect of the theory that he felt it to be immune from the criticism of logical atomism in the *Theaetetus*. This might also help to explain why the Forms are apparently not jettisoned as a result of the criticisms in the *Parmenides*, which I should be tempted to take as an essay, in both its parts, in the folly of taking forms as simple reals and trying to talk about them as such—an essay directed as much perhaps to clearing Plato's own mind as to the instruction of his readers. However this may be, I suggest that the prominence throughout the dialogues of the logos-knowledge-Forms combination merits more attention than it has perhaps received.

Finally, since I have put the theory of Forms very much in the context of language and logic I append without elaboration four considerations which I think should be kept in mind in dealing with Plato:

(*a*) It is clear that there were many puzzles common at the time which at any rate in part were logical puzzles about language—the sort of puzzles raised by Parmenides, Gorgias, Protagoras, Antisthenes, and others; clear also from the *Euthydemus* onward that Plato was familiar with these puzzles.

(*b*) Throughout Plato there are clear indications of the influence of the Socratic elenchus, of the procedure of question and answer as the method of attaining Knowledge. But if this is to proceed, it must proceed by logoi, and the apparatus of simple nameables known by acquaintance seems an alien ingression.

(*c*) Plato was clearly interested in mathematics. But here again logoi and deductive procedures, and not simple entities known by acquaintance, seem to be what is wanted. He himself, for example, in the *Republic* seems to envisage deriving Forms by some process of deductive argument. This would seem to indicate that Forms cannot be simple entities. For how could simple entities be either the premises or the conclusion of any sort of argument?

(*d*) It has to be remembered, perhaps at times with regret, that Plato has an affection for the material mode of speech, and for existential propositions. If we ourselves are to understand his meaning, we must discount these to some extent, though to what extent is a difficult point. It may be that I have over-discounted.

III

LOGOS AND FORMS IN PLATO: A REPLY TO PROFESSOR CROSS (1956)

R. S. Bluck

IN an interesting article in *Mind*, (vol. lxiii, no. 252, October 1954 (see above, II)), Professor Cross raises a problem of considerable importance and says some very interesting things about it, but he is led to propound a view of Plato's Forms that seems to me untenable. To this I should like to reply.

Professor Cross begins by referring to *Tht.*, 202d sq., where Socrates argues that if a logos is simply the names that compose it, and each 'name' is the name of a simple and therefore unknowable element, then the logos is a mere congeries of unknowables, while if the logos is something more, a new linguistic unit, it will itself be a new simple, and therefore unknowable; and he quotes Professor Ryle as saying that 'if the doctrine of Forms was the view that these verbs, adjectives and common nouns are themselves the names of simple, if lofty, nameables, then Socrates' criticism is, *per accidens*, a criticism of the doctrine of Forms, whether Plato realised this or not', and again that 'if a Form is a simple object or a logical subject of predication, no matter how sublime, then its verbal expression will be a name and not a sentence; and if so, then it will not be false but nonsense to speak of anyone knowing it (savoir) or not knowing it'. Cross seeks to avoid the conclusion by denying the premiss, which he identifies with the view (described as 'accepted orthodoxy') that Platonic Forms are 'universals' which 'exist timelessly in their own right apart from the sensible world' as 'real entities' or 'substances', and are known by a kind of immediate apprehension or 'knowledge by acquaintance'.

He gives reasons for abandoning that view, and for interpreting the Forms instead as 'logical predicates displayed in logoi'. That is to say, when in answer to a 'What is X?' question an answer is given (or supposed to be giveable) in the form of the logos (X is so-and-so), the εἶδος or Form is given us in the predicate. 'We might say', says Cross (p. 447; above, p. 27), 'that a Form, so far from being a "substantial entity", is much more like "a formula".'

I wish first to raise certain positive objections to Cross' view of the Forms, and then to consider the reasons that have led him to his new interpretation. I hope to show that these reasons are invalid, and even that in some instances the evidence here too points positively to an opposite conclusion. I shall leave to the last the difficulty raised by Professor Ryle, and then offer my own solution of it.

We may begin by asking exactly what it is that Cross wants to interpret as the predicate of a statement. Is it what Plato calls the εἶδος of something, or is it what Plato means when he talks, for example, about αὐτὸ τὸ δίκαιον? Or is the εἶδος of τὸ δίκαιον the same as αὐτὸ τὸ δίκαιον? Cross insists (p. 448; above, p. 28) that an εἶδος is an εἶδος *of* something, and always requires or implies a dependent genitive; and *this* is what, in his view, should function as a logical predicate and not as a logical subject. That *of which* it is an εἶδος, the logical subject (e.g. τὸ δίκαιον), is something different. But when Cross comes to face the question, 'What then is the logical subject?', he can offer no satisfactory reply. On his theory that 'the logos is not about the Form figure. The Form is displayed in the predicate', he can only suggest that 'when we say that the sentence is about figure or about justice it looks as if what we must mean is that the sentence is about the word "figure", "justice", and so on . . . logical truths about the way we talk about things'. He admits, indeed, that Plato seems clearly to have thought that he was dealing with 'things' (in fact, what we define is an οὐσία, according to *Phaedo*, 78d); but he then leaves this matter as 'in some sense a digression'. Now Plato, I suggest, regarded αὐτὸ τὸ X as being the εἶδος of X, and if so Cross' conception of the εἶδος must be wrong. The identification appears clearly in certain passages. In the *Phaedo*, at 100b, it is suggested εἶναί τι καλὸν αὐτὸ καθ' αὑτὸ καὶ ἀγαθὸν καὶ μέγα καὶ τἆλλα πάντα, and then, immediately after discussion of the causal nature of these entities, we read at 102a–b, ἐπεὶ . . . ὡμολογεῖτο εἶναί τι ἕκαστον τῶν εἰδῶν. Then at 103e, after discussion of πῦρ in conjunction with τὸ θερμόν and χιών in conjunction with τὸ ψυχρόν, we read, ὥστε μὴ μόνον αὐτὸ τὸ εἶδος ἀξιοῦσθαι τοῦ αὐτοῦ ὀνόματος εἰς τὸν ἀεὶ χρόνον, ἀλλὰ καὶ ἄλλο τι. At *Rep.*, 476a we read, καὶ περὶ δικαίου καὶ ἀδίκου καὶ ἀγαθοῦ καὶ κακοῦ καὶ πάντων τῶν εἰδῶν πέρι ὁ αὐτὸς λόγος; and at 597a we find that the carpenter who makes a bed οὐ μόνον αὐτὸ τὸ εἶδος ποιεῖ, ὃ δή φαμεν εἶναι ὃ ἔστι κλίνη, ἀλλὰ κλίνην τινα, while God is responsible for ἡ ἐν τῇ φύσει οὖσα [κλίνη] (597b). At *Hippias Major* 289d Socrates speaks of αὐτό τὸ καλόν as that ᾧ καὶ τἆλλα πάντα κοσμεῖται καὶ καλὰ φαίνεται, ἐπειδὰν προσγένηται ἐκεῖνο [not ἐκείνου] τὸ εἶδος. It seems, therefore, that for Plato (αὐτὸ) τὸ X *is* the εἶδος of X. But it is well known that in his works the 'What is X?' question regularly resolves itself into the question 'What is αὐτὸ τὸ X?'; and it follows from this that in any reply to such a question the εἶδος of X, as being identical with αὐτὸ τὸ X, will be, or rather will be represented by, the logical *subject*. The predicate will describe it, but will not itself constitute the εἶδος. As for Cross' insistence that the word εἶδος implies a dependent genitive, and that therefore an εἶδος cannot function in its own right, I am quite prepared to believe that Plato allowed it to do so for his own purposes, and Ross seems to me to be perfectly justified in his remark (quoted by Cross) that 'the Forms are for Plato simple entities, but that is not what the word *means*'.

Again, the εἶδος, as we have seen above, appears as the divine pattern after which sensible objects and acts are copied (*Rep.*, 597b), as that which makes them what they are (*Hipp. Maj.*, 289d), and as something that deserves to have the same name applied to it for ever (*Phd.*, 103e); and it is a thing of which phenomena partake (*Phd.*, 102b). It looks from all this as though it was more than a 'formula'; and Aristotle certainly took what he calls Plato's ἰδέαι to have been the *objects* of definition (*Met.*, 987b). We may add that according to the *Seventh Letter* the logos of a thing (which, on Cross' view, would contain the εἶδος), so far from being or containing a 'pattern', is incapable of indicating τὸ ὂν ἑκάστου and can do no better than suggest τὸ ποιόν τι περὶ ἕκαστον . . . διὰ τὸ τῶν λόγων ἀσθενές (342a–e). It is an indispensable clue towards the acquisition of knowledge (342d–e), but like the ὀνόματα and ῥήματα of which it is composed it is not βέβαιον but ἀσαφές (343b–c). The *Phaedrus* too, though primarily concerned with speeches and treatises, implies that any fixed formulation of words must be lacking in βεβαιότης and σαφήνεια (275d–e, 277d–e). Further, if we are to take as Platonic doctrine the suggestion in the *Theaetetus* that simple nameables are unknowable, should we not also accept what follows, that a logos consisting of names of unknowables must itself be unknowable? If so, Cross' attempt to show that a Platonic Form is the predicate of a logos does not, after all, save Plato's theory, at least in such a way as Plato might wish. For since Forms alone are objects of knowledge, whatever is presented by the several 'names' that make up a logos will not be knowable; and neither, therefore, in Plato's view, will the logos itself, or any part of it.

Thirdly, the *Meno* and the *Republic* are generally taken to mean that the knowledge which is virtue cannot be taught by rule of thumb. Yet if the εἶδος can be given us in a formula, it is difficult to see why that cannot be done, especially if the sentence of which the formula is predicate is defining merely a 'word'. And fourthly, why should there have been such a fuss in Aristotle about the 'separation' of such things from phenomena, if they were formulae?

I turn now to Cross' arguments in favour of his interpretation. First (after raising the difficulty of the *Theaetetus*, which I shall leave to the end) he examines the *Meno*, and observes (p. 440; above, p. 20) (*a*) that Meno finds no difficulty in the fact that there is something common to a group of particulars which are called by the same name ('on the orthodox view of the theory of Forms, a "universal" '); (*b*) that what he and Socrates *are* interested in is what this common element is; and (*c*) that Socrates illustrates the sort of answer he wants to the 'What is X?' question by defining figure as the only thing which always follows colour (75b) or as the limit of a solid (76a). Now I agree with Cross that Plato's Forms are not 'universals', that in the *Meno* Socrates is asking for a definition of virtue, and that the answer wanted is not simply 'There is a Form of X'. But it does not follow that Plato's Forms are definitions, formulae or predicates of statements. In the first place it is usually supposed that Platonic as opposed to Socratic εἴδη—that is to say, χωριστὰ εἴδη—do not appear until after the time of the *Meno*. But this 'What is X?' question, which admittedly occurs in later dialogues also, need mean no more than that Plato believed a search for definitions to *facilitate* the attainment of knowledge of the Forms. If the Platonic εἴδη were truly knowable only by 'acquaintance', there might still be occasion to employ definition as an aid to Recollection and the practice of Dialectic. Although the nature of any such reality could not be adequately grasped or conveyed by language, human thinking is conditioned by the words we use.

In discussing the vision of the Beautiful Itself in the *Symposium*, Cross remarks (p. 442; above, p. 23), 'We are told that of this there is οὐδέ τις λόγος οὐδέ τις ἐπιστήμη. . . . The suggestion is that it is above knowledge in any ordinary sense, and that with knowledge in its ordinary sense there always goes a logos'. But if there is no logos of αὐτὸ τὸ καλόν, is there then no εἶδος of it either? On the other hand, the existence of an εἶδος τοῦ καλοῦ seems to be implied in the passages quoted above from the *Hippias Major* (289d) and *Phaedo* (102b), and if there is an εἶδος of it, but no logos, the εἶδος cannot be the predicate of a logos. (In fact, however, οὐδέ τις λόγος κτλ. probably only means that the Beautiful Itself does not appear *in the form of* a particular beautiful logos or science, not that there can be no logos or knowledge of it.)

Cross then stresses (p. 444; above, p. 25) how throughout the dialogue knowledge, Forms and logos occur together. This phenomenon is hardly surprising if Plato regarded logoi, although different from and only inadequately representing εἴδη, as an indispensable aid towards the attainment of knowledge of them; and nearly all of the passages that Cross quotes are concerned with Dialectic. *Politicus*, 286a may even be treated as evidence against Cross' thesis: διὸ δεῖ μελετᾶν λόγον ἑκάστου δύνατον εἶναι δοῦναι καὶ δέξασθαι· τὰ γὰρ ἀσώματα, κάλλιστα ὄντα καὶ μέγιστα, λόγῳ μόνον ἄλλῳ δὲ οὐδενὶ σαφῶς δείκνυνται. This can hardly mean that Forms *are* logoi or parts of logoi. If it did, what would the ἀσώματα be? As logical subjects, would they be mere 'words'? They are κάλλιστα καὶ μέγιστα! The sense must surely be that logoi are the only means by which in our converse we can convey any clear indication of the nature of Forms. Cross also quotes *Phaedo*, 78d, αὐτὴ ἡ οὐσία ἧς λόγον δίδομεν τοῦ εἶναι καὶ ἐρωτῶντες καὶ ἀποκρινόμενοι. Here again, if the Form is contained in the logos, what is the οὐσία? Surely not a 'word'? Elsewhere (pp. 441, 447; above, pp. 21, 27) Cross finds *Theaetetus*, 148d (ὥσπερ ταύτας πολλὰς οὔσας ἑνὶ εἴδει περιέλαβες, οὕτω καὶ τὰς πολλὰς ἐπιστήμας ἑνὶ λόγῳ προσειπεῖν) important because 'ἑνὶ λόγῳ is parallel with ἑνὶ εἴδει'. But it would perhaps be a little odd to have the part (the predicate) followed in this way by the whole (the logos), and in any case εἶδος here may perfectly well be taken in its frequent non-technical sense—'in a single class'. Not one of the quotations used by Cross requires that the Platonic εἶδος *must* be contained in the logos, and there is only one that might for a moment suggest that it is so contained. This is from *Parmenides*, 135e, where we read, οὐκ εἴας ἐν τοῖς ὁρωμένοις οὐδὲ περὶ ταῦτα τὴν πλάνην ἐπισκοπεῖν, ἀλλὰ περὶ ἐκεῖνα ἃ μάλιστά τις ἂν λόγῳ λάβοι καὶ εἴδη ἂν ἡγήσαιτο εἶναι. Cross, who wants to connect logos in Plato as closely as possible with 'stating' or 'saying', and to avoid the idea of 'reason' or 'thought', would render the last part of this, 'in reference to those things which are especially grasped by statement', etc. (p. 446; above, p. 27). This is, however, a little awkward, if the things grasped are predicates, and that λόγος in Plato *can* mean 'reasoning' (a process, perhaps, rather than a faculty) is shown by *Republic*, 582e, 'Επειδὴ δ' ἐμπειρίᾳ καὶ φρονήσει καὶ λόγῳ (sc. ἐκρίνετο τὰ κρινόμενα), and to some extent supported, perhaps, by 529d, ἃ δὴ λόγῳ μὲν καὶ διανοίᾳ ληπτά, ὄψει δ' οὔ.

I now come to the problem which gives Professor Cross his starting-point, the difficulty raised by Professor Ryle: if the Platonic Forms are 'simple nameables', an argument which Plato puts into the mouth of Socrates in the *Theaetetus* seems to prove that they cannot be known, and yet Plato still, apparently—and here I agree with Cross—did not abandon his Forms. Before giving my own answer to the problem, I should like to suggest that Cross' solution, reinterpreting the Forms as logical predicates, is unsatisfactory if only because it is incomplete. I have already argued that Plato means by the εἶδος of X the same as he means by αὐτὸ τὸ X, and that in a statement made in reply to the 'What is X?' question this entity would have to be represented by the subject. It may now be added that even if the εἶδος of X *were* distinct from αὐτὸ τὸ X, αὐτὸ τὸ X would itself appear to qualify for description as a simple 'nameable', for Plato himself describes it as incomposite. It is οὐσία ὄντως οὖσα (*Phdr.*, 247c), and may be said εἶναι ὡς οἷόν τε μάλιστα (*Phd.*, 77a); but as being constant and invariable, it is likely also to be uncompounded (*Phd.*, 78c sq.). αὐτὸ τὸ καλόν in the *Symposium* is ἀεὶ ὂν καὶ οὔτε γιγνόμενον οὔτε ἀπολλύμενον (211a), but it is also εἰλικρινές, καθαρόν, ἄμικτον (211e). What is this but a 'simple real'? But *these* entities are knowable (*Phd.*, 75c–d), and Cross does not show how *this* can be reconciled with the *Theaetetus* passage. Certainly *αὐτὸ τὸ* X is not a formula or a predicate of a statement; it is the *οὐσία of which* we give a logos (*Phd.*, 78d).

How then is this problem to be solved? Is Plato inconsistent in not applying the *Theaetetus* theory to his Forms, which are simple entities? Should he not have recognised that that analysis of knowledge is correct, and abandoned his Forms accordingly? Plato indeed could hardly have accepted that analysis, because according to the ideas of his time (or at any rate of the time when he wrote his earlier works) an object of knowledge must be *real*, and only a 'thing' could be real. But this hardly affects the issue, as Plato, I am going to submit, was concerned with something *different* from what we ordinarily call knowledge.

First, what was his view of *ἐπιστήμη*? The *Theaetetus* theory, that what can be known is something that can be stated and that 'simples' cannot be stated but only named, is explicitly rejected in the *Theaetetus* itself. First we have the point that if simple elements are unknowable, complex things composed of them are also unknowable, and then Socrates goes on to see whether the theory could be improved by interpreting logos in a different sense (that is, not simply as an enumeration of parts), but none of the senses adopted is found to help it. True belief (or opining) was found at 201a–c not to be knowledge, and now the addition of a logos, in any of the senses adopted, is found not to help. Cornford in his *Plato's Theory of Knowledge* (pp. 151, 142) points out that the only things here recognised as possible objects of knowledge are concrete individual things, that Socrates argues within the limits of the theory he is criticising, and that none of the senses here given to logos is the sense that it bears in the *Meno* and the *Timaeus*. That Plato's *own* theory was of some kind of *ἐπιστήμη* by direct 'acquaintance' (*connaître*) of simple Forms is a reasonable inference from what is said in the *Phaedo* about the soul in a state of purity beholding pure Forms, from the image of the *ὑπερουράνιος τόπος* in the *Phaedrus*, and perhaps even from the *Timaeus*, where the Demiurge uses the Forms as models. Study of the relationship between Forms and recognition of *κοινωνία* among them may have led Plato to practise *διαίρεσις* and to conclude that even Forms may be in some sense extended (not One but Many); and (probably later still) he seems to have tried to reduce the Forms to more primary elements and reached, as we gather from fragments of Aristotle's Περὶ τἀγαθοῦ (Alex. *in Met.*, 56, 7; 56, 34), the One and the Indefinite Dyad. These are the elements of number and, since Forms apparently are now numbers, the elements also of Forms. But even if we deny that Plato continued to hold his theory of Recollection, as Gulley has recently argued with some cogency that he did (*Classical Quarterly*, N.S. iv [1954], 209 seqq.), the available evidence suggests that he continued to believe in ἐπιστήμη by 'acquaintance' of something self-evident, and that the problem of the simple nature of the objects of ἐπιστήμη did not worry him.

Now whatever we may believe today to be the correct account of intellectual knowledge, we should recognise that Plato looked upon ἐπιστήμη of the Good as something that we might describe rather as spiritual awareness or religious conviction. Our problem then becomes something different: Was Plato wrong in supposing that there is such a thing as spiritual awareness, which comes by direct 'acquaintance'? It is true, of course, that Plato seems to regard all the other Forms also as known, originally, by 'acquaintance'—such indeed is the necessary implication of the doctrine of Recollection, as Ross observes in his *Plato's Theory of Ideas* (p. 25). From *Republic*, 511b it would even seem that all recollected knowledge (which is a thing that must be 'bound fast by an understanding of cause', as we read in the *Meno* at 98a) follows at once upon awareness of the Good, which is, of course, the ultimate Cause. This raises the further question, has Plato confused intellectual knowledge with spiritual knowledge? Even supposing we allowed that knowledge of the Good might be a sort of religious experience, can we grant that all other knowledge is similar? Only, I suggest, if by 'knowledge' of a thing is meant *having an understanding of its teleological purpose*. But that is precisely what Plato had in mind. With his intense interest in teleological purpose he was not concerned with the sort of thing that we generally call knowledge. He was not talking about the same thing at all. What *we* call knowledge, he might say, *is* something that can be opined and therefore stated—ἀληθὴς δόξα, in fact. But some of the reasons that he gives for denying to ἀληθὴς δόξα the title of ἐπιστήμη, that it is not a *complete* understanding of *all* circumstances (*Tht.*, 201a–c) and that it does not embrace a full understanding of *cause* (*Men.*, 98a), of themselves show how different is the thing with which he is concerned from what we ordinarily mean by knowledge; so, too, does his reason for denying that a logos can be known, that the elements composing it will be unknowable—as though he wanted a special sort of ἐπιστήμη (a teleological explanation) even of 'simples', of which his metaphysical Forms may have seemed to allow. Whether the possibility of such an intuitively acquired teleological understanding exists can hardly, perhaps, be proved (as Plato thought it could, because of our notions of perfection) by rational argument, but—and this is the point—we can hardly blame Plato for not treating it in the way in which we might wish to treat something else. If it does exist, we may suppose that it can have a 'simple' as its object quite as easily as a compound entity.

Plato himself undoubtedly believed that ἐπιστήμη (in his sense) of a thing entailed the ability to give a logos of it (*Rep.*, 534b), but only a logos of a special kind: not a definition or description that *constituted* knowledge and so could convey knowledge from one person to another, but an explanatory account of the Form in question that should indicate its relationship to other Forms. To the man who had not 'recollected' any of the Forms to which reference was made, this would still be a congeries of unknowns. That is precisely why language is so unsatisfactory. But such logoi could play an important part in Dialectic, being capable of aiding Recollection because of the kinship of one Form to another; and they might also help to inculcate ἀληθὴς δόξα in the uninitiated.

Two final points. Cross remarks (p. 450; above, p. 30) that in the *Republic* Plato 'seems to envisage deriving Forms by some process of deductive argument. This would seem to indicate that forms cannot be simple entities. For how could simple entities be either the premisses or the conclusion of any sort of argument?' But the procedure referred to is much better regarded as a confirmation, not of various propositions deducted from a statement-premiss, but of our notions (ὑποθέσεις) of the various Forms in the light of a teleological first principle. Cross' final point is that we should remember, 'perhaps at times with regret', that Plato has an affection for the material mode of speech, and for existential propositions, and that we should to some extent discount these. But if the whole object of Plato's χωρισμός of Forms from phenomena was to give an ontological and metaphysical backing to the ideals of Socrates—if his Forms, in fact, were such as I have taken them to be—there is no need to discount a word of what Plato has written.

IV

PARTICIPATION AND PREDICATION IN PLATO'S MIDDLE DIALOGUES (1960)

R. E. Allen

I PROPOSE in this paper to examine three closely related issues in the interpretation of Plato's middle dialogues: the nature of Forms, of participation, and of predication. The familiar problem of self-predication will serve as introduction to the inquiry.

I. SELF-PREDICATION

The significance—or lack of significance—of Plato's self-predicative statements has recently become a crux of scholarship. Briefly, the problem is this: the dialogues often use language which suggests that the Form is a universal which has itself as an attribute and is thus a member of its own class, and, by implication, that it is the one perfect member of that class. The language suggests that the Form *has* what it *is*: it is self-referential, self-predicable.

Now such a view is, to say the least, peculiar. Proper universals are not instantiations of themselves, perfect or otherwise. Oddness is not odd; Justice is not just; Equality is equal to nothing at all. No one can curl up for a nap in the Divine Bedsteadity; not even God can scratch Doghood behind the Ears.

The view is more than peculiar; it is absurd. As Plato knew, it implies an infinite regress, one which he doubtless regarded as vicious. Indeed, if a recent critic, Professor Gregory Vlastos, has analysed the Third Man correctly,[1] it implies still more. We must suppose that Plato could swallow, without gagging, a flat self-contradiction;[2] that the reason for this, presumably, was that the author of the Third Man—one of the more brilliant of philosophical demonstrations—lacked the wit, or perhaps the diligence, to identify the premisses of his argument; that the man who first explicitly distinguished between universals and particulars confused them; and, finally, that a central thesis of his ontology, the doctrine of degrees of being and reality, rests on this elementary mistake.

Such thorough confusion is not lightly to be imputed to any man, let alone to Plato. Common sense and the common law agree that a man is innocent until proved guilty; and common charity dictates that philosophers be not excepted. The amount of evidence required to convict Plato of so puerile a confusion must be immense indeed. I propose in this paper to show that it has not yet been produced, and in the very nature of the case cannot be produced.

Let us be quite clear on what is to be proved. Plato obviously accepts the following thesis: some (perhaps all) entities which may be designated by a phrase of the form 'the *F* Itself', or any synonyms thereof, may be called *F*. So the Beautiful Itself will be beautiful, the Just Itself just, Equality equal.[3] But this thesis does not, *by itself*, imply self-predication; for that, an auxiliary premiss is required.

This premiss is that a predicate of the type '. . . is *F*' may be applied univocally to *F* particulars and to the *F* Itself, so that when (for example) we say that a given act is just, and that Justice is just, we are asserting that both have identically the same character. But this premiss would be false if the predicate were

[1] Gregory Vlastos, 'The Third Man Argument in the *Parmenides*,' *Phil. Rev.*, LXIII (1954), 319–49; below, Ch. XII. For further discussion, see: Wilfrid Sellars, *Phil. Rev.*, LXIV (1955), 405–37; Vlastos, ibid., 438–48; P. T. Geach, *Phil. Rev.*, LXV (1956), 72–82; below, Ch. XIII; Vlastos, ibid., 83–94; below, Ch. XIV; R. S. Bluck, *Class. Quart.*, N. S. VI (1956), 29–37, and *Phronesis*, II (1957), 115–21.

[2] The guilty premisses, in Vlastos' formulation of the argument, are (A3) Self-Predication and (A4) Non-Identity; these are so stated, however, that their incompatibility is not immediately apparent.

[3] Cf. *Prot.*, 330c, 331b; *Phd.*, 74b, d, 100c; *Hipp. Maj.*, 289c, 291e, 292e, 294a–b; *Lysis*, 217a; *Symp.*, 210e–211d.

systematically equivocal, according as the subject of the sentence was a Form or a particular. In that case, to say that Justice is just and that any given act is just would be to say two quite different (though perhaps related) things, and the difficulties inherent in self-predication could not possibly arise. That is, the character of Forms would not be assimilated to that of particulars.

I propose to show that predicates involving the names of Forms exhibit just this kind of ambiguity. The evidence for this conclusion will be drawn from the theory of predication put forward in the *Phaedo* and from the ontology which underlies it.

II. PLATO'S THEORY OF PREDICATION

Plato has no word for 'predication'. Rather he says that particulars are 'called by the same name' (ὁμώνυμον) as their Form.[1] But this is surely a loose way of describing the use of common terms; 'ὁμώνυμον' is Aristotle's usual term for 'ambiguous'; things called by the same name may have nothing in common but their name. But later in the *Phaedo* this terminology is repeated and made more precise:[2]

> Each of the Forms exists, and the other things which come to have a share in them are *named after* them.

The reason for naming particulars after Forms is that they have in them an immanent character defined by their Form:[3]

> Not only is the Form itself always entitled to its own name, but also what is not the Form, but always has, when it exists, its immanent character (μορφή).

Significantly, Aristotle chose to emphasise precisely this feature in his summary of the theory of Forms in the *Metaphysics*:[4]

> Sensible things, [Plato] said, were all *named after* [Ideas], and in virtue of a relation to them; for the many existed by participation in the Ideas that *have the same name* as they.

These passages imply that '*F*' is a *name*, a name whose *prime* designate is a Form: '*F*' names *the F*. But this name is also applied, through what we may call derivative designation, to particulars,

[1] *Phd.*, 78e 2; cf. *Rep.*, 596a 7; *Soph.*, 240a.
[2] *Phd.*, 102b 2; cf. *Parm.*, 130e 5; italics here, as elsewhere, mine.
[3] *Phd.*, 103e; cf. 103b 7 ff.
[4] A 987b 3 ff., trans. by Ross.

which are *named after* the Form in much the way that a boy may be named after his father. The reason for this, the justification for derivative designation, is that particulars have in them the immanent character defined by their Form; or, to put the matter in a slightly different way, they are named after the Form because of their peculiarly intimate relation to it—they depend upon it for their character and their existence.

We have, then, a theory of predication without predicates. What appear to be attributive statements are in fact *relational* or *identifying* statements, depending on the designation of their predicates. In derivative designation, to say of something that it is *F* is to say that it is causally dependent upon *the* *F*. Notice that '*F*' is here not strictly a univocal term, but a common name, applied in virtue of a relationship to an individual, the Form.

On the other hand, when '*F*' is used in primary designation, it is a synonym of 'the *F* Itself' and '*F*-ness'; therefore, to say that *F*-ness is *F* is to state an identity. It follows that it is invalid to infer self-predication from Plato's apparently self-predicative language. In the first place, '*F*-ness is *F*' is not a predicative statement. Second, we cannot mean by it what we mean when we say that a particular is *F*. The function '. . . is *F*' is systematically ambiguous; its meaning depends upon the context in which it is used, the type of object to which it is applied.[1]

If this is true, it follows that Plato's self-predicative language is both intelligible and logically innocuous. Grammatical predicates are names which exhibit a systematic ambiguity according as they designate Forms or particulars; Forms themselves are proper nameables; what appear to be self-predicative statements are

[1] Note that this view of the way words mean is consistent with a well-known feature of Greek syntax. One may always, in Greek, form an abstract noun by using the article with the neuter singular adjective. '*τὸ ἴσον*,' for example, is equivalent to the abstract '*ἡ ἰσότης*'; both mean 'equality'. But this usage is quite ambiguous, since '*τὸ ἴσον*' may also mean 'the equal thing' or 'that which is equal'; in other words, it is normal usage, in Greek, to use 'the *F* thing' to refer to *F*-ness, particular *F*s, and even the class of *F* things. It has sometimes been supposed that this ambiguity was a source of confusion to Plato; I suggest that it rather confirmed a theory of the way words mean, which, in conformity with normal usage, preserved that ambiguity and rendered it intelligible. The use of '*αὐτό*' will always make it clear, should need arise, which type of *F* is in question. '*αὐτὸ τὸ F*' is an identifying phrase.

identity statements; and what appear to be attributive statements are relational statements.

We have a reasonably close analogue to this in English: our own use of predicates where standards of weight and measure are involved. To say of something that it weighs a pound, or measures exactly one yard, is to say that it bears a specific relation—equality in weight or length—to an individual locked in a vault of the Bureau of Standards, an individual arbitrarily selected to define a unit of measurement. Like '. . . is *F*', in derivative designation, the function '. . . weighs a pound' covertly mentions an individual of a type from its argument.

The parallel may be made more exact. We may say of other things that they weigh a pound, but if we assert this of *the* pound, we cannot assert it in the same sense. We can measure other things against a standard; we cannot measure a standard against itself. The predicate '. . . weighs a pound' is capable of exhibiting just the kind of ambiguity that Plato's theory requires. It may be systematically ambiguous; on the one hand it mentions a relation; on the other it may be an identifying phrase, designating an individual.

There is no reason in principle why this analysis should not be extended to other types of statement. Why should we not, for example, read statements like 'this desk is brown' or 'that figure is triangular' as asserting that the desk or figure stands in the relation of colour or shape resemblance to *the* brown and *the* triangle, individuals selected to define standards of colour and shape? There is no internal reason why predicates should not be analysed in this way. If they are, attributive statements will then one and all be translated into relation-to-standard statements.

The analogy of relation-to-standard statements to statements involving names of Forms was drawn advisedly;[1] for Forms clearly function, in the early and middle dialogues, as standards and paradigms. Plato's theory of predication admirably supplements a fundamental thesis of his ontology.

[1] It must be remembered that this *is* an analogy, not a basis for literal explication of the theory of Forms. Forms resemble standards in that they are of a different epistemic order from the class of things they define; but Forms are, as standards are not, also of a different ontological order. This leads to fundamental difficulties if the analogy is pressed; cf. 'Forms and Standards', *Phil. Quart.*, VIII (1959), 164–7.

III. IMITATION AND DEGREES OF REALITY

The theory of Forms involves two fundamental doctrines: (*a*) that the relation between particulars and Forms is that of imitation, of copy to original, and (*b*) that Forms and particulars differ in degree of reality. These theses, the proponents of self-predication maintain, obscured in Plato's mind the distinction between characters and things characterised, a confusion which leads directly to the absurdities of self-predication; and the regress arguments of the *Parmenides*, resting as they do on this mistake, reflect not verbal confusion but a radical and deep-seated incoherence in the theory of Forms.

It is clear that Plato's theory of predication does not entail this incoherence; but it is equally clear that it can do nothing, of itself, to prevent it. Indeed, the theory could have contributed indirectly to produce it, for it provides no clear way either to affirm or to deny that the *F has F*-ness. The very language in which the theory of Forms is expressed makes the issue of self-predicability peculiarly difficult to isolate and analyse. This would account for the fact (if it is a fact) that Plato was unable to identify the premisses of the Third Man and therefore could not mend the flaw in his theory.

But is it true that the degrees of reality and copy theories imply self-predication? In fact, they imply nothing of the sort.

(a) *The Copy Theory*. Plato characteristically describes particulars as copying or imitating Forms, and this seems to imply that particulars resemble Forms. The proponents of self-predication maintain that it implies still more: that if *F* particulars and the *F* Itself resemble each other, they must do so in virtue of being *F*.

This conclusion is one of almost breathtaking eccentricity. My hands resemble each other in being hands. Do they also resemble the Hand Itself in this respect? Clearly not. For the relation of hands to the Hand is analogous, on Plato's account, to the relation between pictures or reflections of hands and hands. Therefore, if 'the logic of Plato's metaphor' implies that *the* Hand is *a* hand, it also implies that the picture of a hand is a hand; which is absurd.

Pictures of hands are not hands, though they may resemble hands in colour, shape, and so on. We must, then, distinguish between substantial resemblance (to use Aristotelian language) and accidental resemblance, between the resemblance of things of the same sort, and the resemblance of things which are merely similar in quality. And when this is done, the argument for self-predication from the copy theory is exposed for what it is: a muddle. The reason for that muddle is not far to seek. When the self-predicationists discuss imitation, they have a peculiar type in mind: one thing may be used as a model on which to fashion something else of the same kind—a shuttle, say, as a model for shuttles. But it is clear that this is not what Plato had in mind; in fact, he may well have denied that this type of imitation *is* imitation.[1]

But even if it is granted that the resemblance metaphor does not imply self-predication, it continues to generate familiar difficulties; for if we grant even so much as accidental resemblance between particulars and Forms, there will be a sense, though a weak one, in which the absurdity inherent in self-predication will recur.

Resemblance is an indirect relation, that is, a relation which holds only in virtue of some common term: if x and y resemble each other, they do so in respect of some common character C. But if the relation of any x to its C is one of resemblance—if particulars resemble Forms—two things follow immediately: there will be an infinite regress of Forms, or third terms in relations of resemblance;[2] and Forms (though, to be sure, not strictly self-predicable) will share classes with particulars and by so much be assimilated to their character.

But does Plato's metaphor commit him even to this? The answer, surely, is No. The objection turns on assuming that particulars resemble Forms, and this assumption is false.

Consider the reflection of a red scarf in a mirror—a good example of what Plato understands by an imitation. It is clearly false that the reflection is a scarf. Is it true that it is red? Or is it only the reflection of a red thing?[3]

[1] Cf. *Crat.*, 389a ff.; *Soph.*, 239d ff. *Tim.*, 28b, appears to entertain this type of imitation as possible. But notice that the hypothesis that the creator could use a generated model in his work implies an infinite regress, though Plato does not explicitly mention this.

[2] This regress could terminate in a C which was self-predicable; but then we would only have laid the foundation of a new regress, resting on a different base.

[3] I do not maintain that the analysis of reflection which follows is the only, or perhaps even the correct, analysis. I do maintain that it is consistent and reasonable, and that, as a matter of historical fact, it is presupposed by the Theory of Forms.

The reflection is not similar in *kind* to the original. Is it then similar in quality? If we say that it is, we face an evident embarrassment; for to say this is to say that we can predicate of reflections, which are essentially adjectival, in just the way we predicate of their originals, things which exist in their own right. Scarves can be bought and sold, lost or stolen, wrapped around the neck in winter; but I would gladly give you every image that has crossed the surface of my mirror, and count myself no poorer for the loss.[1]

The very being of a reflection is relational, wholly dependent upon what is other than itself: the original, and the reflecting medium.[2] It is for this reason that, though you may call the reflection of a red scarf red if you so please, you cannot mean the *same* thing you mean when you call its original red. The function '. . . is red' is, in this case, systematically ambiguous. It follows that you cannot say that the reflection stands in the relation of colour resemblance to its original, since this implies the univocal exemplification of a common quality, presupposed by an assertion of resemblance. The reflection does not *resemble* the original; rather, it is a *resemblance of* the original.[3] This is its nature, and the whole of its nature. 'Resemblances of' are quasi-substantial; relational entities, not relations.[4] They stand to their originals as

[1] This argument may be made more precise. We see reflections in the mirror, and we see the mirror in the room. But 'in' here is ambiguous. Mirrors are physical objects which may be located relatively to other physical objects. But we can locate reflections only relatively to the reflecting medium; otherwise, we would be forced to claim that two things, the reflection and the surface of the medium, may be in the same place at the same time. But given this as a lemma, the following argument seems sound; whatever is red is extended; whatever is extended is locatable with respect to any other thing which is extended; mirror images are not so locatable; therefore, they are neither extended nor red. Rather, they are reflections of an extended red thing.

[2] The mirror of the Forms is of course three-dimensional: the Receptacle. Notice that the fundamental distinction between the Aristotelian and Platonic views of space is explained by their differing evaluation of extended entities. For Aristotle the extended is substantial, real in its own right; and therefore it is for him feasible to adopt a relational view of space, with substances as relata. But for Plato extended entities are reflections, images; space, the medium of reflection, is a precondition of their existence, the receptacle in which Forms are mirrored. It is therefore absolute, not a consequence of the mirroring. Cf. *Tim.*, 50d ff.

[3] The 'is' here is, of course, that of identity.

[4] This distinction between resemblance and resemblances, between relations and relational entities, will no doubt seem strange to those whose

the dependent to the independent, as the less real to the more real. Plato's metaphor of imitation brilliantly expresses a community between different orders of objects, different levels of reality; it does not, as his recent critics have maintained, collapse that order.[1] Their reading of the metaphor can be sustained only by assuming the very thing that must be proved—that Plato viewed imitation as they do.

(b) *Degrees of Reality.* Plato's metaphor of imitation expresses a fundamental thesis of his ontology, that particulars differ from Forms, as resemblances differ from originals, in degree of reality.[2] For particulars 'fall short' of their Forms, and are 'deficient' with respect to them.[3]

In what sense can a particular be deficient with respect to a Form? Only, the proponents of self-prediction have urged, by possessing in merely approximate or comparative degree a character that the Form, which *is* the character, *has* fully. But this assimilates the Form categorically to the class of things it defines; it must possess in pre-eminent degree a character which particulars own only deficiently, and it is therefore itself a particular, albeit, no doubt, a perfect one.

If this interpretation is accepted, it is quite fatal. But it turns

[1] It will be objected that Plato compares particulars with reflections and pictures indiscriminately; that pictures are not merely resemblances of, but stand in the relation of resemblance to, their originals; and that, therefore, the above interpretation cannot be attributed to Plato. But this objection overlooks the nature of his theory of art. The analogy is drawn, not to the picture *as* a picture, but to the art object—a 'man-made dream for waking eyes'. The picture does not differ in type or degree of reality from its original; it is an artifact, an object of *πίστις*; to apprehend it so is to apprehend it *as* a picture; and to be able to compare it, we cannot confuse it with that original. But the artist holds a mirror up to nature; it is essential to apprehending a picture as an art object that we may take it to be, not a resemblance, but the very thing it resembles, as we may mistake a reflection in a mirror for the thing reflected. Viewed as an art object, the picture no longer retains its independent character; it is assimilated to that of a reflection, which is to say that its full meaning is relational, dependent upon the nature of its original.

[2] Cf. *Soph.*, 240a–c; images are not real, but really are images.

[3] *Phd.*, 74d 5–7, e 1–4, 75a 2–3, b 4–8.

---

imaginations are set in the cast of *Principia Mathematica*; but it has a long and honourable history. It has been the root metaphor for most Western degrees-of-reality philosophies which reject the literal inconsistency of the lower orders of being; and medieval exemplarism is unintelligible without it.

on construing the deficiency of particulars as one of quality, rather than of type; they are deficiently something else *of the same sort*, as a blind eye is deficiently an eye, or as one shuttle, modelled on another, may be a defective copy. Yet surely the force of the metaphor of imitation, and of the χωρισμός, is to indicate that the deficiency in question is that of one *type* of thing with respect to something of another type: 'deficiency' is here a category distinction, not a distinction within categories. Particulars are deficient not because they have the characters they have but because they are the kind of things they are—because they are qualified by opposites, because they change, because they are in some degree unintelligible, because they depend for their existence upon Forms and are themselves *not* Forms—because, in a word, they are images. The interpretation of the self-predicationists, though it gains an initial plausibility by interpreting 'deficiently' in the way most obvious *to us*, is impossible, for it assumes (and does nothing to prove) that Forms and particulars are of the same type.[1] But Plato does not say that they are; and he does say that they are not.[2]

If the foregoing analysis has been sound, the arguments offered to show that Forms are self-predicable beg the question: in each case the conclusion is proved only because, implicitly, it has been assumed.

IV. FORMS AND UNIVERSALS

The case for self-predicability rests, in the final analysis, not on Plato's apparently self-predicative language, nor on the logic of his

[1] Note the further difficulty that certain Forms define characters which admit of no logical extreme. There is no largest, or smallest, *possible* thing, a fact which Plato, who was familiar with the Zenonian treatment of infinity, must surely have known. But if the self-predicationists are correct in their interpretation of 'deficiency', Largeness must be the largest thing possible, Smallness smaller than any small thing; at this point, the imagination boggles.

[2] It will doubtless be urged that the Good of the *Republic* (and analogously, the Beauty of the *Symposium*) is 'the best', and better than any good thing. But the question is whether it is 'better' in the *same* sense in which one good thing is better than another. Can we compare things of different ontological status in the way we compare things of the same ontological status? The answer implied to this question by Plato's theory of predication, the imitation metaphor, and the degrees of reality theory, is No; and that answer, as I shall show, is sustained and made intelligible by Plato's theory of participation.

imitation metaphor, nor on supposed systematic presuppositions of the degrees of reality theory; it rests on a false assumption about the nature of Forms, imported bodily into his text by his interpreters. It is to the credit of the proponents of self-predication that they have seen the implications of that assumption far more clearly than the majority of their critics.

It is generally agreed that Forms are universals, and in some sense that is surely true: 'One over Many' is the nub of the argument for their existence. In *some* sense, then; but in *what* sense?

On this question, the verdict of recent scholarship has been almost unanimous. The Form is a *commutative* universal, a character or attribute, a nuclear identity capable of instantiation in diverse material contexts, a pure 'what' which in some mysterious way inheres in and qualifies 'thats'. On this commonly accepted view, Platonism differs from other theories of the commutative universal only in that it is realistic and extreme; the universal exists 'alone by itself', independent of any mind and any instantiation. No one need think of it; nothing need have it. Its existence is intrinsic to itself.

Now commutative universals or attributes clearly cannot be identified with standards and paradigms; for the latter are things characterised, not characters; and if there is confusion on this point, self-predication follows immediately. But Forms clearly function in Plato's ontology as standards and paradigms; therefore, if he also thought of them as common characters or attributes, the result is shipwreck.

But did he? I submit that he did not, that this is an assumption of Plato's critics, not of Plato. For consider its consequences.

To begin with, it wrecks dialectic. With the commutative universal, the relation of genus to species is always that of the more abstract to the more concrete: the genus is essentially poorer than its species, having less content, and this diminution continues as one proceeds upward in the abstractive hierarchy, so that the highest genera are most barren of all. But such a view as this clearly cannot provide a ground for the synoptic vision of all time and all existence, or account for the fact that dialectic ends in an unhypothetical first principle, or provide a basis for the deduction of lower from higher which the downward path of dialectic requires.

Second, this assumption destroys the main point of the χωρισμός. It is of course trivially true that attributes and their instantiations are ἕτερα ὄντα, different sorts of things. It may even be true, granted a few assumptions, that attributes are causes of their instantiations, since they are that by which things are what they are; and also true that attributes may exist 'alone by themselves', independently of instantiation. But it is *not* true—though this is at the heart of the χωρισμός—that an attribute may be instantiated imperfectly or in deficient degree. A crooked line is not an imperfect instantiation of straight linearity; on the contrary, it is a full and complete instantiation of the *kind* of crooked line that it is, and the kind is repeatable, though the line itself is not. In general, things exhibit the characters they exhibit and none other; so far as commutative universals are concerned, to say that something is deficient with respect to one character is merely an awkward way of saying that it quite fully has another. But with paradigms and standards, the language of approximation and deficiency makes perfect sense.

This point is related to a further one. Particulars, unlike Forms, are qualified by opposites. We can form no stable conception of them, 'either as being or as not being, or as both being and not being, or as neither'.[1] The plain meaning of this statement, in its context, is that particulars are both F and not-F, either F or not-F, and neither F nor not-F. If Plato understood F to be an attribute or commutative universal, then he must have believed that particulars are (quite literally) self-contradictory, and supported that absurdity by arguments which are a fortiori equally absurd; whereas, I suggest (though I will not here attempt to prove), if we interpret the negation here involved as that of deficiency or privation, implied by approximation to an entity which stands on a different level of reality, it is possible to construe this discussion in a way that does not make Plato both a skeptic and a fool.

Instantiations do not pursue, or fall short of, or imitate, attributes; they simply have them or fail to have them. Nor are they of a lower degree of reality. On the contrary, the major objection to extreme realism is that it posits a domain of reality so drained of actuality that it is shadow-thin, a ghostly wraith hovering about the verges of existence, powerless even to gibber.

[1] *Rep.*, 479c, trans. by F. M. Cornford.

Forms are not commutative universals.[1] What, then, are they? A thorough attempt to answer that question would far outrun the limits of this paper. But Plato has provided us with an analogy, and that analogy is worthy of attention. Forms are like originals; particulars are like images or reflections. The comparison is significant.

To begin with, it places the One over the Many; there may be many reflections of a single thing, and those reflections gain their community of character from that thing. Second, the analogy expresses degrees of reality; reflections depend upon their original both for their character and their existence; it depends upon them for neither. Third, the analogy illustrates how particulars may approximate to Forms and yet be categorically distinct: reflections may differ in the degree to which they are true to their original, but no matter how faithful they are to it, they can never become it, for it is of a different order than they. Finally, the analogy helps to make clear in what sense Forms are standards and paradigms; in order to know that anything is a reflection, still more to know of what it is a reflection, one must know its original. But the original, then, is a standard or criterion, by which we judge of images and their degree of adequacy.

The metaphor of resemblance is not, of course, fully adequate. Most notably, it sheds no direct light (unlike the imitation metaphor) on the teleological side of Plato's thought, nor on the question of how the reflection of an unchanging object may be in flux. But it brilliantly conveys features essential to Plato's view of Forms and their relation to particulars; and by appealing to what is close at hand and familiar, it provides us with at least an intuitive grasp of how a Many can be unified by a One which is not a commutative universal. Finally, it suggests that Forms

[1] I have not troubled to criticise this view in greater detail simply because it has never, to my knowledge, received explicit defence. At times it is accepted on the basis of an undistributed middle: Forms are clearly universals; by a universal we commonly mean a commutative universal or attribute; therefore, Forms are commutative universals or attributes. But there are hints in the literature of another motive. It seems sometimes to be assumed that every philosophy must (ought to?) hold a theory of commutative universals; therefore Plato must have held such a theory. I find it odd, in the light of the past five hundred years of philosophy, and especially of the last fifty, that anyone should blithely assume the premiss to be true. But true or false, the conclusion is a *non sequitur*.

stand to particulars, not as attributes to instantiations, but as exemplars to exemplifications, and that participation, μέθεξις, is not nearly so mysterious as it has sometimes seemed.

V. PARTICIPATION

The objects of our changing world of sense, though each is different from every other, are in certain fundamental—though varying—respects, the same. In difference we find community of character; in diversity we find unity. How is this to be explained?

The theory of Forms is intended as an answer to this question, and the solution it offers is this. The particular objects of sense are unified by a One which stands on a different level of reality from theirs; their community of character is to be explained by the introduction of Forms. Unity and diversity are reconciled if we posit the existence of two domains, Being and Becoming, a world of particulars, of things unified, and a world of Forms, their unity. To understand the One and the Many, we must understand that the One is *over* the Many.

But if this solves one problem of community, it leads directly to another. In placing the One over the Many, we unify the Many; the next task, clearly, is to unify the Many and the One. The community of particulars is to be explained by the introduction of Forms; but how are we to explain the community of particulars and Forms?

This is the problem of participation: given a diversity of domains, of worlds, to account for their community. It clearly cannot be met by positing a One over the original Many and their One; for this merely supplies us with another Many demanding unification, and with a vicious regress. Being and Becoming must either then be collapsed or infinitely fragmented; but in either case, the problem of community, to which this ontology had addressed itself, remains unsolved.

Paradoxically, we cannot assert that Forms and particulars are related or that they share any common character. For the relation between a Form and a particular must be either a Form or a particular or some third kind of thing. If it is either a Form or a particular, the original question is unanswered, since our problem is to account for the community between Forms and particulars, and that problem cannot be solved by multiplication. But if the putative relation is some other type of thing, a member of some third domain, we must ask what accounts for the community of three domains, not merely of two. Therefore, any attempt to relate Forms and particulars will lead, no matter how that relation is construed, to an infinite regress. It follows that Forms and particulars are not related. But in that case they cannot share common predicates; for if two things share a common predicate they are similar, and similarity is a relation. But here no relation is possible.

Being and Becoming must be distinct and yet together, and their nexus of connection can belong to neither, nor can it be anything distinct. We have here one of the fundamental problems of Plato's ontology. His solution is to be found in the doctrine of degrees of reality.

Particulars and Forms are not merely different types of things; they are types of things which differ in degree of reality, for the one is wholly dependent upon the other. Particulars have no independent ontological status; they are purely relational entities, entities which derive their *whole* character and existence from Forms. Because their being is relational, adjectival, dependent, relations to bind them to Forms are neither possible nor required. To understand the community of Being and Becoming, we need only understand the dependent nature of Becoming.

But this leads to a further difficulty. We must say that particulars are, that they have a kind of existence, though in the same breath we must go on to affirm that they do not have existence in the way that Forms, things which are fully real, do. This is the problem of εἴδωλα: images are not real—yet they really are images. We talk about them, predicate of them, and act with respect to them, for they form the substance of our world. But they are wholly dependent upon their transcendent source, and of immensely less reality; and therefore, though we must say that they *are*, we must also say they *are not*.

We cannot say that particulars and Forms exist in the *same* sense, for that is what the degrees of reality theory denies. Can we then assert their existence in a different sense? But if 'existence' is simply ambiguous, if to say that a Form exists and that a particular exists is to say something wholly different about each, then the community which is fundamental to degrees of reality is abandoned, and we are left with a domain which in no proper sense exists at all. We are committed, not only to maintaining *degrees* of reality, but to maintaining degrees of *reality*.

The solution to this difficulty has already been hinted at in our examination of Plato's theory of predication. Particulars are named after Forms because Forms are their causes. To say of anything that it is *F* is to say that it depends for its existence upon *the F*, that in virtue of which *F*-things are *F*. But the *F* is not merely a cause; it is an *exemplary* cause. Particulars not only depend upon it; they are resemblances of it, as reflections are resemblances of their originals. Like reflections, they differ in type from their originals; they share no common attribute; and yet they exhibit a fundamental community of character. From this analysis it follows that the names of Forms cannot be applied univocally to Forms and particulars, exemplars and exemplifications; diversity of type implies a distinction between primary and derivative designation. But it also follows that the names of Forms are not simply ambiguous; community of character implies that the meaning of a term in derivative designation is defined in terms of its meaning in primary designation.[1]

[1] There is an interesting type of ambiguity involved here, something intermediate between univocity and full equivocity. Aristotle calls it πρὸς ἕν ambiguity, or equivocity by reference. (Cf. *Met.* 1003a 33 ff.; *E.N.*, 1096b 27; *Topics*, 106a 9 ff.; W. D. Ross, *Aristotle's Metaphysics*, vol. i, p. 256; J. Owens, *Doctrine of Being in the Aristotelian Metaphysics*, ch. iii et seq.) It is the peculiar merit of equivocity by reference that it expresses the community of different orders of things without assuming the diverse instantiation of a common universal. It requires no more than some form of dependence-relation in order to be applicable. It is for this reason that this type of equivocity plays so important a role in Aristotle's *Metaphysics*. First Philosophy or Theology has as its object being qua being, and the characteristics which essentially pertain to it. But to speak of the being of a substance and of an accident is to speak of two very different things. τὸ ὂν λέγεται πολλαχῶς; 'being' is said in many ways. A substance 'is' in the full sense; its being is its own. But the being of an accident is adjectival, attributive, in some sense borrowed from that of the substance to which it belongs. It holds its existence, not in its own right, but by virtue of its relation to what is self-existent; and its being is defined by that relation.

It is important to note what this denies: it denies that being is a genus, that is, a universal or common term. (Cf. *Met.*, 1003a 33 ff.; 1053b 22; 1045b 6; *E.N.*, 1096b 27.) Being is not a genus because it can be predicated of everything, whereas a genus cannot be predicated of its differentiae. (See *Met.*, 998b 23; 1059b 31; and Ross, op. cit., ad hoc.) To say that substance and

It also implies that statements such as 'the *F* is *F*', though their form is that of a mere statement of identity or synonymy, play an important function in explicating the theory of Forms; in asserting that the *F* is *F*, we are asserting, not only that it is the cause of *F*-things, but also the peculiar manner in which it is the cause. It is an exemplary cause and, as such, exhibits a community of character with its exemplifications.

VI. THE THIRD MAN

It is easy to show that the regress arguments of the *Parmenides* are powerless against this position. The first (131c–132b) assumes that the Form and its particulars are called by the same name and that that name is applied univocally; the second (132c–133a) assumes that particulars resemble Forms. Both are fallacious. Let 'F_1' be substituted for 'F' when 'F' is used in primary designation, and 'F_2' in derivative designation. Then it is false to say that *F*-things and the *F* are called by the same name, equally false to say that they resemble each other either in respect of being F_1 or F_2. These arguments, because they neglect the systematic ambiguity of the names of Forms, are, it would seem, the results of mere confusion—may be viewed, indeed, as *reductiones ad absurdum* of that confusion.[1]

We may go further. The fundamental difficulty underlying the Third Man is ontological, not linguistic. Not only the regress arguments but all of the objections to participation in the *Parmenides* posit an identity of character between Forms and particulars; the Many and the One are to be unified, in effect, by a further One. These arguments demonstrate conclusively that this supposition is absurd.

Yet they point to a difficulty which is crucial in any exemplaristic

[1] It should be noted that the Third Man does not presuppose the distinction between commutative universals and instances. The argument rests on a categorical or type confusion; it can be generated by confusing exemplars with exemplifications, goals with the things which have them, or standards with the things they measure. This list is not exhaustive.

---

accident both exist is not to say that they share a common character, but that they stand in a certain relation: the one is dependent upon the other. 'Being' is a πρὸς ἕν equivocal; so too are the names of Forms.

ontology. For though there can be no identity between exemplars and exemplifications, there must be community of character; and how is this community to be explained? It can be explained by treating exemplifications not as substances in which qualities inhere but as relational entities, entities in which resemblance and dependence so combine as to destroy the possibility of substantiality. Plato's use of the metaphors of imitation and reflection, and his characterisation of particulars and Forms, indirectly indicate that he accepted this solution.

V

MATHEMATICS AND DIALECTIC IN THE *REPUBLIC* VI–VII (1932)

F. M. Cornford

THIS paper has two objects: (1) to define the mental experiences which Plato distinguishes as *noesis* and *dianoia*; (2) to disentangle certain threads he has woven together in his scheme of higher education. The *Republic* is a long book, and Plato saves space by treating concurrently themes which a modern writer would keep apart. It is hardly too much to say that Plato, at the height of his powers, never wasted a word; whereas many readers of Book VII must have been troubled by an impression, which the commentaries do nothing to remove, that dialectic is described over and over again for no clear reason. I hope to show that each of these descriptions has a special purpose and meaning, which can be distinguished when they are assigned to two programmes, one of education, the other of research, with different aims and methods.

I. 'NOESIS' AND 'DIANOIA'

In setting forth the analogy between the Good and the sun, Plato has drawn the main distinction,[1] already familiar, between the objects of intelligence (νοητά), namely the Ideas—Good, Beautiful, and the rest—and the many things seen or otherwise perceived (αἰσθητά). The diagram of the Line again divides each region into two. There are four corresponding 'mental experiences' (παθήματα ἐν τῇ ψυχῇ, 511d). We are not concerned with the two lowest,

[1] 507a, ἄλλοτε ἤδη πολλάκις εἰρημένα, e.g. at *Phd.*, 78c–79c, of which this passage might be a summary.

confined to perception of, and beliefs about, sense objects, but only with the two highest, *noesis* and *dianoia*, whose field is the intelligible. This is the first place where Plato contrasts two modes of operation of the reasoning part of the soul. The distinction is then allowed to lapse in the long review of the mathematical sciences in VII, where, with Plato's usual avoidance of technical language, νόησις, διάνοια, and λογισμός are synonyms, all meaning reflection or intelligence or abstract thinking.[1] But *noesis* and *dianoia* become distinct again in the subsequent accounts of dialectic (531d–535a). What is the ground of the distinction?

It first occurs in the contrast of mathematics and dialectic (510b–511e). Here it will be convenient to keep apart four elements in the contrast: (*a*) Objects; (*b*) Methods of procedure; (*c*) Movements of thought, deductive and intuitive, shown in the procedures; (*d*) States of mind, characteristic of the mathematician and of the accomplished dialectician.

(a) *Objects.* Where the intelligible section is subdivided, clearly some distinction of objects is meant. I agree with critics who hold that nothing here points to a class of mathematical numbers and figures intermediate between Ideas and sensible things. Further, whatever may be said elsewhere about the extent of the intelligible world, the only Ideas that figure in the whole scheme of education are the moral (507b) and the mathematical (510d) Ideas. These, and truths about them, form, so far as can be seen, the whole relevant content of the intelligible realm. It appears also that the moral Ideas are not a higher class, apprehended by *noesis*, the mathematical a lower, apprehended by *dianoia*; for the mathematical can be objects of *noesis* when seen 'in connection with a first principle' (νοητῶν ὄντων μετὰ ἀρχῆς, 511d). What difference, then, is there in the objects?

The only distinction indicated is not a difference of higher and lower, but lies in the natures of the two classes of Ideas. Mathematics can use 'visible images': a number can be represented by a collection of things, a square by a picture. Such aids have always been employed; the mathematician is not blamed here for using them; he knows he is not thinking of these collections and pictures, but of Ideas (510d). Of moral Ideas there are no visible images; their likenesses (εἰκόνες) in this world are invisible

[1] Cf. παρακαλοῦσα τὴν νόησιν 523b, λογισμόν τε καὶ νόησιν παρακαλοῦσα 524b παρακλητικὰ τῆς διανοίας . . . ἐγερτικὰ τῆς νοήσεως 524d.

properties of souls (402c). Hence it is harder to see the difference between the justice of a particular action or character and Justice itself than to distinguish two apples from the number 2, also represented by other visible pairs. Accordingly, mathematics serves as the easiest bridge from the sense world to the intelligible, and should precede the study of moral Ideas.[1] The distinction of objects is a matter of expediency in teaching and of no further importance for our purpose.[2]

(b) *Procedures.* The contrast of the two procedures, in mathematics and dialectic, does not correspond to the difference, just dismissed, between mathematical and moral Ideas. The dialectical procedure will be found to apply to both fields of objects.

Plato first describes the procedure of mathematics and the condition of the science in his time. The main point is that the prevailing method is deductive, a downward movement from premiss to conclusion: 'the mind is constrained to start its investigation from hypotheses, travelling not towards a beginning (principle) but towards an end (conclusion)' (510b). The geometer, for instance, takes as hypotheses the figures and three kinds of angle, and treating them as known, gives no account of them to himself or to others, as if they were evident to anyone. Starting from these hypotheses, he 'proceeds through all the rest and reaches a conclusion upon the question he set out to investigate'.

We must first fix the meaning of 'hypothesis' in mathematics. Aristotle records two uses of the word, both relevant to Plato's account of mathematics and dialectic. He is writing primarily about logic, not geometry, and we may take it that his definitions of 'hypothesis', 'postulate', 'axiom', etc., were current among mathematicians, and probably formulated in the Academy.

(1) The first is the 'hypothesis relative to the pupil'. The word here bears its old sense of a supposition 'suggested' or 'put to

[1] Nicomachus, *Introd. Arithm.*, I, 3, 6, *κλίμαξί τισι καὶ γεφύραις ἔοικε ταῦτα τὰ μαθήματα διαβιβάζοντα τὴν διάνοιαν ἡμῶν ἀπὸ τῶν αἰσθητῶν καὶ δοξαστῶν ἐπὶ τὰ νοητὰ καὶ ἐπιστημονικά*. The context refers to *Rep.*, vii.

[2] Plato does not say that geometers are 'forced to use sensible diagrams' either because their science 'depends on hypotheses of which they can give no account' or because 'the hypothesis of three kinds of angles has a spatial character' (Burnet, *Greek Philosophy*, i, 229). The word 'forced' (*ἀναγκάζεται*, 510b, 511a) applies only to the use of deductive procedure, and at 511c it is remarked that in studying mathematics we are 'forced' to use abstract reasoning (*διάνοια*), and not the senses.

another person (ὑποτίθεσθαί τινι) for his acceptance as a basis of argument—the sense which we shall meet with again in the technique of philosophic conversation.[1] In the middle of a discussion of the basic truths of demonstrative science (*Anal. Post.*, I, 10), Aristotle recalls this usage. 'That which is capable of proof but assumed by the teacher without proof is, if the pupil believes and accepts it, hypothesis—that is, relatively to the pupil; if the pupil has no opinion or a contrary opinion on the matter, the same assumption is a postulate.'[2] Here the making of an hypothesis is simply an expedient in conversational teaching. Any proposition in the science may, on some occasion, be taken as an assumption by agreement[3] between teacher and pupil.

A special case falling under the head of the 'relative' or *ad hoc* hypothesis is any assumption made with a view to the solution of a problem. This procedure 'by way of hypothesis' is illustrated at *Meno* 86e ff., where the geometer, asked whether a given area can be inscribed in the form of a triangle in a given circle, replies that he does not know yet, but thinks he has a hypothesis that will be useful: only if the given area is of such and such a kind can the inscription be made. 'Accordingly, by using an hypothesis, I am ready to tell you what results—whether the thing is possible or not.' This is an example of διορισμός 'the determination of the conditions or limits of the possibility of a solution of the problem, whether in its original form or in the form to which it is reduced.'[4] The process (to which we shall return later) is analytical, involving the divination of a premiss that must be true if the required conclusion is to follow. The method can be applied to the problems presented by observed facts in nature. Thus Plato is said

[1] Burnet (*Greek Philosophy*, 162) explains ὑποτίθεσθαι as meaning setting before oneself or others a task to be done or 'a subject to be treated'. He appears to me here to confuse the hypothesis with the enunciation (πρότασις) the Q.E.D. or Q.E.F., which states the conclusion desired, not a premiss, of a demonstration or construction.

[2] 76b, 27. Cf. Proclus, *Eucl.* I., p. 76, 6 (Friedl.) Throughout this paper I have made much use of Proclus' Commentary, which, when allowance is made for neoplatonic mysticism, illuminates the Greek conception of mathematical science and its methods.

[3] Cf. *E.N.*, 1133b, 20, coin as an agreed common measure of commodities is 'hypothetical', ἐξ ὑποθέσεως· διὸ νόμισμα καλεῖται, or 'conventional', κατὰ συνθήκην, καὶ διὰ τοῦτο τοὔνομα ἔχει νόμισμα (a 29). The two expressions are here synonymous.

[4] Heath, *A History of Greek Mathematics*, i, 303. Proclus, *Eucl.* I, p. 66.

to have set the Academy the problem of finding out on what assumptions (τίνων ὑποτεθέντων) the apparent irregularity of the heavenly bodies' movements can be reconciled with the real regularity so as to 'save the appearances'.[1] The *Republic* says that the treatment of 'problems' should figure, not only in geometry, but in astronomical inquiry (530b) and in harmonics (531c).

(2) The science itself, on the other hand, has its own hypotheses (in a narrow sense), which are not 'relative', but basic truths (ἀρχαί). Aristotle[2] explains that any demonstrative science must start from necessary truths taken as indemonstrable. Thus geometry takes for granted (λαμβάνει), besides the common axioms, (*a*) the *definitions* of its subject-matter (magnitude) and of certain 'essential attributes' of magnitude, such as 'straight', 'triangular', and (*b*) the *existence* of magnitude and of certain other primary things corresponding to the definitions, *viz.*, points and lines. The existence of everything else e.g., the various figures and their properties, has to be proved by constructions and demonstration. Definitions are not hypotheses: they do not assert the existence of anything, but only state a meaning that must be understood. Hypotheses are assumptions of the existence of things defined.

In speaking of the hypotheses of mathematics (510c), Plato primarily means the 'absolute' kind of hypothesis, not the 'relative'. He seems, moreover, like Aristotle, to restrict 'hypotheses' to assumptions of existence and not to include definitions; a definition in mathematics is itself an 'account' (λόγος) of the meaning of a term, and no 'account of it' can be demanded. His instances are 'odd and even (arithmetic), the figures and three kinds of angles (geometry), and other kindred things in each branch of study' (510c). According to Aristotle, arithmetic and geometry assume the *meaning* (definition) of odd and even, etc., straight and triangular, etc., but the *existence* of these things should be demonstrated. The only things whose existence these sciences are entitled to take for granted as ultimate hypotheses are the unit (arithmetic) and magnitude, points, and lines (geometry). He thus would agree with Plato in condemning mathematicians who should treat as ultimate hypotheses the *existence* of 'odd and even, the figures and three kinds of angles'.

[1] Simplic., *de caelo*, 488, 21; 492, 31 (Heiberg). Cf. Burnet, *Greek Philosophy*, 222.

[2] *Anal. Post.*, I, 10. Cf. Heath, *Thirteen Books of Euclid*, I, 117 ff.

Probably Plato has in mind also the original meaning of ὑποτίθεσθαι, and thinks of the mathematician's assumptions as put to the learner for acceptance in the process of instruction. The whole description would fit the conversational method of teaching. When he says, 'starting from the hypotheses, they go through all the rest and reach a conclusion ὁμολογουμένως', this ambiguous word may mean either that the whole demonstration hangs together *consistently* (though it hangs, so to say, in the air so long as the hypothesis is not proved), or that it rests on *agreement* between teacher and pupil to accept the hypothesis. The same ambiguity recurs at 533c, 'How can such ὁμολογία (consistency or agreement) ever become knowledge?'

Geometry still awaited its codification by Euclid. Solid geometry had 'not yet been discovered' in Socrates' time (528b), and was in process of being discovered at the Academy when the *Republic* was written. The textbook of geometry for the Academy was to be the work of Plato's pupils, Theudius of Magnesia and others; when written, it was a less perfect structure than Euclid's *Elements*.[1] At present the science consisted of a number of theorems, with alternative proofs established by various mathematicians using different hypotheses; the theorem had not yet been fitted together in a single chain of deduction. No one had reduced the primitive hypotheses of the science itself to the smallest possible number, or made out what they were. Plato saw that hypotheses such as those he mentioned ought not to be laid down as 'evident to everyone' or taken as principles of which no account could rightly be demanded. They could be traced back to a higher principle. We should then arrive at the genuine hypotheses (or hypothesis) of the science itself. Thence the whole structure could be deduced in a single chain of reasoning, and the gaps between the scattered theorems filled in. Arithmetic and the other branches will be submitted to the same treatment. This belongs to the programme of research that will be outlined.

Turning from the deductive procedure of mathematics to the

[1] Proclus, *Eucl.* I, p. 66 (after Eudemus): Leodamas, Archytas, and Theaetetus increased the number of theorems and brought them into a more scientific connection; Eudoxus added to the number of universal theorems; Plato's pupils carried the whole of geometry further towards perfection; and Theudius drew up a good statement of the 'elements'. Other improvements are recorded before Euclid completed the structure.

description of dialectic (511b), we find that the ascent to the first principle is part of the task of dialectic, whose procedure in criticising the current hypotheses of mathematics will thus be in the reverse direction. In mathematical proof the mind 'travels' down through an argument limited by the premisses assumed 'as if the mind could not mount above its hypotheses' (τῶν ὑποθέσεων ἀνωτέρω ἐκβαίνειν, 511a). Dialectic includes an opposite movement of thought, upwards, 'treating its hypotheses not as principles but literally as hypo-theses, positions laid down like steps[1] which discourse can mount upon and take off from in order that, advancing all the way to that which rests on no hypothesis[2]—to the principle of the whole—it may apprehend that'. We shall discuss later the scope of research in the dialectical criticism of mathematical hypotheses. Here we must consider the two contrasted movements—downwards in mathematical deduction, upwards in dialectical criticism.

(c) *The Two Movements of Thought*. I shall argue that, where Plato observes a distinction between *noesis* and *dianoia*, *noesis* (in one of its senses) means the upward movement of intuition, *dianoia* (in one of its senses) the downward movement of reasoning in deductive argument.

Plato realised that the mind must possess the power of taking a step or leap upwards from the conclusion to the premiss implied in it. The prior truth cannot, of course, be deduced or proved from the conclusion; it must be grasped (ἅψασθαι, 511b) by an act of analytical penetration. Such an act is involved in the solution 'by way of hypothesis' at *Meno* 86, already quoted; the geometer directly perceives, without discursive argument, that a prior condition must be satisfied if the desired construction is to follow. Now in a certain passage Proclus has been understood to associate Plato's method of dialectical ascent to genuine principles with the

[1] οἷον ἐπιβάσεις τε καὶ ὁρμάς. The metaphor is from climbing stairs, *Symp.*, 211c, ὥσπερ ἐπαναβαθμοῖς χρώμενον, Ar., *Met.*, 990a, 5, ἀρχὰς ἱκανὰς ἐπαναβῆναι καὶ ἐπὶ τὰ ἀνωτέρω τῶν ὄντων. The primary and common meaning of ὁρμή is 'impulse' or 'effort' or 'impetus'. It is nearer to 'spring' than to 'springboard'.

[2] μέχρι τοῦ ἀνυποθέτου, 511b. Mr. Ross notes that Aristotle (*Met.*, 1005b, 14) uses ἀνυπόθετον 'quite in the Platonic sense of the word' of principles 'about which we cannot be deceived, which are best known and rest on no hypothesis, and which must be known if one is to know anything' (W. D. Ross, *Aristotle's Metaphysics* I., 262–3).

method of analysis in geometry. After mentioning a contemporary with an exceptional gift for obtaining the required result from the fewest possible principles, without working by method, Proclus adds: 'Nevertheless certain methods have been handed down. The finest is the method which by means of analysis carries the thing sought up to an acknowledged principle (ἐπ' ἀρχὴν ὁμολογουμένην ἀνάγουσα τὸ ζητούμενον); a method which Plato, as they say, communicated to Leodamas, and by which the latter too is said to have discovered many things in geometry'.[1] Sir Thomas Heath remarks:

> 'Analysis being according to the ancient view nothing more than a series of successive reductions of a theorem or problem till it is finally reduced to a theorem or problem already known, it is difficult to see in what Plato's supposed discovery could have consisted; for analysis in this sense must have been frequently used in earlier investigations [of which examples are given]. On the other hand, Proclus's language suggests that what he had in mind was the philosophical method described in the passage of the *Republic* [511b], which of course does not refer to mathematical analysis at all; it may therefore well be that the idea that Plato discovered the method of analysis is due to a misapprehension. But analysis and synthesis following each other are related in the same way as the upward and downward progressions in the dialectician's intellectual method. It has been suggested, therefore, that Plato's achievement was to observe the importance, from the point of view of logical rigour, of the confirmatory synthesis following analysis.'

No doubt Plato did not invent the method of analysis; but the connection with dialectical method is closer than is here suggested. Plato may well have been the first to recognise as distinct the movement of thought involved in what Aristotle calls the 'analysis of a mathematical diagram'. Describing deliberation, which proposes an end to be achieved by action and then works backwards along the chain of means to that end, till it reaches, as a first link in the chain, an action that can be at once performed, Aristotle compares this regressive process in the solution of a practical problem to 'analysing a mathematical diagram', where the last step in the analysis becomes the first in the construction that follows. The Paraphrast adds a description of the subsequent

[1] Proclus, *Eucl.*, I, p. 211, 18, Sir Thomas Heath's translation (*Greek Mathematics*, I, 291).

deduction: 'the mathematician having reached the last step in his analysis, then assumes that, and, travelling from it through the other steps, so demonstrates the conclusion proposed'.[1]

The process of 'analysing a diagram' is described in a curious passage where Aristotle, with instructive ambiguity, uses the word *diagramma* so that commentators doubt whether he means geometrical proofs (Bonitz) or geometrical constructions (Ross).[2]

> *Met.*, 1051*a*, 21, '*Diagrammata* are discovered by an activity. For it is by dividing (drawing lines in the given figure) that people discover them. If they had already been divided, they would have been obvious; as it is, they are present potentially. Why are the angles of the triangle equal to two right angles? Because the angles about one point are equal to two right angles. So if the line parallel to the side had already been drawn, the reason would have been immediately plain to inspection. . . . Clearly, then, the potentially existing (*diagrammata*) are discovered by being brought into actuality. The reason is that the activity is intuition' (or, reading ἡ νόησις ἐνέργεια with Ross, 'the intuition employed is an activity').

'If they (the "diagrams" = the given figures) had already been divided, they (the "diagrams" = geometrical constructions or proofs) would have been obvious.' Aristotle uses the word *diagramma* to mean: (1) the given figure, in which the divisions exist potentially; (2) the figure completed by making the divisions actual and thus exhibiting the proof in a picture, so that one has only to look at it to see the reason (prior truth) actually displayed in the construction itself; and (3) the proof whose 'elements' are so made obvious to inspection. What concerns us is the process by which the reason or prior truth is discerned. The geometer contemplates the given figure, a triangle, either drawn on paper or in the mind's eye. Knowing already that the angles about a single point are equal to two right angles (*Eucl.*, I, 13), he divines that this prior truth is latent in the given figure (δυνάμει ἐνυπάρχει). He makes it explicit by producing the base of his triangle and drawing the line parallel to the side (△∠). He thus brings this

[1] *E.N.*, iii, 3, 11, ὁ βουλευόμενος ἔοικε ζητεῖν καὶ ἀναλύειν τὸν εἰρημένον τρόπον ὥσπερ διάγραμμα . . . καὶ τὸ ἔσχατον ἐν τῇ ἀναλύσει πρῶτον εἶναι ἐν τῇ γενέσει. Paraphr. καθάπερ ὁ μαθηματικός, πρὸς ὁ ἔσχατον ἀφίξεται ἀναλύων, τοῦτο ὑποτιθεὶς καὶ ἀπὸ τούτου διὰ τῶν ἄλλων ὁδεύων ἀποδείκνυσι τὸ προκειμένον. See Stewart, *Notes, on the Nichomachean Ethics of Aristotle* ad loc.

[2] Cf. Xen. *Mem.*, IV, 7, Socrates thought geometry should not be studied μέχρι τῶν δυσξυνέτων διαγραμμάτων.

'element' in the demonstration into actual existence, making it visible to simple inspection. He has next to demonstrate that he has solved his problem. Having laid bare the 'elements' needed to compose the proof, and ascertained that they are all theorems previously established, he will now frame his demonstration in full discursive form—a deduction starting from the hypothesis, 'Let there be a triangle *ABC*' (*Eucl.*, I, 32). Aristotle speaks elsewhere of the 'elements of *diagrammata* and of demonstrations in general' as analogous to the elements into which bodies are said to be ultimately divisible. They are 'the primary demonstrations *contained in* a larger number of consequent demonstrations'.[1] The title of Euclid's *Elements* preserves this meaning.

Themistius[2] defines analysis as 'assuming a true conclusion and then discovering the premisses by which it is inferred'. Where the problem is a construction, the geometer may start by contemplating a picture of the conclusion desired. In the *Meno* instance, he would draw the given rectangle and a triangle inscribed in the given circle, and then consider what properties his rectangle must have. Those properties are 'elements' in the solution. Thus he takes the construction to pieces. The opposite process is *synthesis*, 'putting together' this element and others in the proper deductive order. So Aristotle says that one may 'analyse a diagram and not be able to put it together again'.[3] Each step in the demonstration is a component 'contained in' the complete *diagramma* (diagram, construction, proof).

Pappus (VII, Introd.) gives a clear account of Analysis and Synthesis, which has been lamentably misunderstood:

'The *Treasury of Analysis* is a collection of material specially

[1] *Met.*, 1014a, 31, τὰ τῶν σωμάτων στοιχεῖα λέγουσιν οἱ λέγοντες εἰς ἃ διαιρεῖται τὰ σώματα ἔσχατα . . . παραπλησίως δὲ καὶ τὰ τῶν διαγραμμάτων στοιχεῖα λέγεται καὶ ὅλως τὰ τῶν ἀποδείξεων · αἱ γὰρ πρῶται ἀποδείξεις καὶ ἐν πλείοσιν ἀποδείξεσιν ἐνυπάρχουσαι, αὗται στοιχεῖα τῶν ἀποδείξεων λέγονται. Cf. 998a, 25. Menaechmus ap. Procl., *Eucl.* I, p. 72, τὸ στοιχεῖον λέγεται διχῶς . . . τὸ κατασκεύαζον ἐστὶ τοῦ κατασκευαζομένου στοιχεῖον, ὡς τὸ πρῶτον παρ' Εὐκλείδῃ τοῦ δευτέρου . . . ἄλλως δὲ . . . εἰς ὃ ἁπλούστερον ὑπάρχον διαιρεῖται τὸ σύνθετον . . ὥσπερ τὰ αἰτήματα στοιχεῖα τῶν θεωρημάτων.

[2] On *Anal. Post.* I, 12 (p. 26, 23, Wallies), ἀναλύειν δὲ λέγω νῦν τὸ τεθέντος τινὸς ἀληθοῦς συμπεράσματος τὰς προτάσεις ἐξευρίσκειν δι' ὧν συνήχθη.

[3] Top., 175a, 27, συμβαίνει δέ ποτε καθάπερ ἐν τοῖς διαγράμμασιν · καὶ γὰρ ἐκεῖ ἀναλύσαντες ἐνίοτε συνθεῖναι πάλιν ἀδυνατοῦμεν. Even in so early a proposition as *Eucl.*, I, 32, a large number of 'elements' are involved, and it is a nice question how many should figure in the demonstration.

provided for those who, after doing the ordinary elements, wish to acquire, in dealing with lines (as distinct from problems in sciences other than geometry), a power of discovering the solutions of problems proposed to them. . . .

'Analysis is the procedure which starts from the desired conclusion, taken as agreed, through *the succession of sequent steps* (διὰ τῶν ἑξῆς ἀκολούθων—steps that in Analysis are traversed upwards, from each proposition to a prior proposition implied in it) to something agreed upon in Synthesis (some proposition previously proved and now admitted). For in Analysis we suppose (ὑποθέμενοι) the desired result to be already accomplished, and look for that (prior proposition) from which it results, and then again for the prior proposition leading to *that*, until, by tracing our steps backwards in this way, we meet with something already known or holding the rank of a first principle. Such a method we call 'Analysis' as being a 'solution backwards' (ἀνάπαλιν λύσιν).

'In Synthesis, on the other hand, reversing the process, we take as already done the last step reached in the Analysis; the steps that followed one another in the former (upward) process (τὰ ἑπόμενα ἐκεῖ) we here put into their natural (logical) order as leading on one to another (downwards), and put them together one after another; so finally we arrive at the establishment of the desired result. This we call Synthesis.'

Analysis, he continues, is either (*a*) *theoretical* (to prove a theorem) or (*b*) *problematical* (to solve a problem of construction). '(*a*) In the *theoretical* kind we assume the conclusion sought as existent and true; and then, through the sequent steps, taken as true and as hypothetically existing (ὡς ἀληθῶν καὶ ὡς ἔστι καθ' ὑπόθεσιν—these assumptions of existence are as yet unproved hypotheses awaiting confirmation in the Synthesis), advance (upwards) as far as something admitted (some proposition, true or false, admitted to be implied, as a necessary premiss or "element", in the conclusion we started from). Then, if (1) that admitted thing is true, the conclusion sought will be true also, and the demonstration will correspond, in the reverse order, to the Analysis (the Synthesis traverses the same series of steps, but in deductive order); but if (2) we come upon something admitted that is false, the conclusion sought will also be false. (*b*) In the *problematical* kind, we assume the (construction) propounded as if it were known; and next advance (upwards) through the sequent steps, taken as true, as far as something admitted (a construction, possible or impossible, admitted to be a necessary element in the desired construction). Then if (1) the admitted thing is possible and obtainable—"given", as the mathematicians say—the construction propounded will be possible too, and once more the demonstration will correspond, in the reverse order, to the Analysis; but if (2) we come upon something admitted that is impossible, the problem also will be impossible.'[1]

It is quite possible to accept the statement that Plato 'discovered' the method of Analysis, in the same sense as Aristotle discovered the syllogism; that is to say, he was the first to reflect upon the process of thought involved and to describe it in contrast with the process of Synthesis. And it is certain that in his account of the dialectical ascent Plato is describing the upward movement of thought which has been illustrated from geometrical analysis. Since he assigns the mental experience called *noesis* to the corresponding section of the Line, it seems justifiable to say that the intuition used in this upward spring of thought is one of the meanings of *noesis*. I cannot point to a passage where the word must have this sense to the exclusion of its more general uses, but that is because Plato constantly substitutes the metaphors of 'grasping' (ἅψασθαι) and 'seeing' (κατιδεῖν, θεᾶσθαι, etc.), for νοεῖν in this sense. The important thing is not the name, but the fact that the intuitive movement is unmistakably recognised. For

[1] I gather from Sir T. Heath's discussion of this passage (*Thirteen Books of Euclid*, i, 138) that modern historians of mathematics—'careful studies' by Hankel, Duhamel, and Zeuthen, and others by Ofterdinger and Cantor are cited—have made nonsense of much of it by misunderstanding the phrase '*the succession of sequent steps*' (τῶν ἑξῆς ἀκολούθων) as meaning logical '*consequences*', as if it were τὰ συμβαίνοντα. Some may have been misled by Gerhardt (Pappus, vii, viii, Halle, 1871), who renders it '*Folgerungen*'. They have then been at great pains to show how the premisses of a demonstration can be the consequences of the conclusion. The whole is clear when we see—what Pappus says—that the same sequence of steps is followed in both processes——*upwards* in Analysis, from the consequence to premisses implied in that consequence, and *downwards* in Synthesis, when the steps are reversed to frame the theorem or demonstrate the construction 'in the natural (logical) order'. You cannot follow the same series of steps first one way, then the opposite way, and arrive at logical *consequences* in both directions. And Pappus never said you could. He added ἑξῆς to indicate that the steps 'follow in *succession*' but are not, as ἀκόλουθα alone would suggest, logically 'consequent' in the upward direction. In the definitions of Analysis and Synthesis interpolated in Euclid XIII (Heath, ibid., I, 138) the phrase διὰ τῶν ἀκολούθων is used in the same way: 'Analysis is a taking of the thing sought as admitted (and the passage) *through the sequent steps* to some admitted truth'. Here again it is translated by Heiberg (Teubner edit., III, 365) '*per consequentias*', and by Heath 'through its consequences'. These definitions may have been copied, with abbreviation, from Pappus' statement.

similar reasons I infer that the deductive reasoning characteristic of mathematical procedure is one of the meanings of *dianoia*. *Noesis* is an immediate act of vision; the ascent is made by one or more sudden leaps. *Dianoia*, on the other hand, is a continuous process; the mind 'journeys' (πορευομένη, 510b) along a path of discourse which the reasoner 'traverses' (διεξιόντες τὰ λοιπά, 510d) from beginning to end.

The next point to be noted is that the dialectical method includes also a downward process following after the ascent to the principle. The description continues: 'having grasped the first principle, turning back again and holding to that which depends on it, then and only then discourse may descend to a conclusion, making no use at all of any sensible thing, but only of Ideas (passing) through Ideas to Ideas, and end with Ideas'. The whole of this first account of dialectic is closely compressed and framed in terms chosen to fit the dialectical treatment either of mathematics or of the moral Ideas. As we shall see later, where the two fields are separately considered, the procedure is not altogether the same in both. But both movements of thought are employed in both fields of objects. Neither the analytical power of *noesis* nor the process of deductive reasoning is limited to mathematical objects; and 'hypotheses' (though of a different sort) are used in the effort to define moral Ideas and are subjected to criticism.

Even in mathematics we can conceive the geometer as dispensing with diagrams, visible or imagined, and contemplating the Idea of the triangle—the essential nature of all triangles (of which in fact no picture can be made without adding irrelevant properties, 'equilateral', 'scalene', or 'isosceles'). This nature is I believe, conceived by Plato and Aristotle as containing implicit in itself all the 'essential properties' that can be drawn out and demonstrated in the indefinite chain of *theorems* about the triangle. The *problem* was something to be done; its solution was the fruit of action (πράττειν)[1] which brought out into actual existence

[1] Proclus, *Eucl.*, I, p. 77, 12. καθάπερ γὰρ αἱ ποιητικαὶ τῶν ἐπιστημῶν θεωρίας μετέχουσι, κατὰ τὰ αὐτὰ δὴ καὶ αἱ θεωρητικαὶ τὰ προβλήματα ταῖς ποιήσεσιν ἀνάλογον προσειλήφασι. *Rep.*, 527a, λέγουσι μέν που μάλα γελοίως τε καὶ ἀναγκαίως · ὡς γὰρ πράττοντές τε καὶ πράξεως ἕνεκα πάντας τοὺς λόγους ποιούμενοι λέγουσι τετραγωνίζειν, κτλ. There are traces of an Academic controversy as to the nature and possibility of 'operations' in mathematics, whose objects are eternal; but this question cannot be pursued here.

the elementary constructions divined by intuition as latent in the given figure, and exhibited them in a completed diagram. The '*theorem*' is the fruit of contemplation (θεωρεῖν), which penetrates by intuition to the latent properties 'contained in' the essence. The 'demonstration' (ἀπόδειξις) is the exhibition of these properties as belonging to the essence, in the form of explicit statements set out in logical sequence, deductive or syllogistic.

Further, not only mathematical Ideas like the Triangle, but moral (and other) Ideas are genera, which can be conceived as containing, potentially latent within them, the species.[1] These species are made explicit in the tabular Division (διαίρεσις), aiming at a *definition* that will isolate the lowest species from every other species. When dialectical method is applied to the definition of an Idea, the ascent is made by the 'synoptic' act of divining by intuition the unity pervading a manifold 'gathered together' (συναγωγή). This unity becomes the 'genus' that must stand at the head of the table. The downward process is 'Division', discerning 'differences' within this unity and arranging them in proper logical sequence.[2] An analogy between these upward and downward movements in obtaining definitions and the upward and downward movements of the geometer's analysis and synthesis in obtaining constructions was perceived by Proclus. Hence the passage above quoted (p. 43) goes on to connect the Platonic Division of genus into species with the solution of a problem by construction:

> 'The second is the method of Division, which divides into its parts (species) the genus proposed for consideration (as a result of previous συναγωγή), and gives a starting-point for the demonstration by means of the elimination of the other elements in the construction of what is proposed, which method also Plato extolled as being of assistance in *all sciences*.'

To Proclus the dialectician's contemplation of the genus proposed for division seemed analogous to the geometer's contemplation of his given figure. The final definition of the species sets

[1] Thus at *Tim.*, 30c, the Idea of Animal embraces within itself (ἐν ἑαυτῷ περιλαβὸν ἔχει), all the 'intelligible animals' falling under the four species of 39e, ἐνούσας ἰδέας τῷ ὅ ἔστι ζῷον.

[2] In the *Sophist* and *Politicus* many rules are laid down for observance in the downward process of Division; but no rules are, or can be, given for συναγωγή. Σύνοψις is an act, not a methodical procedure. It is a case of hit or miss, and you cannot tell which, till you have deduced the consequences.

out in explicit form (λόγος) the elements (differences) contained in the essence defined, as the geometer's completed diagram exhibits the elements in the demonstration. Each, in reaching his results, eliminates, step by step, irrelevant elements: the dialectician, as he selects each *differentia*, rejects its alternative; the geometer retains only the elements that will figure in his demonstration and rejects others that occur to him but are found not to lead to his conclusion.[1]

(d) *States of mind.* It remains to note another use of the words *noesis* (or *nous*) and *dianoia*. Glaucon says he understands the account of dialectic as meaning that 'the field of the real and intelligible as studied by the science (ἐπιστήμη) of dialectic has a clearer truth (σαφέστερον) than what is studied by the mathematical "arts" as they are called, whose hypotheses are taken as starting-points'; and that 'although students are compelled in studying these arts to use abstract reasoning (διανοίᾳ) and not the senses, yet, because they proceed from hypotheses without going up to a first principle, they do not, you think, come to have *nous* (νοῦν ἴσχειν), albeit their objects can be objects of *nous* in connection with a first principle (καίτοι νοητῶν ὄντων μετὰ ἀρχῆς). I understand you to describe the state of mind (ἕξις) of geometers and other mathematicians as not *nous* but *dianoia*, regarding *dianoia* as something between belief and *nous*' (511c–d). Later, the mathematician is said to live in a sort of dream, not seeing reality with waking vision (533b); his so-called knowledge is not science (ἐπιστήμη) but only *dianoia* (533d).

The contrast between the two states of mind may be illustrated from the *Meno*. The slave who is there questioned[2] at first produces false beliefs about the solution of the problem, then true beliefs; but these will become knowledge only when he has been taken through the proof repeatedly and grasped its logical necessity 'by reflection on the reason' (αἰτίας λογισμῷ). The mathematician and his pupil in the *Republic* have done all this, but now Plato will not call their state of mind 'scientific knowledge' or *nous*,

[1] Elsewhere (p. 57, 22) Proclus mentions 'Division of species from genera' as a method also used by geometry in obtaining definitions which figure among its first premisses.

[2] Referring to this experiment at *Phd.*, 73b, Plato uses the phrase ἐάν τις ἐπὶ τὰ διαγράμματα ἄγῃ. The slave is confronted with a given figure and a problem of construction.

because the reason they have reflected upon is an assumption that is not either demonstrated or seen to be indemonstrable. Their intellectual understanding of a coherent, but isolated, piece of deductive reasoning is *dianoia*; they will not 'come to have *nous*' or genuine knowledge until they have gone up to intuitive apprehension of the indemonstrable principle of their whole science. By *nous*, here and later, Plato means the perfectly clear vision, or unshakable grasp, of the completed structure of mathematical truth, through all the ramifications so far discovered, as illuminated from above, by the light of the ultimate premiss, intuitively seen and such that it cannot be questioned. So long as bits of the structure are allowed to depend on questionable hypotheses, there will be an atmosphere of dimness and uncertainty in the state of mind. The structure might fall, should the premisses prove to be unwarranted; and anyhow the truth of the assumptions is not either proved or certainly 'clear to anyone'. The intuition of the ultimate premiss will dispel this mist of uncertainty and irradiate the whole science.[1] The mathematician will then 'come to have *nous*', the state of mind compared to vision, no longer in a dream, but in the light of day.

Conclusions. I conclude that the terms *noesis* and *dianoia*, where a distinction is observed between them, are used in several senses, just as the curious name εἰκασία for the fourth 'mental experience' includes 'perception of images' and 'guess-work' (the prisoners in the Cave *watch* the sequence of the passing shadows, and *divine* which will come next, 516c–d).[2] *Noesis* means: (*A*) generally, as opposed to αἴσθησις or δόξα, the cognition of any objects or truths in the intelligible realm; (*B*) as opposed to *dianoia*, (1) the intuitive act of apprehending, by an upward leap, an Idea or a prior truth implicit in a conclusion (for this sense ἅψασθαι, κατιδεῖν, θεᾶσθαι, etc., are usually substituted for νοεῖν); (2) the state of mind (properly called νοῦν ἔχειν or ἐπιστήμη) of one who sees with perfect clearness a completed structure of truth illuminated by the unquestionable principle. *Dianoia* means: (*A*) generally, 'abstract

[1] Cf. Proclus, *Eucl.* I, p. 27, 13, νοῦ καταλάμποντος ἄνωθεν τὴν ἐπιστήμην·

[2] A knowledge of nature consisting of empirical observations and predictions based on them, is to Plato not 'science' or even 'art', but ἐμπειρία 'merely preserving a memory of what usually happens' (*Gorg.*, 501a) without being able to give any account of the reason, and involving a naïve 'trust' (πίστις) in the reality of the appearance it records.

thinking' (with νόησις and λογισμός as synonyms); (*B*) as opposed to *noesis*, (1) the downward movement of understanding following a deductive argument from premiss to conclusion; (2) the uncertain state of mind of one whose so-called 'knowledge' consists only of isolated chains of reasoning depending on an assumption either not demonstrated or not seen to be indemonstrable. There are many degrees of dimness in this twilight; but, if perfect enlightenment has never been attained, all human knowledge moves in this region of dream. All our own mathematical knowledge still lies somewhere in the vast range between a child's 'true belief' that two and two make four and the perfect comprehension, not yet (I gather) certainly achieved by any human intellect, of all the logical concepts and propositions implied in $2 + 2 = 4$.

II. THE PROGRAMMES OF EDUCATION AND RESEARCH

We need not linger over the allegory of the Cave, symbolising the whole process of education from the most naïve acceptance of any appearance at its face value up to the apprehension of the first principle of reality and truth. Emphasis falls on the need to accustom the soul's eye to the light gradually, by training in mathematics before dialectical canvassing of moral Ideas is allowed.[1]

Next comes the review of the mathematical sciences. Here Plato speaks as head of the Academy, a school of statesmen directed by men engaged in the advance of theoretical knowledge. His two interests—education and research—become distinguishable. Not that they could ever be separated: the researcher is always learning, and in communicating his results he is teaching; while the student who follows those results is exercising the same faculties in rediscovering them. Plato, moreover, with his belief in teaching by conversation, aimed at a closer co-operation of researcher and pupil than can often be achieved in a modern university. In the plan of the *Republic* the interest in education overshadows research. Despite all this, the distinction is clearer in his text than in the commentaries.

[1] 516a συνηθείας δέοιτ' ἄν. It is here that the difference in the objects comes in. The 'visible images' of mathematical Ideas are compared to shadows and reflections in water, which the eye will take in at first more readily than the objects that cast them. Later, it will turn from these (terrestrial) objects themselves to the stars (the moral Ideas).

As each branch of mathematics is considered, its utility in educating the mind to abstract thought is contrasted with the vulgar utility of calculation for counting objects, of geometry for land-measurement, and so on. At the same time, the gap that should be filled by solid geometry is indicated, and the backwardness of research is attributed to the fact that no city holds these studies in honour. The studies are hard and 'researchers need a director (ἐπιστάτου δέονται οἱ ζητοῦντες), without whom they are not likely to make discoveries'. It is not easy to find one, 'and even supposing him to arise, ὡς νῦν ἔχει, men who are inclined to research would be too conceited to follow his guidance' (528b). Plato must have enjoyed framing the studied ambiguities forced on him by his dramatic method. *Socrates* means: '*as things are* (the state taking no interest), a director, even if he arose, would not be obeyed'. *Plato* means: 'and even if a director should arise, *as in fact he has*, he would not be obeyed'. Athens, in a word, would do well to encourage the Academy, and in Plato and his colleagues she has directors of research ready to hand.[1] All through what follows, Plato, while laying down a curriculum of education for the Academy and for the ideal philosopher, at the same time indicates a programme for the advance of knowledge. I shall try, so far as possible, to disentangle the two.

The Curriculum of Mathematical Education (536d–537c). The stages of education up to the point where dialectic begins are set out as follows:

(1) The elementary education in music and gymnastic has already been outlined in II–III.

(2) 536d–537a. All the studies in the mathematical προπαιδεία to dialectic are to be introduced to children up to the age of seventeen or eighteen in the form of play, not of compulsion. (The kindergarten methods of *Laws* 819b ff.—lessons in counting apples and wreaths or in grouping athletes in pairs and byes, lessons in weights and measures, etc.—will be used at the earliest stage. More advanced exercises will gradually wean the mind from dealing with apples and diagrams to thinking about abstract numbers and ideal figures. Then, as ever since, pupils would be taken through operations and proofs already set down in textbooks.)

[1] Cf. Adam's note, ad loc, and Heath, *Greek Mathematics*, I, 12.

(3) 537b. Then follow two or three years of 'gymnastic' training, too severe to allow of intellectual effort at the same time.

(4) 537c. At the age of twenty a select number will be promoted to ten years' study of the same mathematical sciences from a 'synoptic' or comparative point of view. 'They must bring together the scattered pieces of mathematical learning (*τὰ χύδην μαθήματα*) they have acquired as children into a comprehensive view (*σύνοψιν*) of the relationship of these studies to one another and to the nature of reality.' Only so will their knowledge be securely established (*βέβαιος*). Moreover, this test will reveal which of them are capable of going on to dialectic, where a comprehensive view, seeing many things together and finding in them a unity, is essential (*ὁ γὰρ συνοπτικὸς διαλεκτικός*). This passage echoes 531c–d: the labour spent on the pursuit of all branches of mathematics will be profitable only if it leads up to reflection on their interconnection and relationship. No further details are given; but the length of time allowed—ten years—implies that these mature students will be initiated into the results of advanced mathematical research, which, as will be seen, aims precisely at the co-ordination of mathematical truth in all branches. Some might begin to advance knowledge themselves. The training is such as is given to students for honours in mathematics at a modern university. Then, as now, it could consist almost entirely in taking fresh students over ground already explored.

Preliminary Description of Moral Dialectic in Education (531d–532d). The first mention of the 'synoptic' study of mathematics (531d) is followed by a preliminary description of moral dialectic as the final stage of education.[1] The dialectician is one who can 'give and receive an account' of what he knows. He advances like the prisoner taken outside the Cave, who attempts to look at real things, at the stars, and finally at the sun itself. So the dialectician 'attempts, without using the senses, by means of discourse, to start (*ὁρμᾶν*[2]) towards each form of reality, not giving up until he apprehends by pure intuition (*αὐτῇ νοήσει λάβῃ*) the nature of the Good itself'. He will then be 'at the culminating point of the

[1] The second description (537d ff.) which follows the curriculum just outlined will be considered later.

[2] *ὁρμᾶν* is, of course, intended to recall the *ἐπιβάσεις καὶ ὁρμάς* of 511b and to suggest the upward leap of intuition.

intelligible realm' (ἐπ' αὐτῷ γίγνεται τῷ τοῦ νοητοῦ τέλει). This journey, we are told, is dialectic; the earlier mathematical discipline corresponds to the journey up the interior of the Cave and to the habituation of the eye to the daylight by looking first at shadows and reflections in the world outside. The effect of such discipline has been to lift up 'the highest thing in the soul towards the vision of the highest thing in reality'.

Here (532d) there is a pause. Glaucon next asks for a further account of dialectic on the same scale as the review of the mathematical sciences: 'what is the manner of its working, into how many kinds (εἴδη) is it divided, and what are its methods (ὁδοί)?' Socrates replies that Glaucon will not be able to follow him further: 'You would no longer be seeing an image of what we are speaking of, but the truth itself' (αὐτὸ τὸ ἀληθές). The refusal partly means that no complete account of the kinds and methods of dialectic can be given here without going beyond the scope of the *Republic* into a full statement of the theory of Ideas. But Socrates' words recall Diotima's warning on the threshold of the 'Greater Mysteries'.[1] Why 'the truth itself' is represented as mysterious we shall see later. What now concerns us is Glaucon's suggestion that there is more than one kind kind of dialectic, and more than one method. As I read the following context, Plato does in fact briefly describe, so far as necessary limitations permit, two distinct kinds and methods, proper to research (and incidentally to education) in (*a*) the mathematical and (*b*) the moral fields respectively.

(a) *Dialectic in Mathematical Research* (533a–534b). In this section there is no mention of the Good, but only of the truth (τὸ ἀληθές) and reality (τὸ ὄν). It gives a classification of the arts and sciences in an order of merit; describes the perfecting of mathematical science by dialectical criticism of the hypotheses in use; and revives the contrast between the existing mathematician's state of mind (*dianoia*) and the higher condition of illuminated understanding formerly called *noesis* (or νοῦν ἔχειν), now called 'scientific knowledge' (ἐπιστήμη).

[1] 533a, οὐκέτ', ὦ φίλε Γλαύκων, οἷός τ' ἔσῃ ἀκολουθεῖν, ἐπεὶ τό γ' ἐμὸν οὐδὲν ἂν προθυμίας ἀπολίποι. *Symp.* 210 (Diotima) τὰ δὲ τέλεα καὶ ἐποπτικά . . . οὐκ οἶδ' εἰ οἷός τ' ἂν εἴης [μυηθῆναι]. ἐρῶ μὲν οὖν ἐγὼ καὶ προθυμίας οὐδὲν ἀπολείψω. Both places may contain a reminiscence of a (tragic?) passage, of which fragments seem to survive (unrecognised, so far as I know) at *Rep.*, 497d–e, τὰ γὰρ δὴ μέγαλα πάντ' ἐπισφαλῆ and παρὼν δὲ τὴν ἐμὴν προθυμίαν | εἴσῃ', where παρών can only be explained as a quotation.

The drift is as follows. The power of dialectic alone can reveal the truth to one versed in mathematical science: there is no other way. No one will deny that mathematics (as taught deductively in the προπαιδεία) will not suffice to lead to a grasp of the true nature of its objects; some other method is required. None of the other existing 'arts' will be of any use; some are concerned with human beliefs and desires, others with the production of natural or artificial things, or with the care of them when produced. (This covers all the arts practised in the world of appearance: the fine (mimetic) arts, agriculture, manufacture, medicine, gymnastic, etc.) There remain mathematics—geometry and the rest. These 'arts' have been described as 'laying hold of something of reality', but we observe that they are in a sort of dream and cannot see reality with waking vision, so long as the hypotheses in use are allowed to remain untouched and mathematicians can give no account of them. The true first principle is still unknown, and the conclusions and the whole texture (of deductive demonstration) consist of elements that are not known. 'How can such ὁμολογία (agreement or consistency) be called knowledge (ἐπιστήμη)?' The dialectical method alone proceeds, by the abolition of the hypotheses (τὰς ὑποθέσεις ἀναιροῦσα), to the first principle, in order to make itself secure (ἵνα βεβαιώσηται). It makes use of mathematics as aiding in its work of clearing the eye of the soul and gently drawing it upwards. But the mathematical 'arts' in their present condition ought not to be called 'sciences' (ἐπιστήμας). The state of mind of one who only studies existing mathematics is mere *dianoia*—clearer than 'belief', but dimmer than knowledge. Finally, 'knowledge' or 'science' (ἐπιστήμη) is substituted for *noesis* to designate (*in this context*) the highest 'mental experience', *noesis* being recalled to its first general use—cognition of any objects in the intelligible realm, as opposed to δόξα, cognition of the world of becoming.

The whole of this passage is concerned solely with turning mathematics into a genuine science by reducing it from an assemblage of scattered theorems, or chains of theorems, resting on unproved but demonstrable hypotheses, to a single chain depending on a single principle. No other form of science is even hinted at here or elsewhere in these Books. To say that 'such a unification of the sciences *as the Republic contemplates* would require a combination of the reduction of mathematics to logic with the

Cartesian reduction of the *natural sciences* to geometry'[1] is to overlay Plato's simple programme with schemes of which he had, and could have had, no conception. In his view what we call the 'natural sciences' had no existence as distinct from the lower arts (medicine and the rest), which he has dismissed as concerned only with the world of becoming. Further, no science of logic existed; Plato was beginning to discover one, but with no very clear notion of what he was doing. It is fantastic to allege that 'a part, and not the most important part, of what the *Republic understands* by "dialectic" ' is 'just that reduction of mathematics to rigorous deduction from expressly formulated *logical* premisses by exactly specified *logical* methods of which the work of Peano, Frege, Whitehead, and Russell has given us a magnificent example'.[2] If Plato could have conceived such a reduction of mathematics to logic, the world would not have waited two thousand years for Peano and the rest to dethrone the logic of Aristotle.

What is contemplated in the *Republic* is something much simpler though still, for Plato's time, a vision of magnificent range. The task is limited to mathematics, but it covers the whole of that field. Plato always speaks of a single principle at the head of the entire structure, not of such a collection of primitive concepts and assumptions as we find in Mr. Russell's *Principia*. The task of dialectical research is to get back, not merely (as Aristotle would have said) to the genuine hypotheses of *each* branch, but to the single principle of all mathematical deduction, and thereby 'abolish' the indefinite collection of unproved assumptions then in use. The one basic truth (ἀρχή) of all science will itself 'rest on no hypothesis' (ἀνυπόθετος), but be intuitively known with perfect clearness and unshakable certainty.

We can, moreover, state what this ultimate hypothesis will be. Since it is single, all the five sciences must be reducible to a single chain of reasoning, in the order of increasing complexity starting with arithmetic.[3] Now, according to Aristotle, the primitive hypothesis of arithmetic is 'the existence of the unit' (or of

[1] A. E. Taylor, *Plato, the Man and His Work* (1926), p. 293. My italics.

[2] A. E. Taylor, ibid. My italics. 'Example' seems hardly a fair description of one of the most brilliant of modern discoveries.

[3] Cf. Proclus., *Eucl.*, I, p. 75, 6: *τὴν ἐπιστήμην ταύτην τὴν γεωμετρίαν ἐξ ὑποθέσεως εἶναί φαμεν καὶ ἀπὸ ἀρχῶν ὡρισμένων τὰ ἐφεξῆς ἀποδεικνύναι · μία γὰρ ἡ ἀνυπόθετος, αἱ δὲ ἄλλαι παρ' ἐκείνης ὑποδέχονται τὰς ἀρχάς.*

'units').[1] Plato in his latest phase derived numbers from the One and the 'Indefinite Dyad'. The second factor, so far as numbers are concerned, is the principle of plurality: 'Each of the numbers, in so far as it is a particular number and *one* and definite, shares in the One; in so far as it is divided and is a *plurality*, in the Indefinite Dyad'.[2] If plurality can somehow be deduced from 'the existence of a One', we can dispense with the existence of the Indefinite Dyad as a second primitive hypothesis. Now the *Parmenides* (143) contains an argument which does in fact deduce a plurality of numbers from 'the existence of a One', as follows. The hypothesis that 'a One exists' (εἰ ἓν ἔστιν) means that this One has existence or partakes of existence (οὐσίας μετέχει). The One itself, conceived apart from the existence it has, is 'one thing' (ἕν). The existence which it has is other than it—a second 'one thing'.[3] Also 'other' is a third thing, distinct from both.[4] Any pair of these three 'ones' is *two*; add a third, and you have *three*. Three is *odd*, two is *even*. By multiplication of odd and even numbers we can obtain indefinite series of numbers. 'Therefore if a One exists, number also must exist' (144a). Having thus obtained numbers from the single hypothesis 'a One exists', the deduction, as it proceeds, introduces concepts involving space (σχῆμα, 145b), motion (145e), and time (151e), not as independent hypotheses but as if they were all somehow deducible from the original hypothesis. In fact, to obtain 'by way of otherness (negation)', the Indefinite Dyad of spatial magnitude—'greater and less' or 'the unequal'—involves no more difficulty than Plato is prepared to face in obtaining the plurality of numbers from the existence of a One. Any unit of spatial magnitude is equal to itself, and the positive 'equal to' is equivalent to the negative 'neither greater nor less than'. Motion and time can be obtained in similar ways. I do not suggest that the

[1] εἶναι τὴν μονάδα, 76 *a* 35, ἃ λαμβάνεται εἶναι . . . οἷον μονάδας ἡ ἀριθμητική, *b* 5. *Cf.* Proclus, ibid., p. 59, 20, ἀρχαὶ γεωμετρίας μὲν ἡ στιγμὴ προσλαβοῦσα τὴν θέσιν, ἀριθμητικῆς δὲ ἡ μονάς.

[2] This statement is derived, through Alexander and Simplicius (*Phys.*, 454, 22 ff.), from the Lectures on the Good. See Ross, *Metaphysics*, Vol. I, p. lx.

[3] The *definition* of Unity—(say) 'One is (means) that which is indivisible'—does not assert the *existence* of a one. When we add existence in the hypothesis 'a one exists' we are bringing in a second thing (the *meaning* of a second name).

[4] As shown in the *Sophist*, the meaning 'other' figures in every negative proposition of the type 'A is not (= is other than) B'.

whole deduction as stated in the *Parmenides* is intended to be valid, but the first steps seem to be guaranteed by the *Sophist*, which again explains that any proposition such as 'a One exists' involves the recognition of three terms: 'One', 'existence', and 'otherness'. This is used to convict Parmenides of contraction when he asserts the existence of a One and yet denies plurality (*Soph.*, 244 ff.). We note that the hypotheses specified at 510c as illegitimate in arithmetic—the existence of *odd* and *even*—are 'abolished' by deduction from 'the existence of a One' (*Parm.*, 143d). If it is claimed that arguments like the above amount to a 'reduction of pure mathematics to logic', it may be replied that the whole deduction starts from the first hypothesis of arithmetic and falls within the science of mathematics itself.

A passage in Sextus (*Adv. math.*, X., 258–262) may be taken as roughly sketching the ascent to the principle as conceived by those who believe in 'bodiless Ideas, in Plato's sense', having an existence prior to that of bodies. Platonic Ideas, says Sextus, are not the ultimate principles of things; for, though each Idea taken by itself is a One (ἕν), as partaking of one or more *other* Ideas, it is two, or three, or four; so there must be something on a higher level of existence (ἐπαναβεβηκός), namely number; by participation in which 'one', 'two', 'three', and higher numbers are predicable of Ideas. Sextus then describes the ascent from sensible bodies to 'the One'. Prior to sensible bodies are bodiless solid figures; prior to these the surfaces composing them; surfaces, again, are composed of lines, and prior to lines are numbers. The simplest line cannot be conceived without number: as drawn from point to point, it implies 'two'. And numbers themselves all fall under the unit (ὑπὸ τὸ ἓν πεπτώκασιν), 'for the dyad is *one* dyad, the triad is *one* thing, a triad, and the decad is a *single* compendium of number'. Hence Pythagoras was moved to declare that the principle of things is the Monad, by partaking of which each thing is one: considered in its own nature by itself, the Monad is a one, but combined with itself 'in respect of otherness' it produces what is called the Indefinite Dyad, a thing distinct from all the determinate dyads which partake of it. There are thus two principles: the first Monad, by partaking of which all arithmetical units are conceived as units,[1] and the Indefinite Dyad, of which determinate dyads partake.

[1] The numbers below 10 are still called 'units', the ancient μονάδες, followed by the δεκάδες ('tens').

Despite the reference to Pythagoras, all the terminology here is Platonic,[1] though Sextus' manner of deriving the Indefinite Dyad from the Monad is questionable. I quote the passage as illustrating the ascent from sensible bodies through geometry to arithmetic and finally to the ἀρχή of arithmetic, 'the existence of a One'. Plato himself indicates that the most complex sciences of the five—astronomy and harmonics—are to be studied in the form of problems capable of expression in numbers and their ratios (529d–530a, 531c). The *Epinomis* (990c–991b) elaborates this reduction of all the sciences to numerical expression.

The upshot is that the aim of dialectical research in science, i.e. mathematics, is first to ascend by analysis to the sole hypothesis, 'the existence of a One', and then to complete the deduction from it of all mathematical truth so far discovered in a single chain of inference. This is a task which could be accomplished once for all. The path of further discovery in mathematics would then lie in the downward direction, solving fresh problems and extending deduction to fresh conclusions indefinitely. Little is said about the deductive part of the work, though it falls under the description of the downward movement of discourse which 'having grasped the first principle, turns back and, holding by what depends on it, descends to a conclusion' (511b). That is obvious enough, and the main interest is in the ascent. We have now formulated the whole task of research in the scientific field.

(b) *Dialectic in Moral Research* (534b–d). At 534b Glaucon, 'so far as he can follow', agrees to this conception of 'science'. Socrates then starts upon another description of dialectic: 'And by a dialectician you mean one who can take account of the reality of each thing; he who has no account to give to himself and others, to that extent has not *nous* in respect of that thing.—Yes.—And is not the same true with regard to the Good?' Here the Good is introduced as another object of which dialectic must give an account, as well as of the realities and truths of mathematics. We pass, in fact, to the field of moral Ideas. The description of dialectical method which follows, exactly fits the familiar Socratic procedure in attempting to define moral Ideas, and does not fit the procedure of dialectic in the mathematical field, just considered. The dialectician, we are told, must be able to 'formulate a

[1] Sextus' ultimate source can hardly be other than the records kept by Plato's pupils of the Lectures on the Good.

definition of the nature of the Good, isolating it from all other Ideas' (διορισάσθαι τῷ λόγῳ ἀπὸ τῶν ἄλλων πάντων ἀφελὼν τὴν τοῦ ἀγαθοῦ ἰδέαν). He must, 'as it were, fight his way through all *elenchi*, determined to apply the test not of appearance (or belief, δόξα) but of reality, and make his way to the end through all these *elenchi* without sustaining a fall in his discourse'. Otherwise, he will know neither goodness itself nor any good thing, but only lay hold upon images by belief without knowledge, and sleep away his life in a dream, until he passes into that other world where he will sleep for ever.[1] The method is 'question and answer' (ἐρωτᾶν καὶ ἀποκρίνεσθαι).

Every phrase here fits the technique of Socratic conversation—giving and receiving an account by question and answer, in order to reach the definition of a moral term after passing through a series of *elenchi*, and so gaining knowledge in place of mere belief. The objective here is a *definition*, not, as in the mathematical field, a primitive hypothesis or assumption of existence; and the technique of arriving at correct definitions is not the same as that of arriving at the ultimate hypothesis of science. The mathematician exercises his analytical faculty in penetrating to a prior truth; but he will not have to 'fight his way' through a series of *elenchi*. When he 'abolishes' demonstrable hypotheses, he does so by going behind them and showing how they can be obtained by deduction and finally confirmed (βεβαιοῦν). But the 'hypothesis' of moral dialectic is an hypothesis in the original sense—not a true and demonstrable assumption of existence, but an inadequate tentative definition, *suggested* by the respondent, submitted to criticism by the questioner in the *elenchus*, and either amended or abandoned altogether. It is transformed or destroyed by criticism, and never restored or confirmed by subsequent deduction. Such suggestions are mere stepping-stones which are kicked away in the ascent to the correct definition.

In the procedure so often illustrated in the dialogues, the opposite movements of intuition and deductive argument both figure at each stage of the ascent. Suppose the objective to be the true definition of Justice. The respondent puts forward his *suggestion* (hypothesis) that Justice means paying one's debts. He has before

[1] This echoes the parallel description of the mathematician as only 'dreaming of reality' (533b), but adds the consequence of living in a dream with respect to moral Ideas.

his mind a dim vision of what Justice is; he tries to see the nature of Justice and to put it into words.[1] This is an effort of intuition, for which καθορᾶν is often used—an effort to see the unity in a number of things. The formula (λόγος) produced is a bad attempt, an imperfect, one-sided account of the nature of Justice. Here the questioner intervenes with his *elenchus*. Taking the *suggestion* as a *supposition*, he leads the respondent through a deductive argument showing that some consequence results which the respondent will see to be unacceptable as conflicting with other beliefs he holds as strongly.[2] The first hypothesis is now abandoned. The questioner's argument, if skilfully conducted, may have brought to light considerations that will help the respondent in his next attempt; or the questioner may enlarge the 'synoptic' view by an ἐπακτικὸς λόγος, 'adducing' instances that have been overlooked. The respondent, by another effort of intuition, substitutes a second suggestion. This ought to be closer to the true meaning, which he is beginning to discern more clearly. The deductive *elenchus* is once more applied; and so the conversation goes on till, after 'fighting his way through all the *elenchi*', the respondent sees quite clearly the nature of Justice, and can now 'isolate it from every other Idea' and circumscribe it in a formula (διορίσασθαι τῷ λόγῳ). In place of mere belief, he has knowledge, which the two together have reached by using hypotheses as 'positions laid down for discourse to mount upon and take off from' in a series of leaps, each of which 'abolishes' the previous stepping-stone.[3]

[1] Laches well describes the state of mind: 'I seem to myself to have a notion of what courage is (νοεῖν περὶ ἀνδρείας ὅ τι ἐστίν) but somehow it has eluded me so that I cannot catch it and put it into words (συλλαβεῖν τῷ λόγῳ) and say what it is' (*Laches*, 194b).

[2] Cf. *Tht.*, 165d. Theaetetus admits he has been led to a conclusion which is τἀναντία οἷς ὑπεθέμην.

[3] The *elenchus* has some resemblance to the *reductio ad absurdum*, which 'assumes what conflicts with the desired result, then, using that as a supposition (τοῦτο ὑποθμένη), proceeds until it reaches an admitted absurdity and by thus *destroying the hypothesis* confirms the result originally sought (τὴν ὑπόθεσιν ἀνελοῦσα βεβαιώσηται τὸ ἐξ ἀρχῆς ζητούμενον)' (Proclus, *Eucl.*, I, p. 255, 8 ff.). Proclus classes the *reductio* with Analysis as being a method which moves upwards 'towards premisses' (ἐπὶ τὰς ἀρχάς), in contrast with deduction (ἀπὸ τῶν ἀρχῶν); but Analysis (like mathematical dialectic) posits premisses (θετικὴ τῶν ἀρχῶν), while the *reductio* is (like Socratic dialectic) ἀναιρετική, completely destroying the hypothesis, which is false and not to be re-established. At *Phd.*, 101d, Socrates lays down that criticism of a

Even so, however, the respondent has as yet only one piece of knowledge. He must mount further to the supreme Idea in the moral field, and define the nature of the Good. Only then will the full significance of the truth discovered be seen in its relation to the rest of truth. If he stops short, his definitions of Justice and other Ideas, though correct, will be analogous to a mathematical hypothesis that is true but awaits deduction from the first principle. But, if he can reach the Good, he will 'acquire *nous*' (νοῦν ἔχειν 534b), that illuminated vision of the whole field which can only be had from the summit.

The philosopher can then make the final descent: he can 'give an account', not only of one piece of knowledge, but of the whole. He will deduce (presumably in the form of a 'division') all the subordinate moral Ideas, 'descending through Ideas to Ideas and ending with Ideas'. The results of this research, if they could ever be set down in writing, would amount to a complete system of moral philosophy, securely deduced from the definition of Goodness. Such is the complete programme of research in the moral field.

Final Description of Moral Dialectic in the Curriculum of Education. Now that we have clearly distinguished the aims and methods of dialectical research in the mathematical and moral fields, we may return to the curriculum of education which follows next (535a), and consider what place dialectic of either kind has in it.

The mathematical προπαιδεία we have already considered. It ended with ten years' 'synoptic' or comparative study of mathematics. In this field, as we remarked, the task of research at the upper end of the science could be done once for all. The deduction of all mathematical truth already discovered from 'the existence of the One' could be set down in a continuous written discourse for students to study. During his ten years' advanced course, the competent pupil would work over the whole of this ground, rediscovering what was already discovered and perhaps making

hypothesis in dialectic must not begin until the consequences of assuming it have been deduced and it is seen whether they are consistent with one another. When the time comes to give an account of the hypothesis, a second higher (ἄνωθεν) hypothesis must be assumed, and so on until 'something satisfactory' is reached. (If the consequences are inconsistent, we have a sort of *reductio* destroying the hypothesis; if consistent, we continue the Analysis upwards.)

a beginning of research. Mathematical dialectic evidently belongs to this synoptic stage of scientific education.

But the guardians are to be trained also for the practical exercise of moral functions in statesmanship. A select few must be carried further into the field of the moral Ideas. Their training here will occupy the next five years, from 30 to 35 (539c–d). The immediate object of the educator is 'to test them by philosophic conversation and find out which of them are capable of renouncing the eyes and the other senses and advancing in the company of truth towards reality itself' (537d). The demoralising effect of premature questioning of received moral beliefs is described at length; it leads to lawlessness and a taste for eristic disputation.[1] Only mature students of stable character must be admitted. Even so, not everyone tested by this five years' course of dialectic will attain to a full vision of the Good. At 540a the revelation of the Good is separated from the course of moral dialectic by an interval of fifteen years (35–50) spent in subordinate military and civil offices. Then, the few who come through all these tests in education and practical life will be 'brought to the goal'. This is described in mystical terms. They are 'constrained to lift up the light (vision) of the soul and fix it upon that which gives light to all things, seeing Goodness itself'.

The reader has not been prepared to find the vision of Good separated in time from training in moral dialectic. In the programme of research there is, of course, no break. But in the education described in the *Laws* we again find two stages. Only a small number of students will be capable of a really thorough study of arithmetic, geometry, and astronomy (818a). Where the higher education is introduced (965b) the 'synoptic' view is stressed: they must be 'able not only to see the manifold but to press on towards the one (πρὸς τὸ ἓν ἐπείγεσθαι) and, having recognised it, to bring all into order with reference to it in a comprehensive view' (πρὸς ἐκεῖνο συντάξασθαι πάντα συνορῶντα). A thorough study and vision (θέα) of any object is possible only to those who can turn their gaze from the many and dissimilar to the single form. Such will be constrained to see clearly the

[1] Here, as earlier at 498a, Plato virtually admits that Socrates had 'demoralised' some of his young companions by encouraging them to canvass received morality without first undergoing a severe training both in abstract thinking and in practical discipline.

unity (ἕν) which pervades the four great virtues, courage, temperance, justice, and wisdom, and which deserves the single name of *moral goodness* (ἀρετή). They must be able to state the essential nature of this unity—in what sense it is a single thing, or a whole, or both (965b–e). This study, confined to the moral field, may represent the ground covered in the five years' course of the *Republic*. Then the Athenian observes that the same may be said περὶ καλοῦ τε καὶ ἀγαθοῦ: the Guardians must know 'in what manner and sense each of these is a unity' as well as a manifold; and they must be able to express their knowledge of *all forms of goodness* (περὶ πάντων τῶν σπουδαίων) in explicit discourse (966a–b). This wider knowledge, going beyond moral virtue to include all forms of goodness, may correspond to the final vision of the Good reserved in the education of the *Republic* for the age of 50, as well as to the goal of research earlier described as 'defining the nature of the Good'.

We have reached a stage where the distinction between education and research can hardly be maintained. Plato would not hold that the results of research in the moral field could, like the results in mathematics, be set down in a textbook, even of 'teleological algebra'.[1] Each generation of philosophers would have to be led to the goal through living intercourse with others who had attained it or come nearer to attaining it. They must all fight their way through the *elenchi* of conversation and discover for themselves a knowledge that cannot be conveyed by instruction.

The Descent of the Philosopher and the Statesman (540a–b). The descent is briefly described. When the philosopher has seen the Good itself, he will for the rest of his life divide his time between research (φιλοσοφία) and the practical duties of the supreme ruler. In mathematical research he will work at extending and perfecting the structure of mathematical science. In the scientific and the moral fields alike, as educator he will train others like himself to succeed him (ἄλλους ἀεὶ παιδεύσαντας τοιούτους). As statesman, he will legislate, like Moses when he came down from

[1] The existence of such a science was first recognised by Burnet (*Greek Philosophy*, 230): 'the whole of a science would thus be reduced to a sort of teleological algebra', and seems to be accepted by Prof. Taylor (*Plato*, 294); but its nature will remain obscure until some proposition in the science is produced.

the vision on Sinai bearing the tables of the law.[1] Using the nature of the Good as a 'pattern', he will create order (κοσμεῖν) in his city and in his own soul and the souls of others. (This is the Pythagorean reproduction in the soul and in society of the cosmic order disclosed in research and education.) Finally, he will be worshipped after death as a *daemon*, or at least as εὐδαίμων and a 'divine' man.

PROGRAMME OF RESEARCH	AGE.	PROGRAMME OF EDUCATION.
	–17 (18)	Music and Gymnastic. Elementary Mathematics.
	17 (18)–20	Gymnastic only.
ASCENT (outside the Cave)		
MATHEMATICAL DIALECTIC: criticism of hypotheses, ascending to the genuine *hypothesis* ('the existence of a One').	20–30	Comparative Mathematics and MATHEMATICAL DIALECTIC.
MORAL DIALECTIC: study of moral Ideas, ascending to the *Definition of the Good*	30–35	MORAL DIALECTIC: criticism of received belief, leading to the *Unity of moral goodness.*
	35–50	Subordinate office.
	50	*Vision of the Good.*
DESCENT		
of PHILOSOPHER		of STATESMAN (into the Cave)
↓ *Theoretical Deduction* of all pure Mathematics; ↓ *Theoretical Division* of all moral Ideas	50–	*Practical* legislation, rule, and training of successors.
		Death and *daemon*-worship.

The Unity of the Good. The above table shows the results of disentangling the threads of Plato's web. The object has been to

[1] Florus in Plutarch (*Quæst. Conv.*, VIII, 2, 2) remarks that the Socrates of these Books of the *Republic* has an admixture of Lycurgus as well as of Pythagoras, as Dicaearchus thought: *Πλάτων . . . ἅτε δὴ τῷ Σωκράτει τὸν Λυκοῦργον ἀναμιγνὺς οὐχ ἧττον ἢ τὸν Πυθαγόραν, ὡς ᾤετο Δικαίαρχος.* Not the historic Socrates!

bring out two points: (1) that the programme of research, which is progressive, can be distinguished from the programme of education, which is recurrent—each new generation of students being taken over so much of the course as they are fit for; and (2) that dialectical procedure is not the same in the mathematical as in the moral field, though the exercise of intuition and deductive reasoning is common to both. When the threads are kept apart, there seem to be three conceptions of the goal of knowledge: (*a*) the apprehension of 'the existence of the One' as the single hypothesis from which all mathematical propositions can be deduced; (*b*) the formulation of the definition of the Good, as the supreme Idea from which all subordinate moral Ideas can be derived; (*c*) the vision of the Good, as an experience comparable to the ἐποπτεία of the religious mystery.[1] But, by weaving his threads into one pattern, Plato means that the three goals are really one.

In the first place, the mathematical and moral Ideas are not so sharply distinct in Plato's mind as in ours. They meet in the conceptions of rhythm and harmony. Man is the only creature that attains to the consciousness of order (τάξεως αἴσθησις), which in the motions of the body is rhythm, and in the organisation of vocal sound is harmony: the two are combined in χορεία (*Laws*, 664e). The aim of early education in music and gymnastic is to create εὐαρμοστία εὐσχημοσύνη εὐρυθμία εὐήθεια, the physical and moral rhythm and harmony that 'steal into the soul' through music (*Rep.*, 401d), and that reasonableness (εὐλογία) which is the beginning of intellectual understanding (411d). These words are recalled as a preface to the review of mathematical training in VII. That early schooling in music and gymnastic was a training by habituation (ἔθεσι παιδεύουσα), communicating, as regards harmony and rhythm, only εὐαρμοστία and εὐρυθμία, not knowledge; and in discourse (λόγοι) only a corresponding habituation (ἔθη, customary intellectual and moral beliefs, accepted on authority), not any form of study that will lift the eye of the soul to see reality (522a). Then, at the end of the mathematical curriculum, in the account of astronomy and harmonics, there emerge the two conceptions of συμμετρία (530a) and συμφωνία (531a–c), as manifest in the proportions and consonant ratios of numbers, illustrated

[1] Plut., *Quæst. Conv.*, VIII, 2, 1. Geometry draws us from the sense-world, ἐπὶ τὴν νοητὴν καὶ ἀίδιον φύσιν, ἧς θέα τέλος ἐστὶ φιλοσοφίας οἷον ἐποπτεία τελετῆς.

by the rhythmical movements of the heavenly bodies and the audible harmonies of music. These conceptions are common to the scientific and the moral fields; it is as leading to them that mathematics is 'useful for the inquiry after τὸ καλὸν καὶ ἀγαθόν (531c), the principle which pervades all forms of physical, moral, and intellectual beauty and perfection' (*Symp.*, 210). The *Laws* (967d–e) connects the enlightened study of astronomy with the fundamental truths of morality and religion. No man can be 'securely god-fearing' who does not know that soul is immortal and prior to the bodies it rules, and also discern the intelligence (νοῦς) revealed in the motions of the stars, together with the necessary preliminary sciences (the rest of the mathematical προπαιδεία). He must also observe what these have in common with Music (synoptic study), and turn his knowledge to harmonious uses (συναρμοττόντως) in the establishment of moral practice and institutions (the descent of the statesman); and he must be able 'to give an account of everything of which any account can be given' (the dialectical descent of the philosopher from the principle of which no account can be given). These places and many others reveal the intimate connection between the intellectual and moral phases of truth and reality in the cosmos. They explain why Plato can speak of the mathematician's ascent to the existent unity of 'One Being' as if it were the same as the dialectician's ascent to the unity pervading all forms of moral goodness, or the definition of τὸ καλὸν καὶ ἀγαθόν.

Why is the apprehension of the first principle called a vision or revelation which comes 'suddenly' (ἐξαίφνης, *Symp.*, 210e)? In the *Symposium* and the *Phaedrus*, as well as in the *Republic*, Plato adopts the language of the Eleusinian mysteries. It is appropriate because initiation ended with the ἐποπτεία, the sight of certain sacred objects 'in a blaze of light', coming after a long process of purification and instruction (λεγόμενα) in the significance of the rites that had been witnessed (δρώμενα). So Plato's course of intellectual instruction by verbal discourse, in mathematics and dialectic, is a passage from darkness to light, and ends with an experience of a different order—a vision. The criticism of mathematical hypotheses led up to the formulation of the genuine hypothesis: 'Let there be a One.' As an object of intellectual understanding, this is no more mysterious than any other proposition in mathematics. Moral dialectic, again, led up to the formulation of a definition (διορίσασθαι τῷ λόγῳ) distinguishing the nature of the Good from all other Ideas. A defining formula is expressed in words; it can be written in a book and intellectually understood, like the definition of any other Idea. By means of it the dialectician can 'give an account' of derivative moral truths, and even teach them to men who will never be philosophers. But the intellectual understanding of formulae expressed in words is not the same as the intuitive vision of the reality which the formulae profess to describe. Plato's whole theory of knowledge is a development of Socrates' conception of the knowledge which is wisdom and virtue—that imperious insight into what is really good for us, which cannot fail to determine will and action. It is not the continent or incontinent man's intellectual 'belief', which tells him truly what he ought to do, but may fail to govern his actions: 'I *know* this is right, but I want to do that.' This is the difference between knowing a thing and and knowing about a thing. Socrates refuses to give Glaucon a definition of the Good or a complete account of dialectic because Glaucon and the readers of the *Republic* have not undergone the severe training required before they could even understand his meaning; still less would they *see* the reality behind the verbal formula: 'You would no longer be seeing an image, but the truth itself.' 'There is not, nor shall there ever be, any writing of mine on this subject. It is altogether beyond such means of expression as exist in other departments of knowledge; rather, after long dwelling upon the thing itself in a common life of philosophic converse, suddenly, as from a leaping spark, a light is kindled, which, once it has arisen in the soul, thenceforward feeds itself' (*Ep.*, VII, 341). Aristotle, in a much misused passage, says that 'the initiated do not need to understand something, but to have an experience and be put in a certain frame of mind'.[1] This does not mean that no doctrines were implied or taught in the Mysteries, but that the goal was not to understand the hierophant's discourse but to 'learn by experience' (παθεῖν μαθεῖν) what discourse cannot express, and thereby pass into a new state of mind. Plato's metaphors for the vision were drawn from contact and marriage: the soul finds rest from the travail of desire in union with that which is akin to it; then *nous* and truth are born, knowledge and true life are nourished (490b). It is hard for some to imagine an impersonal passion for truth

[1] Frag. 45, τοὺς τελουμένους οὐ μαθεῖν τι δεῖν ἀλλὰ παθεῖν καὶ διατεθῆναι.

strong enough to warrant such language; and it is only too easy to fall into sentimental anachronism and find the Amor of the *Divine Comedy* in the Eros of the *Republic* and *Symposium*. The experience Plato means is, I believe, rather an act of metaphysical insight or recognition that what we should call a 'religious' experience—certainly nothing of the nature of trance or ecstasy. But the knowledge is of a kind in which the soul is united with the harmonious order it knows, an insight which harmonises the soul's own nature and illuminates the entire field of truth. Up to that moment the philosopher has used his power of intuition and intellectual understanding, but only at that moment does he 'begin to have *nous*'. He becomes a god, knowing the true from the false, the good from the evil, and incapable of error and wrong-doing.

VI

PLATO'S *PARMENIDES* (1939)

Gilbert Ryle

THE following observations are arguments in favour of a certain interpretation of Plato's dialogue, the *Parmenides*. According to this interpretation the dialogue is philosophically serious, in the sense that its author thought that its arguments were valid and that its problem was one of philosophical importance. Further, it will be maintained that he was right on the latter point and predominantly right on the former point. The problem is important and most of the arguments are valid.

It will be suggested that the obvious obscurity of the dialogue is due to a very natural cause, namely that Plato could not with the logical apparatus accessible to him propound in set terms what is the general conclusion or even the main drift of the dialogue. For the construction of the required logical apparatus could not be taken in hand until after the inevitability of the sorts of antinomies which the dialogue exhibits had been realised.

If this interpretation is correct, or even if some interpretation of a kindred type is correct, then the interpretation suggested by Burnet and Professor A. E. Taylor is wrong. My main object is to show what the true interpretation is, but a brief resumé of other reasons for rejecting the Burnet–Taylor theory may not be out of place.

Burnet and Professor Taylor declare the dialogue, or the dialectical part of it, to be a joke. Plato's object was to ridicule certain philosophers or philosophasters by parody. None of its arguments are valid or thought by Plato to be so. And its pretended problem or set of problems is a sham one. The butts of the ridicule are either the philosophers of the Eleatic school or those of the school of

Megara or both. They merited such ridicule because the logic employed by them was vexatious and fallacious. They had exercised this corrupt logic against certain doctrines which Plato accepted; consequently Plato in this dialogue is paying them back in their own coin.

The main objection to such a theory is of course that the arguments of the dialogue are either valid, or else plausible enough for their author to have taken them to be so. Other objections are as follows. If the intended butts of the alleged mockery were Parmenides and Zeno, it is hard to explain why in the two adjacent dialogues, the *Theaetetus* and the *Sophist*, Plato goes out of his way to express his admiration for the former; or why the Zenonian method of argument by antinomy is declared by Professor Taylor himself[1] (I think correctly) to be that recommended to philosophers by Plato in the *Republic* as well as in the *Sophist*.

Moreover, Professor Taylor recognises not only that Plato thought that the Zenonian pattern of ratiocination was valid, but also that it is valid. He recognises, too, that it is important, since by means of it Zeno had shown that there were hidden absurdities in the premisses of Pythagorean mathematics—which absurdities were acknowledged and partly remedied by Plato's own circle.

In the *Sophist* and the *Politicus* the leader of the discussion is described as an Eleatic stranger, and his arguments are notoriously intended to be taken seriously. And the Megarian philosopher Euclides is introduced as a sympathetic character at the opening of the *Theaetetus*. The Eleatic Stranger who conducts the argument of the *Sophist* is expressly praised as a genuine philosopher and not a mere tripper-up of unsubtle persons.

So slight a part does Socrates play in the *Parmenides*, *Sophist*, and *Politicus*, and so slight also is the positive rôle given to any known Socratic theories in those dialogues or in the *Theaetetus*, that the natural inference would surely be that Plato had discovered that certain important philosophic truths or methods were to be credited not to Socrates but to the Eleatics. Zeno is the teacher now and not Socrates.

Doubtless there were (long after the time of Parmenides) Megarian thinkers who loved to lay logical traps and pose logical riddles. Maybe some of them prosecuted this search from motives

[1] In *Plato*, p. 290.

of mischievousness, though generally the collectors of fallacies and puzzles in logic (like Lewis Carroll) do so from the more serious motive of desiring to discover the rules of logic which will provide the rebuttal of the fallacies and the solution of the riddles. But the theme of the *Parmenides* has (unlike Aristotle's *Topics* and *De Sophisticis Elenchis*) no obvious connection with any such posers. Nor could Plato have preserved any historic unities and represented Parmenides as the victim of the posers garnered by this yet unborn band of formal logicians.

But in any case the supposed joke would have been a very poor one. For Parmenides and his followers are supposed to be rendered a laughing-stock by the ascription to Parmenides' own lips of arguments which he never used. He is made to talk nonsense by Plato. Yet this joke would only have succeeded—and then how lamely!—if the words put into his mouth were almost parallel to words which he was known to have uttered. The comicality of the former would be transferred to the latter by the closeness of their analogies. But Parmenides is not known to have produced either fallacious or valid specimens of Zenonian dialectic, and Zeno is known to have produced valid specimens of it. Was Plato perhaps being silly enough to poke fun at a valid method of ratiocination, mistakenly thinking it to be fallacious? This would have made only Plato ridiculous.

Moreover, Parmenides in the dialogue, so far from being an innocent victim, unwittingly entrammelled in an absurd argument, himself draws attention to the untenability of certain of the conclusions of the dialectic. It is he who brings out and draws attention to the contradictions which he has deduced. He underlines the antinomies here as vigorously as Zeno underlined the antinomies which he disclosed as resident in the Pythagorean premisses. He is a poor butt who is both the author of a joke and the commentator upon its absurdities.

It is small wonder that it took two and half millennia before anyone was found to give vent even to a laboured chuckle at the supposed fooling. Further, in the *Sophist*, which is accepted as a sober dialogue, a certain stretch of the dialectic of the *Parmenides* is echoed as a constituent of the argument. Was it conscious sophistry in the *Parmenides* and serious reasoning in the *Sophist*?

Later on we shall see that the central crux of the second part of the *Parmenides* was recognised by Aristotle to have been a serious philosophical puzzle, and one which he thinks he can, with the aid of his logical apparatus, resolve. This will also be evidence that this issue was not a sham issue and the intricacies of the argument not gratuitously manufactured.

The one piece of internal evidence which seems to be in favour of Professor Taylor's theory is the passage where Parmenides prefaces his antinomian operations with the expression 'since we have committed ourselves to the laborious sport'. I think that παιδιά is here 'play taken as exercise or practice' rather than 'fun' in the sense of 'jest' or 'ridicule'. But even if it were taken in the latter sense, the whole alleged joke would be killed. Parmenides could not be the unwitting butt of ridicule while himself recognising that he was being ridiculed. Don Quixote does not say 'Let me pretend for fun to be a gallant knight'. He is a figure of fun because he takes his acts and attitudes seriously.

Finally, the first part of the dialogue, where Socrates is being cross-questioned, is taken by Professor Taylor to be serious. He holds that the arguments which silence Socrates are not really conclusive (in which point I think that he is mainly wrong), but that the discussion is one which has a genuine philosophical problem and moves by a method which is meant to be taken seriously. It is therefore only the second and longer part of the dialogue which has to be construed as a parody. Yet so far from there being any detectable relaxation here in the sobriety of the dialogue, it is generally felt that liveliness and dramatic qualities, not to speak of humour, vanish from the very beginning of this second part.

It reads as if it were sober, professional, systematic, arid and in conformity with set rules—and it reads so, I suggest, because it is so. Moreover, there is a clear connection between the two parts. In the first part Socrates several times over proclaims a challenge, and Parmenides more than once declares that he takes it up. What the challenge is, we shall see later. But if in a serious part of the dialogue a task is set, and if in the second part the task is performed, it is hard to reject the inference that the second part of the dialogue is also serious.

It is now time to give an analysis and interpretation of the dialogue based upon the assumption that Plato thought that it dealt with a real problem and that its arguments were valid. I shall begin with a discussion of the first part of the dialogue, where Parmenides is in discussion with the young Socrates.

Socrates has been listening to the reading of an argument written by Zeno, in which Zeno had been controverting certain opponents of the Monism of Parmenides by demonstrating that their position entailed that one and the same subject had incompatible predicates. Namely, they maintained the existence of a plurality (no matter of what), and Zeno argues that the members of a plurality must exemplify both similarity and dissimilarity; and as these are opposite attributes, it is impossible that there should exist a plurality.

Socrates then urges that Zeno's argument is answerable. For according to the theory of Forms, since Forms and the instances of them are indistinguishable, it is possible for there to exist things which are instances of several Forms at once and even, in a certain fashion, instances of opposite Forms at the same time. Things may exemplify similarity and dissimilarity at the same time, or unity and plurality, as a person is one person but a plurality of limbs and bodily parts. It is to be noticed that Socrates does not try to explode the apparent contradictions by distinguishing relational from other predicates, a distinction of which Plato is well aware in other dialogues. He might have shown that there is no contradiction in saying that something is bigger than one thing while smaller than another, or similar to one thing and dissimilar to another, while there would be a contradiction in describing a thing as having and not having a given quality at the same time. Instead the young Socrates maintains that the apparent contradictions vanish or lose their menace when it is seen that Forms and their instances are to be distinguished from one another and that a particular may, without absurdity, be an instance of several Forms and even opposing Forms at the same time.

However, Socrates repeats four times between 129b and 130a that he would be gravely perturbed if it were shown that not the instances of Forms but Forms themselves underwent opposite predicates. And we shall see that in the second part of the dialogue Parmenides takes up just this challenge.

Meanwhile, however, Socrates' theory of Forms has to undergo an examination. And as Socrates has proposed to upset Zeno's assertion that the existence of a plurality entails that the members of such a plurality would have opposite predicates, by referring to the relation between Forms and the instances of Forms, it is to this alleged relation that chief attention is paid.

Socrates accepts as specimens of Forms similarity, unity, plurality, magnitude, justice, beauty, and goodness. He boggles at the suggestion that there are also Forms of hair-ness, mud-ness and dirt-ness, and is uneasy even about Forms of natural kinds such as men, fire, and water would be instances of. He is advised not to be squeamish, but the general theoretical question is at once embarked on: What sort of a relation is it which holds between instances and what they are instances of? To put it roughly, a Form is taken to be something answering to any general predicate, noun, verb, or adjective, in such a way that any significant abstract noun will be the proper name of such a something. And it is because there exist such somethings that many ordinary objects can be characterised by a common predicate. To ascribe a predicate to something is to assert that this something stands in some relation to a Form. So if a thing is an instance of something, there exist two objects, the instance and that of which it is an instance. And there is the special relation between them which constitutes the former an instance of the latter. For example, my body, being one body, exemplifies or is an instance of unity. This, according to the theory, entails that there exist two things, namely my body and unity, and there obtains too the relation answering to the word 'exemplifies' or the phrase 'is an instance of'. We might say, for nutshell effect, that the theory of Forms is the theory that abstract nouns are proper names or that being-an-instance-of is a proper relation.

What sort of a relation is this relation of exemplification? Socrates essays different answers to this question, all of which collapse. We shall see later that any answer must collapse, since the question itself is logically vicious, which entails that the theory of Forms, in its present shape, is logically vicious.

Socrates first suggests that the relation is that of participation, and Parmenides proceeds to examine the concept expressed by this word taken in its natural and literal sense. To participate in something is to possess or occupy a part of something. You and I participate in a cake if you take half of it and I take the other half. So if to be an instance of something is to participate in it, it must be to possess or occupy a fragment. If a thousand objects exemplify circularity by being circular, then on this literal rendering of 'participation' each must somehow have one-thousandth of circularity. Now it already sounds absurd to speak of fractions of attributes, such as slices of yellowness or quotas of similarity. But Parmenides does better than rely upon our nose for the ridiculous; he explores a set of cases where the notion generates flat contradictions. He operates, namely, upon predicates of magnitude and relative magnitude. For example, the existence of many large things would imply that each possessed a very small fraction of largeness, a fraction very much smaller than that of which it was a fraction. And things equal in size will possess fragments of equality which are much smaller than and so not equal to equality. Smallness will vastly exceed in dimensions the fractions of itself that render their possessors small.

Our reactions to such reasoning naturally take two forms. We object at once that of course concepts like magnitude, equality, smallness and the rest do not themselves have magnitudes. Bigness is not bigger or smaller than anything else, nor equal in size to anything else. It is nonsense to ascribe predicates of size to concepts of size. Attributes such as quantitative dimensions, are not instances of themselves. Indeed, like Professor Taylor and Mr. Hardie, we are ready to declare with confidence that no 'universal', i.e. no quality, relation, magnitude, state, etc., can be one of its own instances. Circularity is not circular nor is proximity adjacent. Nor even are such concepts capable of being instances of other concepts of the same family as themselves. It is nonsense to describe circularity as circular *or* of any other shape; and it is nonsense to describe redness as of *any* colour, or equality as of *any* dimensions. We are right to make such objections. The theory of Forms is logically vicious if it implies that all or some universals are instances of themselves or of other universals of the same family with themselves. And Plato had, apparently, once thought that beauty was beautiful and goodness was good; maybe he had thought that circularity and circularity alone was perfectly circular.

But that such descriptions of qualities, magnitudes, relations, etc., are illegitimate has to be shown and not merely felt. Plato is either showing it or on the way to showing it in this part of the dialogue. The very next stage in the argument proves that no universal can be an instance of itself.

Another objection that we feel disposed to make is that Plato is treating such concepts as smallness, equality, similarity and otherness, as if they were qualities, instead of seeing that they are relations. To be small is simply to be smaller than something, or than most things or than some standard thing. But we are here trading upon the distinction, worked out in part by Aristotle, between universals of different sorts. Yellow is an universal in the category of quality, equality is one in the category of relation. But how do we establish such categorial differences? Not on the authority of Aristotle or by native instinct or whim, but by exhibiting the contradictions or other absurdities which result from treating universals as all of one type. The theory of Forms was logically vicious in so far as it did, unwittingly, treat all universals as if they were of one type. Plato is proving the need for a distinction between the different types of universals.

In 132a Parmenides briefly shows that if instances of largeness and that of which they are instances are alike considered and compared in respect of largeness, an infinite regress is at once set on foot. If largeness is a large something, it must be an instance of largeness Number 2, and this will be an instance of largeness Number 3 and so on for ever. So 'largeness' will not be the name of one Form but of an endless series of Forms. It is only our generalisation of this to say that it is logically vicious to treat any universal as one of its own instances. We shall see that interesting consequences follow from this.

Socrates now toys for a moment, still within the confines of the participation theory, with the conceptualist theory that Forms are thoughts or notions, so that the relation between instances and that of which they are instances either is or is a species of the relation between our thinkings and what we think about. To this Parmenides gives two different but both fatal objections. The thinking of that of which instances are instances must be the thought of something, and that which is the object of such thinking must be real or exist. And this will be a Form, the existence of which will not be the occurrence of that thinking but presupposed by it as its object. Moreover, if universals were bits of thinking, their instances (on the literal participation theory) will be fragments of those bits. So everything whatsoever will be a piece of thinking, unless we are ready to swallow the alternative of saying that there exist thoughts which are never thought. The latter of these objections would not hold necessarily, if some account of 'being-an-instance-of' other than the literal participation account were given.

Socrates now abandons the literal participation theory and suggests in its place the similarity theory. For one thing to be an instance of a Form is for it to copy or resemble it in one or more respects; or if there exist several instances of a Form they all copy or resemble it, and from this resemblance is derived their resemblance to one another. Historically it is probable that this theory had seemed the obvious theory to hold when attention was being focused upon the concepts of mathematics and especially of geometry. The squares and circles which we draw are not exactly square or circular. They are nearly but not quite good copies of ideal or perfect squares and circles, though these never exist in nature. At this stage, probably, philosophers failed to distinguish ideal circles from circularity and ideal squares from squareness. It was only later seen that they are or would be instances of those attributes and so are or would be particulars even though not ones existing in nature.

Parmenides swiftly refutes this theory. Resemblance is a symmetrical relation. If A is similar to B in a certain respect, B is similar to A in that respect. [We must be careful not to say that 'being a copy of' signifies a symmetrical relation, since in the notion of being a copy there is, over and above the notion of resemblance, the quite different notion of origination. A portrait is a copy of a face, but a face is not a copy of a portrait.]

But for two things to resemble each other in a certain respect, both must have at least one common attribute, or both must be instances of at least one common universal. So if a Form and its instances are similar, both must be instances of at least one higher Form. And if their being instances of it entails, as according to the theory it must entail, that they and it have some point of similarity, then all must be instances of a still higher Form, and so on *ad infinitum*. So even if there is some sense in which a drawn circle is rather like an ideal circle, there is no sense in which either is similar to circularity.

Socrates is now bankrupt of any answer to the question, What sort of a relation is being-an-instance-of? But the debate is so far inconclusive that the fact that Socrates cannot answer the question does not imply that there is no answer. Other 'friends of the Forms' might assimilate the relation to some other as yet unexamined familiar relation. I propose here to go beyond my text and argue that there can be no answer to the question, since the question itself is illegitimate.

To show this, it is convenient to consider Cook Wilson's answer to the question. His view is that the relation of being-an-instance-of is a relation *sui generis*, capable of no analysis and in need of none. It is a mistake in principle to look for some familiar relation which holds between one particular and another, and to try to show that the relation of being-an-instance-of is a case or species of that. None the less, there is no mystery about the relation of being-an-instance-of; it is one with which any ability to think presupposes familiarity. Indeed no ordinary relation or quality or state could be familiar to us without our being familiar with this unique relation.

Let us for brevity, call this alleged relation, as Cook Wilson does not, 'exemplification', and ignoring the question whether or not it is assimilable to any other known relation, consider whether the assumption that there exists such a relation contains any logical vice. On this view a thing–quality proposition will assert that a thing is in this relation of exemplifying to the quality; and a relational proposition will assert that the two or more terms jointly exemplify the relation.

Thus every thing–quality proposition will be a relational proposition, and every ordinary relational proposition will be a doubly relational proposition, since it will be asserting that the relation of exemplification holds between the terms and the special relation, say that of being-neighbour-to.

Now, if one thing is in a certain relation to another, the latter will be in some, not necessarily the same, relation to the former. If 'this is green' is more fully expressed by 'this exemplifies greenness', there will be another relational proposition of the form 'greenness is exemplified in (or inheres in) this'. Forms will be the subjects of relational propositions: i.e. there will be significant and irreducible relational sentences each with an abstract noun denoting at least one of the terms in the relational proposition.

Now what of the alleged relation itself, which we are calling 'exemplification'? Is this a Form or an instance of a Form? Take the two propositions 'this is square' and 'that is circular'. We have here two different cases of something exemplifying something else.

We have two different instances of the relation of being-an-instance-of. What is the relation between them and that of which they are instances? It will have to be exemplification Number 2. The exemplification of *P* by *S* will be an instance of exemplification, and its being in that relation to exemplification will be an instance of a second-order exemplification, and that of a third, and so on *ad infinitum*.

(This is not the same regress, though reminiscent of it, as that which Bradley thought he had found in the necessity of there always existing a further relation to relate any relation to its terms.)

This conclusion is impossible. So there is no such relation as being-an-instance-of. 'This is green' is not a relational proposition, and 'this is bigger than that' only mentions one relation, that of being-bigger-than.

There are no genuine simple relational propositions having for their terms what is denoted by abstract nouns. Forms are not terms in relational propositions with their instances acting as the other terms. And if (what is a further point which is not here being argued) Forms are also incapable of having qualities or dimensions or states or places or dates, etc., it follows (what is true) that Forms cannot be the subjects of any simple propositions, affirmative or negative, attributive or relational.

Now when we say such things as that there is no relation between greenness or circularity and its instances, we seem to be saying that there exists an intolerable remoteness or alienation between universals and particulars. It sounds like saying that two men have no dealings with each other, or that two bodies are debarred from ever coming into contact. But this is not what is meant. What is meant is that abstract nouns are not proper names, so that to ask what is the relation between the nominee of such a noun and something else is an illegitimate question. The semantic function of abstract nouns is something other than that of denoting subjects of qualities, states, dimensions or relations. To inquire after the qualities, states, positions, sizes, or relations of circularity or unity or civility is to ask a nonsensical question. Abstract nouns are not the names of entities (solemn word!), for they are not names at all in the way in which 'Julius Caesar' is the name of someone.

So when we say that there is no relation between an universal and its instances we are only saying the same sort of thing as when we say that yellowness has no colour or circularity has no shape. These assertions suggest that yellowness is woefully anaemic and that circularity is gravely amorphous; but what is meant is simply that such sentences as 'yellowness is yellow or green' and 'circularity is circular or square' are illegitimate, since the abstract nouns are not the names of things possessing qualities.

It is important to see that this is all quite consistent with the admission that there are plenty of significant sentences of the noun–copula–adjective or the noun–copula–noun pattern, the grammatical subjects of which are abstract nouns. 'Yellow is a colour' and 'unpunctuality is blameworthy' are significant and true sentences. Only they do not express singular attributive propositions about one entity of which the proper name is 'yellow' and one of which the proper name is 'unpunctuality'.

The theory of Forms maintained that Forms are terms in relational propositions; namely, that about any Form there will be the true proposition that something does or might stand in the relation to it of exemplification. So this was a doctrine of Substantial Forms, for according to it each Form would be a substance, since it would be an 'entity' possessing at least one relational property.

It is commonly said that where the young Socrates went astray was in treating universals as if they were particulars. How does one treat a quality or a relation or a dimension as if it were a particular? Not by falsely asserting of it that it has the quality of particularity, for there is no such quality. Treating an universal as if it were a particular can only be speaking as if there could be significant sentences of the simple, singular, attributive, or relational patterns having abstract nouns (roughly) for their nominatives; as if, for example, given a sentence like 'This has such and such quality or relation or magnitude', an abstract noun could replace the 'this' and leave the resultant sentence significant. And this is illegitimate, partly for the reasons already given by Parmenides, partly for reasons yet to come in the dialogue, and partly for reasons which I have suggested.

The reasons are all of one type, namely that contradictions or vicious regresses arise out of assertions which assume the validity of the practice in question.

Parmenides now produces a general argument against the possibility of there existing any relation between Forms and their instances. I am not sure that the argument is valid; it would certainly require a much profounder inquiry into the varieties of relations than Parmenides supplies to establish the point. The argument is as follows. If instances and that of which they are instances, namely Forms, both exist, they will be existences of different orders. Now when a relation holds between terms, those terms are correlates of each other. And these correlates must be of the same order of existence. A slave-owner is the correlate of the slave whom he owns. He owns a slave and not slavery. The correlate to servitude is ownership, while the correlate to a slave is an owner. If there are the two orders of existence—'existence' and 'subsistence' are the titles recently coined—then what exists is correlated with what exists, and what subsists with what subsists. There is no cross-correlation of something existing with something subsisting.

Thus instances of knowing, namely the cases of knowing which we enjoy, are correlated with their objects, namely instances of truth. But knowledge (that of which cases of knowing are instances) is correlated not with truths but with trueness. Hence if there are Forms, they cannot be what our knowings are knowings of. We cannot know the Forms. And if knowledge—in the sense of that of which knowings are instances—belongs to God, then God cannot know us or any of our concerns. (This step is unwarranted. Parmenides is speaking as if that of which knowings are instances is itself a knowing of something and one which God enjoys. I think he is also assuming or pretending that God, because supramundane, must be a Form, and yet a possessor of knowledge. But if God knows anything, he is a particular, whether supramundane or not; and his knowings will be instances of knowledge.) This last conclusion is rather shocking than convincing; but the general point is of some logical importance, though it is too elliptically presented to carry much weight as it stands. I think that it is true that a relation can only be conceived to hold between terms that are of the same type or level; and if instances and what they are instances of are not of the same type or level, no relation can hold between them. But the notion of types or levels is still a very obscure one, and was much more so in Plato's time when even the much more elementary distinctions of Aristotelian categories had yet to be worked out.

There is now left a big question. It is apparently illegitimate to assert that Forms have this, that or any relation to their instances; it is illegitimate to assert that any quality, relation, magnitude, state, etc., is an instance of itself or of any attributes of the same family with itself. What sorts of propositions can then be asserted about Forms? Are there any cases where it is legitimate to describe one Form as an instance of any other? Are there any attributive or relational propositions about Forms at all? Or is Socrates to be disconcerted in the way in which he repeatedly said that he would be disconcerted by the discovery that propositions about Forms are or entail self-contradictions?

Parmenides says that the young Socrates has got into difficulties because he has not been put through a certain sort of philosophical discipline; namely, he has not learned to explore questions by the Zenonian method of dialectical reasoning. We know well what this method was. Zeno had shown that the premisses of Pythagorean mathematics were illegitimate, since incompatible consequences could be rigorously deduced from them. Those premisses had seemed innocent and plausible, but their hidden viciousness was exposed by the derivation of antinomies from them.

But the method requires a certain expansion. Zeno had shown that certain propositions or hypotheses entailed contradictory consequences; but it is also required to see whether the contradictories of such propositions or hypotheses entail contradictory consequences.

For *prima facie* we should expect that if a given proposition is shown to be logically vicious, its contradictory must be automatically validated. But if both a proposition and its contradictory are logically vicious, both entailing contradictory consesequences, then the viciousness of those propositions is of a more radical order.

For instance, 'Jones is a childless parent' contains a contradiction, but 'Jones is not a childless parent' contains none, though it contains a 'trifling proposition'. But 'a line is an assemblage of a finite number of points' as well as 'a line is an assemblage of an infinite number of points' generate contradictions. There is an illegitimacy common to both which is first revealed when both are shown to entail contradictory propositions.

Parmenides is prevailed on to give a specimen exhibition of

this sort of two-way Zenonian operation, in which he is also to take up Socrates' challenge to show that Forms have incompatible predicates. Namely he is to take up a proposition or hypothesis about a Form, and show that this hypothesis and also the contradictory of it entail that contradictory propositons are true about that Form.

He gets Socrates to allow that it is an integral part of his theory of Forms, that if there exist instances of something, that of which they are instances itself exists and is something other than they. Goodness, similarity, circularity and the rest, are terms of which it is not only significant but true to say that they exist (or are 'entities', if we relish terms of art). It is also taken to be an integral part of the theory that Forms have attributes, i.e. that abstract nouns can be the subject-words in significant and true sentences, of which the predicates signify the having of qualities, relations, magnitudes, states, etc.

Parmenides is going to perform a dialectical operation upon a selected Form; namely, he is going to discover whether a certain hypothesis about that Form as well as its contradictory generate contradictions. Which Form will he choose? The list of alternatives out of which he selects is 'plurality (or manifoldness), similarity, dissimilarity, change, changelessness, becoming, annihilation, existence, non-existence, and unity (or singleness)'. And he picks on the last on the pretext that it was his philosophical perquisite. The proposition which and the contradictory of which he is going to subject to Zenonian dissection both have for their subjects the Form or concept of Unity or Singleness, that namely of which 'all these buildings are one college' embodies an instance.

And here I must differ from Professor Taylor, Mr. Hardie, and many others on a point of translation. For they render τὸ ἕν as 'The One'. Now this phrase is objectionable on other grounds, for any man of sense will be provoked to say 'the one what'? As it stands, the phrase is incomplete and meaningless. However, the suggestion is that we are to take it as analogous to 'the Almighty', i.e., as a terse description of a being of which singleness (like omnipotence in the analogous case) is a leading property. But Plato makes it perfectly clear that τὸ ἕν is the name of a Form side by side with ἰσότης or σμικρότης. The English abstract noun 'Unity' is its proper translation. If the Greek language had possessed the word—as it did later on—ἑνότης would have been employed instead.

The collocation of the article with a neuter adjective is a perfectly familiar way of expressing what we express by an abstract noun, and the only excuse for rendering it by 'the one' in this dialogue is the presupposition that of course Parmenides must be discussing his Monistic theory, for which there is no internal evidence whatsoever.

While on this matter of translation, we may also complain of Professor Taylor's constant use of such phrases as 'the just equal' and 'the just similar' as translations for *τὸ ἴσον* and *τὸ ὅμοιον* or *αὐτὸ τὸ ἴσον* and *αὐτὸ τὸ ὅμοιον*. Actually these phrases are only the equivalent of our abstract nouns 'equality' and 'similarity'; but Professor Taylor's phrases are nearly senseless and quite misleading. When we use the word 'just' adverbially we usually mean 'nearly not', as when I reach the station just in time. Or sometimes we use it in the sense of 'merely', as when I call someone 'just an ignoramus'. If either sense were appropriate, phrases like 'the just equal' would be descriptions of particulars characterised as 'nearly not equal' or 'merely equal'—silly descriptions of nothing at all. But in fact, the Greek phrases are used to denote Forms; they mean 'equality' and 'similarity', and the sentences in which they occur make no sense unless they are so taken.

What then are the propositions or hypotheses about Unity which are to be shown to entail contradictory conclusions? And here, unfortunately, there is a real ambiguity in the Greek.

There are three alternatives:

(1) Each hypothesis is the existence-proposition 'Unity exists' or its contradictory 'Unity does not exist'.

(2) Each hypothesis is the attributive proposition 'Unity is unitary (or single)' or its contradictory 'Unity is not unitary (or single)'.

(3) Some of the hypotheses are of type (1) and some of type (2).

If we are primarily interested in the logic of existence-propositions or in the theory of the substantiality of the Forms, we shall be tempted to render all the hypotheses as of the first pattern. If we are primarily interested in the logical question whether any universal can be an instance of itself, we shall be drawn towards the second.

Both would be natural topics for Plato to explore, after what has already transpired in the first part of the dialogue. The *Theaetetus* and the *Sophist* show that Plato was at this time deeply concerned with the logic of existence-propositions, and they contain no suggestion that he was much exercised about the problem whether a term can be one of its own instances. The prefatory remarks of Parmenides (135–6) strongly suggest that the hypotheses will be of the form 'that so and so exists' and 'that so and so does not exist'. But the internal evidence of the earlier dialectical movements, though equivocal when taken by itself, points as strongly to the second alternative or to the third as to the first.

The difficulty is this. ἐστί can be used as a copula or to mean 'exists'; ἕν can be used as an abbreviation for τὸ ἕν, i.e. substantivally, or it can be used adjectivally, so that it can mean 'Unity' or it can mean 'unitary' or 'single'. And Greek permits the predicate-adjective to precede the copula. So the little sentence ἕν ἐστί can mean 'Unity exists' or 'it (i.e. Unity, which has been previously mentioned) is unitary'.

And this is complicated by the fact that Plato is ready to infer from a proposition of the form *S* is *P* to '*S* exists', since if *S* has a certain sort of being it must have being, i.e. exist (see *Tht.*, 188–9, *Parm.*, 161–2, *Soph.*, 252). That is, an ἐστί in the sense of 'exists' follows from an ἐστί in the sense of 'is . . .'. And conversely, if it is true to say that Unity exists, it is plausible to infer that it is unitary. (This begs a big question—but we cannot say yet that Plato realised that it begs it.)

I am convinced that the correct interpretation is the existential one; that is, that in the first two of the four 'operations' the hypothesis under examination is 'that Unity exists' and in the second two it is 'that Unity does not exist'.[1] When, as sometimes occurs, especially in the first operation, he is deducing consequences from the proposition 'Unity is unitary (or single)', this itself is taken to be an obvious consequence of the original one, 'Unity exists'. It has to be admitted that, especially in the first operation, the Greek does not square any better with this interpretation than with the other. But the following considerations make it necessary, if it is possible.

[1] V. Brochard construes the hypotheses in this way in his essay, 'La Théorie Platonicienne de la participation' in his book *Etudes de Philosophie Ancienne et de Philosophie Moderne*.

The general pattern of the argument is simple. There are two main operations upon the affirmative hypothesis, and two main operations upon the negative of it. Let us label them *A*1 and *A*2, *N*1 and *N*2 ('*A*' for affirmative, '*N*' for negative). Next, *A*1 answers to *N*1, and *A*2 to *N*2, in this way: In *A*1 and *N*1 Parmenides is seeing what propositions *about Unity* are entailed by the hypothesis; in *A*2 and *N*2 he is seeing what propositions *about terms other than Unity* follow from the hypothesis. (There are subordinate divisions within these operations, which do not matter for our present purpose.

Now though the actual formulation of the hypothesis and the development of the argument in operation *A*1 leaves it in doubt whether the hypothesis is 'Unity exists' or 'Unity is single', the formulation of the hypothesis and the argument of *N*1 make it perfectly clear that here the hypothesis is 'Unity does not exist'.

It is fairly clear too, though less so, that the hypothesis of *N*2 is 'Unity does not exist'. But from this it follows that the hypotheses of operations *A*1 and *A*2 must be 'Unity exists', else the promised two-way application of the Zenonian method would be broken. Moreover, this alone is consistent with Parmenides' sketch of the task of the dialectical method in the passages from 135a to 136b. And as I have said, it is corroborated by the facts (1) that in the *Theaetetus* and the *Sophist* Plato is acutely concerned with existence-propositions, and (2) that, as we shall see, Aristotle recognises that there was or had been a major philosophical crux about the two concepts of Unity and Existence. And anyhow later ὑπόθεσις normally meant the assumption of the *existence* of so and so.

Professor Taylor's translation hinders rather than assists us in this matter. For he rings the changes upon such formulations as, 'if it (i.e. the one) is one', 'if there is one', 'if the one is', 'if the one is not' and 'if there is no one'. None of these are consonant with English idiom, and hardly with English syntax; but anyhow the very variety of them is inconsistent with Parmenides' self-announced task. His task is to explore one proposition with its contradictory, and not several. And this proposition and its contradictory must have Unity for their subjects.

Evidence that the single word ἕν is used as a simple substitute for the phrase τὸ ἕν is as follows: καλόν, δίκαιον and ἀγαθόν are so used in 130b and 135c, ἀνόμοιον in 136b. ἕν is indubitably used substantivally at 143b 2, 143c 5–7, 144a 4, 149c 7, 160b 5–7 et seq., 161b 9, 163c 1, 164b 3, 164d and e, 165b 6, 166b 1. Cf. also *Theaetetus*, 185d 1, 186a 8, *Sophist*, 238e 1, 239a 10, *Phaedo*, 76 and 77. On my view there are lots of places in the *Parmenides* where this idiom is employed; but I cannot use most of them as evidence, since it is just the conclusion that it is being employed there for which I adduce these other passages as evidence.

There are, of course, plenty of passages where ἕν is certainly being used adjectivally or predicatively.

Before embarking upon the exegesis of the main drift of the Zenonian exercise, there is a matter of some general interest to notice. Why does Plato make Parmenides choose to operate upon such rarefied concepts as Unity and Existence? Or, when making his selection of his victim, why does he only mention as candidates for the post such rarefied concepts as Manifoldness, Similarity, Dissimilarity, Change, Changelessness, Existence, and Non-Existence? Would not the operations have worked if applied to beauty or justice, circularity or squareness, humanity or animality?

No hint of a reason is given in the dialogue. The answer may simply be that he assumed that what is true of the more generic Forms will cover the more specific ones; the general logical properties of universals will come out most swiftly from an inspection of those which are nearest the peak of the pyramid. That is, Plato may have thought that as Figure is higher than Plane Figure, and that than Triangle, so Similarity, Plurality, Existence, and the rest are higher than Figure, i.e. that they are Summa Genera. If he did think this, he was mistaken. This seems to be Professor Cornford's explanation for the selection; he does not recognise that Existence is not a sort-concept.

In fact, these concepts or most of them, and several others, differ from most ordinary concepts not just in level of generality but in type. They are formal concepts, not peculiar to any special subject matter, but integral to all subject matters. They belong, so to speak, not to this or that special vocabulary of knowledge, but to its general syntax. Now in the *Theaetetus* and the *Sophist* we find Plato recognising just such a feature of certain concepts. The mode of arrangement of letters which constitutes them a syllable is not itself a letter; and Plato uses this analogy to explain how certain concepts like existence and non-existence have a different sort of logical behaviour from most ordinary concepts, just (as I construe him) because they are not terms in the propositions which we think but the forms of the combinations of those elements into propositions. He does not and cannot fully develop this view. But as it is true and important and was in Plato's mind at this period, it is agreeable to conjecture that it entered into his motive for selecting the concepts which he does select for subjection to his Zenonian operation.

As what I wish to show is that the *Parmenides* is an early essay in the theory of types, this suggestion has some relevance to what will be my general thesis. I shall take it up again later on.

Another possible motive should be considered. What were the salient properties of Forms according to the strict theory of them? Plainly two; first, that a Form is single whereas its instances are or might be plural. The whole problem was: How can a plurality of objects different from one another be given one name or be spoken of as if there were one identical something in them? It is the prime business of a Form to be single. And, second, a Form had to be real or existent, in order to infect its instances with such meagre contagions of reality as they enjoy. It is by referring to a Form that we answer the question, What really is this particular?

Now, if Forms, to resolve any of our difficulties, have to exist and to be single, what sort of Forms will these be, namely Existence and Singularity? Will they too be existent and single? Or not? Clearly the menace of an infinite regress or else a flat contradiction stares us in the face. (Cf. *Philebus*, 15.)

For this to have been Plato's motive in selecting for inspection the hypothesis that Unity exists *or* that Unity is single (or their contradictories) he would not have had to suppose that Unity and Existence are Summa Genera, nor yet would he have had to see or half-see that Unity and Existence are not Summa Genera but form-concepts. His concentration upon them would have had the historical reason that just these concepts were the sheet-anchors of the whole theory of Forms. He operates upon them, because the whole argument is an *argumentum ad homines*. I think that in fact, if not in Plato's consciousness, this suggested line of approach is only a special case of the one previously mentioned. For what it is tempting to construe as the essential properties of universals, will in fact turn out (since universals cannot have properties) to be formal features of propositions, in which of course universals will be factors.

The one motive which I feel fairly sure did not much influence Plato is the one usually mentioned, namely that he wished to discuss Parmenidean Monism. This insipid unitarianism has no special bearings on more general question of logic, and I see no reason why Plato should have interested himself much in it, or much evidence that he did so, whereas there is plenty of evidence internal to this dialogue and adjacent dialogues that he was very much interested in the theory of Forms and very much interested also in more general questions of logic.

Parmenides has opted to practise his Zenonian operations upon one selected concept: that of Unity. But he does not suggest that the resultant antinomies are peculiar to this concept. The implied suggestion is, rather, that antinomies of the same type could be shown to result from operations either upon any other concepts or upon some other concepts. Parmenides nowhere says which. Either discovery would provide the young Socrates with the disturbance which he had said would trouble him. Whether it is shown in the case of one concept, or of several, or of all, that contradictions arise in their description, it will be enough to show that the promise of the perfect knowability of the supposed supramundane entities has been delusive.

The most tempting reading of the position is that Plato realised or nearly realised that antinomies necessarily arise from the attempt to make any concept whatsoever (from the most specific to the most categorial) a subject of attributes. To assert or to deny that a concept does or does not exemplify itself or another concept is to assert something illegitimate, no matter what that concept may be. A quality or a relation neither has nor lacks any quality or relation. The name of a quality or relation cannot significantly occur as the subject of an attributive or relational sentence. Abstract nouns cannot assume the rôles of proper names or demonstratives.

In particular, there is a deep-seated irregularity in sentences of which the verb is the verb 'to exist', and the subject is an abstract noun or the name of an εἶδος. Contradictions arise as well from the denial as from the assertion that Unity or any other εἶδος exists. So the hallowed doctrine that it is only of such subjects that we can with knowledge or truth assert that they really exist is baseless.

This, I say, is the most tempting construction of the message of the *Parmenides*. For, for one thing, it is true. And for another thing, it is completely general. And, thirdly, it rounds off very neatly Parmenides' criticism of the young Socrates' simple theory of Substantial Forms. It had been shown already that Socrates could say nothing of the relations between his Forms and their instances, or between his Forms and our knowings and thinkings. And now it is shown that he can say nothing of the relations between one Form and another Form.

None the less, I am not satisfied that this is the message of the dialogue. I think that Plato thought that the antinomies which he exhibits result from the application of the Zenonian operation to certain concepts, and no such antinomies would have arisen from its application to certain others. There is something logically eccentric about certain concepts, such as Unity and Existence, which does not infect all concepts, though it may infect a few others.

I shall try to formulate this interpretation more accurately later on. For the moment I wish to mention the grounds which make me dubious of the truth of the more tempting interpretation. First, the dialogue the *Sophist*, which is certainly closely connected with the *Parmenides* in date and style, and in certain stretches also in method and topic, nowhere handles any general theoretical difficulties in the theory of Forms; but it does deal very intensively with the logical properties of a few concepts which are of a very formal sort, namely, those of existence, non-existence, similarity, difference, change, and changelessness. And it picks up two threads which are already to be found in the *Theaetetus*, namely (1) that there is something logically peculiar about the concepts of existence, and non-existence, and (2) that the modes of combination of elements, like that of letters in syllables or words in sentences, are not themselves elements. And it is suggested that some concepts (but not all) are somehow analogous not to letters or words but to the modes of combination of letters and words, so that the contradictions which perplexed us over these formal concepts arose from the fact that we were trying to treat as 'letters' or 'words' what are in truth modes of combination of 'letters' or 'words'. Or to use the language of Kant and Wittegenstein, we were trying to treat formal concepts as if they were 'proper' or material concepts.

Finally, it seems to me unquestionable that Aristotle (in *Metaphysics*, 1001a, 1003b, etc., *Physics*, 185–7, *Topics* 121a and b, 127a, and *De Sophisticis Elenchis* 182b) is referring to notorious cruces about the special concepts of Unity and Existence—whether he actually has his eye on the *Parmenides* does not matter. There were clearly difficulties about them which were not thought to attach to most other concepts; they were clearly closely affiliated to each other; and something important is thought by Aristotle to be revealed about them when it is said of them not merely that they are not substances (which is true of all Forms alike), but also that they are not genera and do not fall under any one of the categories as opposed to any other, but in some way pervade them all —in which respect they are unlike most concepts.

These considerations suggest to me the following way of rendering Plato's line of thought in the *Parmenides* and the *Sophist* (and in lesser degree the *Theaetetus*).

He was beginning to see that there are different types of concepts. (As always happens, a philosophical problem is, at the start, dominated by a status-question. Later, this status-question surrenders its primacy and even its interest to a network of constitution-questions.) (*a*) One difference between types of concepts, specimens of which Plato explores with almost tedious pertinacity in the *Sophist* and the *Politicus*, is that between generic and specific concepts, or between the more generic and the more specific concepts. Thus, living creature—animal—man, or, figure—plane figure—plane rectilinear figure—triangle—isosceles triangle, are scales of kinds or sorts, which scales exhibit differences in degree of generic-ness or specific-ness. But this sort of difference is not directly important for our purpose, save in so far as the negative point, to which Plato was, I think, alive in the *Sophist*, is relevant, namely that Existence and Non-Existence are not co-ordinate species of a genus, nor themselves genera having each other or other concepts as subordinate species. The same would be true of Unity and Plurality. (*b*) Another distinction, which Plato himself draws elsewhere, is that between qualities and relations. Relational predicates, with the possible exception of identity, require the existence of at least two terms, whereas qualitative predicates only require one. (*c*) A third distinction, which I think Plato never attends to, is that between simple and complex concepts, or between simpler and more complex concepts. Thus, 'danger' is less simple than 'harm', for it combines the notion of harm with that of likelihood. Completely simple concepts would be indefinable, and definable concepts are complex. It is odd that the Socratic hunt for definitions did not lead to the realisation that some concepts must be simple and so indefinable. Perhaps the cryptic theory, expounded and criticised in the *Theaetetus*, that the ultimate elements of what exists are simples which can be named but not asserted, is an indication that somebody had noticed the point. But it is probable that by 'simple elements' Plato understood atomic particulars, like sense-data, rather than elementary concepts like 'yellow'. (*d*) Quite other than these differences of type between concepts is the difference between formal concepts and 'proper' concepts. A formal concept is one which may have a place in a proposition about any subject-matter you please, and some formal concepts or other will be present in any proposition. But non-formal concepts will only occur in propositions with this as opposed to that special topic. 'Triangle' occurs in propositions of geometricians or surveyors, and 'catapult' in propositions describing shooting. But 'not', 'exists', 'some', 'other', 'single', 'several', 'is-an-instance-of', 'and', 'implies' and many others are not peculiar to any special topics.

Such formal concepts are not subject or predicate terms of propositions—they are not 'letters', but rather the modes of combining terms. What the spelling of a word is to its letters, or what the syntax of a sentence is to the words in it, that a formal concept is to the non-formal concepts in a proposition.

So it may be that the laborious operations of this dialogue are intended, perhaps only half consciously, to bring out the difference between formal and ordinary concepts by showing that the logical behaviour of some of the former is anomalous.

I have said that the Parmenidean dialectic contains four main stages or operations which I have labelled *A*1, *A*2, *N*1, and *N*2. Each of these contains two movements. Let us call these *M*1 and *M*2 so that we can refer to a given movement as *A*1 (*M*2) or *N*2 (*M*1), ('*M*' for movement).

The references to them are as follows:

*A*1	(*M*1)	137c 4	*N*1	(*M*1)	160b 5
*A*1	(*M*2)	142b 1	*N*1	(*M*2)	163b 7
*A*2	(*M*1)	157b 6	*N*2	(*M*1)	164b 5
*A*2	(*M*2)	159b 2	*N*2	(*M*2)	165e 2

The general relation between the two movements within one operation is this, that while *M*1 (say) proves that the subject under investigation, namely Unity (or, in the other cases, what is other than Unity), possesses both of two antithetical predicates, the other movement *M*2 proves that that same subject possesses neither of two antithetical predicates. Or rather, in each movement the label of which is *M*1, say, it is proved that there are numerous pairs of antithetical predicates both of the members of all which pairs characterise the subject, while *M*2 establishes that the subject is characterised by neither of the members of these several pairs of antithetical predicates. And in general the predicate-couples considered in *M*1 are more or less the same as the predicate-couples in the corresponding *M*2.

Actually in *A*2, *N*1, and *N*2, the first of the two movements in each case proves that the subject possesses both of the members of the pairs of antithetical predicates, while the second movement proves that it possesses neither; but in *A*1 the order is the other way round, *M*1 proving that it has both.

*A*1 (*M*1)

The first movement of the first operation, namely *A*1 (*M*1), is (according to my interpretation) as follows:

If Unity exists, it cannot be manifold and therefore must be unitary or single. It cannot therefore be a whole of parts. It will not therefore have outer or inner parts, and so it will have no figure. It will have no location and no surroundings and so no change of position or stationariness of position. Change and fixity or relations are forbidden to it. It cannot be numerically different from anything or identical with anything: it cannot be identical with anything else or different from itself for obvious reasons; and it cannot be different from anything else, because being different is different from being single, so that if it is single it cannot be that *and* be different from anything. Equally it cannot be identical with anything, even itself. For unity is one thing and identity is another. [This seems a dubious step. Certainly unity is not the same as either identity or difference. But it does not seem to follow that it cannot *enjoy* identity or difference, save on the assumption that unity is single *and* has no other properties than singleness. However, this point is now affirmed.] If Unity has any other attributes than that of being unitary, then it is *ipso facto* shown to be several things, which severalness is inconsistent with its unitariness. Unity cannot be *both* unitary *and* anything else at all, even identical with itself. Since similarity and unlikeness are identity and difference of attributes, Unity cannot enjoy either similarity or unlikeness, and so neither equality nor inequality of dimensions. So it cannot have equality or inequality of age with anything, and so cannot have an age at all, and is therefore not in time.

Its existence therefore is existence at no date, and this is non-existence at every date. It cannot, therefore, exist, and if it does not exist it cannot carry its alleged special property of being single, since there would be nothing in existence for the property to characterise. So Unity neither exists nor is it single. No name can be the name of it, no description the description of it, and there can be no knowledge, opinion or perception of it. It cannot be talked or thought about (since there isn't any 'it'), which is absurd.

Comment. This, like all the other operations, smells highly artificial. There must be something wrong with the several deductions. We are inclined to say that the starting-point was illegitimate, and to write off 'Unity exists' and 'Unity is unitary' as bogus sentences—the latter for making an universal one of its own instances, the former for tacking the verb 'to exist' on to what is supposed to be a logically proper name. We may also suspect that the argument presupposes that singleness is a quality, when it is nothing of the sort. Doubtless we are correct on all these scores—but how can the illegitimacy of such procedures be established? Not by *prima facie* unplausibility, for the Theory of Forms did seem plausible and did entail (1) that every universal is single; (2) that every abstract noun is not only possibly but necessarily the subject of a true affirmative existence-sentence; and (3) that being single is a case of having an attribute.

The illegitimacy of the starting-point is established by the impossibility of the consequences that must follow if the original propositions are taken to be both legitimate and true. We must not be superior and appeal to sophisticated distinctions between formal and non-formal concepts or to professionalised classifications into 'categories' or 'types' of the various sorts of logical terms; for the necessity of such distinctions and classifications had first to be shown. Plato is showing it, though it may well be that he could not formulate what it was that he was showing. Of necessity he lacked the language of categories and types. That there are different forms of judgement and what their differences are could hardly be familiar at a time when the very notion of 'judgement' had yet to receive its introductory examination, e.g. in the *Sophist*. And little progress could be made in the former inquiry until principles of *inference* became the subject-matter of specialised research.

We can say, glibly enough, that qualities do not have qualities and also that existence and unity are not qualities. For we have been taught these lessons. But what first made it clear to whom that these lessons were true, unless some such ratiocinations as these?

To say that a term is of such and such a type or category is to say something about its 'logical behaviour', namely, about the entailments and compatibilities of the propositions into which it enters. We can only show that terms are not of one type by exhibiting their logical misbehaviour when treated alike. And this is what Plato is here doing.

To complain that the several conclusions are absurd is to miss the whole point. Plato means to prove that the premisses must be illegitimate because the conclusions are absurd. That is the sole and entire object of *reductio ad absurdum* arguments, which is what all these arguments are.

*A*1 (*M*2)

This, the second movement of the first operation, is the longest of them all. And it is insufferably tedious. Its object is to prove that Unity has both of the members of all the predicate-couples, the lack of both of the members of which had been established in *A*1 (*M*1).

If Unity exists, it must partake in or be an instance of existence. So being unitary is one thing and being an existent is another. So the Unity to which existence belongs will be a compound of Unity and Existence, a compound having those two parts or members. The whole containing these parts will itself be unitary and existent, and so also each of its members will be both unitary and existent and thus will be another compound of these two elements over again, and this will continue forever. So if Unity has existence, it must be an infinite manifold.

Next 'Unity' and 'Existence', not being synonymous, must stand for different things. So both will be instances of differences or otherness, which is consequently a third term over and above those original two. We can now speak of one couple consisting of Unity and Existence, another couple consisting of Unity and Otherness, and a third of Existence and Otherness.

And the constituents of a couple are units both of which must be unitary in order to be instances of unit. A couple plus the third unit will make three objects, and as couples are instances of even-ness, and threes of odd-ness, the Forms of Even-ness and Odd-ness are also now on our hands. And as multiplying consists in, e.g. taking couples three at a time, or threes twice at a time, we can get any number in this way. All arithmetical concepts are automatically generated; from the existence of unity the existence of every number follows, i.e. an infinite number of objects must exist. Every number yields an infinity of fractions, so Unity is fractionised by its interlocking with Existence into as many members as there could be arithmetical fractions, i.e. an infinite number.

Being a whole of parts it must contain its parts. There must be a distinction between what is and what is not contained by it. So it must have limits and consequently be finite, for all that there is an infinite number of parts which it contains.

If it has limits or boundaries it must have a beginning and an end as well as a middle: and it must have a configuration or shape. [Parmenides here unwarrantably jumps to the conclusion that it must have a *spatial* configuration.] Being a whole of parts, Unity cannot be a part of any of its parts, nor can it be just one of its own parts. It cannot therefore be one of the things that it itself contains. To be anywhere it must be in something other than itself; yet since everything countable is among its parts, it must be contained in itself. This is supposed, I think invalidly, to imply that it must, *qua* self-containing, be immobile, and, *qua* contained by something else, be mobile.

Next, Unity, not standing to itself as part to whole or as whole to part, must be identical with itself, fully and not partially, and it must also be fully and not partially other than whatever is not Unity. But the next stage seems very paradoxical. For it is to be argued that Unity is *not* different from what is other than it and also is *not* identical with itself.

For a container is not where its contents are, since they are inside it, which it cannot be. Now Unity has just been shown to be both content and container, so it must be elsewhere than itself and so not be identical with itself.

The opposite point, that Unity is identical with what is not Unity, is shown in this way. Otherness cannot characterise anything, for everything is 'itself and not another thing'. So neither Unity nor what is not Unity can possess otherness. And as what is not Unity cannot be either a part of unity or an unitary whole of which Unity is a part, it is only left for Unity and what is not Unity to be identical. [This argument pretends, for the moment, that 'otherness' is the name of a quality. Of course it isn't a quality—but why not?]

Next, since Unity is other than what is not Unity, and *vice versa*, both Unity and what is not Unity must exemplify otherness. But in their both being instances of the same attribute, namely that of otherness, they must be similar in that respect. For that is what similarity is, the possession by two things of the same character. Now identity is the opposite of otherness. But it has been shown, in an earlier argument, that Unity must be identical with what is not Unity (146–7); consequently, as the possession of identity is the non-possession of otherness, there must be this respect of dissimilarity between Unity and what is not Unity. For by this argument a suggested shared property is not shared. It follows that Unity is both similar and dissimilar both to what is not Unity and to Unity itself.

I skip the detail of the next few stages of the argument. It is argued that Unity must be both in and out of contact with itself and with the 'field'; that it must be both equal and unequal to itself and the 'field', that it must be greater and smaller than itself and the 'field' and also older and younger than itself and the 'field', and also be neither of these.

Then, to controvert the end conclusion of *A*1 (*M*1) it is shown that Unity does exist at every time and is there to be named and described, known and thought about.

Finally, since the only way in which a subject can be conceived both to have and to lack a given property is that it *alters*, having the property at one date and lacking it at another, it is argued that Unity changes, develops, decays, and moves as well as being immutable and static, and that the time of its changings and movings must be a time which takes no time—at which time it is in neither of the conditions from or to which its transition is. (This looks like a variant of a Zenonian paradox about motion.)

Comment. Naturally we feel that most of the foregoing assertions, with the arguments leading to and from them, are absurd. Concepts are being played with fast and loose. Those of one type, with one sort of logical rôle, are being made to understudy or deputise for others of quite different sorts. Different concepts should not be treated as if the rules of their co-functioning were all similar. Precisely—but only absurdities reveal the different rules, and the *reductio ad absurdum* argument marshals the absurdities.

*A*2 (*M*1)

Parmenides now inquires: From the assumption that Unity exists, what consequences follow about τὰ ἄλλα? He will argue that this subject too must possess opposite predicates. What exactly does τὰ ἄλλα denote? We have no reason to restrict it, for example, to the objects of sense or opinion; nor yet to the Forms other than Unity. It must be taken to cover all terms whatsoever, of whatever sorts, which are other than Unity. So Circularity as well as Alcibiades, the Equator as well as my present pang of pain, will be members of this *omnium gatherum.* Let us just call it, in racing parlance, 'the field'.

The field is other than Unity, yet it embodies it. For it has members, being a plurality, and so must be *one* aggregate or whole of those members. Moreover, each of those parts or members must be one part or member. A whole is a plurality of units, so it is a unit and each of them is a unit.

But though or because they exemplify it, it is not and none of them is Unity. A thing is not that of which it is an instance. So since the field is not Unity it must be a plurality or manifold. And the argument, which I skip, is developed that such a plurality must be both a finite and an infinite plurality, so each of its members will be so too.

Being both limited and unlimited, the field and its several members are similar to one another, since they all co-exemplify limitedness and unlimitedness; yet since these are opposite predicates, what exemplifies one must be unlike what exemplifies the other, as what is black is unlike what is white. Similarly it could be shown, though it is not shown, that the field and its several members must enjoy both identity and otherness and both change and changelessness, etc.

*A*2 (*M*2)

Unity and the field are an exhaustive disjunction; there can be nothing which does not belong to the one camp or to the other. So there can be no superior camp, to which both these camps are subordinate as members. Hence Unity will have no truck with the field, either so as to constitute it *one* whole of parts, or as an assemblage of *unitary* parts. So the field cannot be a plurality, nor will any number be applicable to it, or to any part or feature of it. So the field cannot possess either similarity or dissimilarity or both at once. For both together would be a pair and each by itself would be single, and these are applications of number. For the same reason the field cannot be identical or different, stationary or mobile, coming into or going out of existence, greater or smaller or equal.

The conclusion of all the movements of both operations *A*1 and *A*2 is thus summed up. If Unity exists it both has every predicate and lacks every predicate, including that of unity. And the same holds good for the field too.

*N*1 (*M*1)

We now turn to the consequences of the hypothesis that Unity does not exist. The proposition that Unity does not exist clearly differs in having a different subject from the propositions that largeness or that smallness does not exist. So we know what 'Unity' denotes and that it denotes something other than what these other nouns denote, whether our judgement is that there does or that there does not exist such a thing. So Unity is something which we apprehend, and it possesses and is known to possess the attribute of being other than the terms which we have distinguished from it. Consequently Unity, for all that it does not exist, is an instance of various things. The word 'it' applies to it. Being distinguished, it has dissimilarities from what it is distinguished from, and as it is not so distinguishable from itself, it must have the opposite of dissimilarity, namely, similarity to itself. [We may grumble at this step. The inference 'I am not unlike myself, therefore I must be like myself' contains a fallacy. But what sort of fallacy? The inference is valid if I am compared with my father, so why does it not hold good in this case? If we say 'because the terms to the relations of likeness and unlikeness must be numerically different', then we are asserting a very special sort of 'must'. Namely we are saying that 'I' and 'like (or unlike)' are terms which are of such formal constitutions that absurdity results from their juxtaposition in this way. And that *is* a discovery about the formal properties of certain sorts of terms. It shows that similarity is not a quality. But the distinction of quality-concepts and relation-concepts is a distinction between types of concepts.]

Being unlike the field, it cannot be equal to it or its members; so it must be unequal to them. But inequality is in respect of largeness and smallness (since for two things to be unequal in size one must be relatively large and the other relatively small). So Unity possesses largeness and smallness [the argument would only prove that it must possess at least one of the two]; but as being big is the opposite of being small, Unity must, by way of compromise, have what is betwixt and between the two, i.e. equality with itself. [This is fallacious—but why?] Unity therefore is an instance of bigness, smallness, and equality.

But if it has all these predicates, Unity must, though non-existent, still enjoy being in existence in some fashion. For if the above descriptions were true, they described it as being what it really is. Unity must be there for us to be able to say or think that it does not exist. But also it must not be there, for its non-existence is change, and change or transition is motion [this is illegitimate, but to see why it is illegitimate is to see something important about the concepts of existence, non-existence, and change.]

Yet since it does not exist it cannot be anywhere or move anywhence anywhither. And the other sort of transition, from state to state, is also ruled out; for if unity changed in this way it would cease to be Unity and become something else.

But to be exempt from movement and change is to be stationary and immutable. So Unity both is and is not mobile, and both is and is not mutable. And it also follows both that it is and that it is not subject to generation and annihilation.

Comment. The interesting parts of this movement are the stages where we find the famous argument that that of which it is true that it does not exist must be *there*, in some sense, to accept this ascription of non-existence and also to be distinguishable from other terms, existent or non-existent. We are enlightened enough to say (with Kant) that 'exists' is not a predicate or (with latter-day logicians) that the nominatives to verbs of existence do not function as demonstratives or logically proper names; but the penalties of not saying so are here exhibited. Doubtless the rules governing the logical behaviour of verbs of existence are still obscure to Plato; but that there are such rules and that they are different from those governing ordinary predicates, is here being realised by him. For absurdities result from treating them alike. Plato seems to be ahead of Meinong here.

*N*1 (*M*2)

If Unity does not exist, it is lacking in all modes, departments or sorts of existence. It can enjoy neither coming-to-be nor annihilation; it cannot be subject to mutation or motion, nor, being nowhere, can it be stationary anywhere.

Indeed, it can have no attributes or properties, neither largeness, smallness, nor equality, neither similarity nor difference. It cannot even be correlated with a field, for its having such a correlate would be a relational property of it. It has no attributes, parts, relations, dates, and it is not there to be known, thought or talked about, perceived or named. There is no 'it' at all.

Comment. It seems to follow from this that all negative existence propositions must be nonsense if they are true, since there is nothing left to support the negative predicate. So the name of the subject of predication is the name of nothing. From this it is a short step, which Plato does not take (any more than Meinong did), to seeing that the nominatives to verbs of existence are *not* the names of anything, and 'exists' does not signify a quality, relation, dimension, or state, etc.

*N*2 (*M*1)

If Unity does not exist, what predicates attach consequentially to the field? Plainly the field must by definition be other, yet it cannot be other than Unity, since this, by hypothesis, does not exist for the field to be demarcated against it. The field must be other in the sense that its members are other than one another.

Yet, since Unity does not exist, the members of the field cannot be unitary or be units; so the field can only be a manifold or manifolds without end. Only of such manifolds can we say that they are other than each other—since there is nothing else to say it of. Each manifold of manifolds will seem to be single, though not really being so. And numbers will seem to be applicable to them, though the seeming will be illusory. Derivatively the concepts of odd and even, greater, smaller and equal, limit and unlimitedness will appear to have application, together with those of unity and plurality, similarity and dissimilarity, etc., etc. Yet if unity does not exist, none of these concepts can really have application to the field.

N2 (M2)

If Unity does not exist, the field cannot be single, nor can it be a plurality, else it would be *one* plurality and its members would be units. Nor could the field seem to be either single or a plurality. For since there is no Unity, there is nothing of the sort for the field to exemplify or participate in in any respect whatsoever. So the field cannot be thought, even, to be single or plural or to be an instance of anything else, such as similarity or dissimilarity, identity or otherness, contact or separation, or anything else at all. The field could not therefore be thought to exist. So if Unity does not exist, nothing exists. So whether Unity exists or not, Unity and the field both have and lack every predicate and its opposite. 'Very true' is the last word of the dialogue.

What is the outcome of all this tiresome chain of operations? First, *ad hominem* it seems to have been proved, in the case of at least one extremely eminent Form, what Socrates was reluctant to believe could be proved, that a Form does undergo hosts of incompatible predicates, and that these disagreeable consequences flow not only from the palatable hypothesis that that Form exists but also from the unpalatable hypothesis that it does not exist.

But what does Plato think to be the important lesson of the whole dialogue? Here we can only make more or less plausible conjectures.

1. Plato might think that the whole argument proves that no

universal can be the subject of an attributive or relational proposition; and he may have confused with this the quite different point that no universal can be the subject of an affirmative or negative existence-proposition. (For he may have thought wrongly, as Descartes and Meinong did, that 'exists' is a predicate of the same category, i.e. with the same sort of logical behaviour, as 'is square' or 'is green'.) Universals are not substances, or abstract nouns are not proper names, and sentences in which we talk as if they were are logically vicious.

This conclusion is true, and relevant to the question of the truth of the Theory of Forms. So it may be what Plato had in his mind.

2. But Plato may be apprising himself and us of a seemingly more parochial discovery, namely that some concepts do not behave in the same way as some others.

He may, for example, be making the discovery that 'exists' and 'does not exist' do not have the same sort of logical behaviour as 'breathes' or 'resembles' or 'is square'. If we consider the concepts which occur in our ordinary descriptions and classifications of things, they seem to fit reasonably well into scales of genera and species. And we can imagine a table depicting all the ladders or pyramids of generic and specific concepts, such that any descriptive or classificatory concept would have its place fixed for it somewhere in one and not more than one such ladder or pyramid. But there are some concepts which can be peculiar to no one ladder or pyramid but must somehow pervade them all. Such are the concepts answering to expressions like 'not', 'exists', 'same', 'other', 'is an instance of', 'is a species of', 'single', 'plural', and many others. Some concepts are 'syncategorematic'.

At first sight we may be tempted to take such concepts, which are obviously of very general application, to be merely highly generic concepts, perhaps actually Summa Genera. But if we do so take them, our enterprise collapses, for just these concepts are again required when we attempt to describe the affiliations or non-affiliations between Summa Genera themselves, and also between the sub-divisions, not of one but of all the sort-hierarchies.

Formal concepts, as we may now call them, differ from generic ones not in being higher than they in the way in which they are higher than specific concepts, but in some other way. They differ from generic concepts not, for example, as 'Even Number' differs from '2', but as '$+$' and '$\sqrt{\ }$' differ from either.

Or again, to pick up again the two analogies which Plato uses in the *Theaetetus* and the *Sophist*, formal concepts differ from generic and specific concepts not as one letter of the alphabet differs from another or as one bunch of letters differs from another bunch of letters, but as the mode in which letters are arranged into a syllable or word differs from the letters which are so arranged: or else as the way in which nouns, verbs, adjectives, etc., are combined to form a significant sentence is different from those elements or even from the way in which one such element, like a noun, differs from another, like a preposition. What a grammatical construction is to the words of a sentence embodying that construction, that a formal concept is to the terms (particulars and ordinary universals) which enter into the proposition or judgment.

Now when we treat a formal concept as if it were a non-formal or proper concept, we are committing a breach of 'logical syntax'. But what shows us that we are doing this? The deductive derivation of absurdities and contradictions shows it, and nothing else can. Russell's proof that, in his code-symbolism, ϕ cannot be a value of x in the propositional function ϕx is only another exercise in the same genre as Plato's proof that 'Unity' cannot go into the gap in the sentence-frame '. . . exists' or '. . . does not exist'.[1]

I feel fairly sure that this is something like the point which Plato was trying to reveal in this dialogue. I feel this partly because the imputed doctrine is true and important and partly because, so construed, the dialogue then links on directly to the later parts of the *Theaetetus* and to almost the whole of the *Sophist*. Whereas the first interpretation which I suggested has no echoes of importance in either dialogue.

Moreover, we know that Aristotle was alive to the fact that there was a special crux about Unity and Existence; and also that these concepts with some others (e.g. Good) did not come under

[1] It is worth noticing that the concept of being-an-instance-of, about which the discussion turned in the first part of the dialogue, is in fact a *form-concept*, and not a proper concept; the contradictions and circles which embarrassed Socrates did arise from his attempt to treat it as if it were from the same basket with ordinary relations. However, Plato does not point this out. We can conjecture that the second part of the dialogue does contain (between the lines) the answer to the problem of the first part; but we cannot say that Plato was aware of it.

any one of the Categories but exhibited themselves in all of the Categories: nor were they concepts of the genus-species sort.[1]

And (in *Met.*, 1003b and 1053b) he uses for both 'existence' and 'singleness' the argument which Hume and Kant used for 'existence', to show that they do not signify attributes; namely that the descriptions of a man and an existent man are not descriptions of different sorts of men.

And lastly I am tempted to prefer this interpretation to the other on the score that it does more credit to Plato's powers of discerning the important in logical questions. There is, indeed, an agreeable sweepingness in that suggested message of the dialogue according to which Plato was proving the general point that universals are not subjects of qualities or relations. But its sweepingness would only be *sanitary*, for it would only be establishing the negative point that there was something wrong with the foundations of the theory of Forms.

It would have small instructive effect on thinkers who had never adopted the belief that abstract nouns are the names of substances.

It would leave open and, worse, it would leave almost unformulated the profounder question, What is wrong with those foundations? *This* question requires the discovery of the difference between formal and non-formal concepts—and this discovery is required for all sorts of logical problems, and not only this special historical one of the nature of the fallacy underlying the special doctrine of Substantial Forms.

One objection to the foregoing interpretation of the dialogue is sure to be made. It is incredible, it will be said, that the central doctrine of Platonism, namely, that Circularity, Unity, Difference, etc., exist, should be shown by Plato himself to be logically vicious, even though he mitigates the cruelty of his exposure of his earlier children by showing that there would be a precisely parallel viciousness in the doctrine that they do *not* exist. On minor points, doubtless, Plato's second thoughts might be expected to be improvements on his first thoughts, but that he should overtly demonstrate the untenability of the very principles of the

[1] And cf. *De Interpr.*, 16b, where Aristotle explicitly says that 'is' and 'is not' only function significantly in the assertion of some synthesis, and cannot be thought except together with what is combined in such a synthesis.

system from which his whole influence upon subsequent thinking derives is too shocking a supposition.

But such an objection does less than justice to a great philosopher. Kant is felicitated for being capable of being awoken from dogmatic slumbers; Aristotle is permitted to be fonder of truth than of Platonism; those of Russell's contributions to logical theory are considered important which belong to the periods after his affiliation to Kant, Bradley, and Bosanquet. Why must Plato alone be forbidden the illuminations of self-criticism?

Moreover, it has long been recognised that in the whole period which includes the writing of the *Theaetetus*, the *Sophist*, the *Politicus*, Plato's thinking is not entirely, if at all, governed by the premisses of the Theory of Forms.

He attends to the theory on occasions, but he does so in a dispassionate and critical way. In the *Sophist* (246) the exponents of the theory of Forms are treated in the same way as are the materialists; neither can answer the Eleatic Stranger's puzzles about existence and non-existence. Similarly in the *Philebus* (15). Moreover, if it is true that the theory of Substantial Forms embodies radical fallacies, to praise Plato as a great philosopher, as we do, would be consistent with crediting him both with the acumen to recognise and the candour to expose them.

But more important than these considerations is this fact. Whatever its sublimity and inspiration-value, the Theory of Forms had been from the start, *inter alia*, a doctrine intended to resolve certain puzzles of a purely logical nature. How can several things be called by one name or be of one sort or character? And how is it that only those systems of propositions express certain knowledge which contain neither the names nor the descriptions of actual instances of sorts or characters—namely mathematics and philosophy?

The Theory of Forms was intended to answer both these questions. It fails to be a satisfactory theory, for the reason, mainly, that exactly analogous questions arise about Substantial Forms to those questions about the instances of Forms which the theory had been intended to resolve. And in so far it was the wrong sort of answer.

But something remains. It remains true that every judgement or proposition embodies at least one non-singular term or element. It remains true that the propositions of mathematics are universal propositions. And it remains true that in some sense, some or all philosophical questions are of the pattern 'What is it for something to be so-and-so'? (where 'being-so-and-so' is an universal).

The criticisms of the doctrine of Substantial Forms given in the dialogue have no tendency to upset these positions even if they do not directly yield an answer to the problem which they raise. But the road is cleared for an answer to them, a road which was blocked by the fascinating but erroneous theory which they dispose of. Nor could the new advances have been begun save by someone who had himself gone through the stage of being at least very familiar with the theory of Substantial Forms.

In particular, I shall suggest, the road is now cleared for the advance which was partially made in the *Sophist*, where for the first time the possibility and the need of a theory of categories or types is realised.[1] The distinction between generic concepts and formal concepts is here seen or half-seen, and logical inquiries are at last capable of being begun.

In fine, on my theory, the *Parmenides* is a discussion of a problem of logic—as part of the *Theaetetus* and most of the *Sophist* were discussions of problems in logic. Not that Plato says 'let us turn back from Ethics, Metaphysics, Epistemology, and Physics and consider some questions belonging to the province of Logic', for these titles did not exist.

But his questions and his arguments in this dialogue should be classified by us as belonging to the same sphere to which belong, for example, Aristotle's theory of Categories, Kant's separation of formal from non-formal concepts, Russell's theory of types, and Wittgenstein's and Carnap's theories of logical syntax.

Whether, if I am right, the dialogue is interesting is a question of taste. The central problem seems to me of radical importance and therefore interesting, potentially, to any philosopher who cares to get down to the roots. But the detail of the argument is arid and formalistic and so sustained that everyone must find it tedious—in the same way as the methodical dissection of Vicious Circle Fallacies is tedious if it is thorough.

I do not think that the dialogue could or should be interesting to a student who is primarily anxious to know Plato's later views about the human soul, or God, or immortality, or physics, or Parmenidean Monism. For, as I read it, the dialogue contains no

[1] I use the word 'category' in a less misleadingly precise way than Aristotle.

references to such topics and no premisses from which conclusions about these topics can be deduced.

The dialogue is an exercise in the grammar and not in the prose or the poetry of philosophy.

To corroborate the foregoing theory about the programme of the *Parmenides*, I append some remarks about the *Theaetetus* and the *Sophist*, in which, I think, the same or kindred lines of thought are to be traced. These dialogues were certainly composed close to the date of the *Parmenides*. The *Sophist*, which is a sort of sequel to the *Theaetetus*, was certainly written after the *Parmenides*, to which indeed it makes one or two undoubted allusions and of which, in an important stretch, it partly echoes and partly presupposes a part of the dialectical operations. The *Theaetetus* was almost certainly in part, and perhaps as a whole, composed after the *Parmenides*, and it contains what is probably a reference to it.

THE *THEAETETUS*

With the main problem of this dialogue I have no special concern. It is an inquiry into the nature of knowledge. It begins with a sustained exposition and criticism of the theory that to know something is to have sense-acquaintance with it or memory of sense-acquaintance with it. It is soon shown that neither this theory nor a more generalised analogue to it can account for our knowledge about the future, or of the truth of theories about what is right or expedient, especially of the truth or falsehood of this theory of knowledge itself, or even of mathematical truths. And it is briefly indicated that even within the field of the objects of sense-acquaintance it will not do. For to know that sense-given objects exist or do not exist, are similar or different, single or plural is to do or experience something more than merely having sense-acquaintance. So a new hypothesis is considered, the gap between which and the previous view is of the greatest importance not only for the theory of knowledge, but also for our special problem. For it is now suggested that to know is to judge, or is a species of judging. And this means—to bring together threads from earlier and later parts of the dialogue—that knowledge requires for its expression not just a name but a sentence or statement. And what a sentence or statement expresses always contains a plurality, at least a duality of distinguishable elements or factors. Knowledge, as well as true and false belief and opinion, cannot be expressed just by a proper name or demonstrative for some simple object, but only by a complex of words which together constitute a sentence.

At this point Socrates does something which at first sight seems to be deserting the direct path in order to follow up a side-track. For he suddenly opens up a prolonged inquiry into the nature of false beliefs or mistakes, and is of necessity at once led to debate how we can either think or state that which is not. How can I either think or describe something which is not there to be the object of a thought or description? But I think that this is in fact no digression at all. For, first, it is true that I can only be described as knowing the same sort of things as I could be described as mistaken about. To know is, at the least, to be under no mistake. And, second, any description of any actual or possible mistake automatically reveals the complexity both of what is falsely judged and, correspondingly, of what would be truly judged. For to mistake is to take something for something instead of for something else.

So a 'simple' could never be the object of a mistake. I could mistakenly think that $7 + 5 = 11$, and unmistakenly judge or know that $7 + 5 = 12$. But 7 could not be the total object of a mistake, and so, by implication, not the total object of a piece of true belief or knowledge either. And this is what was at bottom wrong with the equation of knowledge with sense-acquaintance. This noise or that stench is not the sort of thing that could be described as what I mistakenly believe, and therefore it is not the sort of thing which could be described as what I correctly believe or know. There must be a complex of distinguishable elements as well in what I know as in what I mistakenly or correctly believe. What I know are facts, and facts always have some complexity. So 'simples' could not be facts, though they would be elements in facts. Only a proper name could directly stand for a simple, and only a sentence could state a fact.

Now, without raising for the moment the question what are the simples or elements of which what I know or believe are complexes, or even whether there are any such elements, we can see that a complex of elements must be one of two things. Either it is just a lot of assemblage of elements or it is some sort of union of or fabric embodying them. *Either* the required complex of elements *A*, *B*, and *C* just is *A* and *B* and *C*, so that to know the complex would just be to know *A* and to know *B*, and to know *C*, which would merely be to go back on the result already arrived at and to suppose that what can be named but not stated could be what I know. *Or* the required complex is some sort of an organised whole, of which the principle of organisation is distinguishable from the elements which it combines. And in this case the principle of organisation is something unitary and not to be resolved into a plurality of elements; that is, it is a new 'simple', somehow superadded to the original elements which it organises into the single complex. But if we may not say that simples are what we know, we may not say it either of this new combining simple.

This point is brought out by means of the analogy of letters in syllables. A syllable is a complex of letters, which themselves are not complexes. Now *either* a syllable is nothing but the lot of letters in it, in which case to know it is just to know each of them, an illegitimate hypothesis if what I know must always be a complex. *Or* a syllable is some ordered arrangement of letters. But in this case the order of arrangement *is* not a lot of letters but something unitary and irresoluble. And then it is an extra simple element (though not, of course, one of the same type as a letter). Finally it is argued, on the tacit assumption that by a 'complex' can only be meant either a conjunction of similar elements ('letters') or a conjunction of some elements of one sort ('letters') plus at least one element of a different sort ('order of arrangement'), that in fact such conjunctions or assemblages are not more knowable but less easily knowable than what they are conjunctions of.

If knowing was inventorying collections, certainly simple elements could not be known. But in fact, whatever knowing is, collections are not more accessible to knowledge than their members are. Moreover, inventories are just as well capable of being the objects of true or false beliefs, as of knowledge. So the differentia of knowledge is not to be found in this direction.

Now this discussion reveals at least two extremely important points.

1. It is true that if the universe contains simples, such that for each there could be, in principle, a proper name, the utterance just of this proper name could not be the expression of true or false belief or of knowledge (in the sense of 'knowledge that . . .'). What I believe or know requires a whole sentence for its expres-

sion, and what a sentence states is *in some sense* a complex. It is always possible to find for any sentence another sentence the signification of which is *partly* similar and *partly* dissimilar to that of the given sentence, i.e. what a sentence says contains parts or factors distinguishable from each other and capable of some independent variations by substitution.

Now, though Plato does not make this application, Substantial Forms were supposed to be just such simple nameables. And if we ask ourselves: What would it be like to be knowing Equality or knowing Justice or knowing Existence? and, still more, if we ask: What would it be like to be mistaken about Equality or Justice or Existence?, we find ourselves bothered and bothered for the very reason that Plato here gives, namely that we know that when we describe ourselves as 'believing or knowing so and so', a proper name cannot go into the place of the accusative to those verbs.

Oddly, Professor Cornford, who approves of the refutation of the view that knowing is having sense-acquaintance, since knowing is, or is a species of, judging, still believes that Plato's real theory of knowledge, unexpressed in this dialogue, was that Substantial Forms are what knowledge is of. Yet this would involve that 'Equality' and 'Circularity' do express knowledge, for all that it would be nonsense to assert that any such abstract noun could express either a mistaken or a true belief.

Socrates draws attention to an important affiliated point when he asks how we can mistake one thing for another either when we know both (supposing still that we may speak of knowing 'things'), or when we know one and not the other. And he asks: Who has ever mistaken the number 11 for the number 12 or vice versa, for all that plenty of people have taken 7 + 5 to equal 11? No one has ever told himself that an ox must be a horse or that two must be one, that beauty is ugliness or justice is injustice. By analogy we might ask (though Socrates does not): Who ever told himself the infallible tidings that 11 is not 12 or that 11 is 11, that justice is not injustice or that ugliness is ugliness?

It is tempting to suggest that the moral of this puzzle and of later developments of it is something like this, that while a mistaken or a true judgement must contain some plurality of elements, this requirement as it stands is too hospitable. Not any combination of any sorts of elements constitutes a possible mistake, or in consequence, a possible truth. '7 + 5 = 11' is a possible mistake, but '12 is 11' is not. 'Theaetetus is Theodorus' is not a possible mistake, but 'Theaetetus is the son of Theodorus' is. The elements of what I know or believe will not all be of the same type. But Plato does not here allude to any such lesson.

2. But anyhow it is unquestionable that Plato is in this dialogue alive to the following matters. What I know or truly believe or falsely believe is some sort of a complex of elements, and one the verbal statement of which requires not a name only, nor even a conjunction of names, but a complex expression of which the special form of unity is that of a sentence. What constitutes a complex, like a syllable, a unity is some feature of it other than any one or the mere lot of its elements, such as letters.

That is, Plato is now considering the places and rôles of 'terms' in truths and falsehoods, with his eye on the underlying question of what are the principles of organisation which govern the combination of such 'terms'. He does not say, nor are we warranted in inferring from the contents of this dialogue that he saw, that there are some concepts, namely form-concepts, which cannot do duty for proper concepts or ordinary 'terms', much less that he saw that 'exists', 'not', 'one', 'several', and others do express such form-concepts. But it is clear that he is consciously developing a method of inspecting the formal properties of such complexes of elements as constitute truths and falsehoods. He knows that names are not true or false, that sentences are not names, that sentences are not just assemblages of names or composite names resoluble without residue into several component names; and he knows that nothing less than sentences will express what we know or truly or falsely believe. A mere inventory of nameable simples would not only not be all that we know, or wish to know, it would not even be any part of what we know or wish to know.

In any truth or falsehood there must be some multiplicity of distinguishable factors, and of these at least some perform a different sort of function from some others—the order of arrangement of letters in a syllable does not play the same sort of rôle and so is not the same type of factor as the individual letters. Of course, Plato has not got a substitution-method, or, what this involves, a code-symbolism with which to indicate those similarities and differences of factor-types which sanction or veto particular substitutions. But that there is a co-functioning of distinguishable factors in truths and falsehoods and that their functions are not all similar is, I suggest, a thing which Plato is here clearly realising.

THE *Sophist*

This dialogue begins with an attempt to arrive at a clear definition of what constitutes a Sophist. Its method is that of dichotomous division. Some highly generic concept, which is assumed without proof to be the correct one is divided into two sub-species, and so on until a point is reached where the concept under inquiry is seen to be such and such a sub-sub-species of the original genus. Many commentators regard this method of Dichotomous Division as a grand discovery of Plato, and some even identify it with the Method of Dialectic for which Plato makes his famous claims. It is clear to me that the Method of Dialectic as this is described in outline in the *Republic* and in detail in the *Parmenides*, has almost nothing to do with the Method of Division. The Method of Dialectic has links with Zeno's antinomian operations, or it may just be an expansion of them; but this process of Dichotomous Division is an operation of quite a different sort. In particular, it is not a process of *demonstration*, as Aristotle points out.[1]

Whether Plato did or did not believe that the Method of Division was a powerful philosophic instrument, we can be quite clear that it is not so. No philosopher, including Plato, has ever tried to employ it for the resolution of any serious philosophical problem, and if they had done so they would not have succeeded. For first of all it can only be applied to concepts of the genus-species or determinable-determinate sort, and it is not concepts of this sort that in general, if ever, engender philosophical problems. And, next, most generic concepts do not subdivide into just two polarly opposed species; usually there are numerous species of a genus or sub-species of a species.[2] And the question whether a sort divides into two or seventeen sub-sorts is, in general, a purely empirical question. So nearly any case of a philosopher's operation by Division could be upset by the subsequent empirical discovery of sorts lying on neither side of the philosopher's boundary lines.

[1] In *Prior Analytics*, 46a, *Posterior Analytics*, 91b and 96b.

[2] Cf. Aristotle's criticism of the programme of dichotomous division, *De Part. An.*, 642.

And, finally, there is room for almost any amount of arbitrariness in the selection from the ladders of sorts *en route* for the definition of a given concept. Except in artificial hierarchies, such as library catalogues and regimental ranks, there are few, if any, rigid scales of kinds. So there are many tolerable and no perfect ways of defining most of the sort-concepts that we employ.

Had Plato wished to exhibit these and kindred blemishes in the programme of definition by Dichotomous Division, he could have chosen no more effective procedure than that of exhibiting several definitions of one and the same concept, all achieved by descending different scales of kinds. And this is what in fact he does. He gives six or seven different definitions of 'sophist', all arrived at by different paths. However, he does not say that he is revealing defects in the method, and the subsequent dialogue, the *Politicus*, is another exercise in it; so some of his commentators may be right in believing that Plato thought well of its potentialities.

However, there is a pair of concepts which are forced upon our notice in the course of the operations which turn out to require a very different sort of elucidation, namely those of non-existence and existence. For a Sophist is a pretender who either thinks or says that what is not so is so. The puzzle which arose in the *Theaetetus* arises again here. How can what does not exist be named, described, or thought of? And if it cannot, how can we or Sophists talk or think of it, falsely, as existing? So the question is squarely put: What does it mean to assert or deny existence of something?

What do Pluralists or Monists mean when they assert that there exist a lot of things or that there exists only one thing? What do materialists or idealists mean when they assert or deny that bodies or that Forms are real?

Now, it is of the first importance for our main question to notice certain points. (1) With reference to Parmenidean Monism it is shown that the concepts of Unity and Existence interlock in an important way without being identical. And part of the argumentation of the *Parmenides* is echoed here upon just this matter. (2) No attempt is made to elucidate the concepts of existence and non-existence by the Method of Division. The heroic attempt of Meinong to show that they are co-ordinate species of a generic concept is not anticipated by Plato. And we can see—as perhaps Plato saw—that the Method would not work just because these concepts are not sort-concepts, but that there is an important difference between sort-concepts and these two which is the source of the inapplicability of the Method of Division to them. (3) There are some other concepts, identity, otherness, change, and changelessness which have to be operated upon alongside of existence and non-existence. (4) The procedure of investigating the interrelations of these concepts is called Dialectic—which, I think, is only remotely connected with the operation of tracing out sort-hierarchies which is called Division.

Now in attempting to elucidate the concepts of existence and non-existence, Plato makes use of two analogies, one of which he had used in the *Theaetetus*. Namely, he compares the ways in which some concepts will combine in only certain ways with certain others (*a*) to the ways in which letters will only admit of certain sorts of alliances so as to form syllables, and later (*b*) to the ways in which words will admit only of certain sorts of alliances so as to form sentences.

For a syllable to be constituted vowels must be there as well as consonants, and for a sentence to be constituted a noun must be conjoined with a verb and not a noun with a noun or a verb with a verb. If we like to build metaphors from these analogies we can say that some, but not all, concepts must be 'vowel'-concepts, or that some, but not all, concepts must be 'syntax'-concepts as opposed to 'vocabulary'-concepts. And existence and non-existence are of these new types.

It is further indicated (253, 259, 260b) that these two concepts of existence and non-existence, together with certain others which are associated with them, namely change and changelessness, otherness and identity, are in an important way pervasive—they crop up, that is, in all the Division-scales in which we locate other concepts, in the same sort of way, I take it, as 'non-existence' cropped up in one of the definitions of 'sophist'. We are reminded of Aristotle's assertion that Existence and Unity and Goodness belong to no one of the Categories but pervade them all, though his Categories are not, of course, Summa Genera.

There appears then to be quite good internal evidence in the *Sophist* for the view that Plato was now discerning an important difference between types of concepts or universals, and in particular that concepts of sorts, which can be scaled with or without precision in hierarchies of genera, species, and sub-species, obey very different rules from some others, like existence and non-existence. And the concepts of this latter class perform what I may call a logical rôle which is analogous to the rôle of vowels in syllables or that of syntax-rules in sentences. They function not like the bricks but like the arrangement of the bricks in a building.

Now the interesting thing is that it is true that existence and non-existence are what we should call 'formal concepts', and further that if modern logicians were asked to describe the way in which formal concepts differ from proper or material or content-concepts, their method of exhibiting the rôle of formal concepts would be similar to that adopted here by Plato. But we need not go further than to say that Plato was becoming aware of some important differences of type between concepts. There is no evidence of his anticipating Aristotle's inquiry into the principles of inference, which inquiry it is which first renders the antithesis of formal and other concepts the dominant consideration. There is, consequently, in Plato, no essay at abstracting the formal from the contentual features of propositions, and so no code-symbolisation for the formal in abstraction from the material features of propositions.

There is, of course, always a considerable hazard in attempting to elucidate a doctrine of an earlier philosopher in the light of subsequent and especially of contemporary doctrines. It is always tempting and often easy to read palatable lessons between the lines of some respected but inexplicit Scripture. But the opposite policy of trying to chart the drift of some adolescent theory without reference to the progress of any more adult theories is subject not to the risk but to the certainty of failure. We cannot even state what was a philosopher's puzzle, much less what was the direction or efficacy of his attempt to solve it, unless subsequent reflections have thrown a clearer light upon the matter than he was able to do. Whether a commentator has found such a light or only a will-of-the-wisp is always debatable and often very well worth debating.

Thus I may be wrong in believing that there are affinities between Plato's inquiries in these dialogues and Hume's and Kant's account of assertions of existence, Kant's account of forms of judgement and categories, Russell's doctrine of propositional functions and theory of types, and, perhaps, more than any other, nearly the whole of Wittgenstein's *Tractatus Logico-Philosophicus*. I may be wrong in construing these dialogues as, so to speak, forecasting most of the logical embarrassments into which the infinitely courageous and pertinacious Meinong was to fall. But at least my error, if it is one, does not imply that Plato's puzzles were so factitious or ephemeral that no other serious philosopher has ever experienced any perplexity about them.

AFTERWORD, 1963

1. When I wrote this article in 1939 I had paid no attention to the fact that while Part I of the *Parmenides* is in Oratio Obliqua, Part II, apart from one initial 'he said', is in Oratio Recta. So Plato cannot have composed either Part with the intention that it should be the complement, inside one dialogue, of the other Part.

(*a*) The Parts could, therefore, have been composed at different, and even quite distant dates; and the dramatically impossible junction of the two must have been made at a date later than the composition of either Part. Part I may have remained on Plato's shelf, uncompleted and unpublished, for a long time after he composed it.

(*b*) It follows, too, that my attempt in the article to render the questions canvassed in Part II pertinent to those canvassed in Part I may have been gratuitous. Old Parmenides tells the youthful Socrates that, to become a philosopher, he needs training in the Zenonian exercises, of which he then deploys a protracted exemplar. He does not say that these exercises carry a philosophical moral more relevant to the Theory of Forms than to any other philosophical theory. Certainly Socrates' challenge, at 129a–e, gives the appearance of a special relevance, but this stretch, like the stretch from 135d to 137b, might be the 'knitting-wool' which Plato, when he combined the two Parts, interpolated to provide some, but not all, of the needed continuities.

2. I had also paid no attention to the fact that instruction in the questioner–answerer elenctic duel had become a part of the Academy's curriculum by about the middle of the 350's. Isocrates, who calls 'eristic' what Plato and Aristotle call 'dialectic', tells us this in his *Antidosis* (258–69), of 354/3. Aristotle's *Topics* shows us the sort of instruction that he himself gave in the strategies, tactics, and tricks of the disputation-exercise. In Part II of the *Parmenides* old Parmenides demonstrates the two-way Zenonian

method of argumentation, dressed up in questioner–answerer style. If, as I now think, it was Aristotle who in his early teaching years, introduced the teaching of dialectic into the Academy, partly as a training-exercise for future philosophers, then, some way on in the 350's Plato designed Part II of the dialogue as a pedagogic exemplar for Aristotle's *Topics* classes. It is no accident that Parmenides' young interlocutor is a namesake of the author of the *Topics*.

3. Aristotle frequently, e.g., in the *Topics* (170a–172a), *Metaphysics* (995b) and *Rhetoric* (1358a) separates off one class of concepts from all the rest, namely the class of 'common' or ubiquitous concepts from those which are proprietary to different branches of knowledge. These ubiquitous or topic-neutral concepts are those of *existence*, *non-existence*, *likeness*, *unlikeness*, *identity*, *otherness*, *motion*, *rest*, *coming-to-be*, *ceasing-to-be*, *unity*, *plurality*, *part* and *whole*, and a few others.

Once, in *Metaphysics* III, (998b and 999a), Aristotle calls them not 'common', but 'first' and 'highest'. It is the dialectician's task to investigate these ubiquitous concepts, and his study of them has something to do with the study of inference. Plato seems to treat these concepts in the same way; he calls them 'common' in the *Theaetetus* (185) and 'greatest' in the *Sophist* (254). In the *Sophist* (253) he makes it the dialectician's business to investigate their interrelations.

In the *Parmenides* (129e) Socrates adduces some of these ubiquitous concepts and Parmenides does so too in 136b. In the dialectical Part II the concept operated on is that of *unity* (or *singularness*), but the concepts operated with are, almost entirely, the 'common' concepts of *existence*, *non-existence*, *likeness*, *unlikeness*, *identity*, *otherness*, *coming-to-be*, *ceasing-to-be*, *motion*, *rest*, *part* and *whole*, and *unity* and *plurality* themselves. When more specific concepts are operated with, they are often just specialisations of the ubiquitous concepts, as *equality* is of *similarity*.

However much Plato and Aristotle differed, or had differed about the Ontology of Forms, they seem to be alike in separating off the ubiquitous concepts from all the rest; and in making the ubiquitous concepts the proper subject-matter of dialectic. In Part II of the *Parmenides*, the argument exemplifies just what Plato seems to require in the *Sophist* (253) and what Aristotle requires in the *Rhetoric* and *Topics*. When, in my article, I contrasted 'formal' concepts with the rest, I did not realise how awake Plato and Aristotle were to the contrast, or part of the contrast that I think I had in mind.

4. As regards the detail of Part II of the *Parmenides*, (*a*) I failed to notice that a good deal of the argumentation belongs to the philosophy of arithmetic. Plato is interested in questions akin to those which interested Frege. 'Unity' often seems to be our 'the number One'. (*b*) I failed to notice that a large fraction of the operations are operations with the temporal concepts of *before*, *after*, *alteration*, *older*, *younger*, *getting older*, *starting*, *stopping*, *continuing*, *instant*, as well as of the varieties of past and future tenses.

5. At several points in my article I spoke very loosely of Plato's and Zeno's arguments being 'valid'. Now, in Part II antithetical consequences are drawn from one and the same thesis; so, unless the thesis itself embodies some hidden logical trouble, at least half the deductions from it must be flawed deductions. We can take it that Plato was well aware that something was amiss with some of his deductions, just as he, like all other educated folk, knew that Zeno had not really demonstrated the impossibility of motion. So presumably, like Aristotle, he thought that students of dialectic should inquire into the differences between real and apparent demonstrations, and do this at the highest possible level of abstractness.

The arguments in Part II of the *Parmenides* are not, like some of those in the *Euthydemus*, just tricks and teasers. They are designed to be tasks, and very serious tasks, like those set by Zeno. We have nothing to show that Plato was equipped with the apparatus to say what was wrong with his own, or with Zeno's arguments.

6. I have corrected a few uninteresting mistakes of spelling and printing.

VII

PLATO'S *PARMENIDES* (1959)

W. G. Runciman

MY purpose in adding to the already considerable literature[1] on the *Parmenides* is as follows: I think it can now be satisfactorily established that the dialogue contains no fundamental modification of the theory of forms, but that it nevertheless represents serious expression of Plato's own comments on the theory. Further, I wish to suggest that the second part contains no explicit exposition of doctrinal or metaphysical teaching, but that its moral is to be deduced from the fact that its contradictions are possible at all; that this moral is both more than the need for dialectical gymnastics and less than the abandonment of the theory of forms; that it can be drawn from the consideration of the second part in its relation to the first; and that the dialogue can accordingly be seen as a coherent and serious whole.

I

The dialogue purports to be a reported conversation between Zeno, Parmenides, and the young Socrates. Zeno has been reading

[1] I list some of the more important recent contributions: G. Ryle, 'Plato's Parmenides', *Mind*, N.S. XLVIII (1939), 129 ff. above, Ch. VI; R. Scoon, 'Plato's Parmenides', *Mind*, N.S. LI (1942), 115 ff.; R. Robinson, 'Plato's *Parmenides*', *Class. Philo.*, XXXVII (1942), 51 ff., 159 ff.; Sir David Ross, *Plato's Theory of Ideas* (Oxford, 1951), 86 ff.; A. L. Peck, 'Plato's Parmenides', *Classical Quarterly*, N.S. III (1953), 126 ff.; G. Vlastos, 'The Third Man Argument in the Parmenides', *Phil. Rev.*, LXIII (1954), 319 ff. below, Ch. XII (also W. Sellars, ibid., LXIV (1955), 405–37; Vlastos, ibid., 438–48; P. T. Geach, ibid., LXV (1956), 72–82 below, Ch. XIII; Vlastos, ibid., 83–94; below, Ch. XIV; R. S. Bluck, 'The Parmenides and the Third Man', *Class. Quart.*, N.S. VI (1956), 29 ff.; K. Johannsen, 'The One and the Many', *Classica et Mediaevalia*, XVIII (1957), 1 ff.

a treatise in which he argues that a denial of monism entails that the same subject must undergo opposite predicates. Socrates, however, suggests that on the basis of the theory of forms no paradox arises, since one particular can exemplify several different forms. He would only be surprised if it could be shown that the forms themselves undergo opposite predicates. Parmenides then proceeds to an examination of the theory of forms which occupies the first part of the dialogue. This part (130b to 135c) may be briefly summarised as follows:

Parmenides first inquires what classes of terms Socrates admits to the category of forms, and encourages him not to be hesitant about those of whose status he is doubtful. He then examines the nature of participation between forms and particulars. Socrates suggests three explanations in turn, each of which is refuted by Parmenides. Parmenides concludes his examination by an argument designed to show that if the forms exist they must be unknowable. But he then tacitly admits that the forms must in fact exist.

Before examining each argument separately, we must consider the part assigned in the dialogue to Parmenides. Certain commentators, feeling that Plato cannot have had a greater respect for Parmenides than for Socrates, have held that he would not put into the mouth of Parmenides criticisms of the theory of forms which he (Plato) could not in fact refute. It has further been suggested that Plato intended the dialogue to be an implicit refutation of views which the historical Parmenides might be supposed to have held.[1] However, it is, I think, considerably more plausible to suggest that Plato uses the young Socrates to express views that he either previously held or was still holding at the time of writing, and that he uses Parmenides to present serious comment upon these views. This interpretation may be strongly supported on the following grounds:

The dramatic date of the dialogue presents Parmenides as aged about sixty-five and Socrates as perhaps twenty. It is unlikely that the historical Socrates ever held the views he expresses in the dialogue, and certain that he did not hold them at the age of twenty. Thus there is no initial reason for supposing that Parmenides will argue from the standpoint which he historically held. Indeed, unless the purpose of the dialogue is an anti-Eleatic

[1] This view, already held by Burnet and Taylor, has been revived by Peck.

polemic, we have no cause to suppose it at all. But if Plato's purpose is to discuss certain problems arising out of his theory of ideas, there is no intrinsic improbability in his putting his comments into the mouth of a thinker for whom he is known to have had a very great respect. Further, the historical Parmenides would certainly not have expressed the acceptance of the theory of forms which we find at 135a-d. He does not argue as a monist; and I shall later hope to show that we may reject the suggestion that in the second part of the dialogue it is Parmenidean monism which is under discussion.

There is an additional difficulty which faces those interpreters who hold that Plato expects his readers to detect the fallacies in Parmenides' refutations of Socrates' suggestions as to the relation between forms and particulars. Socrates suggests first participation (*μέθεξις*), then conceptualisation (*νόημα ἐγγιγνόμενον ἐν ψυχαῖς*), then resemblance (*εἰκασθῆναι*). If we consider all of Parmenides' arguments false, are we to conclude that all three different suggestions are sound? We must presumably assume that the refutations are based on a misinterpretation: that is to say, that Parmenides is attacking views which Plato never held in the form in which they are stated. But if this is so, it must be admitted that Plato never does state in what form he really did hold them. For if any one of Socrates' three alternatives is in fact the view that Plato held to be correct, then Parmenides must be wrong in this instance and right in the others; but in fact Plato represents Socrates as driven equally to abandon each argument in turn. The interpreters who find Parmenides' arguments invalid seem to do so on the ground that he is guilty of wilful misconception or deliberate sophistry; thus in the first argument he 'illegitimately' holds Socrates to a rigidly literal interpretation of participation. But this, surely, is precisely the point of the argument. It is designed to show that the relation between forms and particulars is not one of literal participation; and this it effectively does.

That Plato cannot, however, have thought Parmenides' arguments fatal to the theory of ideas is demonstrated by his retention of the theory after the writing of the dialogue. That he did retain it seems to me to be beyond question; and to deny this involves rejecting not only evidence in the dialogues themselves, but also the evidence of Aristotle and of all subsequent tradition. But since certain commentators, including Burnet and Ryle, have sought to minimise or ignore this evidence, I feel that some reference to it is necessary. It is of course true that Plato often uses language which does not make it certain that he thinks of the concepts he is discussing as forms. But the following passages from dialogues generally agreed to be written after the *Parmenides* are to me adequate proof that Plato continued to hold to his belief in the forms: *Timaeus*, 51b–52c, *Philebus*, 15a–b, 16c–e, 58c–59d, 62a, *Theaetetus*, 185d, *Politicus*, 284e–286a, *Sophist*, 249c–d, 253c–254a, *Phaedrus*, 277a, *Laws* 965b–e. I do not cite the evidence of the *Seventh Letter* since its authenticity is not beyond question; but even if spurious it is evidence of a kind for Plato's beliefs, and it is unequivocal in the belief expressed in the existence of forms. Further, the burden of proof must rest on those who maintain that Plato ceased to regard as forms concepts or objects to which he had previously assigned this rank. I do not think satisfactory proof has been offered. The view that Plato was led by the arguments of the *Parmenides* to modify or abandon the theory of forms is made more plausible if we accept the attempt of G. E. L. Owen, 'The Place of the *Timaeus* in Plato's Dialogues,' (below, Ch. XVI) to date the *Timaeus* prior to the *Parmenides*. But the *Philebus* reflects no such modification as is implied by Professor Ryle (whose view I shall discuss more fully later); and most of Owen's arguments have been very strongly disputed by Professor Cherniss, 'The Relation of the *Timaeus* to Plato's Late Dialogues,' (below, Ch. XVII, cf. also '*Timaeus*, 38a 8–b5', *Journal of Hellenic Studies* LXXVII (1957), 247–51.) Not all of Owen's arguments are dealt with by Cherniss, notably Owen's conclusions about the *Politicus*; but the stylometric evidence on the question of hiatus remains perhaps the strongest reason for agnosticism about Owen's suggested dating.

Thus Plato may well have thought Parmenides' arguments not invalid but irrelevant since he believed that the language used to describe the relation between forms and particulars is merely a metaphorical description for some other true and indefinable or as yet undefined relation. But it is a mistake to argue from this, as has been done, that Parmenides' arguments are thereby rendered unsound. In fact, they are more damaging than we can suppose Plato ever to have realised. For we may ask, as Plato and some of his commentators do not, what is the literal relation of which Parmenides criticises the metaphorical expression? Now there is in fact no answer to this question, either in Plato or anywhere else.[1] The relation may be regarded as metaphorical to the extent that the statements 'this partakes of greenness' or 'greenness inheres in this' are synonymous with the statement 'this is green'. But for Plato both forms of statement express a relation between the pre-existent entity greenness (for colour as a form cf. *Epistle* VII. 342d) and the particular concerned. This relation is never adequately defined by Plato. He uses participation in a perfectly legitimate sense in the *Gorgias* at 466a where it is said that rhetoric is a part of flattery.[2] This metaphorical statement we can satisfactorily translate by saying that flatterers employ rhetoric or that rhetoric is a species of flattery. But no such translation may be rendered for the participation in forms of particulars. However, since Plato continued to believe in the existence of the forms, he must have believed that we must not reject them on the grounds that the relation between forms and particulars is not susceptible of precise analysis. Such a relation must in fact exist no matter how difficult it may seem to be to explain.

Finally, if we conclude even one of the arguments to be in fact sound, this must tell strongly against the view that Parmenides is the proponent of a string of fallacious sophisms for which, on this view, it is difficult to find any worthwhile purpose. It may of course always be true that an argument which is in fact sound was not seen by Plato to be so. But if he means to expose the inadequacy of a certain type of criticism of the theory of forms, and if some of this criticism is in fact sound as he himself expresses it, it seems not unreasonable to doubt whether such exposure was his intention. But, as I have said, this does not mean that he thought the criticism though valid to be conclusively damaging. In fact, I think it is now generally accepted that Parmenides' final argument is unsound (I shall examine its purpose later), but that those arguments which deal with the relation of forms to particulars constitute effective criticism of the proffered explanations of this relation. Accordingly I shall now proceed to consider in turn each of the arguments of the first part of the dialogue.

On being questioned by Parmenides, Socrates expresses certainty of the existence of forms of likeness, unity, plurality,

[1] Cf. Arist., *Met.*, 1079b 25–6, where Aristotle justly points out τὸ δὲ λέγειν παραδείγματα εἶναι καὶ μετέχειν αὐτῶν τὰ ἄλλα κενολογεῖν ἐστι καὶ μεταφορὰς λέγειν ποιητικάς.

[2] Cf. *Euthyph.*, 12c, where reverence is described as a part of fear.

justice, beauty, goodness, and 'all such things' (130b). However, he admits that he is puzzled about forms of man, fire, or water, and unwilling to accept hair, mud, or dirt. Parmenides tells him that this hesitation is due to his youth and his deference to general opinion, but that when he becomes more truly philosophically inclined he will be ready to accept all these things as forms.

This argument presents no problems. It was ethical and aesthetic qualities which were the starting point of the theory of ideas, and such ideas as unity and similarity had come into prominence in the *Phaedo* and the *Republic*. However, in the earlier dialogues (*Republic*, 596a, cf. *Phaedo*, 75c–d, *Cratylus*, 386d–e) it had been explicitly stated that the positing of a form is entailed by the application of a common name. The question thus arises whether this axiom is to be exhaustively applied; and we need only consider why in fact Plato should hesitate at all. An answer seems discernible in the language of the early dialogues. Not only were the early ideas considered to be the projection of such concepts as beauty or equality, but Plato appears to have thought of the particulars as in some sense aspiring to attain their perfection. With the moral ideas this seems reasonable enough; we may for instance think of Socrates as aspiring to the perfect form of justice. In the *Phaedo* such language is used of equality which individual particulars are said to desire or to fall short of (e.g. ὀρέγεται 75b). Likewise it is not absurd to think of the craftsman as aspiring to create a bed or a shuttle which should be as good as possible a representation of the ideal form. But when this notion is extended to hair and dirt, the danger of absurdity becomes obvious. Are we to say that all things which are dirty aspire to the perfection of dirtiness? or that all hairs aspire to the perfection of hairiness? Plato seems here to be expressing his awareness of this difficulty. But Parmenides' concluding remark suggests that the difficulty does not damage the theory, and that the young Socrates will come to accept the existence of an idea answering to every common name. The method of diaeresis, which was adopted after and, I shall suggest, in part as a result of the arguments of the *Parmenides*, involves a belief in a natural subdivision of classes, or in other words a belief that forms exist in accordance with a preordained interrelation between genera and species (cf. *Phaedrus*, 255e, *Politicus*, 262b, and the *Sophist* as a whole); and the fullest list of forms is found in the *Seventh Letter* (342d), written (if, as is now widely thought, it is genuine) in the last decade of Plato's life. Moreover, Plato seems in the *Theaetetus* and to a greater extent in the *Philebus* to have come to concede an increasing respectability to the world of empirical phenomena; although, as I have mentioned, I do not think there is adequate evidence for holding that he abandoned his belief in transcendental ideas.

Parmenides now turns to his examination of the relation between forms and particulars. I shall summarise and comment separately on each of the three arguments.

(1) *μέθεξις*. Socrates suggests that the relationship is one of participation. Parmenides then argues that participation entails that each form must be divided into parts and shared among the particulars. Thus largeness will be divided into fragments smaller than largeness itself, equality will be divided into fragments unequal to itself, and smallness itself will be larger than the fragments by which particulars become smaller. Further, if Socrates has been led to postulate largeness by observing it as the common characteristic of large things, it will presumably share with them this characteristic of largeness. From this, an infinite regress is at once engendered.

Comment. This argument is clearly a valid refutation of a literal participation theory. It could only be answered by giving some other meaning to *μέθεξις*, which is never given; and as I suggested above, no satisfactory meaning could in fact be advanced within the premisses of the theory of forms. It is accordingly established that the relation between forms and particulars is not one of participation in any literally analysable sense. Socrates first offered the analogy of the daylight, which is in many places at once. Parmenides rejects this in favour of the analogy of a sailcloth. He never gives any explicit grounds for his rejection, which Socrates accepts. But it is worth remarking why the daylight analogy could not in fact avoid Parmenides' objections. To say that different places all share in the daylight is only to say that many places are illumined by the daylight at the same time. In the same way, to say that many objects at the same time partake of largeness is only to say that there are many objects which are all large. In other words, the relation is not one of participation in its literal sense as in the case of a sailcloth (or a cake or a sum of money), which is all that (for the moment) Parmenides has set out to prove.

The infinite regress (or 'third man') argument deserves separate comment. Analysis of this argument has been much clarified by the comments of Vlastos and his critics. I do not propose to enter the controversy concerning the formal analysis of the argument itself. Whether or not it is refutable by replacing the 'self-predication' and 'non-identity' assumptions by the 'separation assumption in its explicit form', the important fact is that Plato failed to realise that any instance of an attribute must, even if it is a form, have the logical status of a particular. The 'third man' argument exposes an error which, though Plato did not realise it, is fundamentally damaging to the theory of forms. Professor Ryle accordingly concludes that Plato had come to realise the logical illegitimacy of self-predication.[1] But had he been fully aware of it he would have seen (which he never did) that the theory fails because it merely recreates on a different level the problems which it was designed to solve. In fact, although Parmenides later shows that a resemblance theory apparently entails an equally damaging regress, Plato continues to use the language of resemblance in the *Timaeus*, e.g. at 29b, 48c, 49a, 50d —cf. also *Politicus*, 285d–286a echoing *Phaedrus*, 250b—and at *Philebus*, 16d he speaks of the form as being present in (*εὑρήσειν γὰρ ἐνοῦσαν*) the particular. Further, at *Sophist*, 258b–c we find the phrase *ὥσπερ τὸ μέγα ἦν μέγα*; and that it is the form of *τὸ μέγα* which is referred to is shown by the phrase *τὸ μέγα αὐτό* used at 258a. The evidence of relevant ancient literature not only does not reflect any abandonment by Plato of paradeigmatism but offers positive evidence to the contrary; for references see Cherniss, below, Ch.XVII. We must accordingly conclude that Plato found the present passage damaging only to a theory of strictly literal participation, and that he continued to believe in some other indefinable (or at least undefined) relation between particulars and forms. However, that he was aware that problems arise from the consideration of the relations between the forms themselves is shown by Socrates' remarks at 129d–e. Some of these problems he examined in the *Sophist*; and they are relevant, as we shall see, to the second part of the *Parmenides*.

[1] Most notoriously expressed at *Prot.*, 330c where the conclusion that justice is just seems to be arrived at by a fallacious use of the excluded middle: it is clearly absurd to say that justice is unjust, therefore it must be just. Cf. *Phd.*, 74d (equality is equal) and 100d (beauty is beautiful).

(2) νόημα ἐγγιγνόμενον ἐν ψυχαῖς. Socrates now attempts to avoid these objections by suggesting that the forms are thoughts existing in the mind. Parmenides objects that the thought must be a thought of something, namely a form. Thus the problem of relationship has not been solved; further, on the participation theory particulars will have shares in a thought, and will therefore either be pieces of thinking or thoughts without thought.

Comment. It is certainly a part of Platonic doctrine that the forms are objects of thought, since it is by thought that they are apprehended and known. But Parmenides' argument effectively shows that to describe them as such does not solve the problem of their relationship to particulars. However, it has been argued that Parmenides' argument is illegitimate because it is the minds that are thinking about the forms which provide the necessary link.[1] But this would entail a kind of Berkeleyan position which Plato certainly never held. Are we to believe that although, for example, greenness and treeness always exist, green trees only exist when they are being thought about? Unless this is so, the problem remains, and Parmenides can again bring up his argument against the literal participation theory. Socrates accordingly abandons his conceptualist theory as an explanation and offers a resemblance theory in its place.

(3) εἰκασθῆναι (παραδείγματα). Socrates suggests that the forms are fixed in nature and the particulars made in their likeness, so that participation is in fact nothing more than resemblance. Parmenides answers that if two things resemble each other they must both possess at least one common attribute. Thus if a form and a particular are similar, both must be instances of at least one other form; and hence there at once arises an infinite regress.

Comment. This argument, as Vlastos shows (see below, Ch. XII), involves the two inconsistent assumptions that F-ness is F and that anything which is F cannot be identical with F-ness. But it thereby serves to demonstrate, for reasons more damaging than we can suppose Plato to have realised, that the relation between forms and particulars is not one of resemblance. To posit the resemblance theory entails the belief that forms can legitimately undergo the same predicates as particulars; and this

[1] Thus Peck, 136. However, Peck has earlier admitted (p. 134) that forms do not depend on souls for their existence. It must therefore presumably follow that particulars do.

is the central mistake exposed, as we saw, by the first version of the 'third man' argument. It is a mistake which would seem most naturally to arise out of the confusion of forms with ideal particulars which is implicit in the discussion of geometry at *Euthydemus*, 290b or of the bed of *Republic*, 597a ff. But Plato, as we have seen, continued to use the language of resemblance. We must accordingly conclude that he saw that resemblance could not give a complete and satisfactory account of the relation between forms and particulars; but he did not see that the consideration which renders resemblance unsatisfactory is a criticism damaging to the whole theory of forms.

Certain commentators have tried to circumvent the argument on the grounds that the relation is an 'asymmetrical' resemblance as between pattern and copy.[1] But this cannot alter the fact that if there is any resemblance at all it must be a mutual relation; and for the copy to be a copy it must resemble the pattern in some respect, e.g. in colour or shape. Asymmetrical resemblance is a contradiction in terms. If p resembles q in any respect, this logically entails that q will in this same respect resemble p. The common attribute thus designated will on the assumptions of the Platonic theory be a form. Thus, if the relation between forms and particulars is one of resemblance an apparent regress can at once be engendered.

It is accordingly distressing to find that Professor Cherniss (see below, Ch. XVII) still retains his conviction that Parmenides' arguments are invalid and were seen by Plato to be so. He does not repeat his truly astonishing statement (*Aristotle's Criticism of Plato and the Academy*, I, 298) that 'even before Plato wrote the *Parmenides* he must have believed that the "likeness" of particular to idea does not imply that the idea and the particular are "alike".' But he still argues that the παραδείγματα argument is invalid because particulars are likenesses of ideas (originals) and it does not follow from this that both are likenesses of another single original. He further thinks (below, p. 374) that if the argument were valid, 'it would be a general proof that nothing can be a likeness or image of anything whatever'. The fact is, however, that the possibility of resemblance between particular and idea entails the existence of a common characteristic; and to predicate this characteristic of a form is to reduce it to the logical

[1] Among them Taylor, Cornford, Scoon, and Peck.

status of a particular. If whiteness is white (which must follow if white objects are white by resembling it) then whiteness is one of the class of white objects. Any two similar objects need only be likenesses of another original if the existence of a common characteristic is taken to entail the hypostatising of an entity or form by resemblance to (or participation in) which they come to have this characteristic: but this of course is the mistaken supposition which gave rise to the theory of forms. It is only true to say that the regress argument against paradeigmatism is not valid in the sense that the regress is illegitimate before it starts, since it accepts the paradeigmatic assumption that attributes predicable of a particular can (and indeed must) be predicated also of a form. Professor Cherniss argues that the relation of a copy to its original need not presuppose a common resemblance to a further original. Of course it need not, unless we accept the assumption of the theory of forms that common characteristics (which a copy must share with its original to be a copy) are joint resemblances to the same forms. But since this is precisely the *παραδείγματα* theory which is under discussion, the criticism of Parmenides does expose its inadequacy as an explanation of the relation between forms and particulars.

Parmenides now passes to his concluding argument, which may be summarised as follows: The forms exist separately from the sensible world. They will be correlates of each other, not of particulars, and particulars will be correlates of each other, not of forms. Thus mastership is relative to slavery, and master relative to slave. Likewise knowledge in the world of forms is a correlate of the form truth, whereas phenomenal knowledge can only be relative to the particulars of our world. Therefore we cannot have knowledge of the forms. Further, if divine knowledge is true knowledge, it cannot be knowledge of our world.

It may in some sense be true that there can be no relation between correlates of different orders or categories. But Parmenides' argument as it stands is invalid, and he himself indicates as much by tacitly accepting the theory of forms while putting his emphasis on the difficulties of converting the objector (133b, 135e). His two examples are in any case insufficient to establish his contention. It is of course true that mastership is not master of a slave in the way in which a particular master is, nor in the way in which Parmenides wrongly suggests that it is of slavery. But this does not establish that there cannot be any connection between a master and mastership. This conclusion would require a far fuller inquiry into the possible varieties both of correlates and of relations. Similarly Parmenides does not establish that there cannot be any relation between the form of knowledge and our particular acts of knowing, and it is illegitimate to assert that knowledge can know anything (134b). Further, if, as Parmenides suggests, the forms are in God's world, God must according to the preceding argument be himself a form since there can be no relation between the forms and any other category of existence.

What, then, is the purpose of this final argument? Socrates has been shown unable to give a satisfactory description of the relation between forms and particulars. Parmenides has then adduced a separate argument designed to show that any such relation is impossible. Now it is clear that Plato cannot have thought this final argument valid since it would inevitably destroy the whole theory of forms. In fact, we have seen that one of the reasons which make it invalid is that in order to prove his contention Parmenides would have to exhaust all possible varieties of relation. Thus the first part of the dialogue seems effectively to focus Plato's attitude to the problem at the time of writing. He realised that it was apparently impossible to give a complete or satisfactory analysis of the relation between forms and particulars, and this difficulty will appear to lend plausibility to the argument that there can be no relation because the two are entities of a separate category. But this will only be so if all possible relations are shown to be invalid; and in fact, since our minds are capable of apprehending forms as well as sensory particulars, it follows that some relation must exist. Therefore, although this relation is not susceptible of literal description, its indescribability should not be allowed to convince the objector that its existence is impossible.

This analysis is borne out by the remarks that Plato now puts into the mouth of Parmenides. Parmenides reasserts the difficulties involved both in the ascertaining and the expounding of the forms. Socrates agrees. Parmenides then allows that if belief in the forms is rejected because of these difficulties, the validity of both thought and communication will be completely destroyed (135a–c). It is difficult, I think, to dispute that these remarks are an accurate statement of Plato's own views; and as such they need no further comment. Parmenides then suggests that Socrates' difficulties are due to his attempting to define the forms without the necessary preliminary dialectical training. It is an illustration of such training which occupies the second part of the dialogue.

II

Parmenides suggests that a selected form should be subjected to dialectical examination. But he makes two important stipulations. First, the inquiry is not to be confined to the objects of perceptual experience; it is to extend to those entities which are apprehended by dialectic (λόγῳ) and can be considered as forms. Second, not only must those consequences be deduced which follow if the selected form exists, but also those that follow if it does not exist; and further, the consequences must be deduced not only for the form itself but also for those things which are other than the form. In addition to Zeno's original supposition of plurality, the following forms are suggested: similarity, dissimilarity, motion, rest, generation, decay, existence, and non-existence. After a show of protest, Parmenides agrees to perform the demonstration, and he selects unity as being his own hypothesis (137b). Unity is accordingly examined under four separate arguments; but within each argument, directly contradictory conclusions are deduced. We thus find eight arguments set out as follows:

(1) If unity exists, certain specific conclusions can be deduced about itself.

(2) If unity exists, conclusions can be deduced about itself contradictory to the conclusions of (1).

(3) If unity exists, certain specific conclusions can be deduced about everything else.

(4) If unity exists, conclusions can be deduced about everything else contradictory to the conclusions of (3).

(5) If unity does not exist, certain specific conclusions can be deduced about itself.

(6) If unity does not exist, conclusions can be deduced about itself contradictory to the conclusions of (5).

(7) If unity does not exist, certain specific conclusions can be deduced about everything else.

(8) If unity does not exist, conclusions can be deduced about everything else contradictory to the conclusions of (7).

Before proceeding further to examine the purpose and result of this exercise, it must first be established that it is the same concept which is being discussed throughout, and that this concept is the Platonic form of unity. I think that any plausible interpretation of the second part must rest upon this assumption, but the assumption is open to two objections.

First, in the original discussion of Zeno's treatise at the beginning of the dialogue, Zeno himself declares its purpose to be an attack on the pluralists who attempt to ridicule Parmenides' supposition (*ὡς εἰ ἕν ἐστι, πολλὰ καὶ γελοῖα συμβαίνει*). This is the starting-point of all the subsequent discussion of unity. Indeed already (at 128a–b) Socrates has referred to Parmenides' poem in which, he says, 'you assert that the universe is one'. And as we have seen, when Parmenides selects *τὸ ἕν* for the dialectical exercise, he does so on the grounds that its existence is his own original hypothesis.

Second, it has been urged that the ambiguity with which *τὸ ἕν* is discussed makes it impossible for it to be interpreted throughout as the Platonic Form. Cornford (*Plato and Parmenides*, 112) asserts that 'We shall miss Plato's whole intention, if we assume beforehand that "The One" must stand all through for the same thing, and then identify it with the One Being of Parmenides, or the Neoplatonic One (or Ones) or the Hegelian Absolute or the universe, or the unity of the real, or the Platonic Form.' He further maintains that 'the One' is implicitly defined at the outset of the different hypotheses. Wahl posits a combination of the Parmenidean and Platonic senses, suggesting (in his *Etude sur le Parménide de Platon*, 107) that 'L'Un c'est L'Un de Parménide et Parménide lui-même a soin de dire que c'est de son hypothèse qu'il parle. Mais en même temps c'est l'idée Socratique en tant qu'elle est unité.'

However, both these considerations can be effectively rebutted on the following grounds:

(*a*) The dialogue is a historical fiction. There is, as we have seen, no reason to suppose that Plato will put into the mouth of Parmenides anything that the historical Parmenides might have been expected to say; and the Parmenides of the dialogue is in fact made to express views with which the historical Parmenides certainly would not have agreed. Similarly the young Socrates is made to hold views which he certainly did not hold at the age at which he is here pictured.

(*b*) Although certain arguments of the second part could be construed as referring to Parmenidean monism, it is clearly impossible so to interpret them all; and if Plato wished to discuss Parmenidean monism, he would not have done it in this intermittent way. Further, at 142a the conclusion of the first argument is agreed to be unacceptable; and the whole discussion is very remote from the homogenous sphere of Parmenidean cosmology. Finally, what would *τἆλλα* mean to the historical Parmenides?

(*c*) There are good reasons (to which I shall later refer more fully) for rejecting the interpretations of both Cornford and the transcendentalists. But the ambiguities of the second part do not invalidate the contention that it is nevertheless the form of unity which is under discussion throughout. It is clear that for the dialectical exercise to be successful, it will only be possible for the appearance of plausibility to be maintained if a considerable degree of sophistry is employed. But equally it is clear that the exercise loses any point it may have if it is not the same concept from which the contradictions are to be apparently deduced. Parmenides' preliminary descriptions of the form the exercise is to take assumes throughout that it is the same concept which is to be subjected to it, and it is not surprising if he has to treat this concept illegitimately in order to achieve his object.

(*d*) Unity is selected for discussion, as we have seen, out of a list of forms. It has been considered as a form from the moment (129b) when Socrates puts it forward as such. Parmenides accepts throughout the consideration of abstracts as forms. Moreover at 129d, 129e, and 130b unity is mentioned together with at least one other form.

But two further questions still remain. First, what exactly did Plato understand at the time of writing by the form of *τὸ ἕν*? And second, why did he choose this particular form for the dialectical exercise? Leaving aside, for the moment, the meaning which *τὸ ἕν* must bear for the Neoplatonic interpreters, we are left with a certain ambiguity in the way it is treated by Plato. For in addition to the concept of unity or singleness (as contrasted with plurality) it is also the number 1, the first in the series of positive integers; and this mathematical status has, I think, received too little attention from commentators on the *Parmenides*.

The number 1 is somewhat ambiguously treated both by Plato and by Greek mathematics as a whole. For the purpose of calculation it was normally treated like the other positive integers. (The Greeks had, of course, no knowledge of 0 and the negative integers, and regarded fractions as the expression of a ratio between numbers.) Thus at *Laws*, 818c Plato speaks of one, two, and three as on a par with each other. At *Phaedo*, 101b–c he explicitly states that every two is two by participation in the idea of twoness and every one one by participation in the idea of oneness. Aristotle at *Metaphysics*, 1080a counts number as 1, 2, 3. But on the whole one is treated as different and distinct from the rest, as at *Republic*, 524d, *Phaedo*, 104a–b, *Metaphysics*, 987b, 1088a, *Physics*, 207b; cf. Euclid, *Elements* VII, props. 9 and 15. This seems due to the fact that for the Greeks number was a plurality or synthesis of units; cf. Euclid VII, def. 2. However, the term 'unit' was differently understood by Plato from the way in which it was understood by Aristotle or the Pythagoreans. For the Pythagoreans it meant an indivisible material point-unit existing in space; for Aristotle it meant either a concept in respect of which objects are counted, or one of the objects so counted; cf. *Metaphysics*, 1088a. But for Plato the term 'unit' can only be understood in relation to the theory of the ideal numbers and the intermediates. Here we find the same preoccupation with the paradox of unity and plurality. The discussion of arithmetic in the *Republic* seems to suggest a line of argument as follows: No sensible object is truly single since it partakes at the same time both of oneness and of an indefinite plurality; therefore to predicate oneness in relation to any particular is to express a relation of imperfect exemplification between the idea of oneness and the particular concerned. The perfect exemplifications of the ideal numbers are the mathematical numbers. Plato was perhaps led to abstract the mathematical numbers through seeing the inadequacies of the Parmenidean system; cf. *Philebus*, 56c–e, *Metaphysics*, 987b. But he had still to posit above the mathematical numbers the ideal numbers, since there are infinitely many mathematical 1s, 2s, etc. Thus, we have the unique transcendent forms of oneness, twoness, and the rest.

This is not, of course, intended to give a summary of Plato's philosophy of arithmetic, about which there is still no unanimity among Platonic scholars. But I hope it will serve to indicate that τὸ ἕν, although considered by Plato to be more of a philosophical than a mathematical concept, can never be wholly divorced from its somewhat ambiguous mathematical status. Indeed, at *Parmenides*, 143a–144a we find what can be interpreted as an outline proof of the infinity of the series of positive integers, and at 149a–c a recursive proof of the relation between the number of terms and the number of contacts in any finite linear sequence of terms.[1] These passages can hardly accord with a monistic interpretation; but they do not, of course, indicate in any way that Plato did not regard one as different from the other numbers in kind. In the first place it is pervasive in a way that they are not, and is closely affiliated with the concept of existence without being synonymous with it; at *Republic*, 524d Plato explicitly states that the study of τὸ ἕν will guide the soul to the contemplation of true being. Further, even if considered purely mathematically, it is essential as a fundamental concept to any theory of numbers without requiring any such theory for itself. I would accordingly suggest that the form of τὸ ἕν meant at this time both of two things to Plato: first, oneness, by which I mean the form or idea of the number one; and second, singleness or unity. By this I mean what I have called the philosophical rather than the mathematical concept implicit in any proposition concerning an object, concept, or class of objects considered as a single whole and distinguished from any and all other objects, classes, or concepts. Further, I would agree with Professor Ryle that the only feasible translation is not 'The One' but 'Unity'.[2]

[1] On this and the issues referred to above, see A. Wedberg, *Plato's Philosophy of Mathematics* (Stockholm, 1955).

[2] I do not think that it is necessary to consider here what may or may not have been Plato's later views on the form of τὸ ἕν and the ideal numbers as a whole. However we are to understand the accounts of Aristotle, Theophrastus, and the rest, it is clear that the closer Plato came to a mathematical theory of the ideas the more metaphysically important τὸ ἕν became and the more closely affiliated to the Idea of the Good; cf. *Met.* 1091a–b. But there is no evidence that at the time of writing the *Parmenides* Plato had formulated any of these doctrines in the form in which they are later described by Aristotle; nor does Aristotle ever refer to the *Parmenides* in his discussion of them. It is enough to note in the preoccupation of the *Parmenides* a foreshadowing (at most) of Plato's later doctrines.

Why, then, did Plato choose this particular form for the dialectical exercise? We are specifically told at 136e that it is not to be the form of any visible object, since it has already been agreed that such objects exemplify in themselves the paradox of contradictory predicates. The theory of forms was suggested by Socrates at 128e ff. as resolving this paradox; but he has stated at 129b–c that if someone proves to him that unity can be many and plurality one, then he will begin to be surprised. It is precisely this which Parmenides proceeds ostensibly to do. This would seem to suggest the link between the two parts of the dialogue. First, Socrates has suggested the forms of unity, similarity, and other such terms. Parmenides raises certain objections directed against the relation between forms and particulars, but agrees that forms exist; he suggests that Socrates can see no way out because he has undertaken to define the forms too soon, before he has undergone the necessary training (135c–d). He accordingly proposes and carries out his eightfold exercise on the form of unity. Whatever interpretation we may ultimately place upon the exercise, it seems to follow from the first part consistently enough.

The choice of unity is in no way surprising, since the problems and paradoxes of unity and plurality are one of Plato's fundamental preoccupations during this period. Socrates has already raised the question at the outset of the dialogue. In the *Philebus*, Plato again returns to the problem of how the forms can retain their unity yet be present in many particulars. In the *Sophist*, 244b ff., there reappears the paradox of existing unity entailing a duality of unity (oneness) and being. Linked with the problems of unity and plurality are those of the πέρας and ἄπειρον and the great and small, which reappear in the *Philebus* and are shown by the evidence of Aristotle to have assumed increasing importance, together with τὸ ἕν, in Plato's later metaphysics. Thus in the second part of the *Parmenides* we may expect to trace both the reflection of his present preoccupation and the seeds of his future doctrine. But, as we shall see, any attempt to find a positive exposition of doctrine must break down over the layout and content of the eight hypotheses.[1]

[1] This mistake seems to me to be made by Johannsen in his remarks on the *Parmenides*. To say (p. 22) that the second part of the dialogue 'deals with or touches on almost all serious problems in Plato's philosophy' does not make

What, then, is the purpose of the exercise? I clearly have not the space to examine all the various suggestions made by previous commentators. But before considering the more recent interpretations which (rightly, as I believe) draw a positive moral from the ostensible *reductio ad absurdum* of the deliberate eightfold contradiction, I propose to deal briefly with the three principal traditional interpretations.

The parody interpretation. This maintains that the object of the arguments is to parody and so to ridicule the Eleatic dialectic. It is open to the following damaging objections: (*a*) Plato is known to have had a great respect for Parmenides; cf. *Theaetetus*, 183c. Though he may have disagreed with him, he is hardly likely to make Parmenides parody his own methods. (*b*) Parmenides himself at 142a implies that the argument of the first hypothesis is inadmissible; if it is a parody, the parody loses its force at once. (*c*) The Eleatic stranger of the *Sophist* and *Politicus* has never been held to be a parody. (*d*) It is Parmenides himself who speaks of the arguments as παιδιά; if this is translated as 'jest' it loses its point in the mouth of Parmenides. As argued above, it is not a very effective parody if it is the object of the supposed ridicule who declares it to be so. (*e*) Some of the argumentation is in fact sound. (*f*) The parody, if it is one, is not only inefficient but laboriously unfunny.

The transcendentalist interpretation. This finds in the arguments a positive statement of metaphysical doctrine, first expounded by the Neoplatonists. Against this it may be argued as follows: (*a*) Such an interpretation is nowhere stated or implied in the dialogue itself. (*b*) It cannot take account of all the hypotheses, which cannot by any stretch of interpretation all be shown to state (even indirectly) some metaphysical doctrine. (*c*) τὸ ἕν as described in the first hypothesis (i.e., beyond knowledge, opinion, or perception) cannot be equated with the Good of the *Republic*.[1] (*d*) As we have seen, it is implied that the conclusion of the first hypothesis is absurd.

Cornford's interpretation. Cornford finds in the arguments both

[1] Cf. F. M. Cornford, *Plato and Parmenides* (New York, 1939), 131–4.

---

it legitimate to extract from the hypotheses selected doctrinal implications (as opposed to preoccupations) unless the selection is justified by a satisfactory interpretation of the dialectical exercise as a whole.

positive statement of doctrine and exercise in the detection of fallacy. This view is open to the single fatal objection that the one impairs the other and vice versa. Further, it is very surprising to find both together in the mouth of Parmenides, and it deprives of its point the eightfold layout of the arguments. Cornford's whole position is effectively demolished by Robinson, who also deals with the view of Professor Cherniss.[1]

Thus, we must look elsewhere for our interpretation. Broadly, there remain two approaches. First, there is the view upheld by Robinson in the article just cited. This view, originally put forward by Grote and supported by Ross, finds no further purpose in the arguments than dialectical exercise purely for its own sake. Second, there is the contention that some indirect doctrinal lesson is to be drawn from the total contradictions of the ostensible conclusion. This view is the basis of the interpretations of Ryle, Peck, and Scoon. It will be my contention that the most plausible interpretation of the dialogue must fall in some sense between these two approaches. Accordingly before advancing my own view I shall consider individually the interpretations of Robinson, Ryle, Peck, and Scoon.

Robinson's interpretation. Robinson maintains that the second part of the dialogue cannot be interpreted either as a direct or as an indirect statement of either doctrine or method. It is purely and simply an exercise in argument. Parmenides five times speaks of it as γυμνασία. Having advised the young Socrates that he needs further training in dialectic, he proceeds to present him with a series of arguments which require very considerable dialectical skill to unravel. 'The dialogue' (p. 177) 'is addressed primarily to Plato's own supporters.... It is a manifesto for more dialectic and less enthusiasm.' Parmenides is selected by Plato as the most authoritative figure who could be introduced for the inculcation of this lesson. In addition to the arguments which he goes through, he also recommends to the young Socrates the application of the Zenonian method to the assumptions both that an abstract idea is true and that it is false. Ross further draws attention to the *Politicus* (265d) where it is stated that the discussion is less important for its bearing on the problem than for the dialectical training which it affords. 'It seems to me a mistake,' Ross concludes, 'to

[1] Robinson, 181–6; on Cherniss ('Parmenides and the *Parmenides of* Plato', *Amer. Journ. of Philol.*, LIII [1932], 122–38), 166–8.

try to trace grains of positive teaching in the wilderness of paradox which the hypotheses present.'[1]

Comment. This view is difficult to refute conclusively. While it is admittedly hard to find positive grounds for some constructive conclusion, it is impossible to dismiss out of hand the contention that the arguments have no other purpose than to offer a demonstration of dialectical gymnastics. But the gymnastic view remains open to serious objections as follows:

It is strongly implied within the dialogue itself that the dialectical exercise will lead to the discovery of the truth. The *γυμνασία* is orginally recommended by Parmenides as the solution to the inability of Socrates to answer the questions which have been discussed (135c–d). He concludes his description of the form the exercise should take with the words 'if after performing your exercise (*γυμνασάμενος*) you are really going to make out the truth' (136c). Zeno declares at 136e that 'most people are unaware of the fact that it is impossible to come upon the truth and acquire understanding without this comprehensive and circuitous enquiry'.

It does not, of course, necessarily follow from these hints that there will be a direct constructive conclusion from the subsequent arguments. It is still possible that the benefit will come by returning to the original dilemma after the experience gained by following through to their conclusion a series of complicated arguments which are not directly relevant. But this seems on the face of it unlikely. Such a view is further weakened by what Robinson admits to be the defect of the gymnastic theory. 'The second part of the dialogue is not really, as it professes to be, a case of the exercise that Parmenides recommends, but an argument by examining which we who read the dialogue may obtain that exercise.'[2] Robinson is prepared to admit this 'slight incoherence', but accepts it as preferable to any possible alternative. But the situation is worse than he allows. He admits that Parmenides makes serious methodological recommendations: but if this is so, it must at once weaken the gymnastic theory and be weakened by it. If the recommendations are not to produce a constructive conclusion from the dialectical exercise, what is the point of the dialectical exercise? Or if the point of the second half is the gymnastics of the dialectical exercise, why are we given the recommendations?

[1] Ross, 99, 101. [2] Robinson, 178.

Further, if the object of the second part is dialectical training for its own sake only, we may question whether this is the best way of giving it. It is surely curious to perform such training without making clear that it is what it is. In the *Sophist* (259b) Plato expresses his contempt for playing upon contradictions in discussion for their own sake.[1] What is difficult and worth while is the careful and critical examination of such paradoxes. Now it is possible that no further implication need be drawn from this than that such examination is worth while for the sake of practice only. But once again it is surely more reasonable to conclude that Plato recommends such examination for the sake of some constructive results, as opposed to the mere dialectical sophistry of constructing the paradoxes. I do not suggest that this one passage from a dialogue written later than the *Parmenides* can give any conclusive hint towards the interpretation of the second part, but its implications seem to me to point away from the gymnastic theory.

Finally, we may object that Robinson's original exclusion of any other interpretation is not satisfactory. He adduces strong arguments to support his view that the arguments are neither a direct nor an indirect statement of doctrine or method. But none of his arguments in fact controverts any of the three interpretations which I am next proposing to consider. These share a common basis of interpretation, holding that the eightfold operation constitutes in some sense a *reductio ad absurdum*: that is to say, they maintain that a constructive conclusion is to be drawn not from the arguments themselves, but from the fact that the arguments can be laid out as they are. Thus Plato is using the dialectical exercise to point out some implication concerning the behaviour or nature of the concept under discussion. Robinson's dichotomous classification of doctrine and method does not really apply here. Such an implication as I have outlined would, I suppose, be described as an indirect statement of doctrine. But in Robinson's dismissal of the possibility that the arguments are an indirect statement of doctrine, he takes the phrase in a different and limited sense. He considers it to mean 'proving some proposition by reducing its contradictory to absurdity'.[2] But what these interpretations maintain is that Plato is by implication deducing a proposition about a concept (or type of concept)

[1] Cf. *Phil.*, 15d–16a. [2] Robinson, 76.

from the fact that contradictory conclusions can apparently be deduced about it. This method of interpretation does not seem to be considered by Robinson.

Ryle's interpretation. Professor Ryle considers the dialogue as a whole to be an early essay in the theory of types. The arguments of the second part are designed to bring out the difference in logical behaviour between certain types of universal, or between formal and non-formal concepts. This is achieved by pointing out the anomalies of treating Unity as though it were a non-formal or 'proper' concept such as, shall we say, Yellowness or Justice. Socrates has said that he will be surprised if it can be shown that forms can undergo contrary predicates; Parmenides by the use of the Zenonian method demonstrates that Unity can. Ryle rejects the idea that the moral we are to draw is the illegitimacy of treating any universal as though it were a substance or a proper name (although it is of course true that it is illegitimate). But he thinks that Plato wishes to demonstrate only that concepts of different logical or syntactical status cannot be made to behave as though the rules of their co-functioning were similar. In support of this view, Professor Ryle finds indications of a similar awareness of this fact in both the *Sophist* and the *Theaetetus*, and explicit statement of it in Aristotle.

Comment. The one objection to this view is that it is altogether too sophisticated. Ryle is indeed aware of this danger, and claims little more than that Plato was 'beginning to see' the difference in types of concept, which is certainly true enough. But I think it may be disputed whether he ever saw them at all in the form outlined by Ryle. Ryle's whole interpretation implicitly attributes to Plato a knowledge of the distinction between semantics and ontology which Plato never possessed. Now this distinction is obviously relevant to a critical examination of Plato's views, and it is a distinction of which Aristotle was certainly aware. But there is abundant evidence in Plato's dialogues that he himself was not—that is to say, that he was incapable of distinguishing a purely logical or syntactical question as such. Such questions are indeed implicit in both the *Sophist* and the *Theaetetus*, but I do not think it can satisfactorily be demonstrated that they are ever more than implicit.

This is primarily because for Plato such discussions were neither about logic or syntax, but about forms. Now it is possible and indeed likely that in the *Parmenides* Plato may be using the dialectical exercise to point to some conclusion about one or more forms. But from this to assert that he is saying something about the logical behaviour of one or more concepts is at once misleading. Similarly, it is misleading to find in the *Sophist* the discovery of the copula; it is the discovery of the properties of a certain form.[1] Robinson rightly remarks of the *Sophist* in his article, 'Plato's Consciousness of Fallacy', *Mind*, N.S. LI (1942), 114, that 'Not provided with any semantic concepts, and mistaking the ontological nature of his subject matter, Plato has yet contrived to get wonderfully close to certain facts about language.' Some of these facts were stated by Aristotle, but this is no evidence that Plato saw them as such. The description of a hierarchy of forms cannot really be called an exercise in logical syntax. Similarly, although the *Theaetetus* points out that knowledge must be of a complex of simple elements, Plato does not draw the conclusions implicit in this discovery; and indeed Socrates' 'dream' is propounded only to be refuted (202d ff.). Ryle tells us that Plato 'is consciously developing a method of inspecting the formal properties of such complexes of elements as constitute truths and falsehoods'. But this is unwarrantable. It is certainly true that the notion put forward in Socrates' 'dream' has important implications on how we are to interpret such a statement as 'Unity exists'. But Plato does not inquire into such implications. He points out that it is possible mistakenly to believe that seven plus five equals eleven, whereas it is impossible to mistake the number eleven for the number twelve. But he never considers whether the simple elements of knowledge will be of different logical type, or in what way 'unity exists' is a statement of a different order from 'twelve is the sum of seven and five'.

Further, we may object that if Plato had in fact been aware of the considerations which Ryle imputes to him, they would entail a revision of the theory of ideas of a kind which there is no evidence that Plato made. That he was aware that certain forms possess very different properties from others has already been admitted; and the *Sophist* does embody certain modifications of the early theory of forms. But to say that he was aware of

[1] I am, of course, aware of the continuing discussion of this problem. I do not propose to enter this discussion here: but see for example J. L. Ackrill, 'Plato and the Copula: *Sophist*, 251–259', below, Ch. X.

difference in logical status would imply a pervasive recognition of the illegitimacy of treating the forms in a logically anomalous way, e.g. by making them the subjects of predicative statements of the form 'justice is just' as opposed to perfectly meaningful statements of the noun–copula–adjective form such as 'justice is commendable'. There is no evidence, however, that Plato ever fully realised the fundamental antinomy involved in the notion that the ideas are instances of themselves; and as I shall hope to show, it is not necessary to interpret the second part of the *Parmenides* as an implicit recognition of this antinomy. Professor Ryle suggests that some such recognition is likewise implicit in the first part. But the conclusion of the first part surely implies, as I have tried to show, that Plato cannot have seen how damaging this consideration in fact is. Ryle is prepared to dismiss the objection that his interpretation of the dialogue imputes to Plato the overt demonstration of the logical untenability of the very principles of his system. Why, he asks, must Plato be forbidden the illumination of self-criticism? Now clearly there is nothing impossible in itself about the notion that Plato or any other philosopher may make drastic revisions of his own tenets. But in Plato's latest writings there is no evidence of such a drastic revision. As far as we know, he continued long after the writing of the *Parmenides* to hold to some version, at least, of the doctrine of substantial forms. The conclusion seems to be that we cannot accept an interpretation of the dialogue which finds in it arguments (however true) which can only be formulated in the light of later philosophical developments.

Peck's interpretation. This holds the purpose of the arguments to be to show that τὸ ἕν is not a legitimate form. Plato puts into the mouth of Parmenides a sequence of verbal sophistries in order to illustrate the error of positing forms on the basis of deceptive verbal images. The statement 'x is just' is a legitimate example of μέθεξις from which we are entitled to posit the existence of the form justice; 'x is one' is on the other hand an illegitimate example of μέθεξις. No form of 'the One' exists, just as no form of τὸ μὴ ὄν or of θάτερον exists. A particular is not one through participation in the form of 'the One' but through participation in a form which is one. The same is true of 'Being'. Any form exists and is single of its own nature, not through participation in οὐσία or τὸ ἕν. ' "Oneness" is a non-significant abstraction in the sense that "one" means something different in every case just as "other" meant something different in every case. "One man" consists of several parts and *one* man is not the same as *one* leg.' Socrates has stated that he would be surprised if Zeno could show that 'the One itself' is many. Plato demonstrates that this cannot be shown simply because 'the One itself' is not a form. Peck supports this argument by reference to his analysis of the *μέγιστα γένη* of the *Sophist*. He holds that we are to conclude from the *Sophist* that *τὸ μὴ ὄν, θάτερον, ταὐτόν*, and *τὸ ὄν* (*οὐσία*) are not true forms: and we are to draw a similar conclusion for *τὸ ἕν* in the *Parmenides*.

Comment. We must first inquire whether this rejection of *τὸ ἕν* as a form is borne out by Plato's subsequent teaching. In the first place, there is no explicit statement in Plato that *τὸ ἕν* is to be denied the rank of idea, and outside the *Parmenides* nothing which so far as I know has ever been regarded as an implicit statement to this effect. Nor is there any evidence in Aristotle which might support this contention. Within the dialogue itself, unity is referred to among 'the forms themselves, such as similarity, dissimilarity, plurality, unity, rest, motion, and all the other concepts of this kind' (129d–e). Are we then to conclude that these are likewise to be rejected as forms? Similarity is referred to by Parmenides at 131a in the same breath with size, beauty, and justice. At 130b Socrates has expressed equal certainty about the existence of forms of similarity, unity, and plurality and about forms of justice, beauty, and goodness. This does not, of course, prove that Plato's intention was not to recant in part this earlier doctrine of his own which he puts into the mouth of the young Socrates.[1] But if this is so, it is surely surprising to find reference at *Theaetetus*, 185c–186b to existence, non-existence, similarity, dissimilarity, unity, plurality, goodness, badness, beauty, and ugliness as concepts alike distinguished by thought rather than by sense.

But the most damaging objection to Peck's interpretation is what I described above as the mathematical status of *τὸ ἕν*. Here the evidence overwhelmingly demonstrates that not only did Plato believe in a form of Oneness, but that he assigned to it increasing importance. The belief is first explicitly stated in the *Phaedo* that things are one by partaking in the form of oneness.

[1] This is in fact suggested by Peck, 38.

Now not only is there no evidence that Plato abandoned this view; but the *Philebus* (56c–e), which is generally agreed to have been written after the *Parmenides*, seems to confirm the theory of mathematical numbers which we find implied in the *Republic* and the *Phaedo* and which is attributed to Plato by Aristotle. Peck's claim that Oneness is a 'non-significant abstraction' is argued on the grounds that 'one bicycle consists of various parts and the oneness of a bicycle is not the same as the oneness of a wheel'.[1] But it is precisely as a solution to this problem that Plato conceived the notion of the mathematical unit as I have earlier outlined it. It is certainly true that for Plato the oneness of a bicycle would differ from the oneness of a wheel. But as we have seen it is the mathematical one which is the true and perfect exemplification of the ideal one. Are we to infer from the *Parmenides* that Plato abandoned the belief in the ideal numbers? Certain problems do indeed exist concerning Plato's later beliefs as to the relation between the ideal numbers and the other ideas, but there is no evidence that he ever denied them the rank of ideas. However, Peck seems to suggest that it is only oneness which is not a form; if it were a form it is difficult to see how it could generate other forms together with the great and small, whereas in fact any form or particular must of its proper nature exist and be one, not through participation in forms of unity and existence. The objection to this view is not that it is necessarily unsound, but that there is no evidence that Plato held it, any more than that he was aware of the antinomy of the ideas being instances of themselves. An independent consideration of this kind cannot be evidence in support of the view that Plato rejected τὸ ἕν as a form. Peck's view must rest solely on his interpretation of the *Parmenides* itself, and I hope I have said enough to show that here the view must be rejected.

Scoon's interpretation. Scoon maintains that Plato wishes to show the illegitimacy of reasoning with abstract concepts which have no reference to the particulars of experience. He too holds that the ideas with which Parmenides concerns himself in the second part of the dialogue are not forms. Plato is repudiating a rationalism that fails to take account of the visible world, by showing that such a failure allows contradictory and stultifying ambiguities in thought. However difficult it may be to formulate the relation

[1] Peck, 136–7.

of ideas to particulars, it is hopeless to try to consider abstract concepts without reference to particulars at all.

Comment. This view differs from Peck's in one important respect. Peck holds that Plato begins with the assumption that unity and the rest are forms, and then shows by the *reductio ad absurdum* that unity is not. Scoon seems to imply that the assumption is never made, but that the concepts dealt with cannot be forms because they do not have reference to particulars. I do not think this view is tenable. As we have already seen, the implications in the dialogue point strongly to the view that unity is throughout considered as a form. Further, we know that Plato certainly believed it possible to make statements about the ideas in the abstract, if only to say that they are instances of themselves. Now in his writings after the *Parmenides* we seem to find no abandonment of his belief in the transcendental nature of the ideas.[1] In particular the transcendent view is clearly expressed in the *Timaeus*, 51b–52d, where the ideas are considered as pre-existent entities outside space and time. Finally, we may again urge the mathematical status of τὸ ἕν. Here it may be true that number must be derived originally from the perception of sensible particulars; but we certainly cannot say that Plato thought it impossible to formulate abstract truths about mathematics without reference to perceptible objects. It is clearly true that Plato is demonstrating that the discussion of unity in the abstract can apparently lead to contradictory conclusions. But it seems unwarrantable to infer from this that the moral he wishes to point is that all discussion about abstract concepts must be conducted with reference to particulars. This would entail that he believed it impossible to make meaningful predicative statements about forms except in so far as they are immanent in particulars. That Plato did not in fact believe this can be shown from passages taken from all the periods of his writing where the transcendent nature of the forms is clearly expressed, e.g., in addition to the passage from the *Timaeus* already cited, *Phaedo*, 78, *Republic*, 500, *Phaedrus*, 247, *Philebus*, 59.

I am of course aware that the brief treatment I have given them does not do full justice to any of the interpretations which I have outlined. But I hope enough has been said to show that none of

[1] Cf. Harold Cherniss, *Aristotle's Criticism of Plato and the Academy*, I (Baltimore, 1944), 214 n. 128.

them can be regarded as satisfactory. Accordingly it only remains to offer some comments of my own.

The crux of the problem is that we are led to expect that the dialectical exercise will enable us to resolve the difficulties on which our attention has been focused in the first part of the dialogue. But for this, we could without difficulty see the relation of the second part to the first. It could be seen as raising the paradoxes apparently arising from the relation of forms to each other in the same way that the first part raised those apparently arising from the relation of forms to particulars. The conclusion put into Parmenides' mouth at the end of Part I would then be applicable to both parts, namely that in spite of these difficulties the forms must exist since without them the significance of all thought and discourse will be destroyed. The aporetic nature of the dialogue as a whole need not of itself be surprising. In the *Theaetetus* Socrates and Theaetetus are represented as unable to define knowledge; but no one will maintain that Plato, either before or after writing of the *Theaetetus*, believed that there was no such thing. However, the transitional passage of the *Parmenides* suggests that the gymnastic exercise will actually help to circumvent or to solve the problems with which the young Socrates has found himself faced. It is my purpose to suggest how Plato may have thought this to be so.

There is one important hint within the transitional passage. At 135c–d Parmenides attributes young Socrates' difficulties to his having prematurely undertaken to define the forms without the necessary training: *Πρῴ γάρ, εἰπεῖν, πρὶν γυμνασθῆναι, ὦ Σώκρατες, ὁρίζεσθαι ἐπιχειρεῖς καλόν τέ τι καὶ δίκαιον καὶ ἀγαθὸν καὶ ἓν ἕκαστον τῶν εἰδῶν.* This does not mean that the dialectical exercise will explicitly be an exercise in definition. In fact it is a series of deductions not from hypothetical definitions but from an existential hypothesis and its denial. But it is clearly implied that the exercise will throw light on problems arising from premature and misguided definition of forms. I do not propose to discuss the whole question of Socratic definition.[1] But a few remarks are relevant at this point. Definitions are offered and either accepted or rejected in dialogues both before and after the *Parmenides*. But we nowhere have what Plato professes to regard as a complete

[1] On the question in general I am entirely in agreement with the analysis of Richard Robinson, *Plato's Earlier Dialectic*, 2nd ed. (Oxford, 1953), 49–60.

definition of a form as such. At *Theaetetus*, 147c he gives an example of what he would regard as a satisfactory answer to the 'What is X?' question. To 'What is mud?' a satisfactory answer is 'Earth mixed with water'. But Plato clearly would not regard this as a satisfactory answer to the question 'What is the form of mud?' It is certainly not earth mixed with water. But is it earthiness mixed with wateriness? Or is it αὐτὴ ἡ γῆ mixed with αὐτῷ τῷ ὑγρῷ? Since at *Parmenides*, 130c, when young Socrates expressed hesitancy about the existence of a form of mud, he was advised not to be squeamish, we must suppose that Plato thought such a form did exist. Presumably he thought that it stood in some relation to the forms of earth and water, and this relation we may suppose he came to regard as discernible by the method of diaeresis. But that discernment of diaeresis of the interrelations between forms, not descriptive definition of these forms, is the solution Plato hoped to find for young Socrates' dilemma, is, I shall contend, precisely the moral of the *Parmenides*. Definition of the essence whose reality was entailed by Plato's ontological presuppositions was at all stages the object of the vaunted science of dialectic. But after the *Parmenides* Plato adopts an entirely different method. The remarks of young Socrates at *Parmenides*, 129b–e may be taken to show that Plato had become aware of the problems posed by the relations necessarily entailed within the world of forms; and it is diaeresis, not hypothesis, which is brought to bear on these problems in the *Sophist*.

It is arguable both on these and other grounds whether 'define' is the best translation for ὁρίζεσθαι (or ὁρίζειν: I can find no distinction between Plato's use of the active and middle when he is using the verb in this sense). However, I shall be using 'definition' to mean what I think ὁρίζεσθαι meant to Plato; and some further comment is therefore necessary. There are places in the dialogues where 'designate', 'distinguish', or 'determine' appears to be a better translation than 'define'. At *Gorgias*, 470b εἰπὲ τίνα ὅρον ὁρίζῃ seems to mean 'what criterion do you propose?' At *Phaedo*, 104e (ὃ τοίνυν ἔλεγον ὁρίσασθαι) ὁρίζεσθαι seems to mean little more than 'settle' or 'decide'. But the underlying idea is in all cases the search for essential attributes. At *Sophist*, 246b ταὐτὸν σῶμα καὶ οὐσίαν ὁριζόμενοι means not what we should mean by 'defining οὐσία' as σῶμα so much as 'identifying οὐσία and σῶμα'. At *Theaetetus*, 187c where the question is asked, τὴν ἀληθῆ δόξαν ἐπιστήμην ὁρίζῃ; the point is not 'do you propose to designate true opinion by the word knowledge?' but 'is true opinion what knowledge really *is*?' I think that Plato's idea of definition was further reinforced by his confusion of description and reference which we find in the *Cratylus*; cf. esp. 388b, 428e, 435d.[1] Plato thought that to name something was to describe it, and that you could not really say anything useful about it without having grasped its essential nature; for this second point, cf. *Meno*, 86d–e, *Protagoras*, 360e–361a, *Theaetetus*, 196d–e. Thus for Plato a full definition (although he sometimes seems only to want a distinguishing mark, as at *Euthyphro*, 6d–e) must be not any equivalent or synonym but a descriptive account of those essential attributes of the thing itself which make it what it is. This is what Socrates is described by Parmenides at *Parmenides*, 135c–d as having attempted to do without the necessary training. It is clear that in the case of forms this will involve statements describing interrelations existing between forms, to which Plato hints that he has hitherto paid too little attention. It is this that I mean when I talk about 'definition' in the remainder of this article.

We are now in a position to consider how a constructive moral may be implicit in the dialectical exercise. This must first involve the difficult question of how far Plato regarded the argumentation as valid or invalid. If he was clear in his own mind about the relative merits of the deductions, it is possible that we should interpret the exercise as giving a practice in argumentation which, after the fallacies have been successfully detected and weeded out, will leave a residue of sound doctrine adequate to explain the relation of such forms as unity both to the other forms and to particulars. On this view, all possible conclusions are to be drawn from both the existential hypothesis and its denial, in order that those which are sound may be extracted from the rest and accepted as valid. Unfortunately, for reasons which I shall now give, I do not think this is possible. But I also shall hope to show that hypotheses (4) to (8) have an independent value apart from the rest.

It is extremely difficult to distinguish clearly what in fact are the ambiguities on which the arguments of the exercise rest. However,

[1] Cf. Robinson, 'A Criticism of Plato's Cratylus', *Phil. Rev.*, LXV (1956), 324–41, esp. p. 337. Against, Ronald B. Levinson, 'Language and the Cratylus: Four Questions', *Rev. of Met.*, XI (1957), 28–41, esp. p. 37. Levinson's treatment, however, is extremely cursory.

I follow Robinson in concluding that there appear to be three principal fallacies: confusion of identity and attribution; confusion of an adjective with the substantive characterised by it; and the fallacy of reification. To these I would add a misunderstanding of the notion of nonexistence which underlies almost all the argumentation of hypotheses (5) and (6), where deductions are made about the nature of a unity which, *ex hypothesi*, does not exist. Some of the arguments appear so crassly fallacious (Robinson cites, for example, 139d–e, 147c, and 157c–d) that it seems impossible not to feel that Plato saw them to be so. But I am doubtful whether, at least until the time of writing the *Sophist*, he was more than dimly aware of the nature of the fallacies involved. Some hint of a consciousness of ambiguity appears as early as *Euthydemus*, 278b; but τὴν τῶν ὀνομάτων διαφοράν, which is there referred to, seems to mean no more than examples as crass as puns. We may be reluctant to believe that Plato saw nothing wrong with the arguments of *Parmenides*, 146d–e concerning sameness and difference; but his statement at *Sophist*, 256a that οὐ γὰρ ὅταν εἴπωμεν αὐτὴν ταὐτὸν καὶ μὴ ταὐτὸν ὁμοίως εἰρήκαμεν reads more like a discovery than the recapitulation of a recognised ambiguity, nor is there even a hint of it before its occurrence here. Reification and the confusion between an adjective and the substance it characterises are both inherent in the theory of forms itself, but, as I have tried to demonstrate, there is no warrant for holding the *Parmenides* to be a recantation of the theory. The confusion about nonexistence seems blatant at 161c–d. But until he formulated his answer about nonexistence in the *Sophist*, it is not impossible that Plato could not see why a nonexistent unity, being not equal, need not therefore be unequal.

Thus it seems improbable that Plato saw at all clearly where and why the arguments of the exercise are fallacious; and accordingly it is highly unlikely that he expected his readers to be able to do so. The view that he does not distinguish in value between the deductions is reinforced by their layout. Each conclusion appears to be deduced only in order to furnish the requisite antithesis. At 137c it is argued that if unity is one it can have no parts, at 142c–d that it must have the two parts of unity and existence. At 146a existent unity is both at rest and in motion; at 162e nonexistent unity is likewise both at rest and in motion. To cite further examples would merely be tedious. What renders conclusive the view that no residual doctrine can be intended to remain after the detection of fallacies is that on any conceivable view of Plato's awareness of the fallacies it is impossible to see what this doctrine would be. One example will be adequate to illustrate this. At 155d the conclusion that unity is knowable (which Plato must have thought sound) is reached on the curious grounds that it exists in time, therefore there will be something of it (εἴη ἄν τι ἐκείνῳ καὶ ἐκείνου), therefore there will be knowledge and opinion and perception of it. But at 141d–142a it has been shown unknowable because extratemporal, although in the *Timaeus* Plato appears to regard the forms as outside space and time. I accordingly conclude that Plato does not distinguish in logical merit between the different deductions, and that the moral of the exercise must lie in the fact that the contradictions are possible at all.

However, that there is a discernible purpose in the last four hypotheses as a whole is hinted by the discussion at the very beginning of the dialogue (128d). The purpose of the treatise which Zeno has been reading is said to be to show that the denial of a certain hypothesis leads to contradictions worse than those resulting from its assertion. Now the conclusion of hypotheses (4) to (8) is summarised by the assertion at 166b–c, that if unity does not exist then nothing exists (οὐκοῦν καὶ συλλήβδην εἰ εἴποιμεν ἓν εἰ μὴ ἔστιν οὐδέν ἐστι, ὀρθῶς ἂν εἴποιμεν). Plato surely regarded this conclusion as more absurd than the apparent possession by unity and τἆλλα of contradictory predicates. This consideration does not, of course, provide the solution to these paradoxes. But the amplified Zenonian method has at least shown grounds for not concluding from these paradoxes that unity does not exist. Effort to resolve them will still be worth while. It remains to show how Plato may have thought such effort more likely to succeed after the performance of the dialectical exercise as a whole.

I wish to suggest that the moral of the exercise is that forms are not definable by deduction from existential hypotheses. Exhaustive application of this method has been shown to lead as legitimately to one set of contradictory conclusions as to another. This does not of itself resolve the difficulties in which Socrates finds himself, but it shows how these difficulties can arise and hints that some other method is necessary. This method is the method of diaeresis. That it is not expounded in the dialogue itself is not surprising. Parmenides twice (134e–135b, cf. 133b) stresses the length of time and discussion necessary to overcome the difficulties of the theory of forms. But that diaeresis was Plato's answer to the problems of premature definition is shown by a passage in the *Phaedrus*, (277b) where definition is declared necessary to the knowledge of truth and unequivocally associated with the method of diaeresis: Πρὶν ἄν τις τό τε ἀληθὲς ἑκάστων εἰδῇ περὶ ὧν λέγει ἢ γράφει κατ' αὐτό τε πᾶν ὁρίζεσθαι δυνατὸς γένηται ὁρισάμενός τε πάλιν κατ' εἴδη μέχρι τοῦ ἀτμήτου τέμνειν ἐπιστηθῇ. (Cf. 265d–266c.) The gymnastic exercise shows that the properties of unity and its relations with τἆλλα cannot be deduced from the premiss of its existence, although denial of its existence will engender both for itself and τἆλλα contradictions which are at least as absurd. It thus paves the way for a method which defines forms by determining their relations with each other. Indeed, that the forms are in some sense ineffable seems implied by Plato at all stages of his writing; cf. *Symposium*, 211a, *Epistle*, *VII*, 343b, *Republic*, 533a. After the *Parmenides*, however, Plato seems to have been convinced that the best way to attempt to grasp the essential nature of a form was not by hypothesis and deduction of its properties but by location of its place in the hierarchy of forms.

It is, of course, in fact the case that diaeresis does not resolve the difficulties raised in the *Parmenides*.[1] Indeed, as we have seen, they are insoluble, since the theory of forms is logically unsound. But although certain commentators, including Ryle and Cherniss, have sought to minimise its importance, Plato assigns it unmistakable prominence in the later dialogues and makes explicit and extravagant claims on its behalf (most notably at *Philebus*, 16c–e, *Phaedrus*, 266b). The method of dichotomous division[2] is not, of course, the same as that which discovers the relations of the μέγιστα γένη. But both exemplify aspects of the new method which is concerned to distinguish those ontological interrelations which Plato assumed to exist. I do not find it incredible that although

[1] Stenzel appears to have thought it did in his *Plato's Method of Dialectic* (tr. D. J. Allan, Oxford, 1940), 138 ff. He seems also to have thought (p. 135) that all relations between forms are of species to genus. But the relations described in the *Sophist* between the μέγιστα γένη are not of this kind.

[2] It should also be noted that the method is not necessarily dichotomous. This is explicitly stated at *Pol.*, 287c and *Phil.*, 16d.

the method does not resolve the problems inherent in forms Plato should have believed it capable of doing so. The *Philebus* does not (as Stenzel claims it does) resolve the problems of participation by the method expounded in the *Sophist*. But it does at least appear to hint at the existence of a solution to the problem of 'One and Many' which we may suppose Plato to have thought the key to the question of participation; and the *Sophist* does settle some, at least, of the problems of interrelation between forms to which our attention has been drawn in the *Parmenides*. The conclusion of the *Parmenides* is that the forms must exist despite the problems they raise. But they cannot be defined (or described or deduced from) in the way that the young Socrates had thought that they could. The gymnastic exercise, by leading to this conclusion, points the way to a method which will prove useful by charting the interrelations between the forms, which we know must exist.

How far Plato may have been aware of the fallacies in the argumentation and how far he had the method of diaeresis explicitly in mind[1] must remain to some extent matters of speculation. But this does not invalidate the conclusion that the exercise demonstrates that some other method must be found for resolving the difficulties within the world of forms; and it is this new method which Plato brings to bear on the *μέγιστα γένη* in the *Sophist*. It is the thorough performance and examination of the *γυμνασία* which shows the way to a method which does explain or bypass the most important of the contradictions engendered by the method of deduction from existential hypotheses. The conclusion which Plato intended his readers to draw should perhaps be stated no more strongly than as follows: Since apparent contradictions can be deduced from even the simple hypothesis or denial of so fundamental and pervasive a form as unity, it is not to be wondered that the relation of forms to particulars is not capable of being clearly expressed; and a different method must be adopted[1] for the explication of the forms, which although

[1] That the dialogue is an indirect and not very successful recommendation of communion is the interpretation of D. W. Hamlyn, 'The Communion of the Forms and the Development of Plato's Logic', *Phil. Quart.*, V (1955), 295–300. But he holds this on the grounds that the first part shows the dangers of pluralism and the second of monism. That this view is incompatible with my own is, I hope, clear.

knowable to the trained philosopher are not precisely definable. I am myself unable to form any confident opinion as to how far the *Parmenides* should be regarded as the deliberate and conscious precursor of the *Sophist*. But that the *Sophist* does offer some solution to the problems raised in the *Parmenides* is, I think, beyond question. Further, I hope I have shown that the *Parmenides* is best interpreted as to some extent paving the way for this solution. My view, if it is correct, embodies the contention that the purpose of the second part is dialectical training, but it gives this training a relevance lacking to the purely gymnastic interpretation. On any interpretation the exercise is so completely and deliberately exhaustive as to be tediously long. But I hope to have shown that it is likely that Plato intended some moral to be drawn from it, and that the dialogue can accordingly be seen to be both serious in content and coherent in form.[1]

[1] Since writing this article I am indebted to Mr. J. M. E. Moravcsik for pointing out to me that my view of the independent value of hypotheses (5) to (8) closely follows that of Constantin Ritter.

VIII

KNOWLEDGE AND FORMS IN PLATO'S *THEAETETUS* (1957)

Winifred F. Hicken

IN the last pages of the *Theaetetus*[1] Socrates is made to present four[2] versions of a final attempt to define knowledge as true opinion accompanied by logos, and to reject them all; yet in earlier dialogues 'ability to give account', λόγον ἔχειν or λόγον διδόναι δύνασθαι, is closely associated with knowledge, not always,[3] or not necessarily,[4] knowledge of Forms, and in the *Republic* it is said to be the essential mark of the dialectician.[5] These facts are exceedingly hard to interpret. In recent years the passage has been read as an indirect defence of the earlier theory of Forms, as the statement of a problem answered in the *Sophist* by a revision of that theory and as a piece of radical self-criticism. No one of these interpretations seems to me without difficulty, and in this article I shall attempt to argue for yet another solution which owes something to all three.

[1] *Tht.*, 201c 8–end.

[2] *Tht.*, 201c 8–206b 11; 206d 1–e 2; 206e 5–208b 12; 208c 1–210a 7. Unlike others who have written on this passage, e.g. Cornford and Stenzel, I am proposing to count the 'dream' (201c 8–206b 11) as a version in its own right, the first of the expansions of Theaetetus' formula (*Tht.*, 201c 8–d 1). Of the three senses mentioned later (*Tht.*, 206c 8), the first seems to me to be introduced only to get put out of the way an obvious but unhelpful sense of λόγον διδόναι, so that by 'the three main versions' I shall mean the 'dream' and those stated and discussed in 206e 5–208b 12 and 208c 1–210a 7.

[3] *Gorg.*, 465a 2 ff.

[4] *Men.*, 97e 6 ff., if δῆσαι αἰτίας λογισμῷ is a variant for λόγον διδόναι; *Phd.*, 76b 4 ff.; *Smp.*, 202a 5 ff.

[5] *Rep.*, 510c 6 ff.; 531e 4 ff.; 533b 8 ff.; 534b 3 ff.

Professor Cornford,[1] pressing the fact that Socrates draws all his illustrations from the world of concrete things,[2] believes that Plato intended by criticism of the different versions to point the way to an old and invulnerable sense of λόγον διδόναι which implies that the proper objects of knowledge are Forms. This is the statement or understanding of grounds for judgments which in the *Meno*[3] is said to turn true opinion into knowledge. A rather similiar line has been taken by Professor Cherniss.[4] Professor Stenzel[5] thinks that the earlier theory of Forms is vulnerable to Socrates' criticism of what I call 'the first version', the 'dream', but he believes that all three of the later versions 'recover their meaning' when the problem of definition has been solved in the *Sophist* with the help of the method of diaeresis; and so restated they can be shown to apply to particulars as well as to Forms. Mr. R. Robinson[6] argues that in the passage to be discussed, as everywhere else in the dialogue, Forms are left out of account for the very good reason that to limit the objects of knowledge will not help to find out what knowledge is, but he believes that when Socrates refutes the version of the 'dream' he makes a direct attack on the view that knowledge implies ability to give an account, whatever sense be given to the words, and that his criticism of the last two versions tells against two of the most familiar forms of Socratic definition.

I have not room here to do more than indicate why these interpretations seem to me unsatisfactory. The definitions of knowledge attributed to Plato by Cornford and Stenzel seem in different ways too limited to satisfy Socrates' orginal demand for a *general* definition, covering a number of different kinds of knowledge, including, or so we are given to expect, both the science of the mathematician and the skill of the craftsman.[7] Cornford supposes that the only objects of knowledge are supra-sensible

[1] *Plato's Theory of Knowledge* (1935), p. 141 f.

[2] *Tht.*, 201e 1 f.; 207a 3 f.; 208d 1–3.

[3] *Men.* loc. cit.

[4] 'The Philosophical Economy of the Theory of Ideas', see above, Ch. I.

[5] *Plato's Method of Dialectic*, translated and edited by D. J. Allan (1940), pp. 71 ff.

[6] 'Forms and Error in Plato's *Theaetetus*', *Philosophical Review*, LIX (1950), pp. 3 ff.

[7] *Tht.*, 146e 7–148b 7.

Forms, while Stenzel limits the relations grasped in an act of knowing to those between genera and species. Cornford's interpretation, if I understand it, gives no explanation at all of the infallibility of knowledge, while Stenzel's answer to this problem[1] supposes that Plato believed that the content of any given species could be deduced by division from the one above it, and ultimately from the highest genus, Being itself, though in the passage of the *Sophist*[2] which Stenzel believes contains an answer to the problem of the *Theaetetus* Plato appears to recognise a symmetrical relationship between Being and Difference,[3] and indeed between others of the 'great kinds', which forbids us to treat them as species and genus. On the other hand, Robinson's solution leaves unexplained a difficulty inherent in the passage itself: the puzzling fact that Plato chooses to make Socrates and Theaetetus meet with final defeat when they have failed to defend any of a number of definitions of knowledge not one of which, if allowed to stand, seems capable of covering mathematical science or the skill of the craftsman, or indeed that case of knowledge which Robinson finds specially interesting,[4] the knowledge which in one place Plato admits is possessed by eyewitnesses to a crime;[5] and this although it is possible to collect from earlier dialogues[6] other senses of λόγον διδόναι which we might have expected Plato to have taken into account.

The view for which I shall argue is that the final discussion may be interpreted as a rearguard engagement in a moment of defeat. The dialogue reflects a genuine state of ἀπορία: Plato has no answer to Socrates' question. For while still confident that the most illuminating kind of knowledge is dialectical knowledge of Forms,[7] so that no general account can be satisfactory which does not cover this, he no longer finds it possible to distinguish this kind of knowledge from true opinion. He is, and remains,

[1] *Tht.*, pp. 90–3.

[2] *Soph.*, 252e 6–259e 6.

[3] E.g. ibid., 257a 4–6; 258a 7–9.

[4] Op. cit., p. 5.

[5] *Tht.*, 201a 10–c 2.

[6] *Gorg.*, 465a 2–6, where λόγον ἔχει seems to mean 'is able to justify a set of actions by an appeal to general principles'.

Men., 97e 6–98a 5, where δῆσαι αἰτίας λογισμῷ seems to mean 'to give general grounds for the truth of a statement'.

Rep., 534b 3–d 1, where by ἔχειν λόγον διδόναι Plato seems to mean not 'ability to define' but 'ability to justify a definition by argument'.

[7] Cf. e.g. *Phil.*, 58a 1 ff.

convinced that dialectical knowledge, perhaps also by analogy the knowledge of the mathematician and of the 'Socratic' craftsman, who can teach the principles of his craft, *implies* ability to give account,[1] which means to him ability to justify a position, whether statement or definition, by reasoned argument;[2] and as long as he thinks in terms of argument, he finds no difficulty in distinguishing knowledge from unjustified, and so fallible, opinion. But he is also convinced, and continues to be convinced,[3] that *in itself* knowledge is direct intuition of reality, and he can find no way of translating the truths discovered by dialectic into descriptions of objects which will enable him to distinguish an act of knowing from one of no less immediate opinion.

He now finds himself baffled by a problem which once seemed to him merely eristic,[4] to explain how it is possible for a man to have an object before his mind without instantly knowing it. This is a problem which he once hoped to solve with the help of the doctrine of ἀνάμνησις,[5] and in the *Republic* it presented no difficulty because the only fallible judgments in which Plato was then interested could be traced back to ambiguous sense impressions and so directly contrasted with knowledge of determinate and unvarying Forms. But in the apparent digression on the possibility of false opinion[6] it has been presented in a new and more deadly form. Error, it seems, is possible at a purely intellectual level,[7] where there is no question of being misled by imperfect recollection of objects once fully known. This problem Plato solves neither elsewhere nor indeed in the *Sophist*,[8] which deals only with the other of the two difficulties raised in the digression, the one about τὸ μὴ ὄν.[9] His logic has outrun his metaphysics, and he now has things to say about Forms and relations between Forms which make it virtually impossible for him to describe them, except in general terms, as objects at all. He can continue to call them 'divine', 'eternal', and the like, but he cannot show what is 'seen' when a man is said to have knowledge of individual Forms.

What he can do is to show that this is a *general* problem, and

[1] Cf. *Phil.*, 62a 2–5.
[2] Cf. e.g. *Tht.*, 175c 8–d 2.
[3] Cf. e.g. *Sph.*, 254a 8 ff.
[4] *Meno*, 80e 1 ff.
[5] *Men.*, 81a 5 ff.
[6] *Tht.*, 187d 1–200c 5.
[7] *Tht.*, 195c 6 ff.
[8] I.e. *Soph.*, 260b 10–264b 3.
[9] *Tht.*, 188c 9–189b 8.

that those who tacitly limit knowledge to the particular are still further from solving it than those who find it necessary to posit Forms. The three main versions examined, which are all attempts to distinguish knowledge of concrete things from true opinion about them, are not merely refuted but refuted by objections which, in their specific form, it seems possible to meet with the help of the theory of Forms. In each case we find a temporary resting-place from our difficulties in the theory, though the last two of Socrates' criticisms could be restated, and it seems to me likely that Plato realised that they could be restated, in forms dangerous to the theory itself, and all that is secured for the theory by the analysis of the 'dream' is sheer immunity from attack but no definition of knowledge.

In the first version[1] it seems to be suggested that whereas true opinion is an unanalysed impression of a complex particular,[2] knowledge implies ability to analyse such a complex into absolutely simple parts. These elements or 'letters' are sensible but can be made the subject of no judgments whatever, not even of the judgments of opinion. They can only be named, for to make any statement about them involves the use of terms like 'is' and 'each' which are applicable to other things and so cannot describe their peculiar nature. But of the 'syllable' formed from these it is possible to give account, for it is of the nature of a 'logos' to be a complex, *συμπλοκή*, of names, and such a logos is the expression of knowledge.

This version Socrates refutes first[3] by inducing Theaetetus to admit that the syllable is either all its letters or a single indivisible nature, distinct from the letters, which comes into being when they combine. But if we take the first course, we are guilty of the absurdity of supposing that while each of the letters is unknowable, we still know them all; if we take the second, we find ourselves faced by yet another 'simple' of which no account can be given.

This first criticism has been read in two ways, both of which have been thought to tell against Plato's earlier theories. Robinson[4] is, I believe, alone in thinking that it is an attack on the whole notion that knowledge implies giving account, and tends

[1] *Tht.*, 201c 8–202c 5.
[2] So Cornford suggests, I think rightly. Op. cit., p. 145.
[3] *Tht.*, 203d 8–205e 7.
[4] Op. cit., p. 15.

to show that there may be knowledge of what is ἄλογον. The orthodox view is that Socrates refutes only the notion that there may be knowledge of complexes whose elements are simple and so unknowable, but it has been suggested by Stenzel[1] and Ryle[2] that the Forms of the earlier dialogues were simples of just this kind.

Robinson's view seems to me untenable. Plato presents the doctrine of simples in such a way that we expect him to show that it is inadmissible. He uses the device with which in the *Sophist*[3] he attacks the theorists who believe that only statements of sheer identity are logically sound: he describes the simples with the help of words which he later rejects as inapplicable.[4] If we take him seriously, we make nonsense of the whole business of giving things names, which, as Plato assumes in the *Cratylus*,[5] is an act of discrimination, and as soon as we discriminate, we set things in relation to each other and cease to regard them as absolutely simple. It seems to me significant that when in the *Parmenides*[6] the philosopher attempts to separate off such a simple in his first hypothesis εἰ ἕν ἐστιν, he concludes: οὐδ' ἄρα ὄνομα ἔστιν αὐτῷ οὐδὲ λόγος οὐδέ τις ἐπιστήμη οὐδὲ αἴσθησις οὐδὲ δόξα. Moreover, it does not seem to me true that the argument tends to show that 'if elements are unknowable because they have no logos, everything is unknowable'.[7] Everything is unknowable only if everything is a complex of simples. But the attempt to construct complexes of such simples breaks down. We find ourselves confronted either by a mere aggregate or by an ἰδέα ἀμέριστος, itself unrelated to letters, that is by something utterly unlike a syllable. The argument seems rather to imply that if there is to be knowledge of complexes, there must be a sense, necessarily a second sense, in which it is possible to give account of their elements.

The suggestion of Stenzel and Ryle seems to me more plausible. Two quite different issues seem to be raised: (1) are the Forms of the earlier dialogues indivisible? (2) are they intuited *in vacuo* as if unrelated to each other or to anything else? Only if both

[1] *Tht.*, p. 73. ''Αμέριστον and μονοειδές are two of the honourable titles of the Ideas in earlier days.'

[2] See above, Ch. VI. 'Now although Plato does not make the application, Substantial Forms were supposed to be just such simple nameables.'

[3] *Soph.*, 252c 2 ff. [4] *Tht.*, 201e 2–202a 8. [5] *Crat.*, 388b 13 f.

[6] *Parm.*, 142a 3 ff. [7] Robinson, op. cit., p. 15.

questions can be answered affirmatively do we seem justified in believing that they were supposed to be simples in the dangerous sense. For Plato takes special pains to show that the ἰδέα ἀμέριστος is unknowable not simply because it is indivisible but because it is a single isolated object.[1]

The evidence, such as it is, seems to be all indirect. *Prima facie* the first question might seem to be settled by the fact that the epithet μονοειδές, which in other contexts Plato uses to mean 'without parts',[2] and in the *Theaetetus* is treated as a synonym for ἀμέριστον,[3] is in the earlier dialogues applied to Forms.[4] But the term is found in contexts to which the notion that Forms are indivisible seems entirely irrelevant. In the *Symposium*[5] it is used to contrast the Form of beauty with what is beautiful in some contexts and ugly in others; and in the *Phaedo*[6] it is closely associated with the immunity of Forms from change. It seems to mean not 'without parts' but 'uniform', 'invariable', 'without ambiguity', something which comes close in meaning to εἰλικρινές and καθαρόν,[7] 'without trace of its opposite'. If so, it tells us nothing about the simplicity of Forms in the first sense, though it might tell us something about their simplicity in the second, for nothing would seem more surely to guarantee their uniformity than a complete absence of 'context'.

There is indeed one passage in the *Parmenides* which has been thought to show that Plato once held that there was no communication between Forms,[8] *Parmenides*, 129a 6–e 3. But in this passage Socrates does not suggest that he expects Forms to be incapable of 'mingling' but of 'mingling and separation',[9] and by 'mingling and separation' he seems to mean something very like that swing between opposite characters described in the *Symposium*. He is in no way surprised that particulars should be shown to admit of opposites like one and many, but he would be shocked to find Unity and Plurality behaving in that way.[10]

In the *Sophist*,[11] however, in a passage designed to show how

[1] *Tht.*, 205c 4–e 4. [2] E.g. *Rep.*, 612a 3 ff. [3] *Tht.*, 205d 1 f.

[4] *Symp.*, 211b 1 and e 4; *Phd.*, 78d 5; 80b 2; 83e 2. Ἀμέριστον, according to Ast, is used only in later dialogues, unless we are justified in giving an earlier date to the *Timaeus*.

[5] *Symp.*, 210b 2–211b 5. [6] *Phd.*, 78d 1–7. [7] Cf. *Symp.*, 211d 8 ff.

[8] Cf. e.g. Robinson, '*Plato's Parmenides*', *Class. Philol.*, XXXVII (1942), p. 66.

[9] *Parm.*, 129e 2–3. [10] Ibid., 129a 6–b 6. [11] *Soph.*, 254b 7 ff.

there is communication between just the 'kinds' cited as Forms in the *Parmenides*,[1] Plato suggests that there is a sense in which they do admit of their opposites. Movement is the same as itself and different from any other 'kind',[2] and it is easy to develop the argument to show that Unity is a many in that it admits of predicates like Being and Difference, and Plurality a one in that it is one Form. Such relationships present no difficulty once we have been enabled with the help of the notions of ταὐτόν and τὸ ἕτερον to distinguish the 'is' of identity from the 'is' of predication, and in the *Philebus*[3] problems about the unity and plurality of concrete things are described as 'childish and easy and a serious hindrance to discussion'. It is plausible to suppose that in the *Sophist* Plato corrects an earlier view that Forms are unrelated simples, and shows that the difficulty from which their supposed simplicity was to set them free is unreal.

But it seems unlikely that this is a fair inference from the two passages. For in a dialogue generally thought to be later than the *Sophist*, the *Philebus*, Plato is still prepared to describe Forms as ἀμεικτότατ' ἔχοντα,[4] where again, to judge from the context and Socrates' earlier use of the metaphor, he seems to mean 'having unvarying character', 'without trace of an opposite', and so surpassing concrete things in ἀλήθεια, truth to type, as a small quantity of what is pure white surpasses μεμειγμένου πολλοῦ λευκοῦ.[5] It looks as if Plato did not suppose that the 'multiformity' of perceptibles could be explained away and with it the need to posit entities which were μονοειδῆ. The confusion between universals and perfect types which made it possible for him to compare Forms with particulars in this way is still evident in the *Sophist*,[6] where he illustrates the point that no Form can stand in a relation of sheer identity with its opposite by saying that Movement does not rest.

The indirect evidence for the indivisibility of Forms seems to me strong. I can find in the earlier dialogues no trace of a distinction between simple and complex Forms, and yet any definition of a Form which named its parts would imply that it was composed of simpler Forms, for although the number and nature of Forms explicitly mentioned are limited, Plato seems sufficiently

[1] *Parm.*, 129d 8–e 1.
[2] *Soph.*, 256a 10 ff.
[3] *Phil.*, 14d 4–8.
[4] 59c 4.
[5] Ibid., 52e 6–53b 6.
[6] *Soph.*, 255a 10.

aware of their universal character to posit in theory a Form for every general term.[1] Stenzel seems to be right in saying that we have no evidence in the earlier dialogues that he divided individual Forms into genus and species,[2] if indeed he ever did. He is in a sense aware of the relation between genus and species when in the *Phaedo*[3] he points out that ἡ τῶν τριῶν ἰδέα carries with it ἡ περιττὴ μορφή; but it looks as if he thought of them as distinct Forms with an interesting relationship. He may be feeling after the notion of a complex Form in the *Politicus*,[4] where he compares the Form of the Statesman to a syllable, but in the *Sophist*[5] he still seems to have the idea that genera and species are interconnected Forms.

On the other hand the indirect evidence seems to tell against the view that in the earlier dialogues Plato believed that single Forms could be intuited *in vacuo*. The only passage which suggests this is the account of beauty in the *Symposium*,[6] which contains a description of an act of knowing as sheer intuition of a single object[7] and makes no reference to reasoning which might have set it in relation to other Forms. But in this respect it is to be contrasted with the accounts of knowledge of Forms in the *Republic*,[8] and they seem to me right who have argued that Diotima is describing contemplation rather than a typical case of knowledge.[9] Not all Forms seem capable of being 'known' in this way, and in the *Phaedrus*[10] we find a similar account of the vision of single Forms, although when Plato wrote this dialogue he had a lively interest in *diaeresis*, which seems to imply that some Forms at least are related to each other and known only in their interrelation.

I can find no passage in the *Republic* which carries similar implications. For while Plato often speaks of single Forms as standards of conduct,[11] intuition of which enables us to discriminate intelligently between particular cases, he nowhere describes such intuition as knowledge, though he does of course imply that we have knowledge of Forms intuited as standards.[12] If

[1] Cf. e.g. *Rep.*, 596a 5–8.
[2] Op. cit., pp. 70 ff.
[3] *Phd.*, 104d 1 ff.
[4] *Pol.*, 278c 3–e 10.
[5] *Soph.*, 253d 5 ff.
[6] *Symp.*, 209e 5–212a 7.
[7] *Smp.*, 211b 7–d 1.
[8] E.g. *Rep.*, 532a 5–b 2.
[9] E.g. R. C. Cross, see above, Ch. II.
[10] *Phdr.*, 247d 5 ff.
[11] E.g. *Rep.*, 484c 6 ff.; 520c 1–6.
[12] *Rep.*, 484c 6 f.

knowledge is intuition of single Forms, it is hard to see what we are to make of Plato's insistence that dialectic is essentially synoptic, that Forms are fully known only in relation to the Good, and that knowledge of this Form, as of every other, implies ability to give an account.[1] It is unfortunate that Plato tells us so little about this process, and in particular does not explain what he means by saying that the Good is to be abstracted from everything else.[2] It seems unsafe to assume, as Cornford does in his translation, that by 'everything else' Plato means 'all other Forms' so that to distinguish the Good is to set it in relation to all the rest, for he may be thinking primarily of inadequate concepts like health or pleasure, and in the *Symposium* beauty is distinguished from concepts of a similar kind only to be contemplated in itself. But he does suggest that the 'account' is to be defended against criticism by *argument*,[3] and we should expect it to contain some explanation of the way in which the Good is causally related to truth and knowledge, since such is the conclusion we have to make when we are finally confronted by the Good.[4] We have no reason to believe that Plato had at this time tried to work out any schema of relationships between the terms used in definitions, which in the earlier dialogues reflect in their variety the many senses of the question 'What is X?'[5], but that definition means setting one thing in relation to another it seems impossible to deny.

It seems to me, then, that so far from being vulnerable to Socrates' criticism of the first version a case might be made for holding that it is just the virtue of the earlier theory of Forms that it provides us with ultimate units of analysis which are comparable with true parts of wholes. For as Plato recognises elsewhere, most clearly perhaps in the *Phaedrus*,[6] it is of the nature of parts of wholes not to be absolutely simple but to possess a character appropriate to each other and to the wholes in which they combine. That Plato intended us to draw such a conclusion from his examination of the first version it is not possible to disprove, but Socrates' very uncompromising treatment of the distinction between τὸ ὅλον and τὰ ἅπαντα was surely meant to disturb

[1] E.g. *Rep.*, 334b 3 ff.
[2] *Rep.*, 534b 8 f.
[3] *Rep.*, 554b 8 ff.
[4] *Rep.*, 517c 1 ff.
[5] Cf. Robinson, *Plato's Earlier Dialectic*, (2nd ed.) pp. 53 ff.
[6] *Phdr.*, 264c 2 ff.

us, as it did Theaetetus;[1] and in the *Parmenides*,[2] in an apparently straight bit of reasoning, he argues for a distinction between 'all' and 'whole' in words which directly recall those of the *Theaetetus*, and in *Theaetetus*, 203b 2 ff. he makes Theaetetus unconsciously admit that after all it is possible to give some kind of a definition of letters.

Moreover, in his second criticism[3] of the first version Socrates makes a point which invites us to apply the analogy of letters to Forms and in a familiar way. When we learn to read, our crucial task is not to recognise syllables but to recognise our letters without being misled by their arrangement in spoken and written syllables. It seems to be just Plato's contention in the *Republic*[4] that dialectic frees a man from the danger of being misled about justice and beauty by the different contexts in which they are presented in sense experience. He looks beyond the manifold of experience in which beauty is variously associated with actions and bodies and Forms to the single nature by which the concepts drawn from experience are judged. We might express this as ability to recognise letters in spoken or written syllables, except that in the middle books of the *Republic* he will not allow that Forms are really *exemplified* by particulars, which are therefore not strictly comparable with letters. This seems to have been one of the points on which Plato has changed his mind.[5] He may have returned to the position which seems to be reflected in the Third Book of the *Republic*[6] in which he explicitly compares knowledge of Forms with the recognition of letters and represents particulars by words.

The point seems to be further developed in Socrates' criticism of the second of the three main versions,[7] in which he tries to lead directly to the conclusion that knowledge of universals is prior to and implied by knowledge of instances. When we say that, if we are to read and write, we must know our letters, we mean by 'letters' not the sounds we hear or the marks on a particular page but the abstract symbols. Once again it seems to be the virtue of Socrates' analogy that it provides us with means

[1] *Tht.*, 204a 11–b 3 and 204 e 11–13.

[2] *Parm.*, 157d 7 ff.: *οὐκ ἄρα τῶν πολλῶν οὐδὲ πάντων τὸ μόριον μόριον, ἀλλὰ μιᾶς τινὸς ἰδέας καὶ ἑνός τινος ὃ καλοῦμεν ὅλον, ἐξ ἁπάντων ἓν τέλειον γεγονός, τούτου μόριον ἂν τὸ μόριον εἴη.*

[3] *Tht.*, 206a 1–b 11.

[4] *Rep.*, 476a 4–7; 519c 2–6.

[5] Cf. e.g. *Tht.*, 186b 11 ff.

[6] *Rep.*, 402a 7 ff.

[7] *Tht.*, 207c 6–208b 9.

distinguish between 'knowing' something and merely 'opining' it by suggesting that whereas in opinion we give a rough description by enumerating the obvious but still complex parts of which something consists, in knowledge we 'give account' of it in the sense that we analyse it into parts which are no longer absolutely simple but still incapable of further division. In opinion at the best we spell a word by syllables, in knowledge we give it letters. This version Socrates shows will not do by reminding Theaetetus that there is a stage in learning to read and write when we get a letter right in one word and wrong in another. In such cases we 'give an account of' the word in the way suggested, but no one will allow that we have knowledge. This argument seems to lead directly to the conclusion that knowledge of universals is prior to and implied by knowledge of instances. When we say that, if we are to read and write, we must know our letters, we mean by 'letters' not the sounds we hear or the marks on a particular page but the abstract symbols. Once again it seems to be the virtue of Socrates' analogy that it provides us with means whereby we may show that the dialectician more nearly satisfies the conditions of knowledge than one who tries to identify it with any kind of analysis of particulars. For although to equate Forms with universals is to oversimplify in view of the tacit limitation Plato sets to Forms, there seems to be no evidence that he ever consciously distinguished between them.

Socrates' treatment of the last version,[1] that to give an account is to state the mark whereby a thing may be distinguished from everything else, is rather different. No positive point is made which tells in favour of the theory of Forms, but his specific criticism seems relevant only to particulars. For his argument is that if we are to have no more than true opinion about X, say Theaetetus, we must already have distinguished him from everything else or we shall be thinking not of him but of men in general or at the best of men of a certain physical type. But it is nonsense to suggest that the addition of true opinion about the differentia can turn true opinion into knowledge, and if we say that we must *know* the differentia, we argue in a circle. There seems to be no way in which we might select from Forms elements of greater or less generality, unless indeed we suppose that they are complexes made up of genera and species. If, as I believe, this passage does

[1] *Tht.*, 208c 6–210b 2.

contain tacit criticism of the theory of Forms, it is not to be found in the first part of Socrates' criticism.

Examination of the three main versions reveals some of the virtues of the theory of Forms and goes some way to suggest that knowledge cannot be explained without their help, but it has provided us with no 'fourth sense' of λόγον διδόναι; we cannot identify knowledge with understanding of 'intelligible Forms and truths about them'.[1] For the analysis of particulars into constituent Forms has been shown by the criticism of the second version to be less than knowledge,[2] and if we try to restate the first version in terms of Forms and nothing but Forms, and suppose that dialectic gives an account of complexes of Forms in universal propositions, we find that Socrates' criticism of the second version tells against this too. It seems perfectly possible for us to relate a Form correctly in one proposition and wrongly in another. We may correctly affirm that Rest and Movement differ from Being while still aware that there are an indefinite number of puzzles about Being to which we have no answer.[3] In the *Politicus*[4] at least Plato seems to recognise this. For he points out, though for quite another purpose, that we may recognise Combination and Separation in the complex notion of Weaving and yet fail to perceive its presence in the more difficult syllable, Statesmanship.

In some sense, then, the object of knowledge seems to be the 'letter' and not the 'syllable', the Form and not the complex of Forms. We have to find a set of relations, other than those which obtain between parts and whole, which are the permanent possession of Forms, and may be used to distinguish them securely in every one of the complexes in which they may be found. But at once we are confronted by the difficulty raised in the last part of Socrates' criticism of the final version.[5] If we are to make no more than true statements about Forms, we must be already thinking of them as distinct natures, and so be already in some sense aware of the relations which distinguish them from other Forms.

Plato does seem to have provided some sort of answer to the problem of 'knowing' such letters in the *Sophist*,[6] but not in a form which can be reconciled with belief that knowledge is

[1] Cornford, op. cit., 162.
[2] *Tht.*, 207c 6–208b 12.
[3] Cf. *Soph.*, 250c 3–10.
[4] *Pol.*, 278c 8–279b 5.
[5] *Tht.*, 209d 1–210a 9.
[6] *Soph.*, 252e 1 ff.

direct intuition of objects. For there Plato compares dialectic with the art of the grammarian, who, as Theaetetus earlier recognised,[1] knows his letters in a specially satisfactory way. The dialectician secures himself against the danger of mistaking the same Form for a different one or a different Form for the same one by working out the general rules for the combination of Forms just as the grammarian works out the rules for the combination of letters. But knowledge of such purely potential relationships cannot without absurdity be treated as a form of direct intuition of permanent relations between objects. As long as the philosopher thinks in terms of propositions, he can work out the relations of compatibility and entailment which govern the combination of Forms in general statements or definitions, and enable him to give reasons for accepting or rejecting them; but if he tries to translate rules for combination into descriptions of actual relations between metaphysical objects, he has to meet the difficulty raised in *Parmenides*, 131a 4 ff. and others worse. It is not merely that all Forms are shown to 'partake' of Forms like Difference and Being,[2] but that these Forms partake of each other,[3] and on the Stranger's principles Difference itself can be distinguished from other Forms only if we suppose that in some sense it partakes of itself.

Plato's use of such metaphors in the *Sophist*, which seems almost light-hearted after the struggles of the *Parmenides*, would have been inexplicable if the theory of Forms had ever been merely, or even primarily, a metaphysical theory and not a weapon for the clarification of thought. He still finds that he has important things to say with the help of the theory, though he cannot meet his own criticisms, and his failure to justify his earlier view that knowledge is some kind of direct acquaintance with stable and determinate objects is reflected in the way in which in his later dialogues he keeps in the background, when speaking of Forms, the imagery of vision which characterised the *Phaedo* and *Republic*, and explores instead the analogy of γραμματική.[4]

[1] *Tht.*, 163b 1–c 3.
[2] Cf. *Soph.*, 255e 3–6; 256d 11–e 3.
[3] Ibid., 256d 11–257a 6; 258a 7–9.
[4] E.g. *Soph.*, 252e 9 ff.; *Pol.*, 277e 2 ff.; *Phlb.*, 17a 8 ff.

IX

SYMPLOKE EIDON[1]

(1955)

J. L. Ackrill

IT is the purpose of this short paper[2] to consider the meaning and implications of a sentence in Plato's *Sophist*. At the end of the section on *κοινωνία γενῶν* the Eleatic visitor is made to speak as follows (259e 4–6): *τελεωτάτη πάντων λόγων ἐστὶν ἀφάνισις τὸ διαλύειν ἕκαστον ἀπὸ πάντων· διὰ γὰρ τὴν ἀλλήλων τῶν εἰδῶν συμπλοκὴν ὁ λόγος γέγονεν ἡμῖν.* I shall be mainly concerned with the second half of this remark, and shall refer to it, for brevity, as sentence or statement *S*.

Cornford (in *Plato's Theory of Knowledge*, p. 300) translates sentence *S* thus: 'any discourse we can have owes its existence to the weaving together of Forms'. In his commentary he writes: 'All discourse depends on the "weaving together of Forms" . . . It is not meant that Forms are the only elements in the meaning of all discourse. We can also make statements about individual things. But it is true that every such statement must contain at least one Form.' A few lines later Cornford says that the point made by

[1] These papers (Chapters IX and X) are reprinted here without alteration. This is not because I think them incapable of improvement. They have been discussed in print by a number of scholars since their original publication, and some of the criticisms that have been made are certainly weighty. However, I cannot at present undertake a major re-writing, and I think that it is better to leave them in their original form than to make merely minor changes.

[2] This is a shortened version of a paper read to a Colloquium at the Classical Institute on March 14, 1955. The paper was designed to provoke discussion: this fact may help to excuse some over-simplification and some over-statement.

Plato in *S* is 'that every statement or judgment involves the use of at least one Form'; and later (p. 314) he remarks that Plato 'has said that "all discourse depends on the weaving together of Forms", i.e. at least one Form enters into the meaning of any statement.'

Cornford seems to take it for granted that Plato is saying something about Forms being 'contained in' or 'used in' statements. But he notices that not every statement does 'contain' a plurality of Forms—Plato's own examples a few pages later, the statements about Theaetetus, do not do so. So, to avoid attributing to Plato an obvious howler, he construes *S* as meaning not that every statement uses or contains or is about a *συμπλοκὴ εἰδῶν* but that it necessarily contains at least one Form. But this of course is just what *τὴν τῶν εἰδῶν συμπλοκήν* does not mean, as is particularly evident when we take account of the word *ἀλλήλων*, which Cornford omits in his translation. 'Discourse depends on the weaving together of Forms *with one another*.' Who could suppose that this meant merely that at least one Form enters into the meaning of any statement? *If S* says something about Forms being contained in any logos, then what it says must be that a *συμπλοκὴ εἰδῶν* is contained in any logos. If this last is evidently false, as shown by Plato's own examples a moment later, we must question the assumption that *S* does say something about Forms being contained in logoi.

It is worth noticing briefly how Ross (in *Plato's Theory of Ideas*, p. 115) deals with our passage. The Eleatic visitor, he says, asserts 'that all discourse depends on the weaving together of Forms by the speaker or thinker. This is in fact an over-statement, since a sentence may have a proper name for subject, and a proper name does not stand for a Form or universal. But the *predicate* of a sentence normally stands for a Form, and all subjects of statements except proper names stand either for Forms or for things described by means of Forms'. Ross does not pretend that *S* is true; he takes it to mean that every statement involves at least two Forms and shows this to be false. But notice how he proceeds. He does not say: since on our interpretation of *S* it is blatantly false perhaps our interpretation is wrong. Instead Ross glosses over the falsity of *S* (on his interpretation) by calling it an overstatement. But of course Plato is claiming to say something true of *all* logoi (259e 4, 260a 9). So *S*, on Ross's interpretation, is just false, and glaringly false. Misleading smoothness shows itself again a moment later:

talking of the examples 'Theaetetus is sitting', 'Theaetetus is flying', Ross says not that they refute *S* (on his interpretation of *S*) but that they 'do not illustrate Plato's thesis'. If I asserted, rather solemnly, that all philosophers are good-tempered, and immediately went on to chat about the bad-tempered philosophers I know, you would hardly say that my examples were 'not illustrating my thesis'.

Surely then something has gone wrong with the interpretation of *S*. Surely it must not be understood in such a way that the statements about Theaetetus are clear refutations of it. Surely it must not be taken to imply that every statement asserts or is about a relation between Forms (or even 'things described by means of forms'). How then is it to be understood?

Let us look back at what Plato has said before about the συμπλοκὴ εἰδῶν; not at the section in which he investigates connections among various chosen Forms—this is, comparatively, a matter of detail—but at the passage 251d–252e, which seeks to show that there *must be* a συμπλοκὴ εἰδῶν. Statement *S* says something about the necessity of συμπλοκὴ εἰδῶν for all logoi: it is reasonable to try to elucidate this by considering the arguments by which in the first place Plato sought to demonstrate that there must be such a συμπλοκή.

Plato lists, in this earlier passage, three possibilities: (1) that every Form combines with every other; (2) that no Form combines with any other; (3) that while some pairs of Forms do, others do not, combine with one another. By ruling out the first two possibilities he establishes the third; and it is this limited intercommunion of Forms that is subsequently spoken of as the συμπλοκὴ εἰδῶν. The argument for this last consists in effect of the arguments which disprove the other two possibilities.

The first possibility is ruled out on the ground that if it were true such statements as κίνησις ἵσταται would follow. These we can see to be self-contradictory, logically impossible—ταῖς μεγίσταις ἀνάγκαις ἀδύνατον. So if they are entailed by (1) then (1) must be false. To generalise: if a statement in which *A* is asserted of *B* is self-contradictory, logically impossible, then it follows that Form *A* does not combine with Form *B*. Since we are trying to understand what Plato means by his talk of 'combination' there can be no question of challenging the validity of his argument here; we have to take the argument as a clue to what 'combination' means. What emerges so far is that some restriction on the intercommunion of Forms is implied by the fact that some sentences express statements which are self-contradictory.

Plato's refutation of the second possibility—*μηδεμία σύμμειξις*—has two parts. Firstly, if this were true all the theories put forward by philosophers about reality, change, the constitution and behaviour of the world, would be null and void. Pluralists, monists, Eleatics, Heracliteans, all of them *λέγοιεν ἂν οὐδέν, εἴπερ μηδεμία ἔστι σύμμειξις*. Secondly, the very statement of (2) involves a contradiction. Its exponents, in stating it, must combine words into sentences—*συνάπτειν ἐν τοῖς λόγοις*—and in so doing they contradict their own thesis. It does not need others to refute them: *οἴκοθεν τὸν πολέμιον καὶ ἐναντιωσόμενον ἔχουσιν*.

Taking this point first, we must notice exactly how the exponents of (2) are refuted out of their own mouths. It is not of course that they straightforwardly both assert and deny *σύμμειξις*; it is that the statement of (2) necessarily presupposes the falsity of (2). Arguments of a somewhat similar kind are used by Plato elsewhere. In 249c he mocks at those who claim to know for certain the truth of a thesis whose truth would in fact make it impossible for any one to know anything. Or compare *Sophist*, p. 244. The theory that only one thing exists must be false, or at any rate it cannot be true. The statement 'only one thing exists' would have no meaning at all unless there were several different words with different meanings. The meaningfulness of the statement therefore presupposes, as a necessary condition, its own falsity.

The thesis 'no Forms combine with one another' is held to be self-refuting because its meaningfulness presupposes that some Forms do combine. Here then is another clue to an understanding of Plato's talk about Forms combining. That some statements are self-contradictory was taken as proof that some pairs of Forms are irreconcilable; now the fact that a certain statement is meaningful is taken to prove that some Forms do combine with others. Plato's conclusion, that there are connections between Forms, but not between every pair of Forms, rests upon the simple fact that some sentences are meaningful and some are not. The former presuppose the existence of concept-friendships or compatibilities, the latter the existence of concept-enmities or -incompatibilities.

To return to the first part of Plato's refutation of (2): if there were no *σύμμειξις* all the philosopher's accounts of things would be empty, they would not be saying anything at all, nothing significant. This last is how I want to translate λέγοιεν ἂν οὐδέν. This expression can of course mean simply 'to say what is false' or 'to say what is silly'; but it can also mean 'to make no genuine statement at all', 'not to succeed in saying anything'. It seems to me that the argument here demands this last sense: if there were no σύμμειξις, then no statement of any theory could be even significant. For suppose λέγειν οὐδέν here meant just 'to say what is false'. Then (*a*) the argument would be evidently inconclusive. For granted that alternative (2) did entail that all those philosophers' theories were false—well, perhaps they are false. Plato himself remarks that it is hard to decide about the truth of such theories (243a 2–3). To point out that (2) entailed the falsity of the theories listed would convince nobody that (2) was false unless he chanced to be a firm believer in one of those theories. (*b*) Again, on this interpretation of λέγειν οὐδέν, it is completely mysterious why (2)—the thesis that no Forms combine—should entail that the theories are false. For they are certainly not all theories *about* Forms. Empedocles talked about the world and its processes, he did not assert that certain Forms combined. So how would the assumption that no Forms combine make his theory necessarily false? (*c*) If, however, it were claimed that the philosophical theories mentioned did in fact *assert* that Forms combined, the result would be that Plato's argument was not indeed invalid but utterly pointless. For it would amount to this: some Forms must combine; for if none did then all philosophers who said they did would be wrong.

Taking λέγειν οὐδέν to mean 'to speak falsely' we find Plato's argument weak, obscure or pointless. It is surrounded by arguments that are cogent, clear, and highly relevant. This is a good reason to suspect that interpretation. If we take the expression to mean 'to make no genuine statement, to convey no logos whatsoever' the argument falls properly into place. If there were no liaisons among concepts the philosophers' statements (indeed all statements) would be just meaningless. Just as it is a presupposition of there being self-contradictory statements that some pairs of concepts will not go together, so it is a necessary condition of there being significant, non-self-contradictory statements (whether true or false) that some concepts will go together. These, I suggest, are the points Plato is making in his proof that there is a συμπλοκή εἰδῶν. Human discourse is possible only because the meanings of general words are related in definite ways; it is essential to language that there be definite rules determining which combinations of words do, and which do not, constitute significant sentences. To map out the interrelations of concepts (inclusion, incompatibility, and so on) is the task of dialectic (cf. *Sophist*, 253b–e).

I am obviously under an obligation to show that with my interpretation of *S*—as opposed to that of Cornford and Ross—there is no difficulty over the specimen logoi about Theaetetus. I must show that the dictum 'without a συμπλοκὴ εἰδῶν no logos would be possible' is *not* invalidated by the fact that many logoi contain only one general word, together with, for instance, a proper name. A quotation from a recent book on logical theory will help to make this clear (P. F. Strawson: *Introduction to Logical Theory*, 1952, p. 5):

> 'One of the main purposes for which we use language is to report events and to describe things and persons. Such reports and descriptions are like answers to questions of the form: what was it like? what is it (he, she) like? We describe something, say what it is like, by applying to it words that we are also prepared to apply to other things. But not to all other things. A word that we are prepared to apply to everything without exception (such as certain words in current use in popular, and especially military, speech) would be useless for the purposes of description. For when we say what a thing is like, we not only compare it with other things, we also distinguish it from other things. (These are not two activities, but two aspects of the same activity.) Somewhere, then, a boundary must be drawn, limiting the applicability of a word used in describing things.'

Substantially the same point is made by Aristotle in *Metaphysics* Γ. 4, where he argues for the Principle of Contradiction. He admits that it cannot be proved; for any proof would necessarily make use of the principle in question. But he says that you can explain to someone the necessity of this principle,—provided he will say something, something significant, with a definite meaning; for you can then show him that he must intend his statement to rule out something or other, to be incompatible with at least one other statement. A statement compatible with every other statement would tell one nothing. ἀρχὴ . . . τὸ ἀξιοῦν . . . σημαίνειν γέ τι καὶ αὑτῷ καὶ ἄλλῳ· τοῦτο γὰρ ἀνάγκη, εἴπερ λέγοι τι. εἰ γὰρ μή, οὐκ ἂν εἴη τῷ τοιούτῳ λόγος, οὔτ' αὐτῷ πρὸς αὐτὸν οὔτε πρὸς ἄλλον. ἂν δέ τις τοῦτο διδῷ, ἔσται ἀπόδειξις· ἤδη γάρ τι ἔσται ὡρισμένον. To return to Plato: the statement 'Theaetetus is sitting' is a genuine informative statement only because it rules something out ('Theaetetus is not sitting' or, more determinately, 'Theaetetus is standing'). To say that it rules something out is to say that there is an incompatibility (*μηδεμία κοινωνία*) between two concepts ('sitting' and 'not-sitting' or, more determinately, 'sitting' and 'standing'). In studying the relations among concepts a philosopher elicits the rules governing the use of language; that there are some such relations, some such rules, is a necessary condition of there being a language at all: διὰ τὴν ἀλλήλων τῶν εἰδῶν συμπλοκὴν ὁ λόγος γέγονεν ἡμῖν.

These few remarks must suffice to indicate how a συμπλοκὴ εἰδῶν is presupposed by any and every statement, including those about Theaetetus. Plato admittedly does not argue the point in connection with the Theaetetus examples, which are used in the discussion of a different topic. Still it is a related topic since it does involve the incompatibility of two predicates. And I think that if we had asked Plato to reconcile *S* with these examples he would have done so in the way suggested in outline above. This at any rate seems more plausible than to suppose that he follows up *S* by using examples of logoi which he would have been totally unable to reconcile with *S*.

I have gradually passed from talking about Forms to talking about concepts, and I have taken these to be, in effect, the meanings of general words. Correspondingly, I have implied that the task assigned in Plato's later dialogues to the dialectician or philosopher is the investigation and plotting of the relations among concepts, a task to be pursued through a patient study of language, by noticing which combinations of words in sentences do, and which do not, make sense, by eliciting ambiguities and drawing distinctions, by stating explicitly facts about the interrelations of word-meanings which we normally do not trouble to state, though we all have some latent knowledge of them insofar as we know how to talk correctly. To justify all this, and to add the many sober qualifications which it evidently demands, would take a volume. I can here mention, in conclusion, only two small points.

There is a section of the *Sophist* (254b ff.) where Plato is undoubtedly *practising* the dialectic he has previously described.

He first distinguishes certain εἴδη (cf. 253d 1–3) and then determines their inter-relations (cf. 253d 9–e 2). It is important to notice that what Plato does in this section is to appeal to truths too obvious to be disputed, in particular truths which anyone who knows the language must immediately admit. For instance, Being is proved to be different from Sameness by a simple substitution-argument (255b 8–c4): if they were *not* different then to say of two things that they both existed would be to say that they were both the same. But this is not so. In particular, we have agreed that κίνησις and στάσις both *exist*; but it would be different, and indeed absurd, to say that they are both *the same*. The dialectician's statement that Being is different from Sameness merely makes us see clearly (or at a new level) a fact about the meanings of words which we already in a way know. The dialectician makes explicit the rules in accordance with which we all already talk.

Finally, a reference to the *Parmenides*. After his searching criticisms of Socrates Parmenides goes on to imply that the theory of Ideas *is* capable of being salvaged, but that great skill and subtlety will be required for this. He adds (135b): 'if in view of all these and similar objections a man refuses to admit that Forms of things exist, or to distinguish (ὁρίζεσθαι) a definite Form in each case, he will have nothing on which to fix his thought, so long as he will not allow that each real thing has a character which is always the same; and thus he will completely destroy the possibility of significant talk (τὴν τοῦ διαλέγεσθαι δύναμιν)'. This passage may be taken to show that, in spite of the powerful criticisms voiced by Parmenides, Plato did not propose to abandon completely his theory of Ideas. It may be that he thought of himself as maintaining a revised version of the theory whereas we might find it more natural to say that he jettisoned the theory. Anyway the passage quoted strongly suggests that what he is now sure of is *not* that there must be Forms as conceived in the middle dialogues, Forms as ethical ideals and as the metaphysical objects of intuitive and perhaps mystical insight; what he is now sure of is that there must be fixed things to guarantee the meaningfulness of talk, fixed concepts—the meanings of general words—whose rôle is to ensure τὴν τοῦ διαλέγεσθαι δύναμιν. The *Sophist* explains further that these concepts must stand in certain definite relations to one another, and gives the dialectician the task of investigating the boundaries and inter-relations of concepts.

X

PLATO AND THE COPULA: *SOPHIST* 251–259 (1957)

J. L. Ackrill

MY purpose is not to give a full interpretation of this difficult and important passage, but to discuss one particular problem, taking up some remarks made by F. M. Cornford (in *Plato's Theory of Knowledge*,) and by Mr. R. Robinson (in his paper on Plato's *Parmenides*, *Class. Phil.*, 1942).[1] First it may be useful to give a very brief and unargued outline of the passage. Plato seeks to prove that concepts[2] are related in certain definite ways, that there is a συμπλοκὴ εἰδῶν (251d–252e). Next (253) he assigns to philosophy the task of discovering what these relations are: the philosopher must try to get a clear view of the whole range of concepts and of how they are interconnected, whether in genus-species pyramids or in other ways. Plato now gives a sample of such philosophising. Choosing some concepts highly relevant to problems already broached in the *Sophist* he first (254–5) establishes that they are all different one from the other, and then (255e–258) elicits the relationships in which they stand to one another. The attempt to discover and state these relationships throws light on the puzzling notions ὄν and μὴ ὄν and enables Plato to set aside with contempt certain puzzles and paradoxes propounded by superficial thinkers

[1] I shall refer to these two works by page numbers, without repeating their titles.

[2] The use of this term may seem provocative. But whether or not the εἴδη and γένη of the *Sophist* are something more than 'mere' concepts, a good deal of interpretation of 251–9 can satisfactorily proceed on the assumption that they are *at least* concepts.

(259). He refers finally (259e) to the absolute necessity there is for concepts to be in definite relations to one another if there is to be discourse at all: *διὰ γὰρ τὴν ἀλλήλων τῶν εἰδῶν συμπλοκὴν ὁ λόγος γέγονεν ἡμῖν*. So the section ends with a reassertion of the point with which it began (251d–252e): that there is and must be a *συμπλοκὴ εἰδῶν*.

The question I wish to discuss is this. Is it true to say that one of Plato's achievements in this passage is 'the discovery of the copula' or 'the recognition of the ambiguity of *ἔστιν*' as used on the one hand in statements of identity and on the other hand in attributive statements? The question is whether Plato made a philosophical advance which we might describe in such phrases as those just quoted, but no great stress is to be laid on these particular phrases. Thus it is no doubt odd to say that Plato (or anyone else) *discovered* the copula. But did he draw attention to it? Did he expound or expose the various rôles of the verb *ἔστιν*? Many of his predecessors and contemporaries reached bizarre conclusions by confusing different uses of the word; did Plato respond by elucidating these different uses? These are the real questions. Again, it would be a pedantic misunderstanding to deny that Plato recognised the ambiguity of *ἔστιν* merely on the ground that he used no word meaning 'ambiguity', or on the ground that he nowhere says 'the word *ἔστιν* sometimes means . . . and sometimes means . . .'. If he in fact glosses or explains or analyses the meaning of a word in one way in some contexts and in another way in others, and if this occurs in a serious philosophical exposition, then it may well be right to credit him with 'recognising an ambiguity'. I mention these trivial points only to indicate, by contrast, what the substantial question at issue is.

It is generally agreed (e.g. Cornford, p. 296) that Plato marks off the existential use of *ἔστιν* from at least some other use. How he does this can be seen from his remark about *κίνησις* at 256a 1: *ἔστι δέ γε διὰ τὸ μετέχειν τοῦ ὄντος*. This *διά* does not introduce a *proof* that *κίνησις ἔστιν*: this was already agreed without question before and used to establish a connection between *κίνησις* and *τὸ ὄν* (254d 10). Nor, obviously, does it introduce the *cause* why *κίνησις ἔστιν*: it does not refer to some event or state which resulted in the further state described by '*κίνησις ἔστιν*'. The words introduced by *διά* give an expansion or *analysis* of *ἔστιν* as this word is used in *κίνησις ἔστιν*, i.e. as used existentially.

μετέχει τοῦ ὄντος is the philosopher's equivalent of the existential ἔστιν; but, as will be seen, it is not his analysis of ἔστιν in its other uses. So the existential meaning is marked off.

The philosopher's formulation (κίνησις μετέχει τοῦ ὄντος) both elucidates the sense of ἔστιν in κίνησις ἔστιν, and also makes clear —what is not clear in the compressed colloquial formulation—the structure of the fact being stated; makes clear that a certain connection is being asserted between two concepts. The philosopher's formulation contains not only the names of two concepts but also a word indicating their coherence, μετέχει, which is not itself the name of an εἶδος but signifies the connection between the named εἴδη.

There remain two other meanings of ἔστιν, as copula and as identity-sign. The assimilation of these had led to a denial of the possibility of any true non-tautological statements. What is needed in order to deprive this paradox of its power is a clear demonstration of how the two uses of ἔστι differ. By 'demonstration' I do not mean 'proof' but 'exhibition' or 'display'. The way to sterilise a paradox is to expose and lay bare the confusion from which it arises. One can draw attention to the two different uses of ἔστι, point out how they are related, perhaps provide alternative modes of expression so as to remove even the slightest temptation to confuse the two.

Consider how Plato deals, in 256a 10–b4, with the pair of statements κίνησίς ἐστι ταὐτόν, κίνησις οὐκ ἔστι ταὐτόν. These look like contradictories yet we want to assert both. We need not really be worried (οὐ δυσχεραντέον); for we are not in both statements speaking ὁμοίως. Analysis of the statements (introduced again by διά) will show exactly what is being asserted in each and enable us to see that there is no contradiction between them when properly understood. The first statement means κίνησις μετέχει ταὐτοῦ. The second means κίνησις μετέχει θατέρου πρὸς ταὐτόν.

The essential points in Plato's analysis of the two statements are these: (1) where ἔστιν is being used as copula it gets replaced in the philosopher's version by μετέχει; (2) the philosopher's version of οὐκ ἔστιν, when the ἔστιν is not the copula but the identity-sign, is (not οὐ μετέχει, but) μετέχει θατέρου πρός. . . . By his reformulation of the two statements Plato shows up the difference between the ἔστιν which serves merely to connect two named concepts (copula) and the ἔστιν (or οὐκ ἔστιν) which expresses the concept of Identity (or Difference) and at the same time indicates that something *falls under* the concept of Identity (or Difference).

With Plato's procedure here one may compare a passage in Frege's paper *Über Begriff und Gegenstand.*[1] One can just as well assert of a thing that it is Alexander the Great, or is the number four, or is the planet Venus, as that it is green or is a mammal. But, Frege points out, one must distinguish two different usages of 'is'.

> 'In the last two examples it serves as a copula, as a mere verbal sign of predication. (In this sense the German word *ist* can sometimes be replaced by the mere personal suffix: cf. *dies Blatt ist grün* and *dies Blatt grünt.*[2]) We are here saying that something falls under a concept, and the grammatical predicate stands for this concept. In the first three examples, on the other hand, "is" is used like the "equals" sign in arithmetic, to express an equation. . . . In the sentence "the morning star is Venus" "is" is obviously not the mere copula; its content is an essential part of the predicate, so that the word "Venus" does not constitute the whole of the predicate. One might say instead: "the morning star is no other than Venus"; what was previously implicit in the single word "is" is here set forth in four separate words, and in "is no other than" the word "is" now really is the mere copula. What is predicated here is thus not *Venus* but *no other than Venus*. These words stand for a concept.'

Frege explains the copula by talking of something's *falling under* a concept: Plato uses for this the term *μετέχειν*. Frege expands the 'is' of identity into 'is no other than . . .', in which phrase the 'is' is simply the copula ('falls under the concept . . .') and 'no other than . . .' stands for a concept. Plato expands the *ἔστιν* of identity into *μετέχει ταὐτοῦ* . . . (and *οὐκ ἔστιν* into *μετέχει θατέρου* . . .) where *μετέχει* does the copula's job ('falls under') and *ταὐτόν* (or *θάτερον*) names a concept. In offering the analyses that he does it seems to me that Plato, no less clearly than Frege, is engaged in distinguishing and elucidating senses of 'is'.

The claim that one of the things Plato does in *Sophist*, 251–9 is to distinguish between the copula and the identity sign would seem

[1] I quote Mr. Geach's translation, in *Translations from the Philosophical Writings of Gottlob Frege*, edited by Peter Geach and Max Black, pp. 43–4.

[2] One is reminded of Aristotle, *Phys.*, 185b 28: *οἱ δὲ τὴν λέξιν μετερρύθμιζον ὅτι ὁ ἄνθρωπος οὐ λευκός ἐστιν ἀλλὰ λελεύκωται, οὐδὲ βαδίζων ἐστὶν ἀλλὰ βαδίζει.*

to be supported by the following consideration: that this distinction is just what is required to immunise us against the paradoxes of the ὀψιμαθεῖς (251b), and Plato does suppose that his discussion puts these gentlemen in their place. Robinson, however, denies that this consideration has any force (p. 174): 'Plato certainly thought of his Communion as refuting the "late learners". But it does not follow that he thought the manner of refutation was to show that they confused attribution with identity. Nor is there anything in the text to show that he thought this.' Robinson is certainly right to say that it does not *follow*. Still we are surely entitled—or, rather, obliged—to make some reasonable suggestion as to how exactly Plato did suppose himself to have 'refuted' the late learners. If the above interpretation of 256a 10–b 10 is sound, that passage exposes the error of the late learners, who construed every 'is' as an identity-sign; and it would be natural to infer that Plato himself regarded the distinction drawn in that passage (and elsewhere) as the decisive counter-move against the late learners. Moreover, if no *other* reasonable suggestion can be made as to how exactly Plato thought he had disposed of the late learners and their paradox, this fact will be an argument in favour of the interpretation of 256a–b which finds in it an important point which is directly relevant to, and destructive of, the paradox.

Now it might be suggested that it is by his proof that there is Communion among εἴδη (251d–252e) that Plato refutes the view that only identical statements are possible; that it is here, and not in later talk about ὄν and μὴ ὄν, that he supposes himself to be refuting the late learners. But what are the arguments by which he proves there is Communion?[1] The first (251e 7–252b 7) is this: if there were no Communion then philosophers and 'physicists' in propounding their various views would in fact be 'saying nothing' (λέγοιεν ἂν οὐδέν). It is simply *assumed* that this apodosis is false and that Empedocles and the rest were talking sense. But, of course, this assumption is exactly what the late learners, maintaining their paradox, will deny, and an argument based on it is obviously no good against them. Plato's second argument for Communion (252b 8–d 1) is that the theory that there is no Communion cannot be stated without implying its own falsity. As applied to the late learners the argument would be: you say

[1] I have discussed these arguments above, Ch. IX.

only identity-statements can be true; but this statement—'only identity-statements can be true'—is not an identity-statement; so on your own theory your theory is false. Now this argument is certainly formidable and might easily put a late learner to silence; he could hardly be expected to distinguish between first- and second-order statements. Yet as a refutation of the thesis itself it is surely superficial and unsatisfactory. For the thesis was put forward not only by elderly jokers but also by serious thinkers who felt themselves obliged to maintain it for what seemed to them compelling theoretical reasons. Robinson writes as follows (p. 175):

> 'To such more responsible thinkers it is folly to say: "But you obviously can say 'man is good'; and if you could not, all discourse whatever would be impossible, including the paradox that you cannot say 'man is good'." For these thinkers already know that you can say that "man is good", and that the supposition that you cannot immediately destroys all thought and speech. Their trouble is that, nevertheless, they seem to see a good reason for denying that you can say that "man is good". What they want is to be shown the fallacy in the argument which troubles them. They know it must be a fallacy; but they want to see what it is. Now for such thinkers Plato's exposition of his doctrine of Communism is no help whatever. For he merely points to the fact that we *must* be able to say "man is good", because otherwise no thought or communication would be possible. He does not even notice any argument to the contrary, much less show us where they go wrong.'

I agree with Robinson that, for the reason he gives, Plato's proof of Communion cannot be said to dispose satisfactorily of the paradoxical thesis (even though the second argument in the proof is valid against the thesis); for nothing is done to expose the error or confusion which led quite serious persons to embrace the paradox. Surely this passage (251d–252e) cannot be the whole of what Plato has to say in rebuttal of the late learners and their paradox. Surely he somewhere exposes the underlying error, the rotten foundations on which the paradox was built. And he does this, I suggest, for instance in the passage previously discussed, by clearly distinguishing two different uses of ἔστιν, as copula and as identity-sign, and by showing how the two uses are related.

Let us turn now to Cornford. He says that the copula 'has no place anywhere in Plato's scheme of the relations of Forms' (p. 279). The relation between Forms that combine—'blending'—is a symmetrical relation; so it cannot be the same as the relation of subject to predicate in an attributive statement, i.e. the relation indicated by the copula (pp. 256–7, 266).

First a very general point. The relation 'being connected with' or 'being associated with' is a symmetrical relation. But there are, of course, many different *ways* in which things or persons may be associated or connected; and many of these ways involve non-symmetrical relationships. One may say of a group of people, members of one family, that they are all connected. But if one wishes to say *how* they are connected each with the other, one must employ such expressions as 'father of', 'niece of', which do not stand for symmetrical relationships. Now it is agreed by Cornford that the philosopher's task, according to Plato, is to 'discern clearly the hierarchy of Forms . . . and make out its articulate structure' (pp. 263–4). Every statement the philosopher makes in performing this task may be expected to assert some connection or association between Forms. And 'association' is indeed a symmetrical relation. But surely the philosopher could not possibly achieve his purpose without specifying the *kind* of association there is in each case. And he could not do this without bringing in some non-symmetrical relations. Consider the following small extract from a possible 'map of the Forms':

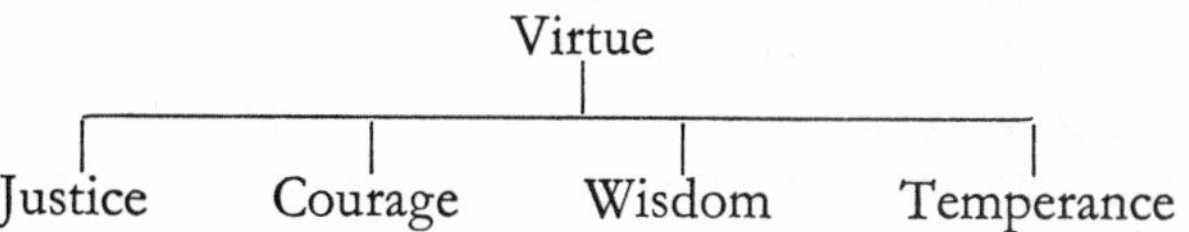

The structure exhibited here must be described by the philosopher; and to do this he *must* advert to a non-symmetrical relationship. In the above diagram the words 'Virtue' and 'Justice' are not merely close together; one is *under* the other. Similarly, Virtue and Justice are not merely connected; they are connected in a particular way: Justice is *a species* of Virtue.

Non-symmetrical relations must then be invoked if the complex structure of the 'world of Forms' is to be described; nor is this something Plato could easily have overlooked. Certainly the analogy he draws with letters and musical notes (253a–b) does not support the idea that the dialectician would, according to him, be satisfied with asserting *symmetrical* relations between εἴδη. If we are to say whether 'f' and 'g' fit together, with the aid of 'i', to make an English word we must obviously specify the *order* in which the letters are to be taken: 'gif' is not a word, 'fig' is. The scale of C major is not just such-and-such notes, but these notes in a certain order. Whatever terminology one uses to state the facts about spelling or scales or Forms, some non-symmetrical relation must come in. But if Cornford's view were right and every Philosopher's statement told of a symmetrical 'blending' of Forms, the philosopher would never be able to express irreducibly non-symmetrical truths, such as that Justice is a species of Virtue. So we may suspect that Cornford's view is not right.

To this it will be objected that the *Sophist*, though it implies that the philosopher will have to study relations between genera and species, does not itself explore such relations; so a proper interpretation of the *Sophist* should leave them aside and concentrate on how Plato proceeds in exhibiting the relations which he does in fact consider. Let us then look at some of the statements of Communion which Plato makes.

Firstly, 'Motion exists' (I retain Cornford's translation; 'Change' would be better). Cornford says (p. 256): ' "Motion exists" means that the Form Motion blends with the Form Existence'; and (p. 279): ' "Motion blends with Existence" is taken as equivalent to "Motion exists".' He also says (p. 278): 'The relation intended (*sc.* by "blending") is not the meaning of the "copula" . . .; for we can equally say "Existence blends with Motion".' Taken together these remarks lead to absurdity. For if 'Motion blends with Existence' means 'Motion exists', then 'Existence blends with Motion' must mean 'Existence moves'. And then, if 'Motion blends with Existence' is equivalent to 'Existence blends with Motion', 'Motion exists' must be equivalent to 'Existence moves'. Plato obviously did not intend this. The trouble lies in Cornford's insistence on the 'blending' metaphor, which suggests a symmetrical relation, to the exclusion of others which do not. What 'Motion exists' is equivalent to is not 'Motion blends with Existence' ('blending' being symmetrical), but 'Motion shares in, partakes of Existence' ('partaking of' being non-symmetrical). Cornford's remarks lead to absurdity because he will not let into his exposition any non-symmetrical expression like 'partakes of' (even though Plato's exposition bristles with this metaphor).

Secondly, 'Motion is different from Rest'. Now this is indeed equivalent to 'Rest is different from Motion'. But before drawing any inference concerning 'Communion' we must put the statement into its 'analysed' form, into dialectician's terminology. We get: 'Motion communicates with Difference from Rest'. The question is whether 'communicates with' in this formulation can be taken to stand for a symmetrical relation. But if it is so taken we must be prepared to say that 'Motion communicates with Difference from Rest' is equivalent to 'Difference from Rest communicates with Motion'; for the 'Communion' asserted in the first statement is evidently between Motion on the one hand and Difference from Rest on the other. But then, since 'Motion communicates with Difference from Rest' is the technical way of saying that Motion is different from Rest, we must suppose that 'Difference from Rest communicates with Motion' is the technical way of saying that Difference from Rest moves. So we shall find ourselves claiming that 'Motion is different from Rest' means the same as 'Difference from Rest moves'. As before, the absurdity results from taking 'communicates with' as standing for a symmetrical relation. If 'Motion communicates with Difference from Rest' means that Motion is different from Rest (as it clearly does), then 'communicates with' must here stand not for 'blending' but for a non-symmetrical relation ('partaking of', 'falling under').

These considerations, it may be said, are still very general and involve too much extrapolation and 'interpretation'. I am not sure how much weight to attach to this criticism. For one must suppose that Plato had something reasonable and consistent in his mind when writing the very taut piece of exposition in *Sophist* 251–9; and if Cornford's account leads, on reflection, to grave difficulties or absurdities this is a sound *prima facie* argument against it. (Even if in the end Cornford's account were to be accepted it would be desirable that the defects in Plato's discussion —as interpreted by Cornford—should be candidly exposed.) However, it is certainly necessary to turn to a closer examination of Plato's actual terminology.

Plato uses a great variety of terms in speaking of relations among εἴδη. While some of them (e.g. συμμείγνυσθαι) seem naturally to stand for the rather indeterminate symmetrical relation 'being connected with', there are others, like μετέχειν, which we expect to be standing for some more determinate, non-symmetrical relation. Cornford denies that this expectation is fulfilled and says that Plato does not distinguish 'partaking' from the mutual relation called 'blending' or 'combining' (pp. 296–7). He does not support this by a detailed study of all the relevant passages. His explicit argument that 'participation' as between Forms is a symmetrical relation (like 'blending'; hence nothing to do with the copula) rests on the one passage 255d, in which Existence is said to *partake of* both τὸ καθ' αὑτό and τὸ πρὸς ἄλλο. Cornford writes (p. 256): 'So the generic Form partakes of (blends with) the specific Form no less than the specific partakes of the generic.' And in his footnote on 255d 4 he says: 'Note that Existence, which *includes* both these Forms (*sc.* τὸ καθ' αὑτό and τὸ πρὸς ἄλλο), is said to *partake of* both. This is one of the places which show that "partaking" is symmetrical in the case of Forms.' I do not know which are the other places Cornford here alludes to; yet the reference to 255d is by itself a very inadequate justification of Cornford's sweeping remarks about 'participation', and of his insistence on symmetrical 'blending' as the one and only relation holding between Forms.

Professor Karl Dürr, in his paper *Moderne Darstellung der platonischen Logik*,[1] assigned precise and distinct meanings to various terms used by Plato in *Soph.*, 251–9, but did not attempt anything like a full justification. More useful for us is the following observation by Sir David Ross:[2] 'Plato uses κοινωνία, κοινωνεῖν, ἐπικοινωνεῖν, ἐπικοινωνία, προσκοινωνεῖν in two different constructions—with the genitive (250b 9, 252a 2, b 9, 254c 5, 256b 2, 260e 2) and with the dative (251d 9, e 8, 252d 3, 253a 8, 254b 8, c 1, 257a 9, 260e 5). In the former usage the verbs mean "share in"; in the latter they mean "combine with" or "communicate with".' I do not think Ross should have added that 'though Plato uses the two different constructions, he does not seem to attach any importance to the difference between them'. For Plato does not use the two constructions indiscriminately or interchangeably. A comparison between the two groups of passages yields a clear result (I leave out of account 250b 9 and 260e 2 and e 5, which are not in the main section on κοινωνία γενῶν). κοινωνεῖν followed by the genitive (e.g. θατέρου) is used where the fact being asserted is that some εἶδος is (copula) such-and-such (e.g. different from . . .);

[1] In *Museum Helveticum*, 1945, especially pp. 171–5.

[2] In *Plato's Theory of Ideas*, p. 111, n. 6.

that is, it is used to express the fact that one concept *falls under* another. The dative construction, on the other hand, occurs in highly general remarks about the connectedness of εἴδη, where no definite fact as to any particular pair of εἴδη is being stated. Surely this confirms—what ordinary Greek usage would suggest —that Plato consciously uses κοινωνεῖν in two different ways. Sometimes it stands for the general symmetrical notion of 'connectedness', sometimes it stands for a determinate non-symmetrical notion, 'sharing in'.

There are thirteen occurrences of the verb μετέχειν or noun μέθεξις in *Soph.*, 251–9. One of these is at 255d 4, in the passage used by Cornford in his argument quoted above. But in all the other twelve cases it is clear that the truth expressed by 'A-ness μετέχει B-ness' is that A-ness is (copula) B, and never that B-ness is (copula) A. For instance, τὸ ὂν μετέχει θατέρου . . . formulates the fact that Existence is different from . . .; it does not serve equally to express the fact that Difference exists,—that is expressed by τὸ ἕτερον μετέχει τοῦ ὄντος. The way Plato uses μετέχειν in all these cases makes it very hard to believe that he intended by it a symmetrical relation.

It is worth attending specially to the passage officially devoted to the statement of certain relations among the five chosen γένη, 255e 8–257a 11. Here the objective is to state definite truths in careful, philosophical terminology; not merely to allude to the fact that there are connections among γένη, but to say precisely what some of them are. Now in this passage Cornford's favourite metaphor occurs once (256b 9), in a purely general reference to the connectedness of concepts (εἴπερ τῶν γενῶν συγχωρησόμεθα τὰ μὲν ἀλλήλοις ἐθέλειν μείγνυσθαι, τὰ δὲ μή). And κοινωνία with the dative occurs once (257a 9), in an equally unspecific context (εἴπερ ἔχει κοινωνίαν ἀλλήλοις ἡ τῶν γενῶν φύσις). The other terms used are as follows. κοινωνία with the genitive occurs once (256b 2) and is used to state the definite relation holding between two named εἴδη (κίνησις and θάτερον); the fact stated is that Motion is different from . . ., not that Difference moves. μεταλαμβάνειν occurs once (256b 6) in a passage whose interpretation is controversial. But the significance of the verb is clear. If it were true to say κίνησις μεταλαμβάνει στάσεως then one could rightly say κίνησίς ἐστι στάσιμος. μετέχειν (or μέθεξις) occurs five times (256a 1, a 7, b 1, d 9, e 3), in each case expressing the relation between two named εἴδη the first of which falls under the second. Thus all the real work of the section 255e 8–257a 11, all the exposition of actual connections between particular εἴδη, is done by the terms μετέχειν, μεταλαμβάνειν, and κοινωνεῖν (with genitive), that is, by the non-symmetrical metaphor 'partaking of' which Cornford is so determined to exclude. And the rôle of 'partakes of' in Plato's terminology is clear: 'partakes of' followed by an abstract noun, the name of a concept, is equivalent to the ordinary language expression consisting of 'is' (copula) followed by the adjective corresponding to that abstract noun.

This examination of Plato's use of some terms, though far from exhaustive, is, I think, sufficient to discredit Cornford's claim that the 'blending' metaphor is the one safe clue to Plato's meaning, and to establish that μετέχειν and its variants, μεταλαμβάνειν and κοινωνεῖν (with genitive), are not used by Plato as mere alternatives for μείγνυσθαι. It may be admitted that in 255d, the passage Cornford exploits, μετέχειν is used in an exceptional way; but one passage cannot be allowed to outweigh a dozen others.[1]

To sum up: I have tried to argue firstly, that the verb μετέχειν, with its variants, has a rôle in Plato's philosophical language corresponding to the rôle of the copula in ordinary language; and secondly, that by his analysis of various statements Plato brings out—and means to bring out—the difference between the copula (μετέχει . . .), the identity-sign (μετέχει ταὐτοῦ . . .) and the existential ἔστιν (μετέχει τοῦ ὄντος).

[1] This is rather a cavalier dismissal of the passage on which Cornford relies so heavily. But it is not possible in the space available to attempt a full study of the perplexing argument of 255c 12–e 1, and without such a study no statement as to the exact force of μετέχειν in 255c 4 is worth much. My own conviction is that even in this passage μετέχειν does not stand for the symmetrical relation 'blending'; but it is certainly not used in quite the same way as in the other places where it occurs in 251–9.

XI

PLATO'S DESCRIPTION OF DIVISION

(1954)

A. C. Lloyd

THERE are many passages in Plato which look as if they alluded to well-worn practices, discussions, or lessons in the Academy. As is natural with allusions, they are often marked by a puzzling brevity or oddity of expression. One need not assume that they are always conscious allusions; for every writer has moments of obscurity which are due not so much to his conclusions as to his reaching them along lines that have been familiar to *him*. To appreciate his whole meaning the reader has then to infer as best he can the writer's train of thought. I wish to suggest that the language in which Dialectic is described in the later Dialogues presupposes a particular and probably familiar method of illustrating it. This was a geometrical illustration of the rules of Division by means of a divided line. By failing to notice it readers have not been led into any important misunderstanding of the Academy's rules. But I hope it will appear that the recognition of it makes Plato's manner of describing Division intelligible to an extent that is otherwise difficult. It is only a tentative suggestion, and would perhaps not have been worth making but for the possibility that some points of interest might at the same time emerge for those who were unconvinced by it.

So much only is the direct intention of this article. But if the suggestion is correct, it has also in my view an indirect importance. For Plato was fascinated by the mathematical puzzles of infinite divisibility. And by the time he wrote the *Parmenides* he considered (I believe) that Zeno's paradoxes indicated a solution of his own paradoxes about the One and the Many. I do not want to defend this suggestion here: but its upshot may be put very roughly and dogmatically in the following equations. The Many = the Indeterminate = the *infinite*, i.e. indefinite, number of parts of a whole. The 'Ones' or species = the *finite* or determinate number of parts into which a whole or genus must be divisible if it is to be an actual whole. For in mathematics magnitudes are infinitely divisible:[1] but such magnitudes are only abstractions; and in reality there are always indivisible parts. And just as mathematical objects are images of the real, so the infinite Many are only appearances (due to inadequate division) of the One. Both horns of Zeno's dilemma are grasped:[2] one accounts for the intelligible, the other for the sensible. Being is shot through with Not-being (or Otherness or Matter): but the first forms a plurality, the second an infinity.[3] Dialectic meant always the discovery of the One in the Many, and in the later Dialogues this consisted of Collection and Division.

In my opinion, then, the illustration of Dialectic by the division of a line into parts would be a natural result of Plato's great imaginative feat—his theory that there was (as we should say now) identity of logical structure between Zeno's continuous magnitude and the world itself as an object of experience and knowledge. And the choice of illustration would help to confirm the interpretation of his metaphysics. It was probably used in the Academy for refuting Zeno. But let me repeat that to show this is only an indirect or secondary purpose here. For the recognition of the illustration does not depend on accepting the metaphysical interpretation. It depends only on an examination of Plato's expressions. And to this I now proceed.

After the *Phaedrus* the chief passages in which the theory of Dialectic is expounded are two. The most generalised account

[1] This is not to be contradicted by Aristotle's statement (*Met.*, 992a 22; cf. 1084b 1–2) that Plato believed in indivisible lines. For there is more than one sort of mathematics according to Plato. *Parm.*, 164c–165d, where magnitudes are infinitely divisible, applies to 'popular' as opposed to 'philosophical' mathematics (v. *Phil.*, 56d–e; *Rep.*, 525d–526a). I hope to offer an explanation of this on another occasion.

[2] Cf. *Parm.*, 142c 7–145a 2.

[3] *Soph.*, 255e, 256e–257a.

is in *Phil.*, 16d ff. It can be divided for convenience as follows:

> *δεῖν οὖν ἡμᾶς τούτων οὕτω διακεκοσμημένων (1) ἀεὶ μίαν ἰδέαν περὶ παντὸς ἑκάστοτε θεμένους ζητεῖν—εὑρήσειν γὰρ ἐνοῦσαν—(2) ἐὰν οὖν μεταλάβωμεν, μετὰ μίαν δύο, εἴ πως εἰσί, σκοπεῖν, εἰ δὲ μή, τρεῖς ἤ τινα ἄλλον ἀριθμόν, (3) καὶ τῶν ἓν ἐκείνων ἕκαστον πάλιν ὡσαύτως, (4) μέχριπερ ἂν τὸ κατ' ἀρχὰς ἓν μὴ ὅτι ἓν καὶ πολλὰ καὶ ἄπειρά ἐστι μόνον ἴδῃ τις, ἀλλὰ καὶ ὁπόσα· τὴν δὲ τοῦ ἀπείρου ἰδέαν πρὸς τὸ πλῆθος μὴ προσφέρειν πρὶν ἄν τις τὸν ἀριθμὸν αὐτοῦ πάντα κατίδῃ τὸν μεταξὺ τοῦ ἀπείρου τε καὶ τοῦ ἑνός, (5) τότε δ' ἤδη τὸ ἓν ἕκαστον τῶν πάντων εἰς τὸ ἄπειρον μεθέντα χαίρειν ἐᾶν. (6) οἱ μὲν οὖν θεοί, ὅπερ εἶπον, οὕτως ἡμῖν παρέδοσαν σκοπεῖν καὶ μανθάνειν καὶ διδάσκειν ἀλλήλους· οἱ δὲ νῦν τῶν ἀνθρώπων σοφοὶ ἓν μέν, ὅπως ἂν τύχωσι, καὶ πολλὰ θᾶττον καὶ βραδύτερον ποιοῦσι τοῦ δέοντος, μετὰ δὲ τὸ ἓν ἄπειρα εὐθύς, τὰ δὲ μέσα αὐτοὺς ἐκφεύγει . . . .*

We are to imagine, as it might be drawn or composed of pebbles on the ground, a line *AB* of unknown length. This is *τὸ ἄπειρον*, though not because it is infinitely divisible but because it is not known of how many divisions it is capable.

(1) We place provisionally[1] between *A* and *B* a point *C*, thereby 'finding' in *AB* a line *CB* (the *μίαν ἰδέαν*). (2) *CB* is divided at *D*, giving us *CD* and *DB* (*μετὰ μίαν δύο*). (3) *CD* and *DB* are similarly divided at *E* and *F* respectively.

A *C* *E* *D* *F* *B*

(4) The divisions of *CE*, *ED*, *DF*, *FB* are continued as far as necessary, i.e. until it is seen how many indivisible lines there are in *CB* (*τὸ κατ' ἀρχὰς ἕν*, the generic Idea). (This is not of course derivable from the diagram; in Dialectic it involves Collection. We shall suppose the process already completed.) This is equivalent to refraining from considering *CB* (*τὸ πλῆθος*) as infinitely divisible (*τὴν τοῦ ἀπείρου ἰδέαν προσφέρειν*) before the exact

[1] *θεμένους* refers not merely to the diagram but to the fact that in Dialectic all Ideas start as hypotheses. For, incidentally, Plato never said there is an Idea corresponding to every general name, although this is now attributed to him by writer after writer. *Rep.*, 596a says *εἰώθαμεν τίθεσθαι*, 507b *τιθέντες*. Cf. *Phdr.*, 237d 1 (*ὁμολογίᾳ θέμενοι ὅρον*) for connection with Socratic method.

number of its components is known.[1] πλῆθος is a word which Plato uses when he means it to be undetermined whether a magnitude is ἄπειρον or πεπερασμένον (cf. 18 b2). The number of lines, viz. *CD*, (*DB*), *CE*, *ED*, *DF*, will be seen to be between (μεταξύ) *AC*, which is the remaining still divisible part (τοῦ ἀπείρου) of the original line, and the last indivisible line, *FB* (τοῦ ἑνός). The objection to this is that τοῦ ἑνός has a different denotation both from that of κατ' ἀρχὰς ἕν and from τὸ ἕν in (6), which, we shall see shortly, cannot be the lowest species. One may reply (*a*) that if Plato visualised a diagram the difficulty would not occur, since the 'one' in question could be pointed to; and (*b*) that (6) is a new sentence in which the thought makes it quite natural to return to the original 'one'. (There is, however, an alternative, which strains the expression a little, but which would avoid the difficulty: the intermediate lines could be conceived metaphorically as 'standing between' *CB as a unit* and the indefinite divisibility of *AB*; for Plato is thinking as much of the understanding of the genus [*CB*] as of the lowest species [*FB*].)

(5) The lines *CD*, *CE*, *ED*, *DF* are then ignored—or, what comes to the same thing, we attend only to *CB*, *DB*, *FB*.

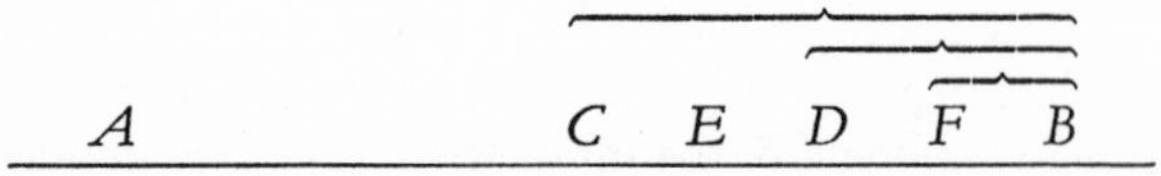

A *C* *E* *D* *F* *B*

CF becomes again indefinitely divisible and we lose *CD*, *CE*, *ED*, *DF*. Two things are to be noticed in this. First, we are now left, as can be seen from the diagram below, with the lowest differentia, the superordinate species and the genus; and this gives us a definition of the lowest species according to the Academy's rules. Secondly, this definition, which amounts to ignoring the left-hand side of a division, amounts also to 'dismissing it into the ἄπειρον'; for the left-hand side contains those things which the contents of the right-hand side (the defining characteristics) *are not* or *are other than*;[2] and the former, the 'others', are, in respect of the otherness, ἄπειρα.[3]

[1] For the use of 'number' where we should say 'number of parts' see *Tht.*, 204d. But it has also an esoteric meaning, as is mentioned below.

[2] *Soph.*, 255 ff.

[3] Ibid., 256e: περὶ ἕκαστον ἄρα τῶν εἰδῶν πολὺ μέν ἐστι τὸ ὄν, ἄπειρον δὲ πλήθει τὸ μὴ ὄν . . . καὶ τὸ ὂν αὐτὸ τῶν ἄλλων ἕτερον εἶναι λεκτέον . . . καὶ τὸ ὂν ἄρ' ἡμῖν, ὅσαπέρ ἐστι τὰ ἄλλα, κατὰ τοσαῦτα οὐκ ἔστιν· ἐκεῖνα γὰρ οὐκ ὂν ἓν μὲν αὐτό

(6) Plato goes on to say that people erroneously reach the limit of division too quickly, i.e. do not put enough points between *C* and *B*, or too slowly, i.e. put too many. In the first case they might, for example, omit *DB* by dividing *CB* only at *F*. (Thinking of Dialectic *only* as definition of the ἄτμητον and of ἄπειρα *only* as individuals, editors have often taken the ἕν in (6) to be the lowest species.[1] But (*a*) μέσα would naturally mean between the ἕν and the ἄπειρα, while if the former is the lowest species there are no such μέσα; (*b*)—more conclusively—it is *not* 'eristic' but correct 'dialectic' to apply the notion of ἀπειρία after the lowest species has been reached. τὸ ἕν is therefore the genus, *CB*.) Such division would be equivalent to 'bad' definition—in Aristotle's example, to defining Man as Two-footed Animal instead of Two-footed Footed Animal as Plato required.[2] This is at once seen if the scheme is represented thus:

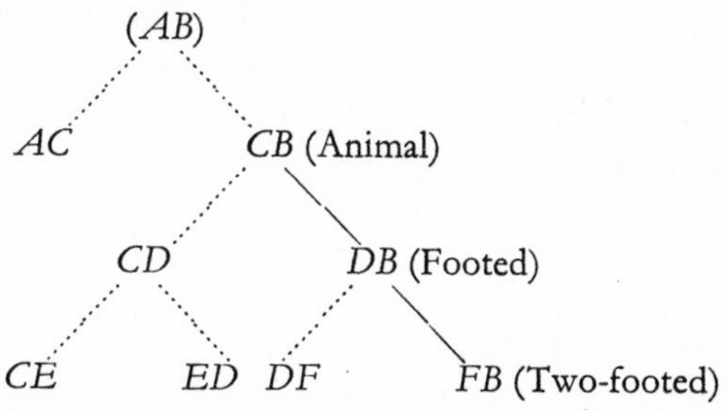

[1] For the error of this view cf. 18c 7–d 1. It is the same reason which has led to suspicion of the text—both καὶ πολλά and βραδύτερον. The latter was thought inconsistent with ἄπειρα εὐθύς. But to suppose too many species is similar to supposing too few: a wrongly supposed species (a μέρος instead of an εἶδος, *Pol.*, 263) is no species at all and therefore ἄπειρον—συναγωγή has simply not taken place. Failure to emphasise this point makes Professor Hackforth's note (*Class. Quart.* xxxiii (1939), 23–4) on this sentence a little unsatisfactory; especially so since his notes (*Plato's Examination of Pleasure*, 23–4) on our (4) and (5) do make the point.

[2] Ar. *Met.*, 1038a 9–25; *De part. an.*, 642b 5–9.

ἐστιν, ἀπέραντα δὲ τὸν ἀριθμὸν τἆλλα οὐκ ἔστιν αὖ. *Parm.*, 158c: οὐκοῦν οὕτως ἀεὶ σκοποῦντες αὐτὴν καθ' αὑτὴν τὴν ἑτέραν φύσιν τοῦ εἴδους ὅσον ἂν αὐτῆς ἀεὶ ὁρῶμεν ἄπειρον ἔσται πλήθει; 159d: οὐδ' ἄρα πολλά ἐστι τἆλλα· ἓν γὰρ ἂν ἦν ἕκαστον αὐτῶν μόριον τοῦ ὅλου, εἰ πολλὰ ἦν· νῦν δὲ οὔτε ἓν οὔτε πολλὰ οὔτε ὅλον οὔτε μόριά ἐστι τἆλλα τοῦ ἑνός, ἐπειδὴ αὐτοῦ οὐδαμῇ μετέχει. Philop., *in Ar. Phys.*, ed. Vitelli, 80. 29 [Lee, *Zeno of Elea*, fr. 3]: εἰ μὴ τὸ ἓν εἴη, φησί [sc. ὁ Ζήνων], καὶ ἀδιαίρετον, οὐδὲ πολλὰ ἔσται· τὰ γὰρ πολλὰ ἐκ πολλῶν ἑνάδων.

This is the more familiar representation, and no doubt it is the one that Plato generally had in mind when he was making applications of *διαίρεσις*. But when he is more concerned with theory—and with the structure of reality as revealed by Division, rather than our piecemeal discovery of it—his language is that of the *Parmenides*; and since the language there is appropriate to the division of lines it is natural to expect it to be so here. Moreover it was from this geometrical point of view that mutual implications were first seen among the concepts of irrationality, indefinability, and infinite divisibility.[1] And the last forms the limiting case of the second possible error, the error of completing the division too slowly. It is what is only prevented from happening, according to Plato, by the fact that if we collected merely particulars even these would have a share in Ideas.[2] So Plato refers to the danger on this side—represented by Protagoras' sensationalism—by describing his opponents as 'crumbling' reality into fragments (*θρύπτειν*).[3] The Eleatics represented the extreme case of the alternative error, for they allowed only a single 'One' to be discovered. The *via media*, advocated by Plato, is that reality is, rather, 'chopped up' (*κεκερματισμένον, κατακεκερματισμένον*).[4] So that he exactly describes the attempt to treat changing particulars as reality by saying, *θρύπτεσθαι δὴ οἶμαι κερματιζόμενον ἀνάγκη πᾶν τὸ ὄν, ὃ ἄν τις λάβῃ τῇ διανοίᾳ* (*Parmenides*, 165b 4–6).

There is one point which presents some difficulty if we do not recognise the suggested illustration. I hope, however, that a discussion may be helpful also to those who do not accept my 'divided line'. In (5) *τὸ ἓν ἕκαστον τῶν πάντων* must refer to all the unities, i.e. Ideas, which have emerged by Collection and Division.

[1] *ὅπου γὰρ ἐπ' ἄπειρον ἡ διαίρεσις, ἐκεῖ καὶ τὸ ἄλογον* (Procl. *in I Eucl.*, ed. Friedlein, p. 60, 15).

[2] For this lesson in the *Parmenides* cf. 158b 2–d 8; 164c 7–d 8; 165a 5–c 3.

[3] Cf. *Soph.*, 246b 9–c 1: the Idealists repudiate the 'reality' of the materialists, *τὰ ἐκείνων σώματα καὶ τὴν λεγομένην ὑπ' αὐτῶν ἀλήθειαν κατὰ σμικρὰ διαθραύοντες ἐν τοῖς λόγοις*.

[4] Ibid. 258d: *ἡμεῖς δέ γε οὐ μόνον τὸ μὴ ὄντα ὡς ἔστιν ἀπεδείξαμεν, ἀλλὰ καὶ τὸ εἶδος ὃ τυγχάνει ὂν τοῦ μὴ ὄντος ἀπεφηνάμεθα· τὴν γὰρ θατέρου φύσιν ἀποδείξαντες οὖσάν τε καὶ κατακεκερματισμένην ἐπὶ πάντα τὰ ὄντα πρὸς ἄλληλα . . .* (cf. 257c 7). It is in respect of its having Being that Not-being is 'chopped up'. The metaphor is, of course, explained by its being used for the division of a genus into species (*Men.*, 79a 10; c 2; *Pol.*, 266a 2).

For to take them as individuals[1] is surely inadmissible when ἕν is just what is being distinguished from ἄπειρον, and when τῶν ἓν ἐκείνων ἕκαστον had denoted species in the previous sentence. Now we are told to dismiss them into the ἄπειρον. But why? All we should be left with is a genus and the arithmetical number (say 4 or 6 or 8) of its species. And if it is important to know *how many* species there are, this can surely only be because we cannot do this without knowing *what* they are. In what circumstances ought we then to forget this latter knowledge? The purpose of Division here may be one or more of the following possibilities: (*a*) to define or understand a genus; (*b*) to define a lowest species; (*c*) to show how a genus (or any divisible Idea) is both a Many and a One; (*d*) as part of an argument (e.g. to refute the thesis, 'Government is necessary, Athenian democracy is government, therefore Athenian democracy is necessary').

But as for (*a*) we do not define or understand a genus by saying that it has *m* species, where *m* is a mere number. In (*b*) to omit the superordinate species from the definition of a lowest species is un-Platonic, as we have seen; and secondly, it is not obvious—except on my (first) interpretation of (4)—that we shall have been left with even a lowest species. (*c*) at least must be admitted here, because Plato explicitly says so (16a–c). He is, for the purpose of this dialogue, fitting his Dialectic into the Pythagorean formula in which τὸ ἕν is the first product of πέρας and ἄπειρον, and in which reality is generated by the imposition of Number or τὸ πόσον on the ἄπειρον. So once the species have been enumerated the genus has been shown to be a Many, and we can return to its unity. And it is to be added that the dismissal of the Many into the ἄπειρον will show how the One and Many together are *also* ἄπειρα—as we were told in (4)—not simply in respect of the lowest species, but all of them.[2] This Pythagorean framework would

[1] As does Stenzel, *Studien zur. Entwicklung, der platonischen Dialektik*[2] (Leipzig–Berlin, 1931), 104, at least in Allan's interpretation ([Stenzel] *Plato's Method of Dialectic*, tr. D. J. Allan (Oxford, 1940) 146). Mr. Allan, who has very kindly read my manuscript, suggests that Stenzel 'could say that ἕν, which has just been used in the dialectician's sense, (4), is then used as a man in the state of πίστις would use it, (5), i.e. "those alleged unities" '. But how many readers would grasp this from Plato's text?

[2] Cf. L. Robin, *Platon: œuvres complètes*, ii (1942), 184 n. 20: 'une fois qu'on est arrivé à l'espèce dernière . . . l'impossibilité de "spécifier" davantage nous met en présence, et de l'individu, avec la multiplicité de ses caractères

explain the emphasis on the mere number of species, for 'the' number has then an esoteric meaning (cf. especially 17c 11–e 6).[1] (*d*) is an aspect to which Hackforth has drawn attention. It too might explain the 'dismissal'. For in our example it is sufficient to know that democracy is a species of government; and if one asks, 'Why the emphasis on the *number* of species?' it could be replied that until the whole division is completed it is impossible to know that any single division was a 'real' one and therefore to be admitted in a genuine, instead of an eristic, argument.[2]

(*d*) is not so important, I think, as (*c*). Nevertheless all four purposes are present to Plato's mind. For it is notable that when he goes on to illustrate the method there is no hint of the 'dismissal'.[3] With the possible exception of the continuation (18b 6 ff.) of the first one, it seems essential in the illustrations to know not only how many the species are, but what they are. The improbability of both (*c*) and (*d*) as explanations could be supported by *Pol.*, 285a–b, where knowledge of all the species was necessary to an understanding both of the lowest species and of the genus. Still more could it be supported by the next page (286c–287a). For there, in an apology for the length of preliminary discussions, μακρολογία and βραχυλογία were also required to be tested against the rules of Division (πρῶτον τὴν μέθοδον αὐτὴν τιμᾶν τοῦ κατ' εἴδη δυνατὸν εἶναι διαιρεῖν). But this criterion was, in fact, the correctness of the definition of the lowest species, viz. the 'royal art'. Indeed when a concrete application of the rules was made (287b ff.), a number of species *were* 'dismissed', namely those on the left-hand side of the division. And these were just the ones which would have been dismissed in our suggested interpretation

[1] Cf. J. Stenzel, *Zahl u. Gestalt* (1924), 7, 13–18; A. Preiswerk, 'Das Einzelne b. Platon und Aristoteles', *Philologus*, suppl.-Bd. xxxii, Heft 1 (1939), 55–6.

[2] Cf. οἱ νῦν τῶν ἀνθρώπων σοφοί of (6) with the νέος of 15d–e, who 'at one moment kneads any argument into one ball, then unrolls it again and chops it into pieces'. Compare also *Phdr.*, 237d.

[3] Nor elsewhere. (*Pol.*, 286e 6, despite Campbell's note, has nothing to do with the present point.)

singuliers, et du nombre infini d'individus auxquels s'étend la notion de l'espèce dernière, avec tout ce qu elle implique et qui constitue la chaîne des intermédiaires.' But his *translation* 'c'est alors que désormais on doit abandonner l'infini et lui dire adieu', is inexplicable.

of the *Philebus* passage, but not on the normal interpretation. The trouble is, in fact, that (*a*) and (*b*) as explanations are incompatible with (*c*) and (*d*). However, this need not rule out the normal interpretation. For one may concentrate on (*c*) and possibly (*d*), and say that both Socrates' examples and the *Politicus* illustrate a use of Division beyond that for which it is introduced in the *Philebus*. This further use would be its more common one in the sciences, and one which had already been alluded to by Socrates in 16c 1–3. An alternative, which I should prefer, is to claim that Plato is trying to combine (*a*), (*b*), (*c*), and (*d*). For he has a habit of combining two levels of thought—of teaching an immediately relevant lesson in method at the same time as an indirect lesson in metaphysics. And it is a habit which is at once idiosyncratic and rather vulnerable to strict logic. To conclude, then, the 'dismissal into the ἄπειρον' is readily intelligible for any of the purposes of Division that may be intended, if the 'divided line' is agreed to illustrate it: but it does not contain sufficient difficulty to make it positive evidence for the illustration.

The second passage which describes the method of Dialectic is in *Sophist* 253d:

> *τὸ κατὰ γένη διαιρεῖσθαι καὶ μήτε ταὐτὸν εἶδος ἕτερον ἡγήσασθαι μήτε ἕτερον ὂν ταὐτὸν μῶν οὐ τῆς διαλεκτικῆς φήσομεν ἐπιστήμης εἶναι; . . . οὐκοῦν ὅ γε τοῦτο δυνατὸς δρᾶν* (1) *μίαν ἰδέαν διὰ πολλῶν, ἑνὸς ἑκάστου κειμένου χωρίς, πάντῃ διατεταμένην ἱκανῶς διαισθάνεται, καὶ πολλὰς ἑτέρας ἀλλήλων ὑπὸ μιᾶς ἔξωθεν περιεχομένας,* (2) *καὶ μίαν αὖ δι' ὅλων πολλῶν ἐν ἑνὶ συνημμένην, καὶ πολλὰς χωρὶς πάντῃ διωρισμένας.*

Especially since Stenzel's work[1] it has been widely agreed that the passage refers to the method of Division. To suppose it merely describes four different kinds of relation between Ideas, two of Communion and two of non-Communion is not at all satisfactory; for instance ἐν ἑνὶ συνημμένην is taken[2] to mean 'remaining on its own' or 'self-sufficient', which does not seem to do justice to the Greek. It is much easier to follow if we think of the same illustration of the divided line—though, once again, only as influencing the

[1] *Studien*, 62–71 [tr. Allan, 96–106].

[2] E.g. recently by B. Liebrucks, *Platons Entwicklung zur Dialektik* (Frankfurt-a.-M., 1949), 148.

expression: it is not necessary to it, and if Plato had thought it necessary he would have made it explicit. But this second passage is closer, of course, chronologically, to the *Parmenides*.

μία ἰδέα (our *CB*) is drawn or stretched across the whole of the shorter lines (πάντῃ διατεταμένην);[1] they are contained by it (ἔξωθεν περιεχομένας), but are still units (χωρὶς διωρισμένας). περιέχειν is the technical term for the relation of a magnitude to its parts,[2] and is contrasted in *Parmenides*, 150 a with δι' ὅλον τεταμένην εἶναι, which is coextensiveness.[3] ἔξωθεν alludes to the paradox of the whole–part relation disclosed by Zeno (v. *Parm.*, 145b–e, and 149d 8 ff., specially 150e 5–151a) and well known in the Academy (v. Ar. *Top.*, vi. xiii; cf. *Phys.*, 210a 16–17).[4] In (2) it is possible that μίαν denotes the generic Idea as it did in (1), and ἑνί the lowest species. But it is preferable to take them the other way about. The emphasis of the first half will then be upon Collection, the emphasis of the second (marked by αὖ) upon Division, and the two will form respective explanations of μήτε ταὐτὸν εἶδος ἕτερον ἡγήσασθαι μήτε ἕτερον ὂν ταὐτόν. ἐν ἑνὶ συνημμένη is a variation from ὑπὸ μιᾶς ἰδέας περιεχομένη and represents the passive of συλλαβών as it was used at 250b 9. . . . But the terms he is employing belong so much to the logic of geometry that the Stranger finds it necessary to explain that all this is the same thing as what the others will already have understood by 'Dialectic'![5]

[1] The collection of parts is mentioned before the Division. Mr. Allan therefore suggests that, if a line is intended, a *discontinuous* one would be more comprehensible:

A *B*

——— . . . ——— . . . ——— . . . ———

'For here some αἴσθησις *is* required to see that μία ἰδέα stretches through from beginning to end.'

[2] Cf. *Parm.*, 145b 8.

[3] This is not to reject C. Ritter's contention (*Neue Untersuchungen über Platon* (1910), 57 ff.) that διατέτασθαι refers to the μέγιστα γένη, like Otherness which is διὰ πάντων διεληλυθυῖαν, and περιέχεσθαι to the species of ordinary genera—though 250b 8 is against it.

[4] Plato's final interest, even in the *Parm.* passages, is not (*pace* Cornford, *Plato and Parmenides*, 179 ff.) in infinite divisibility, but in a whole, i.e. genus, which is, and yet is more than, its parts. Cf. *Tht.*, 201e–205e with Ar. *Met.*, 1041b 9–33 and the neglected passage, *Hipp. Maj.*, 300–2, which looks to me like a set piece of the Academy's Ideal theory.

[5] τοῦτο δ' ἔστιν, ᾗ τε κοινωνεῖν ἕκαστα δύναται, καὶ ὅπῃ μή, διακρίνειν κατὰ γένος ἐπίστασθαι.

There is one other passage to be discussed; for unlike the previous two it does, I believe, provide some *positive* evidence for our suggested illustration. The *Politicus* has a puzzling remark in repeating the rule that dichotomy is to be preferred but, failing that, division into three or more parts:

> κατὰ μέλη τοίνυν αὐτὰς οἷον ἱερεῖον διαιρώμεθα, ἐπειδὴ δίχα ἀδυνατοῦμεν. δεῖ γὰρ εἰς τὸν ἐγγύτατα ὅτι μάλιστα τέμνειν ἀριθμὸν ἀεί (287c).

The usual view of the second sentence is stated by Diès:[1] 'pour la division dans le nombre le plus proche, [cf.] *Philèbe* 16d: μετὰ μίαν (ἰδέαν) δύο, εἴ πως εἰσί, σκοπεῖν, εἰ δὲ μή, τρεῖς ἤ τινα ἄλλον ἀριθμόν. Principe d'économie, âme de toute méthode.' But the *Philebus* passage did not *say* that we should try the lower number first. For the μετὰ μίαν δύο had nothing to do with alternatives. True, Plato regards dichotomy as preferable. But this appears to be for no better reason than the attractiveness of τὸ μέσον.[2] And once the division of mankind by races into *two* parts, like Greeks and Barbarians, is seen to be merely nominal (*Pol.*, 262d–e), it is unlikely to be an economical method to proceed by trying three.

At the same time 'the nearest number' must denote the next number, sc. in the number-series. (It cannot, for example, mean 'nearest to reality', nor, of course, 'the nearest number' in the English sense of nearest the right one.) I suggest that the expression contains a reference to the position of divisions in the line. Thus if *DB* had been divided at *F* and *G* instead of *F* alone, it would not have been divided at the nearest point *to ED* (the last line).

E *D* *F* *B*   *E* *D* *G* *F* *B*

In other words *FB* (the last *definiendum*) should be pushed nearer to *ED*. The result is the same as if Plato had said 'the lowest number'; but the lack of justification for the principle would have been glaring had he been thinking simply of what we call numbers. Pythagorean mathematics would not distinguish, in the absolute

[1] Budé edition, ad loc.

[2] *Pol.*, 262b 6–7; 265a 4. The reason is *not* that which a nominalist logic would give, viz. the exhaustiveness of a class-concept and its contradictory (although this doubtless influenced him in practice, especially in the *Sophist*), for a negative class is likely to be ἄπειρον (cf. *Pol.*, 262d); cf. Ar. *Met.*, 990b 13 and Ross ad loc. (Platonists' denial of Ideas of negations).

way in which ours would, lengths from numbers—which had extension. And I suspect that Plato was thinking too of what would have been at least an exact analogy (and for him perhaps more than an analogy) of this process of Division, namely the generation of numbers by the 'drawing in' of *τὸ ἔγγιστα τοῦ ἀπεί-ρου*.[1]

[1] Ar. *Phys.* 213b 22; *Met.*, 1091a 17; fr. 201 (Rose).

XII

THE THIRD MAN ARGUMENT IN THE *PARMENIDES*[1]

(1954)

Gregory Vlastos

HARDLY a text in Plato has been discussed as much in the last forty years[2] as the two passages in the *Parmenides* purporting to prove that the Theory of Forms involves an infinite regress, which came to be dubbed within Plato's lifetime the 'Third Man' Argument. A flood of light has been thrown both on the meaning

[1] Re-reading this paper in the light of criticisms I have seen in print or heard in discussion, I still find all of its main contentions sound. But were I writing today I would have expressed myself differently on some points. For some improvements in the analysis of Plato's argument I refer the reader to the one offered below in the Addendum; and for degrees of reality in Plato, to an essay I am contributing to a symposium on Greek philosophy edited by Mr. Renford Bambrough (London: Routledge, 1965).

[2] I list the major contributions:

A. E. Taylor, 'Parmenides, Zeno, and Socrates', in *Phil. Studies* (London, 1934); reprinted from *Proceedings of the Aristotelian Society*, XVI (1915–16).

F. Goblot, 'Le Troisième Homme chez Platon', *Revue d'Histoire de la Philosophie*, III (1929), 473 ff.

W. F. R. Hardie, *A Study in Plato* (Oxford, 1936), pp. 88 ff.

F. M. Cornford, *Plato and Parmenides* (London, 1939), pp. 87–95.

G. Ryle, 'Plato's Parmenides', *Mind*, n.s., XLVIII (1939), 129 ff. (especially pp. 136–40). See above, Ch. VI.

R. Robinson, 'Plato's Parmenides', *Class. Philol.*, XXXVII (1942), 51 ff.

H. Cherniss, *Aristotle's Criticism of Plato and the Academy*, I (Baltimore, 1944), *passim*, but especially pp. 231 ff., 284 ff., 375, and 500 ff.

D. Ross, *Plato's Theory of Ideas* (Oxford, 1951), pp. 86 ff.

G. E. L. Owen, 'The Place of the *Timaeus* in Plato's Dialogues', *Class. Quart.*, n.s., III (1953), 79 ff. See below, Ch. XVI.

To works in this list I shall refer hereafter merely by the author's name.

of the text and on its philosophical implications. Yet in spite of this, disagreement continues. Is the Third Man Argument a valid objection to the Theory of Forms? Did Plato believe that it was valid? One can find acute and learned critics on both sides of both of these basic questions. I write as the beneficiary of their controversies, but not in a controversial spirit. If any progress in agreement is to be made at this juncture it must come from some advance in understanding of the logical structure of the Argument. To this end I shall pursue its analysis further than I think anyone has yet found it profitable to push it. This will be the task of Section I. I shall then consider in Section II what this may teach us about the Theory of Forms and also about the state of mind in which Plato held this theory when he turned against it that battery of objections of which the Third Man Argument is the most interesting and the most instructive.

I. ANALYSIS OF THE ARGUMENT

A. *The First Version, Parmenides* 132a 1–b 2

'I suppose this is what leads you to suppose that there is in every case a single Form: When several things seem large to you, it seems perhaps that there is a single Form which is the same in your view of all of them. Hence you believe that Largeness is a single thing.'[1]

This is the first step of the Argument, and may be generalised as follows:

> (A1) If a number of things, *a*, *b*, *c*, are[2] all *F*, there must be a single Form *F*-ness, in virtue of which we apprehend *a*, *b*, *c*, as all *F*.[3]

Here '*F*' stands for any discernible character or property. The use of the same symbol, '*F*', in '*F*-ness', the symbolic representa-

[1] For this and subsequent translations I have consulted Cornford and A. E. Taylor, *Plato's Parmenides* (Oxford, 1934), and mainly followed Cornford. My main concern has been to translate as literally as possible.

[2] I say 'are', where Plato's text above says only 'seem'. But the difference is immaterial to the argument. A few lines later Plato speaks of the large things as 'participating' in Largeness (132a 11), which is his way of saying that they are large (so far as particulars *are* anything at all) and do not merely appear such. Cf. also *Parm.*, 130e 5–131a 2.

[3] In the last clause I merely make explicit an assumption which is implicit throughout the argument and is stated in the second step, 132a 7–8.

tion of the 'single Form',[1] records the identity of the character discerned in the particular ('large') and conceived in the Form ('Largeness') through which we see that this, or any other, particular has this character. On the substantive meaning of the various terms in Plato's statement and in my transcript of it, I have nothing to say just now. Plato's argument professes to be a deductive argument and I propose to treat it as a formal structure of inference from premisses, stated or implied. For this reason, I raise no questions about the Theory of Forms and presume no more information about it than I can extract from the text before me. And what is supplied in its first step is, I trust, fully contained in (A1).

'What then if you similarly view mentally Largeness itself and the other large things? Will not a single Largeness appear once again, in virtue of which all these (*sc.* Largeness and the other large things) appear large?—It seems so.—Consequently another Form of Largeness will appear over and above Largeness itself and the things which participate in it.'

This is the second step:

> (A2) If *a*, *b*, *c*, and *F*-ness are all *F*, there must be another Form, *F*-ness$_1$, in virtue of which we apprehend *a*, *b*, *c*, and *F*-ness as all *F*.

Now merely to compare (A2) with (A1) above is to see a discrepancy in the reasoning which, so far as I know, has never been noticed before, though it leaps to the eye the moment one takes the trouble to transcribe the full content of the two steps in symbolic form. In (A1) we are told that if several things are all *F*, they are all seen as such in virtue of *F*-ness. But (A2) tells us that if several things are all *F*, they are all seen as such not because of *F*-ness, but because of a Form other than *F*-ness, namely, *F*-ness$_1$. To be sure, there is a difference in the protasis of (A1) and (A2), and this is doubtless what has misled patrons or critics of the Argument: (A2) includes, while (A1) does not, *F*-ness, among the things which have the property, *F*. The significance of the assumption which prompts this inclusion will be discussed directly, and will indeed remain the most important single issue throughout the whole of this paper. But if we simply stick to the

[1] That *F* and *F*-ness are logically and ontologically distinct is crucial to the argument. Cf. below, p. 252, n. 1.

logical form of the two statements, the disparity of reasoning[1] as between (A1) and (A2) remains glaringly abrupt and unwarranted.

Is there then no way to get around the difficulty? There certainly would be, if (A2) could be changed to read:

(A2a) If *a*, *b*, *c*, and *F*-ness are all F_1, there must be another Form, *F*-ness$_1$, etc.

Is there any chance that this is what Plato did say, and that I missed it in my transcript of his argument at (A2) above? I think, none. We need only refer back to the text to verify the fact that (A2) and not (A2a), is the information it supplies. All it asks of us is to 'view mentally' Largeness and 'the other large things' and find the Form in virtue of which all of these 'appear large'. It does not invite us to discern a new character, not large, but large$_1$ (whatever this may mean), and having satisfied ourselves that *a*, *b*, *c*, and Largeness are all large$_1$ to infer, *pari passu* with (A1), the existence of Largeness$_1$.

[1] A fastidious reader may be displeased at the vagueness of this expression. I could speak more definitely of a *non sequitur* (and, to simplify matters, will do so hereafter). But this is to understate the faultiness of the reasoning, which can only be fully stated in a proposition whose assertion is not necessary to my argument in the text and whose proof would have exceeded Plato's technical resources: *The joint assertion of* (*A*1) *and* (*A*2) *implies that the protasis of* (*A*1) *and* (*A*2) *are mutually inconsistent*; and since the Argument assumes that both of the latter can be asserted (i.e. that it is true that there are large particulars, and that Largeness and the large particulars are all large), the joint assertion of (A1) and (A2) is absolutely precluded. The proof of the underlined proposition is as follows:

$p =$ *a*, *b*, *c* are *F*.
$q =$ *a*, *b*, *c* are seen as *F* in virtue of *F*-ness.
$\sim q =$ *a*, *b*, *c* are seen as *F* in virtue of *F*-ness$_1$, where *F*-ness$_1 \neq$ *F*-ness.
$r =$ *F*-ness is *F*.
$s =$ *F*-ness is seen as *F* in virtue of *F*-ness$_1$, where *F*-ness$_1 \neq$ *F*-ness.

(It will be noticed that, to reduce the length of the ensuing proof, I have put as $\sim q$ a proposition that is not strictly the negate of q but whose truth value is equivalent to that of the latter, since we may take it for granted that it can not be true that x, y, z are seen as *F* in virtue of *F*-ness and also in virtue of a Form other than *F*-ness.)

Then, (A1) $= p \supset q$.
(A2) $= (p \cdot r) \supset (\sim q \cdot s)$.
But $(\sim q \cdot s) \supset \sim q$; therefore, $(p \cdot r) \supset \sim q$; hence, $q \supset \sim(p \cdot r)$.
But since $p \supset q$, (A1), it follows that $p \supset \sim(p \cdot r)$, i.e., that the protaseis of (A1) and (A2) are mutually inconsistent.

Now it might be claimed that though (A2a) is not what Plato said, it is nonetheless what he meant. This proposal should be advanced, and entertained, with the gravest misgivings, since Plato is anything but a careless writer, and his vocabulary suffers from no limitation which would have kept him from saying (A2a), if he had meant (A2a). Still, the issue being crucial to the whole course of the argument, let us give the proposal its day in court. Would this improvement of the text be an improvement of the argument? The answer is, surely, that it would not. For the purpose of the second step in the Argument is to convince us of the existence of a new Form of Largeness, 'over and above Largeness itself'. This purpose would be defeated if the protasis of the second step were as questionable as its apodosis. And is not this precisely what would happen if the proposal were adopted? The second step would then begin: 'If there are $large_1$ things . . .'; and how could we then help retorting, 'If, indeed,' and ask for reasons why there must? In the case of (A1), the protasis offers no trouble at all; for who would gainsay that there are (or appear to be) a number of large things? But here the matter is absolutely different. Everyone has seen large things; but who has ever seen a $large_1$ thing or set of things? If Plato had meant to offer such an assertion as the *if*-clause of an *if-then* statement, he would surely have seen that it cries aloud for justification, and would never have moved on to the *then*-clause, without stopping to interpolate reasons for the *if*-clause itself. And to do this he would have had to change the whole form of his argument. The burden of the second step would have then become to establish the existence of things that have the remarkable property, $large_1$. I am not saying that such an argument could not be made.[1] All I am saying is that,

[1] It could not be made at all without anticipating the results of Sec. II. If the anticipation be permitted, the argument can be reconstructed as follows: Largeness is large in a different (superlative) sense (which follows from the Degrees-of-Reality Theory in Sec. II) from that in which particulars are large. So:

(i) Largeness is $large_1$. But the large particulars and the $large_1$ Form have something in common; call this—the determinable, of which large and $large_1$ are determinates—$large_2$. It then follows that (ii) Largeness and the large particulars are all $large_2$.

Having completed this detour we would now have warrant for asserting a suitable variant of (A2a), which would now read ($A2a_1$). If *a*, *b*, *c*, and *F*-ness are all F_2 there must be a Form other than *F*-ness, namely, *F*-$ness_2$.

It will be noticed that ($A2a_1$) would no longer be the *second* step of the

had it been made, the second step of the Third Man Argument would have been entirely different from what it is. And since my purpose is to analyse the argument Plato gives us, instead of one he might have given, I have no choice but to consign to the waste basket the suggestion that (A2a) is what Plato meant. We are then left, where we started, with (A2) staring us in the face.

Now if this is all we had to go by, (A1) in the first step, and (A2) in the second, could anyone say that the Third Man Argument was logically valid? Clearly there must have been something more in Plato's mind than the information supplied at (A1), which made the transition to (A2) appear to him not only permissible, but plausible. What could this be? A full answer to this question would send us rummaging into other texts to discover what further assumptions Plato made about his Theory of Forms. But this would have to anticipate Section II. Let us content ourselves now with a more modest question: What are the simplest premisses, not given in the present Argument, which would have to be added to its first step, to make (A2) a legitimate conclusion?

We need, first of all, what I propose to call the Self-Predication Assumption:

(A3) Any Form can be predicated of itself. Largeness is itself large. *F*-ness is itself *F*.

I have alluded to this already. Clearly it is necessary, for were it not true, the protasis of (A2) would be certainly false; if *F*-ness were not *F*, it would be false to say that *a*, *b*, *c*, and *F*-ness are all *F*. The credit for recognising that this is an indispensable, though suppressed, premiss of the Third Man Argument goes to A. E. Taylor.[1] He thereby opened the way to a correct under-

[1] Pp. 46 ff. of his 1916 paper. Most of the later mentions of this vital point acknowledge indebtedness to Taylor, and it is probable that even those which do not are similarly indebted to him directly or indirectly since this insight is missing in all of the earlier discussions.

Argument but, at the very least, the third; the existence of the predicate F_1 would have to be proved not as the common predicate of *F*-ness and the *F* particulars, but as the distinctive property of *F*-ness; and the common predicate of *F*-ness and the *F* particulars would not be F_1, and F_2—all of which is a far cry from Plato's argument in the text before us, and I trust, will convince the skeptic why it should not be taken as 'the meaning' of the second step as it appears in the text.

standing of the Argument, and not only of this but of the whole Theory of Forms, though Taylor, ironically, never realised the implications of his own discovery, for he refused to admit that Plato himself made so absurd an assumption. Of this more later. Here we may remark not only that this premiss is necessary to the argument, but that Plato's actual wording of the second step comes as close to asserting it as one could without actually stating the Self-Predication Assumption: 'Will not a single Largeness appear once again, in virtue of which *all these* (*sc.* "Largeness and the other large things") appear large?' The second clause clearly implies that Largeness, no less than each of the particulars, 'appear(s) large'.

But we need also a further premiss, which I shall call the Nonidentity Assumption:

> (A4) If anything has a certain character, it cannot be identical with the Form in virtue of which we apprehend that character. If x is F, x cannot be identical with F-ness.

This too, though not stated in the Argument, is certainly implied. For think of what would happen if it were not assumed to be true. The transition from the protasis of (A2), 'If a, b, c, and F-ness are all F,' to its apodosis, 'then there must be another Form, F-ness$_1$', would then not be a logical sequence, but the wild and whimsical jump we have seen it to be above. The minimum warrant for passing from 'the large things and Largeness are large' to 'the Form in virtue of which we apprehend the common character of large things and Largeness cannot be Largeness', could be no less than this: If anything is large, its Largeness cannot be identical with that thing. From this it *would* follow that if Largeness is large, then *its* Largeness cannot be identical with itself and must, therefore, be a second Form of Largeness, Largeness$_1$.

In the many modern discussions of the Argument I can find no explicit statement that this Nonidentity Assumption, or an equivalent one, is strictly required in just this way. This may be because the rôle of such an assumption at this point strikes critics more nimble-witted than myself as so obvious that they feel it an insult to their reader's intelligence to put it into words or symbols. However, there are times when the drudgery of saying the obvious is rewarded, and this is one of them. For if one compares (A4) with (A3) above, one will then see that these two premisses, jointly necessary to the second, and every subsequent, step of the Argument, are mutually inconsistent, and that their inconsistency does not need to be exposed through the indirect and elaborate machinery of the infinite regress, but can be shown much more simply and directly. (A3) reads: *F*-ness is *F*. (A4) reads: if *x* is *F*, *x* cannot be identical with *F*-ness. Substituting *F*-ness for *x* in (A4), we get:

(A5) If *F*-ness is *F*, *F*-ness cannot be identical with *F*-ness.

And since the consequent of (A5) is plainly false, because self-contradictory, at least one of the premisses from which it follows —(A3), (A4)—must be false.[1]

Now there is one way of avoiding this particular impasse, and that is to modify (A4), restating it as follows:

(A4a) If any *particular* has a certain character, then it cannot be identical with the Form in virtue of which we apprehend that character. If *x* is *F*, *x* cannot be identical with *F*-ness when, and only when, the values for *x* are particulars, *a*, *b*, *c* . . .[2]

If (A4a) replaces (A4) above, then the inconsistency with (A3) will not arise. For (A4a) does not warrant the substitution of *F*-ness for *x*, and this in spite of the fact that *F*-ness is *F* (A3). What we are now told is that the Nonidentity Assumption holds in the case of particulars; we are not told that it holds in the case of forms, and have no ground for asserting that if a *Form* have a certain character it cannot be identical with the Form in virtue of which it has (and is apprehended as having) that character. But what happens now to the second step of the Argument?—It is no longer a valid inference from our premisses, (A1), (A3), and (A4a). We have now no ground for saying that if *a*, *b*, *c*, and *F*-ness are all *F*, there must be a Form other than *F*-ness, in virtue of which we apprehend that *a*, *b*, *c*, and *F*-ness are all *F*; there is now nothing to keep us from saying that they are all apprehended as *F* in virtue of *F*-ness itself. The existence of *F*-

[1] I am using 'false' here and occasionally hereafter in the broader sense which includes 'insignificant'.

[2] It will be convenient to distinguish hereafter (A4a) from (A4) above, by referring to (A4) as the 'full-strength' Nonidentity Assumption.

$ness_1$ would thus remain unproved in the second step, and, by the same token the existence of all subsequent Forms, F-$ness_2$, F-$ness_3$, etc., would remain unproved. The infinite regress would not materialise.

Let us now see where this analysis of the Third Man Argument has taken us: If we took the second (and crucial) step of the Third Man Argument as a mere inference from what is stated in the first step, it would be a horrible *non sequitur*. To avoid this, further premisses must be supplied, and we could not determine whether the Argument is valid until they were supplied; for to say of any argument that it is valid is simply to say that its conclusions follow correctly from its premisses. And we have now seen what premisses would be necessary for the assertion of (A2):

> the first step of the Argument, (A1);
> the Self-Predication Assumption, (A3);
> the full-strength Nonidentity Assumptions, (A4).

Are they then also sufficient? Certainly, though in a very odd way, for we are working with inconsistent premisses which, as we have seen, have already produced the self-contradictory conclusion at (A5), '*F*-ness cannot be identical with *F*-ness', and we should not be surprised to see them justify all kinds of contradictory conclusions. Since these premisses warrant the proposition that *F*-ness is *not* identical with *F*-ness, they will warrant the proposition that *F*-ness *is* identical with F-$ness_1$, which *is* a Form not identical with *F*-ness, and (A2) will then follow from (A1).[1] And having thus got the existence of F-$ness_1$ at (A2), we can proceed, by the same 'reasoning', to show in the next step the existence of F-$ness_2$, then again, F-$ness_3$, and so on without end. We would thus get a *bona fide* infinite regress, logically vicious, since it is assumed that we discern *F* particulars in virtue of *F*-ness (A1), *F*-ness in virtue of F-$ness_1$ (A2), and so on *ad infinitum*, the discernment of each successive Form being required for the

[1] For we know from (A1) that if a number of things are *F* there must be a Form, *F*-ness, through which they are apprehended as *F*. Whence it follows that (A2b) If *a*, *b*, *c*, and *F*-ness are all *F*, there must be a Form, *F*-ness, through which they are apprehended as *F*. But if *F*-ness is identical with F-$ness_1$, we may substitute F-$ness_1$ for *F*-ness in the second clause of (A2b), which will produce (A2).

discernment of its immediate predecessor, a requirement which can never be fulfilled, since the series is infinite.[1]

And what would we learn from this consequence?—Only that one or more of our premisses is false or void of sense, on the assumption that some vice in one or more of the premisses is the source of the vicious consequence. We could have got the same information by a much more economical procedure: by simply noting the contradiction which follows from the joint assertion of (A3) and (A4), as explained above. And if Plato had even got as far as the explicit assertion of (A3) itself, he would have found good reason for rejecting it,[2] and would thus have been able to

[1] There is a tolerably good explanation of the fact that the Argument does not result in an (unobjectionable) infinite series, but in a (vicious) regress, in Taylor, pp. 47 ff., though I should take exception to the form of his application of the regress to Platonic 'participation' at p. 49. The gist of the matter may be restated as follows: If the Argument simply established an indefinite series of Forms corresponding to each discernible character, no logical disaster would ensue, so long as one (or, at most, a finite number) of these Forms sufficed to do what Forms are supposed to do, i.e., enable us to discern the relevant characters in the particulars and then in the first of the corresponding Forms. All other members of the series could then be ignored as a harmless surplus, though every adept in the use of Occam's razor would itch to lop them off. But what the Argument proves is much worse than this. At (A1) we are told that we apprehend particulars as *F* through *F*-ness. Now if *F*-ness itself must be apprehended as *F*, then it follows from (A2) that we must apprehend *F*-ness through *F*-ness$_1$, and so on. Whence it follows that, since we cannot complete the series, *F*-ness, *F*-ness$_1$, etc., we shall never be able to apprehend *F*-ness in the first place, and thus never apprehend the *F*-particulars; and this *is* disastrous. It may be objected that Plato does not *say* that *F*-ness must itself be apprehended as *F*. Of course, he does not. But what he does say implies it in conjunction with Self-Predication. For if it were true that *F*-ness is *F*, how could it be apprehended except as *F*? However, it is not necessary (and is unwarranted by the evidence) to assume that this distinction between a harmless series and a vicious regress was apparent to Plato himself. He was himself convinced that there was just one Form for each discernible character or kind, and argued (*Rep.*, 597c–d, *Tim.*, 31a–b) that if, *per impossibile*, there were two Forms of anything, there would have to be a third which would be *the* form of that thing. He would, therefore, have regarded even the existence of an infinite series of Forms of any one kind as disastrous for this Theory.

[2] To avoid misunderstanding, I should underline the fact that the Self-Predication Assumption to which I refer throughout this paper is the assertion in (A3) above that *any* Form may be predicated of itself. Absurdity or contradiction inevitably results from this assertion which implies that Forms predicable of particulars are predicable of themselves, as I shall show

nail down the exact source of the trouble that is attested, but not identified, by the infinite regress. But even if Plato had asserted (A3), he could still have saved himself from the disaster of the regress by simply denying (A4) and saying that he had no reason for holding anything more than (A4a).

This result may be summarised, in anticipation of Section II below, as follows: If Plato had identified all of the premisses which are necessary (and sufficient) to warrant the second step of the Third Man Argument, he would not have produced the Third Man Argument at all, unless he were simply pursuing a logical game for its own sake, which is not what he is doing in the first part of the *Parmenides*.[1] In stating the Third Man Argument, and in leaving it unrefuted, he is revealing (*a*) that he did not know all of its necessary premisses, whence it would follow that (*b*) he had no way of determining whether or not it was a valid argument. (*a*) can be independently verified, and it will be in Section II.

B. *The Second Version: Parmenides* 132d 1–133a 6

This is at least as interesting on its own account; and no less so is a third version, supplied by Aristotle.[2] Lack of space forbids altogether a treatment of the third in this paper, and compels me to deal more briefly and more roughly with the second that it deserves. All I shall attempt here is to show that Plato's second

[1] For the best demonstration of this see Robinson, pp. 58 ff.

[2] In his essay *On the Forms*, *ap.* Alexander, in *Met.* (Hayduck), 84.21–85.11; English translation by W. D. Ross, *The Works of Aristotle*, vol. XII, *Select Fragments* (Oxford, 1952), 129; cf. Cherniss, pp. 233–4, and 500 ff. I can only observe here that an analysis of Aristotle's version will show that it too involves, without appearing to notice, the same discrepancy between the first and the second steps of the Argument. While at the first step Aristotle infers the existence of *F*-ness from the fact that *F*-ness is predicated of certain things (in this case, particulars), in the second step he very surprisingly infers the existence of a Form other than *F*-ness from the fact that *F*-ness is predicated of certain things (in this case, the particulars and *F*-ness).

---

in Sec. II-B below. Had Plato merely said or implied that some Forms are self-predicational—those predicable only of Forms, like Logical Self-Identity, Intelligibility, Changelessness, etc.—no obvious absurdity or contradiction would have arisen. On Russell's well-known theory *any* assertion of the Form '*F*(*F*)' is logically illicit; but see, *contra*, A. Koyré, *Epiménide Le Menteur* (Paris, 1947), pp. 36–42.

version of the Argument is similar in logical structure to his first and presupposes both of the inconsistent premisses presupposed by the first.

The first step in the second version:

(B1) The Copy-Theory: If *a* and *b* are similar (in respect of being *F*), there must be a Form, *F*-ness, in which they both participate by way of resemblance: *a* and *b* must resemble *F*-ness, as copies resemble their model.

Moreover:

(B1.1) If *a* resembles *F*-ness (in respect of being *F*), *F*-ness must resemble *a* (in the same respect).[1]

The second and crucial step, whose reasoning is repeated in all subsequent steps:

(B2) If *a* and *F*-ness are similar (in respect of being *F*), there must be another Form, $F\text{-ness}_1$, in which they both participate by way of resemblance: *a* and *F*-ness must resemble $F\text{-ness}_1$, as copies resemble their model.

A comparison of the above with Plato's text will show that the symbolic transcript omits nothing vital to the reasoning, and adds nothing except the parenthetical statements; and these only make explicit the sense of the argument. Clearly, if *a* and *b* are similar, they must be similar in at least one respect; and my parentheses have simply specified the respect with a symbol which is the same as that used for the Form in which they participate. Thus, if *a* and *b* are both white, they resemble each other in respect of being white, the same property which is expressed by the Form, Whiteness, in which they are said to participate by way of resemblance. Again, in the corollary, if Whiteness resembles the white particular, it can only resemble it in the same respect in which the white thing is said to resemble Whiteness, namely, 'white'.

[1] *Not* in respect of being a copy of *a* or *b*—an absurd suggestion, which, of course, is not in the text, though Taylor (p. 87), inexplicably read it into the argument and, therefore, thought he could explode the argument by retorting that the model–copy relation is not symmetrical. The argument only assumes that the relation of similarity is symmetrical which, of course, it *is* (Hardie, p. 96; Ryle, p. 137, above, p. 105; Ross, p. 89; Owen, p. 83, n. 3, below, p. 319, n. 3).

Now a mere glance at my transcript of the argument will show the same discrepancy between the first and the second step that we encountered in the first version. From the premiss that two things are similar in respect of being *F*, (B1) infers the existence of *F*-ness, while (B2) that of a Form other than *F*-ness, *F*-ness$_1$. To be sure, the things which are said to be similar in the protasis of (B1) are once again not the same things which are said to be similar at (B2): *a* and *b*, in (B1), *a* and *F*-ness in (B2). And this protasis in (B2) implies the Self-Predication Assumption:

> (B3) *F*-ness is *F*; for if *F*-ness were not *F*, it would not resemble *a* in respect of being *F*.

But why should the similarity of *a* and *F*-ness in respect of *F* require the resemblance of *a* and *F*-ness to a Form other than *F*-ness? A necessary reason for this is the Nonidentity Assumption:

> (B4) If *x* is *F*, it cannot be identical with the Form, *F*-ness; for if this were not true, there would be no reason at all why *a* and *F*-ness could not both be *F* in virtue of *F*-ness. But (B3) and (B4) are obviously inconsistent, and their joint assertion leads to a contradiction:
>
> (B5) If *F*-ness is *F* (B3), then *F*-ness cannot be identical with *F*-ness; for if anything is *F* it cannot be identical with *F*-ness (B4).

It is worth noting that the two Assumptions of Self-Predication and (full-strength) Nonidentity which are still necessary, as they were in the first version, are still tacit, for neither of them is stated as such; but they are now much closer to the verbal surface of the Argument, for they are both logically implied and even intuitively suggested by the key-concept of the second version, the Copy-Theory of participation. For if an *F* thing participates in *F*-ness, by way of resembling *F*-ness as a copy resembles its model, then (*a*) *F*-ness *must* be *F*, else it would not be resembled by, and resemble, the *F* thing in respect of *F*, and (*b*) the *F* thing cannot be identical with *F*-ness, since a copy cannot be identical with its model. The contradiction at (B5) exposes both the inconsistency of the two tacit Assumptions and the logical vice of the Copy-Theory, for it shows that it implies both (B3) and

(B4) which are mutually inconsistent. Another way of stating the contradiction that follows from the Copy-Theory is:

(B5a) If *F*-ness is *F*, then it cannot be *F*; for the Copy-Theory which, as we have seen, requires that *F*-ness be *F*, also requires that it cannot be *F*, for, if it were *F*, it would have to be, on this theory, a copy of *F*-ness, and nothing can be a copy of itself. And it is further worth noting that the Argument could be collapsed in the second version, exactly as in the first, by rejecting (B4) in favour of

(B4a) If any *particular* is *F*, it cannot be identical with the Form, *F*-ness.

This would avoid the absurd consequences of (B4), (B5), and (B5a), and would ruin the regress by invalidating its second step.

Having learned all this, what is there more to learn about the infinite regress that must start at (B2)? That it does start there, if (B3) and (B4) are supplied, can be easily shown, for (B2) is justified by these premisses in the same queer way in which (A2) was justified above.[1] We have thus got our precious regress once again. But what good is it? As in the first version, its diagnostic value for the logical vices of the Theory of Forms is no better than, is indeed not as good as, the simple statement of the tacit premisses, (B3) and (B4), followed by the simple deduction of the self-contradictory conclusions, (B5) and (B5a) above. If Plato knew that his theory commits him to *these* premisses, he would not need the regress to tell him that his theory is logically moribund and must submit to drastic surgery to survive.

II. THE ASSUMPTIONS OF THE ARGUMENT AND OF THE THEORY OF FORMS

A. *Plato's Ontology*

The question whether or not the Third Man Argument is a valid objection to Plato's Theory of Forms can now be resolved into the far more precise one: Did Plato's Theory of Forms make

[1] (B5) has given us the same remarkable information that we got at (A5) above: *F*-ness is not identical with *F*-ness. Let it then be, once again, identical with *F*-ness$_1$, which empowers us to substitute '*F*-ness$_1$' for '*F*-ness' wherever we please. But from (B1) we deduce (B2a). If *a* and *F*-ness are similar (in respect of being *F*), there must be a Form, *F*-ness, etc. Substituting '*F*-ness$_1$' for '*F*-ness' in the second clause of (B2a), we get (B2).

the two tacit assumptions which are needed to produce the infinite regress? This is what we must now determine. When we have done this, it will appear, I think, that the more complex question, whether Plato himself did or did not believe the Argument to be a valid objection to his Theory, will pretty well answer itself.

The place to begin is with what Plato himself tells about the Theory of Forms, in this very dialogue, before presenting either the Third Man Argument of any of the other objections. 'Tell me, Socrates,' asks Parmenides at 130b, 'have you yourself drawn this division you speak of: on one hand, certain Forms *separately* by themselves and, on the other, *separately*, the things which partake of them? And do you believe that Similarity itself is something *separately* from the Similarity which we possess?' Plato could hardly have been more emphatic in identifying that feature of the Theory which will be the special butt of the attacks that are to follow; and when Aristotle, in his version of the Third Man Argument, as indeed in most of his other polemic, makes the 'separation' (χωρισμός) of the Forms the most objectionable aspect of the Platonic theory he does so with good warrant from at least this Platonic text.[1] But what exactly is Plato saying when he asserts that Forms exist 'separately' from particulars? Only what he had said many times before without using the word 'separately' at all. The solemn announcements of the Theory in the middle dialogues—the *Cratylus*, the *Phaedo*, the *Republic*[2]—are generally put in this form: Beauty (or Justice, or Goodness, etc.) 'is something' (τι ἔστι) or 'is one thing' (ἓν ἔστι). But these expressions are themselves uninformative, nor is there gain in information in doubling the emphasis on 'is', by compounding the verb with its adverbial or substantival derivatives, 'is really' (ὄντως ἔστι), 'is a real (thing)' (ὂν ἔστι), 'is a reality' (οὐσία ἔστι), or even resorting to other adjectives or adverbs, 'is a true (ἀληθὲς) being', or 'is truly' (ἀληθῶς), 'is a pure (εἰλικρινές) being' or 'purely (εἰλικρινῶς) is'.[3] What Plato means by saying, with or without the use

[1] And from many others. See Cherniss, 208 ff., whose thorough refutation of the contrary view makes further argument unnecessary.

[2] *Crat.*, 439c, 440a; *Phd*, 65d, 74a; *Rep.*, 475e, 596a. I am well aware that some scholars believe that the *Cratylus* is one of the later dialogues, but this is no place to argue the point, and nothing of any consequence turns on it for my present purpose.

[3] Detailed documentation is superfluous; these expressions turn up in every context in which the Theory of Forms is asserted, including the

of any other substantive, adjective, or adverb, that 'x is', in the strict sense of 'is', becomes clear only when we see that he understands this to entail:

(i) x is intelligible;[1]
(ii) x is changeless;[2]
(iii) x is not qualified by contrary predicates;[3]
(iv) x is itself the perfect instance of the property of relation which the word for 'x' connotes.[4]

Obviously this is not the place to expound the content of these assertions which epitomise one of the richest and boldest metaphysical theories ever invented in Western thought. Just one or two remarks are called for here.

Perhaps more important than any one or all four of the specific statements which convey the content of the Platonic meaning of the word 'is' is the tacit assumption which underlies them all. Logically, this is the costliest of all the assumptions that Plato made: That the verb 'is' and all its variants (when used in ontological assertions) have a *single* meaning, the one which is jointly specified by the four propositions I have just enumerated. We must not judge him harshly on this account. The Aristotelian axiom that 'things can be said to be in many different senses' was not a commonplace on its own day, but a revolutionary discovery.[5]

[1] In emphatic opposition to 'sensible'. So, e.g., at *Phd.*, 65c ff., *Rep.*, 509d ff., *Tim.*, 51b–e.

[2] E.g., *Crat.*, 439d ff.; *Phd.*, 78d ff.; *Rep.*, 484b; *Phil.*, 59a–c.

[3] E.g., *Phd.*, 74c; *Rep.*, 479a–c, 523b ff.; cf. *Ep. VII*, 343ab.

[4] For this *no* documentation (in the strict sense) can be offered—a point of great importance, to be discussed shortly.

[5] One which, among other things, offers a direct way of tracking down the source of the Third Man Argument, as Aristotle himself clearly saw. In his own language, the confusion of the sense which 'is' has in the first category with its sense in one of the other categories is what 'creates the "third man"', *Soph. El.*, 178b 37 ff.; cf. *Met.*, 1038b 34 ff.

---

passages listed in the preceding note. Those who, like Owen, believe that the Theory of Forms was drastically revised in the later dialogues and who deny the lateness of the *Timaeus*, might be referred especially to *Phil.*, 58a–59d; there the object of dialectic, which consists of the Forms (cf. the 'divine circle and sphere' in contrast to the 'human circle', the 'false circle and rule', at *Phil.*, 62ab), is that which 'really is' (58a 2–3, 59d 4), in explicit contrast to 'this world' of becoming (59a).

Before Aristotle and after Parmenides all the great system-builders —Empedocles, Anaxagoras, the atomists, and Plato himself—had taken it for granted that being had one, and just one sense, whose cardinal feature was changelessness.[1] What Plato did was to draw up a far more systematic, more thoughtful, and thought-provoking list of conditions which anything must satisfy if it can be said to be in the strict sense of the word, a list which was purely conservative in making changelessness definitive of being, but which broke with Ionian and Italian *physiologia* by rehabilitating the Eleatic inference[2] that only the 'bodiless' (ἀσώματον)[3] is wholly real. Plato did not thereby revert to the Eleatic view that the sensible world is wholly unreal. His view was a Degrees-of-Reality Theory which permitted him, in compliance with his native tongue, to say that sensible things are,[4] as logical subjects of assertions of

[1] Empedocles B 8: There is no 'generation' (φύσις) or 'destruction'; 'generation' is only a 'name'; B 17. 35: the only things that strictly *are* the 'roots', and they are 'everlastingly in the same state' (literally, 'ever continuously alike' (ἠνεκὲς αἰὲν ὅμοια). Anaxagoras B 17: 'the Greeks', who think there is such a thing as generation and destruction, are wrong; there *is* no such thing; generation and destruction should be 'correctly called' mixture and separation; hence (by implication) 'things that are' (ἐόντων χρημάτων) are changeless. In the atomists the only things which 'really' (ἐτεῇ, Democritus B 7–10) exist are (the absolutely changeless) atoms and the void.

[2] I should warn the reader that my view that Eleatic Being was incorporeal runs against the general opinion. But it is explicit in Melissus B 9; see *Gnomon*, XXV (1953), 34–5. I believe that it is implicit in Parmenides.

[3] An assumption so basic that Plato does not trouble to spell it out in the earlier statements of the theory, where he only finds it necessary to insist upon the 'invisibility' of the Forms (*Phd.*, 65d 9, 79a 6 ff.), and it is only in the later dialogues that he supplies the further premiss (sc., that the invisible, or not sensible, is the bodiless, *Tim.*, 28b) for the conclusion 'Forms are bodiless', or just states the conclusion by itself (*Soph.*, 246b, the 'Friends of Forms' in opposition to the materialists who 'define reality as identical with body'; cf. *Pol.*, 286a).

[4] And this in the middle, no less than the later, dialogues. Thus the use of 'beings' (ὄντα) to include the world of becoming in the *Philebus* (23c) can be matched perfectly in the *Phaedo* (79a, 'Shall we then assume two kinds of beings (ὄντων), one visible, the other invisible?'). This point spoils one of the major arguments that have been offered by Owen (pp. 85–6) in support of his thesis that the *Timaeus* was written in Plato's middle period: he assumes that a strict dichotomy of being–becoming, which implies a systematic refusal to ascribe being to the world of becoming, is characteristic of the middle dialogues, has been abandoned in the later dialogues, and therefore makes a sure criterion for the earlier date of the *Timaeus*. He ignores the fact that in spite of the harsh being–becoming dichotomy of *Tim.*, 27d–28a,

existence and ascriptions of properties and relations. They were halfway real, 'between the purely real and the totally unreal' (*Rep.*, 478d). The Imitation or Copy Theory incorporates this assumption that the sensible particulars are 'less real' than the Form they resemble. If the bed produced by the carpenter is not 'the real' (τὸ ὄν) Bed, 'but only something which is like it', then 'it would not be right to say that the work of the carpenter or of any other handicraftsman is a perfectly real thing (τελέως εἶναι), would it? We must not be surprised then if this too [sc. the physical bed] is a somewhat shadowy thing as compared with reality' (πρὸς ἀλήθειαν) (*Rep.*, 597a).

B. *Separation and Self-Predication*

We can now ask whether this ontology does or does not include the two tacit premisses of the Third Man Argument. That Plato assumes Self-Predication I already implied in the fourth of the conditions of Platonic being I have listed above. I gave no textual evidence that this was recognised by Plato himself on a level with the other three, for the simple reason that there is none to give. While Plato states and defends conditions (i) and (ii), and (iii), he leaves (iv) not only undefended, but unstated. But if he never stated it, what reason can be given for saying that he did make it after all?—The reason is that it is certainly implied by various things he said and believed. It is implied, first of all, both by his Degree-of-Reality Theory and by his Copy-Theory of the relation of things to Forms. For if an *F* particular is only 'deficiently'[1] *F*, and only the corresponding Form is perfectly *F*, then *F*-ness is *F*. Or if the *F* particular is a copy of *F*-ness and resembles *F*-ness in respect of being *F*, then, once again, *F*-ness is *F*. Moreover, Self-Predication is also implied by quite a different set of statements

[1] ἐνδεεστέρως, *Phaedo*, 74e, 75a; ἐνδεέστερα, φαυλότερα, 75b. Cf. *Rep.*, 529d: the celestial bodies 'fall far short of' (πολὺ ἐνδεῖν) the intelligible Forms whose visible likeness they are.

Plato continues in the same dialogue to stretch being to include the world of becoming; so, e.g. in the psychogony at 35a, which speaks of the 'divisible being (οὐσία) which becomes in bodies', and in the cosmological trichotomy at 52d, where 'being, place, becoming' are said to 'be' (εἶναι). He also ignores the fact that the being-becoming dichotomy is plainly asserted in an indisputably late dialogue like the *Philebus* (59a).

which are not elucidations of the Theory of Forms, but direct and at times, casual assertions about this or that Form. Examples turn up in the earliest dialogues, long before the Theory of Forms had taken shape in Plato's mind.[1] When a man's hairs have turned white, says Socrates in the *Lysis* (217d), 'they have become such as that which is present in them, white through Whiteness': the white hairs are 'such as' or 'of the same quality as' (*οἷόνπερ*) Whiteness; they have the same quality that Whiteness has.[2] Somewhat later, in the *Protagoras* (330c–d) we get an even more striking text which, since first noticed by Goblot in 1929,[3] has become the star instance of Self-Predication in Plato. Here Socrates roundly declares that justice is just and holiness holy. 'What other thing *could* be holy, if holiness isn't holy,' he asks, indignant at the idea that anyone could gainsay that holiness is holy. These two examples would be quite enough to refute Taylor and others who, in the goodness of their hearts, press upon Plato charitable donations gathered from modern analysis. But there are others. In the *Phaedo* (100c) Socrates gives away the same presumption when he indulges in the expression, 'If anything else is beautiful, besides

[1] The contrary view (cf. H. Cherniss, *Riddle of the Early Academy*, (Berkeley, 1945, pp. 4–5) that the Theory of Forms is already present in the early dialogues would simplify my argument. But I do not agree with it, and I cannot argue the point here beyond stating that I cannot consider the employment of certain linguistic expressions as *sufficient* evidence of the concurrent assertion of the metaphysical theory.

[2] Self-Predication is also suggested by Plato's use of the expression 'the x itself' for 'the Form of x' which, as Ross remarks (88), 'treats the Idea of x as one x among others, and implies an x-ness common to it with others'. This expression occurs repeatedly in the *Hippias Major* (Ross, p. 17, n. 1) as well as in the middle dialogues.

[3] P. 473, n. 3. Soon after, it was noticed (perhaps independently of Goblot's paper) by Theodore de Laguna, 'Notes on the Theory of Ideas', *Phil. Rev.*, XLIII (1934), 450–2. De Laguna saw exactly what such a statement implies (and generalised the implication, 'The Platonic idea is a universal, supposed precisely and unqualifiedly to characterise itself') and what is wrong with the implication: 'Justice and holiness are not moral agents; they cannot have virtues or vices.' The next important use of the passage is by Robinson (pp. 62–3) in 1942. Cornford (pp. 87 ff.) in 1939 had seen that Self-Predication is implied right and left in the objections against the Forms in the Parmenides, but still followed Taylor's lead in refusing to credit Plato himself with the Assumption; so too Cherniss. So far as I can recall, Taylor, Cornford, and Cherniss do not notice the Protagoras passage, and fail to see that the Assumption is implied by the Copy-Theory and the Degrees-of-Reality Theory.

Beauty itself.' And in the *Symposium*, while there is no one sentence that says quite baldly that Beauty is beautiful, the whole point of Diotima's speech is that the Form of Beauty is superlatively fair, incomparably more so than fair bodies, minds, or institutions: the universal enters into competition with its instances, and has no trouble at all winning the beauty contest.

Is it possible that man should say, and with the greatest emphasis, 'Justice is just', yet not realise that this is as good as saying that a Form which *is* a character *has* that character? It is perfectly possible. That it is possible to say *p*, which implies *q*, and not think of the implication or even of *q*, is a first principle of inquiry in the history of philosophy.[1] In this case there is a further factor, and a very prosaic one, which may blinker the logical vision of a clearheaded man. It is the fact that 'Justice is just', which can also be said in Greek as, 'the just is just', can be so easily mistaken for a tautology, and its denial for a self-contradiction.[2] I am not suggesting that the Assumption of Self-Predication is just a symptom of the tyranny of language over ontology. The suggestion would not even be plausible, for other philosophers, using the same language, made no such assumption. The assumption has far deeper roots, notably religious ones, which I cannot explore in this paper. What can be debited to language is simply the fact that an assertion which looks like an identity-statement may be taken as having the certainty of a tautology; and the illusion of its self-evidence could very well block that further scrutiny which would reveal that it implies a proposition which so far from being self-evident leads to self-contradiction. Anyhow, whether it be for this or for some other reason, there can be no doubt about the fact that Plato never asserted Self-Predication in any of his writings, and not much doubt that neither did he assert it in oral discussion in the many debates that raged over the Forms in the Academy; for if he had, Aristotle would have known it, and he was not the man to pass over the wonderful polemical possibilities it opens up.[3] Shall we then assume that Plato did know it but kept

[1] No one has stated this so clearly and followed it so rigorously as R. Robinson, *Plato's Earlier Dialectic* (Ithaca, N.Y., 1941), pp. 2–3 *et passim*.

[2] Cornford, p. 87.

[3] In Aristotle's version of the Third Man Argument we see Self-Predication not only at his finger tips but almost in the hollow of his hand: 'and "man" is predicated both of particular men *and of the Form* . . .' ap. Alex., in *Met.*, 84. 29. That he did not *see* what was thus within his grasp is clear from the

the thought locked up in the secrecy of his own mind? This melodramatic possibility can be disposed of fairly simply. Had Plato recognised that all of his Forms are self-predicational, what would he have done with Forms like Change, Becoming, and Perishing, which he did recognise as *bona fide* Forms?[1] Clearly none of these could be self-predicational, for if they were, they would not be changeless, and would thus forfeit *being*. The same could be said of other Forms, not mentioned as such by Plato, but which his Theory would require him to recognise—Forms of the Sensible, Corporeal, Imperfect, indeed of all characters contrary to those which define the conditions of Platonic being. That Plato is never aware of any such difficulty shows that he was not aware of any Assumption which would have made the difficulty as obvious to him as it is to us.[2]

C. *Separation and Nonidentity*

What of the other assumption which I have called Nonidentity in Section I? If the question concerned only the nonidentity of particulars with their homonymous Forms—(A4a), (B4a) above—the answer would seem so obvious as to be trivial. If the Form is

[1] *Parm.*, 136b.

[2] The only Form in whose case one might think that Plato did feel such a difficulty is that of Not-Being. But a careful study of his discussion of Not-Being in the *Sophist* will, I think, show that the real difficulty Plato felt about Not-Being was not *caused* by reasoning that, since all Forms are self-predicational, this Form must also be such, and hence have the character of not being. The difficulty he states at 240a–241b is simply that of thinking what is not, without, by this very fact, being involved in the contradictory assumption that what is not is. His discussion of Not-Being cannot, therefore, be cited as evidence that he understood Self-Predication.

fact that elsewhere he makes much of the point that characters predicable of Forms cannot be predicated of their particular instances; e.g. Changelessness, predicable of (the Form) Man, but impredicable of any man (*Top.*, 137b 3 ff., 148a 15 ff.; and cf. 113a 24 ff. See Cherniss, pp. 1 ff., for a discussion of these passages); and at *Met.*, 1059a 10 ff. he turns this point into an argument against the Theory of Forms. Had he clearly seen that Plato's Forms are self-predicational he would have argued to even better effect that, on this hypothesis, the Forms which *are* predicable of the particulars *qua* particulars (e.g., perishableness, change, mortality) have predicates incompatible with their predicates *qua* Forms (e.g., imperishableness, changelessness, immortality).

what we have seen it to be, how could it help being other than the particulars whose characters it enables us to discern? Indeed, it might be said that Plato is the first Western thinker to make the distinction between a character and the things that have that character a matter of philosophical reflection. For did not his Theory of Forms call attention, and for the first time, to the 'reality' of universals as distinct from that of material existents? This is, of course, perfectly true. But what is no less true is that the Platonic ontology inadvertently blurs the very distinction it was devised to express. It compels Plato to think of the difference between empirical existents and their intelligible properties as a difference between 'deficiently' real and perfectly real things, i.e. as a difference in degree between beings of the same kind, instead of a difference in kind between different kinds of being. To say that the difference between a white thing, like wool or snow, and the universal, Whiteness, is a difference in degree of reality, is to put Whiteness in the same class with white things albeit as a pre-eminent member of that class, endowed in pre-eminent degree with the character which its fellow members possess in variously deficient degrees; it is to think of Whiteness as a (superlatively) white thing, and thus to assimilate it categorically to white things, instead of so distinguishing it from them. For a good example of this I can refer to the closing sentence of the statement of the Separation Assumption I have cited above from *Parmenides*, 130b: 'And do you believe that Similarity itself is something separately from the Similarity which we possess?' Instead of asking the simple question, 'Is the property, Similarity, distinct from any of the things that have that property?' Plato is misled by his Separation Assumption to ask the entirely different question, 'Is the property, Similarity, distinct from the property of Similarity which is exemplified in particular instances of Similarity?'[1] To say, 'Yes',

[1] This is why a symbolic transcript of Plato's statements must distinguish systematically between the substantival form, *F*-ness, and the adjectival or predicative function of the same Form, *F*. Thus, in transcribing the first Man Argument it was necessary to distinguish between Largeness, as *F*-ness and the Largeness of large things, as *F*. Similarly the Nonidentity Assumption must be rendered as, 'If *a* is *F*, *a* cannot be identical with *F*-ness' (A4a), (B4a) above. Were it not for the systematic dualism of *F* and *F*-ness, it could be stated more simply as, 'If *a* is *F*, *a* cannot be identical with *F*', which I take to be the correct statement of this fundamental principle. In the absence of the Separation Assumption we would not need the two symbols, *F* and

to *this* question, is to pass from the distinction between thing and property which every philosophy must acknowledge to the vastly different distinction, peculiar to Plato's ontology, between two grades of reality in things and properties: perfectly real things and properties in the Forms, imperfectly real things and properties in the sensible world.

Among the unintended and unexpected consequences of this distinction is the Nonidentity Assumption in its full-strength form, (A4) and (B4) above, i.e. that the nonidentity of a Form with any of its homonymous instances holds not only when the instance is a particular but also when the instance is the Form itself. Certainly Plato never said any such thing; indeed this is the last thing he would have wished to say. The Separation Theory is clearly meant to separate Forms from particulars, Largeness from large things, not to reintroduce the separation within the formal pole of the Form-particular relation, to split off Largeness from Largeness_1. Yet just this is the nemesis of the Degrees-of-Reality Theory which is part and parcel of the Separation Assumption. For if the Form, Largeness, is superlatively large, while large mountains, oaks, etc., are only deficiently large, it must follow that the single word, *large*, stands for two distinct predicates: (*a*) the predicate which attaches to the large particulars; (*b*) the predicate which attaches to Largeness.[1] Call (*a*), 'large' and (*b*),

[1] If these two predicates were identical, the Form would be indistinguishable from the predicate which attaches to particulars, and the 'Separation' would collapse: *F*-ness would then be the *F* of *F* particulars, and the distinction between, e.g. 'Similarity itself' and 'the Similarity which we possess' at 130b would vanish. Had Plato 'believed that . . . the idea *is* that which the particular *has* as an attribute' (Cherniss, p. 298)—a beautiful statement of what Plato's theory *should have been*—the 'Separation' would have never arisen. This is my main objection to Cherniss' interpretation of the Third

F-ness; the latter would be redundant. To recognise this is perhaps the simplest way of collapsing the Third Man Argument (and, unfortunately for Plato, thereby also collapsing the Separation Assumption). I may add that, though it is language which suggests the distinction between *F*-ness and *F* (by its double furniture of substantives and adjectives or predicative terms), yet neither can this distinction be observed without occasional violence to the linguistic distinction (for we are still forced to transcribe as 'F' any term which refers to the property of a particular: the Largeness of large things or 'the Similarity which we possess' must be taken, on Plato's own theory, as adjectival in sense though they are substantival in linguistic form). A simple linguistic explanation of Plato's theory would be only simple-minded.

'large$_1$'. Now since Largeness is, by hypothesis, the Form of the predicate 'large', it cannot be the Form of the different predicate 'large$_1$'. There must then be two Forms, Largeness and Largeness$_1$ and the full-strength form of the Nonidentity Assumption becomes unavoidable: not only can no large particular be identical with the Form, Largeness, in virtue of which it is seen as large, but Largeness itself cannot be identical with the Form, Largeness$_1$, in virtue of which we see that it is large. The same reasoning which compelled the 'separation' of any F particular from its corresponding Form, F-ness, also compels the 'separation' of any Form from itself, and splits off F-ness from F-ness$_1$.

We can now see why Plato could neither convince himself that the Third Man Argument was valid, nor refute it convincingly. He could do neither without stating explicitly its two implicit assumptions. This he never did; he never looked at either of them in the clear light of explicit assertion, for, had he done so, he would have had compelling reason to repudiate both, since their logical consequences are intolerable to a rational mind. But their repudiation would have been fatal to the Separation Theory and the Degrees-of-Reality Theory, which are central to his explicit metaphysics. He was thus holding consciously a metaphysical Theory whose disastrous implications were hidden from his conscious mind. He was saying and believing things which in self-consistency he would have had to take back, had he clearly understood their true logical outcome.

D. *The Record of Honest Perplexity*

Now it is perfectly possible to be in this state of mind and have no inkling of its insecurity. The run-of-the-mill dogmatist lives in it all his life and never feels any the worse for it. The victims of the Socratic elenchus were cheerfully confident that they knew what they were talking about, and they would have ever remained so had they recited their ignorant certainties to anyone but

---

Man Argument (pp. 293–300): he does not see that the 'perfect reality' of the Forms is incompatible with their *being* the (imperfect) predicates of particulars. If the Forms *were* attributes of particulars, 'Separation' would make no sense, and the Third Man Argument would be not only pure sophistry but so easily refutable sophistry that it would be impossible to understand why Plato takes it as seriously as he does yet leaves it unrefuted.

Socrates. But a great philosopher is not likely to be so thick-skinned and so blind. Perfect catharsis from self-deception is given to him no more than to his fellows. But he is far more likely to become aware sooner or later of the difference between those areas of his thought where he has achieved true lucidity and those where he has not. When he first projects a new theory that succeeds in solving to his immediate satisfaction hitherto unsolved problems and satisfies deep longings of his heart, delight in his creation may produce a kind of rapture that leaves little room for self-questioning. This is Plato's mood in the *Phaedo*, the *Symposium*, and the *Republic*. The Theory of Forms is then the greatest of certainties, a place of unshakable security to which he may retreat when doubtful or perplexed about anything else.[1] But as he lives with his new theory and puts it to work, its limitations begin to close in upon him. He begins to feel that something is wrong, or at least not quite right, about his theory, and he is puzzled and anxious. If he has courage enough, he will not try to get rid of his anxiety by suppressing it. He may then make repeated attempts to get at the source of the trouble, and if he cannot get at it directly he may fall back on the device of putting the troublesome symptoms into the form of objections. He can hardly make these objections perfectly precise and consistent counterarguments to his theory. Unless he discovers the exact source of its difficulties and can embody the discovery, the objections are likely to be as inadequate in their own way as is their target. They will be the expression of his acknowledged but unresolved puzzlement, brave efforts to impersonate and cope with an antagonist who can neither be justly represented nor decisively defeated because he remains unidentified and unseen. This, I believe, is an exact diagnosis of Plato's mind at the time he wrote the *Parmenides*.

I. THE FIRST OBJECTION, *Parmenides* 130e–131e

Of the three formal objections to the Theory of Forms, the first has struck every reader by its patent crudity of expression: if a

[1] Transparently so at *Phd.*, 99c ff.; the 'refuge' metaphor is Plato's own, 99e 5. Another characteristic of this mood is the grandiose schemes which it projects, such as the hope for a complete deduction of all the Forms from the Form of the Good in the closing paragraphs of Bk. VI of the *Republic*, a scheme which is never worked out in the dialogue, doubtless for the reason that it is unworkable.

single Form has many instances, either the whole of the Form must be 'in' each of them, or only a part of the Form; if the first, the Form will be 'in'[1] each instance 'in separation' from itself;[2] if the second, only a fraction of the Form will be in each instance, so that the latter will not be an instance of this Form, *F*-ness, but of another Form, *F*-ness$_1$, which will be a fraction of *F*-ness.[3] The words of the argument force the conception of Forms into the flagrantly inappropriate terms of quasi-physical location, separation, and division. Hence many commentators have drawn the inference that the difficulty they portray is wholly fictitious and that Plato knew that it was such. But this inference is certainly wrong, since as their critics have remarked,[4] Plato reasserts the difficulty in almost identical terms in the *Philebus* (15b–c), though this time not as an objection to his Theory, but as a problem which continues to cause him extreme perplexity and to which he has still to find an answer. Certainly Plato knew that the relation of Form to instance, whatever else it might be, is not that of physical coalescence of either the whole Form or else a part of the Form with any of its instances. And he could easily demolish Parmenides' objection by replying that its very language misdirects it against a man of straw. He did not waste a word to win this cheap dialectical victory because he knew that the difficulty lay at a much deeper level, which he eagerly sought to reach, but which he failed to reach, as the phrasing of the objection shows.

What remained hidden to him becomes clear to us when we note, with Cornford (p. 87), that in illustrating the argument with the Form, Largeness, Parmenides at one point obviously assumes

[1] *Parm.*, 131a 8, ἐν . . . εἶναι, b 2, ἔνεσται. Plato indulged in this way of talking about instantiation in the middle dialogues, as, e.g. at *Phd.*, 103b 8. The Word ἐνεῖναι had a bewildering variety of uses in common speech (see Liddell & Scott, s.v.). But in cosmological and medical usage it had reached a single, definite meaning: '*x* is in *y*' had come to mean, '*x* is a physical ingredient in physical compound *y*', as I have remarked in *Class. Philol.*, XLII (1947), 171 and n. 139.

[2] Here is the immediate nemesis of the *chorismos*, announced at 130b–e, but an intolerably crude one, since it talks of the (physical) 'separation' of particulars from one another and of the (metaphysical) 'separation' of Form from particulars in the same sentence (131b 1–2) as though the word had the same sense in the two cases.

[3] The analogy of the sail dots the i's of the transposition of a metaphysical statement into a physical one.

[4] E.g. Robinson, pp. 59–60.

that Largeness is self-predicational: 'Suppose you divide Largeness itself, and each of the many large things is then large by *virtue of a portion of Largeness which is smaller than Largeness itself . . .'* (131c–d). To say that a 'part' of the Form, Largeness, is *smaller* than Largeness is most certainly to imply that Largeness is large. Less obviously, but no less certainly, the same assumption and the Separation Assumption of which it is a part are involved in, and are of source of, the whole difficulty which the objection seeks to express, and if we put these Assumptions into our question we can state the difficulty without indulging in the irrelevant language of the text: If F-ness is F, and is such in virtue of satisfying requirements which no empirical particular can satisfy, how can any empirical particular be F? If it were genuinely or perfectly F, it would have to be identical with F-ness, which is contrary to the hypothesis that it is not the Form, but a particular. If it were not, it could not be said to be fully F, but only 'deficiently' F, or F in lesser degree; it would then be not F, but F_1, where F_1 is the lesser degree of F instantiated in the particular. This alternative obviously leads to an infinite regress, symmetrical with that of the Third Man Argument:[1] For, by the same reasoning, if F_1 be a character, it can only be perfectly exemplified by the Form, F-$ness_1$, and the particular could not then be F_1, but only F_2, and so on *ad infinitum*. So stated, the objection exposes the self-contradiction of the Separation Assumption when fully explicated to involve both Self-Predication and the Degrees-of-Reality Theory. Plato could not have stated it in this way without stating one of the components of this complex premiss, Self-Predication.

2. THE THIRD OBJECTION, *Parmenides* 133b–134e

Plato faces this one in a more hopeful mood. It could be answered, he says, but only to (and, presumably, by) an extremely competent and persistent thinker.[2] Why then doesn't he answer it? Not

[1] Each of the two regresses exposes symmetrical contradictions in the Theory which may be stated as follows:

(*a*) If the Form be F, then it cannot be F, but F_1 (as we have seen at (B5a) in Sec. 1, above);

(*b*) If the particular be F, then it cannot be F, but F_1.

[2] *Parm.*, 133b.

because he is pressed for time; the second part of the *Parmenides* shows that he has plenty of time. He doesn't, because the answer he would have given to this objection, as to the first, would not have solved the problem which is infinitely more important to him than the defeat of the objector. Nor could he have solved this without, once again, spotting the Self-Predication Assumption which, enmeshed in the Degrees-of-Reality Theory, greets us here at every turn.[1] The argument implies that only the Form, Mastership, can possess 'exactly'[2] the property of mastership and (since the property is a relational one) only in relation to the Form, Slavery, which alone possesses 'exactly' the converse property of slavishness; and that only the Form, Knowledge, can be 'exactly' knowledge.[3] Hence, it infers, you and I cannot *be* Masters or Slaves, since we are men, not Forms, and cannot have the properties of Forms but only less 'exact', or 'human', properties of mastership or slavishness or anything else; nor can we have Knowledge (for this is the prerogative of the Form, Knowledge, and we are not the Form), but only something else which is less 'exact' than Knowledge. Anyone familiar with Plato's Theory of the Soul, which includes his Theory of Recollection, would have known how to talk back to Parmenides at this point. One could discredit Parmenides by telling him that he grossly ignored a part, and a most important and relevant part, of the philosophy he is criticising. But if this had silenced Parmenides, it would have left untouched the logical difficulty, which is precisely the same as in the first objection and raises the same unanswerable question: If only F-ness can be F, how can anything else be F?

[1] So Cornford, p. 98. But he naïvely infers that, because Self-Predication is 'grossly fallacious', Plato saw that it was. Had Plato seen this, he would have said so; and for this he would not have needed 'a long and remote train of argument' which Plato tells us (133b) would be required to defeat the objection; the Greek equivalent of Cornford's single sentence ('It confuses the Form . . . with perfect instances of the Form') would have been enough. And had he done so, Plato would have seen what Cornford fails to see: that this demolition of the objection to the Theory would have demolished the Theory.

[2] He introduces this term only towards the end (134c–d), but the whole argument would have gained precision had he done so from the start. The argument turns on the difference in degree between the exemplification of the Form in the Form and in the particulars: 'exact' Mastership, Knowledge, etc., refers to the former against the latter, to render the sense of 'perfect', 'complete'.

[3] Cf. *Phdr.*, 247d–e.

3. THE THIRD MAN ARGUMENT ONCE AGAIN

Seen side by side with its mates it appears to great advantage. Its language is refined in contrast to the crudity of the first, terse and compact where that of the third is loose and longwinded. The device it exploits, the infinite regress, was the prize product of Greek logical virtuosity, and Plato must have found a bitter delight in turning it against his own Theory. Yet for all its showy elegance it fails as a diagnostic device to locate the exact source of the logical difficulties of the Theory of Forms, for the reasons which I set forth in Section I. And it fails also in its formal purpose, which is to prove that the Theory is logically bankrupt because it involves an endless regress. It could only have succeeded in this, had it been known to be a valid argument; but it could not be known to be this, unless the tacit premisses which alone can warrant the inference from its first to its second step were supplied. I trust it has now become clear that Plato could not supply these and so could not know whether or not it was a valid objection to his theory. This being the case, I can now show that Plato had a perfectly good way of refuting the Third Man Argument as stated by his Parmenides.[1] All his Parmenides has to offer in place of the two tacit premisses is the Separation Assumption in its explicit form, i.e. not understood to imply both Self-Predication and full-strength Nonidentity. But if these implications are not understood, the conclusion of Parmenides' argument is grossly fallacious, and Plato could easily have shown it to be such:

If the Separation Assumption is to be the reason for acknowledging the 'separate existence' of the predicative Form, *F*-ness, from the particulars of which it is predicated, Plato could argue

[1] Other ways of reconstructing Plato's refutation of the Argument abound in the literature (e.g. Taylor, *Plato's Parmenides*, pp. 20 ff.; Goblot, pp. 447 ff.; Cornford, pp. 90 ff.; Cherniss, pp. 292 ff.), but I believe that none of them is free from one or more of the following errors: misunderstanding of the Argument; the view that Plato did not in fact assume Self-Predication; the misapprehension that an argument, somewhat similar in form to the Third Man Argument, employed elsewhere (see above, p. 240, n. 1 *sub fin.*) by Plato to establish the unity of each Form, somehow explodes the Third Man Argument. Ross (p. 87) has an admirably terse refutation of this last misapprehension: 'To show that if there were two Ideas of bed there would have to be a third does nothing to disprove the contention that if there is one Idea of bed, related to particulars as Plato supposes, there must be a second.'

that the same Assumption could not require, but must forbid, the separation of the next predicative Form, F-ness$_1$, from the original Form, F-ness, of which F-ness$_1$ is predicated; and if *this* separation were to fail, the infinite regress would fail. Plato could argue that his metaphysical theory is only intended to separate Forms from particulars, since the ground of the separation is that only the Forms could satisfy the stipulated conditions of being. 'If that is so,' he could ask, 'what warrant is there for saying that F-ness$_1$ is separate from F-ness? Both, as Forms, fully satisfy the conditions of being, both have exactly the same degree of reality, and the ontological separation premissed on a difference of such degree fails completely. Thus Beauty is separate from any beautiful thing of our common experience because its beauty is so different from theirs—an intelligible, changeless, unblemished beauty such as, alas, we have never seen in the world about us, and never will. In what respect then could Beauty$_1$ differ from Beauty? How could the two fail to coincide, if they both designate the highest of beauty?' By such a reply Plato could have stopped the regress dead in its tracks, easily in the first version of the Argument, and also in the second by merely pointing out that the model–copy relation of predicate to instance is meant to hold only when the instance is an empirical particular and not when both predicate and instance are Forms. He could thus defeat the Argument by retreating in effect to the weaker form of the Nonidentity Assumption (A4a), (B4a) above. His objection would stand unless Parmenides could then go on to show why, in spite of it, the Degrees-of-Reality Theory did imply full-strength Nonidentity, (A4), (B4) above.

It is rare enough to find a philosopher employing his best resources to construct an argument which, were it valid, would have destroyed the logical foundations of his life's work.[1] What is rarer still and, to my knowledge, absolutely without parallel in the pages of Western philosophy, is to find a man who faces such an emergency as Plato did. He had every reason to seek to demolish it, for it was believed to be valid, as e.g. by Aristotle,

[1] I believe it is a mistake to think (e.g. with Ross, pp. 87 ff.) that the Argument is fatal not to Plato's Theory, but to the language in which he expressed it. It should now be apparent that the butt of the Argument is no incidental expression whose excision from Plato's text would leave his Theory intact, but the literal, rock-bottom doctrine of his ontology: the Degrees-of-Reality Theory and the Separation Assumption.

and so long as he left it standing it remained an ugly threat to his most original philosophical contribution. And he had a way and, by every rule of disputation, a perfectly fair way, of demolishing the argument, by taking it at face-value and replying not to what it implies but to what it says. His reticence at this point is a remarkable tribute to his perspicacity as a thinker and to his honesty as a man. To study the Third Man Argument in this way is to see the stature of the philosopher rising far above the limitations of his philosophy.[1]

ADDENDUM (1963)

The following analysis of the Third Man Argument avoids a few technical defects in my earlier one:

1. If any set of things are *F*, there exists a unique Form, *F*-ness, in virtue of which each of them is *F*.

1a. *a*, *b*, *c*, are *F*.

From *1* (a fair enough statement of one of the cardinal tenets of Plato's ontology) and *1a* (a commonplace), it follows that

1b. *F*-ness exists.

Now Parmenides goes on (*Parm*. 132a 6–11) to assert that

2. If *a*, *b*, *c*, and *F*-ness are *F*, there exists a second Form, *F*-ness$_1$, in virtue of which *a*, *b*, *c*, and *F*-ness are *F*.

But the antecedent of this hypothetical does not follow from anything said above. *1a*, *1*, and *1b* do not entail that *F*-ness is *F*. To derive this we need a new assumption,

SP. The Form in virtue of which a set of things have a certain character itself has that character.

From this, given *1*, it follows that

3. *F*-ness is *F*.

From *3* and *1a* we can now derive the antecedent of *2*,

2a. *a*, *b*, *c*, and *F*-ness are *F*.

Even so, the consequent of *2* does not follow: what is there to keep *F*-ness itself from being the Form in virtue of which *a*, *b*, *c*, and *F*-ness are *F*? To exclude this possibility we need another assumption,

[1] Max Black has given me generous help with this paper. Though he cannot be held responsible for any statement in it, his advice and criticism have saved me from many mistakes.

NI. The Form in virtue of which a set of things have a certain character is not identical with any of them.

Given this, *1*, and *2a*, we can now infer the consequent of *2*,

2b. A second Form, *F*-ness$_1$, exists, in virtue of which *a*, *b*, *c*, and *F*-ness are *F*.

The existence of a Third Form, *F*-ness$_2$, and so *ad infinitum* would then follow by iteration of the reasoning.

Just three comments:

(1) I pointed out in 1955 (*Philos. Review*, LXIV, 442–3) that Plato supplies us with the materials for two distinct (but complementary) versions of the argument he puts out so briefly in *Parmenides*, 132a 1–b 2: an ontological and an epistemological one. The latter would run as follows (I underline those phrases which mark the differences from the ontological version I have just given above):

1. If any set of things are *F*, there exists a unique Form, *F*-ness in virtue of which each of them is *apprehended as F*.

1a. *1b*: as above.

2. If *a*, *b*, *c*, and *F*-ness are *F*, there exists a second Form, *F*-ness$_1$, in virtue of which *a*, *b*, *c*, and *F*-ness are *apprehended as F*.

SP. The Form in virtue of which a set of things *are apprehended as having* a certain character itself has that character.

3 and *2a*.: as above.

NI. The Form in virtue of which a set of things *are apprehended as having* a certain character is not identical with any of them.

2b. A second Form, *F*-ness$_1$, exists, in virtue of which *a*, *b*, *c*, and *F*-ness are *apprehended as F*.

The textual warrant for this second version is very plain: 'Will not a single Largeness appear once again, *in virtue of which all these will appear large*?' (132a 6–7). How a critic can quote these words and brush them aside with the remark that 'this is not sufficient evidence' for my view (*Phil. Rev.*, 71 (1962), p. 164, n. 8), I find it hard to understand. Nor can I see any justification for the view (expressed by the same critic, p. 164) that 'we do not according to Plato need any Form to enable us to discern that particulars are *X*.' Plato does not, of course, tell us that we need to *know* the

Form, Equality, in order to discern equality in the things we see. But he does hold that we need to *have known* the Form in the prenatal state and to have retained so much of this 'precognition' (*Phd.*, 74e 9) as will enable us to use the Form as the standard to which we 'refer' the things we see and judge to be defectively equal (*Phd.*, 75b). Some sort of apprehension of Equality, however imperfect, then we all must have, since we are all supposed to make such judgements. Nor does this involve Plato in any formal contradiction, since what he calls 'knowledge' is an austere accomplishment, entailing the ability to 'give an account' (*Phd.*, 76b) of the Form in statements which are 'infallibly' (*Rep.*, 477e) true. So he can claim that only dialecticians have 'knowledge' of Equality without denying the rest of humanity that less articulate grasp of the concept which they need to measure correctly, to calculate effectively, and the like. This is the sort of thing Plato evidently has in mind when he speaks of the Form Largeness in this argument as that 'in virtue of which all these will appear (i.e. will be apprehended as) large'. Were it not for the Form, things would neither be, nor appear to be, large. Both assertions are good Platonic doctrine, and Plato would have every reason for putting both into this argument.

(2) 'Self-Predication'. I am not enamoured of this term, and now use it only because it seems well-established in the literature. It should be obvious that when extended from '*white* is white' to 'the Form, Whiteness, is white', *Self-Predication* is used with a certain license. Strictly speaking, what is predicated of itself is the character which things have (and are apprehended as having) in virtue of the Form.

(3) 'Nonidentity'. It has been claimed (R. S. Bluck, 'The *Parmenides* and the "Third Man",' *Class. Quart.*, N.S. VI (1956), pp. 29 ff., on p. 30) that in the full-strength form (in which it applies to Forms no less than to particulars) this assumption 'is not in fact involved in Plato's Theory'. There is at least one passage that proves that it is: the famous argument in the *Republic* (597c) that if there were two Forms of Bed, there would have to be a third, 'whose character both of them would have' (ἧς ἐκεῖναι ἂν αὖ ἀμφότεραι τὸ εἶδος ἔχοιεν). Were it not for this assumption there would be no reason why there would have to be a *third* Form, i.e. why the required Form should not be identical with either the first or the second of the supposed Forms.

XIII

THE THIRD MAN AGAIN

(1956)

P. T. Geach

I AM very much indebted to Professor Vlastos for helping me to interpret the Third Man Argument (*TMA*)—indebted both to his recent article in *The Philosophical Review* (see above, Ch. XII), and to his elucidations in private correspondence. On two main points we are in complete agreement. First, the *TMA* is read by us both as 'the record of honest perplexity'. Plato is not making a merely hypothetical use of an assumption '*p*' in order to infer 'not *p*', which would be a straightforward *reductio ad absurdum*; he begins by *asserting* '*p*', and then states an argument with 'not *p*' as its conclusion—and this argument, if valid, reveals a hidden inconsistency in the premisses, one never tracked down or formulated by Plato himself. Second, we both hold that one of Plato's tacit assumptions is Self-Prediction—that for him a term '*F*' applies not only to 'the many' *F*s but also to the Form that makes them *F*s. I shall allege some evidence for Self-Prediction later; if anything, I take it more seriously than Vlastos does.

There are, however, some important disagreements between Vlastos and myself; and so I have thought it worth while to set out my own interpretation of the *TMA*. First: I cannot believe Vlastos has rightly located the inconsistency in the premisses of the *TMA*. On his view, Plato reaches the conclusion of the *TMA* by using two tacit assumptions: Self-Predication ('*F*-ness is itself an *F*') and Nonidentity ('no *F* is identical with *F*-ness'). Now these premisses are not merely inconsistent; they are formally contradictory, related as '*p*' and 'not *p*'. For 'no *F* is (identical with) *F*-ness' is equivalent to '*F*-ness is no *F*', which is the direct contradiction of '*F*-ness is itself an *F*'. The conclusion of the

TMA would therefore 'follow', as Vlastos himself points out, only in the trivial way that absolutely anything 'follows' when you use '*p*' and 'not *p*' together as premisses. Such a thorough muddle is not lightly to be imputed to Plato; it will be more satisfactory if we can find a set of assumptions each of which Plato may well have made, and interpret the *TMA* as bringing out a buried and unobvious inconsistency of the set.

Second: in formulating Plato's arguments Vlastos continually uses abstract nouns like 'largeness' and '*F*-ness' as designations of Forms. Now, if our aim is to bring out Plato's implicit assumptions about Forms, we had better not call Forms by names that embody a lot of implicit assumptions of our own. Terms like '*F*-ness' have just this disadvantage. The way '*F*-ness' is formed from '*F*' embodies a tacit assumption that something or other stands in a special relation (expressed by the suffix '—ness') to the things that are *F*; and to use '*F*-ness' (as Vlastos does) with the grammar of a singular term embodies a further tacit assumption that there are not several bearers of this relation to 'the many' *F*s. So far, indeed, no assumptions have been brought out that Plato would not have accepted, since he held that there *is* one and only one Form answering to a term '*F*' and standing in a peculiar relation to 'the many' *F*s. But the conclusion of the *TMA* calls in question this very view of his; and we can no more formulate that conclusion properly in terms of '*F*-ness' than we could formulate polytheism by saying 'Allah is many', when the mere use of 'Allah' embodies monotheistic assumptions.

I suspect, moreover, that because of the way philosophy has developed, the use of abstract nouns in English embodies further tacit assumptions, which are less easily brought out, and which would be quite alien to Plato's mind. For one thing, I think the Nonidentity Assumption comes natural to us; to call *F*-ness '*F*' strikes us in most cases as absurd; whereas Plato thought of the Form answering to the term '*F*' as though the term could be applied to that very Form. I cannot, as I said, follow Vlastos in thinking that Plato simultaneously held that the term '*F*' is *in*applicable to the corresponding Form; I conclude that Plato's tacit assumptions about Forms were by no means the same as those which come natural to us when we use abstract nouns.

The English use of abstract nouns, whatever assumption it does in fact induce us to make, certainly tends to conceal from us what assumptions we are making. Plato, of course, himself often used abstract nouns to designate Forms; but the whole question is whether his use of such nouns embodied the same tacit assumptions as ours does. It is easy for us to 'know what we mean' by abstract nouns, ascribe the same meaning to those used by Plato, and elucidate Plato's other ways of designating Forms (which often read oddly in literal translation, and are indeed odd even in Greek) as mere synonymous variants of abstract nouns thus interpreted. But if we take such 'knowledge of what we mean' with us to the reading of the *Parmenides*, we shall be unable to make the critical examination of assumptions that such reading calls for.

I propose to consider, then, not just Plato's use of abstract nouns, but also his other ways of designating Forms. Forms corresponding to names of natural kinds or artefacts are not designated by abstract nouns, but only by concrete nouns with the definite article; Plato speaks of (the) Man and the Bed, not of Manhood and Bedness. (My title accordingly mentions the Third Man, not Manhood-3.) Of course Plato would have had to make up such abstract nouns; but he was quite capable of inventing words (e.g. *ποιότης* for 'quality') when he thought they were needed. Surely his chosen way of speaking of *these* Forms suggests that for him a Form was nothing like what people have since called an 'attribute' or a 'characteristic'. The bed in my bedroom is to the Bed, not as a thing to an attribute or characteristic, but rather as a pound weight or yard measure in a shop to the standard pound or yard. (I owe this insight to discussion with Wittgenstein.) This comparison brings in Self-Predication in a way, because we use the same word 'yard' or 'pound' both of the shopman's weight or measure and of the standard. The explicit Self-Predications 'the standard yard is a yard long', or 'the standard pound weighs a pound', would indeed not ordinarily be made; indeed, we should have some hesitation what to make of such statements. Are we to regard them as trivial tautologies? There is, on the contrary, some ground for regarding them as plain absurdities; the one thing that you cannot measure or weigh against a standard is—the standard itself. But our not using these explicit Self-Predications, and not knowing what to make of them, is all in favour of my comparison; for, as Vlastos emphasises, Plato does not make explicit Self-Predications about Forms, either.

We get further light from Plato's language about Forms that answer to relative terms. At *Parmenides*, 133c 8–d 4 we read that 'correlative Forms have their being in relation to one another, not in relation to their likenesses (or whatever you term them) that exist among ourselves, and are shared by us, and entitle us to the corresponding names; and these, which exist among us and bear the same name as the Forms, are relative to one another, not to the Forms.' These rather puzzling general statements are then explained (ibid., d 7–e 3) by using the relative terms 'master' and 'servant' as examples: 'if one of us is a master or a servant, then he is not a servant of *the* master (αὐτοῦ δεσπότου δήπου, ὅ ἔστι δεσπότης, ἐκείνου δοῦλός ἐστιν), nor is a master master of *the* servant (αὐτοῦ δούλου, ὅ ἔστι δοῦλος), but it is a *man* who is master or servant of a *man*'. The Forms answering to the relative terms 'master' and 'servant' thus bear the same names (cf. d 3) as a man who is *a* master or servant; but such a man, clearly, is not master of *the* servant, nor servant of *the* master, but master or servant of another man. *The* master, on the other hand, will be master of *the* servant, and *the* servant will be servant of *the* master.

Plato indeed goes on (ibid., e 3–4) to designate this same pair of correlative Forms by abstract nouns; 'mastership itself is mastership (literally: is what it is) of service itself, and service itself likewise is service of mastership itself'. This is very odd; surely, we protest, service is service of *a master*, not of mastership. The oddity arises, I should maintain, just because when we use abstract nouns in English we do not mean quite what Plato meant by his abstract nouns. It will be common ground, in discussion of this passage, that Plato used the abstract nouns rendered 'mastership' and 'service', and the concrete expressions rendered '*the* master' and '*the* servant', as synonymous designations of the same correlative Forms. Well then; instead of trying to make out that '*the* master' really means what we mean by the abstract noun 'mastership' (and similarly for '*the* servant' and 'service'), let us try using the concrete expressions to gloss the abstract ones. We then get: '*the* master is what he is (i.e. is master) of *the* servant, and *the* servant likewise is servant of *the* master'. This gives us, as literal translation of the abstract nouns does not, something that has the look and ring of a significant and correct statement; we have in it a peculiar idiomatic use of the definite article—the same use, of course, that we get in '*the* lion (has sharp claws)' and '*the* bed (is meant to lie upon)'. In both sorts of instance, Plato's Theory of Forms would give a very simple account of how the idiom stands to the realities: lions and beds are so called by virtue of their relation to the respective Forms, *the* Lion and *the* Bed; masters and servants, by virtue of their relation to *the* Master and *the* Servant. And *the* Master is to *the* Servant as *a* master is to *a* servant. (In this case, as often elsewhere, Plato uses the pronoun αὐτός with the force of this peculiar article.)

It would be a crude mistake to regard Plato's Theory as just a 'disease of language' generated by what we may call the *hypostatising* use of the definite article; but the presence of this idiom in Greek certainly influenced Plato's way of thinking about Forms, and his Theory was such as to be *aptly* expressed by means of this idiom. Now in Greek Plato can, and frequently does, pass freely between use of a hypostatising definite article with a concrete term[1] and use of the abstract noun corresponding to the concrete term; but in English we do not use interchangeably a pair of expressions so related. It is the Lion, not lionhood, that can be said to have a mane and sharp claws (and in this sort of instance Plato does not use made-up abstract nouns like 'lionhood').

Another case in which our natural assumptions when we use abstract nouns diverge from Plato's is that of abstract nouns expressing plurality. For us, plurality is not plural; nor is equality or similarity plural, though it takes two things at least to be equal or similar. But we find Plato using indifferently, to refer to the same Form, 'the many' and 'multitude' (τὰ πολλά and πλῆθος, *Parm.*, 129b 6–7, d 5–8); and again, 'the similars' and 'similarity' (αὐτὰ τὰ ὅμοια and ὁμοιότης ibid., a 1, a 4, b 1); 'the equals' and 'the equal' and 'equality' (αὐτὰ τὰ ἴσα and αὐτὸ τὸ ἴσον and ἰσότης, *Phd.*, 74a 11–12, c 1, c 4–5). This way of speaking can be explained if we take seriously the conception of the Form as a standard. The Imperial Standard Equality, or Imperial Standard Equals, would naturally consist of a pair of absolutely equal things. (Again I owe this comment to Wittgenstein.)

This doctrine about Forms which involve plurality may well appear in hopeless conflict with Plato's saying that each Form is

[1] I am here treating adjectives, not only substantives, as concrete terms. Cf. Mill's *Logic*, Book I, c. ii, § 4.

one (ἓν ἕκαστον εἶναι). But the immediate appearance of contradiction is only an appearance, which can be easily dispelled. In the realm of Forms, there is *only one* paradigm of equality; but this has to consist of *two* equals, or there wouldn't be equality at all. So far there is no contradiction. Further difficulties can of course be raised, but only, I think, of a sort that affect the Self-Predicative doctrine of Forms generally.

I have argued (like Vlastos) that for Plato the form answering to the term '*F*' is a paradigm *F*, the *F par excellence*; and (in disagreement with him) that on that very account we do best not to use English abstract nouns as names of Forms. There is, however, an English idiom—the hypostatising definite article—well adapted to express a platonistic theory. Let us imagine an English philosopher, Broadman, with a simple-minded view as to the significance of this idiom. Broadman believes in the Lion; he holds that when we say 'the lion has sharp claws and a long tawny mane', this is a true predication about the Lion. Mortal lions are so called only because of their relation to the Lion, whose right to the name is pre-eminent and unqualified. The Lion has whatever properly belongs to lions; a particular lion may have its mane clipped and its claws pared, but the Lion still has a long mane and sharp claws. Broadman's view of the Lion is thus implicitly Self-Predicational —though he might well think it not quite correct to say explicitly '*the* Lion is *a* lion'. It would be vain to urge upon Broadman the absurdity of saying that lionhood has a long mane and sharp claws; he would just reply, 'The word is yours, not mine; and from what you say it is clear that, whatever you mean by it, you don't mean what I mean by "the Lion".' It would be equally vain to protest that the things we call 'lions' have no set of exclusive common properties; Broadman will reply, 'I never said they had; what they have in common is that they all resemble the Lion, more or less, in various ways; that is what entitles them too to the name "lion", in so far as they are entitled to it'.

Another philosopher, Izzard, offers a more serious criticism.

'I suppose, Broadman, your view is this: When you consider the existence of a lot of lions, you think you can discern in them one and the same type; and so you believe there is one single entity, the Lion. This would be your ground for holding that each species is one single thing?'

'Quite so, Izzard; and I call such entities as the Lion, Forms.'

'Well, what about the Lion and the other lions? If you make a similar mental review of all of these, will there not come to light once more a single Lion? and will not this be what makes you take all of these to be lions?'

'I suppose so.'

'Well then, another Lion will have been revealed, over and above "the" Lion and the many mortal lions; and if you consider this Lion along with "the" Lion and the many lions, there will be yet another Lion, by relation to which *they* are all lions; so you won't get just one Form for each species, but no end of Forms.'[1]

Izzard's argument is strictly parallel to the *TMA* of *Parmenides*, 132a 1–b 2. Notice that the plurality to which Izzard argues is a plurality of *lions*—lions that are Forms—not a plurality of properties called 'lionhood', 'lionhood-1', 'lionhood-2', etc. Broadman's initial view is that for each species there is just one archetypal object which can suitably be called by the common name of the species; Izzard drives him into admitting that if there is one there must *pari ratione* be an indefinite number, and thus stultifying the original assertion.

I shall now state in an abstract logical way what seem to me to be Plato's implicit assumptions in the *TMA* (and the presuppositions of the Broadman–Izzard discussion).

(1) There is a set consisting just of the many *F*s that are not Forms.

(2) If *x* is a Form by which *y* is made to be an *F*, then *y* is not a Form by which *x* is made to be an *F*.

(3) If *A* is a set of several *F*s, and *x* is an *F* not belonging to *A*, then there is a set of *F*s containing just the members of *A* together with *x*. (I shall call this set '*A plus x*.')

(4a) Some *F* is a Form by which all other *F*s are made to be *F*s.

(4b) Any set consisting of several *F*s are all of them made to be *F*s by a Form that is itself an *F*.

It needs no argument, I think, to show that Plato assumed (1) and (2). His assuming (1) comes out in his speaking of 'the many large things' (τὰ πολλὰ μεγάλα), which can *all* be mentally

[1] Cf. Wittgenstein's *Remarks on the Foundations of Mathematics*, V, § 29 (pp. 182–3).

reviewed.[1] (1) need not indeed be true for all possible interpretations of 'F'; it is enough, however, if there is *some* interpretation for which it is true. (2) again is continually implied by Plato's language about Forms, e.g. by his talk of 'paradigm and copy'; the relation of an F to the Form that makes it to be an F is always taken to be asymmetrical. From (2) there immediately follows:

(2a) x is not itself a Form by which x is made to be an F.

As for (3), we shall presently see how it is used to get from step to step of the *TMA*.

If we hold that Plato's Theory tacitly involves Self-Predication (4a) will correctly state (part of) what Plato assumes at the start of the *TMA*. (4b) might seem at first sight to follow from (4a) or even to mean practically the same thing. On the contrary: if we add *both* of these assumptions to the set (1), (2), (3), we obtain an inconsistent set. The *TMA* brings out the inconsistency by using first (4a) and then (4b), as we shall see.

We may bring out the difference between (4a) and (4b) by a parallel pair of statements:

(i) There is a man from whom all other men are descended;
(ii) Any set of several men are all of them descended from some one man.

We get (i), (ii), from (4a), (4b), through replacing 'F' by 'man' and mention of the relation *being made to be an* F *by the Form* . . . by mention of the relation *descended from* . . .; the logical parallelism is exact. Here also, (ii) may seem to follow from (i), or even to say much the same thing. If however we add the assumptions

(iii) Any man belongs to a set of several men;
(iv) If x is a descendant of y, y is not a descendant of x;

then we find that the set of assumptions (i), (ii), (iii), (iv), is inconsistent. For (iv) gives us at once: (iva) x is not a descendant of x. By (i), there is a man, Adam say, from whom all other men are descended. By (iii), however, Adam belongs to a set of several men, B let us say. By (ii) there will now be a man x from whom all members of B are descended; and by (iva) x cannot be a member of B, so x is other than Adam; and Adam, being a member of B,

[1] 131d 1. I am assuming that for Plato this phrase is equivalent to 'the other large things', τἆλλα τὰ μεγάλα, at 132a 6.

will be descended from *x*. But then by (iv) there will be a man, namely *x*, not descended from Adam; which is in contradiction to (i), since *x* cannot be Adam either.

Let us similarly consider the consequences of the set (1–4b). From (2) and (4a) we infer (what indeed is asserted at the beginning of the *TMA*, if we interpet τὸ μέγα 'the great', Self-Predicationally):

(5) There is *just* one *F* that is a Form by which all other *F*s are made to be *F*s.

Proof. By (4a) there is at any rate one such *F*. Suppose, if possible, that there are two, *x* and *y*. Then since each is other than the other, it follows from (4a) that *x* is made to be an *F* by the Form *y*, and *y*, by the Form *x*; but this, by (2), is impossible. So there is *just* one such Form. Q.e.d.

On the other hand, from (1), (2), (2a), (3), (4b), we infer:

(6a) There is an unending series of *F*s, each of which is a Form by which the *F*s that are not Forms are made to be *F*s; (6b) there is no *F* that is a Form by which *all* other *F*s are made to be *F*s.

Proof. By (1) there is a set consisting just of the many *F*s that are not Forms. Call this set *W*.

By (4b) there is an *F*, *x* say, which is a Form making all the members of *W* to be *F*s. Being a Form, *x* is not a member of *W*.

By (3), since *x* is an *F* not in the set of *F*s *W*, there is the set of *F*s: *W plus x*.

By (4b) there is an *F*, *y* say, which is a Form making all members of the set *W plus x* to be *F*s. Since *y* is a Form, *y* is not a member of *W*; and by (2a) *y* cannot be *x*, either. So *y* is not a member of the set of *F*s: *W plus x*. And *y* makes all members of the set *W* to be *F*s.

By (3), then, there must be the set of *F*s: (*W plus x*) *plus y*.

By (4b) there is an *F*, *z* say, which is a Form making all members of the set (*W plus x*) *plus y* to be *F*s. Since *z* is a Form *z* is not a member of *W*; and by (2a) *z* cannot be *x* or *y*, either. So *z* is not a member of the set of *F*s: (*W plus x*) *plus y*. And *z* makes all members of the set *W* to be *F*s.

This pattern of argument can be repeated indefinitely; we get an unending series, $x, y, z, \ldots$, of each member of which we can say: It is an F that is a Form making all the members of W (viz. all the Fs that are *not* Forms) to be Fs. This proves (6a).

Moreover, suppose that there were an F that was a Form making *all* other Fs to be Fs. Call this F 'w'. A fortiori, w would make all Fs that were not Forms (all members of W, that is) to be Fs. So (as before) we show (i) that there is the set of Fs: W *plus* w; (ii) that some F outside *this* set is a Form by which all the members of the set are made to be Fs. So *this* F is a Form other than w, making w to be an F. So, by (2), w cannot make *this* F to be an F; contrary to our hypothesis. This proves (6b). Q.e.d.

The above proofs of (5) and (6a) are what I should offer as my formal reconstruction of the *TMA*, or of Izzard's argument against Broadman. (5) and (6a) are not indeed straight contradictories, but a slight modification of the proof of (6a) yields (6b), the contradictory of (5).

What escape from the contradiction offers itself? One way out would be to say that Plato did not really intend to assert (4b), but slipped into arguing as though (4b) were true because he did not distinguish it from (4a). This sort of confusion is very easy and very common, even when a pair of assumptions related like this are put into words—much more so, when they are merely implicit.

This was my original solution; but correspondence with Professor Vlastos convinced me that it would not do. I am now sure that, although Plato did not formulate (4a) and (4b) as distinct assumptions, his thought would be misrepresented if we dropped either of them from an explicit statement of his premisses.

Suppose we assume (1), (2), (4a), and (4b). (5) will then follow as before; and from (5) we can get:

(7) the (one and only) F that is a Form making all other Fs to be Fs is not a member of any set of Fs along with any other F.

Proof. By (5), we may assume the existence of one and only one Form (call it 'w') that is a Form making all other Fs to be Fs. Suppose, if possible, that w belongs to some set B consisting of several Fs. Then by (4b) there is a Form, y say, that is itself an F and makes all the members of B to be Fs. So w is made to be an F by the Form y; and y cannot be w, by (2a), nor, by (2), can y be made to be F by the Form w. But this contradicts our original assumption about *w*. So there can be no such set of *F*s, *B*, to which *w* belongs together with other *F*s. Q.e.d.

This conclusion would of course commit us to dropping assumption (3); and it would break the back of the *TMA*. If the unique *F* that is a Form making all the other *F*s to be *F*s is incapable of being joined in a set of *F*s with other *F*s, then the very first step of the regress, whereby the Lion (say) is grouped with 'the many' lions, becomes illegitimate. (7) might count as a precise formulation of what Plato meant by Forms' being 'separate'; it was, indeed, in order to do justice to this element in his thought that I decided against regarding his implicit use of (4b) as an accidental mistake in logic.

The idea that 'the' *F* cannot be grouped along with 'the many' *F*s in one and the same class of *F*s is, I believe, quite important for the elucidation of certain later developments. As Professor Vlastos has noticed, the scholastic teaching *de divinis nominibus* is intimately related to the Theory of Forms—there is indeed a complete chain of historical derivation by way of pseudo-Dionysius. God is archetypally Wise and Just; and in the real order (though not in the order of our learning to use the words) men can claim to be called 'wise' and 'just' only by participation in the divine attributes. When 'just' and 'wise' are said of God, the predication is only 'analogous' to calling a man just or wise; and yet, it is insisted, God really and truly *is* what we mean by 'wise' and 'just'. There are many difficulties about this doctrine of analogy—some of them parallel to Plato's difficulties as discussed in Vlastos' article. Now the theologians who have held this doctrine would certainly accept the following statement, both as being true and as being a consequence of the doctrine: 'God is wise and just, but no wise or just person other than God can be joined with God as a member of a set of wise or just persons.' When God instead of the Forms is taken to be the exemplar of the perfections found 'among us', then there will be new problems *de divinis nominibus* parallel to the old problems as to what can be predicated of the Forms; so it is natural that a theological statement parallel to statement (7) about the Forms should be a partial explication of the doctrine which was meant to resolve these new problems.

'But is there, in either case, anything at all explained by your "explication"? If the Form (or God) genuinely is *F*, then it is a merely arbitrary, *ad hoc*, solution to deny the possibility of joining "the many" Fs with the Form (or God) in the same group of Fs. If on the other hand the Form (or God) is said to be only analogously F, then really you ought to use a new predicate "F_1" instead of "F". But Vlastos' arguments ought to have sufficiently established what a mire you get into if you do introduce new predicates like this.'

I think I can show, in the first place, that it is not just arbitrary and *ad hoc* to say that 'F' is predicable only analogously of the exemplar F on the one hand and 'the many' Fs on the other. Let us go back to our illustration of the standard pound and 'the many' pounds. The standard pound must weigh a pound; one might say, it weighs a pound no matter what it weighs. But this is assuredly not true of 'the many' pounds; of none of them could one say: it weighs a pound, no matter what it weighs. Just because there is a sense in which the standard pound must be a pound, there is a sense in which it cannot be a pound—not as other weights can be. As I said before, they can be weighed against it, but it cannot be weighed against itself. In this familiar example of a standard and the things measured by the standard, there is nothing to surprise us in the fact that 'pound' is said of the standard pound and 'the many' pounds only analogously, and surely no temptation to replace the analogical use of 'pound' by use of a new term 'pound_1'.

Secondly, if it is objected that 'F' is not genuinely predicable of an exemplar F which cannot be joined in one group of Fs with 'the many' Fs, then it is being uncritically assumed that (at any rate if there are several Fs) the suppositions 'x is an F' and 'x belongs to a set of Fs together with other Fs' are deductively of the same force. A little knowledge of set theory, and of the solutions offered for paradoxes like Russell's,[1] is enough to show

[1] In fact, Frege's suggested way out of Russell's Paradox presents an interesting parallel to my way out of the *TMA* Let 'F' be taken to mean 'class that is not a member of itself'. Frege suggested that there is indeed a *biggest* class of Fs, K say; but that there is one unique F, namely K itself, which is not a member of K—just *because* K is an F, i.e. a class not a member of itself. So here there would be an F that could not be contained in a class of Fs along with 'the many' Fs; and consequently no class would contain *all and only* the Fs. (The parallel is spoiled by the fact that Frege's 'solution' only breeds a new contradiction in other cases; cf. W. V. O. Quine's article 'On Frege's Way Out', *Mind*, April 1955.)

that we are not compelled to assume this. It is admittedly unclear, failing a definite set theory, what consequences will follow from a statement of the form 'x is an F; but x does not belong to any set of Fs together with other Fs, although there are other Fs'. But it is not necessary to treat such a statement as either self-contradictory or equivocating over the use of 'F'. This sort of statement, which I offered as a partial explication of the doctrine of analogy, has far more clear-cut logical features than much that has been written about the doctrine; it is something with which a modern logician can at least make a start.

XIV

POSTSCRIPT TO THE THIRD MAN: A REPLY TO MR. GEACH (1956)

Gregory Vlastos

I FEEL extremely fortunate to have the benefit of comments as acute as those with which Mr. Geach now follows up those previously given me by Professor Sellars (*Philosophical Review*, LXIV [1955], 405 ff.). I have learned much from both. I should like to return the compliment to Mr. Geach, telling him, in Section I, what I believe is wrong with his analysis of the *TMA* and, in Section II, what I think both sound and penetrating in his insight into the Platonic Theory.[1]

I

For the imaginative originality and technical ingenuity of the formal argument which Geach presents in the second part of his paper I have great admiration. But it does not satisfy me as a reproduction, or a restoration, of *the TMA*—the one which, for better or for worse, Plato wrote down in the *Parmenides*. To be sure, some deviation from the text is inevitable since, as we agree, something must be inserted between the first and second steps of the argument recited by Plato's Parmenides (132a 1–4 and 6–11, respectively) to justify the transition. But I wish we could also agree that this expansion of the argument must be kept down to the bare minimum required to span the logical gap; and that the materials should be taken, if at all possible, from the quarry which we know Plato used in other contexts, so that the result will have

[1] But see the Additional Note (1965) on p. 291.

the best chance of matching what Plato himself would have done, had he been able to do the job. When I look at my own efforts through the eyes of the man with the most sensitive conscience in such matters—the philologist—I feel none too confident of my success in preserving the simplicity of the original. But at least I tried to keep intact those chunks of the *TMA* which are in Plato's text and can be transferred to one's own reconstruction with almost no alteration, save that of generalising the statements by utilising symbols wherever possible. Geach seems to have felt no obligation to do the same. There is nothing in his account to answer exactly to the first step in the text. The nearest thing to this is his (5). But this states quite explicitly the assumption of Self-Predication, which is not even implied in the first step of the text. And the reason given in the text why there must be a single Form is not good enough for Geach; so instead of reproducing Plato's reason for it (132a 2–3), he postulates a couple of tacit premisses (2 and 4a) and deduces it from *them*. In the case of the second step, Plato explicitly presents *its* conclusion (the crucial statement that 'another Form of Largeness will appear') as an inference from an explicit statement *in* the second step which, in turn, harks back to the first:

'If you *similarly* view mentally Largeness itself and other large things . . ., a single Largeness will appear once again, in virtue of which all these appear large.'

I italicise 'similarly' because this is what links the second step inferentially with the first. In Geach the second step is swallowed up in the proof of (6a). This is not so objectionable in itself, since (6a) is how Geach writes the conclusion which Plato draws from the second and subsequent steps; so there is some warrant for ingesting the second step in this manner. What is unfortunate is that the explicit inferences which *Plato* makes in arriving at the second step are now lost. The result is that instead of bringing in tacit premisses to *supplement* Plato's own explicit premisses, Geach constructs an argument whose *only* premisses are supposed to have been tacit in Plato's argument. But to say that everything is inferred from unstated premisses is as good as saying that nothing is explicitly inferred. A strange argument this would be.

My second and more important objection is directed not so much to the general form of Geach's analysis as to a matter of substance, a notion which turns up all over his formalisation, most conspicuously at (3) and then later at (7). It makes its first and most innocent appearance at (1), 'There is a set consisting *just* of the many *F*s that are not Forms.' Geach says this 'comes out in his (Plato's) speaking of 'the many large things' (τὰ πολλὰ μεγάλα).' He takes this from an earlier portion of the text (τῶν πολλῶν μεγάλων, 131d 1). What I find in the present text (that of the *TMA*) are not the quoted words but 'several large things' (πολλ' ἄττα μεγάλα) or, more exactly 'several things (which) seem large to you' (132a 2). But this may be of no importance. What is important is the question whether the reference to (i) 'several large things' in the text would warrant the statement that Plato assumed (ii) that there is a set consisting of several large things. I should have thought so. But this is not the point, for this is Geach's axiom-set, and it is what he thinks its statements mean that counts. Now he evidently thinks there is a vast difference between (i) and (ii). He must, else he would not hold that one can 'break the back' of the *TMA* by dropping (3) to pick up (7). For (3) affirms, while (7) denies, that if a Form, *w*, is an *F*, and a lot of particulars are *F*s, there is a set consisting of *w* and the particulars. Suppose, for example, there were just two *F* particulars, *a* and *b*, and an *F* Form, *w*. We would then have three *F* things. Thinking of them we might remark, (i) 'There are three *F*s,' and then again (ii), 'There is a set of three *F*s,' believing, in our innocence, that (i) would be quite enough to justify (ii), unless there were some very special reason to the contrary. But Geach would then tell us we have made a blunder. There is all the difference in the world between (i) and (ii), he would say: (i) could be true, while (ii) is false; knowing that (i) is true we wouldn't have the least warrant for holding that (ii) is also true, unless we are *told* so, as we are at (3). If we weren't told so, then, according to Geach, the contradiction would *not* materialise.[1] So the difference

[1] I say this, judging him by what he does rather than by what he says, for he hasn't quite got the two together. At one point he says he would 'still maintain . . . that failure to formulate and distinguish (4a) and (4b) was what made Plato unable to locate the source of the contradiction'. Thus must be a slip, or a hang-over from his former view. For he now *uses* both (4a) and (4b) in his deduction of the proposition (7) which clears Plato of the contradiction. Thus, on his own showing, Plato could have formulated and distinguished (4a) and (4b), and asserted them to boot, and still kept clear of the contradiction, so long as he refrained from asserting (3). Geach then *must* hold that (3) is 'the source of the contradiction'.

between (i) and (ii) makes all the difference between logical solvency and logical bankruptcy for Plato. But if there is all *that* difference between them, how could we possibly take (i) in the text as evidence for Plato's assumption of (ii)? And if we can't, what other evidence is there to bear out the claim that Plato did assume (1)?—None. And what evidence in the text that Plato assumed (3)?—None.

I have so far asked only for evidence in the text of the *TMA* itself to warrant Geach's claim that the questionable assumption he imputes to Plato *in* this argument is Plato's.[1] But let us now broaden the scope of the inquiry. What is there in Plato's work—all of it, not just this text—to correspond to the notion of the great difference between (i) and (ii) above which leaves one free to affirm or deny at pleasure that an *F* Form and *F* particulars may be joined in a set?—I should be inclined to say, Nothing. Plato never says *that* this or anything like it is true. Indeed, I don't know *how* he would have said it, for the corresponding terms are not in his logical vocabulary. But I don't want to be wooden in a matter as difficult and elusive as this. Even if Plato never talks about sets, does he say anything which *we* could interpret along the lines proposed by Geach? Geach says two things which raise, then dash, my hopes of encountering something of this sort:

(A) He says that (7) might count as a precise formulation of what Plato meant by Forms being 'separate'. Now what Plato means by the latter expression, though not easy to determine, does admit of investigation. The answer I have so far reached was sketched in my original article (see above, p. 246 ff.). To say that a Form 'exists separately' from its homonymous instances is to make several statements about it (I listed four), only one of which need be considered here:[2] that the Form, *x*, 'is itself the perfect

[1] He prefaces his axiom-set by saying, 'I shall now state in an abstract way what seem to be Plato's implicit assumptions in the *TMA*', and makes an effort to connect his (1) and (2) with the text of the *TMA*; but the effort seems to give out after this point.

[2] Because this all by itself is sufficient to show that 'separation' does the exact opposite of what Geach seems to think it does. I suspect he is misled by the *word*, which admittedly is confusing. But it may be worth recalling that Plato scarcely uses it himself; neither the substantive nor the corresponding adjective occur in his text, but only the adverbial 'separately', and this rarely (*Parm.*, 129d, 130b–d).

instance of the property or relation which the word for x connotes'; e.g. that Justice is just and pre-eminently so. But how could *this* be 'precisely formulated' (I should be satisfied with much less) in the statement that Justice cannot be grouped with just men, or be joined with them in a single set? If we want to prevent this illicit union what we surely have to do is to distinguish the respective logical types of Justice and just persons–acts–institutions; and if we do this, what temptation could we possibly feel to join such disparate terms in sets or groups? Geach's (7) would then be at best an innocuous formality; its only use would be against the logical prankster, for no one else would dream of doing what it solemnly forbids. But instead of doing this, Plato's Separation Theory does the opposite. In saying that Justice is pre-eminently just it requires us to do the very thing Geach's (7) is devised to prohibit: to think of Justice as the outstanding member of the class of just individuals.

(B) In the next paragraph Geach says, in effect, that Plato's theory is best understood as saying that a Form is 'only analogously' F, and that this *would* make (7) a reasonable assumption. But this contention leads to a dilemma, of which Geach is aware; he puts a tolerably good statement of it in the mouth of an objector in the antepenultimate paragraph of his paper. It could be made a little more strongly: The difference between '. . . is F' and '. . . is only analogously F' is such as to either (*a*) permit or (*b*) forbid statements to the effect that this Form and that particular are both F. (*a*) If it permits them, we have still to find the reason for the mysterious unjoinability of the F Form and the F particular, and for evidence that Plato believed any such thing. (*b*) If it forbids them, then the mystery is solved indeed, but at the price of calling for drastic changes in our axiom-set. Every reference (open or tacit) to the fact that the (any) Form is F must now be amended to read that the Form is 'only analogously F' or 'F by analogy'. And this will gum up hopelessly the deductive machinery of the axiom set.[1]

[1] Just look, for example, at Geach's first theorem, (5), which must now read, 'There is just one analogously F thing that is a Form by which all Fs are made to be Fs.' How much of the proof of (5) can now be salvaged? It began, 'By (4a) there is at any rate one such F.' But (4a) must now become, 'Something which is only analogously F is a Form by which all Fs are made to be Fs.' Can we then continue with the proof, 'Suppose, if possible, that there are two, x and y, and each is other than the other. Then since each is

At this juncture Geach refers to the extremely interesting analogy of the Standard Pound. But the point of the analogy can hardly be that this and the Platonic Form are 'only analogously' *F*. To say that the Standard Pound is 'analogously a pound' is scarcely permissible in the prose of philosophical discussion except as a preliminary to analysis, and the sort of analysis which would reveal *some* sense in which '. . . is a pound' (*without* the 'analogously') can be said of the Standard Pound. That the ordinary sense will not serve this purpose is obvious. If '*x* is a pound' is to be a statement of weight established by means of the operation of weighing *x* against the Standard Pound, then clearly it would be senseless to say this of the Standard Pound, for it would presuppose the necessarily false statement, 'the Standard Pound has been (or, can be) weighed against itself'. The illusion that it has sense would lead one to re-enact the plot of the *TMA*, conjuring up Standard Pound_1 against which to weigh the Standard Pound, and so forth. So unless we can find something else to justify saying, 'the Standard Pound is analogously a pound,' we would do well to drop it in the interests of clear thinking; since in the ordinary sense of '. . . is a pound' the Standard Pound is *not* like other objects; and the clean-cut way to say so would be to say that it is *not* a pound—where 'is not' means, of course, not that it would be materially false to say that it is, but logically senseless,[1] like saying 'the number, Three, is a pound,' or 'cheerfulness is a pound'.

Nevertheless I would strongly sympathise with those who feel that this cannot be one's last word on the subject, and that to say 'the Standard Pound is a pound' is not *exactly* like—not half as shocking and inexcusable as—saying 'the number, Three, is a pound'. The thing to do then is to find the respect in which the Standard Pound *is* like a pound of coffee, while the number, Three, is not. Obviously this is weight, a property which the

[1] This I take to be Wittgenstein's view, when he remarks that of the standard metre in Paris 'one can say neither that it is one metre long, nor that it is not one metre long' (*Philosophical Investigations*, § 50).

---

other than the other, it follows from (4a) that *x* is made to be an *F* by the Form *y*, and *y*, by the Form *x* . . .' ?—We cannot. For what we now have to show is that there cannot be two different things, *x* and *y*, which are both 'analogously *F*'; and (4a) as now revised is of no help for this purpose: it permits no inference and here *x* is made to be analogously *F* by *y*, and *y* by *x*.

Standard Pound does share with every material object. It would have this property even if no one had thought of conferring on it the dignity of its legal office; and the relative magnitude of its weight to that of other objects would be exactly the same[1] and could be determined perfectly without reference to its conventional status. Thus one could know that this platinum cylinder weighs the same as this bag of coffee without ever having heard of pound units or, for that matter, of any conventional unit of measurement. However, though we could determine this fact, we could not express it in terms of '. . . is a pound' without going back to the Standard Pound as the unit of measurement after all. The best I can do under the circumstances is to accept this necessity and offer the following sense for '. . . is a pound', to fit our Standard Pound: '. . . has the same weight as that of objects which have been (or, can be) found to weigh the same as the Standard Pound'. Since the latter are a pound in the ordinary sense (call this 'pound-*a*'), the Standard Pound could be said to be a pound in the derivative sense (call it 'pound-*b*') of having the same weight as theirs. Is this a good sense for '. . . is a pound'? I feel no missionary zeal to propagate its use. It just happens to be the best I can do to give substance to the persistent feeling one has that there is some sense in which the Standard Pound is a pound after all. But the point of my argument does not depend on the acceptance of this sense, or of any other. What I am arguing for can be put in the form of a second dilemma: Whether or not there is a sense in which it is a pound, the Standard Pound will not provide a parallel for something which *is* an *F* but may *not* be joined with other *F* things. For if there be no such sense, the Standard Pound will not be *F*, and the problem will not arise. And neither does it arise if there be such a sense. For there would then be two sets: one into which the Standard Pound does not go because it is not a pound in the same sense as other objects (the set of pound-*a*

[1] I feel uneasy with the statement that the Standard Pound 'weighs a pound, no matter what it weighs', because it might convey the suggestion (doubtless not intended by Geach) that something *could* be the Standard Pound without having a fixed weight in two quite definite ways: (*a*) the *substance* of which it is made maintaining a physically constant relation to the weight of other objects; (*b*) the *object* made from that substance and officially named 'the Standard Pound' suffering no change of *its* weight (e.g. by having bits of it chipped off by burglar-tourists). Both (*a*) and (*b*) are presuppositions of its *being* the Standard Pound.

things on the above analysis); another into which it does go, because it is a pound in *that* sense (the set of the pound-*b* things, above).[1]

II

The foregoing might give the impression that I have nothing but fault to find with Geach's paper. Let me do something to correct this impression, for even in the matter in which I have criticised him most vigorously the area of agreement is far wider than might appear. That the Form and its homonymous particulars are treated in the *TMA* as forming a single class, seems to me a true and penetrating way of getting at the source of the contradiction; and I quite agree that if this assumption were dropped the contradiction would not arise. All I am arguing for is a procedure for implementing this analysis: Find a sense for *F*—call it *F-a* by analogy with pound-*a* above—in which the Form is not *F*, and present Plato with this sense, telling him that if he will only remember to deny systematically that the Form is *F-a*, he will not be putting Form and particulars into an ill-formed set, and will have nothing to fear from the *TMA*. The next step (for we can't stop here, if we are going to allow Plato to keep assuming that the Form *is F* nonetheless) is to find him another sense—*F-b*—in which Form and particulars *are F*, and go into the same

[1] I may anticipate the following objection: 'That the Standard Pound is a pound-*b* is a necessary statement, while that anything else is a pound-*b* is contingent. It follows that the Standard Pound is not a pound-*b* *in the same sense* as other objects'.—Suppose this *did* follow; we would then be right where we started from, with no sense of '. . . is a pound' common to the Standard Pound and other objects, and the statement that the Standard Pound is 'analogously' a pound still unaccounted for. But *does* it follow? Surely a predicate can have the same sense in a necessary and a contingent statement: 'two' in 'a square has two diagonals' and 'Zebedee has two sons'. If identity of meaning in our predicates did not persist through change of modality in statements in which they are used, how could we draw inferences from modally mixed premises as, e.g. 'All *A* is *B*' (Necessary), 'This is *A*' (Contingent), Hence, 'This is *B*' (Contingent)? Naturally, if one is bent on getting two different senses for pound-*b* here, one *can* concoct two different predicates, 'necessarily pound-*b*' and 'contingently pound-*b*'. But so long as one keeps to 'pound-*b*' without working the modal qualifier into the predicate, I can see no objection to saying that there is *a* sense, 'pound-*b*', which is the same for the present purpose.

set without causing trouble.[1] This is what has to be done. And if we say that the Form is 'analogously *F*' to announce our intention of doing this, I would have no objection to the 'analogously'. Who would object to a promissory note?

But Geach's paper has something far more important to say, and though this was involved in the preceding discussion, it deserves to be noticed on its own account. It is that the Platonic Form is essentially a 'standard' and therefore 'nothing like what people have since called an "attribute" or "characteristic"'. The truth of the matter, in my opinion, is that (within certain limits) Plato wants his Forms to be *both* attributes and standard objects and that their logical distress is mainly the outcome of their having to complete this impossible assignment. But in highlighting one side of this picture Geach performs an extremely useful service. He succeeds at the very point at which free and easy guesses as to what Plato 'must have meant' fail: in producing good exegesis, illuminating in a new and exciting way some portions of Plato's text.

His account of Plato's use of the expression 'the equals themselves' (αὐτὰ τὰ ἴσα, *Phd.*, 74c) in contrast to sensible instances of equality, is the most ingenious and plausible explanation of this puzzling expression that has yet been offered. The only other that does justice to the plural is the one whose latest sponsor is Ross: 'an allusion to mathematical entities which are neither Ideas nor sensible things'.[2] But that the expression does refer to the Form,

[1] But before even starting to look for such a sense (and, more generally, to justify Self-Predication along these lines) we would have to assume that the Platonic Form matches in its own way the crucial feature of the Standard Pound, i.e. the fact that the latter must be a physical object and *have* weight as a condition of serving as a standard of weight. Thus, to get a just-*b* sense, corresponding to pound-*b* above, we would have to assume that Justice names a moral individual and/or a moral institution. I fail to see how we can do this without going further in the direction of particularising the Form than Plato ever did. This way of getting Plato out of the frying-pan of the *TMA* might get him into something worse.

[2] *Plato's Theory of Ideas* (Oxford, 1951), p. 25, and cf. p. 22; but cf. also p. 60, where it becomes uncertain whether Ross means to say this after all: cf. Ackrill's comments, *Mind*, LXII (1953), 553. Burnet's commentary gives us the cheering remark that 'there is no difficulty about the plural' and proceeds to gloss Plato with Euclid; presumably Burnet means that 'the equals themselves' are mathematical equals. This is also the view of the latest commentator, R. S. Bluck, in *Plato's Phaedo* (London, 1955), p. 67, n. 3;

Equality, is proved by the sequel in the text: From the premiss that 'the equals themselves' never even appear unequal, while sensible equals sometimes do, Plato infers that 'these equals [ταῦτα τὰ ἴσα, the sensibles ones] and the equal itself are not the same'. Here 'the equal itself' *must* refer to exactly the same thing as does 'the equals themselves' in the premiss, else the premiss would not justify the conclusion.[1] And since 'the equal itself' obviously refers to the Form, 'the equals themselves' must do so too. Some other interpretation must then be found, for the plural in 'the equals themselves' is not only inconsistent with Plato's linguistic usage (the normal expression for a Form is in the singular) but seems to contradict the doctrine of the *unity* of the Form. Geach's interpretation fills this gap better than any yet offered: it accounts for the plural without imputing to Plato a breach of his own doctrine, for it suggests that if Plato thought of Equality as a 'standard', he would have to think of this *one* Form as consisting of at least *two* equal things. I should like to accept Geach's interpretation, but with two reservations:

(i) I would not wish to say that Plato ever made this thought explicit, i.e. that he ever said any such thing as 'Equality consists of two things'. For had he done so, he would then have had ample reason to ask himself whether, by the same token, the Form, Three, consists of three things, the Form, Half, of half a thing (half of what?), the Form 'greater than' (*Phd.*, 75c 9) of a greater thing (greater than what?), and so on. I cannot pursue this line of thought here. But it is clear that it calls for serious qualification of the thesis that Plato thought of the Forms as 'standards' in Geach's sense. He did, and he didn't—as one can, and does, in the twilight zone of consciousness where one's ideas do not reach clear-cut, hard-edged shape and are not controlled, or are imperfectly controlled, by reflection about them.

[1] There is no suggestion that the argument is elliptical. Socrates is being very explicit throughout this passage.

---

he doesn't think these would be intermediate between Forms and particulars, but neither does he see that the plural 'equals' does refer to the Form, Equality. The most attractive statement of the interpretation of 'equals themselves' as referring to mathematical equals is in Cornford (*Plato's Parmenides* [London, 1939], p. 71): 'Here "equals" means quantities of which nothing is asserted except that they are simply "equal".'

(ii) There is another explanation of 'the equals themselves' here, not inconsistent with Geach's, but complementary to it and logically independent of it. Greek usage does permit the use of the plural form of the (neuter) adjective with the article to signify the corresponding abstract—i.e. as roughly equivalent to (*a*) the abstract noun and (*b*) the same adjectival form in the singular: thus τὰ δίκαια ('the just', in the plural form) can be used to express the same thing as δικαιοσύνη ('justice') or τὸ δίκαιον ('the just', in the singular). Socrates in the *Gorgias* (454e–455a) shifts from περὶ τῶν δικαίων τε καὶ ἀδίκων ('about the just and the unjust,' in the plural)[1] to περὶ τὸ δίκαιόν τε καὶ ἄδικον ('about the just and the unjust', in the singular) and back again, obviously using them as interchangeable expressions. 'The equals' then as an alternate for 'the equal' would be good idiomatic usage, and this would be *one* reason why Plato could slip into it.[2]

I would say the same thing about Geach's parallel interpretation of the plural 'the similars themselves' (αὐτὰ τὰ ὅμοια) and 'the many' (τὰ πολλά) as variants for 'similarity' and 'multiplicity' respectively. And Geach's exegesis of 'mastership itself of service itself' at *Parmenides*, 133e–4 deserves credit not only for offering a solution (a completely adequate one, to my mind), but also for being the first to notice that there is a problem to be solved, i.e. that (and why) there is something logically odd about the *expression* (quite apart from the implied *doctrine*) 'mastership itself of service itself', instead of 'mastership itself of *a* servant (or "servants").'

Geach's thesis leads him to make another original observation of great merit: that the common noun ('Man,' 'Fire') brings out the assumptions of the Platonic Theory (it would be more exact to say: some of them) much better than does the abstract noun

[1] I am not forgetting that he gets the cue from Gorgias' earlier reference to 'those things which are just and (those which are) unjust', 454b. The fact remains that Socrates uses 'the just and the unjust' in the plural to mean the same thing as the same expression in the singular, i.e. justice and injustice.

[2] It may be asked whether this explanation does not make Geach's redundant. It would, *if* this passage were the *only* evidence Geach could offer for his thesis that Plato thinks of the Forms as 'standard'. But since he has, or could find, quite a lot of other evidence for it, one may very well hold that the explanation in (ii) *reinforces* Geach's: the fact that Plato could *speak* of a singular abstract in the plural would make it all the easier for him to *think* of Equality as a pair of two things. See the Additional Note, p. 291.

('Humanity', 'Justice'). His remarks about the 'the Lion' are a suggestive gloss on Plato's talk about the Form, 'Animal' (or 'Living Creature') all through the opening part of the *Timaeus*, as well as on 'Bed' in the *Republic* and 'Shuttle' in the *Cratylus*. On the other hand, if Geach is looking for the 'idiom in Greek . . . (which) influenced Plato's way of thinking about Forms' (and he is), he should have thought of something else whose influence on the Platonic Theory must have been far greater, *sc.* the use of the adjective with the article to designate Forms ('the Just', 'the Beautiful'). We meet this idiom in extreme profusion in Plato's formative (Socratic) period to designate the '*X*' of the 'What is *X*?' question. It is hardly less frequent in the 'middle' period when the Socratic *definiendum* has been elevated into a Form. In both periods Plato's attention is fixed mainly on moral terms (with mathematical ones moving up as close seconds in the middle period); and these, of course, *could not* be expressed by common nouns. Hence *this* idiom is not likely to have influenced appreciably Plato's thinking as he hammered out the Theory and put it to use most confidently and systematically. Forms whose linguistic vehicle is the common noun occur rather infrequently,[1] and seldom move into the focus of Plato's thought in the 'middle' period.[2] A fair commentary on their marginal status in his thought is that at the end of this period, in the *Parmenides* (129b–d), Socrates affirms unhesitatingly the existence of Forms like Similarity,

[1] Thus of all the different instances of Forms mentioned in the *Phaedo* (seventeen on my count) only three are designated by common nouns: Snow, Fire, Soul.

[2] On just three occasions of any consequence: the discussions of the Form of the Shuttle, *Crat.*, 389; of Bed and Table, *Rep.*, 596–7; of Fire, Snow, Soul in the *Phaedo* (103c ff.). I stretch a point to include the ones from the *Phaedo*. No Forms of this kind are mentioned when the Theory is first announced at 65d and reaffirmed with a great roll of drums at 75c–d and 76d. It is only in the last of the arguments for the Immortality of the Soul that Snow, Fire, Soul come in, and even so they are not *tagged* 'Forms'. D. J. Allan even goes so far as to say that 'on the whole' they are not 'treated as forms' (*Phil. Quart.*, II [1952], 370); but I take it as certain that Plato assumes that they are (cf. the introduction to this argument, 102b 1–2). As for the *Republic*, the epistemological and metaphysical heart of the dialogue (Bk. V, 475e ff. to end of Bk. VII) does not include the mention of a single Form designated by a common noun. It is only the appendix at Book X that brings in Bed and Table, and this not so much to illustrate the Theory of Forms as to offer a handle for disparaging the artist at the expense of the artisan.

Justice, Beauty, Goodness, but says he is 'puzzled' as to whether there also exist Forms of Man, Fire, or Water. These are the least securely grounded, for they are shaken by the first tremor of doubt that leaves the others undisturbed. Geach might then have asked himself whether the use of the adjectival form of expression ('the beautiful', etc.) does not exhibit the same assumptions which he thinks are conveyed by the use of the common noun. The answer, of course, is, 'Yes', and for two main reasons:

(i) A grammatical form like 'the beautiful' expresses the notion of beauty by way of referring to a standard member of the class.[1]

(ii) The 'hypostatising definite article', as Geach calls it, is even more in evidence: though the article is not always used even in the adjectival form, it is certainly far more frequently used in this than in the case of the common noun.[2]

[1] Cf. T. B. L. Webster, 'Languages and Thought in Early Greece', *Mem. and Proc. of Manchester Literary and Philosophical Society*, XCIV (1952–53), no. 3, p. 8: 'In its full development . . . the definite article with the neuter participle or adjective signifies (*a*) a particular member of a class, (*b*) any member of a class (and therefore all members), (*c*) a standard member of a class (and therefore very nearly the quality by virtue of which it is a member of the class).' Webster is not thinking of Plato at all in this connection; he is describing the usage of 'the early Hippocratic writings, Anaxagoras, and Thucydides'. His statement is all the more valuable on that account; it outlines the possible senses of this grammatical form in contemporary (or somewhat earlier) usage; and the only one of these that will approximate Plato's (*c*), is the very one that would give grammatical support to the tendency to think of the Form as Self-Predicational. Cf. Bluck, op. cit., pp. 174 ff.

[2] The article is absent in 'Form of Man, Fire, or Water' and of 'Hair, Mud, and Dirt', *Parm.*, 130c; it is omitted in a ratio higher than 5/1 in references to Fire or Snow, *Phd.*, 103c–d and 105c; it is hardly used at all in references to the Forms of Bed and Table in *Rep.*, 596b ff.; it is wholly omitted from the significant expressions, 'that which *is* Bed', 'Bed which really is', *Rep.*, 597a, c, d.

ADDITIONAL NOTE (1965). I now think I erred in endorsing Geach's elucidation of *αὐτὰ τὰ ἴσα* (pp. 287–89). The correct explanation is the one given in (ii), p. 289. For an even better example of the plural neuter used in a perfectly matter of fact way to replace the singular form for an abstract see *Rep.* 520c 5–6 and 538c 6–7 (cf. d 7 and e 2).

XV

A PROOF IN THE *PERI IDEON* (1957)

G. E. L. Owen

IN his lost essay περὶ ἰδεῶν Aristotle retailed and rebutted a number of Academic arguments for the existence of Ideas. Several of these, together with Aristotle's objections to them, are preserved in Alexander's commentary on A 9 of the *Metaphysics*. The first object of the following discussion is to show the sense and the provenance of one, the most complex and puzzling, of these surviving arguments. For several reasons it seems to deserve more consideration than it has yet had.[1] 1. Its length and technicality make it singularly fitted to illustrate the sort of material on which Aristotle drew in his critique. 2. Moreover, Alexander reports it by way of amplifying Aristotle's comment that, of the more precise arguments on Ideas, οἱ μὲν τῶν πρός τι ποιοῦσιν ἰδέας, ὧν οὔ φαμεν εἶναι καθ' αὑτὸ γένος (*Met.*, 990b 15–17 = 1079a 11–13); and the condensed and allusive form of this remark and its immediate neighbours in the *Metaphysics* can be taken to show that here Aristotle is epitomising parts of his περὶ ἰδεῶν that are independently known to us only through his commentator. We shall not understand the objection if we misidentify its target; and another purpose of this discussion is to show that the objection is not the disingenuous muddle that one recent writer

[1] It has been discussed by Robin (who first assigned it to the περὶ ἰδεῶν), *Théorie platonicienne des Idées et des Nombres*, 19–21, 603–5, 607; Cherniss, *Aristotle's Criticism of Plato and the Academy*, I, 229–33, esp. n. 137, and Wilpert, *Zwei aristotelische Frühschriften*, 41–4, each of whom knew only Robin's discussion; and Suzanne Mansion, 'La critique de la théorie des Idées dans le περὶ ἰδεῶν d'Aristote', *Revue Philosophique de Louvain*, xlvii (1949), 181–3, esp. n. 42. I shall refer to these writings by the author's name.

U

labours to make it. 3. But Alexander's report of the argument is a nest of problems, and the same recent writer brands it as almost incredibly careless. To this extent, the success of our explanation will be a vindication of the commentator. But on all the heads of this discussion I am well aware that much more remains to be said.

THE PROOF

In the authoritative text of Alexander[1] (which, with a minor emendation of Hayduck's,[2] Sir David Ross prints on pp. 124–5 of his *Fragmenta Selecta Aristotelis*) the specimen argument that produces *ἰδέας τῶν πρός τι* is given as follows.

I. When the same predicate is asserted of several things not homonymously (*μὴ ὁμωνύμως*) but so as to indicate a single character, it is true of them *either* (*a*) because they are strictly (*κυρίως*) what the predicate signifies, e.g. when we call both Socrates and Plato 'a man'; or (*b*) because they are likenesses of things that are really so, e.g. when we predicate 'man' of men in pictures (for what we are indicating in them is the likenesses of men, and so we signify an identical character in each); *or* (*c*) because one of them is the model and the rest are likenesses, e.g. if we were to call both Socrates and the likenesses of Socrates 'men'.

II. Now when we predicate 'absolutely equal' (*τὸ ἴσον αὐτό*) of things in this world,[3] we use the predicate homonymously. For (*a*) the same definition (*λόγος*) does not fit them all; (*b*) nor are we referring to things that are really equal, since the dimensions of sensible things are fluctuating continuously and

[1] The A of Bonitz and later edd. The version of the commentary in L and F excerpted in Hayduck's apparatus is later in origin (Hayduck, *Alexandri in Met. Commentaria*, pref. viii–ix and ix, n. 2). It modifies the text of our passage in a clumsy attempt to evade the difficulties discussed *infra*, pp. 104–6. (But notice that, where A uses Socrates and Plato as examples, LF at first uses Callias and Theaetetus, reverting then to those in A.) On Robin's attempt (loc. cit.) to assign LF equal authority with AM see Wilpert, n. 38, Cherniss, n. 137.

[2] Cf. p. 107, n. 26 *infra*.

[3] 'We': not of course the Platonists, who make no such error, but generally the unwary or unconverted to whom the argument is addressed. The objector envisaged at *Phaedo*, 74b 6–7, and Hippias (*Hipp. Maj.*, 288a and 289d), see no objection to using *αὐτὸ τὸ ἴσον* and *αὐτὸ τὸ καλόν* of sensible things.

indeterminate. (*c*) Nor yet does the definition of 'equal' apply without qualification (ἀκριβῶς) to anything in this world.

III. But neither (can such things be called equal) in the sense that one is model and another is likeness, for none of them has more claim than another to be either model or likeness.

IV. And even if we allow that the likeness is not homonymous with the model, the conclusion is always the same—that the equal things in this world are equal *qua* likenesses of what is strictly and really equal.

V. If this is so, there is something absolutely and strictly equal (ἔστι τι αὐτόϊσον καὶ κυρίως) by relation to which things in this world, as being likenesses of it, become and are called equal. And this is an Idea. (Alexander, *Met.*, 82. 11–83. 16 Hayduck.)

I shall refer to this report of the argument in the περὶ ἰδεῶν as P. Its gist, if not its detail, seems clear. What is allegedly proved, for the specimen predicate 'equal', is a doctrine familiar from several Platonic dialogues: things in this world can carry the predicate only derivatively, by virtue of resembling a Paradigm that carries it in its own right. The comparison with the *Phaedo* 73c–75d is especially obvious. Both arguments assume that αὐτὸ τὸ ἴσον describes something, and prove that what it describes is no physical thing. But already one characteristic of the author of our argument is clear. As we shall see, he is substantially faithful to his sources in Plato: but he takes pains to sharpen the logical issues they involve. As it stands in P, his proof depends on what must be intended as an exhaustive analysis of the ways in which a predicate can be used without ambiguity.[1] Now it is Alexander's

[1] μὴ ὁμωνύμως in the Aristotelian sense but not, as we shall see, using Aristotelian criteria. Some will detect the influence of Speusippus in P.I, noticing that in it the vehicles of homonymy and its opposite seem to be not things but words, and that this is held to be characteristic of Speusippus by contrast with Aristotle (Hambruch, *Logische Regeln der plat. Schule*, 27–9, followed by other scholars including Lang, *Speusippus*, 25–6. Hambruch contrasts Aristotle, *Cat.*, 1a 1–12, with Boethus's account of Speusippus in Simplicius, *Cat.*, 38.19). Quite apart from doubts about the tradition represented by Boethus, it is clear that Aristotle's usage is far from being as rigid as Hambruch supposes (see e.g. *An. Post.*, 99a 7, 12, *Phys. H.*, 248b 12–21: H. neglects such passages in detecting a book of Speusippus behind *Topics A* 15). Moreover in P.III the ὁμώνυμα are things, not words. All that we can say is that P reflects a general academic usage.

report of this analysis that has perplexed his readers. For it seems plausible to say that the author of the proof cannot have regarded the sort of predication illustrated in I(*c*) as non-homonymous, in the sense initially given to that expression in I, and on the other hand that he cannot have regarded that which is illustrated in I(*b*) as non-homonymous in the sense of that expression required in II; so that the description of these sorts of predication as non-homonymous must be a confusion in P. To lay these doubts is to take a long step towards understanding the argument and establishing the reliability of P.

CRITERIA OF SYNONYMY IN ARISTOTLE AND PLATO

The difficulty in I(*c*) seems both logical and historical. We may say 'That is a man' without ambiguity when pointing to each of two flesh-and-blood men. Or (in a very different case) we may say it when pointing to each of two pictures, and what we say has the same sense of both pictures: in that respect we are still speaking unambiguously. But we are inclined to add that now we are not using the predicate in the same sense as in the first case: otherwise we should be mistaking paint and canvas for flesh and blood. Moreover this is Aristotle's view, and his examples suggest that he has our argument in mind.[1] Yet, as it stands, I(*c*) says just the opposite. The analysis seems to have distinguished cases (*a*) and (*b*) in order to assert with all emphasis that a combination of them in (*c*) imports no ambiguity at all.

The later version of the scholium (*supra*, n. 2) takes a short way with the difficulty, reclassifying I(*c*) as a case of homonymy. Robin (loc. cit.) tried to wrest this sense from the original text; Wilpert (loc. cit.) rejected the attempt but regretted the anomaly. Yet the problem is fictitious. The logical issue can only be touched on here. The fact is that, although the difference between I(*a*) and I(*b*) predication does show an ambiguity of an important type, this is not the sort of ambiguity that can be exhibited by the methods of

[1] *De Part. An.*, 640b 35–641a 3, *De An.*, 412b 20–2, and on the traditional interpretation *Cat.*, 1a 1–6 (cf. Porphyry, *Cat.*, 66.23–8, followed by later commentators, and see earlier Chrysippus fr. 143 (von Arnim). But ζῷον, the predicate cited, is ambiguous in a more ordinary sense: LS[8] s.v. II).

Aristotle and the Academy.[1] It no more proves that the predicate-word has two paraphrasable meanings than the fact that I can point to a portrait and say 'That is Socrates' proves that Socrates had an ambiguous name. This is true, but it is doubtful whether it is the point that our author is making. For the wording of I(*b*) suggests that in its derivative use the predicate *is* to be paraphrased otherwise than in its primary use (i.e. in terms of 'likeness'), though this difference of paraphrase does not constitute an ambiguity. Similarly we shall find (*infra*, 109–110) that the argument of II can be construed as allowing, with one proviso, that a predicate can be used unambiguously of several things even when the λόγος of that predicate differs in the different cases; the proviso is that that different λόγος shall have a common factor. (In the cases distinguished in I this factor is the primary definition of 'man', and in II it is the definition of τὸ ἴσον αὐτό.) If this interpretation is correct our specimen of Academic argument contains an obvious parallel to Aristotle's admission of a class of πρὸς ἓν καὶ μίαν τινὰ φύσιν λεγόμενα which are in a sense synonymous (*Met.*, 1003a 33–1003b 15, cf. *Eth. Eud.*, 1236a 15–20, and n. 37 *infra*).

But Aristotelian parallels are irrelevant to showing the reliability of P. What matters is that the analysis in I would misrepresent its Platonic sources if I(*c*) were *not* a type of unequivocal predication. This is implied by the reference in *Rep.* 596–7 to a bed in a picture, a wooden bed and the Paradigm Bed as τριτταὶ κλῖναι (even when, as in P.I, only one of these is 'really' what the predicate signifies); and more generally it is implied by such dicta as that nothing can be just or holy or beautiful if the corresponding Form is not so.[2] These utterances have no sense unless the predi-

[1] For a connected discussion I can refer now to P. T. Geach in *Phil. Rev.*, LXV (1956), 74, see above Ch. XIII.

[2] See e.g. the instances cited by Vlastos, *Phil. Rev.*, LXIII (1954), 337–8 (see above, 248–250). But Vlastos obscures the point by saying 'any Form can be predicated of itself... *F*-ness is itself *F*'. The very fact that Plato could assume without question that αὐτὸ τὸ μέγεθος is big (e.g. *Phd.*, 102e 5, cf. *Parm.*, 150a 7–b 1 and 131d), whereas in English such an assumption about *bigness* makes no sense, should give us qualms at rendering the title of the Form conventionally in such contexts by an abstract noun (Vlastos' '*F*-ness'). V.'s formula misleads him into assimilating the two regresses in *Parm.*, 132–3. If the first can (but with reservations) be constructed as confusing bigness with what is big, the second requires only that the Form should *have* the character it represents. If the first forces a choice between two possible functions of a form, the second reduces one of these to absurdity.

cate applies without difference of meaning to model and likeness alike;[1] and they are integral to the doctrine that things in this world resemble the Forms. The author of our proof found the latter doctrine in his chief source (*Phd.*, 73c–4c) and remarked that it is illustrated there by the relation between Simmias and Simmias γεγραμμένος (73e), and in paragraph I he tried to do no more than put his original into precise logical shape. We recall Jaeger's suggestion that Aristotle did this very service to Plato in the *Eudemus*. But we had better defer any conjectures on the authorship of our proof.

τὸ ἴσον αὐτό AND τὸ ἴσον

A second puzzle turns on the three occurrences in P of the keyword 'homonymous'. P.I distinguishes three possible cases in which a predicate can be used μὴ ὁμωνύμως, which is shown by paraphrase to mean 'not ambiguously'. But P.II then seems to contend that the predicate 'equal' is used ὁμωνύμως of things in this world, although the explicit conclusion of P as well as the evidence of the dialogues on which P is based prove that such predication would be subsumed under I(*b*). Lastly, P.IV puts the case that the likenesses carry the predicate *non*-homonymously with their model, which squares with I but seems incompatible with II. In fact P.II seems the misfit; and again the later version in LF takes the short way, replacing the ὁμωνύμως of II with συνωνύμως οὐ κυρίως δέ so as to bring the predication in question clearly under I(*b*). Robin's version of the argument (loc. cit.), which covertly reduces it to a *petitio principii* and contradicts the provisions of I, has been criticised by Cherniss (loc. cit.). Mlle Mansion (n. 42) has seized the important fact that P.II is concerned not with τὸ ἴσον but with τὸ ἴσον αὐτό, but I have not understood her claim that the argument is a *reductio ad absurdum* and I do not agree

[1] This is unaffected by the fact that the Forms are standards. 'That is a yard long' has a different use when we are speaking of the standard yardstick and when we are speaking of other things (Geach, loc. cit.), but this does not entail that 'yard' has two meanings. Aristotle commonly treats the Forms as συνώνυμα with their images (cf. *de Lin. Insec.*, 968a 9–10, ἡ δ' ἰδέα πρώτη τῶν συνωνύμων). The objection considered in *Physics* H 4, that συνώνυμα need not be συμβλητά, may well stem from the attempt to safeguard this thesis from the 'Third Man'.

that IV is an interpolation. Wilpert has not considered the problem.

Cherniss has propounded a singular solution (n. 137). He holds that ὁμώνυμος cannot be used in the same sense throughout P; and accordingly he claims that in II it is introduced without warning in a *Platonic* sense, such that the Platonic ὁμωνύμως is compatible with the 'Aristotelian' μὴ ὁμωνύμως in I (which he at once denounces as a 'careless summary' by Alexander of his source). The Platonic sense is identified as 'having the common name and nature derivatively'. So far, the effect is exactly that of the verbal change in LF. But he is then faced with the μὴ ὁμώνυμον in IV. On his interpretation this cannot contradict the other occurrences of the expression, yet he cannot plausibly let himself say that it is a return to the 'Aristotelian' sense 'in the midst of the argument'. Consequently he has to provide a different Platonic sense, equally unadvertised by Alexander, whereby μὴ ὁμώνυμον in IV signifies that 'the image is not *of the same class as* the model'; and this in order that the use of ὁμωνύμως in the first 'Platonic' sense shall be compatible with the use of μὴ ὁμώνυμον in the second 'Platonic' sense and both of these compatible with that of μὴ ὁμωνύμως in the original 'Aristotelian' sense. In face of this it is easy to sympathise with his suspicion that the μή in the third occurrence must be an interpolation.

On the canons of this interpretation I have something more to say, but not until we have reviewed the problem. A closer reading of the text seems sufficient to dissolve it. For what is maintained in II is that τὸ ἴσον αὐτό would be predicated homonymously of things in this world; and τὸ ἴσον αὐτό is expanded in V into αὐτόισον καὶ κυρίως (sc. κυρίως ἴσον, cf. IV: κυρίως καὶ ἀληθῶς ἴσον). Thus the question broached by II is just whether ἴσον can be used κυρίως of things in this world, i.e. as a case of the non-derivative predication illustrated in I(*a*); and the answer is that, except by a sheer ambiguity, it cannot be so used.[1] But this conclusion is perfectly compatible with the conclusion in IV and V that ἴσον

[1] Instead of asking in set terms whether 'equal' can, without ambiguity, be predicated *strictly* of such things, II seems to introduce the compound predicate 'strictly equal' and ask whether this can, without ambiguity, be predicated of such things. This comes to the same thing (in fact the distinction is too hard-edged for the Greek), but it helped to seduce the author of LF into the absurd notion that the compound predicate αὐτόισον could properly be used, in a derivative sense, of earthly things.

without this qualification can be predicated unambiguously of a group including physical things, i.e. that physical things can be called equal by the *derivative* sort of predication shown in I(*b*). The arguments in II are designed solely to prove that, if 'equal' keeps its proper sense, nothing in this world can be called *strictly* equal.[1] III proves the corollary, that no group of things on earth can be called equal even as a case of mixed, I(*c*) predication (which would entail that something in the group *was* κυρίως ἴσον). What is not even considered in II and III is whether physical things can be called equal wholly derivatively, as in I(*b*).

Now IV is concessive in form,[2] and what it concedes is just this third possibility. (Its form does not of course mean that it is surrendering any part of the argument. It is concessive because it forestalls an objection: the objection that the talk of ambiguity in II is misleading and may be taken to apply to ἴσον, not τὸ ἴσον αὐτό.) And, in fact, I(*b*) predication is the only possibility still open to us if we are to keep any unity of sense in our everyday ascriptions of equality. But copies entail models, and this conclusion requires that τὸ ἴσον is predicated κυρίως of something *not* in this world, of which this world's instances of equality are likenesses.

But, finally, IV is only a concessive parenthesis, and it implies (ἀεὶ ἕπεται) that the same result would follow from II and III alone. So it does: for II maintains that when we talk of what is κυρίως ἴσον, what we are referring to (unless the expression is being used ambiguously) cannot be anything in this world. It follows that, unless we call everyday things equal in some sense unconnected with the first, they must be so called derivatively. And since this conclusion is explicitly drawn in V, II, III, and V form a complete argument.

So the form of P is clear and its use of the terminology introduced at the start is, as we might expect, consistent. But it is worth noticing two other considerations which are jointly fatal to Cherniss's account. The gross carelessness of which he accuses

[1] It may be said (I owe the objection to Mr. D. J. Furley) that the argument in II(*a*) is designed to rule out I(*b*) predication as well as I(*a*), since even I(*b*) would presumably require an identical λόγος in the various subjects. But in that case the conclusion of II would contradict V, as well as being a thesis foreign to Plato and never attacked by Aristotle; moreover the difference of λόγοι does not entail ambiguity since, as we shall see, they all have a common factor.

[2] Cf. Alexander, *Met.*, 86.11–12 Hayduck.

Alexander is out of character; he has not remarked that, when the commentator does introduce ὁμώνυμος in the non-Aristotelian sense, he takes pains to explain the ambiguity.[1] Moreover, apart from all particular questions of interpretation (but see nn. 15, 19), the evidence adduced by Cherniss for the existence of his 'Platonic' senses of ὁμώνυμος[2] has no tendency to prove his point; and the reason for this is worth emphasis. Plato does use ὁμώνυμος fairly frequently. It seems clear that he does not use it in the technical Aristotelian sense of 'equivocal'. Sometimes (as at *Tim.*, 52a, *Parm.*, 133d, *Phd.*, 78c) it is *applied* to cases of what Aristotle would doubtless call synonymy. But it does not for a moment follow that the expression *meant* for Plato what is meant by Aristotle's συνώνυμος, any more than it follows that because 'soldier' can be applied to all bombardiers, 'soldier' means 'bombardier'. Elsewhere the same word is used of things that plainly do not have the same λόγος τῆς οὐσίας.[3] This should entail for Cherniss that Plato's use of the word was ruinously ambiguous, but of course it was not. As Plato uses it, what it means, its correct translation, is 'having the same name'; and the argument never requires more than this of it (cf., for instance, the versions of Cornford). The mistake recurs in Cherniss's further comment that 'for Plato ὁμώνυμος when used of the relationship of particulars and ideas meant not *merely* "synonymous" in Aristotle's sense. The particular is ὁμώνυμον τῷ εἴδει, not vice versa, because it has its name and nature *derivatively* from the idea.' Yet elsewhere the word is used of an ancestor *from* whom the name is derived[4] and elsewhere again where there is no derivation either way.[5] Nor does Plato reserve any special meaning for the metaphysical contexts Cherniss has in mind.[6] The fact is that when he thinks it necessary

[1] Alexander, *Met.*, 51.11–15, 77.12–13. Cf. ps.-Alex. *Met.*, 500.12–35, 786.15.

[2] Cherniss, n. 102, citing Taylor, *Commentary on Plato's Timaeus*, 52a 4–5.

[3] *Laws*, 757b; cf. *Phil.*, 57b, which Cherniss (loc. cit.) misconstrues as saying that 'the different mathematics, if ὁμώνυμον, are a single τέχνη' when the point is that although they are ὁμώνυμα, it would be wrong to infer that they are one τέχνη (57d 6–8).

[4] *Rep.*, 330b, *Parm.*, 126c.

[5] *Prot.*, 311b.

[6] That Aristotle, who certainly knew that particulars were 'called after the Ideas' (*Met.*, 987b 8–9), did not recognise a sense of ὁμώνυμος in these contexts such that 'the particular is ὁμώνυμον τῷ εἴδει and not vice versa'

to say that particulars are like the Form in nature as well as name he says so explicitly (*ὁμώνυμον ὅμοιόν τε*, *Tim.*, 52a 5) and when he wants to say that they derive their names from the Forms he says that too (*Phd.*, 102b, 103b, *Parm.*, 130e[1]). The second 'Platonic sense' of the word rests on the same basis.[2]

But why labour this point? Because the thesis in question seems a particularly clear application of one general principle of interpretation, and this principle underlies a well-known theory of the 'unity' (in the sense of fixity) of Plato's thought, to which Professor Cherniss is the distinguished heir. It is often observed that arguments for this theory assume that an expression in one context must carry a special sense determined by its application in quite another setting.[3] And no doubt some of the things to be said in this paper do not square well with that doctrine.

καθ' αὑτό AND *πρός τι*

So far, P keeps our confidence. It remains to discuss it as a digest of Platonic argument and a target of Aristotle's criticism.

On the face of it, P distinguishes two sorts of predicate: those such as 'man', which can be predicated *κυρίως* of things in this world [I(*a*)], and those such as 'equal', which even when they are used unequivocally of such things can be predicated of them only derivatively [II–V]. To all appearance it seeks to provide forms for predicates of the second class by contrasting them with those of the first; and we shall see this impression confirmed by other evidence and by the detail of the argument. This distinction

[1] *Not* however *Parm.*, 133c–d, which Cherniss has misread (loc. cit.): it is not the Ideas that are referred to as *ὧν ἡμεῖς μετέχοντες εἶναι ἕκαστα ἐπονομαζόμεθα* but the 'likenesses-or-what-you-may-call-them' in this world. Since the particulars are nevertheless said to be *ὁμώνυμα*, to the Forms, this sentence alone, if he still takes it as seriously, explodes his thesis.

[2] And a misreading of the text cited, *Phil.*, 57b, cf. 301 n. 3 *supra*.

[3] I can refer now to Vlastos, op. cit., 337, n. 31 above, 299, n. 1; cf. Robinson, *Plato's Earlier Dialectic* (2nd edn.), 2–3.

---

must be proved for Cherniss by *Met.*, 990b 6, which reports that the Form is *ὁμώνυμον* with its particulars: here Cherniss is ready to find 'Plato's sense of the word' (n. 102).

Cherniss tacitly suppresses in his précis of P,[1] and he is accordingly able to find 'no reason to suppose that the argument . . . was not also meant to establish the existence of Ideas in the case of *all* common predicates'.[2] He suggests no reason for this rewriting, unless it is (what is in any case no justification) that the similar argument in *Phaedo* 74–5 is said to apply to all things οἷς ἐπισφραγιζόμεθα τὸ 'αὐτὸ ὃ ἔστι' (75c–d). But to assume that this includes all predicates whatever is to beg the same question. The predicates actually cited there as examples—ἴσον, μεῖζον, ἔλαττον, καλόν, ἀγαθόν, δίκαιον, ὅσιον—are all of the restricted type to which the argument of P applies; in the relevant respect they are all, as we shall see, the logical congeners of 'equal' and not of 'man'.[3] Moreover, the same distinction, which is essential to the argument of P and its sources, is the basis of Aristotle's criticism of these arguments. That criticism gives the rest of our discussion its starting-point and conclusion.

It has come to be agreed that Aristotle's objection to the arguments which 'produce Ideas of relatives' (*Met.*, A 9, 990b 16–17, cf. p. 103 *supra*) is not of the same form as those preceding it in its context. He is not arguing that such proofs as that reported in P can be used to establish Ideas that were explicitly rejected by the Platonists. He is saying that their conclusions contradict a logical principle accepted by the Academy; and the commentary of Alexander enables us, I think, to identify the principle in

[1] Cherniss, p. 230. To do this he omits the illustrations of the three types of predication in P.I. Yet (*a*) without the illustrations the analysis is merely formal and without explanatory force; (*b*) that the predicate cited in the first paragraph of Alexander's source was not ἴσον and was not a 'relative' term is implied by Alexander's remark that at any rate the proof *goes on* to deal with ἴσον, which *is* relative (83. 23–4); and (*c*) in any case the illustration from portraits cannot be excised since it comes from the Platonic source (*supra*, 298). This in addition to the considerations adduced in the following pages.

[2] Cherniss, n. 186.

[3] Similarly those given to illustrate similar formulae at *Phaedo*, 76d, 78d, *Rep.*, 479a–d. The one passage in which Plato seems unequivocally to require a Form for every predicate (*Rep.*, 596a) cannot be ingenuously cited by any critic wedded to the 'unity of Plato's thought' since (even if *Parm.*, 130 is brushed aside) taken literally it contradicts *Politicus* 262a–3e and incidentally leaves Aristotle's criticism of the ἓν ἐπὶ πολλῶν argument valid for every negatively defined predicate (*Met.*, 990b 13: cf. Alexander and Ross *ad loc.*). Readers other than those στασιῶται τοῦ ὅλου are likely to find the comment of D. J. Allan in *Mind*, LV (1946), 270–1, sound and to the point.

question. (But Sir David Ross is one scholar who would not agree with this identification (*Aristotle's Metaphysics*, ad loc.), and in this he is followed by Wilpert.) Namely, Aristotle in this and the following sentence of his critique is turning against the Platonists their own dichotomy of καθ' αὑτό and πρός τι:[1] a dichotomy inherited from Plato and evidently regarded as not only exclusive but exhaustive, since the school of Xenocrates maintained it against the needless elaboration of Aristotle's own categories.[2] Aristotle is objecting that such a proof as P sets up a 'non-relative class of relatives', a καθ' αὑτὸ γένος τῶν πρός τι, and that 'we say' that there is no such class.

The first thing to remark is the wide sense carried by the Academic πρός τι when measured by more familiar Aristotelian standards. This seems to have eluded Alexander: hence, perhaps his reference to P as proving ἰδέας καὶ τῶν πρός τι where Aristotle says only ἰδέας τῶν πρός τι:[3] he seems to have seen that the proof applies, not certainly to all predicates, but to many that fall outside the Aristotelian category. (He reassures himself with the reflection, and the γοῦν seems to prove it his own, that 'anyhow the example used in the proof *is* relative'—sc. in the orthodox sense: *Met.*, 83. 23–4.) In any case he is betrayed by his surprise when in the next sentence of the *Metaphysics* Aristotle argues from the priority of ἀριθμός to the priority not of τὸ πόσον but of τὸ πρός τι (990b 19–21). Here Alexander reports what is certainly the correct explanation (πᾶς ἀριθμὸς τινός ἐστιν, *Met.*, 86. 5–6; cf. Aristotle, *Met.*, 1092b 19, and *Cat.*, 6a 36–7: τὰ πρός τι λεγόμενα are, *inter alia*, ὅσα αὐτὰ ἅπερ ἐστὶν ἑτέρων εἶναι λέγεται. We know that τὸν ἀριθμὸν ὄντος εἶναι was an Academic premiss: Alexander,

[1] Alexander, *Met.*, 83. 24–6, 86. 13–20. The relevance of this dichotomy was pointed out by D. G. Ritchie against Henry Jackson: cf. J. Watson, *Aristotle's Criticisms of Plato*, 32.

[2] *Soph.*, 255e–d, *Philebus*, 51c, cf. *Rep.*, 438b–d, *Charmides*, 168b–c, *Tht.*, 160b. Xenocrates, fr. 12 (*Heinze*) = Simplicius, *Cat.*, 63. 21–4. I am not concerned here with the development and supplementation of this dichotomy in the early Academy, which has been the subject of recent studies. The subsequent conflation of the Platonic 'categories' with the Aristotelian, e.g. in Albinus (Witt, *Albinus*, 62–7), may derive from Aristotle himself (*E.N.*, 1096a 19–21).

[3] Alexander, *Met.*, 83. 17, 22, 85. 7. But the text of 82. 11 (ὁ μὲν ἐκ τῶν πρός τι κατασκευάζων ἰδέας λόγος) should not be amended, for this comes from the περὶ ἰδεῶν and not from Alexander.

Met., 78. 16). But not content with this, he attempts to interpret the anomaly away (86. 11–13);[1] an attempt at once refuted by the amplification of the argument in *Metaphysics* M 1079a 15–17, which makes it wholly clear that Aristotle does intend here to subsume number under *τὸ πρός τι* as a general class contrasted with *τὸ καθ' αὑτό*.

Nor are the sources of such a classification in Plato far to seek. In Republic VII (523a–525a) numbers are classed with such characteristics as *light* and *heavy*, *large* and *small*, on the score that our senses can never discover any of them *καθ' αὑτό*, in isolation (525d 10): in perceptible things they are inseparable from their opposites.[2] For, as Socrates argues in the *Parmenides* (129c–d), what is one of something is any number of something else—one man is many members. We may say, for convenience, that 'one' as we ordinarily apply it to things is an *incomplete* predicate and that, accordingly as we complete it in this way or that, it will be true or false of the thing to which it is applied. Now the same is true, or Plato talks as if it is true, of all those predicates which in the *Republic* and earlier works supply him with his stock examples of Ideas; and conspicuously so of the logical-mathematical and moral-aesthetic predicates for which the young Socrates unhesitatingly postulates Forms in *Parmenides* 130b–d. In this world what is large or equal, beautiful or good, right or pious, is so in some respect or relation and will always show a contradictory face in some other.[3] As large is mixed with small (*Rep.*, 524c), so just and unjust, good and bad, in having commerce with bodies and actions[4] have commerce with each other (*Rep.*, 476a 4–7[5]); and

[1] *Pace*, Wilpert, 109, who cannot think that Alexander would allow himself such an interjection. But see Mansion, n. 79, Cherniss, 301–2.

[2] *ἐναντία*, in a sense that includes any *prima facie* incompatibles (e.g. different numbers).

[3] With *Rep.*, 479a–b, cf. 331c and 538d–e and Shorey, *Republic*, vol. i, 530, n. *a*.

[4] 'actions': but Plato seems to have in mind *types* of action (refs. in last note; cf. *Δισσοὶ Λόγοι* 3. 2–12). The *Symposium* (180e–1a) makes the necessary distinction but here, as elsewhere, seems a step beyond the *Republic*.

[5] The debate on this passage has doubtless lived too long, but the natural sense is surely that given above. The *κοινωνία* of the opposites with each other is a characteristic of those 'manifestations' in the physical world which seem to make a plurality of the Form; this is the only sort of pluralisation in question in the passage (cf. 476b, 479a–b), and any attempt to read

in an earlier context Plato argues that such seeming contradictions are to be resolved by specifying those different respects or relations in which the antagonistic descriptions hold good (436b–7a). Notice how various such specifications will be: some of Plato's predicates are concealed comparatives ('large') or can be forced into this mould ('beautiful' in the *Hippias Major* 288b–9c), some are more overtly relational ('equal' [1]), some are neither ('one'); we have to ask what X is larger *than*, what it is a certain number *of*, what it is equal *to*.[2] Later in the *Philebus* (51c), Plato is ready to say that even of physical things some can be καλὰ καθ' αὑτά and not merely καλὰ πρός τι, but (although what is said of pleasure at *Rep.*, 584d seems a first move towards this) there is no such admission in the *Republic*.

Notice, too, that Plato's treatment of these incomplete predicates makes no essential use of the idea of physical mutability, often though that idea recurs in the characterising of the Forms.

[1] Yet, as many have said, for Plato at this time equality and other relations are attributes of the individual. (It is worth recalling that ἴσον could be used to mean 'of middle size' and in this use is not overtly relational.) Geach's conviction (above, 269) that Plato must have thought of any case of equality, including the Form, as a pair of related terms cannot be justified by the bare αὐτὰ τὰ ἴσα of *Phaedo*, 74c 1. Geach writes that the Form 'has to consist of *two* equals, or there wouldn't be equality at all'; Aristotle in the περὶ ἰδεῶν, discussing the same line of thought in Plato, said 'What is equal must be equal to something, so the αὐτόισον must be equal *to a second* αὐτόισον' (Alexander, *Met.*, 83. 26–8), and whatever we think of Aristotle's methods of polemic *this* would have been absurd if Geach were right. See *infra*, 110.

[2] The argument of *Phaedo*, 74b–c is probably better-construed on these lines, taking the τῷ μέν . . . τῷ δ' οὔ of 74b 8–9 (despite the then misleading dative in 74c 1) as neuter and governed by ἴσα. This at any rate seems to be the sense that the argument in P makes of its chief source (infra, 310). Otherwise it turns directly on relativity to different observers (cf. *Symp.*, 211a 4–5).

---

back the κοινωνία τῶν γενῶν of the *Sophist* into this text simply fits the argument too loosely. Plato is talking in terms of pairs of opposites—the unity of a Form is proved by contrasting it with its opposite, and the same λόγος is said to hold good of the rest (476a)—but the corresponding pluralisation that is marked by the reconciling in one object of such a pair of opposites has nothing to do with the *Sophist*. Good and bad cannot 'communicate' in the *Sophist* sense (*Soph.*, 252d). Cf. rather the κρᾶσις πρὸς ἄλληλα of *Tht.*, 152d 7 and, with due reserve, περὶ ἀρχαίης ἰητρικῆς xv.

Here, it is with the compresence and not the succession of opposites that he is expressly concerned.[1]

With these predicates Plato contrasts others of which 'finger' is an example. A finger can be seen *καθ' αὑτό*: sight never reports it to be at the same time not a finger (*Rep.*, 523d). This predicate, then, breeds no contradictions that have to be resolved by specifying *πρός τι*. And the same is evidently true of 'man', and of 'fire' and 'mud': all those predicates for which the young Socrates is unready to admit Forms.[2] That something is a finger is a matter on which sight is competent to pronounce (523b, 524d), and it is characteristic of the sorts of thing to which Socrates refuses Ideas that they are just what we see them to be (*Parm.*, 130d). The *Phaedrus* reapplies the distinction (263a: cf. *Alcibiades* I, 111–12) when it argues that men disagree not on the use of 'iron' or 'stone' but on that of 'good' or 'right'—or, we can add, on that of 'one' or 'similar'; for Zeno's logical puzzles, like the moral antinomies of his successors, were built on such incomplete predicates, and the *Parmenides* of itself would suffice to show that these two classes of problem lie at the root of Plato's earlier theorising. If we hope to resolve such disagreements by reference to some unexceptionable standard, we shall find that the world which contains unambiguous samples of fire and fingers contains no comparable cases of goodness or similarity or equality *καθ' αὑτό*. If we persist, our unambiguous Paradigms, must be located elsewhere, in a *νοητὸς τόπος*.

Plainly, the exclusion of Forms of such non-relative predicates as 'man' is not characteristic of later dialogues nor even of the last book of the *Republic*. A greater preoccupation with mutability (as in the *Timaeus*) would naturally suggest that in a further sense *all* predicates are incomplete in their earthly applications, for all apply at one time and not at another. This point is already expressly made in a dialogue marked by that preoccupation, the *Symposium* (210e–211a), and the principle which could suggest it is already enunciated in the *Republic* (436b). So doubtless the

[1] *ἅμα*, *Rep.*, 524e 2, 525a 4, 523c 1 and d 5, *ἀεί*, 479b 8, *ταὐτὰ ὄντα*, cf. *Phd.*, 74b 8 with *Parm.*, 129b 6 and *Phd.*, 102 b–c.

[2] *Parm.*, 130c–d. Parmenides' explanation of Socrates' choice, that he rejects Ideas of *γελοῖα*, is applied only to mud, hair, and dirt (130c 5). In any case it is a diagnosis of motive and not a characterisation of the reasons that Socrates could have offered.

argument of P, which ignores this extension of the theory, isolates one strand in Plato's thinking which in his earlier work at least he took small care and had small motive to distinguish sharply or to reconcile with others. The same is true of other arguments collected in the περὶ ἰδεῶν. But what seems beyond serious question is that the earlier accounts of Forms are dominated by a preoccupation with incomplete predicates, in the narrower sense given to that expression.

Man, *fire*, and *water* seem to have remained stock Academic instances of τὰ καθ' αὑτὰ λεγόμενα by contrast with τὰ πρὸς ἕτερον or τὰ πρός τι,[1] and there is small doubt that the broad distinction sketched above between complete and incomplete predicates in Plato lay at the source of the Academic dichotomy as well as of some major arguments for Ideas. The so-called *Divisiones Aristoteleae* preserved by Diogenes Laertius define τὰ καθ' ἑαυτὰ λεγόμενα as ὅσα ἐν τῇ ἑρμηνείᾳ μηδενὸς προσδεῖται and τὰ πρός τι λεγόμενα accordingly as ὅσα προσδεῖταί τινος ἑρμηνείας (67 Mutschmann). Now it seems plain that the same distinction underlies the argument of P. For this explanation of τὰ πρός τι recalls the argument of II(*c*) that the definition of 'equal' does not apply without further specification, ἀκριβῶς,[2] to anything in this world. To explain why one thing is called equal (and here again we have to note that equality is treated as an attribute of the individual thing) is to specify another with whose dimensions those of the first tally. And II(*a*) seems only the other face of this coin, for different cases of equality will require the λόγος to be completed in different ways.[3] [II(*b*) seems to add the rider that, since the dimensions of

[1] Hermodorus apud Simpl., *Phys.*, 247. 30 ff., Diogenes Laertius III, 108, Sextus Empiricus *adv. Math.* X, 263.

[2] = ἁπλῶς, opposed to κατὰ πρόσθεσιν: cf. *An. Post.*, 87a 34–7, *Met.*, 982a 25–8 and 1078a 9–13, *E.N.*, 1148a 11.

[3] Or the sense may be that different cases involve specifying different measurements; but this would leave the senses of λόγος in II(*a*) and II(*c*) unconnected. And II(*c*) may mean just that nothing is equal without being unequal too. But, besides robbing Aristotle's reply of its immediate point (*infra*, 110), these interpretations neglect a parallel of thought and language in the *Eudemian Ethics*. In the discussion of three types of friendship in *E.E.*, VII, 2 it is said that one λόγος does not fit all the cases (1236a 26), but the λόγος of friendship in the primary sense (κυρίως) is an element in the λόγοι of the rest (1236a 20–2: 'the rest' are here of course species and not, as in P, individuals). For whereas friendship in the strict sense is to choose and love a thing because it is good and pleasant ἁπλῶς, friendship in its derivative

sensible things are constantly fluctuating, even to say 'having the same size as A' is to use a description without fixed meaning.] But even in Alexander's possibly condensed version it is clear that II(*a*) and II(*c*) are not duplicates and that their sequence is important. For the point of II(*a*) is that the specification of various correlates can be no part of the meaning of 'equal' if it is not merely ambiguous, and the point of II(*c*) is that when the common core of meaning is pared of these accretions it no longer characterises anything in this world.

Such arguments apply only to predicates which in their everyday uses are, in the Academic sense, relative. They follow Plato in deducing the existence of Ideas from the perplexing behaviour of 'equal' (or *mutatis mutandis* of 'beautiful' or 'good') when this is measured against such unperplexing expressions as 'man'. To this II(*b*) alone might seem an exception, for it can be read to imply (what it certainly does not say) that phenomenal things are continually changing in all respects and so not κυρίως the subjects of any predicates. But such an interpretation would be the death of P. It would contradict P.I, and it would leave the detail of P.II inexplicable, since the special arguments of II(*a*) and II(*c*) would be at once redundant—logically outbidden. Further, it would leave Aristotle's identification of such arguments as producing 'Ideas of relatives' unaccountable. For it seems to be true of all the proofs to which he refers in this context that they produce such Ideas, *inter alia*,[1] so that he can only mean to characterise a further class of argument concerned directly with τὰ πρός τι.

A NON-RELATIVE CLASS OF RELATIVES

The author of our proof is substantially faithful to the class of Platonic arguments he presents but here again he is anxious to sharpen a logical issue. What the dialogues describe as an appeal to an intelligible Paradigm is seen, in practice, to be the application

[1] *Met.*, 990b 11–17. The proofs κατὰ τὸ ἓν ἐπὶ πολλῶν and κατὰ τὸ νοεῖν τι φθαρέντος do so because they are logically unrestricted in scope. For the λόγοι ἐκ τῶν ἐπιστημῶν see Alexander, *Met.*, 79. 13–15.

senses is to do this because it is good πρός τι or pleasant τινὶ. In other words a definition that fits primary friendship without qualification (ἁπλῶς = ἀκριβῶς in P. II(*c*)) needs to be completed to give the λόγοι of the derivative cases. So in P: the similarity of language is very striking.

of a correct definition (e.g. *Euthyphro* 6e). It is in terms of definitions that P is framed. To say that nothing on earth affords an unexceptionable Paradigm of equality is re-phrased as saying that to nothing on earth can the definition of 'equal' be applied, pared of irrelevant accretions. Now this re-phrasing brings out, more clearly than Plato's words, the crucial point at which Aristotle directs his objection—and any success in explaining his reply must stand in favour of our interpretation of the argument. Where a Paradigm is required for a predicate that is incomplete in its ordinary use it must indeed be (as the argument of P faithfully shows) a Standard Case, exhibiting rather than being the character it represents. But more: it seems that the Form and the Form alone, must carry its predicate *καθ' αὑτό* in the sense given by the dichotomy. *αὐτὸ τὸ ἴσον* is indeed equal, but how can we without absurdity ask to what it is equal? It cannot be equal to everything or to nothing (both would engender paradoxes), and it cannot be equal to some things but not others (which would re-import just the compresence of opposites that the Form was invented to avoid: *Parm.*, 129b–130a). The incompleteness which so embarrassingly characterises 'equal' in its ordinary applications cannot, it seems, characterise it when it designates the Form. This is the natural sense of Socrates' warning that the 'equal' he is to discuss is not 'stick equal to stick or stone equal to stone but just *equal*' (*Phd.*, 74a), and it is the main point of the argument in P that unless 'equal' is merely ambiguous the core of meaning common to all its uses must apply to something *ἀκριβῶς* or, as Aristotle puts it in the *Metaphysics*, *καθ' αὑτό*. One aim of the second part of the *Parmenides*, I take it, is to find absurdities in a similar treatment of 'one'. It is the extreme case of Greek mistreatment of 'relative' terms in the attempt to assimilate them to simple adjectives.[1]

This is the point on which Aristotle fastens, and his rejoinder is not the simple deception that Cherniss reads into it.[2] It is developed in more than one place. In the *Metaphysics* he is content to observe that such arguments construct a 'non-relative class of relatives', i.e. a class of non-relative instances of relatives. They require that any essentially incomplete predicate shall in *one* application behave

[1] Cf. Cornford, *Plato and Parmenides*, 78, n. 1, and for a later parallel R. M. Martin, *Phil. and Phen. Research*, XIV, 211.

[2] Cherniss, 279–85.

as though it were complete—yet the Academy's use of the familiar dichotomy recognises no such exceptions (see the *Sophist*, 255c–d). Alexander reports what is in effect the same objection: nothing can be equal that is not equal to something; but this entails that *τὸ αὐτόϊσον* is equal to another *αὐτόϊσον*, and thus the Form is duplicated (*Met.*, 83. 26–8). But even without this corroboration we could be sure of Aristotle's sense. In chapter 31 of the *de sophisticis elenchis* he says: 'We must not allow that predications of relative terms (*τῶν πρός τι λεγομένων*) mean anything when taken out of relation (*καθ' αὑτάς*), e.g. that "double" means something apart from "double of half" merely because it is a distinguishable element in that phrase. . . . We may say that by itself "double" means nothing at all; or, if anything, certainly not what it means in context'—and this rebuts the treatment of 'equal' in P and its sources as applying synonymously to earthly things and to the Form. If 'equal' does not behave as tractably as 'man' in this world, that does not entail that there is another world in which it does: the use of 'equal' is *irreducibly* different from that of 'man'.

The consequence attacked by Aristotle is, I think, implied by the Platonic arguments on which the proof in P relies. But did Plato clearly contemplate the consequence in framing the arguments? That is surely doubtful. It would be easy to overlook it in the case of an asymmetrical relation such as *double-of-half*, where the absurdity of having to give the Form a twin in order to supply it with its appropriate correlate does not arise. And Plato's very use of *καθ' αὑτό*, by contrast with the Academic usage that grew out of it, shows the weakness; for in characterising a case of X as *καθ' αὑτό* he evidently means rather to exclude the opposite of X than to exclude the relativity which gives entry to an opposite (*Parmenides*, 128e and 129d, *Republic*, 524d: notice that the solution of contradictions by specifying *πρός τι* and *τά κατι* is broached in quite a different context of the *Republic*). Nor is the latter exclusion the only means to the former, for where the Idea is overtly or covertly a comparative it can as well be represented as *superlatively* X, X in comparison with everything; so that here the predicate would retain its 'relative' character even when used of the Idea. Between these alternatives the treatment of *αὐτὸ τὸ καλόν* in *Symposium* 210e–211a seems to be ambiguous. But 'equal' and 'one' are not so amenable: their purity is not preserved by making them, in strict analogy, equal to or one of everything. The proof in P does not seem to be mistaken about the implications of its source.

Yet it brings out those implications with a new clarity, and in doing so it plays very neatly into Aristotle's hands. This fact, and the obvious concern of its author with logical reformulations, suggest that here at least we should be incautious in treating our records of the *περὶ ἰδεῶν* as a source of fresh information on Academic arguments about the Ideas. It looks as though Aristotle may be responsible for the representative proof that he produces for refutation. This is not indeed wholly plausible, for by characterising such proofs as *ἀκριβέστεροι* (*Met.*, 990b 15) Aristotle presumably means to commend his opponents and not himself for the logical care with which the proof is developed. And the argument of P is not a mere (even disingenuous) *réchauffé* of extant Platonic arguments, but a new structure of argument in its own right. But is this reason enough to dismiss the suspicion?

XVI

THE PLACE OF THE *TIMAEUS* IN PLATO'S DIALOGUES

(1953)

G. E. L. Owen

IT is now nearly axiomatic among Platonic scholars that the *Timaeus* and its unfinished sequel the *Critias* belong to the last stage of Plato's writings. The *Laws* (including, for those who admit its claims, the *Epinomis*) is generally held to be wholly or partly a later production. So, by many, is the *Philebus*, but that is all. Perhaps the privileged status of the *Timaeus* in the Middle Ages helped to fix the conviction that it embodies Plato's maturest theories.

I want to undermine that conviction by questioning the grounds on which it is commonly based and by sharpening the paradoxes it imports into the interpretation of Plato. No one familiar with Platonic scholarship will claim that these paradoxes could not be explained away, given enough ingenuity. But I think that, once they are seen in aggregate, the cost in such ingenuity should seem quite exorbitant.

This discussion is preliminary to any assessment of Plato's later work. It tries so far as possible to avoid large and controversial interpretations of any dialogue and to canvass a few manageable issues on common ground. Its thesis could have been supported otherwise, by showing how the *Parmenides* and its successors gain in philosophical power and interest when they are read as following and not as paving the way for the *Timaeus*; here I want only to find ground for this approach. And it defers what I take to be proof that the changes of view here ascribed to Plato square with and sometimes elucidate the comments of Aristotle.

THE EVIDENCE OF STYLE

Campbell's pioneer studies in Plato's style[1] were open to attack, partly for their reliance on Ast's *Lexicon*[2] and their uncritical deductions from the statistics of rare and unique words, partly for their assumption that the *Timaeus* and *Critias* could be taken *en bloc* with the *Laws* as Plato's latest writings. And Campbell's pupil Lutoslawski,[3] though he attempted a comparison of the *Timaeus* and *Laws*, still assumed a stylistically uniform *Laws* as the terminal work.[4] He also forgot in practice that, where a dialogue such as the *Timaeus* is unique in its technical range, the originality of its vocabulary cannot be used as a mechanical test of dating. And he discovered, after compiling his much-quoted tables on the opposite principle, that the opportunity for the occurrence of more or fewer stylistic pointers in a work bears no proportion to its volume. His admission that only equal amounts of text should have been compared (p. 185) had the effect of largely invalidating his own and most earlier and later attempts to order the dialogues by relative affinities of style. Stylometrists ignored the warning. But cases arose in which Campbell and Lutoslawski were compelled to exercise their discretion. Their statistics left the *Theaetetus* beside the *Protagoras* (C.) or before the central books of the *Republic* (L.), the *Phaedrus* seemed later than the *Philebus* (C.), the *Critias* earlier than the *Timaeus* (L.). The effect was, reasonably, to discredit mechanical stylometry until it narrowed its field: it was seen to be applicable only to those formal and linguistic features which were wholly independent of the topic and chosen manner of treatment.[5]

[1] *Sophistes and Politicus*, introd.; essays in *Plato's Republic*, (ed. Jowett and Campbell). vol. ii; *Class. Rev.*, x, 1896, pp. 129–36.

[2] Campbell and Lutoslawski, Raeder and Constantin Ritter have at different times written as though, even if Ast does not list all occurrences of a word, he does name all the dialogues in which it occurs; this is quite false (cf. for example, 317, n. 2 *infra*). He does not even list all Plato's words.

[3] *Origin and Growth of Plato's Logic*, chap. iii.

[4] This was the sheet-anchor of stylometrists who were not content with such broad groupings of the dialogues as that accepted by Taylor (*Plato*, p. 19). Yet there is no external or internal evidence which proves that the *Laws* or even some section of it was later than every other work: cf. 335 *infra*.

[5] Here the attempts of Schanz, Dittenberger, and Constantin Ritter to measure the relative frequency of synonyms were theoretically sound. But a

The new search for neutral criteria produced Billig's analysis of the rhythms of Plato's clausulae.[1] He found that 'the *Timaeus* has nothing to do with the rhythms of the *Sophist* digression, the *Politicus*, the *Philebus*, and the *Laws*. Rhythm puts its composition earlier than that of all these works.'[2] And in this he confirmed Kaluscha's earlier study in the same field.[3] Raeder[4] and Taylor[5] drew attention to the finding; Cornford ignored it, but saw a safe stylistic test in the avoidance of 'illegitimate' hiatus.[6] Yet this avoidance gives no rule of thumb for ordering, say, the *Timaeus* and *Theaetetus*. That it is not an automatic test is tacitly admitted by nearly all stylometrists in dating the *Phaedrus* before the *Theaetetus* and *Parmenides* even though the former already shows, as the latter do not, a 'striking rarity of hiatus'.[7] (It clinches the point to construe this as a passing compliment to Isocrates.) And the *Timaeus* is essentially an essay, a 'conscious *tour de force* of style' (Shorey) where

[1] *J. Philol.*, xxxv, 1920, pp. 225–56.

[2] P. 250. The distribution of end-rhythms in the *Tim.* closely matches that in the middle and early dialogues. Thus the rhythms which are dominant (65–85 per cent.) from the *Soph.* digression onwards total 45·6 per cent. in *Tim.*, the same in *Critok*, and 2–3 per cent. below in (for example) *Phd.*, *Rep.* 6 and 10. The graph for later works is interesting (but to be used with care): in the *Phdr.* these rhythms steadily recede; the overall figure (37·7 per cent. or, omitting Lysias' speech, 36·9 per cent.) matches that of the first part of the *Parm.* (38·1 per cent.); in the *Tht.* it rises, reaching 50 per cent. from Protagoras' speech (165e) with brief further rises (e.g. in the discussion of the *κοινά*); the *Crat.*, for those who want it here, is higher (52·4 per cent.), and thereafter the rise is steep. (My figures are approximate to the extent that Billig's rules for assessing interjections are not precise.)

[3] *Wiener Studien*, xxvi, 1904, p. 190.

[4] *Platons Epinomis* (1939), p. 13, n. 1.

[5] *Commentary on Plato's Timaeus*, pp. 4–5.

[6] *Plato's Cosmology*, p. 12, n. 3: cf. now Hackforth, *Plato's Phaedrus*, p. 3; Skemp, *Plato's Statesman*, p. 238.

[7] Blass, *Attische Bered-Samkeit*, p. 458. By Janell's count the figure for the *Phdr.* is little more than half that for the *Parm.* (23·9 and 44·1 per page of Didot, respectively).

---

study of the *Phaedrus* (cf. p. 317 *infra*) proves that Plato adopted the 'late' synonyms in passages of elevated style earlier than elsewhere. In fact, when Plato is said to be dropping one synonym for another he is commonly borrowing from poetry (Campbell, *Republic*, ii, pp. 50–1), and to find these borrowings either in speeches for whose poetic vocabulary Socrates apologises (*Phdr.*, 257a 5) or in a work 'in Inhalt und Form mit der Poesie wetteifernd' (Wilamowitz on the *Timaeus*) is obviously not the same thing as finding them in dialogue proper.

the carelessness of conversation has no place; it may well have been a later decision to adopt such ornaments in writings which make serious use of the dialogue form. (Such warnings patently apply rather to an idiom like the shunning of hiatus, which requires a decision on the writer's part, than to one such as the emergence of dominant prose-rhythms which—as Billig proved for Plato, at least (p. 242)—does not. And we shall see that the rhythms are unaffected by the transition between easy and elevated diction.)

Moreover, I shall try to show why, after an exercise in essay style, Plato should revert in the *Theaetetus* and the opening debate of the *Parmenides* to a conversational form more reminiscent of the early dialogues. For I argue that the *Timaeus* and its sequel or sequels were designed as the crowning work not of the latest dialogues but of the *Republic* group. The project was abandoned from dissatisfaction with certain basic theories, and in the first works of the critical group Plato dropped the confident didacticism of the *Timaeus* to make a fresh start on problems still unsolved. Thus we at once account for the four major characteristics which Taylor singles out as allying the *Timaeus* with Plato's latest writings.[1] The lack of dramatic conversation and the recessive role of Socrates and his scepticism, the predominance of positive teaching and of the periodic essay style, all alike are marks of the doctrinaire assurance with which Plato set himself in the *Timaeus* to expound the system he had constructed. And just as the disappearance of these devices signals the renewal of Plato's doubts, so their readoption in the *Sophist* and its successors marks a new period of assurance which contains his maturest thought. Similarly with many affiliated devices, such as the lack of hesitant and 'subjective' replies (ἔμοιγε, δοκεῖ μοι, etc.) investigated by Siebeck and Ritter. Such features are not, what they are artlessly taken to be, neutral aids to the ordering of the dialogues. They depend directly on the aims and methods of the work in hand.

This point can be proved. For it can be shown that, at a date much earlier than that now assigned to the *Timaeus*, Plato could on occasion adopt an elevated style which by the orthodox tests[2]

[1] *Commentary*, p. 4.

[2] For which cf. esp. Ritter, *Untersuchungen*, pp. 2–33, 56–9 (with corrections in *Platon*, i, pp. 236–7), 70, n. 1; Lina, *de praep. us. platon.*, p. 12; Campbell, *Rep.*, ii, pp. 53–5. But these critics draw no distinctions within the *Phdr.*, and sometimes we shall correct their totals.

tallies closely with that of the *Timaeus*: namely, the style of Socrates' speeches in the *Phaedrus*.[1] There is no need to repeat the broad contrasts between these and the dialogue proper (e.g. the elimination of Socrates' personality, on which Stenzel insisted); but consider the following contrasts of detail.[2] In the speeches ὄντως has ousted τῷ ὄντι (5/0: in *Tim.*, 9/1), while in the dialogue τῷ ὄντι is ubiquitous save where at 260 a 3 its clumsy repetition is avoided by ὄντως. In the dialogue περί c. gen. still exceeds the equivalent περί c. acc. (65/22), ἴσως exceeds τάχα (11/4), and ἕνεκα exceeds χάριν (8/5); but not in the speeches (10/11, 0/1, 2/2: in *Tim.*, 88/116, 0/1, 13/7). Of another group of 'late' forms the speeches show not only κατὰ δύναμιν and εἰς (ἡμετέραν) δύναμιν (as *Timaeus* does) but ὡς δυνατόν (as it does not), and echo the rare καθ' ὅσον δυνατόν of *Timaeus*, 90c; of these the dialogue proper has εἰς δύναμιν once. The proportion of δέ γε / δὲ δή in the dialogue is 5/8, but in the speeches 0/10 and in *Timaeus*, 1/24—a figure otherwise unapproached save in works comparable in form, *Symposium* (1/7) and *Apology* (0/5). καθάπερ, except for the poetic interlude of the cicadas (259a), is confined to the speeches, where its ratio to ὥσπερ (3/5) is over four times that for the whole work. (This is less than in *Timaeus*, but in other 'late' forms the speeches not only surpass *Timaeus*, but carry the dialogue with them, e.g. in the complete ousting of σχεδόν τι by σχεδόν and the frequency of the Ionic dat. pl.) There is further, as Campbell showed, the massing in the speeches of tragic, religious, and medical expressions often coinciding with those of *Timaeus* and *Cratylus* (C. gives some twenty instances peculiar to this group); and Campbell's instances of periphrasis in *Timaeus* (ἡ τοῦ θατέρου φύσις, τὸ τῆς ἀναπλανησέως) are echoed in *Phaedrus* (ἡ τοῦ κάλλους φύσις 254b, τὸ τῆς μνήμης 250a). Other such echoes are πάντη πάντως, πᾶσαν πάντως (246a, 253c). The same conclusion is confirmed by other figures, e.g. for certain uses of τε and for expressions confined to the dialogue proper (τί μήν; γε μήν, δῆλον ὅτι/ὡς, etc.). No one would use these data to argue that the speeches were written later than the dialogue

[1] Lysias' speech, which I shall not consider, tallies by present tests with the dialogue proper.

[2] Ritter's figures, after large corrections in *Platon* and articles in *Bursian's Jahresbericht*, (LXXXVII, 1921) remain untrustworthy: e.g. in *Phdr.* he underestimates cases of κατὰ εἰς δύναμιν (2 excluding 257a 3), ὡς δύνατόν (1), πότερον and πότερα before a vowel (2, 1), εἶπον, etc., in rel. clause (2), δὲ δή (18).

(and no one should have used them indiscriminately to post-date the whole work). What they prove is that, when Plato was still writing dialogue having very close affinities with the *Republic* and *Theaetetus*, he could write uninterrupted prose having equal affinities with the *Timaeus*. This distinction is not touched by the fact that he was not yet prepared to shun hiatus thoroughly in a work of which two-thirds was dialogue (though, equally, in such a work he now refused to give it free rein). What is of quite different importance in this connection, is that the speeches do not interrupt the graph of end-rhythms in the *Phaedrus*. The test of rhythm sustains its claim to neutrality.

Billig went on to ear-mark the few indexes of style other than end-rhythms which seemed to him to have the required neutrality, and his suggestions tell for my thesis.[1] That thesis (to repeat) is that, while the *Timaeus* and *Critias* undoubtedly follow the *Republic* and possibly follow the *Phaedrus*, they precede the ‘critical group which begins with the *Parmenides* and *Theaetetus*. And on the strength of the present discussion and of some clues of diction still to be noted,[2] it seems fair to claim that this reordering tallies well with the admissible evidence of style.[3]

Now for the paradoxes of orthodoxy. In discussing them I follow the order of the critical group.

Παραδείγματα IN THE *Parmenides*

At one stage of the earlier argument in the *Parmenides* (132c 12–133a 7) Socrates defines *μέθεξις* in terms of *ὁμοιώματα* and *παραδείγματα*. Parmenides has no trouble in proving that, if participation in some character *A* is to be construed as resemblance to some *παράδειγμα* in respect of *A*, then, since resemblance is symmetrical, both *παράδειγμα* and *ὁμοίωμα* must exhibit *A* and hence *ex hypothesi*

[1] E.g. in the coining of adjectives in -ώδης and -ειδής the *Tht.* and *Parm.* are characteristic of the late dialogues, and the *Tim.* of the middle period (Lutoslawski, p. 115). Of Billig's other criteria some are discussed above and one, the greater frequency of πέρι after its noun, is not a late form (cf. Lutoslawski, pp. 131–2: in the *Rep.* it is much higher than in the *Tim.* and as high as in the *Soph.* and *Pol.*): B. may have confused this with the predominance of περί c. acc. over περί c. gen.

[2] Cf. see below, p. 321, n. 2; p. 335, n. 1.

[3] Here it seems on stronger ground than recent post-datings of the *Crat.*; but the stylistic evidence on that dialogue (like the arguments so far given for its lateness) can and should be pruned and supplemented.

resemble a further παράδειγμα in that respect. And so on, in regress. Now the suggestion refuted by Parmenides is precisely the account of the relation between Forms and particulars given in the *Timaeus* (e.g. 29b, 48e–49a, 50d 1, 52a, 53c). So commentators, hoping to reconcile a late *Timaeus* with a Plato who saw the point of his own arguments, have laboured to show that the *Timaeus* theory was immune (or at worst thought to be immune) to the objections raised in the supposedly earlier work. But their attempts have failed.

Taylor's contention (after Proclus)[1] that the παράδειγμα and ὁμοίωμα were not related symmetrically by ὁμοιότης was refuted by Hardie,[2] and since it combined a logical fallacy[3] with a disregard for the evidence[4] there was no excuse for its repetition by Cherniss.[5] Cherniss also argued[6] that in the *Republic* (597c) and

[1] 'Parmenides, Zeno, and Socrates', *Proc. Ar. Soc.*, xvi, 1916, pp. 234–89; *Plato's Parmenides*, intro., p. 26.

[2] *A Study in Plato*, pp. 96–7.

[3] That of arguing as though, because the relation between copy and original is not simply resemblance, it does not *include* resemblance; for if it is included Parmenides' regress follows at once. The most one could maintain on Taylor's lines is that, if to predicate *X* of *A* is to assert that *A* is not only like but copied from a Form, then (by definition of 'Form') it is a contradiction to predicate *X* of the Form that *A* allegedly resembles in respect of *X*. But then no such resemblance between *A* and the Form can be maintained, nor *a fortiori* can *A* be the Form's copy; so this serves Parmenides' ends by wrecking the εἰκών—παράδειγμα account of predication. But the evidence is against this line of argument (see next note).

[4] E.g. (i) such uses of the παράδειγμα terminology as at *Rep.*, 501b where the legislator is a painter with his eye on the θεῖον παράδειγμα and able to make a direct comparison between sitter and portrait (cf. *Phd.*, 76e 2); (ii) the fact that on the old theory of Forms the property represented by the Form was predicated without qualms of the Form itself: Justice just, Holiness holy (*Prot.*, 330c–e), Largeness large (*Phd.*, 102e 5), where the predicate-expression is used unambiguously of Forms and particulars, as is proved, for example, by σχολῇ μεντἄν τι ἄλλο ὅσιον εἴη εἰ μὴ αὐτή γε ἡ ὁσιότης ὅσιον ἔσται (*Prot.*, 330d 8); (iii) Aristotle's use of the premiss that the λόγος was common to Forms and particulars (e.g., *Met.*, 997b 10–12; *E.E.*, 1218a 13–15). So Plato did not suppose the paradeigmatic function of the Form of *X*, any more than its being μονοειδές or ἀΐδιον, to rule out the assertion of resemblance between Form and εἰκών in respect of *X*. And this position is not modified in the *Tim.* Hence Parmenides' regress is the exactly appropriate criticism of the theory.

[5] *Aristotle's Criticism of Plato and the Academy*, pp. 297–9.

[6] Ibid., pp. 295–7; cf. Apelt, *Beiträge zur Geschichte der Greichischen Philosophie*, pp. 52–3.

the *Timaeus* (31a) Plato used a regress argument of the type in question (the 'third man') in order to establish the uniqueness of a Form, and hence, since both these dialogues postulate παραδείγματα and εἰκόνες, that Plato thought the argument applicable to relations between Forms but not to those between Forms and particulars. But this is a confusion which seems to arise from the indiscriminate use of the label τρίτος ἄνθρωπος (some of the heterogeneous batch of arguments it covers do not even employ an infinite regress: cf. Alex. *in Met.* 84. 7–21). For neither in the *Republic* nor in the *Timaeus* does Plato use a regress of *similarities*;[1] his premiss is simply that of the ἓν ἐπὶ πολλῶν which is (as Parmenides' interrogation of Socrates shows) neutral as between the resemblance-account of μέθεξις and others. So neither argument shows or requires any awareness of Parmenides' point that, since resemblance is symmetrical, on this version of predication the same account which is given of the particular's participation in the Form must be extended to the Form.

(On this faulty foundation Cherniss built another proof of Aristotle's dishonesty.[2] Aristotle was accused of citing such regress arguments as valid against the old Forms[3] without mentioning that Plato had, or supposed he had, rebutted them. But the reason why Aristotle is as silent as Plato himself on this vital answer is just that no answer existed.[4])

Ross agrees that the apologists have failed and that Parmenides' objection goes home.[5] But, by accepting the lateness of the *Timaeus*, he falls on the second horn of the dilemma. He is forced to suggest that in the *Timaeus* the defeated version of μέθεξις is retained as a 'metaphorical way of describing the relation'; but his own argument refutes this. For in discussing the scope of εἰκὼς λόγος in the *Timaeus* he rightly says that 'in general for his metaphysics,

[1] In the *Tim.* the resemblance of εἰκών to παράδειγμα is introduced to prove not the uniqueness of the Form but that of the οὐρανός, given that of the παντελὲς ζῷον.

[2] Op. cit., p. 293. [3] E.g. *Met.*, 990b 17, 991a 2–5, 1032a 2–4.

[4] As to the answer which Cherniss constructs for Plato, certainly Plato later concluded that the εἶδος should be regarded as '*being* that which the particular *has* as an attribute (Op. cit., p. 298)—the necessary type-distinctions are forced by Parmenides' first regress (132a 1–b 2) and sketched in *Tht.*, 156e, 182a–b; but to expound μέθεξις in the idioms of resemblance and copying is just to show that one has not yet grasped these type-distinctions.

[5] *Plato's Theory of Ideas*, pp. 89, 230–1.

Plato would claim that it is true. That for which he disclaims anything more than probability is not his metaphysics but his cosmology';[1] and he recognises that the metaphysics of the *Timaeus*, save for the Demiurge, centres in the description of παραδείγματα and χώρα and its contents (50c–52c)—a description to which the resemblance of Forms and particulars is integral. Moreover, the distinction between εἰκὼς μῦθος and unshakeable truth is explained wholly by reference to the relation of the physical εἰκών to its Model (29b–d). The explanation (and with it the pointed use of εἰκώς) is annulled if at the time of writing Plato regarded any talk of εἰκόνες in this connection as a mere metaphor which on his own showing could not be pressed without generating absurdities.

In fact, Plato does not again introduce such παραδείγματα to explain predication:[2] in the *Politicus* (277d–278c) he emphasises a different and important function of the expression παράδειγμα; and in the *Philebus* (15b–17a) he either leaves the nature of μέθεξις an open question or, as I think, implies a different analysis.[3] The reasonable solution of the puzzle is to regard the

[1] *Plato's Theory of Ideas*, p. 127.

[2] Ross (ibid., pp. 228–30) has collected occurrences of the idioms by which the relation between Forms and particulars is described in the dialogues. From his data he infers that 'there is a general movement away from immanence towards transcendence' (sc. towards the παράδειγμα-idioms). But his list does not bear this out. Of the dialogues taken to follow the *Phdr.*, the *Tim.* is alone in using the παράδειγμα-idioms, and uses them exclusively and almost exhaustively. *Tht.*, 176e 3–4 is no exception (as Ross agrees, p. 101), for the context (the 'digression') is strongly metaphorical, and the twin παραδείγματα cannot be τἀκεῖ because the ἄθεον ἀθλιώτατον at least has no place in the κακῶν καθαρὸς τόπος which is the soul's proper habitat (177a 5). Ross does not note the following points: (*a*) the special term νόησις used to describe knowledge of the παραδείγματα seems to be confined to the *Rep.* and *Tim.*, except for its occurrence at *Crat.*, 407b 4 and 411d 8 where the particular term is required by the etymology. Since such knowledge was a dyadic relation between minds and Forms, it seems likely that the old expression was shelved when the *Tht.* had proved (199c–200c) that knowledge and error were not a matter of bare recognition and misidentification. (*b*) The term ὁμοίωμα, introduced in the *Phdr.* myth and *Parm.* and subsequently often used for εἰκών, etc., is not found in the *Tim.*, which here too confines itself to the vocabulary of the *Rep.* (e.g. ἀφομοίωμα seems to be peculiar to these two works). But the word occurs in *Crat.*, 434a (Ast omits this, so it has eluded Campbell and Lutoslawski).

[3] Contrast with the refutation of the παραδείγματα the less intimidating arguments brought against the so-called 'immanence' version of μέθεξις

Timaeus as preceding the *Parmenides* and as inheriting from the middle-period dialogues a fallacy which Plato subsequently exposed.

Γένεσις AND οὐσία

The *Timaeus* distinguishes absolutely between τὸ ὂν ἀεί, γένεσιν δὲ οὐκ ἔχον and τὸ γιγνόμενον μὲν ἀεὶ, ὂν δὲ οὐδέποτε (27d–28a); that is, it 'treats γένεσις and οὐσία as simple incompatibles'.[1] It reaffirms this incompatibility by advocating that the expression ἔστι be reserved for pronouncements about ἀΐδιος οὐσία and (by implication) that γίγνεται be left to do duty in statements of contemporary empirical fact (37e–38b). So it has taxed commentators to say why this principle is to all appearances jettisoned in the *Laws* and its immediate predecessors.[2] But the common plea that such departures show merely a venial looseness of language[3]

[1] Taylor, *Commentary*, p. 32. Taylor says that the *Tim.* maintains this incompatibility 'from first to last' in sharp contrast to the *Phil.* theory of γένεσις εἰς οὐσίαν, but contradicts himself in a note on 31b 3 by importing an allusion to the *Phil.* and so leaving the *Tim.* inconsistent on a key doctrine; he is corrected by Cornford ad loc. (*Plato's Cosmology*, p. 42, n. 1). The *Tim.* does not in fact (and does not promise to) adhere always to the special usage proposed in 37e–38b and discussed in this section: naturally, since (as Plato came to see) its adoption is ruled out by logical absurdities. The point is that if he had seen this when writing the *Tim.* the proposal made in 37e–38b would never have been made.

[2] *Laws*, 894a 5–7, *Phil.*, 26d 8, 27b 8–9, 54a–d (cf. *de gen. an.*, 640a 18), *Soph.*, 248a–249b, *Parm.*, 163d 1–2, and passages discussed above. *Phil.*, 59a and 61d–e are not parallels to the *Tim.* disjunction, because the *Tim.* says not only (as the *Phil.* does) that some things exist without changing but (as the *Phil.* does not) that some things change without existing; this step, the outcome of the *Rep.*'s muddles about existence, is not entailed by the commonplace distinction between ὡσαύτως ὄντα ἀεί and γιγνόμενα (μὴ βέβαια, etc.), and it is this which is refuted in the *Tht.*

[3] Cf. Diès, *Philèbe* (Budé), pp. xxviii–xxix.

(*Parm.*, 131a 4–e 5). In the *Phil.* (15b) it is these arguments alone that are quoted as needing an answer if the μονάδες are to be saved. Professor Skemp (*Plato's Statesman*, p. 238) thinks that, since τὸ δημιουργοῦν is explicitly located in the fourfold classification in *Phil.*, 23c–27c, the παραδείγματα cannot have been superseded either. The plain fact, whatever one makes of it, is that this classification of πάντα τὰ νῦν ὄντα ἐν τῷ παντί does make room for the αἰτία and does not make room for παραδείγματα: I do not quote this on behalf of my position, but it scarcely tells against it.

fails, for they are the exact consequence of new arguments in the late dialogues.

First, the *Theaetetus* states and explodes the thesis that γένεσις excludes οὐσία. By a convention which echoes that imposed on contingent statements in the *Timaeus*, Plato eliminates εἶναι in favour of γίγνεσθαι in all contexts (*Tht.*, 157a 7–c 2; cf. *Tht.*, 152e 1 with *Tim.*, 27d 6–28a 1). And then by using the distinction between change of quality and change of place he shows that this convention produces absurdities. Some have wanted to believe that Plato is at this point trying to establish the thesis of the *Timaeus*: namely that, although γίγνεται alone is appropriate to contingent statements, there must be some entities (viz. the Forms) to whose description only ἔστι is appropriate.[1] If Plato had drawn this conclusion from his argument it would have been a sheer blunder;[2] but he does not draw it. He is saddled with it to save the *Timaeus*. What he plainly points out is that if *anything* (and anything in this world, not the next) were perpetually changing in all respects, so that at no time could it be described as being so-and-so, then nothing could be said of it at all—and, *inter alia*, it could not be said to be changing. If an object moves, we can say what sort of thing is moving[3] only if it has some qualitative stability (182c 9–10); conversely, to have complete qualitative flux ascribed to it, a thing must have location. Nor can any quality of the object, such as its whiteness, be claimed as a subject of this unqualified change: any change here would be μεταβολὴ εἰς ἄλλην χρόαν, and to apply 'whiteness' to a colour-progression is to deprive it of determinate sense (182d 2–5). So no description of any process is possible if we can say only that its constituents are changing from or to something and never that they are something (cf. *Tim.*, 37e 5–38a 2, where it is allowed to say only what a γιγνόμενον was and will be; the White Queen offered Alice jam on the same terms).

[1] E.g. Cornford, *Plato's Theory of Knowledge*, p. 101; Cherniss, *Aristotle's Criticism*, p. 218, n. 129.

[2] Cf. Robinson, *Philos. Rev.*, lix, 1950, pp. 9–10.

[3] οἷα ἄττα ῥεῖ τὰ φερόμενα, 182c 10: this argument defeats the lame plea of the *Tim.* (49d–e) that even if we cannot say *what* any mere γιγνόμενον is we can describe it as τὸ τοιοῦτον (cf. *Tht.*, 152d 6). In a similar argument the *Crat.* makes the point so explicitly (ἆρ' οὖν οἷόν τε προσειπεῖν αὐτὸ ὀρθῶς, εἰ ἀεὶ ὑπεξέρχεται, πρῶτον μὲν ὅτι ἐκεῖνό ἐστιν, ἔπειτα ὅτι τοιοῦτον; 439d 8–9) that this alone would vindicate its place in the critical group.

Notice that Plato does not say, as he is reported to say, that knowledge is not perception because the objects of perception are always wholly in flux. He says that the attempt to equate knowledge with perception κατά γε τὴν τοῦ πάντα κινεῖσθαι μέθοδον fails because that μέθοδος is (not false for some things,, but) nonsense about anything. His instances are drawn from the everyday world, not from the world of Forms. And on the strength of this he goes on to ascribe οὐσία to objects of perception (185a, c, 183b ff.) and thereby to demolish the equation of perception and knowledge independently of the theory of flux.[1]

I omit arguments in the *Sophist* and *Philebus* which help to supersede the assimilation of οὐσία and γένεσις to a pair of incompatible qualities. But one other is worth mention. The *Parmenides* introduces (and for its own ends misemploys) the Megarian thesis that any process of change is analysable in terms of a series of particular states of affairs, each obtaining at a different time and none being itself a process (152b 1–d 4). It is validly deduced from this that to the descriptions of the component states of affairs the process-word γίγνεται will be inappropriate and that ἔστι is indispensable to some statements of contingent fact (152c 6–d 2). Now this is Plato's theory, if the analysis of perception in the *Theaetetus* is his; for sensible change is there atomised into a succession of αἰσθητά with correlated αἰσθήσεις (*Tht.*, 156a–157c, 182a–b) and it is correspondingly argued, and made a basis of the perception theory, that a person undergoing change is rather a series of persons (159b–c, e) having no term as long as the change continues (166b–c). (True, in temporarily amalgamating this with the theory of general flux Plato talks of reimporting change into the atoms of change. But this patently self-defeating step is cancelled with the defeat of the ῥέοντες, and before that the right theory is kept very carefully in view: cf. 160b 5–6, 8–10.)

However, this atomistic theory could consistently be denied to be Plato's. But the first argument certainly cannot. It suffices to

[1] Cornford, misconstruing the previous argument, can naturally make nothing of the fact that this final refutation hinges on the οὐσία of αἰσθητά. He is reduced, first to seeing an ambiguity in οὐσία, finally to making the argument turn on the *denial* of οὐσία to αἰσθητά (*Plato's Theory of Knowledge*, pp. 108–9).

defeat the disjunction of γένεσις and οὐσία in the form propounded by the *Timaeus*, and Plato, unlike his commentators, does not resuscitate it.

EUDOXUS

It is commonly agreed that by 368 at latest Eudoxus had brought his school to Athens, and that it was probably at this period that he answered Plato's challenge by producing his pioneer contribution to the mathematical theory of astronomy.[1] Hence it is a familiar puzzle why, if the *Timaeus* is late, Eudoxus' hypothesis has had no effect on its theories. Taylor cited this peculiarity in defence of his thesis that the dialogue was a philosophical archaism.[2] No one has given the simpler explanation that the *Timaeus* was written before Eudoxus' theory was produced (and so quite possibly before the *Theaetetus*, which is now by common consent dated a little after 369). Yet the sole essential difference between the astronomy of the *Timaeus* and that represented by the simple model described in the Myth of Er seems to be that the *Republic* does not provide for the obliquity of the ecliptic.[3] However we expound the ἐναντία δύναμις of *Timaeus*, 38d 4, the expression embodies Plato's continued failure to meet his own challenge (τίνων ὑποτεθεισῶν ὁμαλῶν καὶ τεταγμένων κινήσεων διασωθῇ τὰ περὶ τῆς κινήσεως τῶν πλανωμένων φαινόμενα).[4] For whether the point of it is to ascribe all apparent variations in planetary speed and direction to intermittent voluntary action on the part of the planets[5] or merely to record, without explaining, such variations on the part of Venus and Mercury in particular,[6] the introduction of the Contrary Power is no substitute for an explanation in terms of

[1] Apollodorus sets his *floruit* in 368–365. The theory was in any case presumably published before he left Athens for the final task of legislating for Cnidus (Diogenes Laertius VIII. 88), and this in turn must be some years before his death in 356–353. Cf. Harward on *Ep.*, XIII. 360c 3 (*The Platonic Epistles*, [Cambridge, 1932] 234).

[2] *Commentary*, p. 211.

[3] As this implies, if ἰλλομένην at *Tim.*, 40b 8 signifies a motion I accept Cornford's account of it as compensatory rotation (*Plato's Cosmology*, 130–1).

[4] Eudemus ap. Simpl. in *De Caelo*, 292b 10 (488. 20–4, cf. 492. 31–493. 32).

[5] Cornford, ibid., 106–12.

[6] Taylor, *Comm.*, 202.

'uniform and ordered movements'.[1] Where Plato failed to meet his own requirements, Eudoxus came near to succeeding. Yet his hypothesis is ignored by the ἀστρονομικώτατος Timaeus.

The πλάναι of the five minor planets are πλήθει μὲν ἀμηχάνῳ χρωμέναι, πεποικιλμέναι δὲ θαυμαστῶς (*Tim.*, 39d 1–2), a phrase in which Cornford seems (inconsistently with his main position) to detect a reference to Eudoxus' theory.[2] But for these planets Eudoxus required only twenty component motions (or in effect twelve, since two are shared by all)—a number for which πλῆθος ἀμήχανον would be an absurdly strong expression even in Cornford's weakened version ('bewildering in number').[3] If, on the other hand, we construe the πλάναι as all those apparent anomalies which Eudoxus' supplementary motions were later designed to explain (a clear inference from 40b 6: τρεπόμενα καὶ πλάνην τοιαύτην ἴσχοντα), it is tempting to find Plato's later acknowledgement of Eudoxus' solution in the vexed passage of *Laws* VII (821b–822c) which rejects all celestial πλάναι.[4] Some critics find nothing here to contradict the *Republic* and *Timaeus*. So they can point to nothing which Plato might have learnt in later years (οὔτε νέος οὔτε πάλαι). I am inclined to locate the discovery, not indeed in the whole of what is maintained there, but in the implication that the other planets need no more be supposed to 'wander', in the sense of showing arbitrary variations in speed and direction, than the sun and moon themselves.

THE ALLEGED DEPENDENCE OF THE *TIMAEUS* ON THE *SOPHIST*

So far we have been chiefly concerned with the probability that the *Timaeus* preceded the *Parmenides* and *Theaetetus*. Now, follow-

[1] In fact it represents part of the source of Plato's complaint against empirical astronomy in *Rep.*, 530a 3–b 4—a passage which clearly prefigures the *Tim.*, and not only in introducing the δημιουργὸς τοῦ οὐρανοῦ. Equally, it explains why Plato's astronomy throughout depends for its precise exposition on the manipulation of an orrery (e.g., *Tim.*, 40d 2–3).

[2] *Cosmology*, 116.

[3] Cornford in this connection wrongly quotes the number 27 (which includes the motions of sun, moon, and stars); but even 27 is no πλῆθος ἀμήχανον.

[4] It is sometimes said (e.g. by Professor Skemp, *The Theory of Motion in Plato's Later Dialogues* [Cambridge, 1942], 79) that the *Timaeus*, like the *Laws*, condemns the description of the planets as πλανητά. This is not so. It says merely that they are so called (ἐπίκλην ἔχοντα 'πλανητά', 38c 5–6) and goes on to define the πλάνη (40b 6). Cf. Simplicius in *De Caelo*, 489. 5–11.

ing the order of the late dialogues, we turn to the recent counter-claim that at two points the *Timaeus* presupposes the argument of the *Sophist*.

1. Concerning the psychogony of *Timaeus*, 35a Cornford has maintained, with less reservations than Grube[1] or Cherniss,[2] that 'the *Sophist* (as the ancient critics saw) provides the sole clue to the sense of our passage'.[3] Such arguments for dating can cut both ways: e.g. Cornford has to appeal to the *Timaeus* to support his account (or expansion) of the perception-theory in the *Theaetetus*[4] and of the description of mirror-images in the *Theaetetus* and *Sophist*.[5] But in any case the claim cannot be allowed. Cornford can hardly have supposed that Plato's readers had to await the *Sophist* in order to be informed that any εἶδος existed, maintained its identity, and differed from others (cf. *Phd.*, 78d 5–7, *Symp.*, 211b 1–2, *Rep.*, 597c) or that existence, identity, and difference could be distinguished from each other (this is of course assumed throughout the *Parmenides* and occasionally stated, e.g. at 143b in the case of existence, difference, unity). Yet this is all that he borrows from the *Sophist*.[6] The distinction between divisible and indivisible οὐσία is explained by reference to the descriptions of εἰκόνες and χρόνος in the *Timaeus* and the contrast between ἁπλᾶ and σύνθετα in the *Phaedo*.[7] On the indivisibility of Identity and Difference he is reduced to 'conjecture'[8]—naturally, for there is no enlightening contrast to be found in the divisibility of ἡ θατέρου φύσις in the *Sophist* (257c–258a) which cannot be accommodated within the disjunction of the *Timaeus*. The *Timaeus*

[1] *Class. Philol.*, XXVII, 80–2; *Plato's Thought* (London, 1935), 142.

[2] *Aristotle's Criticism*, 409, n. 337.

[3] *Plato's Cosmology*, 62. The parenthesis hardly deserves refutation. If such 'ancient critics' as Xenocrates and Crantor ever attended to the *Sophist* in constructing their divergent interpretations, it was notoriously not their 'sole clue': cf. Taylor, *Commentary*, 112–15. Xenocrates' importation of motion and rest was presumably grounded in the *Timaeus* itself (57d–e), and attempted to reconcile the *Timaeus* with the definition of ψυχή given in the *Phaedrus*.

[4] *Plato's Theory of Knowledge*, 50 and n. 2: cf. especially his introduction of 'visual fire' and 'fiery particles' which 'interpenetrate and coalesce'.

[5] ibid., 124, n. 2; 327, n. 2.

[6] *Plato's Cosmology*, 59–66.

[7] *Plato's Cosmology*, 62–4, 102. It might have been glossed by the *Phdr.* myth (247c–e) in which the ἐπιστήμη that represents οὐσία ὄντως οὖσα is contrasted with that which is ἑτέρα ἐν ἑτέρῳ οὖσα ὧν ἡμεῖς νῦν ὄντων καλοῦμεν.

[8] ibid., pp. 65–6.

employs an older and simpler schema: the μεριστὴ θατέρου φύσις which is contrasted with the ἀμέριστος is περὶ τὰ σώματα γιγνομένη, and Cornford admits that the *Sophist* does not discuss divisibility of this order.

Consequently I cannot see that Cornford's exposition takes anything from the *Sophist* which is original to the argument of that most important dialogue, or which could not be gathered from such an earlier passage as that in the *Republic* (454a–b) which makes τὸ δύνασθαι κατ' εἴδη διαιρεῖσθαι a mark of διάλεκτος and ascribes it to a failure in διάλεκτος that ἐπεσκεψάμεθα οὐδ' ὁπῃοῦν τί εἶδος τὸ τῆς ἑτέρας τε καὶ τῆς αὐτῆς φύσεως καὶ πρὸς τί τεῖνον ὡριζόμεθα τότε. And, on the other hand, it is noteworthy that, in a highly elliptical context[1] and a dialogue whose ellipses are seldom supplied elsewhere, Plato subsequently offers so full an explanation of this stage of the soul-making (*Tim.*, 37a–c). To go beyond this and pronounce the indivisible Existence, Identity, and Difference 'Forms', as Cornford does, is to manufacture the difficulty (which he ignores) that their role in the psychogony then breaks the law laid down for all Forms in *Timaeus*, 52a 2–3.[2]

2. Perhaps we can settle the order of the *Sophist* and *Timaeus* in the course of rebutting a further claim. Discussing the account of λόγος in the world-soul (*Tim.*, 37a–c), Cornford remarks that the passage 'can only be understood by reference to the *Sophist*. There all philosophic discourse is regarded as consisting of affirmative and negative statements about Forms.'[3] Now this argument would carry weight if the *Timaeus* anywhere presupposed the analysis of negation in terms of θάτερον offered in the *Sophist*. But it does not. It mentions only assertions of identity and difference (37b, 44a), and in this respect shows no advance on the passage quoted earlier from the *Republic*. So it is at least misleading to gloss λόγος ὁ κατὰ ταὐτὸν ἀληθής (37b 3) as 'discourse true in either case, whether the judgements are *affirmative or negative*'.[4]

[1] Cf. the determining of harmonic intervals in the world-soul and the mathematical idioms in *Tim.*, 31c 4, 36c 5–7.

[2] I think Plato may have seen conclusive reasons for excluding παραδείγματα of existence, identity, and difference before he saw the general objection to making the Forms παραδείγματα: then the readmission of existence, etc., as εἴδη in the *Sophist* would mark the revised function of the εἶδος. But this falls outside the present paper. In the *Timaeus* Plato does not commit himself and should not be committed by his commentators.

[3] *Plato's Cosmology*, 96.

[4] ibid., 95, n. 1.

This in itself shows only that in the *Timaeus* the analysis of negation given in the *Sophist* is not presupposed,[1] not that it had not yet been worked out. But this further point can also be proved. For the tenet on which the whole new account of negation is based, namely that τὸ μὴ ὂν ἔστιν ὄντως μὴ ὄν (*Soph.*, 254d 1), is contradicted unreservedly by Timaeus' assertion that it is illegitimate to say τὸ μὴ ὂν ἔστι μὴ ὄν (38b 2–3); and thereby the *Timaeus* at once ranks itself with the *Republic* and *Euthydemus*. Cornford tries to excuse this, but his plea miscarries. He has to say that at *Timaeus*, 38b 2 τὸ μὴ ὄν means 'the absolutely non-existent, of which, as the *Sophist* shows, nothing whatever can be truly asserted'.[2] But what the *Sophist* argues is that any attempt to give this use to μὴ ὄν (we could say, to treat ὄν as a proper adjective) leads directly to absurdities, and that *in the only sense which can consistently be allowed to* μὴ ὄν it is wholly correct to say τὸ μὴ ὂν ἔστι μὴ ὄν.[3] And this formula is echoed insistently and always without the reservation which would be required on Cornford's interpretation.[4] So the *Timaeus* does not tally with even a fragment of the argument in the *Sophist*. That argument is successful against exactly the Eleatic error which, for lack of the later challenge to Father Parmenides, persists in the *Timaeus*.

SECOND THOUGHTS ON GOVERNMENT

1. At the start of the *Timaeus* Socrates alludes to a number of theses canvassed in the *Republic*. They are to be developed and illustrated by Critias in the sequel (*Tim.*, 26c–27b). Some critics, perplexed at the omission of other doctrines found in the *Republic*,

[1] 'Timaeus always talks of the μὴ ὄν in the old undiscriminating fashion familiar to us from the fifth book of the *Republic*' (Taylor, *Commentary*, 32).

[2] *Plato's Cosmology*, 98, n. 4.

[3] To try to give it the former use is to try to say what is ἄρρητον καὶ ἄφθεγκτον καὶ ἄλογον (238c 10); correspondingly ὁπόταν τὸ μὴ ὂν λέγωμεν, ὡς ἔοικεν, οὐκ ἐναντίον τι λέγομεν τοῦ ὄντος ἀλλ' ἕτερον μόνον (257b 3–4). For a further refutation of Cornford's account of the *Sophist* see A. L. Peck, 'Plato and the μέγιστα γένη of the *Sophist*', *Class. Quart.*, N.S. III (1953), 35–8. Though I think Dr. Peck's positive thesis mistaken (viz. that the *Sophist* has primarily the local virtue of beating certain sophists on their own ground) I take it to be at least partly prompted by the very real problem why the *Sophist* differs markedly from the *Timaeus* in its terminology and interests (cf. for example, op. cit., 39, 53). My own answer to this will be evident.

[4] *Soph.*, 258c 2–3, *Pol.*, 284b 8, 286b 10.

have guessed at an implied discontinuity in the argument of the two dialogues instead of insisting, as Plato does, on its continuity. They forget, firstly, that Plato repeatedly takes care to quote the words of the *Republic*;[1] secondly, that the *Timaeus* describes the doctrines it takes over as *κεφάλαια* of Socrates' talk on the previous day and that in the *Politics* (1264b 29–1265a 1) Aristotle summarises the conclusions of the *Republic* in exactly the way adopted in the *Timaeus*, explaining the selection by saying that the rest of the dialogue consists of 'digressions and a discussion of the Guardians' education'. And Plato also calls the central books a digression (*Rep.*, 543c 5). With this emphasis on continuity in mind, then,[2] we can try to connect the abandoning of the *Critias* with the fact that certain doctrines which the *Timaeus* takes over from the *Republic* as a basis for its sequel are rejected outright in the *Politicus*. For the moment we shall set on one side what is said in the *Laws*.

First, some special theses. The *Timaeus* (18b) repeats the prescription of the *Republic* (417a) that the Guardians must have no gold or silver or private property. Breach of this law in the *Republic* marks immediate degeneration from the perfect constitution (547b–548b). But against this the *Politicus* insists (four times in two pages, to show that this is novel doctrine: 292a, c, 293a, c–d) that whether the true ruler has any wealth is wholly irrelevant to the question whether his is the best possible government. Correspondingly, the system of marriages for the Guardians (*Rep.*, 457c–465c, echoed in *Tim.*, 18c–d), which was said to stand or fall with the abolition of private property (*Rep.*, 464b–c), is abandoned by the philosophic statesman in the *Politicus* (310a–311c). Its nearest analogue is the complete elimination of normal marriage and parenthood, by other means, in the non-historical

[1] Cf. Rivaud's notes on *Tim.*, 17c–19a (*Timée* [*Bude*]); he does not remark *Tim.*, 18b 3 = *Rep.* 419a 10 or the deliberate use of *σύνερξις* for the State marriages (a word apparently confined to *Rep.* 460a 9 and *Tim.* 18d 9).

[2] As to dramatic date, surely the reason why the *Timaeus* could not be set after the *Republic* (i.e. two days after the Bendidea) is just that when writing the earlier work Plato had not yet formulated the plan of the later and therefore had not seen the need to introduce any speaker of Timaeus' powers among either Cephalus' guests or Socrates' (presumed) auditors next day. Hence a further recital had to be invented. To infer from this that 'the design of the (*Timaeus*) trilogy is completely independent of the *Republic*' (Cornford) is to invert the natural inference.

time-cycle of the myth (271e 8–272a 1), whither Plato also banishes the lack of private property. Nor can these discrepancies be patched by saying that in the *Politicus* Plato argues only that the abolition of property—and, by implication, of families—is not to be taken as *defining* the government, though it is, in a weaker sense, still a necessary condition of it. Plato does indeed insist that it is not a ὅρος of ὀρθὴ ἀρχή, but what he now denies is that it is a necessary condition at all: this is proved (quite apart from the myth, to which I shall return) not only by the present context (e.g. 293a–b, if a doctor worthy of the name can be rich so can the statesman), but by the suggestion of different and more familiar arrangements for property and the marriages of ἄρχοντες under a scientific government (310a–311c).

But, more important, Plato now jettisons the general principle on which these detailed prescriptions depended: namely the assumption that νομοθεσία, provided it does not become embroiled with minutiae, can be final.[1] In the *Republic* there is no question of changing the original broad νόμοι laid down by Socrates, e.g. those governing the living-conditions and marriages of the Guardians and the ordering of their education. Earlier, the Guardians are permitted merely to obey the laws and 'imitate' them in details of interpretation (458c); later, when there is no longer (as once in 414b) any need or hope of duping them with the Noble Lie, their powers are commensurate with those of the original legislator solely in as far as they now understand why the νόμοι must be maintained (497b 7–d 2) and must be supreme (519e 1–2). Correspondingly, the prime virtue of Critias' model

[1] Barker's paradox, that the *Republic* is 'uncompromisingly hostile to law' and that this hostility is relaxed in the *Politicus* (*Greek Political Theory* [London, 1918], 271), hardly needs refutation. The *Republic* does not repudiate any 'system of law'; it contends only that continuous piecemeal legislation and litigation will be eliminated ἐάν γε θεὸς αὐτοῖς διδῷ σωτηρίαν τῶν νόμων ὧν ἔμπροσθεν διήλθομεν (425e), since then the Guardians will know ὅσα δεῖ νομοθετήσασθαι. Even if the νόμοι of the *Republic* were 'unwritten ordinances', the *Politicus* censures immutability in written and unwritten alike (295e 5); but in fact it is only the σμικρὰ δοκοῦντα εἶναι νόμιμα that will not have written legislation (*Rep.*, 425a–b). No punishment for crime is considered because Plato concentrates on the Guardians, whose crimes will disrupt the constitution and make punishment unavailable and unavailing. If it is true of this πολιτεία that 'its government is the result of its nature' (op. cit., p. 204), it is conversely true that its nature is the result of the παιδεία prescribed by νόμοι which are irrevocable (424b–d).

State is that of Sparta, εὐνομία (*Tim.*, 23c 6, 24d 4), and it is Socrates' νόνμοι which are taken over as the basis of that ἀρίστη πόλις (e.g. *Tim.*, 23e 5). But this whole doctrine of sovereign and immutable laws, asserted in the *Republic* and inherited by the *Timaeus* and its sequel, is denounced in the *Politicus*. No τέχνη (such as statesmanship) can lay down a permanent and universal rule (294b). The scientific ruler will be independent of legislation (294a–301a *passim*), and if for convenience he enacts laws, he is liable to discover that those which were the best possible in past circumstances need to be changed (295b–296a). Only inferior constitutions require laws binding on all members of the State, and such laws must be written records of what is at some time prescribed for the best State (297c–e).

The conclusion is in sight that the *Timaeus*, since it adopts without comment these superseded theories, was written before the *Politicus*; but there are two more steps required to reach it. And in countering the first objection we shall find independent support for our view.

2. It has been argued that the propositions quoted from the *Politicus* do not apply at all to human statecraft. On this interpretation, what the myth in that dialogue teaches is that the ruler with knowledge and independent of the laws is not a human possibility or matter for 'serious political theory';[1] so in the latter sphere, for all that Plato says, the *Republic–Critias* constitution may still rank first. But this is demonstrably a misreading of the *Politicus*,[2] where the argument moves as follows. The initial definition of the statesman as a kind of shepherd of men is pronounced unsatisfactory; it is inferred that by mistake some other σχῆμα βασιλικόν has been defined. The mistake is illustrated by the myth, which brings to light these objections: (*a*) The βασιλεὺς καὶ πολιτικός of the present time-cycle (viz. the historical as opposed to the ideal) must be distinguished from the θεῖος νομεύς of the other cycle: only the divine shepherd is worthy of the original definition, but he is 'higher than a king' (274e 10–275a 2, 275b 4–c 1). And (*b*) the earlier descriptions of the statesman as ruling the whole State must be clarified and amended

[1] Taylor, *Plato*, p. 397.

[2] Probably under the influence of *Laws*, 713a–714a, on which see below, p. 336, n. 1. For another refutation of Taylor's interpretation see J. B. Skemp, *Plato's Statesman*, (London, 1952), 52.

(275a 2–5). The objections are respectively met by (*a*) replacing τροφή by ἐπιμέλεια in the definition and (*b*) analysing the human ruler's ἐπιμέλεια to distinguish it from other functions in the State. The conclusion at once follows that the true statesman independent of laws who subsequently appears in the dialogue is an ἀνὴρ μετὰ φρονήσεως βασιλικός (294a 8): unlike the divine shepherd of the myth, he is a human possibility.[1]

Campbell saw Pythagoreanism in the political theories which are contrasted, under the guise of the divine shepherd, with Plato's own current doctrine.[2] But his evidence is late, and we can come nearer home. When Socrates wishes to see his πολιτεία illustrated in the lives and actions of φιλόσοφοι καὶ πολιτικοὶ ἄνδρες (*Tim.*, 19e 5–6), Critias without qualms establishes it under the guidance of 'divine shepherds' (*Crit.*, 109b 6–c). Then (*a*) if the *Politicus* follows and corrects the *Critias*, it can be read as arguing that the very appropriateness of the *Republic's* institutions to a Golden Age should have removed them from a study of πολιτικοὶ ἄνδρες. And Critias' introduction of the gods and their instrument πειθώ (109c 3) has merely the purpose it seems to have—that of avoiding the difficulties (already envisaged in *Rep.*, 500d–501a, 540d–541a) of establishing by authority a State based on consent.

But (*b*) if the *Critias* follows the *Politicus*, there can be only one inference from Critias' reference to divine shepherds. His whole discourse must then be devoted to illustrating the negative thesis that the institutions taken over from the *Republic* are not a matter of human political theory at all (and this not in the sense that they are a παράδειγμα ἐν οὐρανῷ, as the ideal *human* State may be, but that they are a radically inappropriate model for men). No one, I imagine, would defend this paradox. But two other points make

[1] The possibility is not cancelled by the concession that men do not credit it and that at present no such natural autocrat is to be found (301c–e). At this point Professor Grube's analysis breaks down (*Plato's Thought*, chap. vii). Against Barker he rightly points out that the *Republic* never supposes, what the *Politicus* affirms, that 'the best laws, even those enacted by the philosopher-king himself, are inevitably imperfect' and that law is a δεύτερος πλοῦς (*Pol.*, 300c 2). But he thinks that now the philosopher-king has risen 'so high [sc. above law] as to join the gods' (p. 281), and is consequently puzzled that 'the final definition of statecraft seems to imply the philosopher's knowledge all over again' (p. 284).

[2] *Politicus*, intro., xxi–xxvi.

it intolerable. First, it makes Critias' promise to talk of *θνητὰ καὶ ἀνθρώπινα* (107d 7–8, taking up Socrates' request) a pointless fraud. Next, Critias takes the distribution of the earth among various gods as the setting for his *πολιτεία* (109b 1–2); and the *Politicus* not only relegates this setting to the ideal time-cycle but denies that under these conditions there would be any *πολιτεῖαι* at all (271d 4–6, 271e 8).

3. This weakens in advance a last objection, but it deserves independent discussion. It could be said that in the *Laws* Plato reverts to political theories having a closer affinity with the *Republic*, and hence that the *Timaeus* and *Critias* may equally have been written after the reversion. Now it is easily shown that the *Laws* as a whole embodies no such reversion, and that its inconsistency on a cardinal issue reflects the changes in political theory sketched above.

In *Laws* IV (715c) it is laid down categorically that the ruler must be *τοῖς τεθεῖσι νόμοις εὐπειθέστατος*: here the continuity with the *Republic* is still direct and unbroken by the argument of the *Politicus*. (Contrast, for example, the assertion in 715d, that no State can hope for salvation unless the law is *δεσπότης τῶν ἀρχόντων, οἱ δὲ ἄρχοντες δοῦλοι τοῦ νόμου*, with *Pol.*, 294a: *τὸ ἄριστον οὐ τοὺς νόμους ἐστὶν ἰσχύειν ἀλλ' ἄνδρα τὸν μετὰ φρονήσεως βασιλικόν*.) Curators of the law must also be legislators in order to fill any lacunae, but they must remain *νομοφύλακες* (770a 6, cf. *Rep.*, 458c 2–4): no question here, as in the *Politicus*, of inevitable revision and repeal.[1] But in Book IX (875c–d) there is the first clear echo of the *Politicus* argument in the present sequence of the *Laws*.[2] There it is suddenly conceded that *τάξις καὶ νόμος* are second-best and that *ἐπιστήμη* and *νοῦς* should not be subject to them; but that, since the latter commodities are found *οὐδαμοῦ οὐδαμῶς ἀλλ' ἢ κατὰ βραχύ*, the inadequacies of legislation must be tolerated. Note that previously the 'best state', without

[1] Taylor seems to be right in saying that 'we are apparently to think of the authorities of [Plato's] "city" as needing less than a generation for the experience which would justify them in declaring their institutions definitely inviolable' (*The Laws of Plato*, (London, 1939), xxxii).

[2] There is perhaps another in 12. 945b–948b where certain political abuses described in *Pol.*, 298e–299a are eliminated by arrangements for the election and scrutiny of magistrates. In 6. 773a–c the marriage of complementary characters recommended in *Pol.*, 310a–311a is independently defended. On 4. 713a–714a see 336, n. 1 *infra*.

reservation, has been that whose laws are fixed and supreme: e.g. in 5. 739a–e the πρώτη πόλις (as contrasted with the second best, which is shown in more detail) is that whose laws prescribe a thoroughgoing communism; this is at once the ἀρίστη πολιτεία and the νόμοι ἄριστοι, and Plato calls it the παράδειγμα πολιτείας (cf. *Rep.*, 472d, 592b). Moreover, such legislation is the direct result of power in the hands of a man possessing τὸ φρονεῖν καὶ σωφρονεῖν (711e–712a), whereas in the *Politicus* (294a) it is independence of such permanent and universal νόμοι that marks the ἀνὴρ μετὰ φρονήσεως βασιλικός. On the other hand, the sole difference of view between the passage in *Laws* IX and the *Politicus* seems to be that, whereas the *Politicus* suggests that a ruler with knowledge may well be found (e.g. 293a 2–4, 297b 5–c 2), the *Laws* implies that the search has been and will probably continue to be a failure.

Thus what enters the *Laws* as a παράδειγμα πολιτείας becomes before the end a δεύτερος πλοῦς. And if Book IX imports an internal change of theory which reflects the emergence of new arguments in the *Politicus*, either of two explanations may be given. It may be that the *Laws* as a whole is Plato's latest work and that in it he designed to modify and reconcile political theories which he had advanced at different times. In that case the material is present but (what is evident on other counts too) the work is unfinished. The *Timaeus* and *Critias* show no signs of this late intention. On the other hand, it is arguable that the writing of the *Laws* was concurrent with that of the various late dialogues[1] and that Plato

[1] Suggested by Taylor, Diès, Field, and Ross, *inter alios*. There is no direct evidence that any part of the *Laws* was written after every other dialogue. The work certainly followed the *Republic* (Aristotle, *Pol.*, 1264b 28). But Diogenes' remark that it was left on the wax does not certify even that it occupied Plato to his death, much less that nothing else was written at the same time. (Who would argue that the works which Descartes or Leibniz left in manuscript must have been their last?) The connection of the προοίμια with Plato's work at Syracuse (*Ep.* III, 316a) does not show that the technique first suggested itself to him there or in the year 360 (Taylor, *Plato*, 464–5; cf. Burnet, *Greek Philosophy* (London, 1932), 301. But note that in the *Tim.* (29d 5) the contrast between προοίμιον and νόμος has the musical connotation found in the *Rep.* (531d 8), not the later legal sense). Taylor arbitrarily and inconsistently assumes a 'block' *Laws* in arguing that, if *Laws* IV. 711a–b (describing as if from personal knowledge the powers of a tyrant, which the wise legislator may hope to harness) should be dated after Plato's last return from Syracuse, '*the work* must therefore belong to a date later than 360'

transferred arguments from them to the *Laws* without returning to make the necessary revision of earlier passages in the work.[1] But however the chronology of the *Laws* is decided, our point is made that the dialogue embodies no consistent reversion to the political theories of the *Republic* and that, on the other hand, we shall go astray if we deny the direct continuity with the *Republic* which is stressed in the *Timaeus* and *Critias*. These three dialogues know nothing of the hope (whether inspired by Dion or Dionysius or a new analysis of τέχνη) that a State may be saved by the supremacy not of immutable laws but of an ἀνὴρ φρόνιμος above the law.

CONCLUSION

I hope I have proved that in metaphysics and cosmology, in logic and politics, the *Timaeus* and *Critias* belong to the middle dialogues and ignore salient arguments and theories developed in (or in the case of Eudoxus' hypothesis, concurrently with) the later 'critical' group. No one doubts, I suppose, that the *Timaeus* represents the culmination of a period of growing confidence, a time in which Plato came to think himself ready to expound an ambitious system of speculations. The misfortune is that this crowning work has been tacked on to the latest dialogues, with which it disagrees largely in interests, methods, and conclusions. Its place is at the end of the *Republic* group (allowing a sufficient interval of time for Plato to have developed and co-ordinated the contributory theories). Just as the tripartite soul

[1] This would more easily explain the form of a myth in *Laws* IV. 713a–714a which bears a superficial similarity to that in the *Politicus*. The moral wrongly imported by Taylor into the *Politicus* (namely that the ideal ruler independent of laws is not an historical possibility) is in fact the moral of the allegory in the *Laws*, which can be regarded as a briefer and less sophisticated version corrected, in the light of later political theories, by the *Politicus*. For whereas in *Laws* IV the 'divine shepherd' and the supremacy of law are presented as a simple disjunction (713e–714a) and law is itself the διανομὴ νοῦ (714a 2), the *Politicus* insists on the *tertium quid*, the independent ruler with νοῦς and φρόνησις. And in the *Laws* this possibility does not seem to be entertained before Book IX.

(*Laws*, intro., xii). In any case (*a*) the optimism of the passage hardly accords with Taylor's dating and (*b*) the personal experience (of a tyrant's power to shape a State for good or evil) could clearly have been gained earlier.

is taken over and given a physiological basis in the *Timaeus* (44d, 69c–72d), so the ἀναλογία of the Divided Line is repeated and made a basis of the metaphysics (28a, 29c), the παραδείγματα are put to the service of the δημιουργός, the astronomy of the Myth of Er is developed and refined, and a quasi-historical illustration of the *Republic's* political doctrines is undertaken. (So, too, with details: the *Republic's* proof of the uniqueness of any Form is given a second hearing.) And this provides us with more cogent reasons than those usually given for the abandoning of the *Critias* and the non-appearance of its sequel (supposing a sequel is promised in (*Critias*, 108a–c). Doubtless, if a third member of the group was planned, much of the material for it may now be found in the *Laws*. But we need not suppose that Plato—after repeatedly insisting on his practice of selecting from the available subject-matter (e.g. *Tim.*, 89d 7–e 3, 90e 3–6)—was merely bewildered into shelving his project by the abundance of this material.[1] We can suggest now that some or all of the changes of theory outlined in this paper induced him to turn aside and make the fresh start recorded in the *Parmenides* and *Theaetetus*.

The ordering of the *Timaeus* and *Phaedrus*, whose affinities so far outweigh their discrepancies, cannot be determined by arguments of the sort that I have tried to find. There are, however, some pointers. For instance, it seems that an apologia for the abandoning of the *Critias* may be found in the *Phaedrus*, with its novel denial of βεβαιότης to any written work and its condemnation of the man who 'has nothing more valuable than his own past writings and compositions which he has spent time turning and twisting, welding and censoring' (278d 8–e 1). There is no hint of this revulsion in what the *Timaeus* and *Critias* have to say about types of λόγοι (29b–d, 107a–e); and if the *Timaeus* group was abandoned through dissatisfaction with some now veteran theories, the refusal to waste time 'welding and censoring' gains point after the abandonment but sounds oddly if it comes between the *Republic* and its avowed successor.

Again, there is Plato's apparent inconsistency on the nature of discarnate soul. The *Timaeus*, as from our argument we shall expect, combines the tripartite psychology of the *Republic* with the immortality of νοῦς taught in the *Phaedo* (cf. *Rep.*, 611b

[1] Cf. Cornford's development of Raeder's suggestion, *Plato's Cosmology*, pp. 6–8.

9–612a 6): it excludes passions and appetites from the ἀρχὴ ψυχῆς ἀθάνατος. But this is seemingly contradicted in the *Phaedrus* (246a ff.) and the *Laws* (897a). However, we avoid the conclusion that Plato 'wavered to the end' between these alternatives[1] if we set the *Phaedrus* after the *Timaeus* (and the resulting account of Plato's final views seems to be confirmed if Jaeger and Nuyens are right, as against Themistius, in denying that in the *Eudemus* Aristotle confined immortality to νοῦς). Within the same field there are other pointers. Those who accept Aristotle's literal exposition of the 'creation' in the *Timaeus* can of course argue that the doctrines of that dialogue exclude the definition of ψυχή as αὐτὸ κινοῦν and so ἀγένητον (*Phdr.*, 245c–d). But if we follow Xenocrates here, doubts remain. It is not merely that no mention of the definition occurs in the *Timaeus* (for what is sometimes taken for an oblique reference to it in 46d–e may well contain only its raw material). It is rather that, firstly, when Plato does mention self-motion, he denies it to plants in the same breath as he ascribes to them ψυχή (77b–c: contrast, for example, *Phdr.*, 245e 4–6); that is, he seems to use κίνησις ὑφ' ἑαυτοῦ in an everyday sense innocent of any special doctrine. And, secondly, it does not seem that any attempt to reconcile the disorderly motions in the *Timaeus* with the doctrine that ψυχή is the ἀρχὴ κινήσεως has yet won general credit. But these hints do not add up to a reasonable certainty. In particular, they are weaker than arguments of the type I have so far tried to find because they do not exhibit a precise error or inadequacy correlated with a subsequent precise correction.

On the other hand, I trust the earlier arguments may arouse enough faith to remove one mountain and deliver our interpretation of the critical dialogues from the shadow of the *Timaeus*. It is time, I am sure, to be quit of such ancestral puzzles as that of inserting the Paradigms into the more sophisticated metaphysic of the *Philebus*, and to leave the profoundly important late dialogues to their own devices.

[1] Hackforth, *Plato's Phaedrus*, p. 75.

XVII

THE RELATION OF THE *TIMAEUS* TO PLATO'S LATER DIALOGUES[1] (1957)

H. F. Cherniss

FOR a long time now most Platonic scholars have agreed that the *Timaeus* and its sequel, the unfinished *Critias*, belong to the last group of Plato's writings, that except for the *Laws* and possibly the *Philebus* they are in fact the latest of his works. Some three years ago, however, an English scholar, Mr. G. E. L. Owen, published an article in which he professed to undermine this currently prevailing opinion and to prove that the *Timaeus* and *Critias* were designed by Plato as 'the crowning work of the *Republic* group' and were composed before the group of so-called 'critical dialogues', the *Parmenides*, *Theaetetus*, *Sophist*, and *Politicus*, before the *Cratylus* (which he thinks also belongs to this group), long before the *Philebus* (on the relative lateness of which he holds to the current orthodoxy), and even before the *Phaedrus* (which he would place somewhere between the *Timaeus* and 'the critical group').[2] There is little or nothing under the sun that is entirely

[1] This is the text of a lecture which was delivered at Harvard University in April of 1956. Except for the footnotes here added and one or two changes in the phrasing it is here printed exactly as it was delivered. In this form it is part of a more detailed study of the subject which the author is preparing for publication; but, taken together with the articles mentioned in the notes and one dealing with *Tim.*, 38a 8–b 5 now published in the volume of *J.H.S.* (LXXVII [1957], Part I) dedicated to Sir David Ross, it covers what the author believes to be all the major arguments that prompted the investigation.

[2] G. E. L. Owen, 'The Place of the *Timaeus* in Plato's Dialogues', *Class. Quart.*, N.S. III (1953), pp. 79–95, see above, Ch. XVI. Hereafter referred to as simply 'Owen'.

new in Platonic scholarship. The opinion that the *Timaeus* is one of Plato's latest works is much older than the arguments that established the modern orthodoxy in this matter—it is in fact at least as old as Plutarch;[1] and Mr. Owen's arguments against it also are not so novel as he appears to have believed.[2] Whereas such arguments had hitherto attracted little attention, however, there are clear indications that now, especially in England and among younger scholars, the case as presented by Mr. Owen is coming to be more and more widely accepted as established.[3] This would be reason enough, it seems to me, to subject it as soon as possible to the test of an exhaustive and critical examination.

Such an examination (with all the details of which I shall not try your forbearance) shows, I believe, that Mr. Owen's arguments do not have the cogency claimed for them and do not support the conclusion to which he thinks they inevitably lead. It does not, of course, give positive and ineluctable proof that the *Timaeus* and *Critias* are the latest of Plato's writings except for the *Laws* or the *Laws* and the *Philebus*. The evidence at our

[1] Plutarch, *Solon*, chap. 32: Plato's work on the *Critias* was cut short by death. This may be only an inference drawn from the unfinished state of the dialogue, but it implies that Plutarch too supposed the *Timaeus* to be one of Plato's last writings.

[2] Cf. for example F. Tocco (*Studi Italiani di Filologia Classica*, II [1894], pp. 391–469) who, like Owen, contended that the *Parmenides*, *Theaetetus*, *Sophist*, *Politicus*, and *Philebus* must all be later than the *Timaeus*. O. Apelt held that the *Timaeus* must have been written before the *Sophist* but at the beginning of Plato's latest period, long after the *Parmenides* (cf. *Platons Dialoge Timaios und Kritias* [1919], p. 20; *Platonische Aufsätze* [1912], p. 268, note 1 [first published in 1895], etc.). Even earlier D. Peipers (*Ontologia Platonica* [1883]) had placed the *Timaeus* and *Critias* immediately after the *Republic* and before the *Euthydemus* and *Cratylus* as well as before the 'critical group'; Teichmüller in his writings from 1881 to 1884 placed the *Timaeus* before the *Philebus*, *Parmenides*, *Sophist*, *Politicus*, *Laws* (in that chronological order); and Susemihl (*Woch. für klass. Philologie*, I [1884], cols. 513–24; cf. his *Neue plat. Forschungen* [1898]) contended that after the *Republic* the chronological order of composition was *Timaeus*, *Critias*, *Sophist*, *Politicus*, *Parmenides*, *Philebus*, *Laws*—in which the special interest lies in the place assigned to the *Parmenides* after all the works except the *Philebus* and *Laws* and in the placing of both the *Cratylus* and the *Theaetetus* before the *Symposium*, *Phaedo*, *Republic*, and *Timaeus*. Cf. M. Schanz, *Hermes*, XXI (1886), pp. 439–59 (especially pp. 446 and 454–5).

[3] Cf. e.g. John Gould, *The Development of Plato's Ethics* (1955), p. 202, note 3; D. W. Hamlyn, *Phil. Quart.*, V (1955), p. 290, note 3.

disposal does not suffice for a rigorous demonstration of any such exact relative chronology. It does, however, in my opinion suffice to show 1) that they belong to the latest group of dialogues and so are later than the *Theaetetus* and the *Parmenides*, 2) that they *may be* and probably are later than the *Sophist* and the *Politicus*, and 3) that, even if they were in fact written before the *Sophist* and *Politicus*, Mr. Owen's arguments do not prove the fact nor would the fact make the difference that he thinks it does to the correct interpretation of Plato's thought.

The generally accepted opinion concerning the relative chronology of the *Timaeus* seemed to have been confirmed beyond reasonable doubt by the results of stylometric studies. Owen attacks the assumptions and procedure of those who have applied this method to the study of Plato's writings; and, rejecting its results, he appeals instead to a study of the clausulae in the late dialogues by L. Billig, who concluded that the rhythms occurring at the end of sentences in the *Timaeus* prove this work to have been composed earlier than the *Politicus* and what he calls 'the digression' in the *Sophist*.[1] Many of Owen's criticisms of the stylometrists are well founded, and have often been made before. The more sober practitioners of the method have themselves criticised the shortcomings of the pioneer, Campbell, and the mechanical procedure and excessive claims of Lutoslawski and of von Arnim in his later work in this field.[2]

The criterion upon which Owen relies is open to equally severe criticism, however. Not to mention the more general difficulties that have been raised with regard to the determination of prose-rhythm,[3] Billig's procedure, which Owen adopts, based as it is upon the assumption that the final syllable is indifferent, goes counter to Aristotle's statement concerning clausulae and to the evidence of Plato's own usage;[4] and this by itself justifies the scepticism concerning Billig's statistics and his inferences from them which had been expressed more than twenty years before they were resuscitated by Owen.[5] Moreover, Billig's

[1] *Journ. of Philol.*, XXXV (1920), pp. 225–56.

[2] E.g. H. Raeder, *Platons Philosophische Entwickelung* (1905), pp. 33–44; C. Ritter, *Bursian's Jahresbericht*, CLXXXVII (1921), pp. 130–4 and 170–83.

[3] Cf. e.g. G. Ammon, *Philol. Woch.*, XL (1920), cols. 242 and 248–9.

[4] Aristotle, *Rhetoric*, 1409a 9–21; A. W. DeGroot, *A Handbook of Antique Prose-Rhythm* (1918), pp. 62–4, 191, 221.

[5] Cf. P. Friedländer, *Platon*, II (1930), p. 672, note 1.

statistics in themselves prove that his method is not a safe guide to the relative chronology of the writings. They profess to show that the clausulae of *Sophist*, 236c–260a are approximately those of the *Politicus*, while the clausulae of the parts of the *Sophist* that precede and follow this section are akin to those of the *Timaeus*. From this Billig inferred that *Sophist*, 236c–260a was written much later than the rest of the dialogue and was then inserted into that earlier work. But, in the first place, Plato himself clearly indicates that this so-called 'digression' ends not at 260a, as Billig's statistics require it to do, but four Stephanus pages later at 264b,[1] and the references in the *Politicus*[2] to this same 'digression' prove that it was from the first an integral part of the *Sophist*. In the second place, by Billig's criterion we could as easily prove that the myth of the *Politicus* must have been composed much earlier than the rest of that work, for the incidence of the supposedly late clausulae in this myth is exceeded by their incidence in the rest of this dialogue by a larger proportion than that which is taken to prove the bulk of the *Sophist* to be earlier than its 'digression' and scarcely exceeds their incidence in this so-called 'early' bulk of the *Sophist* itself.[3] Furthermore, anyone who does accept Billig's statistics as proof that the *Timaeus* is earlier than the digression of the *Sophist* should in consistency assert that the *Parmenides* in turn is earlier than the *Timaeus*, since the incidence of these clausulae in the former, whether the whole of the dialogue or only the first part is considered, is appreciably lower than it is in the *Timaeus*.[4]

[1] Cf. *Soph.*, 264c 1 ff., 264d 3 ff.; and H. Bonitz, *Platonische Studien*[3] (1886), pp. 178–9.

[2] *Pol.*, 284b–c, 286b–c.

[3] According to Billig (p. 241) the clausulae supposedly favoured in the late style constitute 48·8 per cent. in the rest of the *Sophist* as against 65·8 per cent. in the digression, a difference of 17 per cent. In the *Politicus* as a whole he calculates them at 70·7 per cent.; but in the myth (268d 8–274e 4) I find that they constitute scarcely 52 per cent., more than 18 per cent. below his average for the whole dialogue, 13·8 per cent. below his figure for the digression of the *Sophist*, and only 3·2 per cent. above that for the bulk of the *Sophist* excluding the digression.

[4] Billig does not consider the *Parmenides* at all; but according to Owen (p. 315, note 2) the rhythms dominant from the digression of the *Sophist* onwards total 38·1 per cent. in the first part of the *Parmenides* (my own count gives 37·5 per cent. for *Parmenides* 126a–137c 3) against Billig's 45·6 per cent. for the *Timaeus*. For the whole of the *Parmenides* Kaluscha's figures would yield a little less than 37 per cent. (*Wiener Studien*, XXVI [1904], p. 196).

To admit this, however, would cancel the significance that Owen sees in his revised chronology.

Billig is not the only scholar who has attempted to determine the relative chronology of Plato's works by means of a statistical study of prose-rhythm. Besides Kaluscha,[1] to whose earlier article both Billig and Owen refer, there are the elaborate studies of A. W. De Groot,[2] whose work is not mentioned by Owen. His analysis and his statistics differ from those of Billig in several significant ways; and, if his percentages of the clausulae favoured and avoided are accepted as a chronological criterion, the *Timaeus* is definitely later than the *Parmenides*, almost as certainly later than the *Sophist*, and possibly later than the *Politicus*. According to this criterion, moreover, the *Critias*, of which Billig takes no account and for which De Groot gives separate percentages, would be the last of all Plato's compositions excepting just possibly Books III, V, and VI of the *Laws*. If the *Critias* was written immediately after the *Timaeus*, however, as Owen assumes it was,[3] it should for the purpose of such calculations be treated along with the *Timaeus* as a single statistical unit; and this unit, *Timaeus–Critias*, would according to De Groot's statistics be still more certainly later than the *Sophist* and the *Politicus*, not to mention the *Parmenides*, although earlier than the *Philebus* and the *Laws*.

If, then, the stylometric methods that Owen rejects have failed to prove positively that the *Timaeus* is later than the *Sophist* and *Politicus*, the statistical analysis of prose-rhythm to which he appeals has so far provided no cogent reason for believing that

[1] W. Kaluscha, *Wiener Studien*, XXVI (1904), pp. 191–204. His work is criticised by De Groot, *Handbook* (see note 2 *infra*), pp. 68–9, 123, 149.

[2] *A Handbook of Antique Prose-Rhythm* (Groningen, 1918) and *Der antike Prosarhythmus* I (Groningen, 1921).

[3] Owen, p. 318. This is the prevailing opinion, and it is strongly supported by *Tim.*, 27a–b and *Crit.*, 106a–b (cf. P. Friedländer, *Platon*, II, p. 602 and L. Stefanini, *Platone*, II, p. 225, n. 1); but not even this obvious connection has gone unchallenged: cf. Wilamowitz, *Platon*, I (1920), p. 592 and II (1919), pp. 256–7; T. G. Rosenmeyer, *H.S.C.P.*, LX (1951), p. 303; F. Kluge, *De Platonis Critia* (1910), pp. 261–3.

Kaluscha did in fact conclude (pp. 202–4) that, while the *Timaeus* and *Critias* antedate the *Sophist*, *Politicus*, and *Philebus*, the *Phaedrus*, *Theaetetus*, and *Parmenides* belong to an earlier period in which Plato took little heed of terminal rhythm.

the *Timaeus* antedates those dialogues and has not even suggested that it was composed before the *Parmenides*.

There is one stylistic characteristic which, while it does not help to determine the relative chronology of the *Timaeus*, *Sophist*, *Politicus*, and *Philebus*, leads to the inescapable conclusion that all these works were written after the *Parmenides*. This is the incidence of hiatus, which divides all Plato's writings into two distinct groups: in one, consisting of the great majority, hiatus occurs on an average ranging from 23·90 times per page of the Didot edition in the *Phaedrus* to 45·97 times per page in the *Lysis*; in the other, comprising only the *Laws*, *Philebus*, *Timaeus*, *Critias*, *Sophist*, and *Politicus*, the average ranges from 6·71 times per page in *Laws* V (5·85 in the *Laws* taken as a whole) to 0·44 per page in the *Politicus*.[1] The variations from dialogue to dialogue within either one of these groups has no absolute chronological significance; but the difference between the lowest average in the first group and the highest in the second is so great that it must reflect a purposeful change of style on Plato's part and a change made without any gradual or tentative transition. It is perfectly clear that he made a consistent attempt to avoid hiatus in *none* of the dialogues of the first group and in *all* those of the second. So much has been admitted almost universally ever since Janell's statistics brought conclusive support to the aperçu of Blass, as it has also been admitted that the second group, which includes the *Laws*, must be later than the first, in which hiatus is not avoided.[2]

Owen contends, however, as he must, that this is not a reliable criterion for determining the chronological relation of the *Timaeus* to the *Theaetetus* or the *Parmenides*. His arguments are two:

[1] Cf. W. Janell, *Jahrbücher für classische Philologie*, Supplementband XXVI (1901), pp. 265–336. For the average in the *Laws* taken as a whole cf. C. Barwick, *De Platonis Phaedri Temporibus* (1913), p. 51. If the pages of formal legislation are discounted, the average for the whole of the *Laws* is only 4·70 per page (Janell, op. cit., p. 306).

[2] Among scholars who had maintained a sceptical reserve with regard to the claims of stylometry see on the criterion of hiatus O. Apelt (*Philol. Woch.*, XXII [1902], cols, 321–3), B. L. Gildersleeve (*Amer. Journ. Philol.*, XXII [1901], pp. 348–9), M. Pohlenz (*Aus Platos Werdezeit* [1913], p. 356), and Cornford, Hackforth, and Skemp cited by Owen, p. 315, note 6. Among others cf. especially H. Raeder (*Platons Philosophische Entwickelung* [1905], pp. 41–3), C. Ritter (*Platon*, I [1910], p. 238), J. Chevalier (*La Notion du Nécessaire chez Aristote* [1915], pp. 220–1), M. Wundt (*Zeitschrift für Philosophische Forschung*, IV [1949], pp. 32–4).

first, that 'nearly all stylometrists' consider the *Phaedrus* to be earlier than the *Theaetetus* and the *Parmenides* although it displays as they do not 'a striking rarity of hiatus'; and, second, that the *Timaeus* is 'a "conscious *tour de force* of style" where the carelessness of conversation has no place'. The latter point presumably implies that Plato at any time during his life would have avoided hiatus in writing the *Timaeus*. But the *Symposium* and the *Menexenus* are equally *tours de force* of style, and in neither of them is hiatus avoided. The avoidance of it in the *Timaeus* (1·17 per page) cannot be explained by the subject-matter or the tone of the work; and that it was not just an isolated stylistic experiment which Plato then abandoned only to adopt again for good after a considerable interval is proved by his rigorous adherence to it in the immediate sequel, the *Critias* (0·80 per page). The first of Owen's arguments is an *ignoratio elenchi*. No one supposes that the dialogues composed without regard to avoidance of hiatus were written in the strict order of the diminishing frequency of the phenomenon; where there is no such concern, the fluctuations of frequency would be the accidental results of other factors and so would not themselves be indicative of any chronological sequence. It is perfectly consistent, therefore, to contend on the basis of other criteria that the *Phaedrus*, in which hiatus appears on an average of 23·90 times per page, antedates other dialogues in which it appears more frequently and at the same time to hold that the great difference in respect of this stylistic characteristic between the first group and the second implies the chronological priority of *all* the former to *any* of the latter. Only by refraining from comparison with this second group can Owen say with any show of plausibility that there is a 'striking rarity of hiatus' in the *Phaedrus*.[1] The incidence in this dialogue (23·90 per page) is, to be sure, lower than in any other work of the first group and only a little more than half as frequent as it is in the *Parmenides* (44·10 per page); but it is very little lower than in the *Menexenus* (28·19 per page), where its frequency struck Cicero as worthy of special remark,[2] and the relatively less frequent occurrence of hiatus in these two works

[1] Owen borrowed the phrase from Blass (*Attische Beredsamkeit*, II[2], p. 458), who applied it specifically to the dialogic parts of the *Phaedrus* in comparison with the *Symposium* and the *Republic* but who proceeded immediately to stress the far greater avoidance of hiatus in the second group, a qualification concerning which Owen maintains a discreet silence.

[2] Cicero, *Orator*, xliv, 151.

has been convincingly explained as the incidental by-product of other stylistic characteristics which they share.[1] What is significant, however, is the great gap between the *Phaedrus* and all the works of the second group. In the *Lysis*, where the incidence of hiatus is highest, its frequency is less than twice what it is in the *Phaedrus*, whereas in the *Phaedrus* it is more than four times what it is in the *Laws* as a whole and more than twenty times what it is in the *Timaeus*; and, taken absolutely, the difference between the incidence in the *Phaedrus* and that in any work of the second group is far greater than the difference between that in the *Phaedrus* and that in the *Symposium*, the *Republic*, the *Theaetetus*, or the *Cratylus*. It is clear that the *Phaedrus*, like the *Menexenus*, belongs to the first group, not the second. Its relatively low frequency of hiatus, which is not remotely an approximation to the Isocratean canon, does not even justify its assignment to a special position chronologically intermediate between the two groups and certainly is no argument against the validity of the inference that the difference in the incidence of hiatus between the first group of works and the second marks a chronological division between the two. So the *Parmenides*, the *Theaetetus*, the *Cratylus*, and the *Phaedrus* too, whatever their true chronological position in the first group may be, cannot be moved below that line of division but must all have been composed before any of the works in the second;[2] and the *Timaeus* and *Critias*, whether earlier or later than the *Sophist*, the *Politicus*, or the *Philebus*, cannot be moved back from the second group, in which these dialogues fall, and so must have been written after the *Cratylus*, *Phaedrus*, *Theaetetus*, and *Parmenides*.

[1] Cf. M. Pohlenz (*Aus Platos Werdezeit*, p. 356); A. W. De Groot (*Handbook*, pp. 75–82); and C. Barwick (*De Platonis Phaedri Temporibus*, pp. 65–6), who shows that the relatively lower frequency of hiatus in the *Phaedrus* is not to be explained as the result of a later revision by Plato, the expedient adopted from Blass by Janell (op. cit., pp. 307–8) and most recently proposed again as a possibility by M. Wundt (op. cit., pp. 54–5).

[2] The *Phaedrus* cannot, then, be placed among the latest works of the second group, where some scholars have recently sought to place it, e.g. E. Hoffmann (*Platon* [1950], pp. 142 and 144), O. Regenbogen (*Miscellanea Academica Berolinensia*, II, 1 [1950], pp. 198–219), D. J. Allan (*Philosophy*, XXVIII [1953], p. 365), G. J. De Vries (*Mnemosyne*, 4 Ser. VI [1953], pp. 40–1). L. Robin, who in 1908 proposed such a late position for it, afterwards withdrew this suggestion (cf. Cherniss, *Aristotle's Criticism of Plato and the Academy*, I, p. 426, note 360).

The eagerness to discover such neutral or objective criteria for determining the relative chronology of Plato's writings, which has induced so many scholars to perform the painstaking and tedious labour of counting particles, syllabic quantities, and occurrence of hiatus in all the Platonic corpus, was prompted not by disinterested curiosity in the variations of his style or in the details of his literary biography as such but by the desire to identify the definitive form of his philosophy and to explain as earlier doctrine—subsequently developed, altered, or abandoned—whatever in his other writings might appear to be at variance with this. Such is also the reason for Owen's concern with the relative chronology of the *Timaeus*. The orthodox opinion of this chronology is responsible, he believes, for what he calls the paradoxes in the interpretation of Plato's ultimate philosophy, paradoxes which he maintains can be resolved simply by revising this opinion. By proving that the *Timaeus* antedates the *Parmenides* he hopes, as he says, to 'deliver our interpretation of the critical dialogues from the shadow of the *Timaeus*', that is from 'the Paradigms'. This 'shadow' cast by the doctrine of ideas he thinks must be dispelled 'from the more sophisticated metaphysics of the *Philebus*' in order that we may 'leave the profoundly important late dialogues to their own devices'.[1]

These phrases of Owen's have their own interest for anyone who has followed the fascinating and perplexing history of Platonic interpretation, which has been so largely a series of insistently charitable efforts on the part of western philosophers and their acolytes, each to baptize Plato in his particular faith—having shriven him first, of course, by interpreting the heresies out of his works. Now, the Analysts of Oxford have succeeded to their own satisfaction in reading the dialogues that they call 'critical' as primitive essays in their own philosophical method. The author of *these* works, they feel, they could adopt as their worthy precursor, if only he could be absolved of the embarrassing doctrine of ideas that he elaborated in all its metaphysical and epistemological absurdity in the *Phaedo*, the *Symposium*, the *Republic*, and the *Phaedrus*. And can he not be shown to have absolved himself of this error? Through the mouth of Parmenides, in the first part of the dialogue named for him, Plato himself presented a whole list of crushing objections to this same doctrine of ideas and

[1] Owen, p. 338 (*sub fin.*).

represented its champion, Socrates, as incapable of rebutting any of them. He must, then, obviously have abandoned the doctrine, which he causes to be thus criticised; and, at least in the form in which he previously held it, it must be absent from the critical dialogues, for these are admittedly later than the *Parmenides*. So in 1939 Professor Ryle could assure the readers of *Mind* that: 'It has long been recognised that in the whole period which includes the writing of the *Theaetetus*, the *Sophist*, the *Politicus*, and the *Philebus*, Plato's thinking is not entirely, if at all, governed by the premisses of the Theory of Forms. He attends to the theory on occasions but he does so in a dispassionate and critical way.'[1] Professor Ryle neglected to say by *whom* this had long been recognised; and, unfortunately for this elegant method of rescuing Plato from himself, he also forgot that the evidence which enabled him to put the dialogues mentioned in a period later than the *Parmenides* had in fact long been recognised by all who had gathered and tested it as proving the *Timaeus* to belong at the end of this very period. In the *Timaeus*, however, that same doctrine of ideas, which the critique of the *Parmenides* is presumed to have demolished, is presented as openly and elaborately as it ever was before and even more emphatically asserted to be true. Dr. Robinson, remembering this, could 'hardly think it wise to say' (as Professor Ryle had done) 'that Plato did not believe in the theory of Forms at this period'; but after this politely muted expression of disagreement he proposed a still more startling way of saving the late Plato for the Analysts and from himself. 'What seems much more probable,' Dr. Robinson wrote, 'is that he still *thought* he believed in it, though in his active inquiries he was in fact beyond it, and it functioned as a theory to be criticised instead of as the rock of salvation it had been in his middle period.'[2] The second part of this sentence suggests that its author had forgotten the *Timaeus* only a dozen lines after he had cited it in evidence against Professor Ryle; as to the first part, if we must resort to such an hypothesis at all, the victim of self-delusion as to what Plato believed is far less likely to have been Plato than Dr. Robinson. It is no wonder that the obvious stumbling-block of the *Timaeus* should obsess, as it has always obsessed, those who insist upon banishing the doctrine of ideas from Plato's so-called 'critical period' and that now one of them should again

[1] See above, p. 134. [2] Richard Robinson, *Phil.. Rev.*, LIX (1950), p. 19.

have resorted to the simple and drastic expedient of redating the work and so purging the period of it. In order to do this, Owen had to reject the validity of the stylistic criteria by which this period itself had originally been established; but, what is more, according to the very stylistic criterion that he would substitute for those rejected the *Timaeus* ought still to be later than the *Parmenides*[1] and would therefore still deny the significance that he and the Analysts see in the objections to the ideas put into the mouth of Parmenides.

Even if we disregard all such stylistic criteria, however, and, contrary to the evidence of them all, allow Owen to assume that the *Timaeus* did antedate the *Parmenides*, we shall find that he has not thereby succeeded in resolving what he calls the paradoxes in the interpretation of Plato's ultimate philosophy and that he is consequently mistaken in asserting that they have been imported by the orthodox opinion concerning the chronology of the *Timaeus*. By 'paradoxes' in this allegation he presumably means contradictions attributable to erroneous interpretations of Plato's statements. For we must reckon with the possibility that Plato even in the ultimate stage of his philosophy, whatever it was, may in fact have enunciated 'paradoxes' in the sense of propositions which in their logical consequences are or seem to us to be self-contradictory or inconsistent with one another; at least acquaintance with the indubitably ultimate expressions of most other philosophers ought to warn us against denying the possibility in his case. And, if by 'paradoxes' is meant tenets contrary to the accepted belief of what is true, then it must be recognised that the fundamental propositions of Plato's philosophy as enunciated in almost any one of his writings are consciously and avowedly paradoxical.

I

Among these conscious paradoxes is the proposition that sensible phenomena are always involved in becoming and never really exist, whereas what really *is* never *becomes* but is unalterably the same and is intelligible but not sensible. With this distinction between τὸ ὂν ἀεί, γένεσιν δ' οὐκ ἔχον and τὸ γιγνόμενον μὲν ἀεί, ὂν δ' οὐδέποτε Timaeus begins his account of the universe.[2] Now,

[1] See above, p. 342 note 4. [2] *Tim.*, 27d 6–28a 4.

according to Owen the assumption that this doctrinal paradox was enunciated by Plato during his 'critical period' involves the exegesis of that period of his thought in an inexplicable paradox of interpretation, which can be completely eliminated simply by recognising that the *Timaeus* was written before and not after the *Theaetetus*, *Cratylus*, and *Parmenides*. For Owen maintains that the principle of the incompatibility of γένεσις and οὐσία is 'the outcome of the *Republic's* muddles about existence' and that it is 'exploded' in the *Theaetetus* and *Cratylus* and is 'jettisoned in the *Laws* and its immediate predecessors'.[1] Yet, if there is such a paradox of interpretation as Owen has here formulated, the device of redating the *Timaeus* would not suffice to eliminate it. For one thing, the distinction in the *Timaeus* between γένεσις and οὐσία to which he objects is enunciated again in the *Philebus*; and, for another, the expressions which in the late dialogues he cites as evidence that Plato had renounced this distinction can all be matched by similar expressions in the works that according to Owen antedate its renunciation.

The former of these two objections to his thesis Owen in part foresaw and tried to forestall by asserting that '*Philebus*, 59a and 61d–e are not parallels to the *Timaeus* disjunction,' because according to the latter 'some things change without existing', whereas the *Philebus* says not this but only that 'some things exist without changing'.[2] This defence fails, however, for in *Philebus*, 59a–b τὰ γιγνόμενα καὶ γενησόμενα καὶ γεγονότα (a 7–9), which constitute the phenomenal world (τὰ περὶ τὸν κόσμον τόνδε—59a 2), are not only sharply contrasted to τὰ ὄντα ἀεί, which are exclusively identified with real existence (58a 2–3, cf. 59c 3–4), but it is emphatically said that none of them ever was or will be or is at any moment free from change (59b 1–2: κατὰ ταὐτά). So the same disjunction between what *really is* and what incessantly *becomes* with which Timaeus begins his account *is* reasserted at the end of the *Philebus*, where the incessant becoming of all phenomena is described in the same terms used of it not only in such so-called 'pre-critical' dialogues as the *Phaedo*[3] but also in those very passages of the *Cratylus* and the *Theaetetus*[4] in which according to Owen it is

[1] Owen, 322–333.

[2] Owen, p. 322, note 2.

[3] *Phd.*, 78e 2–5, 79a 9–10; cf. also *Symposium*, 207d 6–7; *Rep.*, 479a 1–3, 585c 3–5.

[4] *Crat.*, 439e 1–2; *Tht.*, 152d 7–e 1.

refuted. The disjunction also occurs in an earlier passage of the *Philebus* and in one of the *Sophist*, both of which are erroneously cited by Owen as evidence that Plato had renounced it. The former of these[1] is the argument that, if pleasure is always γένεσις and there is no οὐσία of it at all, it cannot be the good, for the final cause of γένεσις is οὐσία, so that there would exist something which is the final cause of this becoming, and that οὐσία, as final cause, not the becoming of which it is the cause, would have the rank of good. Owen apparently thought, as had others before him, that in the statement, γένεσις οὐσίας ἕνεκα γίγνεται, is implied the termination of process in the existence of its subject. This is neither what is said, however, nor what could be meant, for, if it were, pleasure in coming to be would become the good and the argument would obviously reach a conclusion the opposite to that which is stated and intended. As a proof that pleasure is not the good this argument may, as Hackforth believes,[2] be meant only tentatively; but those who cite it as evidence of a change from Plato's earlier attitude towards γένεσις and οὐσία strangely overlook two significant facts about it:

(1) the distinction drawn here between final cause and instrumental process was employed in a similar fashion as early as the *Laches*, the *Gorgias*, and the *Lysis* (and in the *Lysis* used to prove the existence of a real entity different from particular phenomena that are merely simulacra of it);[3]

(2) far from rejecting the disjunction that makes pleasure γένεσις without any οὐσία at all, Plato at the end has Socrates reaffirm his gratitude to those from whom he professes to have heard the argument based upon it.[4]

Nor is the disjunction disavowed in that passage of the *Sophist* in which 'the friends of the ideas' are said to subscribe to it

[1] *Phil.*, 53c 4–55a 11 (but this argument really ends at 54d 7; 54e 1–55a 11 is a subsidiary argument). On the whole passage cf. A. Diès, *Philèbe* (1941), pp. LXII–LXX and my review, *Amer. Journ. Philol.*, LXVIII (1947), pp. 232–3.

[2] *Plato's Examination of Pleasure* (1945), pp. 105–6.

[3] Cf. *Laches*, 185d–e, *Gorg.*, 467c–468c, *Lysis*, 218d–220e (cf. 218c 5–d 5, 220d 8–e 4).

[4] *Phil.*, 54d 4–6.

and which Owen so confidently cites in support of his thesis.[1] The argument of this notoriously maltreated passage is succinctly but exactly the following: The 'friends of the ideas' say that the real being of these ideas, which is always unalterably the same, and not *γένεσις*, which is incessant in its variation, is the object of knowledge.[2] This assertion, however, implies the existence of the action of knowing and therefore of intelligence and life and so of soul, the requisite vehicle of both; and consequently it implies the existence of vital movement that *is* soul and so of real motion.[3] This last, of course, is the *idea* of *κίνησις*, of which the vital motion (i.e. self-motion) is the manifestation. Neither one nor the other is *γένεσις*, which is phenomenal becoming; the neglect of this fact has been a source of multifarious confusion and error in the interpretation not only of this passage but of all Plato's 'later' philosophy.[4] There is in the text no hint of the existence of *γένεσις* and nothing to suggest that the original disjunction of *γένεσις* and *οὐσία* should be rejected or even qualified. On the contrary, the argument proceeds on the assumption that this disjunction is correct and professes to deduce from it—not its contradictory, that incessant becoming is also *οὐσία*, but the existence of a non-phenomenal motion which is entirely different from *γένεσις* and which is implied by the admitted knowability of real being. The 'friends of the ideas' are asked to recognise that they overlook *this* when they restrict action and affection to *γένεσις* alone—*not* that they are mistaken in making the disjunction of *γένεσις* and *οὐσία*; and that this motion, the existence of which Plato thought he had here established, is entirely different from phenomenal becoming is re-emphasised by his statement in conclusion that, if there is to be knowledge, there must exist *νοῦς*, which cannot be immobile, and objects of *νοῦς*, which are in every respect unalterable.[5]

[1] *Soph.*, 248a–249d; Owen (322, note 2 cites only 248a–249b). On 'the friends of the ideas', introduced in 246b 6–c 2, see Cherniss, *Aristotle's Criticism*, I, p. 439, note 376; and on the whole argument ibid., pp. 437–9.

[2] *Soph.*, 248a 7–13 and 246b 7–c 2.

[3] *Soph.*, 248c 11–249b 4.

[4] Cf. De Strycker's comments in his review of my *Aristotle's Criticism*, I, in *Antiquité Classique*, XVIII (1949), p. 105, and *Aristotle's Criticism*, I, pp. 439–54.

[5] *Soph.*, 249b 5–d 5. The text of b 5–6 as printed by Burnet is correct and means: 'So it turns out that no immobile thing can have intelligence of any-

What then of those expressions in the so-called critical dialogues which seem to Owen and have seemed to others before him to be incompatible with this disjunction of γένεσις and οὐσία and so to give proof that Plato had renounced it when he wrote them? In the second part of the *Parmenides* 'becoming' is defined as 'participating in being',[1] and in the *Sophist* 'production' as 'the bringing into being of anything that formerly did not exist'.[2] The *Philebus* speaks of a γένεσις εἰς οὐσίαν which results in what then is called 'being that has come to be' (γεγενημένην οὐσίαν), one of the classes into which Socrates here divides 'all the entities in the universe';[3] and in the *Politicus* one kind of measurement is said to be concerned with τῆς γενέσεως ἀναγκαία οὐσία.[4] Such expressions do seem to imply that being is the termination of becoming and that γιγνόμενα do exist or have οὐσία. Yet, if they do, they are still not evidence of a change in Plato's attitude or his renunciation of the doctrine held in the so-called 'pre-critical dialogues', for those works contain expressions of the very same kind. In the *Symposium* 'production' is defined in terms of the transition from not-being to being, just as it is in the *Sophist*, *Politicus*, and *Philebus*;[5]

[1] *Parm.*, 163d 1–2; cf. also 156a 4–b 1 (not mentioned by Owen).

[2] *Soph.*, 219b 4–6 (not mentioned by Owen). Cf. *Pol.*, 258e 1–2 (. . . συναποτελοῦσι τὰ γιγνόμενα ὑπ' αὐτῶν σώματα πρότερον οὐκ ὄντα) and n.b. that ποιούμενον and γιγνόμενον are identified in *Phil.*, 27a 1–2.

[3] *Phil.*, 26d 8, 27b 8–9; for πάντα τὰ νῦν ὄντα ἐν τῷ παντί cf. 23c 4–5 (not mentioned by Owen).

[4] *Pol.*, 283d 8–9. This is not mentioned by Owen either, who, however, cites in favour of his thesis *Laws*, 894a 5–7. This passage says: 'It is in the process of such change and transformation that anything *becomes*; but when anything abides it is really being (ὄν), and when anything has changed to a different state it has been utterly destroyed.' Now, whatever the meaning of the highly controversial preceding sentence (894a 2–5) to which the 'such change and transformation' in this one refers, Plato certainly does not here say that γένεσις is ὄντως ὄν or that οὐσία is the result of γένεσις. He does not even say that any γιγνόμενον ever ceases from γένεσις. He simply defines γένεσις, ὄντως ὄν, and φθορά in terms of *any* subject and says that a subject that abides or has completed a change is not γιγνόμενον. The implication of this is that a γιγνόμενον is *not* ὄντως ὄν, and so the passage rather tells against Owen's thesis than in favour of it.

[5] *Symp.*, 205b 8–c 1; see the references in note 2, *supra*.

---

thing anywhere', i.e. the knowing subject must have mobility. Then 249b 8–c 5 gives the second part of the conclusion: the objects of knowledge must be immobile.

the definition of *γένεσις* in the *Parmenides* has its parallel in the statement of the *Phaedo* that anything 'becomes' only by participation in the *being* proper to that in which it does participate;[1] and, since in the *Phaedo* immutable being and the incessant becoming of phenomena are called 'two kinds of entities',[2] there can be no novel significance in the use of the phrase, 'all the entities in the universe', to include the world of becoming in the *Philebus*.[3] As to those phrases which in this section of the *Philebus* supposedly express most clearly the new attitude of the 'critical period', *γένεσις εἰς οὐσίαν* and the resulting 'being that has come to be',[4] they have their counterpart in the *Timaeus* itself, where to 'the indivisible and ever immutable being' is contrasted 'the being that comes to be, dispersed in the corporeal sphere'.[5] What is more, Timaeus solemnly asserts that being and space and becoming, all three, *exist*[6] and does so in explicit summation of the argument in which he has distinguished real, immutable being both from space, which always is, and from the sensible world of becoming, which, incessantly in flux, is yet said 'somehow to cling to being'.[7] Even the *Republic*, to whose 'muddles about existence' Owen lays the blame of the disjunction of *γένεσις* and *οὐσία*, not only refers by implication to *οὐσία* which is constantly coming to be and passing away[8] but explicitly states that the world of becoming participates in *both* being *and* not-being and is not properly to be designated as purely and simply either.[9]

So neither Owen's device of revising the chronology of the *Timaeus* nor any other hypothesis of Plato's 'development' can resolve the 'paradox', if such it is, for it exists *within* the *Timaeus*

[1] *Phd.*, 101c 2–4; for the *Parmenides*, see p. 353, note 1, *supra*.

[2] Ibid., 79a 6–10; cf. 78d 1–79a 5 and n.b. *αὐτὴ ἡ οὐσία* (78d 1), *τὸ ὄν* (d 4) contrasted to 78d 10–e 5.

[3] *Phil.*, 23c 4–5 (p. 353, note 3, *supra*). For *γένεσις* here included cf. 25e 3–4, 26d 8, 27a 11–c 1. In both *Phil.*, 23c 4–5 and *Phd.*, 79a 6 *τὰ ὄντα* is probably used as a general term of reference without any philosophical significance, just as the English word 'entities', by which I have rendered it, frequently is (cf. *Charm.*, 175b 3, *Gorg.*, 449d 1–2, *Phd.*, 99d 5 and 97d 7, and P. Shorey, *The Unity of Plato's Thought*, p. 54, note 392).

[4] *γεγενημένη οὐσία*. See references, p. 353, note 3, *supra*.

[5] *Tim.*, 35a 1–3; cf. 37a 5–6 (*οὐσίαν σκεδαστήν* contrasted to *ἀμέριστον*) and 37b 2–3 (*τὰ γιγνόμενα* contrasted to *τὰ κατὰ ταὐτὰ ἔχοντα ἀεί*).

[6] Ibid., 52d 2–4.

[7] Ibid., 52a 1–d 1.

[8] *Rep.*, 485b 1–3 and Adam's note ad loc., *The Republic of Plato*, II, p. 3.

[9] Ibid., 478e 1–3, cf. 479d 9 (*τὸ μεταξὺ πλανητόν*).

itself,—and not only within it but within the *Phaedo* and the *Republic* and within the *Sophist* and the *Philebus* also. The proper questions to ask, therefore, are:

(1) whether Plato gives any indication that he is aware of such a paradox in his treatment of the status of γένεσις and

(2) if he does show such awareness, whether he simply persists in asserting it or attempts in any way to account for it.

The first of these questions must certainly be answered in the affirmative. That is clear even from the passages of the *Republic* just cited, where it is said that γένεσις, since it both *is* and *is not*, is intermediate between being pure and simple and absolute not-being[1] or participates in *both* and is not properly designable as either.[2] It is even more clear from the passage in the *Timaeus*, where in a single breath the sensible world of incessant flux and becoming is denied real being and is said to cling to being and so to exist.[3] This passage of the *Timaeus*, moreover, provides an answer to our second question, since it is the conclusion of a long section which purports to explain how this paradox of γένεσις is possible.[4]

It is the more interesting that, without reference to the argument or the purpose of this section as a whole, Owen has adduced a passage near the beginning of it as positive proof of his thesis. This passage, he says,[5] makes 'the lame plea that, even if we cannot say *what* any mere γιγνόμενον is, we can describe it as τὸ τοιοῦτον', i.e. can describe what is perpetually becoming as 'of such and such a quality'; and this very plea is defeated by arguments in both the *Theaetetus* and the *Cratylus* which prove:

(1) that, if *anything* in this world were perpetually changing in all respects, nothing at all, not even τοιοῦτον, could be said of it; and

(2) that the theory of perpetual change 'is nonsense about *anything*'.

If this second conclusion were stated or implied in the *Cratylus* and *Theaetetus*, Owen's proof of his thesis would have overreached itself: he would have to assume that those dialogues

[1] *Rep.*, 478d 5–7, cf. 477a 6–7.
[2] Ibid., 478e 1–3.
[3] *Tim.*, 52a 1–d 4 (p. 354, notes 6 and 7 *supra*).
[4] Ibid., 48e 2–52d 1.
[5] Owen, p. 323, note 3, on *Tim.*, 49d–e. It is here too that he refers to *Crat.*, 439d 8–9 which he calls similar to the argument of the *Theaetetus* (182c–183c), his interpretation of which is given on pp. 322–324.

repudiate not only the *Timaeus* but the *Philebus* as well, for towards the end of the *Philebus*, as we have seen, it is emphatically asserted that all γιγνόμενα are *in perpetual change in every respect* and for *this* reason cannot be objects of knowledge.[1] This particular embarrassment Owen is spared, however, because his interpretation of the *Cratylus* and the *Theaetetus* is in this respect mistaken. The passage of the *Theaetetus* in question states that the equation of knowledge with sensation is inconsistent with the doctrine that everything is always in motion in every respect, since sensation is then no more sensation than not sensation and so no more knowledge than not knowledge.[2] This neither says nor implies that the theory of perpetual change is 'nonsense about anything', nor even that it is nonsense about all phenomena; it says instead that if there were *nothing* existing but only perpetual change in every respect[3]—a theory obviously different from that of the *Timaeus*—then no intelligible assertion of any kind could be true or, indeed, possible.[4] The same distinction is still more obviously drawn in the passage of the *Cratylus* that has been cited.[5] There the status of phenomena is excluded from consideration.[6] Granting that it is perpetual flux, Socrates argues that still this cannot be the status of *everything*:[7] it cannot be the status of αὐτὸ καλόν or of αὐτὸ ἀγαθόν or of any entity of this kind,[8] for, if *these* entities were perpetually changing, they could not be known[9] and, if *everything* were perpetually changing, so would knowledge itself, which would then be no more knowledge than not knowledge;[10] if therefore there is knowledge, neither the knowing subject nor the real entities that are objects of knowledge can be in flux.[11] The two passages, then, are, as Owen says, similar; but neither denies that the phenomenal world is incessant becoming as distinguished from real being. On the contrary, this is expressly granted in the *Cratylus*, which then argues

[1] *Phil.*, 59a–b; see p. 350 *supra*.

[2] *Tht.*, 182c–183c; n.b. 183c 1–2: ἐπιστήμην τε αἴσθησιν οὐ συγχωρησόμεθα κατά γε τὴν τοῦ πάντα κινεῖσθαι μεθόδον.

[3] Cf. *Tht.*, 181d 8–182a 1. This has been emphasised from the beginning, cf. 152e 1, 156a 5, 157a 7–b 1, 157d 8–9, 160d 8, 180d 5–7, 181c 1–2.

[4] *Tht.*, 183a 4–b 5.

[5] *Crat.*, 439c 6–440c 1 (from which Owen has cited only 439d 8–9 without its context [p. 355, note 5 *supra*]).

[6] Ibid., 439d 3–4.

[7] Ibid., 439c 2–3, 440c 7–8 (cf. 440a 6–7).

[8] Ibid., 439c 7–d 1, d 5–6, 440b 5–7.

[9] Ibid., 439e 7–440a 5.

[10] Ibid., 440a 6–b 4.

[11] Ibid., 440b 4–c 1.

that the possibility of knowledge implies entities other than the phenomenal flux, just as the *Theaetetus* argues that even the equation of sensation and knowledge would have a similar implication.[1]

It is true, however, that explicitly according to the *Cratylus* and implicitly according to the *Theaetetus* what is incessantly changing cannot be designated either as 'that' (ἐκεῖνο) or as 'of such and such a kind' (τοιοῦτον).[2] This *would* contradict *Tim.*, 49d–e, if, as Owen assumes, it were there proposed to designate what is perpetually becoming as τοιοῦτον. But, as has been proved from the

[1] The parallelism of *Crat.*, 440a 6–b 4 and *Tht.*, 182d 8–e 11 is obvious. When Owen proceeds to assert (p. 324) that 'Plato goes on to ascribe οὐσία to objects of perception (185a, c, 186b ff.)', he misinterprets entirely the argument of *Tht.*, 184b–186e. Plato, having shown that the equation of sensation and knowledge, far from being supported by the theory of *universal* flux, is inconsistent with it, now goes on to refute the equation 'independently of the theory of flux', as Owen says; but he does so not by 'ascribing οὐσία to the objects of perception' but by showing that sensation itself involves entities other than the phenomenal 'objects of perception', whatever they are. The οὐσία spoken of in this passage is only the widest of the κοινά and for that reason is especially stressed in the argument (cf. 186a 2–3 and 185c 4–6 and Campbell's note, p. 162, line 6 of his edition); in regard to the question of knowledge and sensation it is no different from any of the other κοινά (ὅμοιον—ἀνόμοιον, ταὐτόν—ἕτερον, ἕν—ἀριθμός, ἄρτιον—περιττόν, καλόν—αἰσχρόν, ἀγαθόν—κακόν, etc. [185c 8–d 4, 186a 5–b 1]). *None* of these κοινά, including οὐσία, is mediated to the soul by the senses; they are all apprehended by the soul functioning without any organ of sense and *reasoning* about the παθήματα (185d 6–e 2, 186a 2–b 10, 186d 2–5, 186e 4–5). As it is emphatically denied that οὐσία is 'perceptible'—even in the παθήματα—or an object of sensation (cf. 186d 2–5, e 2–5), it is clear that οὐσία is *not* 'ascribed to the objects of perception' as such but is an 'object of thought', sensation acting merely as a stimulus to this activity of the soul (cf. my *Aristotle's Criticism*, I, p. 236, note 141); n.b. that even in 185a 8–9 ὅτι ἀμφοτέρω ἐστόν is the result not of perception but of *thought* (διανοῇ, cf. 185a 4, 185b 7). This passage of the *Theaetetus* has a striking parallel in *Rep.*, 524a–d, where Plato, concerned with explaining how 'sensa' are provocative of thought, uses the same example to show that what impinges upon sense ἅμα τοῖς ἐναντίοις ἑαυτοῖς (*Rep.*, 524d 3–4, cf. *Tht.*, 186b 6–7) provokes the mind to ask and answer the question τί ποτ' ἐστί (*Rep.*, 524c 10–11). The close parallel of *Tht.*, 185a 8–d 4, 186b with *Rep.*, 524a–e shows that the attitude towards sensation and the so-called 'οὐσία of the objects of perception' in the *Theaetetus* is the same as that 'already' expressed in the *Republic* (cf. 524e 1, 525a 1).

[2] *Crat.*, 439d 8–9; *Tht.*, 182c 9–d 7. It should be observed that in *Tht.*, 152d 2–6 it is given as a conscious assertion of the doctrine of perpetual change itself, *not* as an inference from that doctrine, that nothing can be rightly called τι or ὁποιονοῦν τι (d 3–4 and 6).

syntax and context of the passage, all such interpretations of it are self-refuting and incorrect.[1] What it does say is nothing at variance with the assertions of the *Cratylus* and the *Theaetetus* but something far different, far more profound, and far more significant. It occurs, as has been said, near the beginning of the section in which Plato introduces the third factor to be assumed in accounting for the physical universe. Up to this point two had been sufficient: intelligible, immutable being, which is the model; and the copy of it, which is visible becoming. For what follows, however, a third must be assumed and explained, the 'receptacle' or 'medium' of all becoming.[2] It is the introduction of this factor that makes a true theory of γένεσις possible.

The substance of what Plato now says in the controversial passage is the following:[3]

> (1) Phenomena cannot be distinctively denominated, because no part of the phenomenal flux is distinguishable from any other. Because it is impossible, by saying 'this is . . .', to distinguish any phase of the flux from any other, it cannot be said of any: '*this* is fire' or '*this* is water' and so forth.
>
> (2) The distinctive names properly denominate in each case not any phase of the flux but 'the such and such, whatever the correct formula may be, that is always identical throughout all of its occurrences'.
>
> (3) Whenever one tries to distinguish any phase of the flux by saying 'this', one always in fact designates *not* any such phase but the permanent, unchanging, and characterless receptacle in which are constantly occurring transient and indeterminable manifestations of the determinate characteristics just mentioned.

Plato then by the use of various analogies illustrates the nature of this 'receptacle' or 'medium',[4] to which he finally gives the formal designation 'space'.[5] What is to be identified by the formula τὸ τοιοῦτον, itself an abbreviation of τὸ διὰ παντὸς τοιοῦτον (i.e. 'what is *always* such and such') and of the still more exact τὸ τοιοῦτον ἀεὶ περιφερόμενον ὅμοιον ἑκάστου πέρι καὶ συμπάντων (i.e. 'the such and such that always recurs alike in each and all cases together') is not a phase, moment, or aspect of the flux, as the διὰ

[1] *Amer. Journ. Philol.*, LXXV (1954), 113–30.

[2] *Tim.*, 48e 2–49a 6.

[3] *Amer. Journ. Philol.*, LXXV (1954), 128–30.

[4] *Tim.*, 50b–51b.

[5] Ibid., 52a 8.

παντός and the ἀεὶ περιφερόμενον ὅμοιον are by themselves enough to prove, but is that which is manifested by coming to be in the receptacle from which again it disappears. These distinct and self-identical characteristics that enter and leave the receptacle are then called 'copies' and 'likenesses' of the eternal entities,[1] and in the conclusion their nature is explained as that of an 'image' of intelligible reality.[2] They are, consequently, not ideas but representations of the ideas, which ideas are emphatically said not themselves to enter into anything.[3] They should not be called 'qualities' either, as they are by many translators and commentators, for they are not confined to qualities (the 'copies' of the ideas, fire, water, earth, air, etc., being on the same footing as the copies of all other ideas)[4] and the use of τὸ τοιοῦτον here has nothing whatever to do with the distinction between 'quality' and 'substance'. On the other hand, they are not the same as the transient phenomena either, for the latter are the *apparent* alterations of the receptacle induced by their continual entrance into it and exit from it.[5] The intensity and limits of these apparent affections of the receptacle are continually changing and so are indeterminable as fire, water, or anything else. Having said that 'what fire is', for example, cannot be identified as 'this' or 'that' phase of the phenomenal flux but only as the perpetually self-identical characteristic that is the determining factor of the affection in itself indeterminable, Plato does not say or suggest either that an indeterminable phase of the flux can be called τοιοῦτον, i.e. 'such as' the self-identical characteristic or that this characteristic can be called τοιοῦτον, 'such as' an indeterminable phase of the flux. These self-identical characteristics are identifiable only by reference to the eternal entities of which they are 'copies' or representations. Consequently, after having distinguished from the phenomenal flux the receptacle and the determinate characteristics that are manifested in it, Plato must defend his crucial assumption of the existence of eternal, intelligible entities of which these characteristics are 'copies'; and this he now does succinctly in a passage[6] the argument of which, as has often been remarked,[7] sums up the results to which

[1] *Tim.*, 50c 4–5, 51a 2.

[2] Ibid., 52c, cf. 52a 4–7.

[3] Ibid., 52a 2–3 and 52c 5–d 1.

[4] Cf. *Tim.*, 51b 5–6 and 51a 5–6.

[5] *Tim.*, 50c 3–4, 51b 4–6, 52d 4–e 1.

[6] Ibid., 51b–e.

[7] Cf. C. Ritter, *Platon*, II, pp. 266–7; Cherniss, see above pp. 8–9 and 11; Ross, *Plato's Theory of Ideas*, p. 103.

the *Theaetetus* has led. He can then assert in the conclusion to the whole section[1] that these characteristics are determinate in meaning by reference to the really existing, intelligible, non-spatial ideas; and, though themselves not really being, 'cling to being' by their entry into space.[2] Their having meaning and their mode of being are both held to be implied in their nature as 'images'; and the theory of space is presented as saving at once the world of becoming and the theory of its relation to being as that of image or semblance to original reality.

II

Now, as we have seen, it is chiefly in order to eliminate from Plato's mature philosophy this theory of the relation between the ideas and the world of becoming that Owen would have the *Timaeus* antedate the *Parmenides*. It is, after all, a fact that this theory is in that dialogue presented by the youthful Socrates and rejected by Parmenides, who argues that, if particulars are 'likenesses' of ideas, an idea and its 'likeness' must be reciprocally 'like' each other and consequently the reason given for assuming the existence of ideas must lead to an infinite regress.[3] This argument, Owen contends,[4] Plato could not have thought fallacious[5] nor, having recognised its validity, could he have continued to use the language of original and likeness as a metaphorical description of the relation,[6] for:

(1) the argument itself *is* valid;
(2) Plato never attempted to answer it; and
(3) nowhere again, if the *Timaeus* be excepted, does he use the idioms of original and likeness for the relation between ideas and particulars.

The last of these three assertions is crucial to Owen's thesis, for, even should the first two be correct, if the third is not, then

[1] *Tim.*, 52a–c. [2] Ibid., 52c. [3] *Parm.*, 132c 12–133a 7.

[4] Owen, pp. 318–322.

[5] Among those who have taken this position Owen attacks specifically A. E. Taylor (*The Parmenides of Plato*, p. 26 and *Philosophical Studies*, pp. 86–90=*Proc. of Aristotelian Society*, XVI) and H. Cherniss (*Aristotle's Criticism*, I, pp. 293–300).

[6] This is the position of Sir David Ross, *Plato's Theory of Ideas*, pp. 89 and 231.

the criticism in the *Parmenides* is no reason for assuming that Plato composed the *Timaeus* before rather than after it, since such a chronological revision would not lift from the later dialogues what Owen calls the shadow of 'paradeigmatism' and would leave Plato's attitude towards that criticism as much a question as it was before. To prove this third assertion false the quotation of a single passage will suffice: 'Most people have failed to notice that, while some of the real entities naturally have certain sensible likenesses (αἰσθηταί τινες ὁμοιότητες) . . ., of the greatest and most precious entities no image (εἴδωλον) has been made clearly perceptible to men. . . .' This statement repeats exactly the thought and the language of the *Phaedrus*,[1] where the 'most precious entities that have no clearly perceptible images' are identified as justice, wisdom, temperance, etc.;[2] as in the *Phaedrus* and the *Timaeus*, particulars are here called 'sensible likenesses' and 'images' of incorporeal entities that are accessible to reason alone;[3] and this passage occurs in the *Politicus*,[4] a dialogue which by its own testimony is later than the *Sophist* and, according to Owen as well as to the 'orthodox opinion', is later than the *Parmenides*. In view of this unequivocal evidence there is no need to review here other passages in the *Politicus* and the other admittedly late dialogues where this language is used and this relation is implied. Two further observations, however, should be made in this connection.

For one thing, even if these later dialogues contained no explicit example of the idioms of paradeigmatism, there would still be strong evidence against the thesis that Plato at any time abandoned the conception implied by them. There is no suggestion or rumour of such a change in the relevant ancient literature, not even in the one passage of Aristotle's *Metaphysics* so often and so uncritically used as evidence for the historical connections of the notions of 'participation' and 'imitation'.[5] Aristotle himself

[1] Cf. *Phdr.*, 250a 6–d 6, 247d–e, 249b 6 ff., 263a–b.

[2] Cf. *Phdr.*, 250b 1–5 and 250d.

[3] Cf. *Pol.*, 286a 5–7.

[4] *Pol.*, 285d 10–286a 7.

[5] *Met.*, 987b 11–14. The historicity of this passage is impugned by all the other evidence of Aristotle himself (cf. Cherniss, *Aristotle's Criticism*, I, p. 109, n. 65; p. 180, n. 103; p. 193); but, if accepted at its face-value, it would imply that in the theory of ideas Plato *at the very beginning* substituted μέθεξις for μίμησις. Tocco had consequently to suppose that he at first substituted μέθεξις

regularly assumes that the Platonic ideas are 'paradigms' and criticises them on that express assumption even in parts of his work certainly written after Plato's death and with the latest expression of Plato's philosophy in mind.[1] Xenocrates defined 'idea' as 'paradeigmatic cause' (αἰτία παραδειγματική) and in so doing professed to be formulating Plato's own doctrine, surely not an 'early' conception that had later been repudiated;[2] even Speusippus called the separately existing decad, which he substituted for the ideas, the 'all-perfect model' of the universe;[3] and Theophrastus testifies to the importance of the notion of 'imitation' in the metaphysics of such Platonists.[4] Moreover, in the *Seventh Platonic Epistle* the phenomena of the world of becoming are expressly and repeatedly called 'images' of the intelligible and truly existing entities.[5] If this passage is authentic, Plato within five or six years of his death solemnly asserted that particulars are 'images' of the ideas; and, if it is not authentic, it still proves that during the generation after Plato's death this could be presented as his own statement of his genuine and ultimate doctrine.

It should also be observed, however, that neither here nor elsewhere is there any evidence for supposing 'paradeigmatism' to have superseded some earlier conception of 'participation' in Plato's development of his theory. A version of this thesis, which has often been maintained by modern scholars, was recently defended by Sir David Ross, who listed the idioms used in the

[1] Cf. for example *Metaphysics* Z, 1034a 2–3.

[2] Xenocrates, frag. 30 (Heinze) = Proclus, *In Parmenidem*, col. 888, 17–19 and 36–7 (Cousin²). For the rest of the definition cf. Cherniss, *Aristotle's Criticism*, I, pp. 256–7.

[3] Speusippus, frag. 4, 16 (p. 54 [Lang]); cf. Cherniss, op. cit., p. 259, note 169.

[4] Theophrastus, *Met.*, 5a 25–8 (Ross and Fobes).

[5] *Epistle* VII, 342b 2 (cf. 343c 1–3) and 343c 7 for εἴδωλον. For αὐτὸς ὁ κύκλος and αὐτὸ ὃ δὴ γνωστόν τε καὶ ἀληθῶς ἐστιν ὄν cf. 342a 8–b 1, 342c 2–3 and 7, 343a 7–8; and for the generalisation cf. 342d 3–8.

---

for μίμησις and later did exactly the opposite (*Studi de Filologia Classica*, II [1894], 465). Owen's hypothesis would require us to believe that the final stage involved still another reversal, the abandonment of μίμησις once again for μέθεξις. Such an improbable hypothesis of vacillation is uncalled for in the face of the evidence of the dialogues supported by all the other testimony, which shows that Plato at *all* times used both idioms as they suited the particular context.

dialogues to describe the relation between ideas and particulars, and from these statistics drew the inference that 'there is a general movement away from immanence to transcendence', that is away from idioms of 'participation' towards those of 'paradeigmatism' and 'imitation'.[1] Owen contends that Ross' list does not support his inference; and in this Owen is right, though not for the right reasons. Had the list been complete and accurate—as it is not—, Owen should have seen that it does not support his contrary thesis either, for he would have found in it such passages as those that I have cited from the *Politicus* and the *Seventh Epistle* (which Ross believes to be genuine) and these should have shown him that the redating of the *Timaeus* will not eliminate paradeigmatism from the later dialogues. What in fact the list even in its present form does prove is that to draw such conclusions as either Ross or Owen does from the comparative frequency of these different expressions is a travesty of statistical method. When, for example, in the *Phaedo* the idea αὐτὸ τὸ μέγεθος is expressly distinguished as that which exists in reality from the μέγεθος that is in us,[2] this evidence for the 'separateness' of the ideas cannot be attenuated by a list of passages from the same dialogue in which 'participation' is mentioned; and it is perverse to count as three scores for 'immanence' Plato's assertion that it is irrelevant whether the causal relation of ideas to phenomena be called 'presence' or 'communion' or any term whatever.[3] In the *Symposium* it is said that the idea of beauty 'exists eternally absolute by itself, a unity with itself, while all beautiful things participate in it in such a way that their coming to be and perishing neither increase nor diminish the idea a whit nor affect it in any way at all'.[4] Ross counts this sentence as one score for 'transcendence' and one for 'immanence'. It is instead clear evidence that the idioms of 'participation' were felt not to involve the ideas in immanence at all but to express the complementary aspect of their 'separateness'. The occurrence of idioms of participation, then, is never in itself evidence that the ideas were not at the same time held to be paradigms; far from

[1] *Plato's Theory of Ideas*, pp. 228–30.

[2] *Phd.*, 102d 6–8 and 103b 4–5.

[3] Ibid., 100d 4–8. The impossible προσγενομένη in d 7 should either be excised or be changed to προσαγορευομένη after Wyttenbach (cf. also Burnet, *Class. Quart.*, XIV [1920], p. 135 and *Pap. Ox.*, XVIII, 2181).

[4] *Symp.*, 211b.

being felt as incompatible, the two kinds of idiom could even be used together to describe the single conception, as in fact they not infrequently are. In the *Parmenides* itself, even after the criticism of paradeigmatism, Parmenides speaks of 'the likenesses—or whatever one calls them—in our world of those entities in which we participate . . .';[1] and later it became common to give as one of the three manners of 'participation' that 'by way of resemblance, as in the case of an image'.[2]

The paradeigmatism of the *Timaeus* is not, therefore, any more than is its treatment of becoming, a 'paradox of interpretation', to be resolved, as Owen supposes, by assuming that the work was written before the composition of the *Parmenides*. On both scores it may safely remain in the latest group of dialogues, where both tradition and the best evidence of modern linguistic research indicate that it belongs.

In any case, Owen's redating of the *Timaeus* would not answer the question of Plato's attitude towards the objection to paradeigmatism in the *Parmenides*. Whatever Plato thought of that objection—and no matter when he wrote the *Timaeus*—it is certain that he was not moved by it to abandon this way of describing the relation of phenomena to the ideas. That being so, it is probable that he considered the objection to be either irrelevant or invalid; and this is not less probable because he gave no direct and explicit refutation of the objection. He makes no such answer to any of Parmenides' objections, and he may have believed that the answers were implied in what he had already said of the ideas elsewhere and that his readers ought to discern this by themselves. After all, Parmenides at the end of all his objections is made to say not that these are unanswerable but that they have confounded the youthful Socrates because of his own deficiency in dialectical training.[3]

Owen insists, however,[4] that to Parmenides' argument against

[1] *Parm.*, 133d 1–2, correctly construed by O. Apelt (*Platons Dialog Parmenides*, p. 63) and by J. Moreau (*Platon, Oeuvres Complètes* par L. Robin, II, p. 203), who saw that ὧν = ἐκείνων ὧν and that its antecedent is not ὁμοιώματα as most interpreters assume.

[2] Alexander, *Met.*, p. 121 (LF version); Proclus, *In Parmenidem*, col. 846, 22–4. Cf. Aristotle, *Met.*, 991a 20–2 = 1079b 24–6 (τὸ δὲ λέγειν παραδείγματα αὐτὰ εἶναι καὶ μετέχειν αὐτῶν τἆλλα . . .), *Eth. Eud.*, 1217b 9–10 (κατὰ μετοχὴν γὰρ καὶ ὁμοιότητα τἆλλα ἀγαθὰ ἐκείνης εἶναι), and frequently in later writers.

[3] *Parm.*, 135c–d.

[4] Owen, p. 319.

paradeigmatism Plato made no reply because no reply is possible. Like Hardie and Ross,[1] he contends that the argument is valid because the relation between copy and original at least *includes* resemblance and to this extent is a symmetrical relation. Yet this symmetry of resemblance does not suffice to justify Parmenides' inference from Socrates' original statement. Socrates had suggested only that the relation of things *other than ideas* (i.e. phenomenal particulars) to ideas is that of images or likenesses to their original;[2] and, even if an idea does resemble the phenomenon that resembles it, it still does not follow from his hypothesis that both are likenesses of a single original, for they are not *both* 'other than ideas', and by hypothesis one is itself the original of which the other is a likeness. This point is explicitly emphasised in one of the Academic demonstrations of the existence of ideas as paradigms that Alexander reports from Aristotle's *De Ideis*.[3] There the conclusion is drawn only after it has been shown that none of the particulars of which a common term is predicated can be either exactly what that term signifies or the paradigm of the others,[4] that is: the inference that similar things are likenesses of a single original depends for its validity upon exclusion of the possibility that any of them is itself the original of which the others are likenesses. This careful formulation would have forestalled Parmenides' objection and may have been intended by its author—whether Plato or one of his associates—for this very purpose; at any rate, against the proof so formulated Aristotle in his attack on it apparently did not try to use the regress-argument of Parmenides.[5]

The saving restriction made explicit in this formulation is obliterated, however, by Parmenides in what is, in fact, the major premiss of his argument, the proposition that *any* two things which are similar to each other must participate in one and the same thing.[6]

[1] W. F. R. Hardie, *A Study in Plato*, pp. 96–7; Ross, *Plato's Theory of Ideas*, p. 89.

[2] *Parm.*, 132d 1–4.

[3] Alexander, *Met.*, pp. 82, 11–83, 17; cf. Cherniss, *Aristotle's Criticism*, I, pp. 230–2.

[4] Alexander, *Met.*, p. 83, 10–12; cf. Cherniss, op. cit., pp. 278–9 and Ackrill, *Mind*, LXI (1952), pp. 108–9.

[5] The objection recorded by Alexander (*Met.*, p. 83, 26–8) is not this regress (cf. Cherniss, op. cit., p. 284).

[6] *Parm.*, 132d 9–e 1: τὸ δὲ ὅμοιον τῷ ὁμοίῳ . . . ἀνάγκη ἑνὸς τοῦ αὐτοῦ εἴδους μετέχειν. Burnet, Diès, and Cornford follow Jackson in excising εἴδους though

To this proposition Socrates is made to assent, though he might have been expected at least to demand that Parmenides express it in the terms of the new hypothesis, the very point of which is the substitution of εἰκασθῆναι—'to simulate' or 'to resemble'—for μετέχειν 'to participate in'. Parmenides' sudden reversion to μετέχειν should alert the reader and may have been intended to do so. If this proposition were expressed in the idiom of the present hypothesis, it would be immediately obvious that it is unacceptable in its universality and that the argument of which it is the major premiss is directed not specifically against the existence of paradeigmatic ideas but against the very notion of original and likeness in general.[1] The shift of idiom somewhat conceals but does not alter the true scope of the argument. If valid, this argument still involves the hypothesis of paradeigmatic ideas in an infinite regress only by so involving the relation of likeness and original as such. According to it, no physical object could have a likeness, since, if it had, it and its likeness, being similar to each other, would have to be so by participation in one and the same thing, which in turn, being similar to the original object and *its* likeness, would along with them both have to participate in still *another* single thing and so on indefinitely.

But the shift of idiom, while it somewhat conceals or diverts attention from the true scope of the argument, all the more clearly signalises the source of its fallaciousness, the fact that the major premiss in its universality implies self-contradiction. If, as Parmenides argues, an original, *O*, and its likeness, *a*, must be similar

[1] If any original is similar to its likeness in so far as the latter is similar to it and if *any* two things that are similar to each other must in that respect be likenesses of (or must resemble—εἰκασθῆναι) one and the same thing, there can be no such thing as a likeness of anything, since, if there were, that thing and its likeness would have both to be likenesses of another original, and this with its likenesses likenesses of still another, and so on indefinitely.

---

it is in all the MSS and was read by Proclus (cf. col. 915, 1 [Cousin[2]]). Excising it would not affect the argument, but there is no reason to doubt that Plato wrote it. It is not 'a premature anticipation of Parmenides' next question' but is used in the neutral sense of 'thing' or 'character' (cf. Cornford, *Plato and Parmenides*, p. 172, n. 1 on 149e 7). Then in e 3–4 'that thing' (ἐκεῖνο) by participation in which similars are similar is identified with the idea itself of Socrates' theory (αὐτὸ τὸ εἶδος, cf. *Phd.*, 103e 3 and Aristotle, *Met.*, 987b 18).

to each other by participation of both in one and the same thing, O^2, and then O and O^2, its original, must be similar to each other by participation in one and the same original, O^3, this must be true of *a* and O^2 as well: both being similar to O in the same respect, they must be similar to each other in that respect and must be so by participation in one and the same thing, O^3. Consequently *a*, O, and O^2 must all be similar to one another by participation in O^3; and so *a* and O are similar to each other by participation in O^3 and by *this* participation are similar to each other in the *same* respect in which, according to Parmenides' original inference, they are similar to each other by participation in O^2. That inference, however, was drawn from the premiss that *any* two things similar to each other in a given respect are so similar by participation in *one and the same thing*. Consequently, O^3 and O^2 must be *one and the same thing*. Yet, if O and O^2 (and *a* and O^2), being similar to each other in this respect, must both participate in O^3, then O^3 and O^2 cannot be one and the same thing, since, if they were, O^2 would participate in itself, which according to Parmenides' assumption is impossible, since, if it were possible, *a* and O could be similar to each other by the participation of both in the original, O, and the regress would not begin.[1] The same contradiction results for O and O^2, if O and each of its multiple likenesses, *a*, *b*, *c*, etc., must be similar to each other by participation in one and the same thing: *a*, *b*, *c*, etc., and O are then similar to one another by participation in O^2, which must be identical with O inasmuch as *a*, *b*, *c*, etc., are similar to one another by participation in O and yet cannot be identical with O inasmuch as it is that by participation in which O is similar to *a*, *b*, *c*, etc.[2]

[1] It is assumed, though not expressly stated, at 132e 3–4 that that by participation in which similar things are similar cannot itself be one of the similar things.

[2] In 132d–133a Parmenides makes no explicit mention of multiple likenesses of a single original but formulates his argument as an attack upon the relation of any single particular likeness to the idea which is supposed to be its paradigm. It is presented, however, as a refutation of Socrates' hypothesis, which is intended to explain the similarity to one another of multiple particulars, as Parmenides himself states at the beginning of the preceding version of the regress (132a 1–4). As a refutation of Socrates' hypothesis, therefore, Parmenides' argument here in 132d–133a must imply the conclusion that the similarity to one another of the particulars, *a*, *b*, *c*, etc., cannot be accounted for on the assumption that they are all likenesses of a single original, O, since that would require each of them and O to be similar

This regress argument against paradeigmatism is, therefore, *not* valid, since its major premiss involves a self-contradiction. The explication of this self-contradiction reveals that if two things are similar to each other in a given respect by the participation of both in a third, then this third and each of the other two, being similar to each other in this respect, cannot be so by participation in a fourth, since this would require the third and the fourth to be and at the same time and in the same respect not to be one and the same thing. Consequently it is not true that *any* two things which are similar to each other must participate in one and the same thing. The relation of original and likeness itself proves that this proposition is not thus universally true, because, if it *is* true of some similars, it *cannot* be true of all. If, then, there are likenesses or images that are similar to one another by participation in one and the same thing or by resemblance to a single original (which is the hypothesis of Socrates), this and any one of the likenesses are similar to each other *not* by participation of both in one and the same thing but just by the latter's representing, simulating, or participating in the former.[1]

Parmenides in formulating his major premiss universally

[1] If *a* is the likeness of an original, *O*, then by definition *a* and *O* cannot both in the same respect be likenesses of another original, O^2. Even if *O* is in turn a likeness of another original, O^2, it is still only by *a*'s being a likeness of *O* that *a* and *O* are similar to each other; and *a* and O^2 are then similar to each other not by both being likenesses of still another original, O^3, but by *a*'s being a likeness of *O* and *O*'s being a likeness of O^2. When Parmenides says that *O* participates in the same thing in which *a*, its likeness, participates, he reduces *O* to a likeness of that of which its own likeness is a likeness. If *O* and *a* are similar to each other by participating in one and the same thing, then *O* is not the original of which *a* is a likeness, not the idea that Socrates posited, but another particular likeness, the original of which is the idea in question; and this idea is similar to its likeness not by participating in that in which the likeness participates but by really being that which the likeness merely represents. If no two things can be similar to each other in this way but only by both participating in one and the same thing, then, quite apart from any theory of ideas, there can be no such thing as a likeness, image, copy, or representation of anything at all.

---

to each other by participation in O^2. That this is not specifically stated only tends to support the suspicion that the argument was originally an argument against the possibility of the relation original-likeness in general and not against the theory of ideas as such.

assumes that any two things that are similar in a given respect—and so also the paradeigmatic idea and its particular likeness—must both in the same sense *have* or *share in* the character or property in respect of which they are similar. To this assumption Plato appears to call special attention when he makes Parmenides conclude his argument by saying that the infinite regress will occur 'if the idea turns out to be similar to that which participates in the idea itself',[1] that is 'to *have* the same character that its participant *has*'. The indispensability of this assumption both to this argument of Parmenides and to the preceding version of the regress, formulated as an argument against the uniqueness of each separate idea,[2] has recently been re-emphasised by Professor Vlastos.[3] In his study, which has started a still-rising flood of literature, intended to clarify Plato's text but tending to whelm it with the symbols of modern logic,[4] Vlastos contends that this, which he calls the 'Self-Predication Assumption', and another, which he dubs the 'full-strength Non-Identity Assumption', are tacit premisses, both essential to both of Parmenides' regress-arguments; that, when these tacit premisses are made explicit, it becomes obvious that they are mutually inconsistent and that therefore both versions of the regress are invalid arguments; but that Plato was never able to explicate these hidden assumptions, that he never felt sure, therefore, whether the arguments were valid or not, and that for this reason he refrained from attempting to refute them.

The 'Self-Predication Assumption' (1) asserts that 'if O is the idea of x, then O is x'; the 'Non-Identity Assumption' (2) that 'if anything is x, it cannot be identical with the idea of x.' In the latter the antecedent means: 'if anything has a certain character x'; and (1) and (2) are declared to be inconsistent on the assumption that in 'O is x'—the consequent of the former—'is x' has the same meaning, that is, means 'has the character x'. Now, Parmenides does indeed assume this premiss (1) and assumes this meaning for it. In fact, at the end of the second version, as we

[1] *Parm.*, 133a 2–3. [2] Ibid., 132a 1–b 2.

[3] G. Vlastos, 'The Third Man Argument in the Parmenides', *Phil. Rev.*, LXIII (1954), pp. 319–49. See above, Ch. XII.

[4] Cf. W. Sellars, *Phil. Rev.*, LXIV (1955), pp. 405–37; G. Vlastos, 'A Reply to Professor Sellars,' ibid., LXIV (1955), pp. 438–48; P. T. Geach, ibid., LXV (1956), pp. 72–82 see above, Ch. XIII; G. Vlastos, 'A Reply to Mr. Geach', ibid., LXV (1956), pp. 83–94 see above, Ch. XIV.

have seen, he appears to call special attention to the fact that the regress depends upon the premiss so understood. This alone would suggest that the implications of this 'hidden premiss' were not hidden to Plato and that he intentionally left them unexplicated in Parmenides' argument. This possibility Vlastos does not entertain, however. On the contrary, he contends that this 'Self-Predication Assumption', while never openly asserted by Plato, is nevertheless necessarily implied in his doctrine of ideas and in certain of his statements, such as 'Justice is just' or 'Beauty is beautiful', so that he must have assumed it without ever having been aware of it and its implications.[1]

Such statements as these quoted by Vlastos and taken by him to imply that Justice and Beauty were assumed to *have* the characters indicated may also mean, however, that 'Justice' and 'just' or 'Beauty' and 'beautiful' are *identical*; and it can be shown that Plato was well aware of the difference between such an assertion of identity and an attribution and in this awareness consciously denied what Vlastos believes he unconsciously assumed without understanding its implications. In the second part of the *Parmenides*, for example,[2] he uses the following argument: If there are parts, since 'each' signifies 'one', each part must participate in Unity (τὸ ἕν); but its participation in Unity implies that it is other than one, for otherwise it would not participate but would itself be one, whereas only Unity itself (αὐτὸ τὸ ἕν) can be one. So each part, like the whole of which it is a part, 'is one' only by participating in Unity. Here Plato clearly distinguishes two meanings of 'is x', namely (1) 'has the character x' and (2) 'is identical with x'; assumes that whatever 'is x' in one sense is not x in the other; and states that αὐτὸ τὸ x and only αὐτὸ τὸ x 'is x' in the second sense.[3] As applied to the statements quoted by Vlastos and to the

[1] For such statements as those quoted Vlastos cites *Prot.*, 330c–d, *Phd.*, 100c 4–6, *Lysis*, 217d, and Diotima's speech in the *Symposium*; he also asserts that αὐτὸ τὸ—for 'the idea of x' suggests Self-Predication. Owen (see above, p. 319, note 4) also cites *Prot.*, 330c–d and *Phd.*, 102e 5 as evidence for Self-Predication in 'the old theory of Forms', presumably meaning that Plato in his 'later theory' abandoned it; but in the *Sophist* itself, which according to Owen represents this 'later theory', there is the statement (258b 10 ff.): ὥσπερ τὸ μέγα (i.e. τὸ μέγα αὐτό [cf. 258a 1]) ἦν μέγα καὶ τὸ καλὸν ἦν καλόν. . . .

[2] *Parm.*, 158a.

[3] The distinction between assertions of identity and attribution is observed elsewhere in the second part of the *Parmenides* also, e.g. at 142b 7–c 2, 143b

doctrine of ideas generally, this is to say: 'the idea of x is x' means 'the idea of x and x are identical and therefore the idea of x does *not* "have the character x" '.

Since Plato formulates this distinction in the second part of the *Parmenides*, it is reasonable to suppose that he was aware of it and its bearing upon the regress-arguments when he put these into the mouth of Parmenides in the first part of the dialogue. We need not rest upon this probability, however, since a passage in the tenth book of the *Republic*[1] shows that he regarded the distinction as essential to the theory of ideas. This passage is a succinct proof that the idea of every plurality is itself unique. Just because this is its purpose, the relevance to the regress in the *Parmenides* that other scholars had seen in it was denied by Ross in a sentence applauded by Vlastos as 'an admirably terse refutation'.[2] 'To show that if there were two Ideas of bed there would have to be a third', Ross said, 'does nothing to disprove the contention that, if there is one Idea of bed, related to particulars as Plato supposes, there must be a second.' Whether it does or not depends, of course, upon the nature of the proof, which neither Ross nor Vlastos deigns to analyse. Plato does not, in fact, argue that there must be only one idea of κλίνη because if there were two, there would have to be a third; that of itself would not show why all three may not be ideas of κλίνη. His proof is instead that there can be only one idea of x just because the idea is ὃ ἔστιν x. God himself could not create more than one idea of x, because if there were even so many as

[1] *Rep.*, 597c.

[2] Ross, *Plato's Theory of Ideas*, p. 87 and pp. 230–1; Vlastos, see above, p. 259, note 1. Owen (p. 320) also denies the relevance of the passage to *Parm.*, 132d–133a on the ground that in the former Plato uses not 'a regress of *similarities*' but simply the premiss of the ἓν ἐπὶ πολλῶν. Each step of the regress in both versions, however, is just the ἓν ἐπὶ πολλῶν; and this is itself an argument from the *similarity* of the πολλά to one another (cf. Alexander, *Met.*, pp. 84, 1–2 and 85, 3–5 and Cherniss, *Aristotle's Criticism*, I, p. 233, n. 138 and pp. 294–5). As will be seen, what Plato does in the passage of the *Republic* is to show why the idea cannot be one of a plurality of similar entities—which is just what Parmenides assumes it is in the first version and seeks to prove that it is in the second—and this is itself the reason why a 'regress of similarities' does not arise.

1–3 (cf. 158b 1–2 and *Soph.*, 245b 7–8); at 149c 5–6 it is said that the others than Unity neither are one nor participate in Unity, at 157b 9–c 2 that they are not Unity but do participate in Unity.

two such entities, they would both *have* the character *x* and so ὅ ἔστιν *x* would be neither of these but would be instead the single entity 'of which they would both *have* the character'.[1] Here is the same distinction between 'what is *x*' and 'what has *x*' that we find drawn in the second part of the *Parmenides*, where it is said that 'What participates in Unity must be other than one, since otherwise it would not *participate* but would itself *be* one, whereas only Unity itself (αὐτὸ τὸ ἕν) can *be* one'.[2] In the *Republic*, however, this distinction is expressly applied to prove that the idea of *x*, since it is identical with *x*, cannot have *x* as a character or property, as it necessarily would if it were one of a plurality of entities alike in 'being *x*', and that such entities, however 'perfect' they might otherwise be, would still be 'particulars' and not ideas of *x*[3] because they would 'have *x* as a character' and therefore would not be 'what *x* is'. This passage clearly shows that, contrary to what Vlastos holds, Plato did *not* confuse the idea of *x* with 'the perfect instance of the property which the word *x* connotes'; and, since he explains that αὐτὸ τὸ *x*, the expression most commonly used for 'the idea of *x*', always means ὅ ἔστι *x*, 'what is identical with *x*',[4] it denies what Ross and Vlastos assert: that this expression makes the idea of *x* one *x* among others and implies an *x*-ness common to it and them.[5] On the contrary, this passage of the *Republic* is clear proof that Plato consciously rejected as false this crucial assumption of Parmenides' regress in both its forms and held that this rejection of it was implied in the very terminology that he used to designate the ideas.

What Plato meant by the formula, 'the idea *is* that which its particular participants *have* as a character', requires a word of explanation, since it has obviously been misunderstood by Owen and by Vlastos alike. According to Owen,[6] this formula that I have imputed to Plato did become his doctrine—but only after he had written the *Parmenides*. Since Owen adopts the orthodox opinion that the *Republic* antedates the *Parmenides*, he must have failed to see that the proof in Book X of the *Republic* rests upon this formula; and this he did because he interprets the formula as a

[1] *Rep.*, 597c 7–9.

[2] *Parm.*, 158a (cf. p. 370, n. 2).

[3] Cf. *Rep.*, 597d 1–3.

[4] *Rep.*, 507b 5–7. Cf. *Rep.*, 490b 3, 532a 7–b 1; *Phd.*, 75c 10–d 2, 78d 1–7; *Symp.*, 211c 7–d 1.

[5] Cf. Ross, *Plato's Theory of Ideas*, p. 88.

[6] See above, p. 320, note 4.

denial of the 'separate existence' of ideas, a change in doctrine that, as we have seen, he mistakenly ascribes to Plato in his 'later, critical period'. Vlastos, rightly denying such a change of doctrine but taking the formula in the same way as Owen does, denies that Plato could ever have adopted it. It would, he contends, have prevented Plato from 'separating' the ideas; and to impute it to him is to fail to see 'that the "perfect reality" of the Forms is incompatible with their being the ⟨imperfect⟩ predicates of particulars'.[1] Vlastos thus explicitly interprets the formula to mean that the ideas are *themselves* attributes or properties of particulars; but this is a complete misapprehension. As the passage in the *Republic* shows, it means that of any character or property, *x*, that a particular *has*, the *reality* is ὃ ἔστιν *x*, which it could not be if it were *had* by anything and which therefore must be independent or 'separate' from all manifestations of itself as a property. The formulation that Vlastos rejects and Owen accepts as a 'later doctrine', then, far from being incompatible, as they both suppose it is, with the independent existence of the true realities, which we call by the conventional but somewhat misleading term 'separation of the ideas', necessarily implies it in asserting that what appears 'dispersed', as the *Timaeus* puts it,[2] in particularisation as a property is in reality an unparticularised entity, indivisible and identical with itself, and so not a property of anything.

Whether or not Plato himself ever took the trouble to point it out to his associates, we have certain evidence to show that by some of them at least the formulation thus made explicit in this passage of the *Republic* was held to be the reason for rejecting as invalid the regress-arguments of the *Parmenides*. This is a passage of Aristotle's *Metaphysics*, the import of which has long gone unremarked, perhaps because of an old corruption in the text, which Ross in his revised edition has now removed, although by a strange inadvertence he has left unchanged and so made irrelevant and unintelligible his old exegetical note on the passage.[3] There

[1] Vlastos, see above, p. 253, note 1. [2] *Tim.*, 35a 1–7, 37a 5–b 2.

[3] *Met.*, 1079b 3–11. Shorey showed that in b 7 τὸ δ' οὗ ἐστι must be an error for τὸ δ' ὅ ἐστι (*Class. Phil.*, XX [1925], pp. 271–3). This correction Ross adopted in the second edition of his translation of the *Metaphysics* (Oxford, 1928); and in the corrected reprint of his text and commentary of *Aristotle's Metaphysics* (Oxford, 1953) he corrected the text accordingly, but the

Aristotle, after having tried to involve the theory of ideas in the regress by arguing that each of the ideas and its participants must *have* the same property in common if ideas and particulars are not merely unrelated homonyms,[1] recognises as the Platonists' reply to this argument the contention that this premiss of the regress is rendered invalid by their addition of ὃ ἔστι to terms designating ideas. This is the explicit application to Parmenides' regress of the formulation used in the proof of the *Republic*; and it is noteworthy that Aristotle testifies to its force when in his rejoinder to it he abstains from arguing that the idea does *have* the property its participants have, thereby silently admitting that as ὃ ἔστιν *x* the idea cannot be treated as an 'eternal particular' or a 'perfect instance of *x*', and attempts instead to establish a new kind of regress, based not upon the relation of the idea to its particulars at all but upon the isolation of this ὃ ἔστι, treated as a common predicate of all the ideas, which he contends must therefore imply a separate idea of ideality.

I take it therefore as proved not only that both versions of the regress are invalid arguments but also that when Plato put them into Parmenides' mouth he believed them to be invalid and invalid for reasons which he felt himself to have indicated satisfactorily for anyone who would compare the assumptions of these arguments with what he had already said concerning the nature of the ideas. In any case, so far as certainty can be assured by the evidence of his own writings and by that of all relevant ancient testimony, he certainly continued to the end of his life to maintain the doctrine that the ideas are paradigms or originals, of which particulars are copies, images, or representations—the doctrine, in short, which according to Parmenides' argument implies an infinite regress.

Now, that argument, as we have seen, is in fact much more than a refutation of the doctrine of paradeigmatic ideas. If it were valid, it would be a general proof that nothing can be a likeness or image of anything whatever; and it is probable that this was the scope and

[1] *Met.*, 1079a 32–b 3.

exegetical note on the passage there (Vol. II, p. 423) still stands as it was written for the impossible reading οὗ. On the reading here, the passage as a whole, and its relation to A, chap. 9, where it is lacking at 991a 8, cf. Cherniss, *Aristotle's Criticism*, I, p. 308–13.

purpose of the original argument, which, as presented in the *Parmenides*, is merely adapted *ad hoc* to refute the specific use of 'likeness' in the theory of ideas. There is evidence elsewhere in Plato's writings that he knew such general arguments against the existence of images or likenesses and that he was interested in the challenge of such arguments to define the way in which a likeness is at once distinguished from its original and related to it. When, for instance, Cratylus, in the dialogue named for him, maintains that words are images of the things they name[1] but that the words must be exact manifestations of those things or not be images of them at all,[2] Socrates explains at some length that an image *as such* cannot be exactly what that is of which it is an image.[3] The position of Cratylus he connects with the notorious doctrine that no statement can be false, since it is impossible in saying anything not to say what is (τὸ ὄν);[4] and in the *Sophist* this same notorious doctrine is said to be the basis of the sophistic contention that there is no such thing as an image, a likeness, or a semblance.[5] This contention, it is said,[6] the sophist will support by challenging Theaetetus to give a definition of 'image'; and, when Theaetetus responds by defining it as 'that which by having been assimilated to the real thing is another such thing' (τὸ πρὸς τἀληθινὸν ἀφωμοιωμένον ἕτερον τοιοῦτον), he is asked whether this means 'another *real* thing' or what it is to which 'such' (τοιοῦτον) in his definition refers. He protests that it means not 'real' (ἀληθινόν)—otherwise, of course, he would have defined instead of 'image' an exact double, indistinguishable from that of which it is supposed to be the image—but 'like' (ἐοικός); and he is then forced to admit that he cannot meet the sophist's challenge, since according to his own definition the being of an image or likeness implies its not really being. This passage in its context is part of the aporetic introduction to the proof that 'not being' can be meaningfully used in the sense of 'otherness' or 'difference'; and, with this established, the sophist can, despite his objection, be defined as one kind of maker of images. The plan and purpose of this dialogue do not require that Plato should here return to explain

[1] *Crat.*, 430a 10–b 2, 439a 1–4; on all that follows in the text see my paper, '*Tim.*, 52c 2–5' in *Mélanges Diès* (1956), pp. 49–60.

[2] Ibid., 431e 9–432a 4.

[3] Ibid., 432a–d.

[4] Ibid., 429b–430a.

[5] *Soph.*, 264c 10–d 1 referring to 239c ff.; cf. 236e 1–237a 4 and 238d 4 ff.

[6] Ibid., 239d–240c.

specifically whether the definition of image offered by Theaetetus is itself saved by the proof that 'not-being' in the sense of 'otherness' exists and, if so, how that definition accounts for the puzzling relation of likeness to original. For us, however, it is important to emphasise that he does not do so in the *Sophist* and that for enlightenment we must turn again to the *Timaeus*, to that passage in which, as I have already said, the theory of space is presented as saving at once the world of becoming and the conception of its relation to being as that of image or semblance to original reality.

The phrase in Theaetetus' definition that had led to his discomfiture was ἕτερον τοιοῦτον 'another such thing'. 'To what does τοιοῦτον refer', he was asked; and the only answer that he could give made the being of an image imply its really not being. Now, an image really is not, of course, that by reference to which the τοιοῦτον that characterises it is meaningful; and this, which gives rise to the perplexity of Theaetetus, is in our passage of the *Timaeus* made to explain the distinctive nature of an image. In this passage[1] Plato summarises in concise, doctrinal language the relations to one another of the three factors: the immutable intelligible reality which is the ideas; the transitory sensible γιγνόμενα, images of the former; and space, the medium in which the continual coming-to-be and passing-away of these images occurs but into which the ideas themselves never enter, as *it* never enters into *them*. The relevant words for our purpose here assert that: not even that very thing that an image signifies belongs to the image itself, but an image is always a transitory adumbration *of* something other than itself; and consequently it must be coming to be *in* something other than itself and thus cling precariously to being or else itself be nothing at all, whereas what really is cannot be *in* anything other than itself or anything else *in* it.[2]

The point of the crucial explanation here is not, as various interpreters have said, that 'the being of an image *qua* image is not self-related' or that 'an image is not its own image' or 'its own original' but that any particular image stands for something, refers to something, means something and that this meaning the image has *not* independently as its own but only in reference to something else apart from it and not dependent upon it but of which, as the parallel and complementary clause says, the image is always a

[1] *Tim.*, 51c 6–52d 1.

[2] Ibid., 52c 2–d 1. Cf. my paper referred to in p. 375, note 1 *supra*.

transitory adumbration. So, for example, a human image is not itself *human*; but it is a human *image* precisely because it does not have as its own the 'humanity' that it signifies. Or, to take an example from this section of the *Timaeus* itself, an igneous or aqueous image, one of those μιμήματα which, as we saw, are to be designated by the formula τὸ διὰ παντὸς τοιοῦτον, is such because, not having as its own what fire or water is, it signifies or means fire or water. It is because the meaningfulness of an image is its reference to something other than itself that the image is essentially τοιοῦτον. As such, it implies a τι, something that *is itself that* by reference to which the image is τοιοῦτον. Bare τοιοῦτον, however, is not any*thing* itself and so, to be at all, must have some external basis (ἕδραν—52b 1) for being, which it can have only by coming to be in something else. Therefore, because an image is what it is '*of* something other than itself', it must, even to be itself, come to be '*in* something other than itself' also, whereas true reality, since it *is itself what it is* independently of anything else, is τι and *not* τοιοῦτον. The medium too, in which the image must come to be if it is to have even the being of an image—this medium, which is space, immutable in its own nature, must also be τι and not τοιοῦτον. So true reality and space can neither one be *in* the other, since they cannot be at the same time both two and one identical thing.[1]

Thus the ἕτερον τοιοῦτον in the definition of image, which reduces Theaetetus to perplexity in the *Sophist* and of which no further explicit account is given later in that dialogue, appears in the *Timaeus* as a fully elaborated explanation of the nature of an image in its relation to the original; and here, moreover, with the explication of this relation is intimately connected the additional factor of the spatial medium which alone is said to make possible the *existence* of an image.

This in itself would be a plausible reason for believing the *Timaeus* to be a later work than the *Sophist*; and the plausibility of such a relative chronology could be reinforced by a comparative study of many other passages, some of them—like those examined here—passages which Owen has mistakenly adduced in support of his own thesis. But, if there were time to examine them all, the result

[1] Cf. Aristotle's argument (*Met.*, 1039a 3–14) that one substance cannot be actually present in another, because what is actually two can never be one, and the example, ἢ γὰρ οὐχ ἓν ἡ δυὰς ἢ οὐκ ἔστι μονὰς ἐν αὐτῇ ἐντελεχείᾳ.

would only increase the *plausibility*; and the highest degree of plausibility is still far different from proof. With this firmly in mind, I would therefore emphasise the following distinctions:

(1) All the evidence we have or are likely ever to have requires us to recognise that the *Cratylus*, the *Parmenides*, and the *Theaetetus* were composed before the *Timaeus*.

(2) Mr. Owen has adduced no evidence—nor to my knowledge has anyone else—that proves the *Timaeus* to have been composed earlier than the *Sophist*, the *Politicus*, or the *Philebus*; and on the contrary there are plausible reasons for believing that at least the *Sophist* and the *Politicus* antedate the *Timaeus*.

(3) Whatever may be the true relative chronology of this group of dialogues, the philosophical doctrine expressed in the *Timaeus* is certainly not at variance with that expressed in any of the others of this group and is not repudiated, abandoned, or in any essential point even modified in any of them.

XVIII

THE DISORDERLY MOTION IN THE *TIMAEUS* (1939)

Gregory Vlastos

SO much has been written on this vexed issue,[1] that one hesitates to reopen it. Yet one has no other choice when one finds scholars accepting as generally agreed a view which rests on altogether insufficient evidence. I propose, therefore, to examine the main grounds on which recent authorities interpret the disorderly motion of *Timaeus*, 30a, 52d–53b, and 69b as a mythical symbol. They are four:

I. That the *Timaeus* is a myth;
II. The testimony of the Academy;
III. That motion could not antecede the creation of time;
IV. That motion could not antecede the creation of soul.

[1] For references to opposing authorities in the last century see Zeller, *Plato and the Older Academy* (English trans., London, 1876, p. 364, n. 5). Some recent authorities who take the view that the pre-existing chaos must not be taken literally (For later works see pp. 401–402 below):

Wilamowitz, *Platon*, vol. i, 1917, pp. 597–8.
C. Ritter, *Platon*, vol. ii, 1923, pp. 415–17.
W. Theiler, *Zur Geschichte der teleologischen Naturbetrachtung*, 1924, section on Plato.
A. E. Taylor, *Plato*, 1926, pp. 442 ff., and *Commentary on the Timaeus*, 1928, pp. 66–9 *et passim*.
P. Frutiger, *Les Mythes de Platon*, 1930, *passim*.
Léon Robin, *Platon*, 1935, p. 191.
G. M. A. Grube, *Plato's Thought*, 1935, pp. 168 ff.
F. M. Cornford, *Plato's Cosmology*, 1937, pp. 37, 176, 203 *et passim*.

I

In what sense is the *Timaeus* a myth? A comparison with the *physiologoi* suggests itself at once. The *Timaeus* corrects their views in their own universe of discourse. Empedocles' cosmology starts with the four ῥιζώματα.[1] Plato disagrees: 'These are products, not *archai*. I cannot give certain knowledge of the true *arche* or *archai*. But I can give an account which is a good deal more probable than any physicist's.'[2] So when he fulfils this promise, going back of the four 'elements' to describe in 52d–53b the winnowing movement out of which they were formed, what he gives us is not more mythological than Empedocles' mingling of the elements in the original harmony of love,[3] than the primordial ἠρεμία of Anaxagoras' ὁμοιομερῆ,[4] or Leucippus' and Democritus' world-forming δίνη.[5]

Thus the *Timaeus* is unique among Plato's myths. It is a mistake to put it on a level with the great myths of the *Gorgias*, *Phaedo*, *Republic* X, the *Phaedrus*, and the *Politicus*.[6] The *Timaeus* uses none of the devices by which all of these disavow the scientific seriousness of major features of their accounts.[7] The speaker is the

[1] Diels B. 6, where, significantly enough, these physical substances are given the names of divinities. Conversely, the anthropomorphic elements, Love and Strife, are conceived as corporeal forces. See Cyril Bailey, *The Greek Atomists and Epicurus*, p. 31; and Cornford, in chapter xv of vol. iv of *Cambridge Ancient History*: 'In Empedocles Love and Strife belong at once to the world of mythical imagery and to the world of scientific concepts.' This ambivalence of myth and science, very different from didactic metaphor or allegory, is the proper mood of the *Timaeus*. It was used unconsciously by Empedocles, consciously by Plato. Cf. μῦθος in *Soph.*, 242c–8ff.

[2] Summarising in paraphrase, *Tim.*, 48b 1–d 4.

[3] Cyril Bailey, op. cit., pp. 31, 32.

[4] Aristotle, *Phys.*, 250b 25, 26.

[5] Diogenes Laertius, ix, 31, 32; Aristotle, *Phys.*, 196a 24.

[6] Anyone tempted to make much of the label 'myth' might note its absence in the first two, and its very casual use at the end of the third (μῦθος ἐσώθη, *Rep.*, 621bc, a quasi-proverbial expression, applied elsewhere to the 'saving' of a philosophical thesis: *Phil.*, 14a, *Laws*, 645b, *Tht.*, 164d).

[7] In the *Gorgias* the story begins with ὥσπερ γὰρ Ὅμηρος λέγει (523a); Homer's witness is called in again in 525e. The story contains such figures and places as the Isles of the Blessed and Tartarus; Minos, Rhadamanthys, Aeacus; Tantalus, Sisyphus, Tityus. In the *Phaedo*: λέγεται δὲ οὕτως . . . (107d); . . . ὡς ἐγὼ πέπεισμαι (108c); λέγεται (110b); καὶ χρὴ τὰ τοιαῦτα ὥσπερ ἐπᾴδειν ἑαυτῷ . . . (114d). The detailed geography is clearly mythological. In

ἀστρονομικώτατος Timaeus (27a), who, in Socrates' estimation, has reached the highest summit of all philosophy (20a). The sober, systematic, prosaic tone of his discourse contrasts sharply with Critias' earlier reminiscences. This all but irrelevant introduction sets the fanciful myth over against the scientific myth. It is stuffed with mythological material: Atlantis, the deluge, Phaethon's flight, and the genealogy of Phrononeus, Niobe, Deucalion and Pyrrha which even the Egyptian priest declares to be mythology (23b). None of this sort of thing comes into Timaeus' story; and its omission has the force of conscious restraint in view of the wealth of poetic allusions suggested by his grandiose theme.[1] When the creation of the stars forces him to say something about the popular gods, he is dry, hasty, ironical.[2] He accepts the traditional accounts in a mood that suggests Hume's, 'Our most holy religion is founded on Faith.'[3] Sacred mythology of this sort he treats elsewhere with the deepest respect.[4] He has no use for it here. The topography of the under-world, described in such detail in the *Phaedo*, is left unmentioned. The chthonian deities, whose worship is an integral part of the state-cult,[5] pass unnoticed. Nor is there any place here for the mediating *daimonic* entities, who

[1] Except in verbs describing the activity of the Demiurge, where he is forced into anthropomorphism, Timaeus indulges rarely in poetic metaphors. The κρατήρ of 46d is the only important one; and there it occurs with the scientist's characteristic carelessness for literary detail: he thinks he has used it before (ἐπὶ τὸν πρότερον κρατῆρα) when he actually has not. Expressions which he knows to be poetic Timaeus expressly qualifies as similes: ἐμβιβάσας ὡς ἐς ὄχημα (41e); this is a vestige of the imaginative figure of the *Phaedrus*, where it had been used *without* qualification: Ζεύς, ἐλαύνων πτηνὸν ἅρμα (246e); θεῶν ὀχήματα ἰσορρόπως εὐήνια (247b); there the mood is mythology, and to qualify would be pendantry.

[2] About irony: see especially Taylor's *Commentary*, on 40d 6–e 2.

[3] *An Enquiry Concerning Human Understanding*, x, ii, 100.

[4] I.e. that he accepts the forms of traditional worship, and wishes to preserve them intact, without the slightest alteration (*Laws*, 738b, c; cf. also *Rep.*, 427b, c, and *Laws*, 716c–718b; 759a–760a; 828a–d).

[5] I.e. *Laws*, 717a; 828c; 958d.

---

the *Republic* we get an Ἀλκίνου ἀπόλογον (allusion to the *Nekyia* of *Od.* XI: cf. Arist., *Poet.* 1455a 2, *Rhet.*, 1417a 13), the tale of Er, the Armenian. In the *Politicus* the reversal of the celestial revolutions is connected with the tale of Atreus and the golden lamb (268e, 269a), the age of Cronus and the γηγενεῖς (269a–b), and said to account for 'innumerable other [events], still more marvellous' (269b). For the *Phaedrus* myth note 265b 6–8.

figure invariably in Plato's supernatural hierarchy[1] and are conspicuous in the cosmology of the *Epinomis* (984e, 985a).

Why should the cosmology of the *Timaeus* exclude figures whose reality is vouched for by the law of the state? Because they fall below its standard of scientific probability.[2] Commentators often pick the expression εἰκότα μῦθον out of Timaeus' epistemological introduction (29b–d), and use it as though the emphasis were on μῦθον instead of εἰκότα. This is certainly wrong. Εἰκός is the important word. It is used thrice explicitly (29c 2, 8; 29d 2), and once implicitly (29b εἰκόνος . . . συγγενεῖς). Of these four, it is used thrice as an adjective of λόγος, once of μῦθος. In the seventeen echoes of this introduction throughout the rest of the dialogue, μῦθος is used thrice,[3] while εἰκός, εἰκότως, etc., are used sixteen times.[4] Εἰκότα λόγον is used eight times; εἰκότα μῦθον twice. And it is a pretty commentary on the 'mythological' connotations of εἰκότα μῦθον that it is used both times of a purely scientific opinion: 59c, of the composition of metals, and 68d, of colour-mixture.

A *mythos* is a tale. Not all tales are fictions. 'What is the meaning of this *mythos*?', asks Socrates of a 'Protagorean' doctrine (*Tht.* 156c). His tone may not be free from condescension; but neither does he mean to prejudge its claim to truth. The typical *mythos* is mythological. But there is none of this in the discourse of *Timaeus* where only the *eikos* is tolerated. And what *eikos* means in this context is carefully defined: the metaphysical contrast of the eternal forms and their perishing copy determines the epistemological contrast of certainty and probability.[5] Thus 'the element of falsity lies, not in the mode of exposition, but in the object described, which is only a fleeting image of the real.'[6] All of what we hopefully call 'science', Plato relegates to verisimilitude. But verisimilitude is not fiction, for the visible cosmos is not fictitious. If within the dream-world of the senses[7] we draw pretty definite lines between the reality of people we see and hear

[1] *Rep.*, 392a; 427b; *Laws*, 717b; 734d; 818c; 910a.

[2] ἄνευ τε εἰκότων καὶ ἀναγκαίων ἀποδείξεων λέγουσιν (40e).

[3] 59c, 68d, 69c.

[4] 30b, 34c, 44d, 48c, 48d, 49b, 53d, 55d, 56a, 56d, 57d, 59c, 68d, 72d, 90e.

[5] The account is 'akin' to the 'image' it describes: εἰκόνος εἰκότας (sc. λόγους) 29c.

[6] F. M. Cornford, *Cambridge Ancient History*, vol. vi, chap. xi, p. 330.

[7] *Tim.*, 52b, c: ὑπὸ ταύτης τῆς ὀνειρώξεως. . . .

and, say, Hesiod's γηγενεῖς (our sanity depends on it), so scientific probability must be kept clear from didactic fictions. So the presumption must be that every element in the *Timaeus* is probable, and none fanciful, unless we are given further instructions or hints to the contrary. Of the latter there are none for the pre-existing chaos. In their absence we are so far driven to accept it as a serious, though only probable, hypothesis of the origin of the material world.

II

It is not then Plato, but Xenocrates who supplies us with the suggestion that, as Aristotle put it in *de Caelo* 279b 32–280a 1, the expressions about the generation of the world are a kind of diagram, given διδασκαλίας χάριν. This passage of the *de Caelo* is 'a plain allusion to the interpretation of the *Timaeus* given by Xenocrates'.[1] In none of our sources is it said that Plato thus construed the *Timaeus*; or even that Xenocrates contended that Plato thus construed it. All we hear is that Xenocrates and Crantor, or 'Xenocrates and the Platonists', supplied this interpretation.[2] Of course, we have Xenocrates' teaching at second, or rather at *n*th, hand. It may be that Xenocrates did make this very claim. But this is not in our evidence. Xenocrates is, therefore, of

[1] A. E. Taylor, *Commentary*, p. 69. So much is clear from the Greek commentaries, listed by Heinze, *Xenokrates*, pp. 179–80:

Simpl. *de Caelo* 303, 34–35: δοκεῖ μὲν πρὸς Ξενοκράτην μάλιστα καὶ τοὺς Πλατωνικοὺς ὁ λόγος . . .

Schol. cod. Coisl. 166: τοῦτο πρὸς Ξενοκράτη εἴρηται ἀπολογούμενον ὑπὲρ Πλάτωνος . . .

Schol. cod. Parisiens Reg. 1853: ὁ Ξενοκράτης καὶ ὁ Σπεύσιππος ἐπιχειροῦντες βοηθῆσαι τῷ Πλάτωνι ἔλεγον . . .

and from Plutarch, *de animae procreatione in Timaeo*, 1013a, where the reference is by implication to Xenocrates, Crantor, and their followers.

[2] Taylor (*Commentary*, p. 69, n. 1) and H. Cherniss (*Aristotle's Criticism of Plato and the Academy*, n. 356) add Speusippus and Theophrastus. The textual authority for the former is frail: the scholion in the Parisian MS. of the *de Caelo*; no mention of Speusippus in Plutarch, Proclus, or Simplicius. As for Theophrastus, his remark, as quoted in Proclus is, τάχ' ἂν γενητὸν λέγοι σαφηνείας χάριν and the τάχα ('perhaps, to express any contingency from a probability to a bare possibility,' Liddell and Scott, *Lexicon*, s.v., II), is understood by Taurus to mean 'possibly' (ἴσως) in this context (Theophrastus, frag. 28). Cherniss does not explain why he favours 'probably' instead (loc. cit., and 610).

little help at this point. For the rest, there are excellent reasons why an apologist and systematiser of Plato's thought should wish to put just that construction upon this troublesome doctrine of the *Timaeus*. For the same reasons the Academy would conserve it. Yet their minds could not have been altogether easy about it, or we could hardly have had Plutarch, Atticus, and ἄλλοι πολλοὶ τῶν Πλατωνικῶν,[1] reverting centuries later to the literal interpretation. So I cannot put as much weight on the 'all but unanimous testimony of the Academy'[2] as Professor Taylor seems to do.

On the other hand, we have Aristotle, who knows Xenocrates' interpretation and also knows something of Plato's oral teaching. So far from attributing this interpretation to Plato, his references to the *Timaeus* imply the very opposite.[3] There can be no question here of 'mere polemical "scores" got by pressing the mere words of a sentence'.[4] His references are too detailed and too serious for that. He tells us that:

(*a*) In teaching the generation of time Plato stood alone against the unanimous opinion of previous thinkers;[5] while

(*b*) he (Aristotle) was the first to teach the beginninglessness of the *ouranos*;[6] that

(*c*) Plato, with Leucippus, taught the everlastingness of motion,[7] yet

(*d*) Plato held that the world and the soul were generated.[8]

Of these statements *a* and *b* might be, and *a* and *c* or *c* and *d* would almost certainly be taken as mutually inconsistent. To see that they are not, implies conscientious recording and thoughtful distinctions. To be sure, every reference to Plato is

[1] Proclus, quoted by Taylor, *Commentary*, 68.

[2] Taylor, *Commentary*, 69.

[3] I.e. *de Caelo* 280a 29, *Phys.*, 251b 14, *Met.* 1072a 2. Cf. *de Anima* 406b 26, καὶ ὁ Τίμαιος φυσιολογεῖ τὴν ψυχὴν κινεῖν τὸ σῶμα, associating the account of the soul's ability to move the body in the *Timaeus* 'with the mechanical explanation of Democritus' (Cherniss, op. cit., n. 314), and thus with a genre of thought which is the polar opposite of mythology (cf. Epicurus, *Ep.*, 2, 87).

[4] Taylor, *Commentary*, 69.

[5] *Phys.*, 251b, 14–19.

[6] *de Caelo*, 279b 12, 13. cf. Cherniss, op. cit., 415–16.

[7] *Met.*, 1071b 31–33.

[8] *de Caelo*, 280a 29, 30; *Met.*, 1072a 1–3.

the prelude to a crushing refutation. But crushing refutation would be singularly inept against mythology. There can be no question here either of ignorance or carelessness. If we are to discount Aristotle's testimony we must charge him with deliberate misrepresentation. It is hard to believe that Aristotle, with all the limitations of his subtle and unimaginative mind, was capable of quite that.

III

We now come to the more difficult part of the discussion: to the contradictions in which Plato would seem to involve himself on a literal interpretation of the pre-existing chaos. Here we must make sure of the canon of criticism on which we are to proceed. Shall we assume at the start that Plato's philosophy is immune from contradiction? This would be wishful thinking. Every great thinker has sought consistency, and none has perfectly attained it, except in the minds of slavish disciples who know the answers so well that they never think of the problems. One thing only we can reasonably assume about a great philosopher: that he is never carelessly or needlessly inconsistent. In the present instance Plato himself has warned us of rough sailing ahead. This is physics, not metaphysics; his physics must have a fringe of inconsistency and inexactness (29c 6), at the risk of belying the metaphysics. In fact Plato has much too cheap an insurance against misadventures in the *Timaeus*. He can always say, 'I told you so. What can you expect of the image of an image that is in constant flux'? We cannot treat him quite so leniently. To meet his inconsistencies with easy-going tolerance would be as shallow as to hide or explain them away. We must insist on the question: Where is the source of the inconsistency? Is it a mere accident of the physics, or can it be traced back to a weakness in the metaphysics? And of the pre-existing chaos we must ask further: Is it the cause of metaphysical inconsistency, or its symptom? If the latter, then to remove it as mythology would be needless exegetic surgery.

Let us being with the most formidable of these inconsistencies:

> 'No sane man could be meant to be understood literally in maintaining at once that time and the world began together (38b 6), and also that there was a state of things, which he proceeds to describe, *before* there was any world.'[1]

[1] Taylor, *Commentary*, p. 69.

But was the contradiction as obvious to Plato as it is to Professor Taylor? And was it avoidable?

Aristotle was a 'sane man'. He records both of these Platonic doctrines: that motion is everlasting (*Met.*, 1071b 31–33), while time is not (*Phys.*, 251b 14–18). He interprets the latter literally. Yet he sees no immediate contradiction between the two. He does indeed hold that 'all change and all that is in motion is in time' (*Phys.*, 222b 30, 31), and that time has no beginning (*Phys.*, 251b 14–28), but he finds it necessary to establish these propositions independently.[1] They are not immediate logical inferences from the self-contradictoriness of 'before the beginning of time'. To convict him of inconsistency Aristotle has to go farther afield and bring in the additional premiss that Plato, who 'sometimes' attributes the cause of motion to the soul, could not consistently make the generated soul cause of beginningless motion.[2] Why is it, one wonders, that Aristotle should resort to such a roundabout argument, weakened as it is by the 'sometimes' in the first premiss, when he could offer the simple and fatal objection that 'before time' is nonsense, since 'before' presupposes time?[3]

The answer is in the 'tradition running throughout the whole of Greek thought, which always associated Time with circular movement'.[4] Aristotle justified this belief by arguing:

(*a*) Time is the number of motion (*Phys.*, 223a 33);
(*b*) there is only one time (*Phys.*, 223b 2–12); therefore,
(*c*) time must be measured by one determinate motion (*Phys.*, 223b 12–18);

[1] He proves the first as follows:

(i) θᾶττον or βραδύτερον is predicable of every motion;
(ii) θᾶττον implies the idea of πρότερον;
(iii) πρότερον implies distance from 'now';
(iv) 'now' implies time (τὰ νῦν ἐν χρόνῳ) (*Phys.*, 222b 31–223a 8).

He proves the second:

(i) time can neither be nor be conceived apart from 'now';
(ii) any 'now' is a μεσότης between past and future;
(iii) any past is a 'now';
(iv) therefore, any past has a past (*Phys.*, 251b 19–26).

[2] *Met.*, 1072a 1, 2.

[3] *Phys.*, 223a 4–8; 251b 10, 11.

[4] F. M. Cornford, *Plato's Cosmology*, 103, q.v.

(*d*) this must be the motion whose number is 'most knowable' and that is the uniform (ὁμαλής) circular motion of the heavenly bodies (*Phys.*, 223b 18–21).

Note the implications of this argument: What would happen if you eliminated the uniform circular motion of the heavenly sphere? According to Aristotle there would be no other uniform motion.[1] Without uniform motion time cannot be numbered, and if it cannot be numbered is it still time? A number that cannot be numbered would be a contradiction in terms. Thus, if Aristotle adhered strictly to this assumption that time is the measure of a determinate motion, he should have been hard put to it to show any inconsistency whatever in Plato's doctrine that motion is eternal while time is not. So long as there is only irregular motion, there would be no time in this strict sense of the word. It is only when the regular motion of the heavenly bodies comes into being that time begins.[2] This is in fact the hypothesis of the *Timaeus*.

On this hypothesis we should have to reject the validity of the argument of *Phys.*, 222b 30–223a 15 (summarised p. 386, n. 1), which attempts to establish that time is coeval with motion. For the first premiss in that argument is that θᾶττον and βραδύτερον is predicable of every motion (222b 31, 32); and to define θᾶττον Aristotle employs the idea of uniform (ὁμαλήν) motion,[3] which is contrary to the hypothesis of the *Timaeus*. So Aristotle could not—and does not—use the argument of *Phys.*, 222b 31–223a 8 against the *Timaeus*. To dislodge Plato he has to fall back on another argument: that of *Physics*, 251b 19–26. Here his logic is sound. But he is no longer using the same concept of time as

[1] He holds that rectilinear motion is not uniform, 'since (according to him) when it is κατὰ φύσιν it becomes faster as bodies near their proper place, and when it is παρὰ φύσιν it becomes slower as the impressed force becomes exhausted. The circular motion of the heavenly bodies is the only change which by its nature proceeds uniformly'. Ross, *Aristotle's Physics*, p. 612. Hence his doctrine that ὁμαλῆ (sc. κίνησιν) ἐνδέχεται εἶναι τὴν κύκλῳ μόνην, *Phys.*, 265b 11.

[2] And we could add: If it should ever happen that the heavenly revolutions should cease, so would time. Cf. Marlowe's *Dr. Faustus*.

Stand still, ye ever-moving spheres of heaven,
That time may cease, and midnight never come.

This is good Aristotelian (and Platonic) doctrine.

[3] *Phys.*, 222b 33–223a 2: *Λέγω δὲ θᾶττον κινεῖσθαι τὸ πρότερον μεταβάλλον εἰς τὸ ὑποκείμενον κατὰ τὸ αὐτὸ διάστημα καὶ ὁμαλὴν κίνησιν κινούμενον.*

before; he is not working with the cyclical time of *Physics*, 223b 12–224a 2, but with the more general concept of a 'now' which is always a *μεσότης* between past and present.

This excursus on Aristotle enables us to understand:

(*a*) Plato's concept of cyclical time;[1]

(*b*) how such a concept seemed compatible with the supposition of a disorderly motion going on in the absence of time.

b needs no further argument. It is a simple inference from the belief that time essentially implies periodic motion; no periodic motion, no time. *a* requires further comment. The doctrine of time in the *Timaeus* is a stronger version of the cyclical time of *Phys.*, 223b 12–224a 2. If Aristotle takes the heavenly revolutions as a necessary condition of time, the *Timaeus* seems to identify them with time. It not only tells us that sun, moon, and the other five planets were *ὅσα ἔδει συναπεργάζεσθαι χρόνον* (38e),[2] and were made *ἵνα γεννηθῇ χρόνος* (38c), but even that the 'wandering' of the planets *is* time.[3] Nights, days, months, and years are 'parts' (*μέρη χρόνου*, 37e),[4] and 'was' and 'shall be' (the most general categories of temporal succession) are 'species' (*εἴδη*, 37e 4, 38a 8) of cyclical time (*κυκλουμένου*, 38a 8).

Now time so conceived is not the contrary of timeless eternity, but an approximation to it: its likeness (*εἰκόνα*, 37d 6), its imitation (38a 8). Time is a finished product, the end result of a raw material which the Demiurge works over with the definite purpose of making it as much like eternity as he possibly can.[5] What is this raw material? Plato tells us in 52d 3: it is *γένεσις*. This distinction between raw *γένεσις* and created *χρόνος* is the key to the whole account. It shows that it was just as necessary for Plato to hold that the Demiurge did not create the first, as that he did create the second. It is the nature of the Demiurge to make his work more like the eternal model, not less like it. So the one thing he could not possibly do is to bring the factor of change and

[1] For a correction on this see pp. 409–410 below.

[2] Cf. 41e 5 and 42d 5: *ὄργανα χρόνων, ὄργανα χρόνου* of mon and other stars.

[3] 39d: *χρόνον ὄντα τὰς τούτων πλάνας*. Cf. Aristotle's statement in *Phys.*, 218a 34, *οἱ μὲν γὰρ τὴν τοῦ ὅλου κίνησιν εἶναί φασι* (sc. *τὸν χρόνον*), where *οἱ μὲν* are identified with Plato by Eudemus, Theophrastus, and Alexander (*Simpl. Phys.*, 700. 18–19).

[4] For the true sense of this and further correction see p. 409 below.

[5] 38b, c; also 37c, d.

decay, of 'perpetual perishing', into existence. That is a necessary condition for his work. Given that, he can proceed to inform it with periodic motion. Since he did not create it, it must antecede creation. It must exist not as a bare nothing, but as change, though disordered change: κινούμενον πλημμελῶς καὶ ἀτάκτως.

But it is not utterly disordered change. Wholly devoid of form it would be, on Platonic standards, wholly devoid of Being; i.e. nothing at all. But obviously it is not that. It is something. This must puzzle Plato, who thinks of πέρας and ἄπειρον as two distinct entities, requiring the imposition of the one upon the other through the mediation of a third ordering entity.[1] The theme of the *Timaeus* is this informing of formless change by the Demiurge. If this dominating idea were false, the *Timaeus* would be not only mythology, but nonsense as well. Yet how conceive of γένεσις which lacks form and being altogether? The more γένεσις is denuded of stable οὐσία, the more it will be true that it *is* γένεσις: ἔστι γένεσις, which sounds like a contradiction in terms. This is the deep-lying difficulty that is mirrored in the problem of pre-temporal motion. Plato could not have been entirely unaware of it. In the *Sophist* he faced squarely an analogous logical difficulty, and showed that ἔστι μὴ ὄν involves no contradiction. But the metaphysical problem he never cleared up in the same way.[2]

[1] This idea is not peculiar to the *Timaeus*. E.g. *Phil.*, 30c: ἄπειρον . . . ἐν τῷ παντὶ πολύ, καὶ πέρας ἱκανόν, καί τις ἐπ' αὐτοῖς αἰτία. Notice the force of ἐπ' αὐτοῖς. Notice also how distinct is αἰτία from πέρας: πρὸς τρισὶ καὶ τέτταρτον . . . γένος (26e). τὴν αἰτίαν ὡς ἱκανῶς ἕτερον ἐκείνων δεδηλωμένον (27b).

[2] I cannot agree with Brochard's bold attempt to identify matter with the Other of the *Timaeus* and thus with the non-being of the *Sophist*. (Brochard et Dauriac, *Le Devenir dans la Philosophie de Platon*, Cong. Int. de Phil., 1902.) This is hardly the place to argue the matter out. But his assumption that the κοινωνία of Being, Same, Other, Motion, and Rest in the *Sophist* covers the relation of forms to material things is effectively answered in Cornford's *Plato's Theory of Knowledge*, 297. Robin's thesis that 'la distinction de l'intelligible et du sensible se fonde sur la pureté ou l'exactitude plus ou moins grandes des relations qui les constituent, et que ce n'est, par conséquent, qu'une différence de degré' (*La Physique de Platon*, Rev. Phil., Vol. 86, 1918, second half, p. 398), is attractive, but, I think, much too Leibnizian an interpretation of Plato. The difficulty with it appears in such a harmless little phrase as 'à la complexité infinies et perpétuellement instables' (p. 410), which Robin uses to describe sensible things. Why 'instables'? Does mere increase of complexity cause instability? Why should it? To establish his thesis Robin should be able to explain how Plato's doctrine of process can be reduced to a doctrine of increasing complexity of formal relations.

And it is doubtful if he could, without recasting his whole philosophy to end the ontological dichotomy of τὸ ὂν ἀεί, γένεσιν δὲ οὐκ ἔχον and τὸ γιγνόμενον μὲν ἀεί, ὂν δὲ οὐδέποτε (27d–28a).

Short of such a drastic remedy Plato had to compromise and say: the chaos is disorderly, but not altogether so; it contains 'some traces'[1] of order. This is a makeshift. Even as a metaphor it is self-contradictory, for 'traces' could only be a result, not an anticipation. Yet it is the best that Plato could do in the case of spatial order. And, I submit, it is the best he can do in the case of temporal order. He would have to say: Just as the pre-existing chaos had 'certain traces' of spatial configuration which justify us in speaking, with studied vagueness, of the Receptacle's becoming 'watery' and 'fiery' before water and fire had yet been created, so it might have 'traces' of temporal order which might enable us to speak in similarly indefinite, uncertain, terms of priority and succession in its occurrences even before the introduction of that sharply precise chronological order for which we reserve the name of 'time'.

This is, of course, a most unsatisfactory expedient. But the cause of the trouble, I repeat, is not the disorderly motion as such. It is the idea of *γένεσις*. Γένεσις, it now turns out, is not the protean state which Plato believes it to be, formless till it be 'likened' to the model by the charitable intervention of the Demiurge. On the contrary, quite apart from any order impressed upon it by the Creator, it has a precise, inalienable order of its own: an order of before and after, inherent in the mere fact of passage. I do not see how Plato could face *this* difficulty without rewriting not only the part of the *Timaeus* which deals with the disorderly motion, but much more of the *Timaeus*, and a good many parts of other dialogues as well.

IV

We have the final perplexity: According to the well-known teaching of *Phaedrus* 245c–246a and *Laws* X, all motion is caused by soul. The disorderly motion would then imply an irrational world-soul. But no such soul is mentioned in the *Timaeus*. Since this is offered as an argument against the pre-existent chaos, a fair way of meeting it is to ask: Just what does it mean for the contrary hypo-

[1] 53b 2: ἴχνη . . . ἄττα.

thesis (i.e. that chaos is only the residual disorder ever present in the world)? Professor Cornford answers:

> 'Since no bodily changes can occur without the self-motion of the soul, the other factor present in this chaos must be irrational motions of the World Soul, considered in abstraction from the ordered revolutions of Reason. The disorderly moving mass must be conceived as animated by soul not yet reduced to order, but in a condition analogous in some ways to that of the infant soul described above (43a ff.).' (*Plato's Cosmology*, p. 205).

Yet—

(*a*) Of 'irrational motions of the World Soul' we know nothing in the *Timaeus*. On the contrary, we are told at its creation: *Θείαν ἀρχὴν ἤρξατο ἀπαύστου καὶ ἔμφρονος βίου πρὸς τὸν σύμπαντα χρόνον* (36e).

(*b*) The analogy with the infant-soul, apposite as it is,[1] is unfortunate for Professor Cornford's hypothesis: It does not tell us how an irrational soul originates irrational motions, but how irrational motions throw out of order the infant's soul. There is nothing the matter with the rationality of its soul. The trouble is with the 'flowing and ebbing tide of the body' (43a, Cornford's translation), and the violent motions that break upon it from the outside.[2] As Professor Cornford himself comments on this passage: 'Contrast the World Soul, which, as soon as it was joined with its body, began an "intelligent life" (36e), not being exposed to external assaults' (op. cit., 149, n. 5). That is surely the difference. There are no external assaults to throw the motions of the world soul out of gear.[3] And, unlike the infant, it is free from the six 'wandering motions'.[4] What else could induce disorder upon

[1] The *ἀτάκτως καὶ ἀλόγως* of the infant's disorder reminds one most forcefully of *πλημμελῶς καὶ ἀτάκτως* (30a) and *ἀλόγως καὶ ἀμέτρως* (53a) of the world-chaos.

[2] Note the force of *τὰ τῶν προσπιπτόντων παθήματα* (43b), *πυρὶ προσκρούσειε τὸ σῶμα . . . διὰ τοῦ σώματος αἱ κινήσεις ἐπὶ τὴν ψυχὴν φερόμεναι προσπίπτοιεν* (43c), . . . *σφοδρῶς σείουσαι τὰς τῆς ψυχῆς περιόδους* (43d). Note the repetition of *ἔξωθεν* 44a 1, 5.

[3] For the very good reason that there is nothing outside it. The world was made one to exclude violent incursions upon it *ἔξωθεν*, which *προσπίπτοντα ἀκαίρως λύει καὶ νόσους γῆρας τε ἐπάγοντα φθίνειν ποιεῖ* (33a). For *νόσος* as disorder of reason see 86b, d; 88a, b.

[4] It has only the motion *τῶν ἑπτὰ τὴν περὶ νοῦν καὶ φρόνησιν μάλιστα οὖσαν* (34a vs. 43b).

it? The only other possible factor mentioned in the *Timaeus* is bad breeding (86e), which, of course, would be absurd for the world soul.

More important than any specific conclusions that we might draw from this argument is the general way in which we put the problem when we look at it through the eyes of the *Timaeus*. We have just been asking, What induces disorder in the soul? But how ask this if you assume that all motion is caused by soul? It is strictly meaningless for you, except in so far as it might suggest that disorder in one soul might be explained through disorder in some other soul. Any other kind of disorder would be irrelevant; for, on this hypothesis, there is no disorder not caused by soul. I do not see how anyone can make head or tail of the *Timaeus* on this assumption. For instead of tracing back all chaos to some spiritual source, the *Timaeus* generally assumes the opposite. This apparent contrast between *Laws* X, and the *Timaeus* is striking, but not inexplicable. It derives from the totally different basic problems to which the two treatises are severally addressed:

Laws X, is simply and purely an exercise in apologetics. It must establish the existence of the gods. It does not raise any issue which will not assist in the proof of this conclusion, so urgent for religion, so essential for the State. The argument turns on one question: Is soul prior to body? This question too is stripped to fighting-weight. It is not encumbered with the additional problem: What kind of soul—good or bad? Experience can decide this.[1] Only when he has proved to his satisfaction that 'all things are full of gods' (899b), does he feel free to broach the problem of evil. Even there his object is not to explain the origin of evil, but to provide religious comfort for the troubled soul, through the assurance of the universal plan in which all things work together for good.[2] Individual souls have in them 'a cause of change' (904c); but this operates only within the framework of

[1] 898c. The whole of 896d to 898b is nothing more than an elaborate propounding of the question: 'If soul is cause of everything, good and bad, and order implies a good soul, whereas disorder implies an evil soul, consider the *ouranos* and decide: Does it suggest the best soul or its contrary?' Therefore, it is a mistake to quote any part of this passage in support of the view that Plato believed in an evil world-soul.

[2] πρὸς τὴν σωτηρίαν καὶ ἀρετὴν τοῦ ὅλου παντ' ἐστὶ συντεταγμένα (903b ff.). It is the organic principle ('the part exists for the sake of the whole'), the same in the order of the universe as in the order of the state. Cf. *Rep.*, 420d 4, 5.

the universal plan already assumed. It explains the just punishment of injustice, not the occurrence of injustice itself. The ominous words *κατὰ τὴν τῆς εἱμαρμένης τάξιν καὶ νόμον* do slip in (904c). But what is this *εἱμαρμένη*? Is it the will of the 'king' or its limiting condition? The question is not raised in the *Laws*. But the *Timaeus* cannot avoid it.

The *Timaeus* is no manual of political theology. It is 'esoteric' philosophy: the private discourse of like-minded philosophers (20a), so much more leisurely and tentative than the defensive vehemence of *Laws* X. It can thus open up the really tough questions of theodicy, without fear of unsettling the faith of the simple or exposing vulnerable flanks to atheistic opponents. It comes soon to the creation of the soul, which the *Laws* had assumed,[1] but prudently refrained from presenting as a problem. To us, with our Hebrew–Christian heritage, the doctrine of creation suggests at once the doctrine of the fall. But Plato is just as much a scientific, as a religious, thinker. He stands in a line of physiological psychologists, who have discovered that elementary cognition involves physical contact with the material world. So two difficulties must be solved at once:

(*a*) How the creature of a perfect creator is so imperfect; and
(*b*) how an immaterial soul can be affected by material things in sensation.

Plato's solution is that though soul does not consist of material articles, it is nevertheless in motion.[2] It can move, and it can be moved. Because it can be moved it is subject to sensation, desire,

[1] *Laws*, X, 892a, c; 896a; 904a; XII, 967d. And cf. p. 414, n. 1, below.

[2] Soul has no part in fire, air, water, earth, the constituents of the world of 'second' causes, though it does partake of the *περὶ τὰ σώματα γιγνομένη μεριστὴ οὐσία* (35a). That the soul is a motion is plain from the account of its creation. It consists of the revolving strips of the Same and the Other. A mental event is always a motion for Plato:

αἱ τοῦ παντὸς διανοήσεις καὶ περιφοραί (90c, d).
τὰς . . . ἐν τῇ κεφαλῇ διεφθαρμένας περιόδους ἐξορθοῦντα (90d).
στρεφομένη, θείαν ἀρχὴν ἤρξατο ἀπαύστου καὶ ἔμφρονος βίου (36e).
ἡ τῆς μιᾶς καὶ φρονιμωτάτης κυκλήσεως περίοδος (39c).
ἵνα τὰς ἐν οὐρανῷ τοῦ νοῦ κατιδόντες περιόδους χρησαίμεθα ἐπὶ τὰς περιφορὰς τὰς τῆς παρ' ἡμῖν διανοήσεως (47b).

Those who 'don't use their heads': *διὰ τὸ μηκέτι τὰς ἐν τῇ κεφαλῇ χρῆσθαι περιόδους* (91e).

pleasure and pain, and passions of every sort.[1] And for the same reason it is prone to disease and disorder.[2] Thus disorderly motion may cause evil in soul. To exculpate God of responsibility for evil it is no longer enough to say, *αἰτία ἑλομένου*. When you find a physical cause for irrational choice,[3] you must exculpate God of the disorderly motion that has caused it. And you cannot stop short of the primitive chaos. This ultimate cause of evil must exist, uncaused by God, and (short of reopening the problem all over again) uncaused by soul.

That is why we may dispense with Plutarch's well-meaning hypothesis of the primordial evil soul.[4] Apart from his forced interpretation of *Laws*, 896d,[5] Plutarch's mainstay is the myth of the *Politicus*. Now when we examine the context of his quotations, it becomes plain that the cause of the 'counter-revolution' in the myth is not soul, but body:

> Ξ. . . . *τοῦτο δὲ αὐτῷ τὸ ἀνάπαλιν ἰέναι διὰ τόδ' ἐξ ἀνάγκης ἔμφυτον γέγονε.*
>
> Ν.Σ. *Διὰ τὸ ποῖον δή;*
>
> Ξ. *Τὸ κατὰ ταὐτὰ καὶ ὡσαύτως ἔχειν ἀεὶ καὶ ταὐτὸν εἶναι τοῖς*

[1] *ὁπότε δὴ σώμασιν ἐμφυτευθεῖεν ἐξ ἀνάγκης, καὶ τὸ μὲν προσίοι, τὸ δ' ἀπίοι τοῦ σώματος αὐτῶν then* follow sensation, eros and the passions (42a). In 69c, d again pleasure, passions, sensation come to the immortal soul with the subsidiary *mortal* soul which, in turn, comes with the *mortal* body: . . . *θνητὸν σῶμα αὐτῇ* (i.e. *τῇ ἀθανάτῳ ψυχῇ*) *περιετόρνευσαν* . . . *ἄλλο τε εἶδος ἐν αὐτῷ* (i.e. *τῷ σώματι*) *ψυχῆς προσῳκοδόμουν τὸ θνητόν*. Sensation occurs when *διὰ τοῦ σώματος αἱ κινήσεις ἐπὶ τὴν ψυχὴν φερόμεναι προσπίπτοιεν* (43c), whence Plato derives *αἴσθησις* (is it from *αἴσσω*, which Cornford thinks the more probable of those given by Proclus? Or from *ἀσθμαίνω* suggested by J. I. Beare in *Greek Theories of Elementary Cognition*, 1906?). See also 45d 1, 2 and 64b 4–6, and cf. with *Philebus*, where sensation is a 'tremor' of soul and body (33d), and note its formal definition of sensation in 34a. (*σεισμός* is the word used in the myth of the *Politicus* of the chaotic disorder of the counter-spin: 273a 3, 6; and in the *Timaeus* of the primitive chaos: 52e, 53a.)

[2] *νοσοῦσαν καὶ ἄφρονα ἴσχειν ὑπὸ τοῦ σώματος τὴν ψυχήν* (86d). Further 87a: phlegms and humours blend their vapours with the motion of the soul: *τὴν ἀφ' αὐτῶν ἀτμίδα τῇ τῆς ψυχῆς φορᾷ συμμείξαντες*. Notice the force of *προσπίπτῃ* in 87a 5, and cf. with use of same word in 33a 4, 5 and 43b 7 and 43c 5.

[3] E.g. in 86c, d, where we are given a definite physiological cause for *ἑλεῖν ἀκαίρως*.

[4] In *de animae procreatione in Timaeo*.

[5] This is presumably the reference of *ἐν δὲ τοῖς Νόμοις ἄντικρυς ψυχὴν ἄτακτον εἴρηκε καὶ κακοποιόν*, ibid., 1014e. *Per contra*, see above, p. 392, n. 1; Taylor's *Commentary*, 116; and Robin's *Platon*, 226–7.

πάντων θειοτάτοις προσήκει μόνοις, σώματος δὲ φύσις οὐ ταύτης τῆς τάξεως (269d).

That is the trouble with the *ouranos*, the speaker proceeds: κεκοινώνηκέ γε καὶ σώματος (269d, e). Plutarch's strongest text is 272e 5, 6. But εἱμαρμένη is plainly enough the ἀνάγκη of the *Timaeus*,[1] the realm of secondary causes;[2] σύμφυτος ἐπιθυμία may only mean that the drag of the primitive disorder is *now* felt, deep in its nature, as a rebellious urge.[3] How can we then escape the plain words, *à propos* of the gradual fading of the Creator's influence upon the creature: τούτων δὲ αὐτῷ τὸ σωματοειδὲς τῆς συγκράσεως αἴτιον, . . . ὅτι πολλῆς ἦν μετέχον ἀταξίας πρὶν εἰς τὸν νῦν κόσμον ἀφικέσθαι (273b)? So far from substantiating Plutarch's hypothesis, the myth of the *Politicus* corroborates the doctrine of the *Timaeus* and the *Phaedo* that the soul's partnership with the body is the source of its aberrations;[4] though its chief value for an account of the origin of evil is the explicit way in which it traces it all back to the primitive disorder: παρὰ δὲ τῆς ἔμπροσθεν ἕξεως, ὅσα χαλεπὰ καὶ ἄδικα ἐν οὐρανῷ γίγνεται, ταῦτα ἐξ ἐκείνης αὐτός τε (sc. ὁ οὐρανός) ἔχει καὶ τοῖς ζῴοις ἐναπεργάζεται (273c).

The *Timaeus* completes the picture. It mentions circumstances in the creation of the soul which account for its susceptibility to irrational motion: and the περὶ τὰ σώματα γιγνομένη . . . οὐσία (35a) has been built into it. Motion is inherent in this γιγνομένη οὐσία which is one of the soul's ingredients. One could hardly attribute the origin of *this* motion to soul without circularity. On the contrary, the *Timaeus*' mechanical explanation of motion makes it quite unnecessary to postulate a bad soul to set the

[1] Cf. ἐξ ἀνάγκης *Pol.*, 269d 2, 3.

[2] *Tim.*, 46e. Plutarch himself puts no stock on εἱμαρμένη but refers to it as ἀνάγκη. Clearly εἱμαρμένη in *Pol.*, 272e cannot be the will of the 'captain', for he has just let go of the helm; it is the disorder he had kept under control which is now asserting itself. That the realm of secondary causes includes a necessary element of disorder when separated from the overlordship of *nous* is clear from *Tim.*, 46e 5.

[3] The same applies to 273b 1, 2: the 'instruction' was not given to a primitive bad soul, but to the god-made soul that marked the end of chaos and the beginning of cosmos.

[4] For the *Timaeus* see above, 394, nn. 4 and 5. For the *Phaedo* see especially 66a–d. The soul of the philosopher must be 'released' from the 'fetters' of the body (67d; cf. *Rep.*, 515c); it must be 'purified' from the 'contamination' of the body (*Phd.*, 67c 5 and *Tim.*, 69d 6; cf. *Symp.*, 211e 1, 2, and *Rep.*, 611c 3). The body is a 'tomb' (*Phdr.*, 250c; *Gorg.*, 493a).

primitive chaos in motion: κίνησιν δὲ εἰς ἀνωμαλότητα ἀεὶ τιθῶμεν (57e).[1] Chaos contains, by definition, the minimum of ὁμαλότης, ὁμοιότης.[2] It must, therefore, and for purely mechanical reasons, be in constant motion. When the creator steps in to reduce the indefinite heterogeneity of the chaos to the definite homogeneity of the five regular polygons, the question arises whether we may not get too much likeness, in which case motion would cease altogether. The Demiurge solves this neatly by introducing variety into the sizes of the atomic triangles (57d). Thus he never has to think of starting motion, but only to keep it going. Likewise, when he creates the 'body' of the universe: there is no question of pushing it off to a start, but only of *subtracting* from it the six 'wandering' motions.[3]

Is it then possible to reconcile this teaching of the *Timaeus* with *Laws* X?[4] Remembering the special limitations of the task to which *Laws* X, is devoted, we need not find that its teaching, taken as a whole, contradicts the cosmology of the *Timaeus*. The crucial tenet of *Laws* X, the priority of soul over all material motions, is not strange to the *Timaeus*, 34b, c. Yet once Timaeus has given it fulsome acknowledgement, he makes no specific use of it. *Because* the soul is 'older', the soul must 'rule'. Chronological priority is hardly more than a vindication of ontological priority, in line with a deep-rooted ethical and political dogma that the older must rule the younger.[5] To press it further would be embarrassing in view of the *Timaeus*' doctrine of time.

Why then does *Laws* X, make so much of this very temporal priority which seems hardly more than a pious formality in the *Timaeus*? Precisely because it has been contradicted by the atheistic materialists. It is they who make, alas, only too good sense of

[1] Cornford comments in a footnote: 'Obviously the mover cannot be the soul, which belongs to a higher order of existence. It could not be spoken of as either heterogeneous and unequal, or homogeneous and equal, with the moved.' Op. cit., 240. Cf. also 58c 2–4 and 57a 2–4.

[2] Cf. the phrase of *Pol.*, 273d, e τὸν τῆς ἀνομοιότητος ἄπειρον ὄντα πόντον to which the world would revert if it persisted in its 'counter-revolution'.

[3] 34a: τὰς δὲ ἓξ ἁπάσας κινήσεις ἀφεῖλεν καὶ ἀπλανὲς ἀπηργάσατο ἐκείνων.

[4] I should now [1964] make it clear that I no longer believe that the primordial motion in the *Timaeus* can be 'reconciled' on these terms with the uncompromising doctrine of *Laws* 896a–b and *Phdr.* 245c–e that soul is the 'source' of all motion.

[5] See *Rep.*, 412c for the axiomatic belief that the old must rule. The whole of the *Laws* is dominated by this idea.

the temporal priority of matter. To refute them Plato must meet them on their own ground. And so he does, retaining the ambiguity of ἀρχή and ἄρχει,[1] and arguing its cosmic primogeniture.[2] In the course of this argument he propounds the bare possibility that primary causation might rest with the evil soul. But this is forthwith declared to be contrary to fact, and the speaker can go on to complete the case against the atheists, without digressing to explain how primary causation through the evil soul is, in fact, inexplicable save through collision with material, secondary causes. That is why Aristotle, years later, writes that Plato '*sometimes*' declares the soul the *arche* of motion (*Met.*, 1071a 1). The expression is a compromise between the apparent contradiction of *Laws* X, and the *Timaeus*.

On this interpretation the proposition that the soul is πρῶτον γενέσεως καὶ φθορᾶς αἴτιον (*Laws* 891e) merely denotes the supremacy of the soul's teleological action *within the created universe*. Its polemic resources are fully exploited in *Laws* X. But it is not offered as a substitute for the cosmologic teaching of the *Timaeus*. Only here, where Plato gives us a complete picture of the relations of teleology to mechanism, can we find an intelligible meaning of the 'firstness' of the soul: Soul belongs with the 'first', good, intelligent, divine causes—not in the realm of necessity, but of purpose (46e, 68e). The 'worse' motions are externally impressed; the 'best' are self-initiated (89a). Soul is inherently of the 'best'; though it is not immune from assaults by the 'worse'.

This is a serious qualification of the apparent meaning of the doctrine that soul is ἀρχὴ κινήσεως (*Laws* 896b; *Phdr.*, 245c).[3]

[1] E.g. 896c: ψυχὴν μὲν προτέραν, σῶμα δὲ δεύτερόν τε καὶ ὕστερον ψυχῆς ἀρχούσης, ἀρχόμενον κατὰ φύσιν, whence it follows in 896d: ψυχὴν δὴ διοικοῦσαν καὶ ἐνοικοῦσαν ἐν ἅπασι . . . καὶ τὸν οὐρανὸν διοικεῖν.. Again 895b: ἀρχὴν . . . καὶ πρώτην . . . ἀναγκαίως εἶναι πρεσβυτάτην καὶ κρατίστην. The double-edged meaning of precedence is always assumed, never argued. E.g. 892a: ὡς ἐν πρώτοις ἐστί (simple assertion of precedence, immediately broken into temporal priority) σωμάτων ἔμπροσθεν πάντων γενομένη (and ontological supremacy) καὶ μεταβολῆς τε αὐτῶν καὶ μετακοσμήσεως ἁπάσης ἄρχει παντὸς μᾶλλον.

[2] *Laws*, 892c: ἐν πρώτοις γεγενημένη.

[3] I am leaving out of this discussion the additional complication that in the *Phaedrus* the idea of the soul as ἀρχὴ καὶ πηγὴ κινήσεως serves at once to prove that the soul is ungenerated: εἰ γὰρ ἔκ του ἀρχὴ γίγνοιτο, οὐκ ἂν ἔτι ἀρχὴ γίγνοιτο (245d). In the *Laws* the soul is still the ἀρχὴ κινήσεως (e.g. 896b 3), but the same conclusion is *not* drawn, as is clear from the frequent references of the *Laws* to the soul as generated (see below, p. 414, n. 1). Ἀρχή is a 'weasel-

Are we mutilating the *Laws* to force conformity with the *Timaeus*? I think not. We are trying to make sense of the statement taken by itself. Forget the *Timaeus* altogether for the moment. How much could Plato mean when he says that the soul is the cause of all becoming and perishing? At its face-value this asserts that the soul is itself the cause of the instability of becoming; that apart from soul reality would be untroubled by transience.[1] But this is grotesquely un-Platonic. When Plato does ask himself, 'Is soul more akin to being or becoming?', he can only answer, 'It is in every way more like being' (*Phd.*, 79e). The one thing he cannot mean in the *Laws* is that soul is the source of Heracleitean flux. Γένεσις must be presupposed. It must be 'there', before soul can supervene to 'rule' it. But if it is 'there', it must involve motion of some sort; not teleological motion in the absence of soul, but disorderly mechanical motion.[2] Thus, quite independently of the description of the disorderly motion in the *Timaeus*, we should be forced to supply something like it in order to make sense of the doctrine of *Laws* X, that soul is the first cause of becoming.

Does this clear up all the difficulties of the disorderly motion? Hardly. How does the Demiurge act upon the disorderly motion?[3]

[1] Note that the hypothesis of the universal standstill (*Laws* 895a, b), against which Plato's argument of the soul as first mover is so effective, is enemy territory. It was they (οἱ πλεῖστοι τῶν τοιούτων), not Plato, who 'dare' affirm it. Likewise in the *Phaedrus* the supposition of all motion of heaven and earth coming to an absolute stop is the apodosis of a *per impossibile* hypothesis.

[2] We must never forget that Plato thinks of mechanism as disorderly, except in so far as it is teleologically ordered: e.g. *Tim.*, 46e, where the 'second' causes, unmistakably identified with mechanical causes in 46e 1, 2, are said to be ὅσαι μονωθεῖσαι φρονήσεως τὸ τυχὸν ἑκάστοτε ἐξεργάζονται. That mechanism nevertheless does contain an order of its own is part of the contradiction in Plato's thinking noted above, p. 390.

[3] An easy solution is to animate the chaos; then the Demiurge would only need to 'persuade' its bad soul, and this would seem to make better sense of such expressions as 48a 2, 4, or 56c 5. But this is only postponing the

---

word' in Plato. It may mean any, or all, of (i) beginning, (ii) source, (iii) cause, (iv) ruling principle, (v) ruling power. It should be noted that the mythological interpretation of the pre-existing chaos and of its associated doctrine of creation could take the chronological 'firstness' of the soul no more literally; cf. Plutarch: εἰ γὰρ ἀγένητος ὁ κόσμος ἐστίν, οἴχεται τῷ Πλάτωνι τὸ πρεσβύτερον τοῦ σώματος τὴν ψυχὴν οὖσαν ἐξάρχειν μεταβολῆς καὶ κινήσεως πάσης. *de an. proc. in Tim.*, 1013 f.

Indeed how does any 'first' cause act upon a 'second' one? Aristotle's complaint that Plato gives no explanation of the soul's κοινωνία with the body it inhabits (*de An.*, 407b 12–19) can be pushed further: How is it that material impact upon the soul can and does take place,[1] even though the soul is not a material body? And, conversely, how is it that the immaterial soul acts and 'masters' the discordant motions of the body?[2] How does one pattern of motion act upon another pattern of motion, though one is the motion of material particles and the other is not?

It is no accident that Plato has avoided such questions. They point to deep-lying difficulties or, at least, obscurities in his categories of material reality. But their further discussion lies beyond the limits of this paper. Our task is done if it be reasonably clear that such difficulties cannot be escaped by the all-too-easy device of relegating the disorderly motion to the status of a mythical symbol.

[1] See above, p. 391, n. 2. [2] *Tim.*, 42b 2.

difficulty. If the Demiurge persuades the evil soul, the reformed soul would then have to persuade its disorderly body—and the difficulty turns up again. At some point final cause must meet efficient cause. To insert intermediary souls only puts off the inevitable encounter of soul with body.

CREATION IN THE *TIMAEUS*: IS IT A FICTION? (1964)

'The Disorderly Motion in the *Timaeus*' (to which I shall refer hereafter as '*D.M.T.*') was written in 1938. It is here reprinted with minor changes in text and notes.

Five years after the appearance of *D.M.T.* came *Aristotle's Criticism of Plato and the Academy* by Harold Cherniss. This truly great work, which has enriched so many aspects of Platonic thought, dealt extensively with the topics treated in *D.M.T.*[1] Had I written after its publication I would have been saved several mistakes. But I do not believe I would have altered my earlier conviction, developed initially in the face of stiff opposition from Cornford.[2] In any case, I have felt no inclination to change my position after absorbing all that Cherniss has had to say about it. So I shall continue to argue for it. But I would urge those who are less concerned with the fortunes of a debate than with the determination of the truth to read and weigh for themselves his side of the case, since my space here is so limited that I could not begin to deal with all he has had to say on and around this question.[3] They might also read a number of other works which have taken different positions from Cherniss on one or more

[1] For specific criticisms of *D.M.T.* see especially notes 314, 362, 364, 365, 366, 385, 392.

[2] *D.M.T.* was an expansion of one or two talks I had with Cornford on the *Timaeus* in the spring of 1938. The paper convinced him no more than did my oral arguments. But it was published with his encouragement.

[3] *Aristotle's Criticism*, 392–457 and notes; 'The Sources of Evil According to Plato' (hereafter 'S.E.'), *Proc. of American Philosophical Society*, 98 (1954) 23–30; review of A.-J. Festugière, *La Révelation d'Hermes Tismegiste, II: Le Dieu cosmique* (Paris, 1960), in *Gnomon*, 22 (1950), 204–16.

points relevant to this controversy.[1] The ones from which I have learned the most are 'Bewegung der Materie bei Platon', by H. Herter (*Rheinisches Museum* 100 [1957], 327–47), and 'Plato's Cosmogony', by R. Hackforth (*Classical Quarterly*, N.S. IX [1959], 17–22.)[2]

I

That the cosmos was not always in existence, but 'has been generated, having started from some ἀρχή' (28b 6–7) is not merely asserted in the *Timaeus*, but demonstrated, and from premisses which give every appearance of expressing firm metaphysical doctrine. It is argued at 28b 4–c2 that the cosmos must have been generated, because

(1) it is corporeal and as such is an object of sense perception and belief, while

(2) all such objects 'are in process of becoming and have been generated'.[3]

[1] The most important of those known to me are: M. Meldrum, 'Plato and the ἀρχὴ κακῶν,' *Journal of Hellenic Studies*, 70 (1950), 65–74; G. R. Morrow, 'Necessity and Persuasion in Plato's Timaeus', *Philos. Review*, 59 (1950), 147–63; see below, Ch. XIX; A.-J. Festugière, work cited in n. 4 above, Ch. V, and Vol. II: *Les Doctrines de L'Ame* (Paris, 1953), XII–XIV; F. Solmsen, *Aristotle's System of the Physical world* (Itnaca, 1960), 50–1; 65, n. 170; F.-P. Hager, *Die Vernunft und das Problem des Bösen in Rahmen der Platonischen Ethik und Metaphysik* (*Noctes Romanae*, 10: Bern, 1963), 230 ff.; Th. Gould, *Platonic Love* (London, 1963), Ch. VII. I should also mention an older book not known to me when I wrote *D.M.T.*, P. Thevenaz, *L'Ame du Monde, le Devenir et La Matiere Chez Plutarque*, (Paris, 1938), 91 ff.

[2] My debt to Herter would have been more apparent if I had tried to deal with broader aspects of the topic. Hackforth's paper, published posthumously, was written late in 1956, as I know from correspondence with him. Previously he had subscribed to the mythological interpretation: *Plato's Phaedrus* (Cambridge, 1952), 67. To Hackforth's paper and to all the other works mentioned in notes 1 and 2 I shall refer hereafter merely by the author's name.

[3] γιγνόμενα καὶ γεννητὰ ἐφάνη, c1–2. ἐφάνη ('have been shown to be', Cornford) refers to 27d 6–28b 7, where γένεσις has been allocated to sensible-opinables in contrast to intelligibles. The word γεννητά is not used in this earlier passage, but γένεσιν σχεῖν is used of them at b 5–6, evidently with the same meaning as γεννητὸν εἶναι. γεννητά is rendered by 'can be generated' in Cornford's translation. This cannot be right in this context. Cornford himself translated γεννητῷ παραδείγματι a few lines earlier (28b 1) as 'generated model' (not, 'model which can be generated'). Cf. also γέγονεν, 28b 7, in the demonstrand, taken as demonstrated (γενομένῳ) at c2.

As Hackforth has pointed out (19) no metaphorical or figurative language infiltrates this sequence of propositions.[1] Εἰκὼς μῦθος is not even mentioned until later (29d 2). And metaphor does not enter the texture of Timaeus' discourse until the reference to the 'Maker and Father of this universe,'[2] i.e. until after the generation of the world has been proved. So just from the opening paragraph of the discourse we could derive a clear-cut, No, to our question—*unless* there were reason to think that Plato thinks there is something wrong about the argument: that one or both of its premisses are false; or that the inference drawn from them is invalid. Could this be so?

That the inference is invalid would be widely granted today. Some would attack it along Kant's lines: even if both premisses were true of each and every object in the world, it would not follow that the conclusion is true of the world as a whole. Others would point out, in still more modern vein, that an aggregate whose every member has a beginning need not itself have a beginning. But no one would suggest that *Plato* would have faulted the argument on these or similar lines.

Would he then have indicted the premisses? Not (1) obviously. Nor can I see any good reason for doubting his confidence in the truth of (2). The only one ever offered, to my knowledge, is the following by Zeller:

> ... this assumption involves us in a series of glaring contradictions. For if all that is corporeal must have become, or been created, this must also hold good of Matter; yet Matter is supposed to precede the creation of the world and (30a) is represented in this its pre-mundane condition as something already visible.[3]

[1] He stressed this in a letter to me: 'The fact that some part, maybe the greater part, of the dialogue is in some sense a myth is irrelevant. For the passage on which the whole issue hinges, viz. 27d 5–28c 3, is in no sense mythical, but straightforward logical argument.... There is no trace of myth before 28c 3.'

[2] Before this we hear only of a 'cause' of generation (28a 4–5), and of a δημιουργός who imitates an eternal model (a 6–9); nothing metaphorical here, unless one takes the core of Platonic ontology to be itself a metaphor (with the αἴτιον here which is a δημιουργός cf. *Phil.*, 27b 1–2, τὸ πάντα ταῦτα δημιουργοῦν, ... τὴν αἰτίαν).

[3] *Plato and the Older Academy*, Engl. transl. (London, 1888) (hereafter 'Zeller'), 365. (Cf. *Aristotle's Criticism*, n. 361.) Though Zeller speaks of a 'series' of contradictions this is the only one he mentions.

Now Plato's cursory reference to the primal chaos in 30a as 'all that was visible' is one of the most obscure of his remarks about that all too obscure concept. A little later he says flatly that nothing is visible unless it has fire in it (31b 5). But chaos had only an inchoate antecedent of fire which did not have the nature of fire but only 'certain traces' of it (53b 2). How, and in what sense, this would, or could, be 'visible' Plato does not explain. So how are we to tell if something answering to this unspecified and problematic sense of 'visible' would share with *bona fide* 'objects of sense-perception and belief' the property of having been 'generated, having started from some ἀρχή'? There is good reason to think that it would not: The ground of Plato's confidence that the objects of our sense-experience have been created is that intelligible structure of theirs which, he thinks, they could only have derived from an intelligent cause; as we know from the *Philebus* (23c ff.) it is the imposition of 'limit' on the 'limitless' by an ordering Mind that results in 'generated existence' (γεγενημένη οὐσία, 27b). But limited structure is just what fire lacked before the Craftsman 'ordered [it] with forms and numbers' (*Tim*, 53b); lacking this it could not be γεγενημένη οὐσία: it would be engulfed in that limitless flux where there is process, but no generation from an ἀρχή. This, to be sure, is a reconstruction. Suppose then it were rejected on the ground that we do not know how Plato would have answered our question as to whether or not a thing so perplexingly 'visible' as pre-formed fire qualifies as a proper 'object of sense-experience and belief'. Even so he would escape Zeller's charge by the very silence he observed on this as on so many other points relating to the primal state. We might then blame him for his silence.[1] But we cannot say he contradicted himself, 'glaringly' or otherwise, since all he left us is, on one side, the perfectly clear-cut statement that the cosmos 'has been generated, having started from some ἀρχή', and, on the other

[1] I.e. for withholding information material to the adjudication of his critics' charges. In my own case, the crux of my contention is that Plato's view that all precise order in the material world is teleologically imposed order founders on the fact that no material can be ordered teleologically unless *it already* has non-teleological order of its own (cf. *D.M.T.*, Section III, last paragraph) and that if Plato himself had made more explicit his own conception of the pre-cosmic state he would have seen that it had to have just such order (both spatial and temporal) as the precondition of receiving the more specific order impressed on it by the Craftsman.

side, no unambiguous contradictory, but an unexplicated obscurity.

And there is a second, quite independent, reason why Zeller's charge falls flat: If it were true, it would put Plato in the position of palming off on his readers falsehoods in the major premiss and conclusion of our syllogism. Believing that it is quite false that all objects of sense-perception and belief are generated, and also false that the world was generated, Plato would be making his mouthpiece, Timaeus, assert the first and join it to a true premiss to engender a false conclusion. Is this at all likely in this context? At the very least, it would be singularly lacking in dramatic fitness, since his spokesman is not a sophist nor yet a philosophically naïve or confused cosmologist: when Timaeus expounds philosophy (46c ff., 49b ff., 51b 6 ff.) everything he says is true Platonic doctrine, with never a false note. How could he then be made to start off his discourse by asserting in a context which is solemnly, even reverently,[1] didactic propositions which Plato believes to be the very opposite of the truth?[2]

II

But let us suppose for the sake of argument that Plato did plant a false premiss into the dialogue at this point and that he went on to narrate in such detail the generation of the world, time, and soul believing all the while that, on the contrary, world, time, and soul are as beginningless as they are endless. Since Plato cares, and cares deeply, for the communication of truth, he would not wilfully mystify, still less mislead, his reader. All parties to this dispute then would agree that he would not write '*p*', while intending to get across 'not-*p*' to the reader, without providing him with clear and unambiguous signs that the latter is his intention. Where are these signs? I shall devote the rest of this paper to

[1] Cf. the invocation to the gods, 27c, followed by Timaeus' vow to 'give the clearest expression to [his] thinking on the subject'.

[2] Zeller says that 'the dogmatic form . . . argues little; for the point is primarily to show, not a chronological beginning, but an Author of the world,' 305. If that is the point, why the assertion of a chronological beginning and its deduction from a false premiss? Zeller cites *Polit.*, 269d–270a, ignoring the fact that everything there is premissed on notorious mythology (see *D.M.T.* above, Section I, p. 380, n. 7) while here the premisses of the argument are, to all appearance, metaphysical doctrine.

just this question. Here to begin with are five supposed disclaimers of creationism which I did not take up in *D.M.T.*:

(i) The order of exposition does not always follow that of the 'mythical' cosmogonic sequence.[1] But a historical account, though normally keeping pace with the events it narrates, need not always do so. Witness the backlashes in Herodotus and even in Thucydides. How then could the reader be expected to draw from the fact that items X, Y, supposed to have occurred in that order, are related in a different sequence, the inference that Plato wants him to understand that both of them are coeval with a beginningless universe? Cherniss refers us to the apology at 34c 2–4 that there is 'too much of the casual and the random' in our speech. But why should that be taken as an apology for any defect other than the one it mentions: the failure to put first in the story an item (the creation of the soul) which came first in the course of events?

(ii) At 42e Plato says that 'having made all these arrangements', the Craftsman 'continued to abide by the wont of his own disposition (ἔμενεν ἐν τῷ ἑαυτοῦ κατὰ τρόπον ἤθει)'. Taking ἤθει here (with Archer-Hind and Cornford) to mean 'nature', Cherniss sees in this phrase an expression of 'the doctrine that god must be unchangeable (*Rep.*, 381c)', and adds that (1) 'if this be taken seriously, the relation of the demiurge to the world must always be and have been the same', which (2) would be contradicted by the very notion of his having created the world.[2]—I fail to see that (2) follows from (1). The constancy of god's ἦθος would comport with any amount of world-making, provided only his behaviour as Craftsman remains consistent with his character as god. In *Rep.* 381c, the point of the statement that 'it is impossible for a god to wish to change himself but, as is only right, each of them being as fair and excellent as it is possible to be, abides for ever absolutely in his own character', is not that god does not act at all, but that he does not act in undignified and wicked ways: he does not lie, masquerade, etc., like the Homeric deities; he never causes evil, only good (379b–380c). Since the world-creation is an act of supreme beneficence (30ab), it would imply no shift of nature or character in this 'best of causes' (29a), but rather a fitting expression of it.

[1] Cf. Zeller, 364; Cherniss, *Aristotle's Criticism*, 424–25, and n. 358.

[2] *Aristotle's Criticism*, 425.

(iii) The Craftsman is no doubt himself a soul.[1] Would it be a 'contradiction'[2] to think of soul creating soul?—I can see none that would arise in the Platonic scheme because of just this. What precisely would contradict what? Why should the Craftsman's soul-making powers be cramped by the assumption that he is himself a soul? If we are to grant him, without logical strain, so many other marvellous potencies, why should our reason take offense at this one? (And cf. p. 415 below).

(iv) According to Cornford, we must understand τὸ γιγνόμενον ἀεί at 27b–28a to mean 'that which is everlastingly (i.e. *beginninglessly* no less than endlessly) in process of change'.[3] But ἀεί is as indeterminate as to the duration over which it extends as is the English 'always' (which is the way Cornford himself renders ἀεί in his translation of the phrase). In this context it could cover just as well, *A*, a duration which has no beginning and end, as *B*, one which does have a beginning but goes on for ever after.[4] How then could it be taken as telling the reader that the former is meant? How could Plato be expected to communicate, '*A*, not *B*,' by flashing a signal which could be read as either '*A*' or '*B*'?

(v) We read at 37d 2–7:

> Now the nature of *Animal* (ἡ τοῦ ζῴου φύσις: the essence or Platonic form) was αἰώνιος and it was not possible for a generated thing to attain this (character) fully (παντελῶς). So he took thought to make a sort of moving image of αἰών: simultaneously with his ordering of the Heaven he makes of αἰών which abides in unity an αἰώνιος image proceeding according to number.

Cherniss comments (I intersperse the numerals): 'Since in this very sentence Plato says that (1) the copy could not be αἰώνιος as the model is (37d 3–4), it appears (2) to be an undisguised self-contradiction to call time an αἰώνιον εἰκόνα, "eternal image" (d 7).' He infers that (3) Plato used this phrase 'with the intention of putting special emphasis upon some characteristic of time which the form of his exposition is inadequate to describe. The

[1] Cf. *Aristotle's Criticism*, Appendix XI.

[2] *Aristotle's Criticism*, 426. Cf. Zeller, 405, n. 40: he thinks there is 'contradiction' (without explaining why) in supposing that the soul of the Demiurge is everlasting while all other souls are created.

[3] P. 26. Cherniss apparently reads the ἀεί at 28a 1 in the same way, *Aristotle's Criticism*, 420.

[4] Cf. Hackforth, 19.

most obvious characteristic of this kind would be unlimited duration, i.e. duration without beginning as well as without end.'[1]—To begin at (1): Plato does not say that the image is not *αἰώνιος*, but that it is not 'fully' or 'perfectly' so. This makes a difference. To say, 'James is not fully educated' is (usually) not the same thing as to say, 'James is not educated.' Plato is alive to this difference. When he says in the *Republic* that no sensibles are *παντελῶς* (or *εἰλικρινῶς*)[2] beautiful, etc., he is not denying that e.g. Helen is beautiful. There is, therefore, (2) no more of a contradiction between saying that time is an *αἰώνιος* image of *αἰών* than there would be in saying that Helen is a beautiful image of Beauty, immediately after admitting, indeed stressing, that she is not *παντελῶς* beautiful. Hence there is no good reason for the inference at (3).[3]

[1] *Aristotle's Criticism*, n. 350.

[2] 477a 3–479d 5. The two terms are used interchangeably for the purpose of the argument of this whole passage: cf. e.g. 477a 3 with a 7, 478d 6–7, and 479d 5, where the same point is being made, *sc.* that only the Form, F, is F *παντελῶς* or *εἰλικρινῶς*, while *F*-particulars are-and-are-not F.

[3] I should add that I cannot believe that Plato had now so changed his use of *αἰώνιος* (cf. *μέθην αἰώνιον*, *Rep.*, 363d) as to reserve it for timelessness in contradistinction to perpetual duration. Plato had indeed now glimpsed—probably for the first time in Western thought—the notion of timeless eternity (H. Cherniss, 'Timaeus 38a 8–b 5,' *Journal of* Hellenic Studies 77, Part I [1957], 18–23, and n. 46). But there is no evidence that he has now made *αἰώνιος* its vehicle, any more than he has put *ἀίδιος* to such a use: he applies *ἀΐδιος* to the created star-gods (37c, 40b) no less than to the timeless ideas (37e). *αἰώνιον* is applied to the gods in *Laws* 904a 8–b 1, if it is read, 'that (human) body and soul are (each of them: cf. b 1–2), when generated, indestructible, but not (as a composite unity) everlasting, as are the legal gods,' which I take to be the most likely reading: As England says *ad loc.* it is 'simplest' to take *καθάπερ οἱ κατὰ νόμον ὄντες θεοί* 'as applying only to *αἰώνιον*. 'The gods of the established religion were, like men, souls with a bodily shape, but in their case no dissolution was possible,' referring to *Tim*, 41b and 43a 2. There is point in contrasting men with gods in this respect in this passage, where transmigration (union with different bodies in the course of a single soul's *αἰών*), a fatality afflicting men but not gods, is in the offing (904c 6–905a 1). It is hard to see what point there would be in coupling men with gods as indestructible-but-not-eternal, on one of the alternative readings (Bury, Diès), or in coupling men with gods as indestructible, while disclaiming eternity for men without reference to the gods (Apelt, Taylor), on the other. It is worth remembering that the sense of an extended duration (as distinct from durationless eternity) would be hard to dislodge from *αἰώνιος* (= 'lasting for an *αἰών*'); a human lifetime had been the typical instance of

III

What then of motions, etc., occurring before the creation of time? Is there not a deliberate contradiction here?—I said, No, in *D.M.T.* (Section III), and I stand by that answer. I can now make it clearer and rid it of some minor errors. I echoed there uncritically Cornford's ascription of a 'cyclical concept of time' to Plato. This is a treacherous expression which can mean two quite different things:

(i) that time is 'conceived, not as a straight line, but as a circle' (*Plato's Cosmology*, 103):
(ii) that it is 'inseparable from periodic motion' (ibid.).

Here (i) is false: though time is *imaged* as a circle (κυκλουμένου, 38a 8),[1] it is not so *conceived*: Plato did not believe that, e.g. yesterday's happenings will happen again at some time in the future. On the other hand, (ii) is both true and fundamental. Let me restate what this implies:

Time 'proceeds according to number' (37d 6–7), i.e. its passage, or flow, can be numbered. But what does that mean? To number a discrete aggregate, like a herd of cows, is to count it. But time is a continuous magnitude. How could this be counted?—Only if first broken up into discrete units. If these are contiguous and of uniform length their count would measure the temporal length they compose. Plato gives us three sets of such units: day-nights, months, years,[2] corresponding to conspicuous heavenly periodic motions. These motions he connects so closely with time that, as I said in *D.M.T.*, he 'seems to identify them with time'. Cherniss objected,[3] and rightly so. When Plato speaks of the stars

[1] As the context shows, the 'circling' is done not by time itself, but by its measures, the celestial revolutions. The same thing, in spite of some unclarity of expression, is said by Aristotle in *Phys.*, 223b 24–33.

[2] He calls these 'parts' (μέρη) of time, 37e 3, meaning that any given temporal interval would be made up of the number of contemporaneous day-nights or months or years whose count gives us the interval's measure.

[3] *Aristotle's Criticism*, 418, and n. 349.

αἰών (cf. Liddell and Scott, Lexicon, *s.v.* αἰών). Cf. E. Fränkel's gloss on τὸν δι' αἰῶνος χρόνον in *Agamemnon*, 554, *Aeschylus' Agamemnon*, II. (Oxford, 1950), 278.

as created 'to mark off and preserve the numbers (i.e. the numerable measures) of time' (38c 6), he is certainly distinguishing (though only implicitly)[1] the siderial clocks from time itself as measures from the thing measured. But neither could we ascribe to him the sort of distinction which would imply that the thing measured could exist in the absence of its measures: everyone would agree that a Newtonian notion of 'absolute, true, and mathematical time, (which) of itself, and from its own nature, flows equably without relation to anything external'[2] is far from his thoughts. He could not have spoken, even loosely, of the stars 'producing time' (38e 4–5) or being 'made that time might be generated' (38c 4) unless he was taking it for granted that the very existence of uniform time-flow depends on the existence of uniform periodic motions which could serve as its measures.[3] This then is what the Craftsman brought into the world: *uniform and measurable time-flow*. Let us call this 'time(U)'.

Now to say that *this* is what the Craftsman created is a very different thing from saying that he introduced temporal succession, or time-flow as such, into the world. This possibility is absolutely excluded by the statement that the Craftsman made time in order to make the world 'still more like the (eternal) model' (37c 8):[4] had there been no temporal passage before creation, matter would have been totally immune from flux and

[1] The distinction becomes explicit in Aristotle: in *Phys.*, 219a 8–9 we have the disjunction, 'time is either motion or something that belongs to motion (τῆς κινήσεώς τι),' but the first disjunct is eliminated at b 1–3: 'For this is time: the number of motion with respect to before and after. Hence time is not motion but that in virtue of which motion has number (ἀλλ' ᾗ ἀριθμὸν ἔχει ἡ κίνησις),' and at 220b 8–9, 'But time is a number—not that with which we number, but that which is numbered.'

[2] *Philosophiae Naturalis Principia Mathematica*, Scholium to the first seven definitions, *ad init.*

[3] In this respect Plato's conception of time is vastly more modern (though also vastly vaguer) than Newton's. On the other hand, he would not have said that 'the question of uniform time (is) not a matter of cognition, but of definition. . . . There is no really uniform time; we call a certain flow of time uniform in order to have a standard to which we can refer other kinds of time-flow' (H. Reichenbach, *The Rise of Scientific Philosophy* (Berkeley, 1951), 146–7). Plato would insist that there *is* uniform time—the one defined by the standard fixed for us by the Demiurge when he established the celestial revolutions. Aristotle would have agreed.

[4] And a 'moving image of eternity' (37d 5), imaging it, obviously, not in its incessant change, but in the invariance of its rate of change.

would thus have had the absolute stability of the Ideas;[1] and in that case the creation of time would have made it far *less* like the Ideal model, than it would otherwise have been. But *could* there be temporal passage in the absence of time(U)?—Certainly. We can conceive perfectly of a state of affairs where events exhibit the irreversible order of past and future (so that, e.g. if X is in Y's past, nothing in X's past can occur in Y's future) but where uniform periodic motions are non-existent and time cannot be measured (if A, B, C, are successive instants we would have no means of telling if the interval, AB, is as long as the interval, BC, or longer, or shorter). This is precisely Plato's primitive chaos: no regular motions there, hence no temporal yardsticks, hence no time(U); but there is still *irreversible temporal succession*, which we may call 'time(S)'. Had Plato drawn this distinction and stuck to it he could have asserted the creation of time (i.e. of time(U)) without running afoul of that contradiction 'no sane man' could commit which made Taylor so sure that creationism could not be seriously meant.[2] So far as I can see, there is no contradiction in any of these suppositions: that disorderly motions occur *in the absence of time*(U); that they occur *prior to* time(U); that time(U) was brought into existence by a creative act which did not itself occur *in* time(U).

Did Plato see all this? To be more precise: did he see, and see clearly, the crucial proposition that time(S) is instantiable in the absence of time(U)?—Let me begin by pointing out that, at any rate, he *did not deny* this proposition. There is one sentence from which one might easily get the impression that he did mean to deny it: '. . . and "was" and "shall be" are generated characters of time (χρόνου γεγονότα εἴδη), which we do wrong to transfer unthinkingly to the eternal essence' (37e 4–5). Are we to take this to mean that the difference between past and future comes into existence only when 'time' (i.e. time(U)) is made?—If so, we would be going beyond what the text strictly tells us: that past and

[1] A hypothesis which would violate the first axiom of Platonic metaphysics that the sensible is, of its very nature, in constant flux (reasserted emphatically in the *Timaeus* 27d 6 ff., 48d, 52a). So I cannot understand why Cherniss should hold that, in the absence of soul, the reflections of the Ideas on space would be purely 'static' (*Aristotle's Criticism*, 454). How so, if as he himself remarks, 'the continuous flux of sensible phenomena is a *datum* of Plato's philosophy from first to last . . .' (ibid., 438, his italics)?

[2] Cf. his *Commentary to the Timaeus*, 69. Cf. p. 385 above.

future come into existence when (but not *only* when)[1] time does so, as attributes of time. To say that *F* and *G* come into existence as attributes of *x* when *x* comes into existence is uninformative as to any prior instantiation of *F* and *G*. The statement would be true regardless of whether *F* and *G* have been instantiated millions of times earlier (as e.g. the sweetness and redness 'generated' in this ripe cherry *and* in innumerable others in times past) or never before (as in the case of certain destructive features of the Hiroshima bomb). It is the context then that must decide for us whether by χρόνου γεγονότα εἴδη here Plato means both (*a*), 'generated now as attributes of time(U)' *and* (*b*), 'never generated as attributes of anything prior to time(U),' or just (*a*). The context tells for the latter on two counts:

(i) In the preceding period (e 1–3) features of time(U) which did not exist prior to its creation—day-nights, months, years—were specifically acknowledged as 'not existing before the heaven was generated.' Had Plato wanted to say also that past and future did not exist πρὶν οὐρανὸν γενέσθαι he would have surely said so then, or brought them in thereafter under the same description. It is most unlikely that Plato would have wanted to slip in unobtrusively a thought so novel and so momentous as that the distinction between 'was' and 'shall be' did not apply to events anteceding the creation of our cosmos.

(ii) As Hackforth (22) reminded us, the purpose of the present sentence (37e 4–5) is to contrast time not with the pre-cosmic state of matter but with the timeless eternity of the Ideas; its point then could not be the inapplicability of 'was' and 'shall be' to antecedent occurrences (to which the sentence makes no reference) but to the eternal essence (to which the reference is direct and emphatic). Hence to stress as strongly as possible that 'they are properly used of becoming which proceeds in time' (38a 1–2), in contrast to the being which is not in process in time, could not be meant to be saying that they are improperly used of what is in process prior to time.

There is no good reason to think then that Plato was *rejecting* the

[1] Not 'only' in 37e 4–5, nor yet in 38a 1–2, 'while "was" and "shall be" are fittingly spoken [not of the eternal essence, but] of becoming which proceeds *in time*—for they are motions.' Cherniss paraphrases, '. . . "was" and "will be", because they are κινήσεις, are properly predictable only of γένεσις which goes on in time' (*Aristotle's Criticism*, n. 362); he does not explain how he got the 'only'.

instantiability of time(S) prior to the creation of time(U). But neither do we have reason to say that he *affirmed* it. He does not say so. Nor is there any evidence that he had made the analysis that would have enabled him to do this by revealing how time (U) was both different from, yet related to, time(S). He is perfectly capable, certainly, of thinking and speaking of time in other contexts in terms of the past/present/future distinction without explicit reference to measurable time-flow: he does so in the *Parmenides* (151e–157b). But there is no indication there, or anywhere else, that he saw precisely how these two concepts are related. We would do well to keep in mind that no one in antiquity succeeded in seeing this—not Aristotle, for example, who wrote more extensively on time, with greater analytical thoroughness, and with knowledge of what Plato had already contributed to the partial exploration of this difficult concept. As I suggested in *D.M.T.* (Section III), the very arguments Aristotle uses against Plato reveal the limits of his own insight. Anyone who thinks he can refute Plato's notion that time had a beginning by arguing, as Aristotle does in *Phys.*, 251b 19–26, that since every 'now' has a 'before', there could be no first 'now', shows that he is unaware that this proves (at most)[1] the beginninglessness of time(S). This of itself suggests that the true relation of time(S) to time(U) has eluded him. And the suggestion becomes a certainty when we note that just before this little argument Aristotle speaks of time as 'either the number of motion or a sort of motion' (251b 12–13),[2] i.e. as time(U), without the slightest indication that, while this is precisely the concept of time whose beginning is asserted by Plato, the one whose beginningless he is about to prove is not this, but time(S).

A similar deficiency of analytic insight mars Plato's account of the creation of time. This is, of course, a far cry from that gross, blatant, and wilful contradiction which could be read by the contemporary reader as a coded message advising him to discount creation-talk as picture-talk. But it is still a blemish, as I stressed in *D.M.T.* (on the basis of a less precise diagnosis of the trouble) and wish to stress again, readverting to what I then took to be the

[1] The premiss that *every* 'now' has a 'before' wants proof. There is no logical reason why time must extend infinitely into the past; if it did not, one 'now' (the first) would have had no 'before'.

[2] Cf. p. 410, n. 1 above.

metaphysical block that helps explain Plato's failure at this point. Had he made the time(U)/time(S) distinction he would have been able to clear up the obscurities of his account to our complete satisfaction—but, unfortunately, not to his. For the idea that the material universe could (and would) have this precise form of temporal order (the transitive, asymmetrical, irreflexive order of a one-dimensional continuum) before creation would have jarred on one of his fixed convictions: that the material universe would have been orderless were it not ordered by a designing Mind. So the most he would have been willing to admit by way of temporal order for that godforsaken nonworld would have been, as I suggested in *D.M.T.*, some sort of vague and unspecified approximation to time, 'traces' of it, a quasi-time as it were.

IV

The creation of soul in the *Timaeus* is in flat contradiction with the doctrine of the *Phaedrus* (though not of the *Laws*)[1] that the soul is uncreated, and appears to contradict also the doctrine of

[1] The *Laws* speaks of the soul as 'the first genesis' (896a 6, 899c 7), 'eldest of all the things that partake of generation' (967d 6–7; for the sense of *γονῆς μετείληφεν* here cf. *γένεσιν παραλαβοῦσα* 966e 1–2, which makes it clear that *γονῆς* = *γενέσεως*, *pace* Cherniss, *Aristotle's Criticism*, n. 365); it says that the soul *προτέραν γεγονέναι σώματος . . . , σῶμα δὲ δεύτερον καὶ ὕστερον*, 896c 1–2. It thus says the same thing (and in the same language) which was said in the *Timaeus* (*γενέσει . . . προτέραν καὶ πρεσβυτέραν ψυχὴν σώματος*, 34c 4–5), where there can be no doubt that the meaning is that the soul *was generated* prior to the body. I cannot see how this can be explained away by arguing with Cherniss, loc. cit., that, as used in the passages in the *Laws*, *genesis* does *not* mean 'generation', but has only the weaker sense of 'process': that Plato should continue to retain in the *Laws* the very language he had used in the *Timaeus* to assert *generation*, but expect it to carry an entirely different meaning which would express a thought *incompatible* with that expressed by the same words in the *Timaeus* is most improbable; I know of no parallel for such behaviour in the Platonic corpus. But even if we were to accept the weaker sense proposed, it would still be impossible to see how Plato could maintain in the *Laws* that the soul is the first process, eldest of things in process, prior in process to the body, if he believed (as Cherniss holds) that both soul and body are beginningless. Moreover, *γένεσιν παραλαμβάνειν* is asserted of the 'motion' of the soul in 966e 1–2, and this can only mean that the motion of the soul was generated (*γένεσιν παραλαμβάνειν*, as asserted of a *κίνησις*, would be a pure redundancy, if *genesis* here meant only 'process'); and since self-motion is of the essence of the soul, if its motion was generated, then *it* was generated.

both the *Phaedrus* and the *Laws* that the soul is the first cause of all motion. Could either of these discrepancies be taken as 'don't-believe-my-creation-talk' signals addressed by Plato to the readers of the *Timaeus*?—That they could not should be all too obvious in the case of discrepancies between the *Timaeus* and the *Laws*. Assuming that Plato knew, when writing the *Timaeus*, that *he was going* to contradict some proposition in it in a later work, he could scarcely have hoped to use this unpublished intention as a means of telling the immediate public of the *Timaeus* to disbelieve that proposition! And the chances of his counting on contradictions between the *Timaeus* and the *Phaedrus* to serve the same purpose are surely not much greater. Could anyone claim in all seriousness that Plato thought his readers would be so certain of the immutability of his philosophical views that if they should happen to find him saying *p* in one work, the mere fact that he had said not-*p* years earlier in another work would give them to understand that he did not really mean *p* when he said *p* in the later work? No one to my knowledge has made such a claim, and I cannot imagine that anyone would. Our inquiry then can be reduced to just this question: Are there any contradictions internal to the *Timaeus* which the reader of this dialogue would find inexplicable on any hypothesis other than that they were planted there to warn him that the creation of the soul is a didactic fiction? There is just one idea in the *Timaeus* that could be thought to produce such contradictions: that the soul is a 'self-moving' thing. This might be taken to contradict

1. the creation of the soul, and
2. pre-cosmic motions uncaused by soul.

I wish to argue that there is no such contradiction in either case.

The reader of the *Timaeus* who remembered how much Plato had made of the soul's power of self-motion in the *Phaedrus* would see that he continues to ascribe the same power the soul. There are several references to it: the thoughts of the World-Soul go on within 'the thing that is self-moved' (37b 5); vegetables are 'fixed and rooted' because their psyche, passively sensitive, but not actively thinking (77e 5–c3), 'has been deprived of self-motion' (77c 4–5); a man wants to induce the most salubrious motions in his body should remember that 'the best of motions is that produced in oneself by oneself, for this is most akin to the movement of thought and of the universe (i.e. of the World-Soul), while motion (produced in one) by another is worse' (89a 1–3). In all three of these texts the soul's power of self-motion is being taken for granted and used, as needed, in a very matter of fact sort of way.[1] The same idea is also implied in 46de, in that important passage where Plato reveals the methodological orientation of his cosmology:

> But the lover of intelligence and knowledge should seek intelligent causes as the first, and only as second (causes) those which, being themselves moved by others, of necessity set yet others in motion (46de).

The latter—inanimate causes, exemplified by 'cooling and heating, compacting or rarefying' (d 2–3)—are identified as *moved-by-others*. Hence the reader of the *Timaeus* would infer at once that the intelligent causes are all *self-moved*.[2]

Would this reader then have cause to find anything which leads to either of the above contradictions? Surely not the first, unless he confused two entirely distinct propositions:

A. The Craftsman generates self-moving souls.
B. He generates the self-motions of self-moving souls.

B is obviously self-contradictory, since the very description of the motion of a given soul as a 'self-motion' entails, in Plato's scheme, that it is caused by just that soul and by no other individual in the universe—hence, *a fortiori*, not by the Demiurge. But *B* is never mooted in the *Timaeus*, where the Craftsman creates souls and then leaves them alone to do their own self-moving for ever after. How then could *A*, once it is clearly distinguished from *B*, involve a contradiction? What is there to keep the Demiurge (assuming he has the wonderful powers of world-creation) from creating entities that have the power of self-moving and, once created, go on to exercise this power to their heart's content?[3]

[1] Cherniss (*Aristotle's Criticism*, 428) speaks of these three texts as 'hints or veiled reminders' of self-motion; they make no such impression on me.

[2] The Aristotelian *tertium quid*, the *unmoved* mover, had not yet been invented.

[3] I cannot see, therefore, that 'had (Plato) declared that the soul is self-motion, he would have ruined the whole structure and form of the *Timaeus*' (429), except (at most) for readers who would assume that he still believes everything he said about the self-motion of the soul in the *Phaedrus*; though

The possibility of the contradiction we are looking for is then narrowed down to the second (2 above). This is where it has been recently found:

> If *psyche* is self-generating motion and thus the first cause of all motion (46e 1), how can the world body be in some motion, however irregular, before the *psyche* is housed in it?[1]

Must psyche be 'the first cause of all motion' if it is 'self-generating motion'? Plato certainly says so in the *Phaedrus* and the *Laws*. But that is not to the point here. What we are now asking is whether *the reader of the Timaeus* would have any reason to think that this is asserted or implied in this dialogue. Professor Gould evidently thinks so, since he refers us, in support, to the lines from 46de I cited above. But these do not say, or imply, that the intelligent causes *generate* or *originate* all the motions of those senseless, soulless causes which we must think 'second'. This never happens in the case of human agency, from which Plato extrapolates his theory of cosmic causation. If the billiard player, *P*, picks up a cue, *C*, to hit a ball, *X*, and thereby cause motion in another ball, *Y*, it might look at first sight as though the 'first' cause here—the self-motion of *P*'s soul—generated all the motions of the 'second' causes (*X* moved by *C* moved by *P*'s hand) which serve as the *συναίτια* of the 'first' cause. But though the cue and the two billiard-balls were motionless to begin with, *P*'s body was not: all

[1] Gould (work cited in n. 5 above), 129.

---

even on readers who had such sublime faith in the unalterability of his views the effect could hardly be catastrophic, since Plato, as Cherniss recognises, does refer three times to the soul's self-motion in the *Timaeus*. (Such readers, if such there were, were heading for a terrible shock: in the *Laws*, where he is no less insistent on self-motion as the 'essence' of the soul [895e–896a] then he was in the *Phaedrus*, Plato speaks of the soul as generated [p. 414, n. 1 above], while in the *Phaedrus* he had derived its uncreatedness from its self-motion [246a].) In any case, Cherniss' own construction of the facts—when writing the *Timaeus* Plato, believing that the soul's self-motion implies its beginninglessness, suppresses a declaration of self-motion which would remind the reader of this implication, expecting 'that this suppression itself, especially when set in relief by his hints at the doctrine suppressed, would make the mythical character of the creation all the more obvious to his audience', ibid., 431—is hard to square with another fact, of which Cherniss, with admirable candour, reminds us in this context: Xenocrates, the protagonist of the mythical interpretation, completely missed this signal (loc. cit., and n. 366).

sorts of motions were taking place within it, which the self-motion of his soul did not originate, but was able to control and redirect so as to make the body execute the desired movement of the cue. What then of those cosmic 'first causes' which explain the constitution of our world and all its creatures? These are presumably the self-motions of the Craftsman's soul. Are *they* supposed to originate the motions of their physical *synaitia*? If Plato wanted to say any such thing he could have said it perfectly within the framework of his 'myth': he need only have pictured the Craftsman starting off with a motionless, inert, lump of matter.[1] He chooses instead to have this raw-material in ceaseless agitation before the Craftsman 'ordered it with forms and numbers' (53b). The self-motions of his soul then, no less than ours, supervene on material motions which he does not generate but only harnesses to the fulfillment of his creative purposes.

Would we have any cause to find this in contradiction with what we were told in 46de? How could we? The injunction we were given there—to pursue intelligent causes as the first, and inanimate ones as the second—works perfectly within the created world, where intelligent causes are always at work. But when, at Plato's bidding, we venture beyond the world to the antecedent chaos, we see that the injunction is useless: it is no use looking for intelligent causes as 'the first' in an area in which they do not exist. Here we must content ourselves with a purely physical cause of motion, *sc.* the 'irregularity' (ἀνωμαλότης) of the material medium. This may cause us disappointment and annoyance, since Plato's methodological maxims have accustomed us to believe that only when an intelligent cause is located will a fully intelligible explanation be achieved. But can we complain of contradiction? Has Plato told us that *every* motion admits of a fully intelligible explanation?—Quite the opposite. Immediately after distinguishing the two kinds of causes, Plato went on to tell us that the causes of the second type, 'when isolated from intelligence, produce particular effects which are random and without order' (μονωθεῖσαι φρονήσεως τὸ τυχὸν ἄτακτον ἑκάστοτε ἐξεργάζονται) 46e 5–6. So there must be some occurrences which are not fully susceptible of rational explanation, and we are to expect these whenever the second type of cause operates in isolation from the first. And this is precisely the condition of the primal chaos, since

[1] As Gould himself points out, loc. cit. and n. 44. Cf. Herter, 331.

it is as 'isolated from intelligence' as anything could possibly be. Hence it *must* frustrate our ideal of perfect intelligibility and *must* fall within the exclusive domain of the second type of cause. Hence the origination of its motions by the self-motions of soul, so far from being implied by what is said in 46de, is positively excluded by it.

In his little book, *Plato* (London, 1908), A. E. Taylor had voiced the conviction that

> Plutarch is right in maintaining that the theory of the eternity of the world can only be read into Plato by a violent and unnatural exegesis which strains the sense of the most obvious expressions in the interest of a foregone conclusion (143).

I would not myself so speak of a hypothesis which has commended itself to the finest Platonic scholarship of the second half of the nineteenth century and the first half of the twentieth. I have never thought of it as a pre-conception forced on the facts. I would readily grant that Zeller, Cornford, Cherniss and others[1] gave it their allegiance only because they thought it the hypothesis which makes the best sense of our difficult textual data. All I have done here and in *D.M.T.* is to offer reasons why, for all its undoubted merits, the hypothesis is probably false.

[1] Including Taylor himself in his *Commentary*—just twenty years later!

XIX

NECESSITY AND PERSUASION IN PLATO'S *TIMAEUS*[1]

(1950)

Glenn R. Morrow

> The generation of this cosmos came about through a combination of necessity and intelligence, the two commingled. Intelligence, controlling necessity, persuaded her to lead towards the best the greater part of the things coming into being; and in this way this universe was constructed from the beginning, through necessity yielding to intelligent persuasion.—*Timaeus* (48a).

THIS passage is generally recognised as asserting something of central importance in Plato's cosmology. But precisely what it intends to assert is not at first sight clear. The language is suggestive of mythology, with its latent personification of Ananke, Peitho, and Nous. We are told at the beginning of Timaeus' discourse that the story of creation is a myth. Perhaps, then, this passage is merely a poetical reference to a problem that needs to be solved, rather than the statement of a solution. For if we take it literally it presents a paradox. What has persuasion to do with the processes of nature? And what kind of necessity is this that can be persuaded? I believe, however, that these difficulties largely disappear and a clear-cut doctrine emerges from this passage when it is understood in the light of the problem with which Plato is confronted in the *Timaeus*.

Any conception of the cosmos that makes teleology fundamental, as Plato's does, has to meet two somewhat different types

[1] Read before a meeting of the Fullerton Club, in Bryn Mawr, October 8, 1949.

of criticism. There are difficulties of faith, and again there are logical difficulties. Plato, as we know, thinks of this cosmos as 'the fairest of creations'. It is for him a living, intelligent being, consciously imitating in space and time the divine and supersensible world of Ideas. Being a creature in space and time, it cannot, of course, be a perfect imitation of the supersensible pattern; nevertheless it exhibits its likeness to that pattern in the orderliness of the celestial movements and in the mathematical perfection of its spherical form. These regular celestial circuits are a 'moving image' of that eternity that characterises true being. Likewise the lesser parts of this visible cosmos, including man, are fashioned 'with a view to the best'. Man is endowed with an intelligent soul, akin to the soul of the cosmos. Man's soul is lodged in a bodily frame that exposes him to innumerable distractions and passions, yet still provides means to facilitate the victory of intelligence over disorder. Thus the organs of vision are given to man that he may behold the courses of the heavens and so attain to philosophy, 'than which no greater gift has been or could be conferred by God upon the mortal race'. Speech and hearing have similar ends; they serve as allies of reason against the disorder within and without us, so that we may be able to imitate the divine craftsman by bringing into order and harmony that portion of the visible world that is under our control.

These are some of the more important elements of what I should call Plato's cosmic faith. The *Timaeus* is an impressive record of this faith; it is, as Shorey has said, 'the chief source of cosmic emotion in European literature'.[1] And its appeal is little affected, for those to whom it does appeal, by the change from the finite spherical universe of the ancients to the still finite but unbounded and perhaps expanding universe of modern physics. It would seem, however, rather futile to argue much with those to whom it does not appeal. Final convictions on such matters depend so much on conceptions of value and on ultimate attitudes towards the world—whether of trust or mistrust, of loyalty or defiance—that probably no parade of empirical evidence will ever be adequate to justify the belief of those who believe or overcome the objections of those who doubt.

But there is another kind of problem raised by the *Timaeus* which is both more fundamental and more susceptible of philo-

[1] *Platonism Ancient and Modern*, p. 92.

sophical argument. Plato thinks of this cosmos as the product of intelligent design. Now if intelligent design is a genuine cause of natural processes, how are we to formulate its relation to the other causes involved in these processes? Nature, as her picture is being drawn for us by modern science in increasing fullness of detail, is a texture of events, each of which is determined by antecedent events, or at least follows upon antecedent events in accordance with causal laws that have a high degree of statistical reliability. This picture of nature affords no little satisfaction to our minds; it is intelligible. If a designing intelligence is also involved in all this or in any part of it, we should be able to fit its operations into the picture without destroying the intelligibility of the whole. The problem, to state it pointedly, is how to make the working of intelligence intelligible. The difficulty of this problem, as well as its importance, is well attested by the numerous attempts to solve it in modern philosophy and by the lack of any assured and accepted solution. This, I believe, more than any absence of cosmic emotion or cosmic faith, is the real reason why philosophers and scientists today are reluctant to make commitments to teleology. Whatever may be our beliefs about the beneficence of the world order, we can have no clear title to them if we cannot show that design is at least thinkable alongside of causal sequence.

And it should be remembered that this problem concerns more than the validity of our beliefs about the presence or absence of *cosmic* purpose. By the same argument we are not entitled to believe in the efficacy of purpose in any part of the natural order unless we can show that purposive activity is thinkable. When the tailor makes me a suit of clothes or the mechanic repairs my automobile, I cannot really say that there is any purpose, or intelligent design, in these activities until I have shown, at least to my own satisfaction, how intelligent design *can* enter into events. Conversely, if we can form an intelligible picture of the working of purpose in these familiar spheres of design, then cosmic teleology cannot be ruled out, as it sometimes is, merely on the ground that purpose is incompatible with the causal order. We all do in fact believe that intelligent design occurs, at least in human affairs. An age that is addicted, as ours is, to thoughts of 'planning' cannot be described as committed to a nonteleological version of nature—for man, we also believe, is a part of nature. There is a pathetic confusion in contemporary thought. We talk confidently about a 'design for living', a 'planned economy', and 'social engineering', while our theories of nature and human nature are steadily making less conceivable the control by intelligence which these visions presuppose.

But this confusion is not a peculiarly modern phenomenon. A similar dilemma confronted Plato's contemporaries, and it is Plato's appreciation of this dilemma that underlies his cosmology in the *Timaeus* and gives point to the solution at which he arrives. The succession of pre-Platonic cosmologists, from Thales to Democritus, has been described, not unfairly, as exhibiting a steady development from 'animism' to 'mechanism'. The interest in the mechanics of nature was by no means universal among these thinkers, nor was the conception of mechanism always clear to those for whom it was the predominant concern. Yet it does receive clear formulation and exclusive importance in the latest of these pre-Platonic cosmologies, that of Leucippus and Democritus. The atomic theory which they set forth pictures the cosmos as the necessary and undesigned result of the collisions of eternally moving particles of solid being. In this world everything happens 'of necessity', as Democritus says, and all purpose is excluded. Now Democritus also constructed an ethical system, which so far as we can understand it has very little connection with his physics. He advises us to moderate our desires, to choose the pleasures that lead to cheerfulness, and to follow a number of other precepts that credit us with a degree of freedom and intelligent self-control that his physics would rule out. Democritus, we see, exhibits the same order of confusion that may be found in almost any well-bred scientist of today.

If we require evidence that Plato saw this confusion, we need only turn to the well-known passage in the *Phaedo* (96a–99c) where Socrates gives an account of his early interest in these 'inquiries into nature' and expresses his eventual dissatisfaction with them because they took no account of the good'. This passage contains most of the principles that Plato was later to use in the *Timaeus*, and therefore it is well to state them systematically. First there is the distinction (99b) between the 'real cause' (*τὸ αἴτιον τῷ ὄντι*) and the conditions or factors 'without which the cause would not be a cause' (*ἐκεῖνο ἄνευ οὗ τὸ αἴτιον οὐκ ἄν ποτ' εἴη αἴτιον*). For example, Socrates' bones and muscles are necessary conditions, but not the true cause, of his conduct during those last days; the true cause is the fact that he deemed it 'better' to remain and drink the hemlock (98e). Secondly, there is the recognition that an explanation in terms of necessary conditions is true and important, though not adequate. 'If you say,' says Socrates, 'that without these things, i.e. bones and muscles and the like, I would not be able to do what seemed best to me, you would be speaking the truth' (99a). In other words, these secondary causes are necessary; and it is implied that a knowledge of them would often be a good thing to have. Thirdly, there is the emphatic analogy between explaining Socrates' actions and explaining the cosmos. Just as bones and muscles are insufficient to account fully for Socrates' being in prison, so also in cosmology we need more than the 'vortex' (δίνη) of Anaxagoras (99b–c). In the one case as in the other, it is necessary to take account of the good if we would fully understand. And lastly, there is the pregnant assertion with which the passage closes—that the good operates by 'binding things together' (99c)—a phrase which will become clear from the *Timaeus*.

The distinction made in the *Phaedo* between the true cause and the conditions without which it could not operate becomes in the *Timaeus* a distinction between two kinds of causes. The true cause, sometimes called the divine or intelligent cause, is an agency working for the best. This agency is described as a craftsman (δημιουργός)—a designation that has often been regarded as primarily poetical or mythical, but which, as will be shown, has a very literal meaning. But like any other craftsman, the cosmic demiurge uses materials; and these materials and their natures are obviously an important factor in determining what kind of product he can fashion from them. They also are causes, but in a secondary sense —συναίτια, 'auxiliary causes' they are designated in the *Timaeus* (46c–d).[1] 'We must deal with both kinds of causes,' says Timaeus, 'on the one hand, those that are intelligent artificers of the good and beautiful, and on the other hand those that without intelligence produce in every case disordered and chance effects' (46e).

This is the programme of inquiry which Timaeus actually follows and in a manner so emphatic as to show itself in the very structure of the dialogue. In the first part of his discourse, Timaeus is primarily concerned with the operations and intentions of the demiurge. He discusses why the creator created a world at all,

[1] Cf. also 68e, 76d.

why he made it one and spherical and endowed it with a soul guided by intelligence. Then he describes the operations of this world soul and the mathematical proportions that give it its character. Then follows an account of the generation of man and of the benevolent intentions of the demiurge manifested in man's bodily frame and in the harmonious proportions of his soul. So far the materials on which the creator works have been taken for granted, without analysis. Only at the end of this section, in the discussion of vision and the bodily mechanism through which it takes place, do the secondary or auxiliary causes begin to receive attention. At this point (48a) Timaeus breaks the course of his exposition and makes what he calls a 'new beginning', in order to take account 'of the nature of fire, and water, and air, and earth, such as they were prior to the creation of the heaven'. These are, of course, the primary bodies out of which Plato's predecessors had constructed their worlds. Whether they are really primary or not remains to be seen; but Plato accepts them provisionally and attributes to them certain inherent qualities or powers (δυνάμεις), as his predecessors had done. These materials and their inherent powers are the auxiliary causes with which the demiurge works and whose co-operation with him he has to effect. They constitute what Plato calls 'necessity' or 'the things that occur of necessity' (τὰ δι' ἀνάγκης, 47e). Finally, after the analysis of these primary materials is completed, comes the third part of the dialogue (69–92), in which Timaeus brings together the auxiliary and the intelligent causes and shows how they co-operate, the former in the service of the latter, to produce the more complex structures in nature, particularly the human body.

Let us now see how Plato conceives of these materials and their powers and how they operate when not under the influence of intelligence. To one who knows the speculations of Plato's predecessors, it is a familiar world that presents itself to the demiurge when he begins his ordering activity. It is a world of powers in unstable equilibrium and in continuous motion, a world of things being pushed by others and being compelled, since there is no void, to push others in turn. We find the four traditional primary bodies—earth, air, fire, and water—and the familiar 'opposites' of pre-Socratic thought—the wet and the dry, the hot and the cold, the dense and the rare. As a result of the continuous motion, the dense and heavy things tend to become segregated from the rare and lighter things. More particularly, each of the primary bodies has a tendency to move, or be thrust, towards its kindred element. Aggregates in turn are dissolved through the working of the powers thus brought into play against one another. There is indeed one factor of considerable novelty in Plato's account. He advances a theory that the differences between the four primary bodies are due to differences of geometrical configuration. If this be true, the ultimate elements are not the four primary bodies, but the triangular plane surfaces of which they are composed. This theory enables Plato to explain the apparent transformation of air, fire, and water into one another; and this transformation in turn explains why it is that all the air and all the water and all the fire and all the earth are not segregated into four separate regions of space, as would naturally result from the forces hitherto mentioned.

These are the materials and powers that constitute what Plato calls the 'works of necessity'. What is the meaning of this designation? The term necessity was chosen, so it seems, because that is the name of the cause which Plato's predecessors—in particular Leucippus and Democritus—had found here. But it was not simply a convenient, because familiar, designation. For Plato also this world of earth, air, fire, and water in perpetual motion and interchange was a realm of genuine necessity, as Democritus understood the term; it was a world in which effects follow regularly upon certain known forces at work. Given *A*, then we can expect *B*. The attempt has been made[1] to show that what Plato meant by necessity here was that special sense of the term which Aristotle calls 'hypothetical necessity'. For example, if a saw is to cut, it must be made of iron. If *B* is to occur, we must have *A* first. According to this interpretation, the necessity that characterises this world before intelligence comes into play is simply its necessity as a means to the ends that intelligence would produce. Now there is no doubt that Plato did think of these materials and forces as necessary means for the realisation of the creator's intentions. But this cannot be all that he meant. What this

[1] Baeumker, *Das Problem der Materie in der griechischen Philosophie*, pp. 115–26 (cf. especially pp. 120–1). This discussion is cited with approval by Taylor, *Commentary on Plato's Timaeus*, p. 303. Other discussions of Plato's 'necessity' will be found in Cornford, *Plato's Cosmology*, 161–77; and in Rivaud's edition of the *Timaeus*, pp. 64–5. Of these various views, that of Cornford comes nearest to the interpretation advanced in this paper.

interpretation overlooks is that definite dependable structure and behaviour must be a characteristic of these means if they are to be usable for the creator's ends. It is the presence of these dependable natures and the regularity of the effects they produce upon one another that Plato means by necessity.

The proof that Plato means this is the thoroughness with which he analyses these powers and their effects. From page 48 to the end of the dialogue, the greater part of the *Timaeus* is concerned with the analysis of these 'works of necessity', in all sorts of combinations. Indeed one reason for the greatness of the *Timaeus*, as compared with most idealistic cosmologies, is the seriousness and thoroughness with which Plato treats of the auxiliary causes. He shows how they produce the motions of the primary bodies and the transformations of these bodies into one anther; and how they give rise to the variety of fluids, metals, and other earthen materials. He traces their operation in the phenomena of melting and cooling, of freezing and thawing, in the production of the qualities of hot and cold, heavy and light, as well as tastes, odours, sounds, colours, and the feelings of pleasure and pain. He shows how they are involved in the structure of the human body, with its bone, marrow, flesh, and sinews. Through them he explains the mechanism of respiration, the movement of the blood and other body fluids, and the various diseases that afflict the human frame. Crude as these explanations often are, when compared with the more refined natural science of our time, there is an unmistakable quest for precision in Plato's procedure. In dealing with these natural processes, whether they occur with or without the guidance of intelligence, he tries to picture as clearly as possible the particular way in which the operating powers produce, or could be conceived as producing, the observed effects. In short, the world on which the creator sets to work is characterised by necessity in the sense that specific effects follow regularly from specific causes. It is because this is true that the creator can use these works of necessity for his purposes.

But how does the intelligent cause use the works of necessity to accomplish his purposes? Here we must come to terms with the metaphor of the craftsman. This is indeed a metaphor, and a bold one, when applied to cosmic design. But it ceases to be a metaphor when we recall that intelligent design has its humbler manifestations. The fundamental philosophical problem, as was insisted upon earlier, is to explain the relation of intelligent purpose to the causal order; and the activity of any craftsman, in the literal sense of the term, is just such an instance of what we are in the habit of calling intelligent design. Plato's statement of the case, then, springs from universal and familiar human experience in guiding the works of necessity to an end we regard as good. How can this experience be made intelligible? If we can show that craftsmanship is possible anywhere, in however humble and limited a measure, we have removed what is probably the main philosophical obstacle to the assumption of cosmic purpose.

Remembering then that the demiurge is not merely a cosmic metaphor, but the simple description of a prima facie fact, let us repeat our question. How does intelligence enter into the stream of events? Plato's answer is that intelligence 'persuaded' necessity.[1] This looks like another metaphor and at first sight a very inapt one. It appears to go haltingly, if at all, with the idea of craftsmanship, which is certainly fundamental. But let us see. Persuasion is of course contrasted with compulsion.[2] Every competent craftsman knows that he cannot force his materials to take on forms or perform functions that go against their nature. But an intelligent craftsman makes no attempt to do the impossible. What he does is to select among the materials available those best adapted to his purpose; and these he handles with discrimination, utilising certain of their powers, while ignoring or subordinating the others. When he has to use materials with undesirable properties, he may introduce other materials with opposite powers to counteract the unwanted ones. It may be objected that there is, nevertheless, compulsion. Does not the carpenter use force when he saws wood into appropriate lengths or hammers boards together with pegs? This is true; but to see the situation correctly we must extend the scope of our analysis. When sawing or hammering, the carpenter uses tools with definite powers. These tools he cannot force; he has to rely upon the severing power of sharpened steel, the flattening and impelling power of the hammer head.

[1] Besides the passage quoted at the beginning of this paper, cf. also 56c, 75b.

[2] This and the following paragraph are an expanded version of an interpretation advanced in my introduction to an edition of the *Timaeus* published by the Liberal Arts Press. Certain sentences and phrases are reprinted here with the permission of the publisher.

He is bringing one set of powers into play against others. But, we may ask again, what about the motion of the saw and the hammer? Here the carpenter is using still other powers distinct from intelligence, this time the powers of his own body—his arms and hands and their intricate leverages moved by muscular contractions. This is another set of powers resident in the materials at his disposal and brought into the context of the event. The result —the mast or the spear shaft—is the product of intelligence, but certainly not of any constraint by intelligence. Rather, it comes about easily and naturally from the co-operation of all these forces each of which produces the effects that could be expected from the nature it has. So much at least is suggested by the metaphor of persuasion.

But persuasion is a term that suggests rhetoric, and we know that in the *Gorgias* Plato was severely critical of the so-called art of persuasion cultivated by the sophists and politicians of his day. He says, in fact, that it is not an art at all, but a mere sham, fundamentally immoral in its effects. But this was not his final word on the subject. In a later dialogue, the *Phaedrus*, he himself sets forth the principles of a genuine art of persuasion, as distinguished from the insincere and superficial 'art' expounded in the usual manuals of rhetoric. Two things the orator must have, Plato says, if he is to be a master of his art. He must know the good, the end he wishes to accomplish; and secondly, he must know the souls of his hearers, so as to appeal effectively to their particular interests and purposes. Rhetoric is psychagogy, the art of leading souls. There follows (270d–272b) a discussion of the types of souls, of how necessary it is for the orator to be able to distinguish these types and to know what kind of arguments to use for each, and when and on what occasion to use each of these arguments. When a man knows all this, then, and not till then, is he a master of the art of persuasion. Is there not more than an analogy between this art of psychagogy and the procedure of the intelligent craftsman in dealing with his materials? As the latter must know his wood and stone and metal tools if he wishes to use them intelligently for his ends, so the orator must know his human auditors, so as to employ effectively the motives in them to further the purpose he wishes to see realised. Persuasion, in its broadest sense, is the technique of intelligence. It is the proper means for accomplishing what we will with others—whether inanimate materials or thinking men—by understanding them so thoroughly that we can use the forces inherent in them to bring about the end we desire.

To say, then, that the cosmos comes about by persuasion means that it results from the working of the powers inherent in the materials of which it consists, each of them bringing into being the effects natural to itself, and none of them being under any constraint by a power outside nature. Nowhere within the series of events will we find any place where intelligence operates as a *deus ex machina* to subvert the natural sequence or replace the natural powers by powers or agencies of a different sort. There are stresses and conflicts within the system of nature, where one natural force is met and counteracted by another natural force; but there will not be conflicts between nature and intelligence. Precisely because the world has come about in this fashion, it is easy to assume that intelligence is not a factor, just as the work of art produced by a master seems to spring from the very nature of the material, and just as the playing of a well-coached team appears to be but the inevitable result of the spontaneous powers of the several players.

Where, then, is the rôle of intelligence? The answer is already obvious, and I believe it is the answer that Plato clearly indicates. Intelligence is responsible, not for the specific effects of any given power or set of powers, but for bringing together these specific powers into such juxtapositions and collocations that their joint natural effects are good, or at least better than would have been the isolated effects of the powers working in separation from one another. As our account of the carpenter shows, what the craftsman does is to bring together into the context of one event a variety of powers that would, in isolation, produce unrelated and irrelevant effects; but together they produce, with equal necessity, an object that expresses his purpose. If this is the way intelligence works in the region of everyday craftsmanship, there is no call to imagine a cosmic intelligence, if there be any, as operating in any different fashion.

Let us see whether this interpretation fits what Plato says elsewhere about the working of intelligence. He frequently describes the activity of the intelligent cause as bringing about order in what was before a disordered world. 'Finding the whole visible world . . . moving in an irregular and disorderly fashion, out of disorder he brought order' (30a).[1] This language seems strange when we remember that these materials and their powers are also called the works of necessity. But there can be no doubt that Plato means this realm of necessity is also, in a certain sense, the realm of disorder. Necessity is called 'the wandering cause' (ἡ πλανωμένη αἰτία, 48a); it 'produces chance effects without order' (46e). Yet it is clearly not Plato's idea that this world of materials and powers is chaos, a bedlam in which anything could follow from anything else. This interpretation is excluded, as I have argued above, by the very thoroughness with which Plato has treated of these various powers and their effects. Furthermore, no intelligence that we know of could operate upon such materials, of which nothing had any determinate and reliable character, and no predictions of any sort could be depended upon. We must allow for the imperfections of human knowledge, of which Plato is well aware; but, with this reservation, he is evidently saying that effects follow regularly from observed causes and that expectations based upon such observed sequences are reliable. The reason why this world on which the creator works is called disorderly is not that it lacks causal connections, but that it also exhibits chance (τύχη). The causes at work in it, 'being devoid of intelligence, produce chance effects, without order' (46e). There is a parallel passage in the tenth book of the *Laws*, where Plato is describing the materialist cosmologies of his predecessors; and here we find the same emphasis upon chance as a feature of the materialists' necessity. The primary bodies are moved by 'the chance of their several powers'; and all other things are mixtures of these bodies, resulting 'by chance, and of necessity' (κατὰ τύχην ἐξ ἀνάγκης) from the coming together of opposite forces (889b). It is clear that for Plato both chance and necessity characterise the world prior to the entry of the intelligent cause.

What did Plato understand by chance? He gives us no analysis of this term; but Aristotle analysed it in the second book of his *Physics*, and his analysis may help us to an understanding of Plato's views. The *Physics* is one of Aristotle's earlier works; and this part of it was written, in all probability, before Aristotle left the Academy. Furthermore, there is no hint in this analysis that he is combating Plato or the Platonists. His analysis is evidently directed against popular thought, which tended to make chance a

[1] Cf. also 69b–c.

cause of events, and also against Democritus and Empedocles, who assumed that purposive sequences could be explained without teleology, i.e. by chance. Aristotle's analysis may be summarised as follows. There are some sequences that are invariable, and other sequences that hold 'for the most part'. These two types of sequences are the only ones that can be the subject matter of scientific inquiry; hence chance is excluded as a cause. What then is it? Suppose we have two regular sequences: *A* followed always or usually by *B*, and *C* followed always or usually by *D*, and suppose that on a particular occasion they occur together. Suppose also that this simultaneous occurrence of *B* and *D* is something that serves a purpose and might have been the product of more or less conscious design. This conjunction of *B* and *D*, each the result of its own independent cause, is what constitutes chance.

This analysis shows clearly how Plato could think of both chance and necessity as characters of the world on which the creator works. Necessity is represented by the causal sequences; chance, by the intersection or conjunction of these causal sequences. Aristotle is inclined to use the word τύχη to denote only those conjunctions of effects that are positively desirable or undesirable, just as we use the word luck, or fortune, to mean primarily good luck or bad luck. But the numberless conjunctions that escape our attention, because they neither aid nor hinder us in our purposes, are also examples of chance. Plato's references to the world of necessity suggest this broader conception of chance as any collocation of caused effects, whether relevant to an end or not. The world of necessity is a world of regular causal sequences, a world in which determinate effects follow regularly from specific causes, but a world in which the joint results of these causes are unplanned. What happens when intelligence enters is that certain sequences which we have no reason to regard as necessarily connected with one another do as a matter of fact occur together, and occur together habitually, producing jointly effects which could not have been expected or predicted from any of the individual sequences, but only from their collective occurrence. These joint results are the work of intelligence, and the production of these results is what constitutes the 'ordering' that Nous brings about. Thus to understand the actual world of becoming we need to know not merely the reasons for the effects produced in the several causal lines, but also the reason for the 'convergence'—as we may call it—of these separate lines. The reason for this convergence is the good of the effect produced. Of such an event constituted by converging causal lines, it is quite literally true to say, as Plato had said in the *Phaedo*, that it is the good that 'binds things together', since it is the good that provides the ground for the conjunction of otherwise independent causal sequences.

Such, it would seem, is Plato's conception of the relation of the ordering intelligence to necessity. I have cast it in somewhat modern terminology in order to indicate its relevance to contemporary issues, though without, as I believe, doing violence to Plato's thought. If this be his conception, then the order brought about by intelligence is not a subversion or contravention of the works of necessity. The actual world of concrete becoming is, so to speak, the result of a selection, from among the various possible collocations of causes, of those particular collocations which will most readily serve his purposes. The actual world is only one of many possible worlds, any one of which might have come about by a variation in the modes of co-operation of the works of necessity—just as the spear shaft made by the carpenter is only one of the possible objects that could have resulted from the co-operation of his muscles, his tools, and the wood on which they exert their effects. In none of these possible collocations would there be involved any suspension of causal connections. The actual world is a product of necessity, as Plato says, but of necessity 'yielding to intelligent persuasion'.

Is this an intelligible account? It will perhaps be objected that the convergence of these causal lines cannot occur without some contravention of the causal sequences present in the works of necessity. It will be said that to bring them together into the context of one event is to violate their pre-existent order and mode of operation; and if this is true, the ordering brought about by intelligence is after all a violation of necessity. Let us note precisely what this objection presupposes. It rests on the assumption that the order and arrangement of these primordial forces at any given moment is so related to all other events in the universe that, given the state of affairs at that moment, there is at any other moment of time, whether past or future, only one state of affairs compatible with the given state. This assumption in effect denies that there are independent lines of causation. From the state of the world at any given time, a truly penetrating intelligence could predict, not merely the effect of cause *A* under determinate circumstances and the effect of cause *B* under determinate circumstances, but also the future collocations of *A* and *B* (or more precisely, collocations of empirical instances of *A* and *B*) and the effects of these collocations. In short, the whole future of the world is necessitated in the present forces and their present arrangements. If this is the character of the world on which intelligence operates, then obviously the ordering activity Plato describes as the work of intelligence is ruled out.

This assumption has appealed strongly to both scientists and philosophers in modern times. It would be difficult, however, if not impossible, to show that it is a necessary assumption. It can hardly be regarded as a necessary *a priori* principle, nor again does it seem required as a working principle of scientific inquiry. For Plato, it was not necessary in any sense; on the contrary, it is an assumption incompatible with his basic distinction between the sense world and the intelligible world. To assume that all the events of the cosmos, through all its becoming in time, could be inferred from a temporal cross section would be to ignore both the particularity of things and events and the element of becoming. A world deducible in all its parts from a portion of itself is a world of universals, not particulars—a timeless world, not one in process. Plato believes that the sense world imitates such a timeless world, but is not itself such a world; it is a world in which contingency and real possibility are not only present but inevitably present. In thus regarding strict necessity as a relation, not between things but between ideas, and in insisting on the distinction between the intelligible world and the world of facts and events Plato really seems to be nearer to us than the nineteenth-century determinists. He at least would understand fully Hume's momentous distinction between matters of fact and relations of ideas, as they apparently did not.

Let us return to persuasion. I have tried to show that Plato's use of this term to describe the ordering activity of intelligence is an apt characterisation of the way in which a planned world, as he believes this to be, could be brought about through the works of necessity. It implies that the plan realised in the world process is not one imposed from without, but one that is elicited from the materials involved. It implies just that insight into ends, that understanding of materials, and that manipulation of necessities that characterise genuine craftsmanship. And I have tried to show just what kind of necessity it is that can thus be subject to persuasion. Besides this, there are certain overtones in the term that add to the richness of its significance and throw further light on Plato's cosmology. Persuasion is a slower, but much surer, process than compulsion. Plato's view has been presented, for the sake of simplicity, as if it might imply a single act of intelligent persuasion, effecting a cosmos at one stroke; but the generation of the cosmos is obviously a more prolonged process than this. What we have in the *Timaeus* story is a sequence of ordering acts, beginning with the initial ordering of the four primary bodies, whereby they took on, 'so far as they could be persuaded' (56c), geometrical shapes that would facilitate their transformation into one another, and continuing on to the ordering acts that produce the most complex of organic structures. Now if each of these acts of the creator represents, as I have said, a selection from among the possibilities open to him, we can see that every act of persuasion inevitably reduces the range of future choices, while rendering more secure the basis for future persuasion within the range of possibilities left open. For example, of the multitude of triangles open to his choice, the creator selected two—the halved equilateral triangle and the isosceles right triangle—to be the surfaces of bodies. Once the primal materials have been persuaded to take on these forms, they are henceforth limited in their movements and possible combinations by these acquired shapes. At the same time their behaviour, so to speak, becomes more reliable; and the creator is able to direct his persuasion toward more complicated forms of co-operation. Thus the genesis of the world is the story of successive acts of persuasion, whereby the 'things coming into being' at each step are 'led towards the best', so far as possible, and furnish in turn new possibilities of further acts of intelligent persuasion.

There is also, Plato suggests at several points in the *Timaeus*, an intrinsic good realised by persuasion, a good distinct from the end which the collocation of forces brings about. Persuasion is a process of eliciting co-operation among powers and forces that were previously indifferent, if not hostile, to one another. The creator makes them 'friends' (32c, 88e) and thus produces, not merely a more stable foundation for higher ends, but also an intrinsic good, the kind of good that is essential to any community.

The *Timaeus*, we should remember, was intended to be the first of a trilogy of dialogues; and the two later ones were to deal with human history and politics. The problem of the statesman is essentially a problem of bringing about order and co-operation among his human materials; and he will succeed, Plato tells us repeatedly in the *Laws*, only if he uses persuasion. The divine craftsman therefore sets the example and provides the setting for the activity of the intelligent statesman, by bringing into being a cosmos built upon the friendly co-operation of its varied parts.

Finally, commentators on the *Timaeus* have often wondered about the source of the disorderly motions that prevail before intelligence begins its work. It seems to be a cardinal point in Plato's later philosophy that all motion has its source in soul. The soul is the self-moving, the source of motion, the ἀρχὴ κινήσεως: this is the definition given in the *Phaedrus* and reiterated in the *Laws*. We do not find this doctrine stated in the *Timaeus*, though we are told that soul is present throughout the cosmos, not merely in man and in the celestial bodies, but also as an all-embracing world soul. Furthermore, Plato explicitly distinguishes between intelligent soul and soul devoid of intelligence, and says that irrational soul came into being first. The natural inference is that the disorderly motions upon which intelligence works are due to the irrational parts of the world soul. If this is Plato's intent, then intelligence, in its demiurgic function, is dealing with motions and forces that spring ultimately from soul; and it employs, therefore, the only means of producing a permanent and beneficent effect upon a soul, viz., persuasion. The craft of the demiurge is after all the art of psychagogy.

XX

PLATO'S THEISM

(1936)

R. Hackforth

IN the ontology of the *Philebus* (23c–30e) νοῦς is the αἰτία τῆς συμμίξεως, the cause (called also τὸ δημιουργοῦν and τὸ ποιοῦν) that combines πέρας with ἄπειρον into the mixture called γένεσις εἰς οὐσίαν or γεγενημένη οὐσία: correspondingly in the *Timaeus* the Demiurge, ὁ ἄριστος τῶν αἰτιῶν (29a), brings order into unordered chaos by 'Forms and Numbers' (διεσχηματίσατο εἴδεσι καὶ ἀριθμοῖς 53b). In the *Philebus* the Universe has a Soul, discriminated from the νοῦς that causes it (30b, where it is argued that we cannot imagine that the αἰτία, while it provides our human bodies with a soul, does not 'devise that which is fairest and most precious' in the body of the Universe: οὐ γάρ που δοκοῦμέν γε . . . ἐν τούτοις δ' οὐκ ἄρα μεμηχανῆσθαι τὴν τῶν καλλίστων καὶ τιμιωτάτων φύσιν): correspondingly in the *Timaeus* the Demiurge devises (ἐμηχανήσατο 34c) a soul of the world, as well as its body.

We can hardly avoid drawing the conclusions that (*a*) the Demiurge is to be identified with νοῦς, i.e. he is the 'mythical' equivalent of νοῦς, (*b*) νοῦς is a more ultimate principle than the ψυχὴ τοῦ κόσμου. What I want to consider is how these conclusions square with that section of *Laws* X, in which Plato works out a theological argument designed to refute atheists. It is often said, and is probably the orthodox view, (1) that ψυχή is there treated as an ultimate principle of things and (2) that there is a hierarchy of ψυχαί amongst which one ἀρίστη ψυχή is God in the sense of a single spiritual Being who rules the world with providential care and wisdom. For example, Professor Taylor says (*Commentary on Plato's Timaeus*, p. 82) 'God, in the dialogues, is the ἀρίστη ψυχή . . . the Demiurge of the *Timaeus* is exactly the "best ψυχή" which is said in the *Laws* to be the source of the great orderly cosmic movements, that is, he is God, and if we are to use the word God in the sense it has in Plato's natural theology, the only God there is'.[1]

A careful reading of the *Laws* will, I think, convince us that there is just the same relation implied between the World-soul and νοῦς as in the two earlier dialogues, and further that Plato says nothing to warrant the conception of a hierarchy of souls culminating in a single supreme soul. It is commonly (though not universally) admitted nowadays that Plutarch was wrong in finding in the *Laws* a single 'Devil' or evil World-soul; what has not, I think, been seen, or at all events not emphatically and prominently stated, is that there is no single God or best World-soul either to be found amongst ψυχαί.

The problem is complicated at the outset by Plato's very wide applicaton of θεός. As M. Diès says,[2] many things are called 'Gods' or 'divine': the Demiurge is a θεός, so is the created Universe (*Tim.*, 34b, 92c), so are the stars and planets (*Tim.*, 40d) and the gods of popular theology (*Tim.*, 40e), and the (possible) plurality of good souls in *Laws* X; the adjective θεῖος is commonly applied to the Forms, and if the reading at *Timaeus*, 37c, τῶν ἀιδίων θεῶν γεγονὸς ἄγαλμα, is to be kept, the Forms which are comprised in the νοητὸν ζῷον are actually called gods.[3]

What then shall be our criteria for deciding who, or what, if anything, is Plato's God in the sense in which the word is used by Theists? What is it, if anything, that makes Plato what we call a Theist? I propose to answer this question very dogmatically: 'God' must (1) have independent, not derivative, existence, and (2) be the source, or cause, of all in the Universe that is good,

[1] Cf. Burnet, *Greek Philosophy*, p. 335.

[2] *Autour de Platon*, p. 555. 'Tout est dieu ou divin chez ce trop divin Platon.'

[3] On the assumption, which seems universal, that ἄγαλμα is a mere synonym of εἰκών. But Prof. Cornford suggests to me—and he is surely right—that the οὐρανός, being as yet only a framework of circles or movements, is called the ἄγαλμα of the stars and planets (οὐράνιοι θεοί) which are subsequently to be set in the framework: for the ἄγαλμα of a god is a token or assurance of his presence to the worshipper. This appears to be meant by Proclus when he explains ἄγαλμα as that which 'is filled with deity' (*in Tim.*, III, p. 4, Diehl καθ' ὅλον οὖν ἑαυτὸν ὁ κόσμος πληροῦται θεότητος καὶ διὰ τοῦτο ἄγαλμά ἐστι καθ' ὅλον ἑαυτὸν τῶν νοητῶν θεῶν). The νοητοὶ θεοί are of course a Neoplatonist figment, but there is no difficulty in taking ἀιδίων θεῶν to mean the heavenly bodies in view of 40b, where the fixed stars are called ζῷα θεῖα καὶ ἀίδια.

orderly and rational, but not of what is bad, disorderly and irrational. For this second criterion I may appeal to the first of the *τύποι περὶ θεολογίας* in *Republic*, 379b–c, a principle which there is no reason to suppose that Plato ever abandoned. I do not of course suggest that these two criteria furnish a definition of God: they are no more than *ὅροι*, marks or criteria; but as such I hardly think they can be contested.

Now in virtue of (1) we must, if Plato's language is to be taken seriously, rule out *ψυχή*, or an individual *ψυχή*, for *ψυχή* is again and again asserted to be, or to have, *γένεσις*. Nobody will think of denying this as far as the *Timaeus* is concerned; in the *Laws* we have 892c *εἰ δὲ φανήσεται ψυχὴ πρῶτον, οὐ πῦρ οὐδὲ ἀήρ, ψυχὴ δ' ἐν πρώτοις γεγενημένη, σχεδὸν ὀρθότατα λέγοιτ' ἂν εἶναι διαφερόντως φύσει*: 896a *ὀρθῶς ἄρα . . . εἰρηκότες ἂν εἶμεν ψυχὴν μὲν προτέραν γεγονέναι σώματος ἡμῖν* . . . 892a *ψυχὴν . . . ἠγνοηκέναι κινδυνεύουσι μὲν ὀλίγου σύμπαντες οἷόν τε ὂν τυγχάνει καὶ δύναμιν ἣν ἔχει, τῶν τε ἄλλων αὐτῆς πέρι καὶ δὴ καὶ γενέσεως, . . . σωμάτων ἔμπροσθεν πάντων γενομένη* . . . In *Laws* XII, where the religious doctrine of X is recapitulated, we have 967d *οὐκ ἔστιν ποτὲ γενέσθαι βεβαίως θεοσεβῆ θνητῶν ἀνθρώπων οὐδένα, ὃς ἂν μὴ τὰ λεγόμενα ταῦτα νῦν δύο λάβῃ, ψυχή τε ὡς ἔστιν πρεσβύτατον ἁπάντων ὅσα γονῆς μετείληφεν* . . . In this last passage the word *γονή* seems to have disquieted the commentators (although it means no more than *γένεσις*) to such an extent that they interpret in a linguistically impossible fashion: England 'would take the superlative as equivalent to a strong English comparative—"far older than all" ': and Taylor follows him by translating 'until he has grasped the two truths we are now affirming, the soul's dateless anteriority to all things generable . . .' Similarly Diès (op. cit., p. 567) with reference to this passage says 'L'Ame, d'ailleurs, n'est antérieure qu'à tout ce qui "participe à la génération" '.

The words can in fact only mean 'eldest of all things that are generated'. Why anyone should feel troubled by this, in view of the passages I have quoted from Book X is hard to understand. But let me substantiate the linguistic point. The substitution of superlative + genitive for comparative + genitive is a common idiom, but it is always so used as to leave no ambiguity, for the genitive is always such, in itself or in virture of some appended word, as to make it clear that the class A with which x is brought into relation does not include x. The examples given in

Kühner-Gerth, II, 1, 23 all illustrate this principle: I need only quote Sophocles, *Antigone*, 100 κάλλιστον τῶν προτέρων φάος, Thucydides, I, 1, ἀξιολογώτατον τῶν προγεγενημένων, id., I, 10, μεγίστην τῶν πρὸ αὐτῆς. In Homer the idiom is very common with ἄλλων. A few pages later in this same book of the *Laws* we have 969a ἢ . . . κλέος ἀρῇ μέγιστον κατασκευάσας αὐτὴν ὀρθῶς, ἢ τό γε ἀνδρειότατος εἶναι δοκεῖν τῶν ὕστερον ἐπιγιγνομένων οὐκ ἐκφεύξῃ ποτέ.

Soul then is a γένεσις or a γεγονός, or 'participates in birth'. That does not of course mean that it is created in time, that there was ever a time when no soul was, any more than the emphatic γέγονε of *Timaeus*, 28b means that the Universe was created in time. The meaning in both cases is that they are derivative existents, things whose being depends on something more ultimate. Hence there is no real inconsistency with *Phaedrus*, 245d and e, where ψυχή is said to be ἀγένητον in the sense of having no beginning of its existence.

The reason why scholars have disregarded, or explained away, this attribution of γένεσις to ψυχή is doubtless that they have assumed that the god or gods whose existence *Laws* X sets out to prove is or are an ultimate principle or principles. But we must remember that Plato is not concerned to give us the whole of his metaphysics, or even of his philosophy of religion, in the *Laws*; his object is to lay down the necessary minimum of philosophical doctrine required for a sound basis of religion and morality; and from that point of view it was not necessary to go into the difficult question of the relation of νοῦς to the Universe, or (what is the same thing) the relation of νοῦς to ψυχή, the principle of movement in the Universe. Indeed it would have been unreasonable to expect Cleinias and Megillus, or the citizen body to whom the 'preambles' to the laws are addressed, to follow him if he had. As Timaeus says (28c) τὸν μὲν οὖν ποιητὴν καὶ πατέρα τοῦδε τοῦ παντὸς εὑρεῖν τε ἔργον καὶ εὑρόντα εἰς πάντας ἀδύνατον λέγειν. Why should that be 'impossible' in the *Timaeus* if it can be done by straightforward scientific argument in the *Laws*?

What then, precisely, does the argument of *Laws* X, establish? This, that all the processes of the physical Universe are dependent upon, and controlled by, non-physical processes or movements, that is by souls, some good some bad. It is not decided whether there is one good soul or many, nor whether there is one bad soul or many, but merely that there must be at least two souls, one good and one bad. It is not said that the good soul or souls control or rule over the bad soul or souls; but it is laid down (897c–898c) that the regular movements of the heaven and 'all that is in it' (viz. the stars, sun, moon, and planets) are controlled by ἡ ἀρίστη ψυχή (897c), or by 'one soul, or more than one, possessing all excellence' (898c). Here is no warrant for attributing to Plato the doctrine of a single supreme deity; τὴν ἀρίστην ψυχήν, both times that the words are used (897c 6, 898c 4), must mean, as England has seen, 'the best kind of soul'.[1] At the most, he regards it as only *possible* that there may be only one 'best soul', and he almost goes out of his way to underline his doubt, or his unconcern, by repeating the words μίαν ἢ πλείους, which he had used in reference to soul as a whole at 896e, in reference to *good* soul at 898c.[2] And at the end of this section of the argument (899e) all that is claimed to have been established is that 'a soul or souls' are the causes of the movements of the heavenly bodies, and so of the 'years, months and seasons', so that we are justified in saying (with Thales) that 'all things are full of gods'. If this is Plato's complete philosophy of religion, we must believe that he was indifferent to, or found it impossible to answer, the question of one God or many Gods. That is surely not easy to believe, though some scholars appear to believe it; if the *Timaeus* myth means anything about God, it surely means that he is one and only one. However, whether we believe this or not, it is certainly not the case that *Laws* X, asserts the doctrine of one God, viz. the best soul.

It appears then, from the evidence of *Philebus*, *Timaeus*, and *Laws*, that ψυχή does not satisfy our first criterion. Does it satisfy our second? At first sight it would seem that it does. The movements belonging to ψυχή itself—the πρωτουργοὶ κινήσεις contrasted with the δευτερουργοί at *Laws*, 897a—include wish,

[1] The phrase is in fact a mere variant of τὸ φρόνιμον καὶ ἀρετῆς πλῆρες (sc. ψυχῆς γένος) 897b.

[2] The astronomical theory behind this passage is difficult, if not impossible, to determine. By leaving open the question whether there is only one, or more than one, orderly or beneficent soul, he seems to be deliberately avoiding the settlement of the problem whether the revolution of the circle of the fixed stars does or does not carry round with it those of the planets—a doctrine implied in the myth of *Rep.* X. I do not think there is anything in the text to suggest that the bad or maleficent souls have anything to do with planetary movements.

deliberation, tendance (*ἐπιμελεῖσθαι*), true and false judgement, love and hate, etc.; and the best kind of soul is said *ἐπιμελεῖσθαι τοῦ κόσμου παντός*. But the Stranger is careful to make it clear that good soul is discriminated from bad soul by its 'association' with *νοῦς* (897b); that is to say, Soul in its own nature is ethically neutral: the good soul owes its goodness to *νοῦς*, the bad soul its badness to its lack of *νοῦς*. Now if we set this doctrine beside two closely similar passages of the *Philebus* and *Timaeus*, we can see clearly enough what Plato means us to understand to be the relation between *νοῦς* and *ψυχή*. I have already quoted the passage, *Philebus*, 30b, where it is said that the *αἰτία* 'devises' *ψυχή* in the Universe; now at 30d the question is put *οὐκοῦν ἐν μὲν τῇ τοῦ Διὸς ἐρεῖς φύσει βασιλικὴν μὲν ψυχήν, βασιλικὸν δὲ νοῦν ἐγγίγνεσθαι διὰ τὴν τῆς αἰτίας δύναμιν*: and at *Timaeus*, 30b we have *δεῖ λέγειν τόνδε τὸν κόσμον ζῷον ἔμψυχον ἔννουν τε τῇ ἀληθείᾳ διὰ τὴν τοῦ θεοῦ πρόνοιαν*. Reason then, as well as Soul, is found in the Universe and is due to the action of God, who is himself identified with Reason. In other words, the Universe is rational and good in so far as God's rational nature and goodness are imparted to it: it is irrational and bad in so far as God's rational nature and goodness are not wholly imparted to it. The same doctrine is expressed earlier in the *Timaeus* (29e), where it is said that the Demiurge, because he was good, desired all things to be so far as possible (*ὅτι μάλιστα*) like to himself.[1]

So far, then, the three dialogues have been found consistent in discriminating *νοῦς*, as an ultimate principle, from *ψυχή* as a derived principle. We are, however, told both in *Philebus* and *Timaeus* that *νοῦς* cannot 'arise' apart from a soul: *Philebus*, 30c *σοφία μὴν καὶ νοῦς ἄνευ ψυχῆς οὐκ ἄν ποτε γενοίσθην*, *Timaeus*, 30b *λογισάμενος οὖν ηὕρισκεν . . . νοῦν . . . χωρὶς ψυχῆς ἀδύνατον παραγενέσθαι τῳ*. Again, in *Sophist*, 249a it is argued that if *τὸ παντελῶς*

[1] Incidentally it may be added that this passage gives no ground for identifying the Demiurge with his model, the *νοητὸν ζῷον*, even in the partial identification adopted by Diès (op. cit., p. 550: 'Allons-nous donc identifier totalement le Démiurge et le Modèle? Nous serions très excusables de les identifier en tant qu'ils représentent ou symbolisent la Divinité suprême. Mais nous sommes contraints de les distinguer en tant qu'ils représentent l'un, l'Objet par excellence, l'autre, le Sujet par excellence'. The words *ὅτι μάλιστα παραπλήσια ἑαυτῷ*, on which alone, so far as I can see, this doctrine has been built, are not intended to suggest the relation of copy to model; they are equivalent merely to *κατὰ δύναμιν ἄριστα*.

ὄν has *νοῦς* it must have *ζωή*, and that it can only have *νοῦς* and *ζωή* in a soul.[1] But in all these passages Plato is speaking of the Universe, not of its 'Creator' or cause, of that which *has νοῦς*, not of that which *is νοῦς*.[2] The language of the *Sophist*, although it makes no reference to *νοῦς* as cause, is perfectly compatible with the distinction drawn in *Phil.*, 28d between *τὰ ξύμπαντα καὶ τόδε τὸ καλούμενον ὅλον* and the *νοῦς καὶ φρόνησίς τις θαυμαστὴ συντάττουσα* which 'steers its course'. It is not relevant to the argument of *Sophist*, 249a, the object of which is to establish the existence of *κίνησις* as an element in reality, to anticipate what the *Philebus* and *Timaeus* are to tell us of the cause behind the Universe. And not only are we not entitled, on the strength of these passages, to infer that the *νοῦς* which is God or cause must be 'in a soul', but we shall make havoc of the *Philebus* ontology and the *Timaeus* cosmology if we do.

To this it may be objected that Plato's God is hereby deprived of personality, that he is no longer a living being, but has become an 'impersonal thought'; indeed this conclusion seems to have been drawn by Zeller,[3] who maintains that the personality of God is a question which hardly presented itself to Plato in a definite form. I can only reply that Plato may well have wished to attribute to God a mode of personality, and of life, different from that known to our experience, but have wisely refrained from the attempt to define it; and although the activity of God certainly meant for him something very different from what it meant for Aristotle, he might well have agreed with the latter's words (*Met.*, Λ 1072b 26) *καὶ ζωὴ δέ γ' ὑπάρχει* (sc. *τῷ θεῷ*)· *ἡ γὰρ νοῦ ἐνέργεια ζωή, ἐκεῖνος δὲ ἡ ἐνέργεια.*

Plato's meaning is, as I understand it, that if God is to impart his goodness to the world—and to do so is an essential part of his goodness—if Reason is to penetrate this world of *κίνησις* and

[1] *ἀλλὰ ταῦτα μὲν ἀμφότερα ἐνόντ' αὐτῷ λέγομεν, οὐ μὴν ἐν ψυχῇ γε φήσομεν αὐτὸ ἔχειν αὐτά; —καὶ τίν' ἂν ἕτερον ἔχοι τρόπον;*

[2] Cf. Zeller[4], 715, Note 1: 'Es handelt sich hierbei (i.e. *Tim.*, 30b; *Phil.*, 30c) nicht um die Vernunft in ihrem überweltlichen Sein sondern um die Vernunft wiefern sie dem Weltganzen (mythisch ausgedrückt: der Natur des Zeus) inwohnt, von dieser innerweltlichen Vernunft aber wird die überweltliche noch unterschieden, wenn es heisst, Zeus besitze eine königliche Seele und einen königlichen Verstand *διὰ τὴν τῆς αἰτίας δύναμιν*'.

[3] Zeller[4], p. 714 ff.

γένεσις, it must be through ψυχή, the principle of movement.[1] It is in the regular movements of the heavenly bodies that Plato finds the closest approximation to the activity of God, just as Aristotle was to find it in the eternal revolution of the πρῶτος οὐρανός. Plato calls the activity of νοῦς a κίνησις, but he seems on the verge of formulating Aristotle's distinction between the minimal κίνησις of the First Heaven and the ἀκινησία of the πρῶτον κινοῦν in the passage (*Laws* 897d–898b) where he discusses the question 'What is the nature of the κίνησις of νοῦς?' The answer that he gives is that we can only describe it in an image: 'let us beware of creating a darkness at noonday for ourselves by gazing, so to say, direct at the sun as we give our answer, as though we could hope to attain adequate vision and perception of wisdom with mortal eyes. It will be the safer course to turn our gaze on an image of the object of our quest'; and the conclusion is that 'if we say that intelligence and movement in one place are both like the revolution of a well-made globe, in moving regularly and uniformly in one compass about one centre, and in one sense, according to one single law and plan, we need have no fear of proving unskilled artists in imagery'.[2]

The question which Plato is asking here is that which Aristotle attempts to answer by his doctrine of God as νόησις νοήσεως, namely what God is *in himself*, regarded in abstraction from that outgoing activity which is his in relation to the Universe. He cannot, or will not, answer it directly, just as he cannot, or will not, directly describe the Form of Good in *Rep.* VI.[3] Nor is it a question that need trouble the legislator of the *Laws*; his concern is that his citizens should recognise the divine as revealed in the Universe.

I do not propose to raise here the much-discussed question of the relation of Plato's God to the Form of Good, or to the Forms in general. Whatever be the precise philosophical meaning of calling the Forms the παραδείγματα to which the Demiurge looks,

[1] Cf. Proclus *in Tim.*, I, p. 402 (Diehl) εἰ ἄρα δεῖ τὸ πᾶν ἔννουν γενέσθαι, δεῖ καὶ ψυχῆς· ὑποδοχὴ γάρ ἐστιν αὕτη τοῦ νοῦ, καὶ δι' αὐτῆς ὁ νοῦς ἐμφαίνεται τοῖς ὄγκοις τοῦ παντός, οὐχ ὅτι δεῖται τῆς ψυχῆς ὁ νοῦς· οὕτω γὰρ ἂν ἀτιμότερος εἴη τῆς ψυχῆς· ἀλλ' ὅτι τὰ σώματα δεῖται τῆς ψυχῆς εἰ μέλλοι (? μέλλει) νοῦ μεθέξειν.

[2] Professor Taylor's translation.

[3] In *Tim.*, 42e he is content to say of the Demiurge, when his work of creation is finished, ἔμενεν ἐν τῷ ἑαυτοῦ κατὰ τρόπον ἤθει.

I believe with Professor Taylor that there is no warrant for identifying him with the Forms, or for regarding them as his thoughts. It seems to me probable that Theism became part of Plato's philosophy, as distinct from his religious belief at a later period than that of the *Republic*; but however that may be, my main purpose in referring to this question of the nature of the *κίνησις* of *νοῦς* is to point out that it confirms, as seriously meant, the discrimination of *νοῦς* from *ψυχή* and the identification of God, not with Soul or 'the best Soul', but with Reason. It is, in short, *νοῦς*, and *νοῦς* alone, that satisfies both the criteria that we put forward.

The importance of our conclusion can be perhaps best realised by a comparison with Aristotle's theology expounded in *Metaphysics* Λ. Aristotle's God is external to the Universe which depends on him, and is connected with it only inasmuch as he is the object of its desire (*ὡς ἐρώμενον*). Plato's God is external too, in the sense that he is the perfect spiritual activity implied by, but nowhere fully revealed in, the Universe: at the same time he is immanent, in the sense that the life of the Universe is *his* life just because his activity is necessarily (unlike that of Aristotle's God) one that goes outside himself, is necessarily a projection of himself. To identify him with *ψυχή* would be to deny his transcendence or externality, since *ψυχή* is a principle operative only in the realm of *κίνησις* and *γένεσις*: and thereby to deny his perfection, since perfection does not and cannot belong to *κίνησις* and *γένεσις*.

In declining to raise here the problem of the identity of God with the Form of Good I have of course declined the attempt to fit Plato's theology into his metaphysical system; but I think it is not unhelpful to add, in conclusion, that his transcendent-immanent God is a conception very similar to his transcendent-immanent Forms. Each Form is the Form of its particulars: though external to the particulars it is part of its nature to be imperfectly represented in them, just as it is part of God's nature to be imperfectly represented in the Universe.

INDEX LOCORUM

The figures in normal roman type refer to Stephanus's edition of Plato and the italic figures to pages of the present book.

International Library of Philosophy & Scientific Method

Editor: Ted Honderich
Advisory Editor: Bernard Williams

List of titles, page two

International Library of Psychology Philosophy & Scientific Method

Editor: C K Ogden

List of titles, page six

ROUTLEDGE AND KEGAN PAUL LTD
68 Carter Lane London EC4

International Library of Philosophy and Scientific Method
(Demy 8vo)

Allen, R. E. (Ed.)
Studies in Plato's Metaphysics
Contributors: J. L. Ackrill, R. E. Allen, R. S. Bluck, H. F. Cherniss, F. M. Cornford, R. C. Cross, P. T. Geach, R. Hackforth, W. F. Hicken, A. C. Lloyd, G. R. Morrow, G. E. L. Owen, G. Ryle, W. G. Runciman, G. Vlastos
464 pp. 1965. (2nd Impression 1967.) 70s.

Armstrong, D. M.
Perception and the Physical World
208 pp. 1961. (3rd Impression 1966.) 25s.

A Materialist Theory of the Mind
376 pp. 1967. about 45s.

Bambrough, Renford (Ed.)
New Essays on Plato and Aristotle
Contributors: J. L. Ackrill, G. E. M. Anscombe, Renford Bambrough, R. M. Hare, D. M. MacKinnon, G. E. L. Owen, G. Ryle, G. Vlastos
184 pp. 1965. (2nd Impression 1967.) 28s.

Barry, Brian
Political Argument
382 pp. 1965. 50s.

Bird, Graham
Kant's Theory of Knowledge:
An Outline of One Central Argument in the *Critique of Pure Reason*
220 pp. 1962. (2nd Impression 1965.) 28s.

Brentano, Franz
The True and the Evident
Edited and narrated by Professor R. Chisholm
218 pp. 1965. 40s.

Broad, C. D.
Lectures on Psychical Research
Incorporating the Perrott Lectures given in Cambridge University in 1959 and 1960
461 pp. 1962. (2nd Impression 1966.) 56s.

Crombie, I. M.
An Examination of Plato's Doctrine
I. Plato on Man and Society
408 pp. 1962. (2nd Impression 1966.) 42s.
II. Plato on Knowledge and Reality
583 pp. 1963. (2nd Impression 1967.) 63s.

Day, John Patrick
Inductive Probability
352 pp. 1961. 40s.

International Library of Philosophy and Scientific Method
(Demy 8vo)

Allen, R. E. (Ed.)
Studies in Plato's Metaphysics
Contributors: J. L. Ackrill, R. E. Allen, R. S. Bluck, H. F. Cherniss, F. M. Cornford, R. C. Cross, P. T. Geach, R. Hackforth, W. F. Hicken, A. C. Lloyd, G. R. Morrow, G. E. L. Owen, G. Ryle, W. G. Runciman, G. Vlastos
464 pp. 1965. 70s.

Armstrong, D. M.
Perception and the Physical World
208 pp. 1961. (2nd Impression 1963.) 25s.

Bambrough, Renford (Ed.)
New Essays on Plato and Aristotle
Contributors: J. L. Ackrill, G. E. M. Anscombe, Renford Bambrough, R. M. Hare, D. M. MacKinnon, G. E. L. Owen, G. Ryle, G. Vlastos
184 pp. 1965. 28s.

Barry, Brian
Political Argument
382 pp. 1965, 50s.

Bird, Graham
Kant's Theory of Knowledge:
An Outline of One Central Argument in the *Critique of Pure Reason*
220 pp. 1962. (2nd Impression 1965.) 28s.

Brentano, Franz
The True and the Evident
Edited and narrated by Professor R. Chisholm
218 pp. 1965, 40s.

Broad, C. D.
Lectures on Psychical Research
Incorporating the Perrott Lectures given in Cambridge University in 1959 and 1960
461 pp. 1962. 56s.

Crombie, I. M.
An Examination of Plato's Doctrine
I. Plato on Man and Society
408 pp. 1962. 42s.
II. Plato on Knowledge and Reality
583 pp. 1963. 63s.

Day, John Patrick
Inductive Probability
352 pp. 1961. 40s.

International Library of Philosophy and Scientific Method

(Demy 8vo)

Edel, Abraham
Method in Ethical Theory
379 pp. 1963. 32s.

Flew, Anthony
Hume's Philosophy of Belief
A Study of his First "Inquiry"
296 pp. 1961. 30s.

Goldman, Lucien
The Hidden God
A Study of Tragic Vision in the *Pensées* of Pascal and the Tragedies of Racine. Translated from the French by Philip Thody
424 pp. 1964. 70s.

Hamlyn, D. W.
Sensation and Perception
A History of the Philosophy of Perception
222 pp. 1961. (2nd Impression 1963.) 25s.

Kemp, J.
Reason, Action and Morality
216 pp. 1964. 30s.

Körner, Stephan
Experience and Theory
An Essay in the Philosophy of Science
272 pp. 1966. 45s.

Lazerowitz, Morris
Studies in Metaphilosophy
276 pp. 1964. 35s.

Merleau-Ponty, M.
Phenomenology of Perception
Translated from the French by Colin Smith
487 pp. 1962. (2nd Impression 1965.) 56s.

Montefiore, Alan, and Williams, Bernard
British Analytical Philosophy
352 pp. 1965. 45s.

Perelman, Chaim
The Idea of Justice and the Problem of Argument
Introduction by H. L. A. Hart. Translated from the French by John Petrie
224 pp. 1963. 28s.

Schlesinger, G.
Method in the Physical Sciences
148 pp. 1963. 21s.

International Library of Philosophy and Scientific Method
(Demy 8vo)

Sellars, W. F.
Science, Perception and Reality
374 pp. 1963. 50s.

Shwayder, D. S.
The Stratification of Behaviour
A System of Definitions Propounded and Defended
428 pp. 1965. 56s.

Smart, J. J. C.
Philosophy and Scientific Realism
168 pp. 1963. (2nd Impression 1965.) 25s.

Smythies, J. R. (Ed.)
Brain and Mind
Contributors: Lord Brain, John Beloff, C. J. Ducasse, Antony Flew, Hartwig Kuhlenbeck, D. M. MacKay, H. H. Price, Anthony Quinton and J. R. Smythies
288 pp. 1965. 40s.

Taylor, Charles
The Explanation of Behaviour
288 pp. 1964. (2nd Impression 1965.) 40s.

Wittgenstein, Ludwig
Tractatus Logico-Philosophicus
The German text of the *Logisch-Philosophische Abhandlung* with a new translation by D. F. Pears and B. F. McGuinness. Introduction by Bertrand Russell
188 pp. 1961. (2nd Impression 1963.) 21s.

Wright, Georg Henrik Von
Norm and Action
A Logical Enquiry. The Gifford Lectures
232 pp. 1963. (2nd Impression 1964.) 32s.

The Varieties of Goodness
The Gifford Lectures
236 pp. 1963. (2nd Impression 1965.) 28s.

Zinkernagel, Peter
Conditions for Description
Translated from the Danish by Olaf Lindum
272 pp. 1962. 37s. 6d.

International Library of Psychology, Philosophy, and Scientific Method
(Demy 8vo)

PHILOSOPHY

Anton, John Peter
Aristotle's Theory of Contrariety
276 pp. 1957. 25s.

Bentham, J.
The Theory of Fictions
Introduction by C. K. Ogden
214 pp. 1932. 30s.

Black, Max
The Nature of Mathematics
A Critical Survey
242 pp. 1933. (5th Impression 1965.) 28s.

Bluck, R. S.
Plato's Phaedo
A Translation with Introduction, Notes and Appendices
226 pp. 1955. 21s.

Broad, C. D.
Ethics and the History of Philosophy
Selected Essays
296 pp. 1952. 25s.

Scientific Thought
556 pp. 1923. (4th Impression 1952.) 40s.

Five Types of Ethical Theory
322 pp. 1930. (8th Impression 1962.) 30s.

The Mind and Its Place in Nature
694 pp. 1925. (7th Impression 1962.) 55s. See also Lean, Martin.

Buchler, Justus (Ed.)
The Philosophy of Peirce
Selected Writings
412 pp. 1940. (3rd Impression 1956.) 35s.

Burtt, E. A.
The Metaphysical Foundations of Modern Physical Science
A Historical and Critical Essay
364 pp. 2nd (revised) edition 1932. (5th Impression 1964.) 35s.

International Library of Psychology, Philosophy, and Scientific Method
(Demy 8vo)

Carnap, Rudolf
The Logical Syntax of Language
Translated from the German by Amethe Smeaton
376 pp. 1937. (6th Impression 1964.) 40s.

Chwistek, Leon
The Limits of Science
Outline of Logic and of the Methodology of the Exact Sciences
With Introduction and Appendix by Helen Charlotte Brodie
414 pp. 2nd edition 1949. 32s.

Cornford, F. M.
Plato's Theory of Knowledge
The Theaetetus and Sophist of Plato
Translated with a running commentary
358 pp. 1935. (6th Impression 1964.) 28s.

Plato's Cosmology
The Timaeus of Plato
Translated with a running commentary
402 pp. Frontispiece. 1937. (4th Impression 1956.) 35s.

Plato and Parmenides
Parmenides' *Way of Truth* and Plato's *Parmenides*
Translated with a running commentary
280 pp. 1939 (5th Impression 1964.) 32s.

Crawshay-Williams, Rupert
Methods and Criteria of Reasoning
An Inquiry into the Structure of Controversy
312 pp. 1957. 32s.

Fritz, Charles A.
Bertrand Russell's Construction of the External World
252 pp. 1952. 30s.

Hulme, T. E.
Speculations
Essays on Humanism and the Philosophy of Art
Edited by Herbert Read. Foreword and Frontispiece by Jacob Epstein
296 pp. 2nd edition 1936. (6th Impression 1965.) 32s.

Lange, Frederick Albert
The History of Materialism
And Criticism of its Present Importance
With an Introduction by Bertrand Russell, F.R.S. Translated from the German by Ernest Chester Thomas
1,146 pp. 1925. (3rd Impression 1957.) 70s.

International Library of Psychology, Philosophy, and Scientific Method

(Demy 8vo)

Lazerowitz, Morris
The Structure of Metaphysics
With a Foreword by John Wisdom
262 pp. 1955. (2nd Impression 1963.) 30s.

Lean, Martin
Sense-Perception and Matter
A Critical Analysis of C. D. Broad's Theory of Perception
234 pp. 1953. 25s.

Lodge, Rupert C.
Plato's Theory of Art
332 pp. 1953. 25s.

The Philosophy of Plato
366 pp. 1956. 32s.

Mannheim, Karl
Ideology and Utopia
An Introduction to the Sociology of Knowledge
With a Preface by Louis Wirth. Translated from the German by Louis Wirth and Edward Shils
360 pp. 1954. 28s.

Moore, G. E.
Philosophical Studies
360 pp. 1922. (6th Impression 1965.) 35s. See also Ramsey, F. P.

Ogden, C. K., and Richards, I. A.
The Meaning of Meaning
A Study of the Influence of Language upon Thought and of the Science of Symbolism
With supplementary essays by B. Malinowski and F. G. Crookshank.
394 pp. 10th Edition 1949. (4th Impression 1956) 32s.
See also Bentham, J.

Peirce, Charles, *see* Buchler, J.

Ramsey, Frank Plumpton
The Foundations of Mathematics and other Logical Essays
Edited by R. B. Braithwaite. Preface by G. E. Moore
318 pp. 1931. (4th Impression 1965.) 35s.

Richards, I. A.
Principles of Literary Criticism
312 pp. 2nd edition. 1926. (16th Impression 1963.) 25s.

Mencius on the Mind. Experiments in Multiple Definition
190 pp. 1932. (2nd Impression 1964.) 28s.

Russell, Bertrand, *see* Fritz, C. A.; Lange, F. A.; Wittgenstein, L.

International Library of Psychology, Philosophy, and Scientific Method

(Demy 8vo)

Smart, Ninian
Reasons and Faiths
An Investigation of Religious Discourse, Christian and Non-Christian
230 pp. 1958. (2nd Impression 1965.) 28s.

Vaihinger, H.
The Philosophy of As If
A System of the Theoretical, Practical and Religious Fictions of Mankind
Translated by C. K. Ogden
428 pp. 2nd edition 1935. (4th Impression 1965.) 45s.

von Wright, Georg Henrik
Logical Studies
214 pp. 1957. 28s.

Wittgenstein, Ludwig
Tractatus Logico-Philosophicus
With an Introduction by Bertrand Russell, F.R.S., German text with an English translation en regard
216 pp. 1922. (9th Impression 1962.) 21s.
For the Pears-McGuinness translation—*see page 5*

Zeller, Eduard
Outlines of the History of Greek Philosophy
Revised by Dr. Wilhelm Nestle. Translated from the German by L. R. Palmer
248 pp. 13th (revised) edition 1931. (5th Impression 1963.) 28s.

PSYCHOLOGY

Adler, Alfred
The Practice and Theory of Individual Psychology
Translated by P. Radin
368 pp. 2nd (revised) edition 1929. (8th Impression 1964.) 30s.

Bühler, Charlotte
The Mental Development of the Child
Translated from the German by Oscar Oeser
180 pp. 3 plates, 19 figures. 1930 (3rd Impression 1949.) 12s. 6d.

Eng, Helga
The Psychology of Children's Drawings
From the First Stroke to the Coloured Drawing
240 pp. 8 colour plates. 139 figures. 2nd edition 1954. (2nd Impression 1959.) 25s.

Jung, C. G.
Psychological Types
or The Psychology of Individuation
Translated from the German and with a Preface by H. Godwin Baynes
696 pp. 1923. (12th Impression 1964.) 45s.

International Library of Psychology, Philosophy, and Scientific Method

(Demy 8vo)

Koffka, Kurt

The Growth of the Mind

An Introduction to Child-Psychology

Translated from the German by Robert Morris Ogden

456 pp. 16 figures. 2nd edition (revised) 1928. (6th Impression 1952.) 45s.

Principles of Gestalt Psychology

740 pp. 112 figures. 39 tables. 1935. (5th Impression 1962.) 60s.

Köhler, W.

The Mentality of Apes

With an Appendix on the Psychology of Chimpanzees

Translated from the German by Ella Winter

352 pp. 9 plates. 19 figures. 2nd edition (revised) 1927. (4th Impression 1956.) 25s.

Malinowski, Bronislaw

Crime and Custom in Savage Society

152 pp. 6 plates. 1926. (7th Impression 1961.) 18s.

Sex and Repression in Savage Society

290 pp. 1927. (4th Impression 1953.) 21s.

See also Ogden, C. K.

Markey, John F.

The Symbolic Process and Its Integration in Children

A Study in Social Psychology

212 pp. 1928. 14s.

Murphy, Gardner

An Historical Introduction to Modern Psychology

488 pp. 5th edition (revised) 1949. (5th Impression 1964.) 40s.

Paget, R.

Human Speech

Some Observations, Experiments, and Conclusions as to the Nature, Origin, Purpose and Possible Improvement of Human Speech

374 pp. 5 plates. 1930. (2nd Impression 1963.) 42s.

Petermann, Bruno

The Gestalt Theory and the Problem of Configuration

Translated from the German by Meyer Fortes

364 pp. 20 figures. 1932. (2nd Impression 1950.) 25s.

Piaget, Jean

The Language and Thought of the Child

Preface by E. Claparède. Translated from the French by Marjorie Gabain

220 pp. 3rd edition (revised and enlarged) 1959. (2nd Impression 1962.) 30s.

International Library of Psychology, Philosophy, and Scientific Method *(Demy 8vo)*

Piaget, Jean *(continued)*

The Child's Conception of Physical Causality
Translated from the French by Marjorie Gabain
(3rd Impression 1965.) 30s.

The Moral Judgment of the Child
Translated from the French by Marjorie Gabain
438 pp. 1932. (4th Impression 1965.) 35s.

The Psychology of Intelligence
Translated from the French by Malcolm Piercy and D. E. Berlyne
198 pp. 1950. (4th Impression 1964.) 18s.

The Child's Conception of Number
Translated from the French by C. Gattegno and F. M. Hodgson
266 pp. 1952. (3rd Impression 1964.) 25s.

The Origin of Intelligence in the Child
Translated from the French by Margaret Cook
448 pp. 1953. (2nd Impression 1966.) 42s.

The Child's Conception of Geometry
In collaboration with Bärbel Inhelder and Alina Szeminska. Translated from the French by E. A. Lunzer
428 pp. 1960. (2nd Impression 1966.) 45s.

Piaget, Jean and Inhelder, Bärbel
The Child's Conception of Space
Translated from the French by F. J. Langdon and J. L. Lunzer
512 pp. 29 figures. 1956 (3rd Impression 1967.) 42s.

Roback, A. A.
The Psychology of Character
With a Survey of Personality in General
786 pp. 3rd edition (revised and enlarged 1952.) 50s.

Smythies, J. R.
Analysis of Perception
With a Preface by Sir Russell Brain, Bt.
162 pp. 1956. 21s.

van der Hoop, J. H.
Character and the Unconscious
A Critical Exposition of the Psychology of Freud and Jung
Translated from the German by Elizabeth Trevelyan
240 pp. 1923. (2nd Impression 1950.) 20s.

Woodger, J. H.
Biological Principles
508 pp. 1929. (Reissued with a new Introduction 1966.) 60s.

867 PRINTED BY HEADLEY BROTHERS LTD 109 KINGSWAY LONDON WC2 AND ASHFORD KENT